Praise for *The Canadian Rangers:*

"This is a great story of the Rangers, whose program is the most cost-effective method for providing a physical sovereignty presence in the Canadian Arctic. They live there, they know their environment, and they have a vested interest in protecting it. Rangers are sentinels of the North and some of most loyal and patriotic soldiers I have met in my thirty-three-year career."

♦ Colonel (Ret'd) Pierre Leblanc, former commander of Canadian Forces Northern Area

"The Canadian Rangers, with their red hoodies and Lee-Enfield rifles, have become as much an icon of the Canadian North as the tundra and sea ice they safeguard. Here, Lackenbauer not only examines their history and how their image was cultivated but also the contradictions of their mission. As Canada continues to define its relationship to Aboriginal people, this book provides a sterling example of one program that has worked for everybody. Maybe there's a lesson here."

♦ Bob Weber, Arctic affairs specialist, the Canadian Press

"In 1991, I joined the Rangers and became a member of a special extended family of remarkable northern men and women. I met Whitney Lackenbauer on 'K-1' (as us 'bush Rangers' call Operation Kigiliqaqvik). His understanding and interpretation of Rangers and the North is outstanding. This book should be mandatory reading for any Regular Force personnel working in the North."

♦ Ranger Sergeant John Mitchell, Dawson Patrol, 1 CRPG

D1558699

STUDIES IN CANADIAN MILITARY HISTORY
Series editor: Dean F. Oliver, Canadian War Museum

The Canadian War Museum, Canada's national museum of military history, has a threefold mandate: to remember, to preserve, and to educate. Studies in Canadian Military History, published by UBC Press in association with the Museum, extends this mandate by presenting the best of contemporary scholarship to provide new insights into all aspects of Canadian military history, from earliest times to recent events. The work of a new generation of scholars is especially encouraged, and the books employ a variety of approaches – cultural, social, intellectual, economic, political, and comparative – to investigate gaps in the existing historiography. The books in the series feed immediately into future exhibitions, programs, and outreach efforts by the Canadian War Museum. A list of the titles in the series appears at the end of the book.

P. Whitney Lackenbauer

The Canadian Rangers
A Living History

UBCPress · Vancouver · Toronto

21 20 19 18 17 16 15 14 13   5 4 3 2 1

Printed in Canada on paper that is processed chlorine- and acid-free.

Library and Archives Canada Cataloguing in Publication

Lackenbauer, P. Whitney
    The Canadian Rangers : a living history / P. Whitney Lackenbauer.

(Studies in Canadian military history series, ISSN 1499-6251)
"Published in association with the Canadian War Museum".
Includes bibliographical references and index.
Issued also in electronic format.
ISBN 978-0-7748-2452-1 (bound); ISBN 978-0-7748-2453-8 (pbk.)

    1. Canada. Canadian Armed Forces. Canadian Rangers – History. 2. Canada – Armed Forces – Native peoples – History. 3. Canada – Armed Forces – Canada, Northern – History. I. Canadian War Museum II. Title. III. Series: Studies in Canadian military history

UA602.C29454L33 2013   355.3'70971   C2013-900236-7

Canada

UBC Press gratefully acknowledges the financial support for our publishing program of the Government of Canada (through the Canada Book Fund), the Canada Council for the Arts, and the British Columbia Arts Council.

This book has been published with the help of a grant from the Canadian Federation for the Humanities and Social Sciences, through the Awards to Scholarly Publications Program, using funds provided by the Social Sciences and Humanities Research Council of Canada.

Publication of this book has been financially supported by the Canadian War Museum, St. Jerome's University, and the Walter and Duncan Gordon Foundation.

UBC Press
The University of British Columbia
2029 West Mall
Vancouver, BC V6T 1Z2
www.ubcpress.ca

This book is dedicated to
Ranger Lieutenant the Right Reverend
John Reginald "Jack" Sperry (1924-2012)

and to the other men and women
of the Canadian Rangers, past and present

You make me proud to be Canadian

Contents

Maps

Acknowledgments

❋ My first exposure to the Canadian Rangers came while I was an undergraduate co-op student working at the Department of National Defence for the director general Aboriginal affairs in 1996. One of my first jobs was to help organize the Aboriginal Awareness Week display at National Defence Headquarters. The exhibit consisted of historical photographs and a "living history" display by two Canadian Rangers who were visiting from Northwest Territories. The Rangers built a Styrofoam igloo and, in their quiet and reserved way, explained to military officers and civil servants what they did. As they packed up at the end of the week, one of them handed me a red sweatshirt that had been transported in a crate with a muskox blanket. "It smells like sick cow," my then-girlfriend (now wife), Jennifer, who grew up on a dairy farm, told me. She proceeded to work on a master's degree in rural planning and development the next year, and for one of her course papers she examined the proposed Junior Canadian Rangers program as a component of northern community development. I was intrigued and decided that I would someday write the larger history of the Rangers, a success story according to popular media accounts, but one about which so little was known.

This book is a living history. It reflects collaboration with the Canadian Ranger Patrol Groups and Rangers from across the country and is grounded in the documentary record, interviews, and participant observation. It reveals how the military and residents of isolated coastal and northern communities built relationships based upon cooperation and accommodation of diversity in ways that scholars seldom emphasize. I have seen this first-hand in my travels, from coast to coast to coast, over the last decade.

My journey began in the documentary record. Without archivists and librarians, historians would be lost. At the Directorate of History and Heritage, Department of National Defence, Dr. Stephen Harris and Major Paul Lansey suggested leads and facilitated access to documents, while Dr. John MacFarlane shared interviews with several Canadian Rangers. Robin Weber at the NWT Archives in Yellowknife offered friendly assistance, as did the staff at the Esquimalt Military Museum and various other museums and archives across Canada. Thanks also to the former director general Aboriginal affairs at National Defence, Rem Westland, and to Caroline Kern, director of Aboriginal policy, for introducing me to this subject.

The true inspiration for this book came from the many Canadian Rangers and other members of the Canadian Forces – past and present – who shared their experiences, insights, and wisdom. The bibliography provides a comprehensive list, but several individuals warrant specific mention. Colonels Pierre Leblanc, Kevin McLeod, and Norris Pettis, as well as Brigadier-Generals Chris Whitecross, David Millar, and Guy Hamel, all supported my research during their tenures as commander of the Canadian Forces Northern Area/Joint Task Force North. Major Conrad Schubert has proven a stalwart supporter of my research since we met in 2002, and he generously shared historical material and facilitated research trips and interviews. This book could not have been written without his support. During trips to Yellowknife, Captain (now Major) Chris Bergeron, Sergeant Denis Lalonde, Captain Rob Marois, Sergeant Tim Stanistreet, and Captain Neil Whitmann were all wonderful hosts. In Victoria, Warrant Officers Pete Malcolm and Dan Hryhoryshen were similarly generous. Captain (now Major) Terry Stead, Master (now Chief) Warrant Officer Lou Kendall, Sergeant Rory Innes, and Sergeant Mike Rude literally kept me on track in Labrador. Ranger Cyril Abbott showed me eastern Newfoundland and arranged meetings with Rangers along the way. In northern Quebec, Warrant Officer Frank Duchesneau and Sergeant Antoine Duff shared their insights during annual training with the Inukjuak patrol while Major Guy Lang and Captain Réjean Plourde invited me to tag along on a helicopter trip to visit patrols along the Lower North Shore. Major Guy Ingram, Captain Mark Rittwage, and Sergeant Peter Moon were engaging hosts at Camp Loon in Geraldton, Ontario. Public Affairs Officer Eric Cameron arranged for a group of academics to visit the Rangers on Operation Nunalivut at Eureka, Ellesmere Island, in 2008, and to observe Operation Nanook in 2008 and 2009. Sergeant Tim Stanistreet led a training exercise in Tuktoyaktuk in January 2009 in which I participated, and 1 Canadian Ranger Patrol Group (CRPG) allowed him to arrange interviews and escort me on a trip through Yukon that June to discuss my ideas with Rangers. Lieutenant-Colonel Tim Byers agreed to several interviews and invited me along for the Saskatchewan-Manitoba leg of Exercise Western Spirit. Brigadier-General (now Major-General) David Millar, always an inspiring host, invited me to visit the Rangers at Alert as they concluded Operational Nunalivut in 2010. Captain Elizabeth Tremblay-Lewicki not only invited me to Resolute for Operation Nanook 2010 but also secured permissions so that I could be embedded in a platoon of the Arctic response company group when it headed to Pond Inlet and Bylot Island. Master Warrant Officer Bruce Dunn at the Canadian Rangers National Authority in Ottawa has been a source of inspiration and know-ledge, challenging my ideas and encouraging me to look at developments from various perspectives. So too have Lieutenant-Colonel Ian Pedley, Major Jim Mills, Chief Warrant Officer Dave Mahon, Warrant Officer Annie Brassard, and Warrant Officer Pat Rizzo who commented on parts of the manuscript. Conversations with former Ranger lieutenant the Right Reverend John Sperry (who passed away in February 2012), Ranger sergeants Mike Powaschuk and John "Mitch" Mitchell, Ranger corporals Chuck Syme and Doug Stern, and Rangers Eli Weetaluktuk, David Nasogaluak, and Paul Attagootak not only shaped this book but also the way that I understand the world.

I am a firm disciple of Harold Innis and his philosophy of "dirt" experience – you need to travel extensively in Canada before you can write about it with any sense of intimacy. My deepest thanks go to the Canadian Rangers who allowed me to observe and participate in annual training exercises or sovereignty patrols, tolerated my endless questions, and shared their stories and survival tips with me. These experiences have influenced me profoundly. Special thanks to the members of the Ross River (2004), Gold River (2005), Inukjuak (2006), Cape Freels (2008), Tuktoyaktuk (2009), and Nain (2012) patrols who allowed me to participate in annual training exercises. The Ross River patrol made me an Honorary Ranger in 2004, which was an unexpected and cherished honour. The patient Rangers who taught me how to ride a snowmobile (and kept me alive!) during exercises Goose Bay to Saglek (2006) and Western Spirit (2009) deserve sainthoods.

Conducting any study in northern and isolated regions is difficult to organize and often prohibitively expensive. This study could not have been completed without the generous support of several organizations and individuals. A Social Sciences and Humanities Research Council (SSHRC) Queen's Fellowship and the Killam Trust supported a preliminary research trip to Yellowknife and Rankin Inlet in 1999-2000. Canadian Forces Northern Area and 1 CRPG generously provided logistical support for research in 2000, 2002, 2004, and 2009; 4 CRPG (BC Detachment) in 2005; 5 CRPG in 2006; 2 CRPG in 2006 and 2007; and 3 CRPG in 2008. Professor Jim Miller hosted me as a postdoctoral fellow through his Canadian Research Chair in Native-Newcomer Relations from 2003 to 2004 and provided a generous research stipend that allowed for northern research. Professor Terry Copp, director of the Laurier Centre for Military Strategic and Disarmament Studies, covered some travel costs in 2006, as did a St. Jerome's University Faculty Research Grant. A Canadian International Council fellowship freed up the time and money needed to undertake research trips in 2008-09, and SSHRC public dissemination grants allowed me to "ground truth" my ideas with Canadian Ranger patrol groups and Rangers in 2009-10 and 2012-13. The final stages of writing were facilitated by a Fulbright grant in the fall of 2010 and ArcticNet funding for a project on the emerging Arctic security environment.

Other colleagues and friends have contributed to this research in important ways.

Moving to Saskatoon in November 2003 without my family for a year of postdoctoral research was daunting, but my supervisor, Jim Miller, and his wife, Mary, kept my spirits high. I had the pleasure of living with Ian and Lorraine Toombs during that year, and their gracious hospitality and generosity made the long distance bearable. In Calgary, David Bercuson, Rob Huebert, Bob Williamson, and Mark Dickerson shared insights and offered encouragement during the formative stages of the research. In Waterloo, Terry Copp, Ken McLaughlin, Ryan Touhey, Peter Kikkert, Dan Heidt, and Tim Winegard have been supportive colleagues and cherished friends. Lisa Beiler superbly compiled newspaper and magazine coverage of the Rangers. Friends and colleagues Harry Borlase, Ryan Dean, Matthew Farish, Richard Goette, Chris Madsen, and Scott Sheffield provided feedback and support. The scholarship on Canada's Norths by Ken Coates and Bill Morrison, with whom I wrote the book *Arctic Front,* illuminated much of the terrain that this study explores. Finally, although often unacknowledged, conference participants who make comments and ask questions play an important role in suggesting avenues for further research and refinement.

UBC Press expressed enthusiasm and supported the project from the onset, and I am pleased that Dean Oliver agreed to support it as part of the Studies in Canadian Military History series. A special thanks as well to the Federation for the Humanities and Social Sciences' Awards to Scholarly Publications Program, St. Jerome's University's Aid to Scholarly Publication Fund, and to Tom Axworthy and Sara French at the Walter Gordon Foundation for financial contributions that helped to facilitate publication.

Last but foremost, thanks to my family. Jennifer Arthur feigned interest as I discussed every twist and turn in my various research adventures, and her critical comments and editorial guidance on papers and chapter drafts, maps, and photographs were brilliant. Even more importantly, she kept the ship afloat during my absences. She, Harrison, Rendall, and Pierce provide me with abundant energy, support, and affection. I love and thank them with all of my heart for allowing me to embark on my Ranger adventures.

I am grateful for permission to incorporate material from the following publications:

P. Whitney Lackenbauer. "Canada's Northern Defenders: Aboriginal Peoples in the Canadian Rangers, 1947-2005." In *Aboriginal Peoples and the Canadian Military: Historical Perspectives,* ed. P. Whitney Lackenbauer and Craig Mantle, 171-208. Kingston, ON: CDA Press, 2007.

−. "The Canadian Rangers: A Postmodern Militia That Works." *Canadian Military Journal* 6, 4 (2005-06): 49-60.

−. "The Canadian Rangers: Sovereignty, Security and Stewardship from the Inside Out." In *Thawing Ice – Cold War: Canada's Security, Sovereignty, and Environmental Concerns in the Arctic,* ed. Rob Huebert, 61-79. Bison Paper 12. Winnipeg: University of Manitoba Centre for Defence and Security Studies, 2009.

−. "Guerrillas in Our Midst: The Pacific Coast Militia Rangers, 1942-45." *BC Studies* 155 (2007): 95-131.

−. "Teaching Canada's Indigenous Sovereignty Soldiers ... and Vice Versa: 'Lessons Learned' from Ranger Instructors." *Canadian Army Journal* 10, 2 (2007): 66-81.

The Canadian Rangers

Introduction

✤ CAPE ISACHSEN, ELLEF RINGES ISLAND, Nunavut, longitude 78°8' N, latitude 103°6' W, 18 April 2002. It was a biting minus thirty-six degrees Celsius with wind chill when the Canadian Forces Northern Area commander and his entourage, including me, stepped off the yellow Canadian Forces Twin Otter plane. The serious faces of twenty-nine Canadian Rangers, lined up in rows behind their snow machines, greeted us. They had just conquered the magnetic North Pole. Ten days before, these Rangers and four soldiers from 1 Canadian Ranger Patrol Group (CRPG) Headquarters in Yellowknife had left the community of Resolute Bay. Operation Kigiliqaqvik Ranger, named after the Inuktitut word for "the place at the edge of known land," covered more than 1,600 kilometres of rough sea ice, pressure ridges, rocky river valleys, and breathtaking expanses of tundra. Each Ranger drove a snow machine that pulled a sixteen-foot *komatik* (sled) laden with up to 675 kilograms of supplies. They endured wind chill temperatures below minus fifty degrees Celsius, near whiteout conditions, and twenty-four-hour sunlight.[1]

The patrol had travelled more than 800 kilometres when it was forced to stop on the sea ice north of Ellef Ringes Island. Two kilometres ahead lay a huge, impassable lead – a crack in the sea ice over 400 kilometres long and 5 kilometres wide. By attaining 79°N latitude, the expedition technically could claim that it had reached the magnetic pole – the point where Earth's magnetic field points vertically downwards, "wobbling" in an oval up to 200 kilometres in a single day. Ranger Sergeant Peter Moon reported that

[a] small iceberg was selected as the symbolic centre of the Pole and Rangers ran to it whooping and shouting and waving two big Maple Leaf and Canadian Ranger flags, as well as the flags of the three territories and their home communities. They hugged, shook hands and slapped high fives.

[Major Yves] Laroche [the commanding officer of 1 CRPG] sat quietly on his snowmobile amidst the jubilation and thought about the 18 months of planning that had gone into the event, the longest, furthest and largest sovereignty patrol in Canadian history. In a short speech to team members he said, "You know, guys, usually I don't say too much, but today is outstanding. Today, you made history. You should all be very proud."[2]

The Rangers on the patrol, all part-time members of the Canadian Forces Reserves based in communities across Canada's remote regions, expressed their excitement. These men and women, many of their weathered faces burned by frost and exposure, loved and lived the land. In this group, I saw a microcosm of northern Canada. They came in all shapes and sizes. Some were Inuit, some Dene, some White. Ranger Paul Guyot from Fort Simpson emphasized one common characteristic: "they are all tough."[3] He took me back to the tent he was sharing with three Inuit Rangers. The group exuded a spirit of camaraderie. Over bannock and cups of "cowboy coffee," visitors coming and going, the Rangers swapped stories. They told me about the trip, but the conversation soon shifted to their personal encounters with polar bears. These were stories about survival – what Margaret Atwood has identified as the dominant theme in Canadian culture and identity.[4] Lounging comfortably on a polar bear skin, despite the frigid temperature outside, I realized that the Rangers' stories were not about victimization, nor simply about surviving. These tales celebrated living on the land and waters, their homeland, as northerners and as Canadians.

The Rangers reflected on patriotism and service: "We don't want other people intruding on our land without us knowing about it," Ranger Sergeant Darrel Klemmer of Tulita explained. Operation Kigiliqaqvik Ranger demonstrated the Canadian Forces' ability to patrol the outermost reaches of the country. The exercise also offered Rangers from different areas a chance to share their experiences. "You get 30 different Rangers together and they'll have 60 different ways of doing the same thing," he noted. "But we talk about our families and our communities and tell stories of the old ways. Everybody has hunting in common. Everybody likes to hunt." Ranger Sergeant

The Rangers conquer the magnetic North Pole, 2002. Photo by Julian Tomlinson, courtesy of
1 Canadian Ranger Patrol Group

John Mitchell of Dawson observed: "the Rangers are one of the things that link the whole North."[5] A quiet patriotism underlay their statements. "It's always been a national thing, you know, to wave the Canadian flag here," Mitchell told a reporter. "I think what everybody ... got was a sort of personal understanding of sovereignty as it pertains to them. You know, it became a personal thing."[6]

The political profile and extensive media coverage of the operation highlighted the Rangers' contributions to Canadian sovereignty. While we were visiting, Prime Minister Jean Chrétien and Art Eggleton, the defence minister, telephoned from Ottawa to congratulate the Rangers on their operation.

"This sovereignty patrol is a continuing example of the service and dedication of the Canadian Rangers over the past 60 years," Eggleton told the press. "It illustrates their unique skills and vital contributions, not only to their own communities, but to Canada. Canadian Rangers, who are masters of operation in Canada's harshest environment, are an invaluable component of the Canadian Forces."[7] The media reported that the exercise provided Canada with "crucial ammunition" for its northern sovereignty disputes. "It's all about sovereignty here," Captain Rick Regan, the deputy commanding officer of 1 CRPG, explained. "The Rangers are the ones letting us know what's going on in our own backyard."[8]

This national profile revealed one face of the Canadian Rangers. Their other face was well known by the residents of the nation's sparsely settled northern coastal and isolated areas. "We rarely make notice of the Rangers, but they are the ones we see at the cenotaph every Remembrance Day. But more than sombre figures to remember the ones that have fallen, the Rangers are here to provide us all vital service," an editorial in *Nunavut News/North* noted on 18 October 1999. "When search and rescue teams are required, the Rangers are trained, ready and willing to deploy on a moment's notice. When emergency situations call for help, our Rangers are there first. We don't often notice them and we hope we never need them, but we can all sleep a little better at night knowing they're out there ready if the unexpected happens."[9]

Sombre evidence of the Rangers' contributions came on New Year's Eve 1999 in Kangiqsualujjuaq, a small village on the George River and the easternmost settlement in Nunavik. About 300 of the 650 residents attended the New Year's festivities at the Satuumavik school gymnasium, which doubled as the community's meeting hall. At midnight, everyone gathered outside the building to watch ten Rangers fire their usual ceremonial salute. Minutes later, the community returned to the gym and formed their customary circle to welcome one another into 1999. Moments after the handshake ceremony ended, they watched in horror as snow from the steep hill beside the building smashed through the wall. People frantically dug with their bare hands, trying to rescue friends and family, many of whom were buried completely by the avalanche. The local Rangers' gunshots had not caused the slide, but the Rangers were vital to the response. They helped pull dozens of injured men, women, and children from the carnage throughout the night and the following day. The deaths of four adults and five children testified to the "horrible nightmare."[10]

Despite being geographically expansive, Nunavik is a close-knit community. When Rangers from northern Quebec heard about the avalanche, they responded. Sergeant Vallee Saunders of Kuujjuaq recounted:

> Since the weather was a whiteout, we had heard the news at around 2:30 A.M. by telephone. Then at 7:30 A.M. the chief of the fire department came to my house to notify me to get my Ranger group ready to go. I started calling my patrol and I managed to get 18 of my Rangers ready by 11 A.M. Then we took a civilian aircraft and arrived there at around noon on Jan. 1.
>
> They were expecting us and a school bus picked us up at the terminal and drove us to the community centre. We saw what we had never expected to see. Many Ski-Doos were all over the place like dinky toys. I saw Ford pickup trucks crushed like sardine cans.
>
> Then we were told they had recovered six bodies but were missing three more. Even though this event was a real emotional tragedy, the people who had been digging all night were very happy to see us because we were there to help them out.
>
> We were handed shovels and we started digging. The condition of the snow was unbelievably hard because it just dropped and didn't travel a lot.
>
> We had to break the snow first to shovel it. We dug for about six hours before recovering the first body. This woman had a baby (with) her in the traditional parka for carrying a baby. Once we found the lady's body, the Surete du Quebec came in to take care of the body.
>
> We didn't proceed digging until the body was removed. We were also told she had a second baby with her. We started digging some more and about 30 to 45 minutes later we recovered the last body, the woman's second child.
>
> The experience was very hard to go through. Two Rangers from that community died in the avalanche and we all knew them.[11]

Members from eleven of the fourteen Ranger patrols in Nunavik assisted in the Kangiqsualujjuaq disaster. They controlled access to the school building, provided honour guards and security when the prime minister and the premier visited the community, carried handmade plywood coffins containing the victims, and reassured the community when weather conditions delayed funeral arrangements. Rangers from as far as Coral Harbour provided

Ranger Sergeant Vallee Saunders with Prime Minister Jean Chrétien after the 1999 avalanche. Courtesy of 2 Canadian Ranger Patrol Group

the disaster site with emergency supplies and food such as freshly harvested caribou.[12] This extraordinary cooperation resulted in the chief of the defence staff awarding 2 CRPG with a Canadian Forces Unit Commendation for their efforts.[13] More importantly, the Rangers' response to the avalanche reaffirmed their leadership role in Canada's remote communities.

SOVEREIGNTY. SECURITY. STEWARDSHIP. These terms lie at the heart of debates about Canada's contemporary Arctic policies.[14] They are also essential to understanding the Canadian Rangers and their contributions to their communities, the Canadian Forces, and their country – past and present.

Canada's extensive coastlines and vast northern expanses have presented security and sovereignty problems since the Second World War. These regions have some of the lowest population densities in the world combined with some of the most difficult climatic and physical environments in which to operate. Maintaining a conventional military presence is prohibitively expensive. As a result, the Canadian Rangers have played an important but unorthodox role in domestic defence for more than six decades. Often described as the military's "eyes and ears" in remote regions, the Rangers have come to represent an important success story for the Canadian Forces. They are a flexible, inexpensive, and culturally inclusive means of having "boots on the ground" to demonstrate sovereignty and to conduct or support domestic operations. The Rangers successfully integrate national security and sovereignty agendas with community-based activities and local stewardship. This practical partnership, rooted in traditional knowledge and skills, promotes cooperation, communal and individual empowerment, and crosscultural understanding.

This book explains how and why the Canadian Rangers took shape, how cycles of waxing and waning support influenced the form and pace of their development during the Cold War, and how the organization has grown and gained national attention over the last three decades. Defence officials defined the Canadian Ranger concept in the early postwar period and based it on the model of the Pacific Coast Militia Rangers created during the Second World War. Since 1947, popular, political, and military interest in the Rangers has mirrored surges of military interest and involvement in the North.[15] Oscillating cycles of disinterest and commitment reveal that the historical relationship between the Rangers and the military establishment was marked as much by uncertainty and neglect as by support and respect.[16]

Historian Bill Waiser reminds us that distance is both a physical reality and a state of mind. "The hard facts of distance" (both getting to and travelling in remote regions) are complemented by distance as a mental construct (the distance between the land and the observer).[17] Defence officials conceived the Canadian Rangers as an inexpensive way to carve out a military space for citizens who live in isolated coastal and northern communities and who would not otherwise be suitable for or interested in military service. The army's early expectations were low and its support limited. Over the last six decades, however, the Rangers have come to occupy a middle ground – an interactive space where residents of remote regions are actors and partners in defence rather than simple pawns of outside forces.[18] The military now understands that residents of remote regions can make meaningful contributions to both national defence and their communities, without leaving their homelands. The history of the Rangers reveals how accommodation and acceptance of cultural diversity can generate and sustain a low-cost military presence that supports sovereignty, military operations, and nation building. The Rangers represent a bridge between the military and civilian realms, spanning different physical and cultural geographies.

Although I characterize the Rangers as a postmodern military unit, they were created in the midst of Cold War modernism. They may just as easily be characterized as pre-modern citizen-soldiers, more akin to the militia of New France than to the primary reservists of the early twenty-first century.[19] The Canadian Rangers are not an anachronism, however. They are a unique form of military service created and adapted to Canada's remote regions. Their evolving roles and practices reflect the interplay between the military's expectations, practical skills, traditional knowledge, and the needs of local communities.

Defence officials and politicians have debated the Ranger concept since the early postwar period. Enduring questions help to frame this history. What should the Canadian Rangers be expected to do? Where should they be located? Who should participate? How should they be organized? And how does Ranger service fit within evolving military and civic identities?[20]

Expectations

This book reveals a long-standing debate about what the military could or should expect of the Canadian Rangers. The Rangers' basic mandate – "to provide a military presence in sparsely settled northern, coastal and isolated areas of Canada that cannot conveniently or economically be provided for by other components of the Canadian Forces" – has remained remarkably consistent since 1947. The tasks that the Rangers perform to support this mission have changed and become more complex. They focused initially on supporting national security – protecting their communities from enemy attack in the early Cold War. By the 1970s, their role dovetailed with general military responsibilities to assert Canada's sovereignty in the Arctic. Since the 1990s, the Rangers have also played a more visible nation-building and stewardship role in remote regions, particularly in Aboriginal communities.

Policy makers framed the original concept around the idea that the Rangers would be the armed forces' eyes and ears in sparsely settled regions. Postwar realities dictated new responsibilities for continental defence, and politicians and defence planners had no desire to position garrison forces across Canada's northern expanse. They sought less resource-intensive solutions. Military officials had debated the usefulness of minimally trained and largely unsupported forces even before the organization formed in 1947. The Rangers' primary role was to detect and report anything unusual while they went about their daily lives. In wartime, they would serve as coast watchers, guides, and guerrillas to prevent the enemy from securing a foothold on Canadian soil. Their tactical role was limited. Because they had no training, they would engage the enemy only until regular troops could respond. Their contribution was modest, but so was their cost. "As an exercise in risk management," one report concluded, "the establishment of the Rangers was a sound and well thought out mitigation strategy. Although the likelihood of invasion was not high, the consequences of a successful invasion were significant."[21]

The early debates about whether the Rangers should focus on surveillance and reconnaissance or be trained in guerrilla tactics and equipped for combat persist. Even though senior decision makers repeatedly denied that the Canadian Rangers resurrected the wartime Pacific Coast Militia Rangers, the Canadian Army's Western Command pushed for a strong operational and tactical role throughout the 1950s. By contrast, liaison officers in Quebec and Eastern Commands worried about a combat emphasis, believing that this would set up false expectations about the organization's purpose and capability. Instead, they emphasized grassroots surveillance and reconnaissance.

These debates were unique to the Rangers, but they paralleled the experiences of other formations within the armed forces. Military historian Bernd Horn's analysis of Canada's airborne forces in the early Cold War offers some striking similarities with the early history of the Rangers. To "defend against help" from its American neighbour, Canada had to show that it was capable of guarding the northern approaches to the continent against an ill-defined Soviet threat. The Mobile Striking Force offered an inexpensive solution to Canada's sovereignty and security problem, but the paltry resources dedicated to manpower and training made it a paper tiger. In due course, the government's inability to rationalize the role, structure, and relevance of airborne forces contributed to their decline after political and military leaders downgraded the idea of the North as a gateway to invasion in the mid-1950s.[22]

The Rangers faced similar problems, and the lack of a clear, credible requirement led to the organization's decline in the 1960s. As the nature of the nuclear threat shifted, so did perceptions about what citizens and soldiers could contribute to defence. The military value of the Rangers' surveillance and tactical roles became less apparent, paralleling trends in Canadian militia service and civil defence planning more generally. Training regimens, which focused on national survival tasks, proved unpopular, and the bureaucratization of civil defence planning pushed out grassroots community organizations.[23] The Rangers' practical roles as coast watchers, advisers, and guides to the military remained, particularly along the Atlantic coast. By the 1970s, however, officials gave more weight to their importance as a simple military presence in northern regions than to their potential to engage a foreign adversary with guerrilla tactics.

The Rangers, as Canadians representing the military in remote parts of the country, had always served an implicit sovereignty function. The government's growing preoccupation with the need for a symbolic military presence in support of sovereignty accentuated this role. The Rangers provided an inexpensive answer to the government's perceived lack of "boots on the ground." To claim sovereignty, popular logic suggested, a government must know what is happening in its territory and be able to respond when required. When Canadians worried about sovereignty over the Arctic, the Rangers offered a fitting example of control over isolated areas through their presence and as advisers to southern troops sent to demonstrate "effective occupation."[24]

Critical theory that broadens and deepens the definition of security and acknowledges discursive, temporal, and cultural contexts also helps to explain the Rangers' growth and success in recent decades.[25] In the 1970s, Nils Ørvik drew a link between northern development issues and the military, economic, and political components of security. He outlined the need for governments to respond to northern Aboriginal peoples' desire to achieve "equality" with southern Canadians while implementing development "methods and measures that could prevent a general adoption of the southern model from disrupting or destroying the values and traditions of the native society." A decentralized approach would allow northern peoples to stay close to their lands and maintain their identity (and thus their personal security), but it would also entail additional money.[26] Although his work focused on resource and political development, his articulation of security concerns beyond the narrow realm of military confrontation sheds light on the sociopolitical climate of the Canadian North and provides a useful theoretical and contextual framework for assessing military activities.

Ørvik's insights have particular relevance when applied to the post–Cold War period. In the late 1990s, Arctic security issues changed significantly. The effects of military operations on northern peoples and ecology became central considerations, and Canadian defence activities in the Arctic focused on sovereignty rather than on conventional military security.[27] Debates about the militarization of the Arctic illuminated its damaging effects, and policy makers could no longer ignore the human-security dimensions of their decisions. Canada's unofficial security discourse shifted from defending the integrity of the nation-state to protecting essential individual and group rights.[28] This shift helps explain why sociopolitical and human-security considerations validated the expansion of the Canadian Rangers in remote regions alongside commitments to traditional security and sovereignty.

While the Canadian Rangers were increasingly celebrated as sovereignty soldiers, military officials, journalists, and politicians began to acknowledge in the late 1980s that they also had a social impact that extended beyond their military presence. Many Rangers enjoyed prominent positions within their communities, which respected and valued the patrols as grassroots organizations that provided essential services in cases of emergency. Rangers regularly took leadership roles in local search-and-rescue activities and were held up as role models. Most surprisingly, given the popular assumption that military activities pose a threat to Aboriginal people and their homelands, Aboriginal leaders repeatedly acknowledged that the Rangers contributed to healthy communities.[29] The creation of the Junior Canadian Rangers in 1998 formalized the organization's nation-building role by using the Rangers to support a culturally appropriate youth program in remote communities.

Ongoing debates about the appropriateness of the Rangers' role and responsibilities reflect the relative weight that commentators give to the organization's operational and representational functions.[30] They value the Rangers for their military contributions to sovereignty, national security, and domestic operations, and some pundits believe that they should have more formal military training and responsibilities to ward off potential enemies. Other commentators believe that the Ranger's sociopolitical value is paramount and that resources should be redirected to enhance their contributions to Aboriginal communities.

Location

The mystique of the "Arctic Ranger" – a misnomer popularized by ill-conceived political statements in recent years – has dominated media and policy debates since the 1970s.[31] The Canadian Rangers, however, have a presence from coast to coast to coast and throughout the provincial norths. Over the years, the Rangers' geographical parameters – "sparsely settled northern, coastal and isolated areas" – have been interpreted in different ways by different people in different contexts. Simply looking at the Rangers as an Arctic organization obfuscates much of their history.

In an important think piece, historian Ken Coates advocates reconceptualizing the study of the Canadian North by focusing more broadly on remote regions. In sharing the fundamental characteristic of remoteness, coastal areas and communities beyond the main population belt, whether northern or non-northern, share "a particular set of structural relationships with the dominant sources of power" not defined by latitude.[32] This insight is particularly appropriate to the history of the Rangers, which does not conform to a fixed, unchanging geographical conceptualization of "the North" or "remoteness."

There is no single definition of *Arctic, North,* or *remote regions* (see the note on terminology at the end of this introduction). Geographer William Wonders observed that a "long-established practice by governments of arbitrarily selecting a particular degree of latitude to define the North still continues despite its artificiality." Nationally, the southern boundaries of the northern territories were set at latitude 60° north. Provincial definitions usually begin their "norths" at latitude 55° north. Even dividing the North into Arctic and Subarctic components oversimplifies tremendous physical and cultural diversity.[33] Louis-Edmond Hamelin's regionalization of the North and measures of nordicity create mental maps in which to situate the Rangers' expansion throughout the Middle, Far, and Extreme Norths over the last seven decades.[34] Scholarship on the northern territories as Canada's colonies and as the provinces' forgotten norths also help to place the Rangers' history in appropriate regional contexts.[35]

The Canadian Rangers provide a military presence along Canada's three coastlines. The Pacific, Arctic, and Atlantic seaboards are diverse, yet coastal communities share commonalities – with one another and with isolated northern communities. The Coasts Under Stress research team recently observed that coasts represent cultural, political, and ecological edges, boundaries, or interfaces depending on the perspective of the viewer. Coastal residents, from their "peripheral" location, produce information that is distinct from perspectives emanating from the continental or political centre. They also face daunting challenges as members of distressed, staple-based communities that are highly vulnerable to external pressures.[36] Fortunately, important studies on Quebec's Lower North Shore, outport Newfoundland and Labrador, and BC's remote coastal areas help situate the Rangers' evolution in temporal- and place-specific contexts.[37]

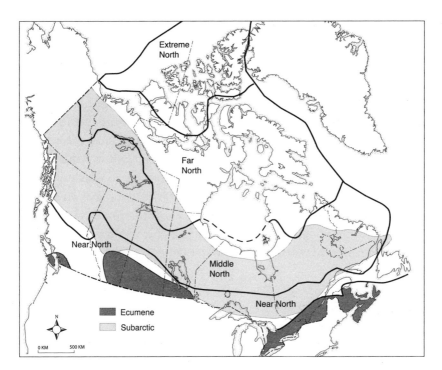

Louis-Edmond Hamelin's Canadian Nordicity Index and the three northern zones

Sources: Based on Robert Bone, *The Geography of the Canadian North: Issues and Challenges* (Toronto: Oxford, 1992) and Louis-Edmond Hamelin, *Canadian Nordicity: It's Your North Too,* trans. by W. Barr (Montreal: Harvest House, 1978)

Although national in scope, the Rangers have developed distinct regional and local cultures. The Pacific Coast Militia Rangers flourished in British Columbia and Yukon during the Second World War, which explains why Western Command created the first peacetime Ranger units. Distinct approaches to organizing units and the roles assigned to them reflected the priorities of regional army commanders, demographic and socioeconomic realities, and geographical constraints. By the 1950s, the Ranger footprint extended across the territorial and provincial norths, along the Newfoundland coastline, and into the High Arctic. Limited resources exacerbated challenges related to organizing units and sustaining relationships. Regional commanders supported the Ranger units with varying degrees of commitment, and local activities and success depended upon the company or platoon commander's initiative and creativity.

The Ranger organization contracted in the 1960s and early '70s, when it was divided between a new Northern Region Headquarters in Yellowknife and Maritime Command (the navy) in Halifax. The composition of Ranger patrols in Northern Region became increasingly Aboriginal and focused on sovereignty while the predominantly non-Aboriginal companies and platoons of Maritime Command concentrated on coast watching. When another Arctic sovereignty crisis renewed interest in the Rangers in the 1980s and prompted expansion, military officials debated whether growth should be directed North of 60 (where they believed the Rangers had a clear operational role in support of sovereignty) or South of 60 (where Rangers were making visible sociopolitical contributions). Despite the popular association of the Rangers with Inuit, the most vigorous growth in the last two decades occurred with the re-creation of the Rangers in British Columbia, northern Ontario, and in the northern prairie provinces. This expansion has enriched the demographic diversity of the organization.

Participation

Participation in the Rangers offers an alternative form of military service to those Canadians who live in remote areas, do not want to join the Regular Force, but still want to serve their country and their communities. The perceived military value of Rangers has always been linked to civilian experiences and practices. The basic premise is to recruit individuals who have lived in an area for a long time; who are intimately familiar with the local people, terrain, and weather conditions; and who possess skills and expert local knowledge.[38] There is no upper age limit so long as the recruits can perform their duties. The army will not deploy Rangers overseas and does not expect them to serve outside of their local areas (with some recent qualifications). This makes Ranger service distinct from Regular Force and Primary Reserve Force units.

The media overwhelmingly associates the Canadian Rangers with romantic stereotypes of Inuit hunter-trappers patriotically defending their homeland. Although true in many contexts, this book contextualizes this popular imagery by explaining how and why it became politically relevant and important. The iconic status of Inuit in the Rangers has generated a persistent misconception – perpetuated through the media and political statements – of the Rangers as an Aboriginal *program*. In reality, the Rangers are a subcomponent of the Canadian Forces Reserves with a high degree of Aboriginal participation. Most Rangers today are of Aboriginal descent, but until the 1980s the majority were not. Misrepresenting the organization as an Aboriginal program fails to acknowledge the diversity of the Rangers and their historical experiences.

The military's evolving perceptions about the contributions that Aboriginal people in remote regions can make to national defence correspond with an expanding literature on indigenous people and military service in the twentieth century. Although the Rangers' history includes some examples of racism, marginalization, and neglect,[39] the dominant narrative reveals a growing military acceptance of Aboriginal people and their role in defending Canada and asserting sovereignty. In her study of military workfare in Canada, geographer Deborah Cowen observes a "shift from an explicitly colonial project of civilizing or 'integrating Indians,' to a complicated military mobilization of social justice discourse and specific celebration of Native rights and tradition in order to increase enrolment."[40] This observation applies to the Rangers, but in this case the military made no sustained attempt to acculturate Aboriginal people. Early critics, particularly Major-General Chris Vokes, questioned whether First Nations and Inuit could make a meaningful contribution to the military. Other officers supported Aboriginal involvement (generally under non-Aboriginal leadership) because they recognized the value of traditional knowledge, survival skills, and land use patterns. Close observers such as Captain Ambrose Shea in Eastern Command embraced this "otherness" and promoted Ranger service as a culturally appropriate way to sustain a military presence in remote communities.

New sovereignty and security discourses made efforts to accommodate Aboriginal peoples in the armed forces all the more significant by the late 1970s. During exercises, military officials saw the operational value of traditional skills. They began to see diversity as a force multiplier – a way to increase a combat force's operational effectiveness – rather than as a liability.[41] Over the last three decades, this acceptance of diversity has allowed the Rangers to flourish in remote regions and has attracted significant positive media attention for the military. Acceptance not only fosters positive Aboriginal-military relations but also allows the Rangers to support self-governing and sustainable communities in unexpected ways.[42]

As the Aboriginal profile of the Rangers has grown, non-Aboriginal contributions to the organization – particularly in British Columbia and Yukon, along the Lower North Shore, and in Newfoundland – have been pushed to the margins of popular awareness. This shift reflects larger political and historiographical trends. Efforts to write Aboriginal people into regional histories have unfortunately led scholars to downplay other residents, and studies of non-Aboriginal people in remote regions have declined precipitously in recent decades.[43] As historical geographer Rosemary Ommer reminds us, remote coastal communities are also homelands to a diverse non-Aboriginal population with a strong sense of place.[44]

Ken Coates observes that northern or remote regions are characterized by "a culture of opposition" that prevents networks of support from developing both within and outside of the region. Theoretical approaches that emphasize core-periphery relations predict that powerful agents of external control will dictate the future of remote areas.[45] Although defence officials in Ottawa and in regional headquarters factor heavily into this study, they are not the whole story. Rangers have never been coerced into service, cannot be employed against their will, and have leveraged their own social power to negotiate a distinctive place within the military system.[46] If there is little conceptual space in the existing literature for intimate co-operation between residents of remote regions and the Canadian state, as Coates suggests, the history of the Canadian Rangers reveals a more positive picture.

Organization

The unique organizational forms that the Canadian Rangers have assumed reflect dynamics at (and across) national, regional, and local levels.[47] On the national scale, political and military priorities have always shaped the Rangers. Politicians set the broad political direction for the military, determine budgets, and help to frame popular expectations for the armed forces. In this particular case, general threat assessments and high-level political and military decisions about how much interest and effort the military should devote to the defence of remote regions had a direct bearing on expansion and enhancement plans. Since 1994, political and national media interest in the Rangers has ensured sustained growth, with emphasis on Aboriginal service. Broader efforts to restructure the military in light of shifting geopolitical, economic, technological, and sociocultural environments also influenced the form and pace of Ranger development.

At National Defence Headquarters, senior officials have long deliberated over where the Rangers fit into the broader direction of national defence and how the organization can meet operational and political objectives without draining budgets or losing overall coherence. Various organizations have executed command and control of the Canadian Rangers since 1947: the army; Maritime Command (the navy) and Northern Region Headquarters/ Canadian Forces Northern Area; the vice chief of the defence staff through the Land Force Areas; and, recently, the chief of the land staff. In practice, central authorities devolved responsibilities for the Rangers to the regional level, where area commanders charted the course for their companies, platoons, and patrols with shoestring budgets and little national direction.

This book devotes significant attention to regional developments in order to reflect the Rangers' decentralized nature. National authorities intervened in debates about the Rangers' role and policy, but they recognized that a one-size-fits-all mentality would suffocate the regional commanders' ability to generate and sustain the Rangers' interest in their area. Officers outside of the national capital therefore had ample creative leeway to interpret national directives. This flexibility accommodated diverse human and physical geographies, and over time it allowed training and operations to adapt to local conditions and priorities. Contrary to the common notion that decentralized, community-based partnerships in remote regions are prohibitively costly, the Rangers were inexpensive compared to other military options. The formal reorganization of regional elements into Canadian Ranger Patrol Groups in 1998 marked a continuation of this long-standing regional evolution, and the groups remain in place today.

This decentralized approach has, however, generated concerns that the Rangers lack coherence as a national organization. Rigid management and the misalignment of structure and socio-environmental realities can lead to an organization's decline or collapse. Unfettered growth and liberal interpretation and implementation of mandates when there is no central coordination and stability can be equally damaging. A military review noted in 2003 that, over the preceding six decades, the Rangers had spent more time "as a number of regional entities than as a national program. Patrol Groups were simply set up to suit their own natural environment, cultural makeup, operational needs and political situation at the time." Although many of these differences were, according to the review, perfectly valid (particularly the accommodation of cultural differences), in other cases regional commanders had simply taken "different paths to achieve an end or have interpreted guidelines or even directives differently."[48] The challenge has been in balancing flexibility and diversity with coherent direction and constraints to preserve the credibility and sustainability of the overall organization.

At its core, the Canadian Ranger organization is rooted in human relationships. Ranger instructors and Ranger liaison officers have provided the critical link between the military hierarchy and the Rangers since the 1950s. They have translated vague directions into practical training programs adapted to local conditions, responded to evolving sociocultural and operational needs, and ensured that the military has credibility at the grassroots level. With few military resources dedicated to the organization, their bottom-up approach to building and sustaining relationships with local communities has been essential to its success.

The Rangers must be understood as both a local, grassroots force and as a nationally or regionally directed military formation. The organization has changed over time, yet the basic principle of rooting it in local populations has remained constant. The original company-platoon structure, overseen by officers from the local area, reflected a traditional military structure – on paper. In practice, however, the characteristics of local leadership, widely dispersed units, and loose relationships with the military hierarchy proved highly unorthodox. As northern and coastal residents concentrated into settlements, the Rangers developed a simplified patrol structure. This structure encouraged community-based stewardship, ensuring that military practices reflected the needs, aspirations, and values of local people.

The Canadian Rangers have no parallel in the military world. Other countries have created unconventional military units to defend remote regions, but most are formally trained and serve requirements more comparable to Canada's Regular or Primary Reserve Forces than the Rangers.[49] This uniqueness means that the Rangers remain an enigma to defence planners who do not comprehend why or how they have taken their particular form. Repeated attempts to reconstitute the organization into a typical or formal military structure have been stymied by fiscal constraints, high-level military restructuring, and debates about feasibility and desirability. Consequently, most organizational change has been incremental and slow. Although unintentional, this pace allowed the Rangers to develop an inclusive governance structure that balances national and regional direction from headquarters staff with elected leadership at the patrol level. The ongoing search for balance between local, regional, and national priorities allows the Canadian Rangers to operate simultaneously on multiple scales, in ways that most casual commentators pushing for "modernization" fail to appreciate.

Ranger Service and Evolving Military and Civic Identities

Hedda Schuurman defines community as a conscious bond that unites people with shared traditions such as experience or language. Community is also "a consciousness that motivates people to work for a common good."[50] Over time, the Rangers have formed a unique community. How and why did this occur, and what are the ties that bind them to the Canadian Forces and the Canadian state, given the culture of opposition prevalent in remote regions? How do the Rangers fit within the broader military community and, in turn, how does the military fit within the broader network of societal relations in remote regions?

The relationship between civilians (people without arms who constitute a society at large) and the military (people with arms established as a separate body to protect that society) in Western democracies has been influenced by national history, sentiment, and tradition. Sociologist Giuseppe Caforio notes that, for centuries, "the military world and the military mind-set have constituted a quite different, quite separate environment from other institutions, groups, and aggregates of civil society, and in part they still do."[51] Proponents of a divergence model insist on the need for a sharp distinction between civilian (political) and military (apolitical) spheres: military power must be contained so that instruments of state-sanctioned violence remain in the hands of legitimate civilian authorities who govern according to democratic principles.[52] Other scholars promote a convergence model that draws the military closer to mainstream society as it incorporates broadly accepted social values. Through this process, military organizations become more decentralized and have more autonomous commands at lower levels.[53] Proponents of a segmented model try to bridge the divide between the divergence and convergence models by characterizing modern militaries as pluralistic organisms in which sectors bearing characteristics of civil society coexist with sectors that preserve a more traditional military *habitus*.[54] This long-standing debate raises questions about how cultural values, attitudes and symbols inform not only the nation's view of military roles but also the military's own view of that role. How do citizens interact with the military? Is there agreement over the role of the military in society?[55]

This book carries the study of civil-military relations beyond the national centre by exploring military engagements with civil society in remote regions. The Rangers' place in broader defence planning and practices partly reflects broader perceptions about professional soldiers and amateur *citizen-soldiers* in modern Canada.[56] The emergence of a profession of arms in the nineteenth century, in which the state trained full-time soldiers to provide it with specialized services, explains why scholarly debates on civil-military relations deal primarily with political power and the relationship between the state and the professional officer corps.[57] Less work has been dedicated to amateur forces – the militia and other reservists.

Historian James Wood argues that Canada's militia myth, created in the aftermath of the War of 1812, "fostered a sense of complacency on the part of the Canadian people" that lasted more than a century. According to this logic, ordinary Canadians would simply volunteer, take up arms as citizen-soldiers, and meet any military crisis. This mentality survived the Great War and the interwar period but died during the Second World War and Cold War. "In an era when 'the next war' was likely to be won or lost in a matter of weeks rather than years," Wood explains, historians (and professional soldiers) found the militia myth dangerous. Consequently, they tended to depict "amateur soldiers as slightly comical anachronisms, holdovers from an earlier, pre-industrial era when war could be approached as a hobby or seasonal occupation."[58] Scholars, preoccupied with military professionalism, overlooked reservists – particularly peculiar subcomponents such as the Canadian Rangers.

In the late 1980s, sociologist Terrence Willett examined this bias towards professionalism, which downplayed the connection between reservists and their local cultures and communities. In his assessment, the Canadian Forces Reserves are a social and civic institution on par with full-time professional soldiers. In some situations, reservists could contribute more than Regular Forces because of their knowledge of and links to their host community. Although professional soldiers often dismiss social defence roles such as responding to natural disasters and other crises as if they are not "proper soldiering," these responsibilities expose soldiers to the same risks and stresses they would encounter in wartime and reinforce the public's perceptions that "a useful body of disciplined men [and women]" has civic relevance at home.[59]

If reservists are citizen-soldiers who embody the link or bridge between the military and civil society,[60] then their perception of where they fit within Canada is integral to understanding their sense of patriotism and civic responsibility. Political scientist Alan Cairns emphasizes the centrality of citizenship to the modern democratic state. He describes citizenship as an instrument that socializes individuals to take ownership of the state, support it, and grant it legitimacy.[61] Other scholars have observed how conceptions of citizenship have broadened from the political to include economic and social dimensions (emphasizing rights rather than obligations), and they have noted the effects of diversity and pluralism on feelings of solidarity, social harmony, and civility.[62] These broader societal trends have shaped how politicians, defence officials, community members, and the Rangers themselves understand the Canadian Rangers' role.

Modern military institutions are quintessentially assimilationist. Uniforms, systems of rank and promotion, and standardized training-and-operating procedures reinforce hierarchy and collective identity. Traditional military socialization seeks to supplant individual difference with a sense of shared loyalty and commitment to the traditions of the unit and the nation.[63] The Canadian Rangers do not fit this description and require a different analytical framework. Military sociologists Charles Moskos, J.A. Williams, and David Segal ascribe five fundamental characteristics to postmodern militaries. First, the civilian and military spheres interact on the structural and cultural levels. Second, postmodern militaries place less emphasis or differentiation on service, rank, and specialization. Third, missions focus less on combat and more on low-intensity humanitarian and constabulary missions. Fourth, postmodern forces carry out missions with multilateral rather than unilateral authorization. This idea extends to the fifth characteristic: the internationalization of military forces.[64]

Applying these theoretical traits to a domestic-oriented force such as the Canadian Rangers requires creative interpretation, but these traits do help to explain the organization's vitality and success in recent decades. The Rangers' history certainly reveals the permeability of the civil and military structures, the erosion of martial values, and the degree to which democratization has been driven by internal rather than external considerations.[65] The organization does not divorce defence and security activities from cultural survival, sustainable community development, and civic or indigenous rights. If traditional theory typically casts military service as "selective, exclusive, and high normalizing in its sweep,"[66] the Rangers stand as an important exception, blurring the line between the citizen-soldier and the citizen-server.[67]

As Canada's political self-image has shifted to a multicultural mosaic, military personnel policies have changed accordingly.[68] Cowen observes that "efforts to moderate the demands of discipline, conformity, and even nationalism have been under way, and new images of military service have been constructed on the grounds of global justice, multicultural leadership, and service to self through education and improvement."[69] Strategic documents emphasize that the Canadian Forces must be a visible national institution, one that reflects the country's geographic and cultural diversity.[70] If cultural pluralism is now the main criterion by which to judge the acceptability of the armed forces' social composition,[71] the Canadian Rangers fare very well.

Accommodating and accepting pluralism also implies official recognition that "identities are not like hats" – people wear multiple identities at the same time. In addition to national identities, people often have limited ones that are local or regional or that reflect ethnic, gender, occupation or class, and familial or clan affiliations.[72] By encouraging Canadian Rangers to function in a manner appropriate to diverse cultural and environmental conditions, the military has accommodated local and individual identities. The organization also reflects regional identities in its training, operations, command structure, liaison efforts, and representational activities. The over-arching national identity of the Canadian Rangers is more elusive: a cliché such as "Unity in Diversity" may apply best.[73]

Multiple imagined communities can, fortunately, occupy the same space simultaneously. In *A Genealogy of Sovereignty,* Jens Bartelson explains that sovereignty has both external and internal dimensions – it can signify something over a territory and within a given territory. As the parergonal divide between the international and the domestic spheres becomes increasingly blurred, it is difficult to classify phenomena as either inside or outside of the state.[74] Aboriginal self-government, for example, blurs the lines between governmental and "national" jurisdictions within the country. Although the Rangers do not constitute an Aboriginal program, they represent an important example of intertwined categories and contexts of citizenship, belonging, and identity. Mary Simon, speaking as a representative of Inuit Tapirisat of Canada in 1994, stressed that "the Inuit agenda for the exercise of our right to self-determination is not to secede or separate from Canada but rather that we wish to share a common citizenship with other Canadians while maintaining our identity as a people, which means maintaining our identity as Inuit."[75] When Rangers set out on exercises, they represent both their local and regional communities and the Canadian Forces.

Although the high rate of Aboriginal membership in the Canadian Rangers is well known, scholars have not explored its broader significance. They typically depict Aboriginal peoples' relations with the state as power contests. Anthropologist Paul Nadasdy warns that even current efforts to restructure Aboriginal-state relations, which appear empowering, may have the opposite effect, "replacing local Aboriginal ways of talking, thinking, and acting with those specifically sanctioned by the state."[76] Echoing the final report of the Royal Commission on Aboriginal Peoples, many commentators insist that the federal government should adopt a "two row wampum" model in which Aboriginal nations are treated as distinct from the Canadian citizenry.[77] With little common ground connecting Aboriginal peoples to Canadians, anthropologist Colin Scott insists that "the goal must be the creation of autonomous spaces within which Aboriginal peoples can give full play to their own cultural dynamics, reproduce their own social orders, and engage in innovations according to their own cultural genius." This framework emphasizes the capacity of Aboriginal communities "for solid resistance and sustained action."[78] Scholars such as Taiaiake Alfred, who hold up warriors resisting the Canadian state as authentic, organic expressions of timeless indigenous values,[79] simply deny legitimacy to Aboriginal people who participate with the state.[80]

A framework that privileges autonomy and denies the possibility of complex Aboriginal identities that include Canadian citizenship cannot explain the Canadian Rangers' success or even its very existence. The "citizens plus" school, first articulated by the Hawthorn-Tremblay Report in the mid-1960s, offers a more useful framework to explain the organization's success.[81] Rejecting assimilation as a policy goal, the report proposed that Indians should instead be regarded as citizens plus, as "charter members of the Canadian community" who could benefit from Canadian citizenship while also maintaining rights guaranteed through Indian status and treaty arrangements.[82] Proponents of a citizens plus approach recognize the need for Aboriginal nations to govern themselves within Canada rather than to see themselves as international actors interacting with a foreign state.[83]

In essence, the Canadian Rangers have become *citizen-soldiers plus* – members of the Canadian Forces who serve in their home areas with no expectation that they sacrifice their cultural and political identities. This book traces how the Rangers evolved to serve a vital function in remote communities, a function that transcends military, sociopolitical, economic, and cultural realms. Their history reveals that military activities designed to assert sovereignty need not cause insecurity for Aboriginal peoples. Managed on a community scale, a Ranger patrol draws on the indigenous knowledge of its members rather than "militarizing" and conditioning them through conventional training regimes. Flexible, cost-effective, and culturally inclusive, the Canadian Rangers support sustainable Aboriginal communities.

Discussions of Aboriginal-state friction, which dominate most theoretically oriented scholarship, are strikingly absent in documents and oral testimonies pertaining to the Rangers. Rangers are not simply a counterhegemonic response to hegemonic forms; instead, the organization accommodates diverse social and political orders and encourages its members to exercise their culture-based rights in a modern context.[84]

In her landmark book *Ethnic Soldiers,* Cynthia Enloe explores how states use ethnicity to maintain political order and authority by manipulating the form and conditions of military service. Even though authorities publicly deplore ethnic divisions, she argues, they exploit them militarily.[85] By contrast, the history of the Rangers suggests an acceptance (rather than a conspiratorial exploitation) of diversity. When, why, and how did the Canadian Ranger organization develop into a middle ground – a civil-military community – embraced by residents of remote regions as a source of connectedness to one another, to the Canadian Forces, and to the Canadian state? Their unique form of military service, which has evolved since the origins of the Pacific Coast Militia Rangers during the dark days of the Second World War, extends across Canada from coast to coast to coast. At the magnetic North Pole in 2002, Ranger Sergeant Darrel Klemmer emphasized that the Rangers had much in common, regardless of whether they called the forest or the bush, the Subarctic or the treeless tundra home. Ranger Sergeant John Mitchell agreed that the Rangers linked not only the whole North but also northerners with the south. "People don't realize how far we are from the nation's capital," he explained, standing at one of the remotest reaches of Canada's High Arctic. "The Rangers make you feel more like you're a Canadian."[86]

A Note on Terminology

For the purposes of this book, *Arctic* has two meanings. Geographically, the region encompasses the territory and permanent ice north of the treeline, which roughly corresponds to Inuit Nunangat – the homeland of Canada's Inuit, comprising the land and marine areas of the Nunatsiavut, Nunavik, Nunavut, and Inuvialuit land claims settlement areas.[87] This area includes the Arctic Archipelago, the islands and waters that lie to the north of the Canadian mainland. Politically and militarily, the term *Arctic* refers to either this topographical or cultural area or to Canada's Territorial North (Yukon, Northwest Territories, and Nunavut – also referred to as "North of 60").[88]

The phrase *the North* is more inclusive than *the Arctic* and is used in various senses. The Canadian North includes the territories and the northern regions of British Columbia, Alberta, Saskatchewan, Manitoba, Ontario, Quebec, and Labrador. In this book, the term *northerners* includes the people of Yukon, Northwest Territories, Nunavut, and (where stated) Nunavik and Labrador.

I adopt the generic term *Aboriginal peoples* to refer collectively to the three groups recognized in the Constitution Act, 1982: Indians (Status, Non-status, and treaty), Inuit, and Metis. I use the term *Aboriginal peoples* synonymously with *Native peoples* and *indigenous peoples*. Military and civilian officials used the term *Indian* in accordance with the Indian Act and the Constitution. Given the stereotypes and ideological baggage associated with the term, people replaced *Indian* with *Native* and then *First Nation(s)* to refer to both individuals and groups (previously bands or tribes). *Eskimo* is now considered pejorative in many circles (being associated with the discredited etymology "one who eats raw flesh") and has been replaced by *Inuit* (the people) in Canada and Greenland. *Eskimo* is still used in parts of Alaska and in anthropological and archaeological contexts.[89] I adopt language consistent with the documentary record, particularly in direct quotes, as well as current and preferred terms. Geographical names reflect those used during the periods under study, supplemented in parenthesis (where appropriate) with current names. Although changing nomenclature may confuse the reader, the process of renaming communities reflects evolving political and social identities.[90]

I also use military terminology appropriate to its historical context. The generic term *Regular Forces* refers to Canada's full-time professional military forces. The land force components have been called the Canadian Army Active Force (Active Army), Canadian Army (Regular), Forces Mobile Command, Land Force Command, and the Canadian Army. *Reserves* or *reservists* refers to part-time components of the Canadian Forces. The term *Primary Reserve* refers to soldiers, sailors, and air personnel who are trained to the level of their Regular Force counterparts. The term *militia* refers to the land forces (army) reserves. Area or regional commands also changed over time. For example, the Canadian Army regional command structure changed after the creation of Mobile Command in 1964. Land force area commands, comprising all regular and reserve army units, were created in 1991 in anticipation of the reorganization of the Canadian Forces in 1997 and the creation of Land Force Command. Since the creation of Canada Command in 2006, land force areas are co-located with regional Joint Task Force Headquarters, responsible for coordinating all army, air force, and navy components in domestic and continental operations. In another example, Northern Region Headquarters in Yellowknife became Canadian Forces Northern Area in 1992 and Joint Task Force (North) in 2006.

1

The Pacific Coast Militia Rangers, 1942-45

He's so gaunt and old that he walks like a wishbone. His suit bags. His white mustaches are the "Alf and 'Arry" kind.

But he topped the rocky ledge ahead of me like a goat. Below us lay the wildest country on this continent: British Columbia. Deep canyons, tangled forests, no roads. We'd come up an old Indian trail.

"You see, Ma'm," he said, "the ruddy little Japs could never make it. You'd pick off a hundred yourself from this ledge, – and you could stop for tea, at that ... Let 'em come. Hit'd be the second time I was servin' 'Er Majesty." That's Victoria to you. He likes to pretend she's still around because he was in her Royal Horse Artillery, Boer War. He's 75. But a recent Sunday at the Rifle Club he popped the bull's eye 92 out of 100. He's never dimmed his eyes with a lot of needless reading.

Now he's one of the Pacific Coast Militia Rangers – the oddest "army" on the Continent.

– "BC Has 6,000 Rangers Ready to Welcome Japs,"
Vancouver Daily Province, 22 May 1942

✤ If war came in the Pacific, William Strange explained in his 1937 book *Canada, the Pacific and War,* Canada would be involved by virtue of its ties to the United States and Britain. Geography and history determined Canada's fate in more ways than one. "The best defence of the Canadian Pacific Coast, beyond doubt, is the nature of the coast itself," he consoled readers. "It is extremely rugged. It possesses an intricate system of islands and channels, and the tide-rips are treacherous. To shoreward the country is difficult to the point of seemed impregnability."[1] Indeed, British Columbians – like most Canadians at the time – viewed their country, to borrow Senator Raoul Dandurand's famous phrase, as a "fireproof house far from inflammable materials." Canadians supported their prime minister and British leaders' appeasement strategy. The best defence was to simply avoid war, and Canadians celebrated their successful coexistence with the United States as a model for the world.

The winds of war were too strong, however, and they blew through Canada in early September 1939. The so-called Phony War in Europe precluded an immediate threat to North America, but Prime Minister William Lyon Mackenzie King's limited-liability war effort died with the Nazi conquest of western Europe in mid-1940. As Britain braced for invasion, concerned citizens across Canada formed local volunteer units to defend their communities against sabotage or invasion. These paramilitary organizations had no official military status or support, but their establishment highlighted Canadians' desire for active, practical measures to protect their homeland.[2] After all, private citizens preparing to ward off invasion had a long history in Britain, and irregular forces such as frontier rangers were entrenched in North American military lore.[3] British Columbians had organized paramilitary groups in the past, and thousands had served as part-time citizen-soldiers in reserve units before the war. The temperament of the population outside of urban areas, however, precluded formal militia participation. Most men who worked in staple industries such as forestry, fishing, and mining could not gather for summer training, and they found the idea of rigid discipline particularly unappealing and unsuited to frontier conditions.[4] Although the idea of a citizenry at arms seemed anachronistic, given modern military technology and tactics, it appealed to a society haunted by the spectre of spies, saboteurs, and Asian hordes waiting to flood their homeland.[5]

In 1941, Axis advances in the Far East drew the attention of defence planners to British Columbia. By October, the Canadian military had established a single Pacific Command to oversee operations in British Columbia, Alberta, Yukon, and the District of Mackenzie. Journalists speculated about the prospects of a Japanese offensive in the southwest Pacific and even aggression in the North. The chief of the general staff in Ottawa assured the minister of national defence that if war broke out with Japan, the forces on the Pacific Coast would be "adequate for the purpose of meeting the anticipated forms and scales of attack."[6] Defence officials stationed infantry battalions in Prince Rupert, New Westminster–Vancouver, and Victoria-Esquimalt; established a general reserve at Nanaimo; and placed Veterans Guard platoons at Royal Canadian Air Force (RCAF) bases on the Coast.[7] When Japan began offensive operations in December 1941, concerned citizens worried that these forces would not meet their security needs. Popular pressure, not military threat assessments, forced the hand of politicians in Ottawa.

If the threat of Japanese forces establishing themselves in North America was "far-fetched militarily," it was also "politically all too real."[8] Coastal air raid precautions suddenly seemed inadequate. Daily headlines about Japanese forces overwhelming Allied possessions in Southeast Asia fuelled fears. The navy expanded the Fishermen's Reserve Service (known popularly as the Gumboot Navy), a reserve unit of volunteer fishers who conducted patrols in their own vessels along the Coast.[9] Citizens covered their windows and shut off their lights, businesses shut their doors early, and radio stations went off the air to hinder navigation by a would-be invasion force. Victoria's mayor reported that the Japanese were off the Aleutian coast (long before the Japanese actually captured Attu and Kiska in June 1942) and warned of imminent invasion.[10]

Popular Demand for BC Defences

In early 1942, the unthinkable occurred: Britain's Asian colonies fell. Parliamentarians such as Howard Green observed that Japan had gained control of the Pacific in seven weeks, and he predicted bombings and an invasion of British Columbia. With only unarmed reservists providing security, he warned, the generals would be forced to surrender the Coast and its people unless the federal government bolstered its defences and organized home guards. Although the chiefs of staff believed that the Japanese could mount nothing more than hit-and-run raids, the prime minister was besieged by editorials, letters from citizens, and citizens' defence committee resolutions demanding action.[11] British Columbians flocked to enlist in army units and demanded home defence formations. Residents in outlying areas, anxious to "protect themselves and their loved ones," polished their sporting rifles, pooled their arms, and imagined mounting grassroots defences. Without official approval or support, voluntary organizations throughout

Why bother learning guerilla tactics? Can it happen here? These are questions we can well ask ourselves often.

In what way could Rangers fight should Japanese forces obtain footholds in Canada?

The art of ambushing, harassing and annoying an enemy, if worth learning at all, is worth learning well.

Diagrams on the black-board and lectures will not teach everything. "Get out and rehearse" is good advice. Experience teaches. Few guerrillas ever learnt their trade from books!

Have you surveyed every road and trail in your area? and selected various ambush points? Have you rehearsed an ambush or two at any point?

"Why Bother?" *The Ranger,* May 1943

the province began to train and drill.[12] "There are thousands of men in civil life – war veterans, loggers, miners, fishermen, shipyard workers etc., who are hunters and capable marksmen, who could form the nucleus" of a proper home guard, one observer noted in the *Victoria Daily Colonist.* Men between the ages of sixteen and sixty-five could volunteer and act as a guerrilla force. The *Vancouver Sun* interviewed "informed civilians and former military officers" and proposed a "Civil Defence Corps in every town, city and village in BC."[13]

A careful balance had to be struck. Ottawa had to demonstrate its commitment to communities along the West Coast, particularly towns and villages in exposed coastal areas. In a total war setting, the federal government would also need to manage its human and material resources carefully. The Allies faced war on several fronts, and Canada could ill afford to redirect expeditionary forces to defend against a potential attack on the West Coast when "the ultimate object [was] the defeat of Germany."[14] Even if the number of Canadian Army Active Force troops were increased substantially, military authorities recognized that they could not cover all vital points. Journalists also noted that soldiers, if rushed to BC from the East, would not possess enough knowledge about the region to defend it adequately.[15] Even the province's reserve units, limited to settled areas, did not have the organization, knowledge, or operational experience to function outside of their immediate areas.

Politicians and journalists in BC also suggested that Japanese fishers along the Coast, who knew the area intimately, would serve the enemy. This logic – equating Japanese Canadian sympathies with those of the Japanese enemy – was problematic.[16] But these rhetorical justifications reflected the alarmism and fear that had gripped the province. "In the present situation it is considered most important that everything possible be done on the West Coast to satisfy public opinion in respect to military security, provided it can be done without prejudice to our major war effort," Lieutenant-General Kenneth Stuart, the chief of the general staff in Ottawa, explained to Pacific Command in January 1942.[17] The latter point could not be stressed enough. The solution could not drain the human and financial resources needed to wage war overseas.

Defence officials recognized that local volunteers could be useful auxiliaries – civilian volunteers supporting a main military force. Their grassroots knowledge would be vital in the case of an invasion and, equally important, their service might lessen the requirement for Regular Forces in remote areas. National headquarters envisaged Home Guard platoons with uniforms and rifles at various points along the coasts of Vancouver Island and the Mainland. General Stuart knew this modest force "would be very popular on the West Coast and would not interfere with our major effort."[18]

The British Home Guard provided an obvious model. When the Low Countries and France fell to the Germans in mid-1940, a Nazi invasion of the British Isles became a real possibility. Winston Churchill took to the airwaves and asked for local defence volunteers. The Home Guard units exceeded 1 million British men by the end of June. Composed initially of individual volunteers serving in vital wartime occupations, or men who were too young or too old to serve in the regular army, the members carried whatever arms were available. If spies and saboteurs threatened domestic security or if German airborne units tried to land, these "people in arms" would be expected to delay their advance until regular army units arrived. As local defence units they received little training and had an unclear role, but the British Home Guard provided citizens with an opportunity to serve their nation.[19]

Pacific Command initially proposed the establishment of coast defence guards, who would serve in places where it was impossible to establish reserve army units. The guards' value would be threefold. First, they would help calm the populace by providing a visible response to public demands for action. Second, they could pass on information about suspicious individuals, vessels, and activities. Third, if a raiding party attacked their local area, they would "take action against them in defence of their own homes and community." The premier and the provincial police commissioner agreed wholeheartedly with this proposal. The regional army commander, Major-General R.O. Alexander, met with members of the BC Legislative Assembly who represented coastal ridings and received their unanimous support. The politicians suggested that the guards wear armbands instead of military uniforms, that they serve as unpaid "defenders of their own homes," and that training be "in accordance with the local situation as regards place, type of country and type of men forming the unit." General Alexander agreed that uniforms would be inappropriate and that a traditional military structure, medical examinations, and qualifications would hinder rather than help the new organization. Ideally, men in about fifteen coastal communities would serve as auxiliary police, carrying sporting weapons issued to them as members of civilian rifle associations.[20]

This proposal violated military law. Local civilians or police could not defend their homes and communities against a military attack without being liable to punishment as unlawful combatants. Consequently, the guards needed formal military status. Steel helmets, distinctive armbands, and some training would legitimize the units. Although the final structure remained uncertain, British Columbia's daily papers announced on 23 February that subunits of the Canadian Army (Reserve) would guard every coastal town and strategic point in the Interior. The units would vary in strength depending on the strategic importance of the place they were defending.[21] The existing reserve structure did not cover extensive areas with low population densities, so the new model would exploit the local experience of prospectors, trappers, loggers, and fishers.

Creating the Pacific Coast Militia Rangers

The task of turning vague concepts into organized reality fell to Lieutenant-Colonel Thomas Alexander Hatch Taylor, a staff officer at Pacific Command Headquarters. Born in Montreal in 1891, "Tommy" Taylor had returned from an extended land survey in the interior of British Columbia in October 1914 to discover the British Empire at war. He enlisted in the Canadian Expeditionary Force in Vancouver and joined the 29th Battalion as a lieutenant. He was promoted to temporary captain with the Canadian Rail Troops before commanding the 6th Canadian Machine Gun Company in Europe.[22] Between the wars, he continued to work in land surveying, timber cruising, and railway construction. He therefore appreciated the diverse geography and people of the province. This appreciation in turn influenced his wartime approach to organizing for home defence. "Only experienced men accustomed to rugged, timbered country could adequately undertake much of the work required if the [Japanese] gained a foothold," the skilled outdoorsman insisted. His force required hardy woodsmen with strength of character who populated the Coast and the Interior. "Strangely enough," Taylor explained, "the initiative and energy possessed by many of these men would not fit them for the life of an ordinary soldier where unified action is imperative."[23] Their ability to work independently and creatively would be essential to the proper functioning of the new irregular force.

The name of the force helped to correct some of the distortions propagated in the media. Military and newspaper sources declared that the government was forming guerrilla units for local defence in BC. Guerrillas – members of independent, irregular armed forces that adopt harassment and sabotage tactics to resist a stronger foe – had no protection under military law. The name of the new corps, therefore, would have to reflect its official military status. Taylor's early designation, "(Civilian) Auxiliary Defence Corps," was vague and uninspiring. After a Pacific Command staff officer met with senior officials in Ottawa in mid-March, the name changed

The Pacific Coast Militia Rangers' cap badge. Photo by P. Whitney Lackenbauer

from "Guards" to "Rangers." During a visit to Victoria the next month, the minister of national defence chatted with Taylor and became convinced that the new designation was fitting. After all, the new corps would range over the coastline and Interior rather than guard fixed points. Use of the word *militia* would prevent the corps from being construed as a civilian organization. Military authorities settled on the name "Pacific Coast Militia Rangers" or "PCMR." Members simply referred to themselves as "the Rangers."[24]

The Ranger label tapped into archetypal North American images of hardy frontier defenders protecting hearth and home through improvisation and necessity. Like the militia in New France, who adopted tactics of *la petite guerre* (the little war of raiding, skirmishing, and ambushes) to combat American and Iroquois raids, the first Rangers had emerged on the colonial scene in late seventeenth-century New England in response to indigenous tactics to undermine European models of war.[25] Members of so-called backcountry communities supported these unconventional practices, and Anglo-American Rangers became ubiquitous symbols of the Indian-fighting frontiersman. After the British Conquest, the Ranger mystique remained alive in the works of authors such as James Fennimore Cooper and Francis

Parkman. It also fit the pervasive myth that Canadians fighting in defence of their homes made the best soldiers.[26]

In spring 1942, Art Boyd of Jordan River, a tiny logging community on southern Vancouver Island surrounded by old-growth rainforests and sandy beaches, expressed his sense of the local situation just before the Rangers were organized: "There are several, probably about 20 to 30 men, in this immediate area who are preparing themselves for an attack by the Japs. They are experienced woodsmen and hunters. Some are veterans or guides ... They have acted individually in this matter – for their own self interest as much as for any reason – there is no organization – some have guns and ammunition, maps and other equipment but others are lacking in rifles and none of them have any authority or even recognition from the military or public." In his opinion, the situation demanded action. The small village of Port Renfrew to the west offered a potential landing spot, but the Regular Forces would be helpless without local assistance. "It is almost beyond belief, that the troops out here can be so green," Boyd wrote. "They are Ontario boys and can't even make a beach fire. If they went [fifty feet] from the highway they would be lost." He wanted to secure military status, rifles, and ammunition for local residents, as a unit of guerrillas, but he did not know where to turn. After all, he warned, army headquarters at "Work Point [Barracks in Victoria] is a maze of red tape and buck passing."[27] His concern about an overly bureaucratic process was understandable. Armies, their complex organizations laden with unwieldy administrations and hierarchical control, seemed anathema to a community-based citizen-soldier force.

Defence planners did not envisage the Pacific Coast Militia Rangers as *ad hoc* companies thrown together by local residents to react to Japanese invaders. They imagined them as part of the official defence establishment. In mid-March 1942, Taylor distributed a memorandum that described the organization in detail. Duties, the memorandum outlined, would not conflict with the Rangers' civilian jobs unless they were called out on active service in an emergency. Their operational role was threefold. First, the Rangers had to "possess up-to-date, complete and detailed knowledge of their own area," which they could provide to Pacific Command Headquarters and to local military commanders if required. Second, as the eyes and ears in their areas, they would report suspicious vessels and any unusual occurrences that might be subversive or fifth-column activities. Third, in case of emergency, they would repel an enemy invasion or attack from the sea or air, by themselves or in conjunction with Active Army units.[28] If necessary,

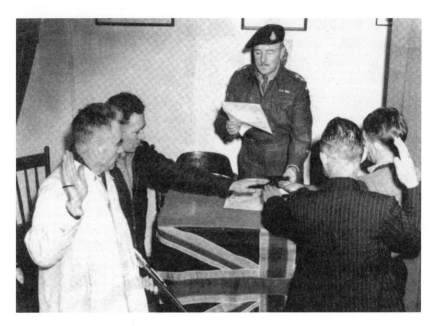

Lt.-Col. T.A.H. Taylor taking the oath from new Rangers. *The Ranger*, January 1944

they would take anti-sabotage measures and employ guerrilla tactics to delay enemy advances. In the Interior, PCMR units would also protect vital lines of communication such as major railways and the Trans-Canada Highway from Chilliwack to Golden.[29]

The PCMR focused initially on coastal communities, where the threat of invasion seemed most acute.[30] Once notice of the Rangers hit newspapers, applications for local units flooded in from throughout the province. Taylor called on community leaders to organize meetings of local citizens. Within two weeks, about forty companies, with a paper strength of more than four thousand Rangers, had taken shape. When General Stuart assumed command, he referred to the groundswell of popular support as the Ranger Movement.[31] To reward his zeal and competence, Major Taylor was promoted and appointed special officer in charge of the PCMR. He continued to strengthen his Ranger empire for the duration of the war.

Within the PCMR, local leaders wielded tremendous power over their units. Deliberately elastic, the organization allowed for local variance to capture the personality of a community.[32] The basic Ranger unit – the company, commanded by a captain – followed the infantry model to reinforce the PCMR's military nature. In turn, each company contained

The PCMR's chain of command. *The Ranger*, January 1944

detachments led by a lieutenant. Detachments were further subdivided into groups, units roughly equivalent to infantry sections and led by a non-commissioned officer. Although the original plans provided for companies with a maximum of five detachments and seven officers, the arrangement did not always meet the PCMR's requirements, and the staff at Pacific Command adapted the regulations creatively in the interests of "keeping the number of companies to a minimum and making a more compact organization."[33]

Brendan Kennelly, a former guerrilla warfare specialist with the Irish Republican Army and the PCMR's training officer for its first sixteen months, criticized Taylor's haphazard method of organizing units and selecting leaders. Taylor wanted to encourage the spread of the Rangers throughout British Columbia, Kennelly recalled after the war, "regardless of the tactical importance of each area and in direct contradiction to the policy laid down by General Alexander." Taylor sent out officers to brief community members and drum up "interest and publicity." These organizers then interviewed the most influential (or at least the most vocal) individuals until one consented to act as a local Ranger captain. "Many of these selectees proved excellent officers," Kennelly observed, "but many, too, were misfits." When poor leaders secured control, a unit failed – regardless of the quality of the personnel. Kennelly reminisced: "The Regiment is what a Commander makes it! Ranger companies were even more susceptible. The Ranger Captain was 'god' – too often a 'tin god.' If he was a misfit he picked personnel about him who were equally misfit and what good men he might have gravitated downwards and dissipated their talents in obscure positions. This could have been altered in devious ways. Competent seconds-in-command would have been provided. However, badly-led units were allowed to remain badly-led."[34] Whether Kennelly's sour assessment simply reflected his strict military expectations is unclear.

Retaining Rangers over the long term nevertheless depended on local leadership and creativity. After all, this form of military service offered few material benefits. Rangers received no pay and a limited scale of issue. The original directive recommended only armbands and steel helmets to distinguish Rangers from ordinary civilians. Furthermore, the military did not provide them with horses, vehicles, clothing, or regimental equipment. It expected Rangers to use private assets for transportation and subsistence. The volunteers would receive a limited supply of arms and ammunitions,[35] but service rifles were in short supply in 1942. The Rangers fell in line behind active or reserve units on the waiting list.[36]

Membership and Training

The PCMR's meteoric growth reflected the recruits' eagerness to defend their homes. Almost ten thousand members – the equivalent of a division of soldiers – enlisted by the end of May 1942. "Throughout the whole province, Rangers set to [work] with a will and made the best of what was at hand," a triumphant article in *The Ranger* magazine declared. "For sheer ingenuity in overcoming equipment shortages and for their ability to 'scrounge' necessary material, PCMR men gained enviable prestige in the eyes of military authorities."[37] Despite the obvious bias of this magazine, which was created for and circulated to the Rangers as a training guide, it provides insight into the Rangers' self-identity and ethos.

Journalists, caught up in the Ranger hype, published a flurry of publicity stories. They cast the Rangers as "BC's Rugged Defenders," BC's "Guerrilla Sharpshooters," or "Cariboo Commandos" and used terms such as *colourful, ingenious,* and *experienced* in their descriptions.[38] Their anecdotes fixated on the most unlikely military characters in the Rangers' ranks: loggers, trappers, hunters, and veterans – men with legendary skills in bushcraft.[39] "The organization is one that places a premium on individual drive and resourcefulness," Lieutenant-Colonel Taylor explained to one reporter. The Pacific Coast Militia Rangers had to, "above all else, be self-sufficient, ready to act on the dictates of their own common sense, and prepared to operate for indeterminate periods without the assistance of supporting services."[40] The archetypal Ranger was undaunted by inclement weather or swarms of mosquitoes, could stealthily manoeuvre in some of the "roughest, wildcat terrain in the world," and had a "horse-sense" about his local environment.[41] His world was not the sportsman's modern wilderness engineered so middle-class urbanites could selectively encounter nature.[42] The Rangers occupied a military theatre in which all but the most knowledgeable would perish in the face of Japanese invasion. British Columbia's self-identity embraced stereotypes of a rugged, individualist, frontier masculinity.[43] The Rangers embodied this identity in practice.

Men ineligible to serve in the Regular Forces for reasons of age or employment found a chance to exercise their patriotism through the Rangers. General Order 320, which had created the organization, stated that "membership will not be limited as to age or physique, but will be open to any who are considered suitable or can be of use."[44] Recruits did not need to take a medical examination: if they could carry out Ranger duties, they were acceptable. Marion Angus, a reporter, discovered that the Rangers included former Canadian Expeditionary Force officers Colonel "Cy" Peck, V.C. (Victoria Cross), and Brigadier E.J. Ross, M.C. (Military Cross). Other volunteers included "a fur trader with fifteen years bush training, familiar

Rangers on patrol in what the photographer described as "typical terrain," in which "these men may spend three of four days 'on the trail' without blankets, sleeping in improvised shelters," November 1942. Department of National Defence, Photo WRC-2955

with Indian (BC and prairie) dialects and northern transportation methods, whose hobby is amateur radio"; an eighteen-year veteran of the Royal Navy whose familiarity with small sea craft and gunnery suited his community; and an "aggressive and reliable" thirty-five-year-old Coast Indian who had been a councillor in his village for a decade and who was a "captain of a fish-packer and [knew] the coast waters like a book." The PCMR also included bakers, heavy equipment operators, game wardens, fishery inspectors, cowboys, loggers, and farmers.[45] The youngest member was thirteen and the oldest eighty-six. The median age of the Rangers in 1943 was nearly fifty.[46]

Underage boys anxious "to prove their readiness for action" found an outlet for their energy in the Rangers.[47] Young lads in outlying areas proved extremely valuable, an official summary recognized. "'Boys' of 15 years and up proved to be good shots, could handle an axe, and were valuable as guides to city-bred men."[48] Several Ranger companies used "boys platoons" as runners (or bicyclers), signallers, and messengers.[49] David Whittaker, a former Ranger, explained that he and his friends were "socialized into the role of men ... and into the role of soldiering, and the adventure and the excitement ... We felt part of the world of men, and it gave us a lot of self-confidence in terms of adolescents wanting to belong."[50] Exposure to military life and training motivated many to join the regular army. Major-General J.P. Mackenzie, the army inspector for western Canada, noted during a visit to Chilliwack in December 1943 that "[q]uite a large number of Rangers are graduating into the Armed Forces and their younger Brothers, in many cases, are joining the [PCMR] as soon as they are old enough so that they can follow the example."[51] In the end, more than twelve hundred Rangers volunteered for general service overseas.[52]

On the other side of the demographic spectrum, older men ineligible for overseas service still had skills that would allow them to outpace and outsmart potential enemies. The knowledge they had amassed during imperial campaigns in Asia and Africa, or during the Great War, was integral to the Ranger organization. Indeed, South African War veterans had been strident lobbyists for BC commando units in the months after Pearl Harbor.[53] "I think that we were lucky ... that we had the old vets of the First World War," Ranger Lloyd Cornett recalled. "They had many years in the trenches ... and many of them had decorations for bravery ... They were very fine guys who knew the hard end of soldiering and they passed those skills and attitudes along to us [younger Rangers] and we benefited greatly." The Rangers gave these veterans "a chance to feel involved again ... to return to that spirit of comradeship that every military organization has."[54] The aged veteran, a man of wisdom and experience, became the Rangers' quintessential stereotype. One newspaper reported, "On autumn Sundays, dignified businessmen can be seen crawling on their stomachs in a manner reminiscent

Rangers capitalizing on the natural advantages of the Pacific landscape: enjoying a cup of tea in a burned out cedar, November 1942. *Left to right:* prospector Dunc Powell, ballistics expert "Pop" McKelvie, and high school student Eric Gard. Department of National Defence, Photo WRC-2950

of long ago boyhood days when they played Indian scouts ... They shinny over waterfalls or ford streams with the elasticity of youth."[55] Their bodies rendered them too old for the battlefields of Europe, but experience made them more than suitable home guards.

Rangers understood their home turf, but they needed training to communicate with military planners. To provide the army with vital intelligence, they needed to speak the same language. Early training, held in community halls, Legion halls, and church basements, was informal. The local Ranger captain got "the boys" together and identified individual members with expertise in a given subject area. Nearly every company included veterans of the Boer War and the Great War, for example, and these men possessed specialized (if antiquated) knowledge about military subjects. Engineers and ham radio operators shared their expertise, while former navy signallers revealed the secrets of Morse code and semaphore.[56] Although British Home Guard units were ordered not to produce homemade weapons because of several tragic accidents,[57] Canadian officers actively encouraged the Rangers in British Columbia to do so. Machinists furnished weapons in their spare time, using scrap metal and facilities offered by machine shop owners. Men interested in electronics improvised signalling equipment, bird enthusiasts trained their own homing pigeon messengers, and chemists concocted homemade hand grenades, Molotov cocktails (out of empty beer bottles), and tracer bullets. Inventive members of 29th Company in Chilliwack built a "Sten electric ray gun" out of scrap metal. The gun, which used photoelectric cells to fire light instead of bullets, facilitated indoor practice without wasting precious ammunition.[58] Ranger units built training facilities on their own initiative and generally out of their own pockets. Before the war, BC had 5 military-owned rifle ranges; by war's end, the Rangers had constructed another 163.[59]

Creativity and resourcefulness were important, but modern combat demanded more professional training than local initiative alone could provide. Taylor received permission to hire a small staff to help with administrative responsibilities at Pacific Command Headquarters. Major W.S. Bartson, a Great War veteran, was appointed his assistant in late March 1942, and Lieutenant Brendan Kennelly, who had trapped in the Peace River district, assumed the role of training officer. That June, Pacific Command authorized travelling instructors to visit companies and detachments and to conduct field training. In due course, Taylor selected six field supervisors to oversee the organization throughout the province. He based his selection on criteria that matched his vision for the force. All had experience working in the province, and all had served overseas during the First World War. Captain George Baldwin, MC, was a forest ranger; Captain B.T. O'Grady, MC, was a civil and mining engineer; Captain S.M. Gillespie was a timber cruiser and surveyor; Captain B. Harvey was a game warden; and Captain J.B. Acland was a former brigade staff officer and member of the tank corps.

The travelling instructors, who eventually numbered eight, found it difficult to reach every Ranger, so Taylor and his staff encouraged preparedness in other ways. Members of the three regular services and the Canadian Legion supplemented Ranger training, as did special lecturers such as Bert "Yank" Levy. A forty-five-year-old, Canadian-born soldier of fortune, Levy had spent six years in jail for armed robbery before fighting as a Loyalist guerrilla leader in Spain and becoming a Home Guard instructor in Britain and the United States.[60] In September 1942, headquarters began distributing *The Ranger* to every member. Featuring regular columns on irregular warfare and bush craft, the magazine taught reconnaissance, map reading, field sketching, first aid, and aircraft recognition. It stressed that the foremost weapons in the Rangers' arsenal were "common, garden horse-sense; a sense of values in relationship with an everyday knowledge of the world and its people and resources; determination to apply themselves to their task; and the ability to combine these three consistently without faltering or fumbling."[61] Even in the harsh winter months, Rangers trained indoors in local schools, community halls, and private residences.[62]

Officers recognized the Rangers as men of action ill-suited to the classroom or the drill hall, and they emphasized realistic outdoor training.[63] The Rangers prepared for bush warfare because they understood that BC's dense forests would provide cover and concealment, allowing them to neutralize even large enemy forces. Coastal platoons practised with naval and combined operations units while others pondered urban warfare. Training in signals, map reading, and direction finding provided practical skills that the men felt they could use in their civilian lives. According to popular stereotypes, even those with white-collar jobs were "outdoor men by practice and inclination," and most training replicated forms of recreation.[64] Born and raised outside of cities, these men "from fishing banks, from logging camps and from tiny coastal stump farms" had "owned fire-arms since childhood."[65] Venturing into the bush was not a bourgeois distraction from their daily lives but the very essence of it.[66] "Many British Columbians had made 'guns' their hobby for years," a *Ranger* article noted in 1944, while others had been bitten by the so-called signalling bug or were interested in explosives, engineering, or map reading. The hobby appeal of Ranger training, combined with patriotic responsibility, helps explain the recruits' keen interest and creativity.[67]

When asked by a reporter whether patriotism was a primary motivation, the staff officer-in-charge of the PCMR replied, "Rubbish. These men are banded into a close-knit body with a single purpose – actual defense of their own homes."[68] The Japanese occupations of the Aleutian Islands of Attu and Kiska in June 1942 might have been "stepping stones to nowhere," but the Western Hemisphere had been breached, at least symbolically. That same month, a Japanese submarine had broadcast its presence in Canadian waters by torpedoing a lumber schooner southwest of Cape Flattery and then by shelling the lighthouse at Estevan Point, on the west coast of Vancouver Island.[69] Marion Angus, who observed the Coquitlam Rangers in July 1943, reported: "After [the company exercise] was over, I asked one of the men, 'Why have you joined the Rangers?' 'To defend my home,' he said simply. 'My home and my family.' A minute later three small tots came running up and a childish treble piped, 'Did you get the Japs, Daddy? Did you kill them?'"[70]

The Rangers, regardless of their motivation, became a key part of wartime social life in small cities, towns, and work camps. They organized Victory Loan drives, supported road-breaking treks, joined in church parades, searched for lost children, and even hunted wolf dogs when they terrorized the community of Haney.[71] The detachment at Moosehide, near Dawson City, Yukon, hosted a fundraising "War Dance" that featured "Native war dances, old-time square dances" and a "red river jig." Local Tr'ondëk Hwëch'in children sang "God Save the King" in their "Native tongue."[72] As a grassroots force, the Rangers were inextricably bound to the social fabric of their communities.

No single unit exemplified the PCMR. Companies and platoons were as diverse as the communities of British Columbia and, as they extended northward, Yukon. "There will be no 'stab-in-the-back' through Canada's northern back door," a zealous journalist proclaimed. "White clad Rangers in the frozen Yukon are on 24-hour alert with their dog teams, their sleds, their rifles and Sten guns."[73] Residents of the colourful frontier town of Dawson, made famous by the Klondike gold rush, viewed their territory as an unlikely combat zone.[74] Nevertheless, the army authorized No. 135 Company in February 1943. Charles Hathaway "Chappie" Chapman, the

135 Company, PCMR, on parade in Dawson, 1945. Yukon Archives, Bill Hare fonds, #6941

manager of Northern Commercial Co. who had five years service with the Mounties, assumed command.[75] Major-General J.P. Mackenzie, the army's inspector general in western Canada, visited the company the following year and applauded its strong local leadership and support. Captain Chapman enjoyed a good reputation with the local citizens, who viewed him as "extremely enthusiastic," an "excellent woodsman," and a strong leader. All five sergeants were veterans and responsible businessmen. The eighty-eight men of other ranks worked for trading and gold-mining companies, had considerable bush experience, and were good rifle shots. "A percentage of them earn their livelihood trapping in the winter time and gold-mining in the summertime," the inspector learned, "which makes them all the more useful to the P.C.M.R."[76]

Dawson's civic support for its Rangers impressed Mackenzie. When he inspected the unit in the community hall (where the Rangers paraded up to three times per week, attended lectures, and viewed training films), "the entire city of Dawson turned out," including the superintendent of the Yukon, the stipendiary magistrate, and the manager of a gold company who had delayed summer operations so the Rangers could attend the parade. The enthusiasm was contagious. The Boys platoon, using bicycles and carrying rifle slings, relayed messages to the various outposts.[77]

Although the Rangers in Dawson demonstrated their shooting proficiency on a rifle range they built at Bonanza Creek, Ranger J.J. van Bibber's wife won all the shooting prizes in competitions.[78] She could not be a Ranger, however, as the logic of the day held that guerrilla warfare was no place for "the gentler sex." Women nevertheless "played no small part in the Ranger scheme of things," official publications trumpeted. Women looked after "farm, ranch or office when their men were away training or out on some Ranger activity."[79] Cartoons in *The Ranger* might have depicted the angry housewife armed with a rolling pin, but the Rangers themselves emphasized cooperation. "On many occasions," one writer reminisced, "the Ranger, returning cold and damp from creeping through rain-wet bracken, has been cheered by a welcome cup of coffee."[80] Women drove cars and delivered supplies, volunteered with the Red Cross in mobile canteens, and helped organize dances to raise money for the Rangers and the war effort more generally.[81]

Ethnic lines were less clearly drawn than gender ones. The military excluded British Columbians of Japanese descent from serving in the PCMR. The prohibition reflected the biases, prejudices, and concerns of British Columbians before and during the war.[82] Other ethnic groups were well represented. For example, the Rangers welcomed and celebrated the contributions of Chinese Canadians, Native peoples, and other "allied" ethnic groups who were strongly invested in the war effort. "The threat of Japanese aggression probably bulks very large to a Chinese, may be more so than [to] the average white Canadian," *The Ranger* stated. "Perhaps the Chinese Ranger has known the grim details of Japanese brutality across the Pacific, and rape, murder and torture mean more to him than it might to the rather complacent people who live behind the barrier of the Rockies." British Columbians, united by a common Japanese threat, would fight together. Accordingly, Chinese Canadians such as storekeeper Wong Toy and his sons could readily participate in domestic defence.[83]

". . . And I'll give you some lessons you won't forget if you come around here again with your blankety-blank street fighting!"

◀ Contrasting views of women and the PCMR. *Top:* The irate, rolling pin–wielding housewife as depicted in *The Ranger,* November 1943. *Bottom:* A woman sharing her tea ration with Rangers Ken Vidal and Frank Smith, November 1942. Department of National Defence, Photo WRC-2946

Journalists warmly embraced Aboriginal people as "natural" Rangers. Their dispersed reserves placed them at key strategic points along the province's periphery, and their patriotism was held up as a model for all Canadians. Newspapers mobilized popular stereotypes to trumpet Aboriginal people's loyalty and participation in the war effort.[84] "Up and down the length of British Columbia's Coast, both on the main reservations and at many an isolated inlet and forest hamlet besides, the Indians have taken a very keen interest in the war," a *Victoria Colonist* editorial proclaimed on 3 April 1943. "Indicative of the way the Indians are backing the war effort," another reporter described, "was the 102-year-old Dog Creek Indian who offered his services as a guide or marksman and pointed back to a long, successful career as suitable qualifications." In appreciation, the Rangers made him an honorary member of their organization.[85]

Aboriginal peoples' support for the Rangers reflected their wartime experience. Although Canadian First Nations men served in higher numbers per capita according to national statistics,[86] high rates of voluntary enlistment among BC bands were confined to southern areas. When the government invoked conscription in 1942, the bands insisted that they had no obligation to serve because of historical promises and their legal status as wards. The government maintained that Indians could be conscripted, but the authorities had trouble finding individuals in isolated northern and coastal areas, never mind registering them. Consequently, the government eventually gave up in its efforts to conscript BC Indians.[87] Aboriginal people feared, however, that the PCMR might be an underhanded way to enlist them for overseas service.[88] Once Ranger organizers dispelled these rumours, Native people's inhibitions disappeared. Queen Victoria's representatives had once told Tsimshian at Port Simpson, Kitkatla, and Metlakatla that "they would never have to fight unless they wanted to." Once staff officers and instructors assured them that this would remain the case, they volunteered in high numbers and were "very proud of their Ranger association."[89]

The Nisga'a, who had lived on the Northwest Coast since time immemorial, wanted to defend their villages in K'alii-aksim Lisims – the resource-rich Nass Valley. Their homeland happened to be "the closest part of the Canadian

The mystique of the stalwart Native Ranger guarding his homeland is clear on this cover of *The Ranger,* January 1945.

mainland to Japan and a long way from the cities to the south." Nisga'a representatives approached the Indian Agent at Prince Rupert in mid-1942 and requested a PCMR company.[90] The military complied. When instructor Brendan Kennelly arrived by boat at Kincolith Bay in February 1943, he was greeted by eighty "Kitkatla" Rangers flying the Union Jack, a twenty-five-piece brass band, and forty members of the Indian Women's Red Cross society. Arthur Nelson, a fisherman and the officer commanding the "all-Indian" Ranger company, marched the procession through "the village to the sounds of martial music & the beating of drums." Although local leaders had stridently opposed conscription for overseas service, the "Indian chiefs of their respective districts" proudly served as Ranger officers.[91]

Kennelly reported that "[a]ll the Indians of these parts are strongly and enthusiastically ... for the Ranger organization." Over thirty men joined during his visit, bringing the Kincolith unit's strength to over two hundred. The leaders of the Aiyansh (Gitlakdamix), Greenville (Laxgalts'ap), and Canyon City (Gitwinksihlkw) Rangers wanted to discuss guerrilla tactics with the instructor, who pleased them when he stated that they trained "Rangers to fight like 'Indians' and not like soldiers." In response, the Nisga'a "began to recall their forefathers' days of fighting with the Alaskan and outer island tribes."[92]

Aboriginal men had intimate, ancestral ties to their homelands, and the Rangers valued their skills.[93] Despite being disempowered by the Canadian political system, Native peoples enjoyed a measure of self-government in their units. In the Nass River communities, Rangers elected their own officers and noncommissioned officers by secret ballot, and the Indian councils and the Indian Agent approved the appointments.[94] Aboriginal people made up a minority of the PCMR's total membership, but they were celebrated members and exemplified the extent to which Ranger service could transcend deep-rooted racial barriers.

Articles published during the war proclaimed that the Rangers also transcended class lines. Historian Kerry Steeves, who used local data to analyze Ranger membership, concluded that the organization was representative of the entire population. For example, No. 73 Company (Yale), located at the southern entrance to the Fraser Canyon in one of southwestern BC's oldest communities, included members from all social strata and various occupations.[95] Major-General Frederic Franklin "Worthy" Worthington, the commander in chief of Pacific Command at war's end, asserted that "the PCMR was of necessity a great 'leveller' – the labourer and the banker worked together. The logging boss found himself in a group or detachment commanded by one of his truck drivers ... They were 'Rangers' – all working together toward the one common end." In a final flourish, he declared that "a fellowship of man was created in the Rangers and it will carry on."[96] Although his celebratory rhetoric could be dismissed as self-serving, reporters frequently described men from all backgrounds coming together for a single purpose. Hyperbolic excess aside, the Ranger ideal was one of unity and camaraderie.

Colonel Taylor considered this strong sense of communal identity the most important ingredient in the PCMR's success. "The fact that each unit was made up of men who lived in the same district, and therefore understood each other, made it all the more easy for 'esprit de corps' to develop," *The Ranger* magazine exulted in early 1944. "The common bond established through the Ranger organization even brought together people who had had personal grievances for years. Those who had got along well with others in their community now had even more reason for long-lasting friendships."[97] Although surely exaggerated, this image reflected strong unit cohesion and personal connections. Corps morale and satisfaction could translate into a greater sense of individual self-worth. Ranger "Andy" Rigors, who wrote a regular column in the *Kamloops Sentinel,* observed that the Rangers bolstered confidence in his community: "There seems to be no doubt about it: members are looking and walking better than ever before as a result of the self-imposed training. Sparkling eyes, shoulders thrown back, clear complexions, and talking with an enthusiastic vigor they did not possess previously, are sure signs of ... a new lease on life, which by the way, is the most valuable thing on the face of the earth: a possession that can easily be wasted, especially in the evenings, by 'collapsing' in an easy chair."[98]

The Changing Context

It took less than a year for the PCMR to become an integral part of Pacific Command. The corps strength peaked in August 1943 at 529 officers and 14,320 other ranks. At scant cost to the public purse, the Rangers helped keep isolated parts of BC and the Coast under surveillance. They searched for lost planes and people in the mountains, and they even tracked down escaped prisoners of war and army deserters.[99]

When the Japanese threat waned, the Rangers felt the reverberations. That fall, Pacific Command reduced its troop strength and capped the PCMR at ten thousand members in 123 active companies. Official statements rationalized the measure as a way to increase efficiency by raising standards and forcing units to drop unsuitable individuals and those too busy to attend

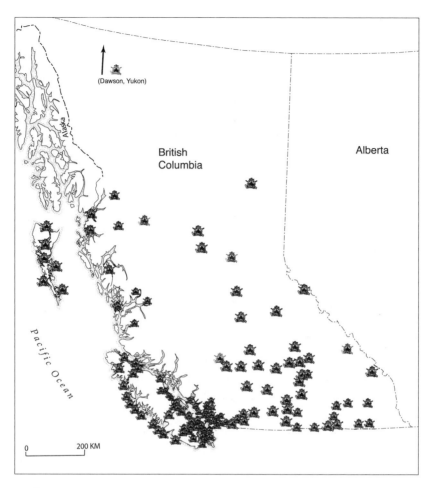

Pacific Coast Militia Ranger company locations, 1944

training.[100] When rumours circulated that the cap had been imposed to save money, journalists recalled Colonel Taylor's earlier statement that "not since the days when settlers organized to protect themselves from Indians has there existed such an economical form of defence."[101] This logic staved off deeper cuts until December 1944, when Allied offensives in the European and Pacific theatres pushed the Axis powers back on their heels. The minister of national defence then approved a proposal to disband all but twenty-nine Ranger companies located in Yukon and on Vancouver Island, the Queen Charlotte Islands (Haida Gwaii), and the northern Mainland coast.[102]

Ranger units received a circular indicating the cuts, but no action was taken because of a new threat. In reaction to Allied advances, the Japanese tried to bolster national morale by launching bomb-bearing balloons designed to fall on North America. The first operational balloons landed in the United States, and in mid-January 1945 one of these delivery systems released several bombs near Minton, Saskatchewan. There were no Canadian casualties, but the incidents reminded people that the war was not over – and thus saved the PCMR from being abolished. In cooperation with the Royal Canadian Mounted Police, provincial police, forest rangers, trappers, and bomb-disposal squads, the Rangers detected and reported balloons through formal military channels, ensuring that they were safely disarmed or destroyed. The fear that balloons could carry biological agents made this a serious assignment, and the transmission of sensitive information that they conveyed through formal military channels made it their crowning achievement.[103]

By August 1945, the Allies had defeated the Nazis in Europe, and the diversion of more forces to the Pacific promised victory over Japan. The newly appointed chief of the general staff, Lieutenant-General Charles Foulkes, recommended disbanding the PCMR, and the minister agreed. Japan formally surrendered on 2 September, and at the end of the month the Rangers held an official "stand down" ceremony in Vancouver. Individual companies across the province held parades and then disbanded.[104] General Worthington, who had visited each company as Pacific commander-in-chief, "hated to see them disperse." He saw the Rangers' value in peacetime and "advocated retaining a nucleus on which to rebuild" should the security situation in the Pacific deteriorate. Senior army officials in Ottawa rejected his recommendation.[105] Instead, in recognition of their voluntary and unpaid services, Rangers who had served for more than ninety days were allowed to keep their uniforms and could purchase their rifles for the nominal sum of five dollars.[106]

✤ WHEN THE JAPANESE OVERRAN Pearl Harbor, Singapore, and Hong Kong in December 1941, British Columbians felt besieged. Suddenly, the comfortable notion that "it couldn't happen here" no longer applied. There had been war scares in the past (from Americans and Russians in the nineteenth century and from Germans during the Great War), but technology and the disconcerting state of the Allied war effort made the threat in early

1942 seem particularly acute. Although senior military authorities advised the federal government that the province's defences were adequate to meet any probable attack, popular hysteria demanded more visible measures. "Cabinet listened to the frightened voters of British Columbia instead of to its military advisers," official army historian C.P. Stacey observed. As a result, the military dedicated significant manpower and equipment to West Coast defences rather than to the pivotal European theatre.[107] Although events would prove that the military's assessment had been better grounded than popular fears, political considerations often outweigh military opinion when it comes to formulating and implementing defence policy.

The Pacific Coast Militia Rangers, although a product of this same wartime pressure, should not be included in Stacey's dismal assessment. This unpaid force recruited men from rural and remote coastal areas who could not, for reasons of age, disability, or occupation, serve overseas. Although no Japanese invasion took place, the Rangers served various military and social functions in wartime British Columbia. The PCMR assuaged the public's demand for grassroots defences, and the Rangers' limited equipment and low costs helped ensure that the defence of the province did not consume more military resources (financial and personnel) than necessary.

In her journal, painter Emily Carr reflected that "war halts everything, suspends all ordinary activities."[108] In reality, everyday living carried on. Miners mined, fishers fished, and loggers logged. Essential industries remained essential, and the men who served with the PCMR from 1942 to 1945 stayed in their communities.[109] Concerns about enemy sabotage and infiltration translated into few tangible threats (balloons notwithstanding) on the West Coast, and the Rangers were never called out on active service. Nevertheless, the PCMR played an important – if modest and peculiar – part in British Columbia's home defence and surveillance network. It allowed young and old men, and those in vital economic sectors, to make a contribution that freed other people for overseas service. "What each unit accomplished depended almost entirely on the initiative of its members," *The Ranger* boasted in January 1944. "Success was measured by willingness."[110]

If the PCMR's primary objective was to meet the public demand for action, it served this purpose admirably. General staff statements in early 1942 stressed that "everything possible be done on the West Coast to satisfy public opinion in respect to military security." Authorities recognized that active force troops could not adequately cover all the ground and that reserve army elements were concentrated in metropolitan areas. As a staff summary succinctly noted, the military needed "an organization of men with a knowledge of British Columbia born of experience from living in the rocky country along the rugged coast line, and the thick, barely penetrable bush" of the Interior's timberlands.[111] The Rangers had this knowledge and provided a sense of security. The threat of enemy operations on Canadian soil had changed the outlook of British Columbians. They no longer viewed the military as an abstract expeditionary force. By its very nature, the PCMR provided "contact between 'Mr. Citizen' and the military," which had not existed before and "which no amount of ordinary propaganda ... can produce."[112]

The Rangers offered an unorthodox model for homeland defence. Their organizational structure and philosophy encouraged an inexpensive military presence in remote regions rooted in ingenuity and self-sufficiency. "While the Rangers are now being disbanded, the Ranger idea will not die," the final issue of *The Ranger* proclaimed in 1945: "If this land of ours is ever again threatened, to make it solid again in total defence, it will be the Rangers who will fill the gaps and supply the link to fit the regular soldier to this rough, rugged country which we love."[113] The emergence of the Cold War led defence planners to resurrect the Ranger concept much sooner than most British Columbians would have anticipated.

2
Setting the Stage, 1946-47

We don't want, and we don't need, further organized military bodies supplementing Active and Reserve Forces but what we need is that small groups of specially adapted people take an interest in the defence of their country in order that we may derive the greatest benefits from their knowledge and particular facilities and it is necessary that they be organized to some extent; but I am afraid that if we try to make them too military we will certainly stand to lose by it. I can understand that the "powers that be" wish to retain the strictest possible control over anyone with firearms, particularly when issued by the Department [of National Defence] and I can see the reason for it but I also suggest that if the ... interest [is] taken by the respective Commanders, that the organization can be kept in line and a great deal of benefit will accrue to the [Canadian] Forces and the country in general.

    – Lieutenant-Colonel Bob Keane, Western Command,
    to Colonel L.M. Chesley, Army Headquarters, 9 July 1947[1]

❦ CANADIANS LOOKED FORWARD to the anticipated peace dividend promised in return for their wartime sacrifices. The armed forces demobilized rapidly, and veterans returned home to their families, made babies on their Veterans' Land Act grants, and welcomed the return to so-called normalcy. The atomic bombs dropped on Hiroshima and Nagasaki secured a quick

Allied victory in the Pacific and ushered in the new atomic age. The Canadian delegates at the San Francisco Conference who helped create the United Nations tried to replace the psychological burdens of wartime fear with the optimism of peace. But early postwar optimism quickly gave way to fear. In late 1945, Igor Gouzenko's suitcase of secret documents revealed that our Soviet ally had established an elaborate spy network in Canada, the United States, and Britain. For well-established political, cultural, economic, and military reasons, Canadians knew in which camp they belonged: the West. Yet the prime minister, William Lyon Mackenzie King, still hoped the grand alliance would survive, obviating the need for national defence preparation. If the Americans and the Soviets became rivals, he would seek to avoid increasing tensions between the two.[2] A house sandwiched between two dominant superpowers was no longer fireproof.

The Canadian military had first considered the possibility of a Soviet air attack over the pole during the early stages of the Second World War. A strategic assessment (made on the basis of a *National Geographic* polar projection map) found little cause for alarm.[3] "On the Dominion's northern territories those two famous servants of the Czar, Generals January and February, mount guard for the Canadian people all year round," C.P. Stacey wrote in his 1940 study of Canadian defence policy. He noted that aircraft may make the Arctic and Subarctic regions more strategically significant but concluded that they did not pose an immediate, practical threat.[4]

It was not the enemy but the tempo of Allied activities in the North that generated anxieties about sovereignty and security in remote regions. American soldiers poured into northwestern Canada to undertake megaprojects such as the Alaska Highway, the Northwest Staging Route, and the Canol pipeline.[5] Northern nationalists worried that Canada's laissez-faire approach to northern governance was not only insufficient but also irresponsible.[6] "The [Americans] have apparently walked in and taken possession in many cases as if Canada were unclaimed territory inhabited by a docile race of aborigines," asserted Vincent Massey, the Canadian high commissioner to the United Kingdom. Mackenzie King shared these concerns about American encroachments and fretted that "Canadians were looked upon by Americans as a lot of Eskimos."[7] Officials therefore began to look "down

Military development in northwestern Canada during the Second World War ▶

Source: William R. Morrison and Kenneth A. Coates, *Working the North: Labor and the Northwest Defense Projects, 1942-1945* (Anchorage: University of Alaska Press, 1994). Reprinted with permission.

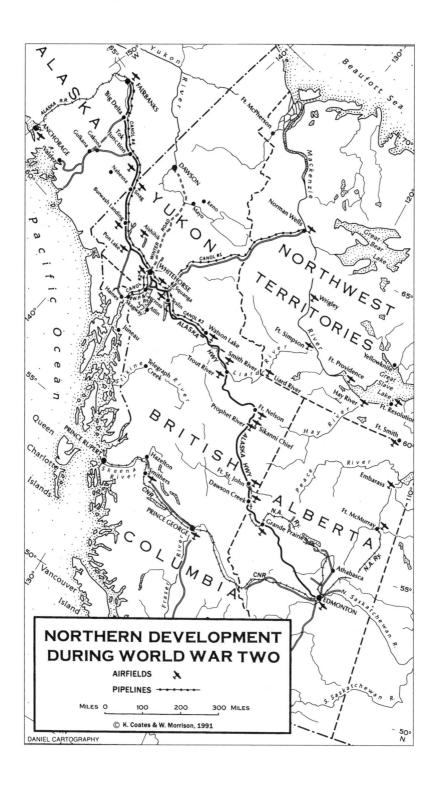

NORTHERN DEVELOPMENT DURING WORLD WAR TWO

AIRFIELDS ✈

PIPELINES ┅┅┅┅┅

MILES 0   100   200   300 MILES

© K. Coates & W. Morrison, 1991

DANIEL CARTOGRAPHY

north," took steps to assert jurisdiction (appointing a special commissioner to oversee northern defence projects in 1943), and made it clear that joint plans and activities to bolster continental defence did not give the United States any continuing rights after the war. The victory and a return to peacetime in 1945 brought a short respite. Ottawa proceeded to reimburse the United States for the infrastructure it had built in northern Canada, and the American troops went home. Their withdrawal allayed short-term worries about sovereignty but left a military vacuum in the region that soon demanded attention.[8]

Cooling East-West relations forced Canada to re-evaluate its geostrategic position. "To the Americans the defence of the United States is continental defence and that includes us, and nothing ... will ever drive that idea out of their heads," General Maurice Pope, Canada's representative on the Permanent Joint Board of Defence, explained in 1944. "What we have to fear is more a lack of confidence in the United States as to our security, rather than enemy action ... If we do enough to assure the United States we shall have done a good deal more than a cold assessment of the risk would indicate to be necessary."[9] He cogently summarized Canada's need to defend against help. If the United States made overly pessimistic assessments of the Soviet Union in the early postwar years compared to "less alarmist" Canadian reports of Soviet intentions and capabilities,[10] defence and foreign policy makers still faced a series of unavoidable questions. If Canada alone did not have sufficient resources to protect the northern flank of North America to the satisfaction of the Americans, what did it need to contribute to a continental defence partnership to preserve its sovereignty?[11] In short, if Canada could not or would not defend the North, the Americans would do it themselves. Canada's closest ally could pose the greatest threat to Canadian sovereignty.

American interest in northern roads, airfields, and potential weather and radar stations resurfaced in 1946. Tremendous advances in air power opened the North American continent to foreign threats, and the North was its most vulnerable front.[12] Joint planning committees discerned little immediate threat, but when (not if) the Soviets got the atomic bomb, the obvious danger would be airplane attacks. The likelihood of a massive land-based invasion sweeping through the Arctic was remote, but incursions to pin down American and Canadian forces and divert attention from the European heartland seemed more plausible. In the short-term, the Soviets could still plant agents for subversion and sabotage, mount clandestine attacks with chemical and biological agents, and use sea- or airborne irregular forces to establish lodgements in northern Canada, Labrador, or Alaska.[13] If the Americans acknowledged a potential threat, then Canada also had to recognize the possibility and take action.

Senior decision makers in Ottawa recognized that a rash response to these new security concerns was neither appropriate nor feasible. Postwar military cutbacks precluded large-scale mobilization to protect remote regions, despite government officials' belief that "to retain sovereignty in the Far North, Canada must do more than she has done in the past – with special reference to effective occupation."[14] When Brooke Claxton took over as minister of national defence in early December 1946, the prime minister told him that his responsibilities were "clear and simple – consolidate and save money." He also had a national duty to sustain viable armed forces with a realistic mission, however modest the budget. Claxton recognized that Canada needed to cooperate with the Americans, but he advocated that it should do as much as it could to defend its North.[15] The press derided what they called a Maginot Line mentality, a reference to the allegedly impregnable defensive line that France had erected during the interwar years and that the Germans had simply flanked to conquer the country in 1940. Reporters considered large standing forces for continental defence wasteful, particularly when military exercises demonstrated that Canada still had much to learn about its polar regions.[16]

At the time, neither the military nor the media contemplated Inuit as potential northern allies.[17] On the eve of Operation Musk Ox, the most public postwar northern exercise, a reporter with the *Winnipeg Free Press* quipped, "There's a lonesome Eskimo in Queen Maud Gulf, Arctic Ocean, who may also be a mighty surprised man one of these weeks." The military planned to airdrop supplies at Perry River, about eleven hundred kilometres northwest of Churchill. "However, the Arctic native who can't read or write and has no radio, won't know about the plan unless a dog team ... gets there first."[18]

The military operation was ambitious but lacked indigenous expertise. In the winter of 1946, forty men on ten snow machines traversed five thousand kilometres of rough northern terrain in ninety days, from Churchill on the coast of Hudson Bay to Cambridge Bay in the Arctic Archipelago, before heading west and south to Edmonton. The exercise grappled with scientific and tactical questions as well as with the simple question of whether a modern military could sufficiently tame the hostile Arctic environment to complete a major mission.[19] The platoon-size force required a special air supply unit of 224 men and nine aircraft, with two advanced bases accommodating another 230 men. The final tally: nearly five hundred troops to support a forty-man force operating in a nontactical setting.[20]

As a governmental spectacle traversing the vastness of the Arctic, Musk Ox generated unprecedented publicity about northern operations. It also refocused attention on the military aspects of Canada's remote regions. The 1946 Canadian-American Basic Security Plan required the Canadian armed forces to prepare for Arctic operations.[21] American threat assessments anticipated diversionary attacks, but Canadian decision makers saw no need for costly Regular Force garrisons. For financial reasons, Prime Minister Mackenzie King emphasized that Canada should "adopt measures of more modest proportions."[22]

Measures of Modest Proportions? Western Plans to Resurrect the PCMR

It fell to the regional commanders to figure out which "measures of more modest proportions" were appropriate. Major-General F.F. "Worthy" Worthington, who became the general officer commanding Western Command after the war, worked to bolster civilian support for the military in his region. In particular, he focused on using community-based reservists to establish a military presence in remote areas.[23] In early 1946, he informed army headquarters in Ottawa that northern residents wanted to contribute to Canadian defence but that transportation, communication networks, and the community demographics would not suit typical reserve units. Worthington suggested rifle clubs. The vice chief of the general staff remained skeptical: the military would have difficulty controlling these clubs and training possibilities would be limited.[24] Worthington had to consider alternatives.

Another proposal came from Tommy Taylor, the strong-willed and energetic wartime empire builder. In April 1946, he formed and incorporated a civilian PCMR Association. As managing director, he strove to "perpetuate the ideals and activities" of the Pacific Coast Militia Rangers in peacetime, and he appealed to National Defence to support Rangers as a "civilian rifle association" that would span the same geography as the wartime organization. Taylor had already arranged affiliation with the BC Rifle

Lieutenant-Colonel Thomas Alexander Hatch (Tommy) Taylor. *The Ranger,* January 1944

Association and negotiated a search-and-rescue role with Western Air Command. He lobbied the director of military operations and plans for support and promised that any wartime friction between the Rangers and the Reserve Force would not reappear. He instead tried to convince senior officers that his association would drum up support for "a well founded, well supported Reserve Army." If the military granted the PCMR status as an official rifle association and provided its members with ammunition for training, Taylor insisted that everyone would benefit.[25]

Military officials knew that Taylor's plans were untenable. The PCMR had disbanded in 1945, and the association's civilian status legally precluded it from receiving a military designation. Furthermore, postwar officials had specifically suspended military support to civilian rifle associations. Until they sorted out organizational plans, muddying the mix made no sense.

Taylor, however, continued to recruit BC politicians to his cause and bombarded cabinet ministers and parliamentarians with appeals to secure military recognition for his organization. Senior military officers held firm. Taylor's association could continue in its civilian form alongside any newly established military units, but it could not and would not have official military status.[26]

Despite their refusal to sanction Taylor's grand dreams for a resurrected Ranger organization that would span all of BC, senior officers did use the PCMR as a template for cost-effective northern defence. When Worthington visited Yellowknife that summer, a local delegation proposed forming a Reserve Force or Ranger unit. Community members insisted that the military would have no difficulty raising "a considerable number of able-bodied officers and men" in the territorial capital. In Yukon, Dawson City's representatives also lobbied for a Ranger unit. Their city had boasted a thriving PCMR company during the war, and they wanted to see it resurrected. Because these proposals fit with Worthington's ideas and brought up positive memories, he passed them along to Ottawa.[27] Since the Department of National Defence had a mandate to foster and develop public interest in the postwar army and to encourage citizen engagement, tapping into local expertise made sense.[28] This time, however, any PCMR-like organization would be national. It would include the northland and both coasts, and it would focus on small, isolated communities along the "fringe." In this way, the Militia Rangers – the proposed name – would not compete with existing reserve units.[29]

The director of military operations and plans, Major-General Churchill Mann, started the ball rolling. In June 1946, he informed the general officers commanding the military districts across Canada that they would discuss organizing new units for remote coastal and northern regions at their annual fall meeting. His preliminary working paper, titled "The Canadian Rangers," outlined the problem of creating and training a part-time, volunteer organization. Mann began by trumpeting the value of the PCMR. Although the reserve army had played a role similar to the Rangers in Eastern Command, it was highly unlikely that "a great portion of the Reserve Force" would be used for home defence. A nation-wide Ranger organization could perform various wartime roles, but command and control would require more than the single staff officer who had overseen the entire PCMR. Mann anticipated complications in organizing, administering, and issuing equipment to a far-flung force. He saw three options:

(a) To organize the force completely. Theoretically this would seem to be desirable to obtain the greatest value in war. However, the training and administrative implications of such a solution must be fully realized and plans be devised which are practicable.

(b) To organize a nucleus of such a Corps to form the basis of expansion in time of war. Here again problems will arise but their solution will present less difficulty.

(c) To limit any action to the preparation of plans for organization in war, which could be kept under review and implemented in the event of an emergency.[30]

He passed these thoughts on to army commanders across Canada for comment.

Worthington vigorously supported the idea of organizing Rangers in peacetime. He notified his subordinates in Western Command of the "secret" plans to create a volunteer body similar to the PCMR and ordered a systematic survey to jump-start planning in his area. Presuming that the new force would adopt the PCMR's model of companies with detachments in outlying areas, Worthington also solicited suggestions for unit locations. Worthy assumed that the new Ranger force would incorporate Taylor's PCMR Association *en masse,* so Military District No. 11 (which spanned BC and Yukon) would be "amply covered." By contrast, in the "virgin ground" of the Alberta military district and the Northwest Territories, he envisaged Ranger companies at strategic points throughout the Rocky Mountain defiles, along the Northwest Highway, and in northern Alberta. He requested information on the western Canadian population (White, Indian, and Inuit), the general nature of their work or native activities, and their "tribal" characteristics. Finally, he asked district commanders to identify equipment needs. During the war, the Rangers west of the Cascade Mountains had received different equipment than those to the east. Worthington assumed the same logic would apply, and he imagined a flexible force that could accommodate regional and local needs.[31]

Officials in Ottawa were less enthusiastic. Brigadier W.H.S. Macklin, the vice adjutant general, had served for eighteen months in senior administrative and staff positions at Pacific Command Headquarters during the war and knew the PCMR's drawbacks first-hand. In his view, the wartime Rangers had become a formal militia that competed with the reserve army. "In areas like the Okanagan the PCMR were nearly as much of a nuisance

Major General Frederic Franklin Worthington, nicknamed "Worthy" and "Fighting Frank" during the war.
The Ranger, August 1945

as they were a help," he recalled. Because the Rangers were not constrained by the same controls imposed on the reserve army, boys as young as fourteen were drawn into the force. Macklin did not approve. He acknowledged the PCMR's wartime relevance "when the Americans lost control of the Pacific for a time, and there was a great risk of an actual invasion of Canadian territory." But why would any enemy want to attack a remote part of Canada in 1946? Before any organizing occurred, Macklin insisted that the military "be perfectly clear as to the military necessity for it and the precise military functions it would carry out, and its relation to the other Armed Forces, especially the Reserve Army." In his assessment, with the exception of "acting as guides, or as hunters of small enemy [detachments] in the immediate vicinity of the Rangers' homes," the Regular Forces could perform every one of the Rangers' proposed roles better.[32]

Where Worthington urged action, Macklin urged restraint. Untrained forces did not benefit a professional army, he insisted, and if the Rangers did not receive adequate training, the results could be disastrous. Coast watching sounded like a simple role, but he recalled "a couple of general alarms in Pacific Command because coast watchers reported 'submarines' that turned out to be whales." Bad intelligence squandered resources and drew attention away from real threats. In Macklin's view, the proposed elementary aircraft recognition training was "nothing less than a menace."

"In fact, there is no such thing – you either recognize the aircraft or you don't! Guesswork is no help." Macklin recommended that the army focus on consolidating and improving the reserves. If, after two or three years, the military "clearly and logically demonstrated" a need for Rangers, then it could organize them.[33]

Widely Divergent Solutions: Regional Views on the Ranger Concept

In early October 1946, the chief of the general staff's office distributed a questionnaire on General Mann's proposed "semi-military" Canadian Ranger organization to the general officers commanding. Senior defence officials anticipated widely divergent solutions, and they were correct.[34] Not only did the regional commanders' enthusiasm for the overall concept vary, they also held different views on organizing, equipping, training, and paying for the organization – core questions that persisted for the next six decades. Regional variance became a permanent characteristic of the Ranger organization, and it helps explain why and how units differed across the country.

Although the regional commanders concurred with the proposed roles, they disagreed about whether the Rangers should be organized fully, partly, or only in theory. Western Command, the most enthusiastic, recommended complete organization akin to the PCMR. If this was not practical in peacetime, Worthington advocated fully organized units in key locations and a "nucleus" of Rangers in other places that could expand if necessary. He insisted that only a regional commander and his staff could make informed decisions about the units' placement and enrollment. In Northwest Territories, for example, full-scale units at Aklavik and Norman Wells could expand to whatever size the local Aboriginal populations allowed. At larger centres such as Port Radium and Yellowknife, prospective Rangers would be screened carefully and a "very definite limit" imposed on unit size. Detachments of 3 or 4 men could span the sparsely populated Alaska Highway, while Dawson City and Mayo could accommodate companies of up to 150 Rangers. Taylor's PCMR Association would play a role in BC. Worthington prioritized flexibility and opposed any "age or category limitations" on Rangers. "The best man in the North that I know of to organize a detachment is sixty years old," he noted. "He has lived in the country for forty years, is strong and hearty, and capable of great endurance. I know also of a one-armed man who would be invaluable to the organization."[35]

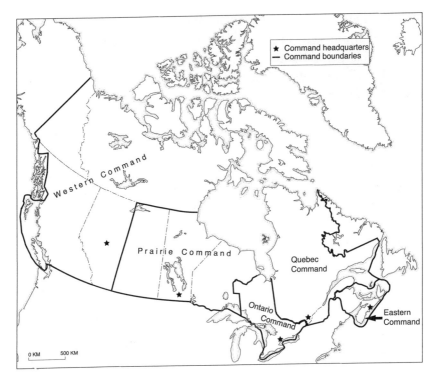

Military commands in Canada, 1946

The other commanders promoted a more modest "nucleus" of Rangers to balance practical realities with peacetime requirements. Central Command favoured establishing Ranger units in appropriate areas but wanted to limit membership to "the best types" who could then educate and mobilize the population in time of war. Prairie and Quebec Commands advocated a similar approach. Brigadier M.H.S. Penhale proposed a "loosely described" organization, one that would "NOT conform to any rigid pattern of war establishment." Major-General E.J. Renault supported a force built around Hudson's Bay Company (HBC) or Royal Canadian Mounted Police (RCMP) posts, places where Rangers could mobilize on short notice. On the one hand, he argued, paper planning would not prepare the Rangers to respond to an actual emergency; on the other, full-scale organizing would not suit a "constantly changing" civilian environment. Across the country, officers emphasized flexibility – a common refrain that continues to be relevant.[36]

Major-General Harry Foster of Eastern Command offered the one dissenting voice. He believed the investment of scarce defence resources into

Major-General Harry
Wickwire Foster.
Department of National
Defence, Photo ZK-943-7

even a modest Ranger establishment would be a waste. "It would be extremely difficult to maintain interest under peacetime conditions even for a nucleus of such a Corps," he asserted. "The problem of administration and training would create an added load for the small staffs available for such work and would be out of proportion to the results obtained." Like Macklin, Foster took a critical view of the PCMR. The Rangers had been "extremely enthusiastic and performed a useful function" while the Japanese posed an immediate threat, but "interest fell off and the organization became somewhat top heavy with administration" as the threat diminished. He saw little value in sustaining a Ranger organization during peacetime and recommended, at most, confining the Rangers to "paper planning." His headquarters would maintain a list of key individuals willing to serve in an emergency, but he had no interest in trying to recruit or train them. He insisted that existing Reserve Force training requirements already exceeded available budgets and that the Rangers "should NOT be formed" or trained at their expense.[37]

Most commanders did not see the necessity of ongoing, formal training. The Rangers would be self-sufficient, and a simple military liaison would keep them engaged. Prairie Command insisted that it would be neither practical nor possible to train recruits to a uniform standard. Weapons and field-craft training would be wasted on individuals who spent their lives handling guns and living off the land. Nevertheless, Rangers could learn aircraft recognition, report writing, and military topography through correspondence courses. At certain times of the year, Ranger personnel could also gather to receive training from a specially selected instructional team, or selected Rangers could attend courses at corps schools to get general or advanced military training. Quebec Command suggested holding two operational schemes each year, one in winter and one in summer, similar to British Home Guard exercises during the war. Lumber companies, forestry associations, RCMP posts, and HBC personnel could "easily" take part without expense to the public. Both Renault and Penhale agreed that standardized training was inappropriate given the varied backgrounds and expectations of the Rangers.[38]

Only Western Command, the home of the former PCMR, proposed an expansive training program. Because "practically one hundred percent of the adults would be accustomed to hunting, and in consequence, skilled shots and familiar with weapons," Worthington suggested training in rescue work, information collection, preparing basic plans to protect vulnerable points, establishing communication systems, and participating in exercises with Active and Reserve Force units. His command proposed a small grant to cover local expenses incurred by instructional teams and to publish a magazine. "These men live in remote places in many cases and are avid readers of anything they can get hold of," Worthington noted. "I know from personal experience the Ranger magazine was read and re-read continually, and where small groups live together, such as in lumber camps, each item was discussed over and over again."[39]

Most of the commanders agreed that Rangers should not be remunerated for day-to-day service. Western Command emphasized that their unpaid status would dissuade individuals interested only in pay from signing up. If the military assigned the Rangers specific tasks such as mountain rescues or guiding other army units, however, they should be paid like any other military personnel doing the same job. Worthington insisted that this "would be the exception rather than the rule."[40] In contrast, General Foster in Eastern Command did not understand how the army could maintain interest or exercise "any meaningful control" over unpaid Rangers. This perspective, so contrary to the philosophy of voluntarism espoused by the other commanders, reinforced how out of sync the view from Halifax was with the rest of the country.

The question of equipping the Rangers generated a similar split. General Foster stated that it was difficult enough to control the equipment allotted to scattered reserve units, never mind "isolated groups such as the Rangers." Without constant supervision, he asserted, people in remote communities had "too great a tendency" to use equipment for private purposes. In his view, they should not be trusted with military kit. In stark contrast, Worthington had no reservations about giving equipment to Rangers. The military had a large quantity of obsolete US 30.06 sporting rifles and ammunition, which he felt, "should be issued on a liberal scale." In Northwest Territories, where most men already owned a rifle and "would not wish to be burdened with a second weapon," the military could issue appropriate ammunition through local training posts. Each Ranger detachment should have compasses, mapping material, stationary, and first-aid or rescue kits. The Rangers would also need some form of insignia to identify themselves. Worthington suggested changing the name on the PCMR's badge but retaining the "proud" emblem. The Rangers could receive "dry-back" clothing, which was already the "recognized uniform of the Rangers" across the Northwest. In winter, however, "the inhabitants would prefer to wear their own type of clothing, as no two men appear to agree on the best type of garment and would certainly disagree with anything that the Department would provide." All told, he thought the local units could account for their equipment periodically. Monitoring an individual working on his trapline for several months was ridiculous. Armed with positive wartime memories, Worthington had few concerns: "I believe that men would take care of ... [the equipment] issued to them because again, in the case of the PCMR, they kept their rifles in perfect condition without any supervision, which is more than can be said for many soldiers."[41]

Other commands had more modest expectations. Central Command suggested a sporting rifle, two hundred rounds of ammunition each year, a pack, a bedroll, aircraft recognition charts, and area maps. Prairie Command argued that Rangers would need equipment only for specific missions or in times of war, particularly some form of wireless communication to transmit information "without the necessity of long journeys in time and place." Quebec Command likewise saw the need for communications equipment so that the Rangers could provide a "covering screen" at key points, and it was willing to consider issuing rifles, light machine guns, ammunition, and personal equipment. With the regional commanders divided, it fell to central authorities in Ottawa to devise a national plan.[42]

Debating the Concept in Ottawa

On 30 October 1946, the director of military operations and plans prepared a document in which he tried to reconcile conflicting views on the proposed organization. The Canadian Rangers would "be formed, on a restricted basis, across Canada for the purpose of operating in the thinly populated parts of the country which are not normally traversed nor under surveillance and where it is impractical to organize units of the Reserve Force." The volunteers would form part of the reserve militia – the part-time army. Units would report to regional army commanders responsible for implementing the overall policy devised by army headquarters. The document reiterated points made in earlier papers. Rather than forming a standard Ranger establishment, the military would focus its practical efforts on creating a nucleus of Rangers led by "key personnel ... selected from the permanent residents of established ports or communities." They would not be organized along "fixed military lines," nor trained as soldiers, and training would "be best given under their own arrangements." The Rangers would have relaxed physical standards and age limits, and they would receive only a sporting rifle, annual ammunition, and an armband. "Normal service" would go unpaid, but when they participated in manoeuvres with other military units or attended military schools, they would receive standard Reserve Force remuneration.[43]

An unclear northern defence policy ensured a mixed reception for the concept at National Defence Headquarters. Several senior military staff registered their concerns and objections. Brigadier Macklin continued to question "any military necessity for a nationwide Ranger [organization]." Would men of the Ranger type not guide the military in an emergency regardless? Would trained soldiers, sailors, and airmen not be better coast watchers than untrained amateurs who did not know what to look for and lacked the communications or training to report properly? Finally, why should the military get involved in civilian and police functions such as counterespionage, reporting on aircraft, and participating in rescue parties? The organization would cost money, absorb time and effort, and bring few appreciable gains to the military. Macklin believed Tommy Taylor was the real "moving spirit behind the proposal" and that the Rangers' potential, even in BC, was "very limited." He could not help but pen a final postscript on his memo: "In short I rather feel this is another instance of making the plan and then desperately trying to make the appreciation fit it." The adjutant general agreed.[44]

Others shared their concerns. Brigadier S.F. Clark, the deputy chief of the general staff, observed that

> folk-lore attributes many qualities to outdoor people and especially to natives (such as Indians and Eskimos) which, in fact, they do not possess. It is common belief that Indians and Eskimos, and to a lesser degree trappers, in our Canadian hinterlands possess special qualities of sense of direction and as such would be extremely valuable as guides to Military parties during operations. One of the most experienced Arctic travellers, Vilhjalmur Stefansson, states that invariably he found that Indians and Eskimos were reasonably good guides in country with which they were familiar but that as soon as they were taken into unfamiliar country, they displayed no "sixth sense of direction" but were, in fact, less able to find their way about than an experienced Anglo Saxon.

Inaccurate or unreliable information was as bad as having no information. "Assuming for the moment that one cannot rely on such personnel as guides and topography intelligence officers," Clark noted, "what then is the value of a handful of men widely dispersed and equipped with sporting rifles?" If the military decided that the Rangers would have real use, "they should either be trained or not trained. There should be no half-way measure." In any case, how would they report from isolated areas? They could not simply walk up to a telephone booth or use a "footling little wireless set" – it would have to be "a man-sized piece of equipment costing a very great deal of money, be technically complex and *not* capable of being man packed." With a wireless system in place, anyone could do the job. All told, Clark questioned the need for Rangers at all.[45]

Optimistic assessments by senior officers who saw the Rangers as an inexpensive way to gather intelligence in remote regions offset these negative reactions to the concept. Major-General J.H. MacQueen, master general of the ordnance, confirmed that the costs of a rifle, two hundred rounds of ammunition per man annually, and an armband would be negligible. Woodsmen and fishermen would have suitable clothing and did not need uniforms.[46] If everything was kept on a reasonable scale, the Rangers might prove useful. After all, the experiment would cost next to nothing.

This argument resonated most of all. When the Conference of Commanders met in Ottawa on 5-6 December 1946, the participants agreed to create a national Canadian Ranger organization.[47]

From Vision to Reality

During an inspection of West Coast defences in early April 1947, Minister Claxton announced the formation of the Canadian Rangers "on a restricted basis" throughout the country.[48] After the military ironed out some minor legal wrinkles, Order-in-Council P.C. 1644 officially created the Canadian Rangers as a corps of the reserve militia on 23 May 1947. During war, they would have the following duties:

(a) Provision of guides to organized troops within own area.

(b) Coast watching.

(c) Assistance to the RCMP and/or Provincial Police in the discovery, reporting and apprehension of enemy agents or saboteurs. The reporting of other suspicious activities.

(d) Immediate local defence against sabotage by small enemy detachments or saboteurs and to assist and augment civilian protective arrangements against saboteurs, within the area in which the organization is authorized to operate.

(e) Reporting, locating and rescue work, including first aid treatment in connection with aircraft distress.

In peacetime, they would have a similar but more limited role:

(a) Provision of guides to troops on exercises, when required.

(b) The preparation of local defence schemes referred to in (d) above.

(c) Collection of detailed information concerning their local area likely to be of assistance to them in carrying out their roles in war and the documenting of such information with any necessary sketches.

(d) Provision of rescue parties for civilian or military purposes, where required.[49]

In short, the Rangers would use their indigenous knowledge of local areas to act as guides and scouts for the regular army, they would report suspicious activities to civil authorities, and they would counter local threats by enemy saboteurs. These roles bore remarkable similarity to those of the PCMR, even though the Rangers would cover a much wider geography.

Translating these roles into a general staff policy statement revealed salient differences between senior officials in Ottawa and regional staff officers. In terms of personnel, the original draft included the proviso that the Reserve Force's standard age and health restrictions would apply. This clause missed the essential point, Western Command insisted. "The type of man who makes the best Ranger is often one who, through physical disability, great age, or immature age, is more or less chained to his particular locality," explained Lieutenant-Colonel Bob Keane. "It is conceivable that some of the most valuable recruits may range in age from twelve or younger to eighty or older ... It is the man's knowledge and intelligence rather than his physical fitness that makes him valuable to such an organization." Keane noted that during the war "half of our NHL hockey stars could not pass the Army medical." These potential recruits, deemed unfit for overseas service, could certainly perform useful functions on the home front.[50]

The original draft statement also missed the mark regarding roles. The primary rationale for the Rangers was to collect local intelligence, not to act as an organized military force compensating for insufficient Active or Reserve Forces. Their role, Keane explained, would be "peculiar to the men themselves." Even in war they would remain in their local areas, serving as "the eyes, ears and feelers of all services in the more isolated portions of the country." Their uniqueness had inherent benefits and limitations. "It might be necessary in extreme cases to ask for the assistance of the Rangers for aid to the civil power," he noted, "but this is considered to be very dangerous in that the discipline of the Ranger organization will not be of the same type or standard to enable them to take action against their fellow men." He added that "the probability of local politics and partisanship entering into the picture" made the Rangers "a very poor risk, in fact a liability," if anyone expected them to assist civil authorities in quelling a local disturbance. They would provide a unique service, not a watered-down version of

Lieutenant-Colonel
Robert A. (Bob) Keane.
Thunder Bay Historical Museum
Society, 984.1.474

other military elements. The key was to acknowledge their local knowledge and existing skills without attempting to make them too militaristic.[51]

By the summer of 1947, the Canadian Ranger organization that existed on paper had morphed into Keane's ideal. Defence officials presented a general staff policy statement that August. The department would organize units in sparsely populated coastal areas and in the area north of Canada's main population belt where reserve units did not exist. The criteria for membership in the Rangers placed a premium on local residence, and they placed no age or physical limitations on officers or other ranks. Recruits would receive armbands and obsolescent Lee-Enfield No. 4 Mk. 1 rifles.[52] Training would include elementary topography, message writing, the use of wireless, and other basic essentials but not close-order or arms drills. The "most suitable and desirable" Rangers would not resemble other militia or Regular Force personnel. A substantial portion of any Ranger unit would comprise men unlikely to serve any other element of the army. Furthermore, most personnel would remain in their home area during both peace and

TABLE 1
Military commands and authorized Canadian Ranger strengths, 1947

Command	Military districts	General description	Authorized Rangers
Western Command	11, 13	BC, Alberta, Yukon, and Northwest Territories	2,600
Prairie Command	10, 12	Manitoba, Saskatchewan, and western Ontario	1,490
Central Command	1, 2, 3	Ontario (less districts of Thunder Bay, Rainy River, and Kenora)	300
Quebec Command	4, 5	Quebec	550
Eastern Command	6, 7	Nova Scotia, New Brunswick, and Prince Edward Island	60
TOTAL			5,000

Source: General Order 21/1946, 28 January 1946, and General Order 74, 28 March 1946.

wartime. These features distinguished the Rangers from other elements of the reserves.[53]

The Rangers would have a flexible structure to accommodate regional diversity. Variations in roles, location, terrain, and demographics, as well as communication challenges, precluded the formation of a standard establishment. The largest unit would be a company commanded by a reserve militia captain responsible for control and administration of up to five platoons. Each platoon, commanded by a reserve militia lieutenant, would have up to thirty other ranks, divided into sections commanded by sergeants. These Ranger officers and sergeants – "well established men permanently located in local areas" – would command only Rangers unless called out or placed on active service, in which case they would assume a status junior to men of equivalent rank in the army. In peacetime, the Rangers would be a modest force compared to the PCMR. The overall strength would be limited to five thousand, all ranks, with more than half concentrated in Western Command (BC and the northern territories) and most of the remainder in Prairie Command.[54]

✤ In July 1946, Lester Pearson wrote in *Foreign Affairs* that "it is for the Great Powers to decide, by their policies and their plans, whether [the development of the Canadian Arctic] can be conducted in an atmosphere of friendly cooperation between all the Arctic nations, and with a resultant benefit to all, or whether the Northern Hemisphere is to become an area of national rivalries, fears and ambitions ... Canada will certainly do its best to ensure the former, for to no country would the consequences of the alternative be more disastrous. In 1946, there is no isolation – even in the Arctic ice."[55] Later that year, the US ambassador to Canada, Ray Atherton, identified home security as a foremost concern and stated, "it is now necessary for us to consider not the *probability* of action on the part of a potential enemy but its *possibility*." The Americans would not be caught unawares as had the British in 1934 when they failed to pay heed to Baldwin's warning that "the Rhine is our frontier." Britain, in turn, worried that Canada's and the United States' emphasis on defending North America might be detrimental to their overseas commitments. Atherton reiterated that "Canada and the United States could not go to anyone's assistance either in the Middle East or elsewhere unless the Arctic were secure."[56]

Circumstances placed Canada in a challenging position. Politicians and senior public servants considered the United States' estimates of a potential Soviet attack overblown. As historian Kenneth Eyre astutely notes, "neither the United States nor Canada looked on the North as a place to be protected because of some intrinsic value. It was seen as a direction, an exposed flank."[57] Senior decision makers recognized that Canada had to take steps to preserve the northern flank of North America; otherwise, the United States might be forced to act unilaterally.[58] This new northern imperative framed the deliberations that led to the creation of the Canadian Rangers in 1947.

Military officials decided to create this new subcomponent of the Reserve Force at a time when the Department of National Defence was in a state of flux. Minister Brooke Claxton's sharp sword cut the armed forces to a size in line with the King government's fiscal sensitivities. In peacetime Canada, the military defined its role based upon what it could accomplish within a limited budget. Stationing Active or Reserve Forces in remote regions simply cost too much. The military also had to frame its activities as civilian contributions to avoid provoking the Soviets or generating adverse public reactions in North America.[59] Caution, not boldness, defined the early postwar era. That policy makers authorized a Ranger corps in this climate is a testament to the idea's political saleability. The Rangers were an inexpensive form of national defence – ideal for an austerity-minded government.

The Rangers concept did, however, provoke debate. Despite western boosterism, significant doubts remained in Ottawa and in the east about the utility of a Ranger force. Some senior defence officials questioned the logic of having a partially or untrained corps with no precise military function. Could the Rangers fulfill their role? Was that role, as defined, even a military priority? These debates revealed the extent to which Canada's militia myth had lost its hold on the military's imagination. The war had reaffirmed the importance of professionalism, not amateurism. The operational relevance of the Reserve Force remained vague, never mind that of small ancillary units in remote regions.[60]

According to the decentralized concept adopted in 1947, regional army commanders throughout the country would create and maintain the Ranger units and soothe any growing pains. These preliminary discussions, however, revealed differing perceptions about the Rangers' role, location, and training. Western Command envisaged an expansive postwar organization built upon the wartime Ranger concept; other commands imagined a more modest nucleus of Rangers placed in strategic locations throughout the country. These divergent points of view led to regional variations in the form and pace of the Rangers' development in the years ahead. As planners predicted, regional commanders encountered serious problems related to funding, command and control, developing reliable communications with isolated communities, and maintaining interest in the Rangers as a peacetime force.

3
"Teething Troubles,"
1947-49

There will undoubtedly be some teething troubles in getting the
Rangers organized, but they should be settled without undue difficulty.

– Colonel L.M. Chesley to Lieutenant-Colonel R.A. Keane,
24 July 1947[1]

❧ SENIOR DEFENCE OFFICIALS created a basic framework for the Canadian
Rangers by August 1947. Paper planning was one thing; translating ideas
into an actual organization another. The minimalist concept that governed
organizing, training, and uniforms and equipment devolved most responsibilities to regional army commanders. Their visions and interests determined the Rangers' form, shape, and growth. The challenges they encountered
reflected the nation's diversity and drove home the importance of flexibility.
These challenges also revealed the importance of managing local, regional,
and national expectations to allow the Rangers to evolve beyond an embry-
onic stage.

Ranger policy dictated that units be organized "in the sparsely populated
coastal areas and areas to the north of the main belt of population across
Canada." To set firmer guidelines, defence planners in Ottawa analyzed
statistics to figure out how to distinguish between north and south and
isolated and populated. On a map, they drew a line that wound its way
across the provinces between the fifty-fifth and fiftieth parallels. They then
superimposed another map of Reserve Force units and areas they considered

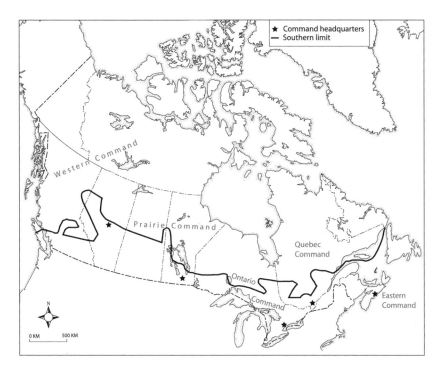

The southern limit of areas in which Ranger units could be formed or raised,
June-July 1947

capable of supporting a unit. The Reserve Force's northern boundary constituted the southern limits of the Canadian Rangers, excluding the Maritime provinces and much of BC's southern Mainland and Vancouver Island, areas where Pacific Coast Militia Ranger (PCMR) units had flourished during the war.

Western Command criticized such simple boundaries. In July 1947, Lieutenant-Colonel Bob Keane stressed that setting an arbitrary southern limit would unnaturally constrain contributions to defence. Why prevent Rangers from forming in the bottom two-thirds of Vancouver Island, which would be vulnerable in wartime? An enemy would certainly not "pay any attention to any lines that we may draw upon maps and will, as has been the custom in the past, take advantage of every loophole that he may find." Why insist on large distances between Rangers and other military units when the former could help the latter? Ambiguity would allow for flexibility. Although officials in Ottawa retained a general demarcation line to prevent the Rangers from sprawling into the BC Interior, they assured Keane that they would make exceptions for coast watchers on the Pacific and Atlantic seaboards.[2]

Western Command wanted to interpret the official description liberally. Its initial plans stretched farther south than anyone in Ottawa had intended. When asked to identify where Ranger units could be formed, Worthington supplied a full list of PCMR Association subunits along the West Coast, as well as interested citizens in Northwest Territories, Yukon, northern Alberta, and the Peace River district.[3] These plans, if carried out, would re-create the wartime empire and bore the unmistakable imprint of Tommy Taylor. Worthington stressed that the Rangers represented "the very essence of 'defence consciousness' and voluntary service," a spirit he wished to inculcate throughout BC. For an annual grant of $20,000 for training and ammunition ("the equivalent of 10 privates in the Active Force") he boasted that he could generate a membership of ten thousand men.[4] Although legal considerations trumped Taylor's proposals, defence officials noted that the association's members certainly could help to create Ranger units and join the force – as long as there was a "clear division of status" between the two organizations.[5]

Missing the distinction, Taylor relished the prospect of reclaiming a re-invigorated Ranger empire. Buoyed by press releases in March 1947 that proclaimed "Canada Plans Ranger Units" and "Coast Defence Corps Planned," Taylor offered to dissolve his association once the army authorized a Ranger force in BC. He also told the chief of the general staff that he was "ready to serve" in "whatever capacity required."[6] But Taylor would not play a central role in the new organization. Worthington met with him in Vancouver and disabused him of the notion that National Defence would pay him as secretary of the PCMR Association. "I knocked that idea out of his head once and for all," the commander explained. That the association would likely fold as a result did not concern Worthington. Overzealous enthusiasts, fuelled by a champion such as Taylor, would compete with the Reserve Force, undermining broader military support for the new organization. "I do not want any Ranger Units within fifty miles [eighty kilometres] of any Reserve Unit," Worthington explained, quashing Taylor's dream to re-create his wartime organization.[7]

The postwar Canadian Rangers would not replicate the PCMR, nor would they enjoy the same meteoric growth. Worthington was cautious and wanted to ensure that the process was done right. His command scrupulously followed the organizing process laid out by army headquarters, first identifying company and platoons areas and then sending its recommendations to Ottawa for approval. It then selected company, platoon, and section commanders to manage the Rangers' growth in their areas. Rangers could not elect their own company and platoon commanders, as some PCMR units had done during the war. The police carefully screened all volunteers, and Worthington allowed only those "whose integrity is above question" to become officers.[8] The commands then authorized the local recruitment of other ranks.

Western Command placed its highest priority on finding the right leaders. If men "of known loyalty" who were respected in their communities headed up companies and platoons, officers realized that the Rangers would have a firm foundation. "Such men are not hard to find on our frontiers, but it is important that he is the right man," explained Lieutenant-Colonel M.R. Dare, commander of the BC area. "Furthermore, the leader must fully understand that there is no financial remuneration nor synthetic glory. He and his compatriots will be rendering Canada a service above the price of gold." Once a Ranger leader assumed command, he would select outdoorsmen for his detachments, "whether they be white men, Indian, or Eskimo," who knew their local area like "the palm of their hand." Suitable individuals would simply be sworn in and "pledged to keep their counsel."[9]

The First Canadian Ranger Companies

The prior existence of a PCMR unit in Yukon, coupled with the territory's unambiguous northernness, made it a prime setting for the first companies. Dawson City, centre of the Klondike gold rush, had declined. Although it remained the territorial capital until 1952, its derelict downtown core and abandoned cabins testified to its former glory. Whitehorse was heading in the opposite direction. It had been a small seasonal transportation town until the Second World War. The construction of the Alaska Highway through southern Yukon brought a deluge of American workers who transformed Whitehorse into the territory's most populous settlement. Growth continued even after the Americans left. Whitehorse's population tripled between 1941 and 1951. The balance of power shifted from the "City of Gold" to the "transportation hub."[10] The presence of the army and air force after the war also signalled Whitehorse's status as a military hub.

Despite its falling fortunes, Dawson City came to boast the first Canadian Ranger company. Several community members contacted Western

Ranger Captain Charles Hathaway (Chappie) Chapman. Courtesy of Sergeant John Mitchell, Dawson patrol

Command about forming a unit in 1947. Worthington paid a personal visit and secured the support of "the leading personalities," including the controller of the Yukon and the local magistrate, who unanimously recommended Captain "Chappie" Chapman to reorganize the Ranger company. Chapman, the former PCMR captain, had served with the Royal Canadian Mounted Police (RCMP) and operated a general store in Dawson. These credentials, as well as his status as the brother-in-law of the local RCMP officer, ensured a speedy security clearance. Howard W. Firth, a former adjutant of the local PCMR, became his second-in-command. Chapman travelled frequently throughout the area while Firth was permanently resident when trappers and prospectors came in for outfitting.[11] Worthington approved their commissions on 22 September 1947. "My hearty congratulations at your being the first officer appointed and in command of the first Ranger Co[mpan]y in Canada's newest defence organization," he told Chapman in a telegram. "It is also gratifying to me that an old RCMP officer leads the van and I am confident No. 1 Dawson City Co[mpan]y will be first in many other things under your guidance and direction."[12]

On paper, the Dawson platoons were listed at Mayo, Keno, and Selkirk. In practice, the Ranger units were even more dispersed. Fort Selkirk, a dwindling trade and supply centre just north of the confluence of the Yukon and Pelly rivers, was too small to support an entire platoon. It combined, however, with Stewart to form a "Yukon River Platoon," a more appropriate label. Trappers "scattered up and down the Yukon river" who traded at the two posts joined the platoon, and Indians of "a very good type" contributed a section. Mayo, the centre of trapping and mining activities on the upper reaches of the Stewart River (and the site of Canada's lowest-ever recorded temperature during the previous winter), had been dormant during the war years, but families returned when the silver mines reopened. Gordon MacIntyre, a well-known government agent, was unanimously selected as platoon commander, and he chose former reservist Reginald Beaumont as his second-in-command. The "floating population" at the Keno mining camp would have its own platoon headquartered at Mayo.[13] The Dawson company was far more expansive than a single dot on a map suggests.

No. 2 Canadian Ranger Company in Whitehorse soon followed. In an earlier report, Worthington had observed that Whitehorse might not be suitable for a Ranger unit because the army and the Royal Canadian Air Force (RCAF) had a sizeable presence there. Given the military significance of southern Yukon, however, he decided the Rangers still had a role to play. The Canadian government had assumed responsibility for the Alaska Highway on 1 April 1946. Beyond the road network, the government had less control. Muskeg, swamps, and lakes dotted the rolling countryside between Watson Lake and Whitehorse, and high mountains flanked the road near Teslin. To the west, the road followed the Takhini and Dezadeash river valleys, dominated by mountain ranges, to the US border. Ranger platoons at Burwash Landing, Teslin, and Carcross provided modest coverage of the area. F.O. Meet, a decorated RCAF veteran and the local Indian Agent, travelled a great deal throughout the area. He was the logical company commander, and ex-PCMR Captain J.P. Stewart, a game warden at Lower Post, BC, joined him.[14] Together, they began organizing the Whitehorse company.

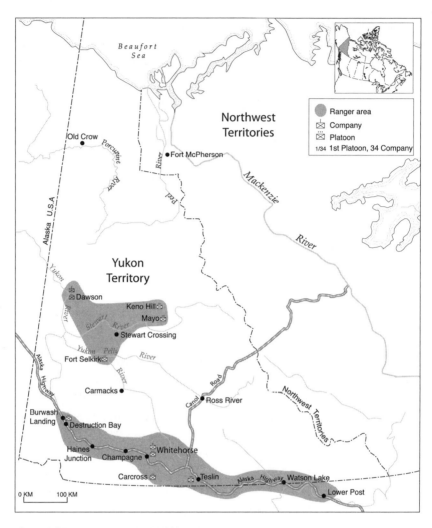

The initial Ranger companies in Yukon, 1947

"In the winter of 1947 a good bus load of us joined with Whitehorse," Ranger Alex van Bibber recalled. He had worked on the gold dredges in Dawson until 1942, when he moved to Whitehorse. "The boom was on," and he got a job with the US army doing survey work by packhorse. He was working for the Inco mining company at Burwash when the Canadian Army conscripted him in 1944. He never made it overseas. He spent six months in quarantine at Camp Debert, Nova Scotia, after contracting the

Ranger Alex van Bibber recalled this early exercise in which "we went out brush camping for about five days" at a place called Joe Creek (now Manyhaul Creek) in Yukon. Photo by Alex van Bibber, courtesy of 1 Canadian Ranger Patrol Group

mumps. After the war, he moved to Champagne, a small Native settlement at Mile 974 on the Alaska Highway between Whitehorse and Haines Junction, where he trapped, guided big-game hunters, and assisted with government geological surveys and mining exploration. He brought a diverse skill set to the Rangers and a deep knowledge of the territory. Like others who joined the fledgling unit, he welcomed the chance to train outdoors and serve his country.[15]

Buoyed by its success in creating the first two companies, Western Command made tentative plans to expand its Ranger footprint. Anxious to proceed but not wanting to "rush the jumps," Worthington discussed his plans with RCAF and navy officials before deciding on other unit locations. In contrast to the PCMR movement, which had been propelled by

Taylor and the war, the Canadian Rangers' ranks grew slowly in the months following their creation. Worthington deliberately moved "quietly and effectively," without publicity, and ensured that the Rangers recruited men of absolute integrity.[16]

Worthington did not want to expand as fast or as far as the PCMR. He focused on strategic areas "where it would not be economical or desirable to station operational troops in the event of an emergency." He planned thirteen more companies to cover the Mackenzie River and Alaska Highway areas, coastal locations with poor communications, and vulnerable points along interior communication lines. Senior defence officials approved his plan in principle but rejected proposed units along the Fraser Canyon. Full-time RCMP guards had watched over rail bridges during the Second World War, and reliable communications connected this region with the rest of BC. Ottawa emphasized two points to set Worthington on track. First, northern and coastal areas particularly needed Ranger units. Second, the military's budget provided no funding for organizing and recruiting Rangers.[17] The Rangers' success would depend on civilian knowledge and resources – in this case, the corporate and public sector.

Building Partnerships

The Rangers' success also depended on the organization's relationship with the RCMP. Potential Ranger officers had to be selected and screened, and the police represented the federal government in remote areas.[18] The army considered the Mounties ideally suited for identifying prospective individuals, but police officials disagreed. "RCMP Headquarters flatly refuses to allow their Officers Commanding to suggest men in areas who would be suitable or desirable for the Rangers," a military intelligence officer reported in 1947. Army officers could ask police detachments for background information on potential individuals, but the police would not serve as recruiting officers or help organize the force.[19]

Major C.R.R. Douthwaite of Western Command found the RCMP's stance "short-sighted and unreasonable." The Mounties were "supposed to act in an advisory capacity to other branches of the government." In his view, the RCMP should have offered "a little practical inter-departmental co-operation," particularly since the Rangers' duties included assisting police. Douthwaite reminded his superiors in Ottawa that "[w]hen all is said and done, the Rangers are NOT working on behalf of the Rangers alone."[20] The RCMP, however, instructed its field officers not to recommend anyone to army personnel.[21]

Corporate citizens proved more obliging. In the fall of 1947, Sir Patrick Ashley Cooper, the governor of the Hudson's Bay Company (HBC), expressed his surprise to Dr. Omond Solandt, the chairman of the Defence Research Board of Canada, that the army had not approached his company to assist with organizing the Rangers. Western Command officials met with HBC executives in early 1948. The company agreed to allow its factors at isolated posts to act as platoon commanders.[22] The HBC had a history of "showing the flag" alongside the RCMP in the North, and it enjoyed a long-term relationship with Aboriginal peoples. Post managers had a "sense of mission as inheritors of empire," and the company's presence and operations had kept government costs in northern regions low through the first half of the century.[23] The army recognized the tangible benefits of working closely with the HBC. The company's network of 215 posts acted like "hubs of a wheel from which trappers and guides work out into the surrounding area, like spokes." HBC staff travelled frequently, knew "every inch of ground in their area," were "expert riflemen," and had continuous contact with northern peoples. Factors at each post operated radio equipment and regularly performed intelligence functions for commercial needs, such as weather reports and local activities. Their local connectedness and influence made them natural candidates to serve as platoon commanders.[24]

Prairie Command simply superimposed its proposed Ranger organization on the HBC's trading-post network because the company's Central Division corresponded roughly with the command boundaries. Why not commission the HBC's section commanders, who visited their posts three or four times each year, as Ranger company commanders and appoint the head of the company's Fur Trade Department a zone commander? The military could exploit the company's existing supply routes and wireless communications. Defence headquarters in Ottawa concurred that this was probably the most efficient way to produce a functioning Ranger organization in the provincial norths but worried about forging an overly intimate relationship with any corporation. Prairie Command's plans would amount to handing the HBC a private army, which it could then use as political capital to embarrass the federal government. In addition, automatically making HBC officials company and platoon commanders was tantamount to placing control of these military appointments in private hands. The informal practice of appointing them as "the best available individuals" in an area would not.[25]

The Rangers developed close links to the private sector throughout the country. The Canadian National and Canadian Pacific railways helped form Ranger detachments at small stations along their lines and suggested potential company and platoon leaders to Ottawa. In Quebec, Canadian Pacific Airlines, Hollinger Mining Corporation, large paper companies, Catholic and Protestant clergymen, and representatives from the departments of Transport and Indian Affairs also helped with planning.[26] Without their contributions, the Rangers' initial growth would not have been possible.

The North Shore and Northern Quebec

Soon after the first companies formed in Yukon, Quebec Command established units along its isolated coastlines. When German U-boats menaced shipping in the Gulf of St. Lawrence in 1942, residents of isolated communities along the North Shore mobilized into reserve units and trained for a shore patrol role. Although German Admiral Karl Dönitz called off the "Battle of the St. Lawrence" at the end of the 1942 season when Canada strengthened its defences, local residents had internalized the threat.[27] Nearly five thousand civilians in the province served as unpaid volunteers in the RCAF Aircraft Detection Corps, formed in 1940 to provide advance warning of aircraft movements, submarines, and possible enemy activity. Along the North Shore, all of the telegraph officers from Tadoussac, Quebec, to Red Bay, Labrador, participated in the corps.[28] This ground-observer warning system was dismantled when the end of the war in Europe removed direct threats to Quebec's coastal communities. The need for modest defences still remained at the Mingan, La Tuque, and Fort Chimo (Kuujjuaq) airfields, as well as at the large power developments at La Tuque and along the St. Maurice River. Consequently, token military representation at HBC posts and in small communities in the interior of Quebec, as well as in isolated and exposed coastal localities, seemed appropriate.[29]

Defence officials recognized that the Rangers would reduce demands on the military to commit better-trained – and more expensive – soldiers to these areas. By late 1947, Quebec area unveiled tentative plans for four Ranger companies (eleven platoons) at Mingan, Sept-Îles, La Tuque, and Fort Chimo. "These companies were to be distributed and located in such a way that their sphere of influence would be ... the greatest possible portion

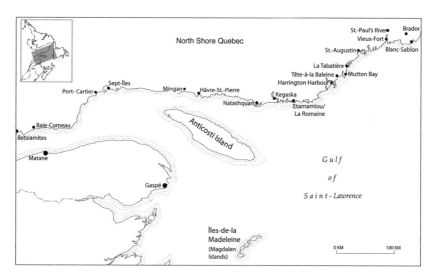

North Shore Quebec, ca. 1947

of the sparsely inhabited areas in the Province," Captain A. Gaumond, the eastern Quebec area intelligence officer, noted after his visit to the North Shore in August 1948. As in Western Command, initial organizing of the Rangers revolved around selecting company and platoon areas, appointing commanders, and recruiting local units up to strength.[30]

During the first phase of Operation Rangers, Gaumond focused on organizing platoons on the North Shore, the 1,050-kilometre stretch along the Gulf of St. Lawrence from Saguenay (Tadoussac) to Blanc-Sablon at the Labrador border.[31] Trapping, hauling logs, and cod and seal fishing dominated the local economy.[32] In the winter, residents lived in houses on the mainland at the end of a bay or at the mouth of a river, where they took shelter from the elements and had access to wood. In the spring, they loaded their boats and left for the headlands or islands closer to fishing grounds.[33] The first company (No. 3) was located at Mingan, which was nestled behind a picturesque archipelago of limestone islands and islets and boasted one of the finest harbours on the North Shore. Mingan had three distinct communities: a US Air Force station with more than two hundred civilian and military personnel and a good communications system; Longue-Pointe-de-Mingan, which had seven hundred people; and the town of Mingan itself, accessible only by boat or plane and inhabited by 35 Whites and 150 Indians who frequently travelled north. The senior US officer nominated one of his civilian employees, James Patrick Whelan, company commander. Whelan, his second-in-command, and a platoon commander then recruited one section of Indians and another of Whites from Longue-Pointe-de-Mingan.[34]

Officials based the other platoon in Harrington Harbour, a fishing village of about four hundred people. Unlike the upper section of the North Shore, bare and rocky coastline dominated the lower stretch. Harrington, surrounded by countless outer islands, was difficult to approach, but it offered shelter against the wind from every direction. A rock-walled "entry passage" protected the small village, and boardwalks led pedestrians over boggy stretches underlain by solid bedrock. Few residents travelled outside the region. "This was an area where silence reigned supreme, where ballot boxes reached their destination the day after scheduled elections," Father Gabriel Dionne wrote upon his arrival in 1948. Only the monthly transit of the time-worn steamer *The North Voyageur* linked the Lower North Shore with Canada. Newcomers commented on the "extreme slowness of communications" and the "fickleness of the weather" which complicated travel between villages, particularly by dog team and *komatik* (sled) in the winter.[35]

The platoon, once established, would focus on coast watching and aircraft spotting along the linear community between Natashquan and St. Augustine River, which included the settlements of Kegaska, Wolf Bay, Cape Whittle, Etameamin River (Etamamiou), Pointe au Maurier, Whale Head, Mutton Bay, and Tabatière.[36] Seen as simple dots on a map, platoon locations do not fully reflect the dispersal of Rangers on the ground.

Gordon Jones became a Ranger in 1948 and remained one for thirty-six years. Born and raised in Harrington Harbour, he served with the Black Watch in Belgium, Holland, and Germany during the war. After he returned, he married a woman from Kegaska in 1947. The following year, an officer recruited Jones, who worked as a game warden along the coast between La Romaine and St. Augustine. Jones recalled that he had "no real reason for joining – I was just asked. Because I was going around in a boat, it just made sense." He enlisted without signing any forms or start-up training. He simply received a rifle, a web belt, and an armband. The officer instructed him that, if a plane came down in the district, he should "do what he could."[37]

What officers encountered on the ground during their visits influenced how plans for practical units took shape. Quebec Command proposed the headquarters for the second Quebec company (No. 4) at Sept-Îles, but plans changed when Captain Gaumond met with Henry Arthur Sewell, a former captain of the 42nd Highlanders of Montreal, the woods manager for the Quebec North Shore Pulp and Paper Company, and the mayor of Baie-Comeau. Sewell convinced him that his company town was a "more logical" choice for company headquarters. Baie-Comeau was larger and had better communications, and many local veterans would be interested in joining. Furthermore, the town had an appropriate local commander: Maurice Lebon, an ex-paratrooper who had fought with the Canadian and American armies in the Aleutian campaign and sustained serious injuries during the battle for Anzio in Italy. After the war, he became the sports officer for the pulp-and-paper company. Lebon enthusiastically agreed to serve his country once again, and he organized the company in Baie-Comeau. Given that most men in the area travelled north in fall and winter, the headquarters' location had little bearing on regional coverage.

Gaumond was optimistic about his accomplishments along the Lower North Shore. The communities warmly welcomed the Rangers idea, newly appointed officers were keen, and "important" local figures had pledged their support. Gaumond anticipated that the company would "expand to its proposed strength, cover a considerable expanse of territory and serve the purpose for which it is being created."[38]

The demographics of "Nouveau Quebec," the Ungava Peninsula covering the northern two-thirds of the province, differed significantly from the North Shore. The 7,500 miles (4,660 miles) of coastline from Cape Jones on Hudson Bay to Cape Childley at the northern tip of Labrador had a largely Inuit population. The 2,500 Inuit who lived in the region meant a ratio of more than 3 miles (5 kilometres) of coastline and 57 square miles (148 square kilometres) per Inuk.[39] The area's vastness, sparse population, and limited communications and transportation infrastructure posed significant problems for defence planners. Not all trading posts had airstrips, there was no land communication during the summer season, and dog teams remained the only means of communication between trading posts in the winter. With no budget, army staff could not visit all of the potential sites. Major Guy Grenier, the regional intelligence officer, had little information when he flew to Fort Chimo (Kuujjuaq), Sugluk, Port Harrison (Inukjuak), Rupert House (Waskaganish), Nichicun, and Chibougamau to establish platoons in August 1948.[40] At most, he could select officers and start the recruiting process. Although the records relating to this visit no longer exist, memories of it linger in oral histories. Johnny Tookalook was not quite sixteen years old

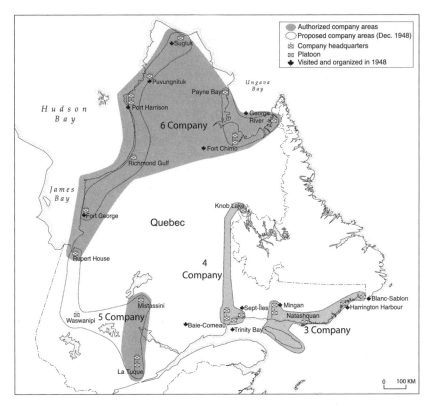

Proposed locations for Rangers units in Quebec, January 1948

when a *qallunaaq* (White man) arrived from Port Harrison and gave him a rifle, twenty rounds of ammunition, and an armband.[41] (Amazingly, he was still serving with the Sanikiluaq patrol sixty-three years later.)

Once the officers flew back to Montreal, they had little contact with the companies or platoons. Army organizers prepared written instructions for newly commissioned Ranger officers that explained the force's function and the qualities sought in prospective Rangers. They were particularly interested in local communication networks – amateur radio operations and companies with wireless sets – because they offered the only means of contacting units. Everything at the local level depended on the Ranger officers' initiative, since the military offered little in return. "You will NOT receive any arms or ammunition before the summer of 1949," Captain Gaumond advised the platoon commanders. "However, in the meantime it is expected that you will carry on recruiting and making plans for your area."[42]

The few individuals who had already enlisted took their role seriously. Lieutenant Douglas Rowsell, the platoon commander in Harrington Harbour, owned and operated the only store in town and served as the town's schoolteacher, church warden, and postmaster. On 31 October 1948, he reported that a suspicious man had crossed the Strait of Belle Isle from Newfoundland (still a separate colony from Canada at the time) and had been slowing working his way along the coast by small boat. The man, giving himself different names at different places, had arrived in the community the night before with no baggage of any kind, and had booked himself passage to an unknown destination. Rowsell wanted instructions on what to do. Headquarters in Eastern Quebec Area told him that the man probably belonged to the Royal Air Force but asked local Rangers to keep an eye on him.[43]

The media emphasized the Rangers' tactical role when it publicized the "sprawling network of trappers, hunters, farmers and lumbermen" serving as "Canada's first line of northland defence in event of a military emergency." In March 1948, both the *Globe and Mail* and the *Montreal Gazette* picked up the story of the "arctic guerrillas" – "a far north home-guard of minutemen" – armed with rifles and automatic weapons who would "stand guard on towns, mines, roads and airfields until regular combat troops are sent north." The author reported that vital points such as the Eldorado uranium mines on Great Slave Lake would receive protection on short notice and that patrols and guards would oversee the "vital communication route of the northwest highway." The article cited only one specific unit – the Whitehorse company – for good reason: unbeknownst to readers, the Whitehorse company was the only functional unit in the country.[44]

Western and Prairie Commands

A slow start did not discourage officials in Western Command. The dictates of peacetime required only "a small nucleus at key points."[45] Central planners promoted measured growth, and Ranger organizers received a national directive in January 1948 to concentrate on northern areas.[46] Yellowknife, the metropolis of Northwest Territories and the main supply and transportation centre for most of the Territorial North, was a logical choice.[47] Major L.W. Nelson, who oversaw the NWT and Yukon Radio System in town, had already recruited prospective Ranger officers in October 1947. Their pedigrees revealed the impressive range of military experience and practical

Ranger Captain Jake Woolgar's shoulder pips. Courtesy of 1 Canadian Ranger Patrol Group

skills that northerners would bring to this grassroots military force. Jake Woolgar – a bush pilot, prospector, and ex-RCAF flight lieutenant who had flown Spitfires, Hurricanes, and Mustangs through Italy, North Africa, and northwest Europe – became a captain. Frank Megill, an ex-Royal Canadian Army Service Corps brigade officer, and Jim Elliott, an ex-Royal Canadian Navy (RCN) lieutenant, rounded out a tri-service leadership cadre. Two additional lieutenants, field engineer Henry Denis and bush pilot Ernie Boffa, reinforced the local connection. Anxious to proceed, the intelligence officer in Vancouver wanted the men to swear in before the formal security vetting. He believed this would "cut down overall expenses." His superiors disagreed and ordered him to work through the proper channels.[48] Even in Northwest Territories, there was no avoiding red tape.

More than six months later, matters remained in limbo. Senior officers attributed the delay to the changeover of company names from territorial to numeric designations – a transition undertaken for security reasons. With the new system in place in May 1948, the military created No. 7 Company (headquartered at Yellowknife, with platoons at Snare River, Fort Providence, Fort Simpson, and Wrigley) and No. 8 Company (headquartered at Fort Smith, with platoons at Fort Resolution, Hay River, Chipewyan, Embarras, and Fort McMurray). By the time the official announcement came, however, the prospective company commander in Fort Smith had lost interest.[49] Jake Woolgar, having spent the spring prospecting in the bush, was more accommodating, yet even he did not wait around for his commission. Within forty-eight hours, he left for the east end of Great Slave Lake, where he prospected until early September. He received mail at regular intervals but was otherwise out of contact with the outside world. If Major Douthwaite wanted to visit him to discuss Ranger matters, Woolgar wrote, there would be room at his camp, provided Douthwaite brought his own sleeping bag. Woolgar did not have one to spare.[50]

Official delays also slowed the Rangers' expansion in BC. In mid-1947, the intelligence officer at area headquarters set to work to identify company and platoon locations in northern and coastal areas. Meetings with provincial officials and members of the army's sister services buoyed his optimism. The Royal Canadian Navy was interested in sea-rescue operations and the RCAF in air-sea–rescue operations.[51] Meetings between the BC police, industry officials, and former PCMR officers in communities along the Coast suggested tremendous interest in the Rangers. By mid-1948, sixteen potential platoon commanders stood ready. The vast majority had been captains or lieutenants in the PCMR during the war and had extensive local connections as businessmen or government workers.[52]

The first five companies in the Pacific province, authorized on 28 June 1948, focused on coast watching. During the war, operational troops had been stationed at Ucluelet, Sooke, and Terrace, and the chief of the general staff argued that the presence of Ranger units at these isolated posts would help offset demands for military personnel in an emergency. Companies headquartered at Tofino and Alert Bay would provide coverage for Vancouver Island, while those in Bella Coola and Ocean Falls would oversee the exposed Mainland coast.

The new BC Ranger network also extended into the Interior. Subunits of No. 13 Company, based in Terrace, stretched along the main communication arteries to Prince Rupert, including the Canadian National Railway, Cariboo Road, and Skeena River. Western Command also located an isolated platoon at Telegraph Creek, a small hub for an agricultural and mining area accessible only by paddle steamer from Alaska but connected to Terrace by telegraph line.[53] In July, the army authorized Ranger companies in Smithers and Prince George to cover the main communication axis connecting Prince Rupert with provincial centres in the south and the Interior. Platoons in remote agricultural settlements and communities along the railway – such as Hudson's Hope, Ootsa Lake, Nazko, and McBride – formed a modest web of coverage.[54]

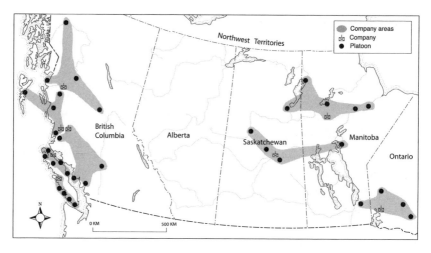

Ranger companies in Western and Prairie Command, September 1948

Prairie Command selected locations for four companies and eighteen platoons that summer after extensive discussions with the RCMP, the HBC, and railway companies. The Rangers would span the provincial norths, with company headquarters at Nelson House and Norway House in Manitoba, Carrot River in Saskatchewan, and Kenora in Ontario. The latter company infringed on the reserves' territory, but the commander reasoned that the region had vulnerable communication lines and that the Rangers would "be older and of the trapper, guide and hunter class." Although the lack of road and rail access, coupled with spring flooding, delayed organizing, Ottawa authorized four companies by September 1948.[55]

Status Report: Fall 1948

"Canada, in her national defence, is like a well-co-ordinated athlete – lean, alert and clean-muscled," the *Toronto Star* proclaimed in October 1948, quoting from a US army report. The Canadian Army's Active Force leadership was small but high-spirited, self-confident, and experienced. Among the public, the article continued, "the military carries public prestige, and soldiering is accepted as a profession essential to the emotional content of the nation, as well as its security." Canadians were well served by conventional intelligence methods: RCMP and air patrols, aerial photography, radar and radio networks, and military personnel working on meteorological projects and testing equipment. "Supplementing the reserve force," readers learned,

"Canada is organizing another militia force, the Canadian rangers – trappers, woodsmen and farmers who are to be on the lookout and do search and rescue work in isolated localities."[56] According to this story, Canadians could rest assured that the force would be another strong appendage to the defence corps.

The Ranger organization grew, on paper, to include nineteen companies by September 1948. In reality, the entire force had only forty-four officers and fifty-seven men of other ranks. Four-fifths of them belonged to Western Command.[57] This imbalance mirrored national trends. Canadians had "stayed away from recruiting centres in droves" the preceding year, forcing total active strength far below authorized levels.[58] When a *Toronto Star Weekly* reporter asked to write an article about the Rangers, the director of military operations and plans expressed concern about revealing locations or the "present strength and state of efficiency of the Rangers," which might give "a false impression of the corps."[59] Indeed, officials in Ottawa worried that the entire scheme had to be reviewed and drastically altered or the Ranger organization would probably "die of its own inertia."[60]

Not everyone was pessimistic about the Ranger concept. Brigadier W.J. (Bill) Megill had worked in the North before the war, and although he found the strength returns disappointing, he characterized the organizational structure as a notable success. A large percentage of "outpost" residents had not signed up, but this lack of enthusiasm fit with "the habits of the average Canadian." In war, he anticipated that they "would come in 100%." Issuing uniforms and additional equipment (binoculars, compasses, and simple wireless sets) and paying the Rangers for training might generate interest, but Megill counselled against these steps. The army intended the Rangers to be individuals who reported and acted on information acquired through their normal, civilian tasks. Only in an emergency would they be expected to act as a "formed body." He cautioned that jitters over strength returns at this preliminary stage should not upset the Ranger's underlying philosophy.[61]

Official statistics reflected restrictive policies rather than a lack of interest. For strategic reasons, the Rangers factored little in overall defence planning and received no military resources. Peter Wright, a lawyer and former army officer, proposed a robust force of three corps that would cover the Canadian North to stir the public's imagination and regenerate interest in the army. Senior defence officials scoffed. A "strategic concept of defence" would relegate a corps such as the Rangers to "a useful but minor role." General Charles Foulkes, the chief of the general staff, soberly explained that Canada's main military effort would have to be directed to "first class well trained units capable of countering enemy forces similarly equipped rather than loosely organized irregulars." Professional soldiers, not amateurs, were the mainstay of Canada's defences. The probability of a major battle in North America was remote, and Canada's most useful contribution to defence came through collaboration with its British and American allies to defeat an enemy "away from our shores."[62]

Although Canadian defence planners shared Foulkes's belief that the Soviets would not likely attack the North, they recognized that they had to contribute to continental defence. The 1946 Canada–United States Basic Security Plan required it. Nonetheless, stationing large numbers of troops in static defences in any one region of a vast country was dangerous, even ridiculous. Regular Forces based in the south but trained and equipped to counter an enemy lodgement on Canadian soil made more sense. Rapidly deployable airborne or air-transportable units were politically expedient, and the military introduced the Mobile Striking Force concept in 1948. This interest in airborne capabilities reflected American concerns that the most likely avenue of enemy invasion passed through Canada's northern regions. Canada needed to counter accusations that it was lethargic in fulfilling its continental defence commitments, so Canadian paratroopers began training in Arctic operations to prevent Soviet airborne forces from seizing forward bases that could be used by strategic bombers.[63] The symbolism was more important than the substance.

"If the Mobile Striking Force's gestation was at best tenuous," historian Bernd Horn notes, "its existence was nothing short of ethereal."[64] The same observation holds true for the Rangers. Both forces existed in emergency plans for the defence of Canada, but both were paper tigers. In theory, the striking force would reduce enemy lodgements and respond to enemy raiders on the coasts. As set out in a general policy statement, the Rangers played a supporting role. Their ability to perform it, however, remained as unclear as that of the Mobile Striking Force. The Rangers still had a skeletal force after ten months, but defence planners expressed little concern. Although "the overall state of efficiency of the Canadian Rangers cannot be considered high," the emergency plan noted, "this situation should improve on the progressive basis."[65]

The Rangers fit with broader plans for domestic defence, but their future remained uncertain. In November 1948, Foulkes explained to the minister of national defence that the previous year had been dedicated to organization, made inherently difficult by time, distance, inaccessibility, and the need to carefully vet all personnel. Progress had been slow but for good reason and to useful ends. Selecting leaders and recruiting would still take time but could now proceed on a solid footing. His thoughts turned to maintaining interest in the Rangers once they were fully organized.[66] He asked each of his regional commanders in early December on how best to proceed.

Almost all of the reports submitted by the general officers commanding claimed that the Rangers could fulfill their assigned roles. Major-General Chris Vokes in Central Command was the exception. He discouraged the formation of Ranger units in northern Ontario for two reasons. First, he saw no need for a Ranger-type organization. "Nothing goes on in the James Bay area which is not quickly known through the natural curiosity of the natives," Vokes explained. "The Hudson['s] Bay factor and the missionaries plus the RCMP pretty well know everything which goes on ... through the moccasin telegraph and their private wireless." Second, Vokes, in his usual blunt and crude fashion, dismissed Aboriginal people as unworthy contributors to Canadian defence: "The population is for the most part CREE Indian, some with Scottish names and blue eyes who exist by trapping and guiding for goose and duck hunters in the Autumn. They are most indolent and unreliable and born lazy. Hunger is the only motivating force, plus the propagation of their race, at which they are very adept ... I doubt the value of these Indians in a para military organization ... You could never train them for anything except to fit into an early warning system or observer corps, and that exists in fact already, without pre-empting their services."[67] If Ottawa insisted on having a military presence in northern Ontario, he would turn to the HBC factor and missionaries to establish small units at Moosonee, Moose Factory, and Fraserville. Although he had "met the odd young Indian who had served in the Canadian Army," Vokes had no appreciation for Aboriginal people's high rates of enlistment and wartime contributions.[68]

In Quebec Command, Major-General Geoffrey Morton surmised that "it would never be easy to keep in touch with the other ranks, many of whom were Indians and Eskimos of migratory habits." In contrast to Vokes, however, Morton believed Aboriginal people's traits and lifestyles would suit the Rangers. After all, "the Eskimos and Indians living in isolated communities were excellent marksmen and probably would use the annual

Major-General Chris Vokes. Department of National Defence, Photo ZK-843

100-round allotment of ammunition (the only remuneration they received) for hunting seal and reindeer."[69] The HBC and RCMP, who cut back flour and sugar allotments and gave out boxes of munitions to encourage Inuit in Quebec to hunt instead of settling around posts and relying on handouts,[70] would also welcome the Ranger rifles and ammunition.

Rather than fixating on negative stereotypes, Morton highlighted the potential benefits of integrating Aboriginal people with intimate knowledge of the land and northern survival skills into the Rangers. Lieutenant P.M. Wright, the Ranger officer at Fort Chimo, had recently passed along a report from Inuit claiming that an eight-foot-long rocket had landed near their camp at Whale River. Wright had asked the local missionary to investigate. Morton saw this as an ideal model for information gathering. Local hunters and trappers were already out on the land, and even if they did not possess the language or technology to communicate their observations to the military, missionaries and factors at trading posts did. In his view, the Rangers were already proving their worth.[71]

There was more going on along the north shore of the St. Lawrence River and north of the fifty-second parallel in Quebec than the available statistics could show. Officers had been appointed and platoon recruitment was well underway in the four companies. The strength returns did not reflect this activity because ordinary mail came only once a year to posts in northern Quebec and only twice per month along the North Shore.[72] Although Quebec Command headquarters placed its highest priority on communications and had established a radio network to reach all Ranger platoons in the province, company headquarters had no way to contact their platoons directly. In what would become a frequent refrain over the next four decades, Quebec Command requested radio sets so that its Rangers could communicate with one another and practise relaying messages. National headquarters decided against it: sets were in short supply and could not be maintained in remote areas, and the Rangers would not make full use of them until they organized completely. Regional officers also found that the vast distances between company headquarters and platoons made it more feasible to administer and supply platoons from Montreal. Although this broke with army protocol and undermined the company-platoon hierarchy, defence planners in Ottawa agreed that the change was inevitable given the nature of the Ranger organization.[73]

While the Rangers took shape in Quebec Command, planning in Eastern Command never left the drawing board. Although Major-General Harry Foster had dismissed the Ranger concept in his 1946 report, he changed his tune two years later. In Nova Scotia, retired naval officers with the federal Department of Fisheries embraced the Ranger idea. They informed local fishermen, many of whom had participated in the civilian Aircraft Detection Corps during the war, about their prospective duties. "We have not issued any rifles or ammunition because these men already possess their own firearms and are not particular in that respect of it," Foster explained, but the men did want uniforms. In New Brunswick, representatives from the fisheries department and the larger lumber companies sought a similar organization.[74] This newfound enthusiasm triggered a response in Ottawa. Army headquarters increased the authorized Ranger strength in Eastern Command to three hundred – even though the entire area fell within Reserve Force territory.[75] Then, for no clear reason, senior officials scuttled these plans, and Ranger units never formed in the Maritime provinces. Only after Newfoundland and Labrador entered Confederation in 1949 would the Rangers establish a presence along the Atlantic seaboard.

Western Command, an enthusiastic proponent of the Canadian Rangers, likewise experienced growing pains. Seven companies awaited the appointment of commanders, and only the companies in Dawson and Yellowknife showed signs of activity. Staff officer Lieutenant-Colonel M.R. Dare believed that the army's organization efforts had been premature, but he advised that disbanding the units would appear "rather weak" and indecisive. He instead identified several core problems that needed to be addressed. First, it was unfair to leave new recruits to their own devices, even if their locations made travel difficult, costly, and time-consuming. He urged Western Command to appoint an officer to establish ongoing, personal contact with far-flung units. Second, the force needed funds. Officers had taken the concept of a low-cost organization too far. Company and platoon commanders needed money to travel around their areas to recruit personnel "and preach the gospel," and it was unfair to expect them to do this out of pocket. Dare also believed that National Defence should pay the Rangers for limited annual training to make them "feel they are doing worthwhile work during peace time." He encouraged the army to include them in Active and Reserve Force exercises. Third, the Rangers needed to publicize why they were necessary and what they were expected to do. The *Toronto Star* had already inquired about visiting the Rangers in Whitehorse, but the army rejected their proposal because the organization was so thin on the ground. "Knowing the Star's love of sensational reporting," Dare predicted the journalist would probably criticize the force when he found few "operational types peering from bushes." The army needed to shield the fledgling Ranger organization from media scrutiny, but the minister and the chief of the general staff could aid recruiting and reinforce the Rangers' perceived importance by making statements about their valuable role in remote regions.[76]

Major-General Matthew Penhale, who took over as general officer commanding Western Command, also emphasized the need to "glamourize" the Rangers. Undeterred by concerns about the corps' existing strength, he believed the Rangers would "pay off in time of emergency just as did the Pacific Coast Rangers in the last war." After all, even a few reliable individuals or small groups scattered at outlying points would allow the Rangers to fulfill their tasks in an emergency. He explained to Ottawa that "the reasons for slow progress are not hard to seek." Personnel in all but the largest centres spent months each year in the bush as prospectors, trappers, and surveyors. An officer from Western Command Headquarters would have to visit units at least twice a year to guide and encourage them. The task demanded a full-time position, given the tremendous distances and time involved. Ottawa had refused an earlier request to hire such an individual, but the chief of the general staff promised to look into it further. The first Ranger liaison officers took up their positions soon afterwards.[77]

As for glamour, the minister himself had used the word with Penhale to stress that he should think up ways to capture the public's attention. Publicity and promotion would take time, money, and effort – and they would depend on the Rangers having distinctive clothing. The armband, which he considered useless, "would seldom be worn." The Rangers needed a uniform akin to the Mounties' Red Serge. Distinctive uniforms and insignia would signal that the Rangers stood "for qualities of integrity, endurance, service and patriotism." Penhale proposed caps, a summer shirt, winter sweaters and parkas, and a large, prominent badge to make the Rangers' presence better known.[78] The venerable red sweatshirt and other accoutrements that did just that would not arrive, however, for several decades. Officers had to generate interest with more modest material inducements.

Relationships on the Ground

While decision makers contemplated policy and worried about administrative burdens, the regional commanders worked to build practical relationships. This depended on vesting the right local people with leadership responsibilities. In early 1949, Penhale met with Ranger officers in Yellowknife, Coppermine, Whitehorse, Port Radium, and Dawson City. He noted that "things are beginning to tick over quite nicely."[79] While in Yellowknife to organize No. 7 Company, for example, he had witnessed the value of tapping into local knowledge networks. Captain Woolgar, the company

Ranger Ernie Boffa in the cockpit window of his Norseman floatplane.
Prince of Wales Northern Heritage Centre, NWT Archives, Busse Collection, N-1979-052-2400

commander, impressed the general. "He is a prospector, young, married, educated, excellent type and is well thought of and respected by everybody in the north ... Formerly a fighter pilot, he seems to be imbued with a serious purpose and love of the North." Penhale briefed Woolgar thoroughly on how he wanted him "to conduct Ranger business."[80] He seemed eager to organize the unit and had the contacts to make it happen.

Woolgar enjoyed excellent support. Penhale convinced Ernie Boffa, a well-known bush pilot whose flights took him over much of the company's territory, to act as a liaison officer, collecting and transmitting information from outlying points. In turn, Boffa asked Rev. Harold Webster, a missionary with extensive contacts among the Caribou Inuit, to organize a Ranger platoon in the Coppermine (Kugluktuk) area. Rather than trying to micro-manage the process himself, Penhale sent a stack of forms so local officers could enrol the people they had in mind. The general also worked with authorities at the Eldorado mine to secure Captain H. Lake, a retired military engineer, as platoon commander in Port Radium. Penhale espoused direct, informal contact between the military establishment and Ranger officers: "I think it best wherever contact has already been [established] to keep Ranger business upon an informal basis. Certainly papers, I know, must be signed, but generally speaking, all communications should be accompanied by a covering note, couched in friendly terms and wherever I have personally made contact, these are to be signed by myself. This is to be regarded as a firm direction. I have found by experience that this method of approach is the best in dealing with this type."[81]

Woolgar, inspired to create a first-class unit out of Yellowknife, signed on "fifteen good men" by April and promised at least ten more once he could "corner them to fill in the forms." Transportation in Yellowknife, a sprawling city with expensive taxis and overloaded flights to remote areas, posed the biggest obstacle to progress. Woolgar asked whether the Rangers could access RCAF and other government-operated planes to get around. What if the Rangers had identity cards and movement orders from headquarters authorizing them to "fly all over the area at no expense to the government"? When Western Command authorized Woolgar to form an air reconnaissance unit, he immediately contacted pilots and selected an ex-RCAF pilot as platoon commander.[82]

That spring, Major Douthwaite, the intelligence staff officer in Western Command, expanded the Ranger network. He hitched a ride with an Indian Health Services doctor x-raying Inuit throughout the western Arctic. (Incidentally, Ranger Ernie Boffa flew the chartered Norseman plane.) Douthwaite had set out to establish platoons or sections in new areas, but Penhale assigned him a broader mission: to photograph as much of the land as he could from the air, to note the appropriateness of the terrain for vehicles or use as airborne drop zones, and to record all local resources of military significance. The Rangers now fit within a broader military picture. Douthwaite successfully established a platoon at Coppermine and enlisted Rangers at Bathurst Inlet (Gingaut), Cambridge Bay (Iqaluktuuttiaq), Gjoa Haven (Uqsuqtuuq), Spence Bay (Taloyoak), Read Island, and Holman Island (Ulukhaktok). All had radio communications with one another and would serve as the "ears-to-the-ground" type of Rangers. Geographic dispersal allowed a relatively small number of Rangers to provide a "fairly complete 'intelligence screen'" across a vast territory.[83] Ranger Captain Frank McCall, a forest warden with the Department of Mines and Resources, received instructions to organize a company out of Aklavik with possible platoons or sections at Banks Island, Arctic Red River (Tsiigehtchic), Reindeer Depot or Kittigazuit, and Pearce Point. Western Command stressed that it did not intend to organize large units up to maximum strength but to enlist "carefully selected personnel at strategic points." Given the North's demography, this could mean platoons as small as one or two men.[84]

Douthwaite's main priority was to organize special home guard units at Norman Wells (Tłegóhłı̨) and at the Eldorado uranium mine at Port Radium. Both locations had been strategically significant during the war, the former as a secure source of petroleum for Alaska and the latter for its uranium. The Canadian government had purchased the mine in 1942 and ran it as a Crown corporation, and the United States had recently asked Canada what steps it had taken to protect it. Although the Canol pipeline was dismantled in 1947, the well and refinery at Norman Wells still produced 1,500 barrels of fuel oil per day (to feed the mine at Port Radium) as well as aviation fuel. Imperial Oil's field superintendent was concerned about "a small Communist minority" among the refinery employees and expressed "some relief" that the military would provide protection. Frank Willock, the assistant superintendent, immediately signed on as a Ranger and identified "twelve to eighteen sound men" in whom "he could place full confidence." He also promised to recruit a few old-timer trappers to serve as "knowledge-of-the-country type" Rangers. The men would oversee the surrounding valley, as well as the hills to the north, which "would provide an excellent covered approach for either the enemy, or ourselves if the need arose."[85]

Western Command requested special authority to issue automatic weapons to the platoons at Norman Wells and Port Radium so they could perform like a local home guard. The platoon at Port Radium, composed entirely of employees of the Eldorado Mining and Smelting Company, had orders to defend the mine in an emergency. Equipping the local Rangers with Bren guns and Sten guns would "reassure the Americans that protection of this [vital point] was in hand and might save ourselves from the necessity of deploying a special guard unit at the site." Most of the platoon members were veterans with combat experience, and General Vokes (Penhale's successor at Western Command) assumed they would know how to train and take care of the weapons.[86]

Aerial view of the Eldorado Mining and Refining mine site, Port Radium, 1946.
Prince of Wales Northern Heritage Centre, NWT Archives, Busse Collection, N-1979-052-3340

Norman Wells proved trickier. Western Command initially envisaged Rangers protecting the refinery, storage tanks, and wells in an emergency. General Simonds refused to authorize automatic weapons because government policy did not allow for the protection of privately owned vital points such as the Imperial Oil refinery. Vokes, however, reminded him that Norman Wells included an RCAF landing strip, aviation fuel storage tanks, and radio and weather stations. The airstrip was vital to the Mobile Striking Force, and the stations' communications crucial to northern defence. Simonds changed his mind and granted authority in June.[87] Once again, Ranger policy had been made to be broken.

Confusion and Disillusionment

In late 1949, Graham Rowley, head of Arctic research at the Defence Research Board, learned from the NWT Council of disturbing developments at Port

Harrison (Inukjuak). When the supply ship had arrived that summer, more than one hundred service rifles were distributed to local Inuit in the Ranger company, with one hundred rounds of ammunition per gun. "Unfortunately these rifles had never been 'zero'ed,'" Rowley reported, "and the apparent lack of accuracy seems to have encouraged the Eskimo to modify them to be more efficient by filing down the sights, as well as lightening them by shortening the stocks, etc." However deep the Rangers' disappointment in the guns, the former musketry instructor doubted these modifications would increase their performance. Rowley closed his correspondence by asking that the military inform the NWT Administration about the creation of any future Ranger companies in the North. The administration, responsible for all Canadian Inuit, "would be happy to assist defence interests."[88]

When Quebec Command looked into the matter, it admitted "a certain lack of control of these stores." It wanted to send an officer to Port Harrison to clean up the mess, but the area did not have adequate landing facilities for RCAF aircraft, and chartering a private aircraft was too expensive. Officials instead analyzed the army's paper trail and contacted local authorities. Further investigation revealed that two hundred rifles had been sent to northern Quebec: roughly one per man in a thirty-man platoon. Thirty had been sent to Port Harrison, but their whereabouts were unknown because Lieutenant Kerr had left the community in August without informing the army. Quebec Command wanted the RCMP to investigate the situation because a military officer could not visit the community until the following summer.[89]

Officials in Ottawa wondered why such a large number of weapons had been sent north given that the platoons would not reach full strength "for some time – if ever"? Asking the RCMP "to pull [the army's] chestnuts out of the fire" seemed inappropriate. They wanted to deal with the matter internally and recall the damaged rifles. When the general officers commanding next met in Ottawa, this example of the difficulties associated with distributing military equipment to Rangers, and accounting for it, was an obvious topic for discussion.[90]

Other Ranger companies expressed frustration because they had not received equipment. Some fledgling units had done their best to open lines of communication with headquarters, but military officials had not reciprocated. Lieutenant Roswell of Harrington Harbour complained to headquarters in Montreal in early 1950 about the military's lack of commitment. He had enlisted fourteen or fifteen Rangers and forwarded the application forms to the Commanding Officer at Mingan. Along with the applications, he asked if he should enlist more men to bring the platoon up to full strength. After several months, he had still not received a reply. "Some of the men I enlisted have been asking for the Rifle and ammunition that was promised to them," he explained, and because they had not received it, they began to believe that "the whole thing has been called off." He wanted headquarters to tell him if he was supposed to proceed. If so, when would his men receive the promised weapons and ammunition?[91]

At Dawson City, when Rangers who had previously served with the PCMR explained that they had felt isolated and cut off from headquarters during the war, Western Command promised closer liaison in the postwar Ranger system.[92] Chappie Chapman sent letters to all of the Rangers in his company and tried to secure official support for a rifle range.[93] In February 1950, he asked the army representative on the Arctic Research Advisory Committee to pass along several concerns to Ottawa. First and foremost, because the army had not authorized any activities or training for the Rangers, interest in the unit had waned. Second, Chapman felt the Rangers should have participated in Exercise Sweetbriar, a massive and much-lauded exercise carried out by the US and Canadian armies in southern Yukon. The military had also overlooked the Rangers when it conducted searches for missing aircraft.[94] Third, Chapman asked why the Rangers had been issued rifles of lesser quality than most members already owned. Finally, he requested army wireless sets to establish closer communications with platoons or sections in outlying areas. The Regular Force officer called Chapman "a capable and conscientious officer," indicating that his concerns should not be dismissed.[95]

✳ THE GROWING PAINS ANTICIPATED by Colonel Chesley did not pass quickly, and officials continued to have mixed opinions about the Rangers. Lieutenant-General Guy Simonds, the new chief of the general staff, noted in April 1948 that "[t]he response from all concerned with the North country in connection with this organization of [the Canadian Ranger] Corps has been most gratifying and far beyond expectations."[96] The Rangers had taken basic shape. Regional commanders had identified appropriate company locations and suitable leadership at the local level and had established twenty-one companies in Western, Quebec, and Prairie Commands.[97] They had laid the foundation for future growth, but the other senior officials did not share Simonds's optimism. They lamented that the Rangers remained a skeleton force of less than five hundred. Lack of funding, inconsistent directives from senior officers, and chronic delays had inhibited progress.

The failure to recruit to authorized strength should not have caused alarm. Defence officials had not intended to achieve overall coverage at this stage. Most regional commanders wanted to create a nucleus of Rangers that could expand in an emergency. Furthermore, the armed forces in general faced a recruit shortage throughout the late 1940s, despite an "extensive and expensive advertising campaign" unavailable to the Rangers.[98] A viable Ranger organization would depend on securing the acceptance of Canadian citizens in remote regions and on building relationships with the private sector.

Success would also depend on having a champion at the national level. Major-General "Worthy" Worthington, who retired from the army in late 1947, supported the Rangers ardently. Indeed, the adjutant general in Ottawa attributed whatever success the Rangers enjoyed to Worthington's personal interest. Brooke Claxton therefore recommended that Worthy be made honorary colonel commandant of the corps. He accepted the appointment in May 1948, considering it "a high honour to be associated with an organization destined to play a vital role in home defence."[99] After sending a Christmas circular to all Ranger captains and receiving only two replies, Worthington reminded the minister of national defence that "[a] point which must be borne in mind when dealing with these people is that they are not military and must be regarded as partisans. I am convinced that a great value can be obtained providing they are handled right which will not take a great deal of time, but they must not be left simply to hibernate with nothing to do. Furthermore, such administration as they may have must be simple to a degree as writing is not one of their strong suits."[100] Claxton agreed and recommended that a manual or field guide be prepared and issued to all Rangers to provide them with a basic sense of military direction.

National Defence Headquarters, however, offered little encouragement. Brigadier George Kitching, the senior staff planner responsible for ground defence of Canada, warned that transportation and communication problems would only become more acute as the Rangers expanded.[101] This concern connected to his general defence plan. The military "was far too small a force to have to deal with the millions of square miles of our northland," Kitching explained. "Furthermore, it was spread in penny packets across the country with each packet under command of a different senior officer." In his assessment, effective operations depended on coordinated planning both within the army and with the air force.[102] In practice, overall coordination proved particularly difficult.

Within the Rangers, regional commanders had already taken the organization in distinct directions. Western Command, which had the largest concentration of Rangers, pushed for more equipment, money, liaison, and training. It clung to the belief that the Rangers could and should serve as home-guard units. Quebec Command had devised a solid communications and organization plan focused on surveillance, but the plan suffered from delays. Prairie Command developed its Ranger network on paper, but staff officers in Ottawa worried that they would rely too much on the HBC. Central Command lacked enthusiasm, and Eastern Command had only expressed its intent to form units. In light of the mixed reception, the vice chief of the general staff imposed a "go slow policy" in early 1949 and commissioned more studies before committing additional resources to the organization.[103]

Authorities at the national and regional levels did not share a common vision. Regional commanders, who had invested considerable effort into planning for Ranger expansion, knew nothing about the "go slow" directive or the high-level review. Ottawa officials exchanged ideas without input from the regions, where staff officers pursued their own policies. There was no guarantee that the Rangers would survive the review process. The director of military operations and plans, Colonel J.E.C. Pangman, argued strongly in May 1949 for abolishment:

(1) The Canadian Rangers are not, at present, of any real military value.

(2) It is extremely doubtful if they can *ever* become well enough organized, trained and equipped to fulfill their assigned missions, to be an asset to the national defence and to be a credit to the Army.

(3) It is a certainty that the above will *never* occur without intensive support by the Army in terms of time and effort, funds, equipment and personnel.

(4) It is apparent that [Army] Headquarters is not in a position to give adequate support in all the above categories.

(5) The inescapable conclusion is, therefore, that the Canadian Rangers are not now and will never be of significant value to the national defence.

(6) The existence of a semi-military organization as poorly organized and impotent as the Rangers constitutes a reflection on the efficiency of the entire Army.

(7) It is therefore considered that, from a military point of view, the Rangers are a failure and therefore should be abolished.[104]

Minister Claxton received Pangman's recommendation only after the army had completed a more formal review. Meanwhile, Ottawa withheld authorizations for new companies and told regional commanders to delay implementing their organization plans.[105]

Ottawa, ironically, imposed constraints on Ranger growth out of concern for the organization's viability just as momentum picked up at the regional level. National inertia notwithstanding, the Ranger corps grew quickly in the years ahead, expanding across the country and into the new province of Newfoundland and Labrador. As the Rangers became more diverse, the challenges of maintaining coherence in an organization driven by regional interests grew apace.

4
The Formative Years,
1950-52

✤ *HOUSE OF COMMONS, OTTAWA, 9 JUNE 1950.* "Probably no one in the house would have thought it possible two or three years ago that within less than five years of the end of the fighting Canada would be faced with the necessity of appropriating at least half a billion dollars ... for defence purposes," Conservative member of Parliament Howard Green noted during Question Period. The division of the world into two rival blocs had precipitated this sorry trend. Green did not share the minister of national defence's optimism that Canada would be "far away from the centre of activity" when another war broke out. Despite joint Canadian-American exercises to test preparedness in the northwest, he feared "that Canadians, from the Minister of National Defence down, are still European-minded – or perhaps I should say Atlantic-minded."

Green referred to early 1942, when West Coast journalists and citizens had been forced to convince Ottawa that the defenceless Pacific required attention. Had the Americans not defeated the Japanese in the Battle of Midway, he argued, North America "might well have been invaded." In the postwar world, Canada was more vulnerable, and Russia was a "much tougher opponent" because it reached to "within a few miles of Alaska." The Russians, familiar with fighting in northern climates, boasted an undefeated Siberian army.

Canada had to prepare to defend its northwestern territory with air forces, coastal patrols, and a more robust Reserve Force. Green also suggested expanding "the Canadian militia rangers" and recalled the halcyon days of the Pacific Coast Militia Rangers (PCMR). "I have never seen anything finer since the days of the Canadian corps in the first war," he trumpeted. The wartime Rangers in "all the hamlets up and down the west coast and right into the interior were very proud of the part they were playing, and if there had been an invasion they would have been of inestimable value to Canada." The Canadian Rangers, he stated, had been re-established in peacetime and "would be excellent leaders in any guerrilla type of warfare." The opposition MP clearly had no idea of the Rangers' strength or range, for he recommended that units be set up in BC, Yukon, and Northwest Territories.

Brooke Claxton, the minister of national defence, concurred that the Pacific was vulnerable, and the outbreak of the Korean War two weeks later proved his instincts correct. "As to the Canadian Rangers, we have twenty-one companies organized," Claxton informed Parliament. "I have seen the location of the various groups of men, and I can assure the hon. member they cover every place in the north all the way up to the extreme Arctic as well as in British Columbia, Alberta, Saskatchewan, Manitoba and north-western Ontario where there is more than a handful of people." He could also have mentioned Ranger platoons in Newfoundland and Labrador. Claxton failed to impress Green, who reminded him that there had been more than one hundred companies in BC alone during the war. The defence minister retorted that the Rangers now had larger groups,[1] but he did not disclose that the military hesitated to publicize the Rangers for fear of embarrassment.[2] Although Claxton could claim that the force extended across the Canadian North, the Rangers remained a skeleton crew – more impressive on paper than in reality.

The Cold War Heats Up

On the strategic level, Canadians had few reasons to panic in the early postwar years. Claxton believed that any enemy attack on North America would be diversionary, designed to create panic and tie up Canadian and American armed forces.[3] Since any assessments of Soviet intentions or military strength were inherently speculative, Canadian officials anticipated and planned for the kind of war that fit their budget. In the late 1940s, the Department of Finance's priorities had a more practical influence on actual defence policy than did the military's strategic analyses.[4] The Rangers, which cost virtually nothing, fit the paltry budget.

The government's tune changed in the early 1950s. The Soviet detonation of an atomic bomb in 1949 and the outbreak of the Korean War in 1950 seemed to confirm the inevitability of armed conflict between the communist and capitalist worlds. Senior bureaucrats acknowledged Canada's continental neighbour as the leader of the Western world and recognized that if Canada did not rearm and help to defend its territory and airspace, the United States would do so unilaterally, with obvious implications for Canadian sovereignty. Multilateral security agreements meant that Canada needed to put boots on the ground as part of its membership in the new North Atlantic Treaty Organization (NATO). Canada organized an air division to serve in Europe and sent an expeditionary force to the Far East the next year. In fall 1951, 5,500 Canadian troops returned to Germany to join the British Army of the Rhine. Defence expenditures grew to consume more than 50 percent of the federal budget in the early 1950s.[5]

Senior defence planners knew that the enemy would attempt to spread panic among the civilian population and tie up forces in a home defence role. A top-secret memorandum written in May 1950 explored the conditions that had led Canada to squander precious resources this way during the Second World War. In July 1943, the army had deployed more than eighty thousand troops in Canada to deal with a possible enemy raid of no more than five hundred men. The document emphasized one positive initiative: the Pacific Coast Militia Rangers. "Although never called upon operationally," the wartime Rangers were "a good public morale builder." Had they been called upon for combat, "they would have acquitted themselves well." A peacetime Ranger force would cost little and could help with anti-sabotage and coastal patrols, activities that had tied up Reserve Force units during the last war. "The raising of the status and efficiency of this organization in peacetime might well be considered," the document suggested. "While a nucleus organization is now in existence its future depends on a more aggressive approach." The memorandum recommended that the Rangers not only continue but also be "expanded, encouraged and publicized."[6]

The chief of the general staff discussed the Rangers' with his regional commanders in early 1950. A staff paper attributed the organization's poor progress to a lack of enthusiasm and initiative at army headquarters and at the underfunded, understaffed commands. "There appears to be a definite feeling at a very high level that the Ranger Organization should be allowed to become more or less dormant," the document noted. Fortunately, a majority of the regional commanders still supported the Ranger concept and argued that they could expand it to "ten times its size" if "pressed to do so." Simonds advised, however, that "no changes were contemplated" and that "the organization should remain as simple as possible."[7]

If senior officers remained cautious, reporters did not. On 23 June 1950, G.R. Stevens of the *Montreal Star* expressed dismay that "Mr. Claxton's Rangers" had not been discussed during the House of Commons debates on the minister's defence estimates. "The enlistment of Arctic trappers and rivermen as special service troops" should have triggered debate, Stevens suggested, because "there is no subject upon which qualified military opinion is more divided than upon the wisdom and profit of arming civilians for detached operations." Deliberately provocative, he likened the Rangers to guerrilla forces in North Africa, Burma, Greece, and the French Maquis. Stevens concluded that

> [t]he difficulty with special service forces, whether in uniform or not, whether at home or in a foreign land, is threefold. They are difficult to control, they are expensive to maintain and they afford the enemy the opportunity to break the rules of the game. There should be a difference in status between regular guerrillas, such as Long Range Desert Group [in North Africa during the Second World War] and civilian partisans, such as the French Maquis. But to an enemy they are birds of one feather ... There therefore would seem to be a basis for arguing that the special service category does not justify itself. It might be better for Mr. Claxton to enlist his woodsmen and rivermen of the far north in regular formations, in which they would fulfil normal military functions in reconnaissance groups, in sapper, signals or other specialist units. Therein they might accomplish more than if given a wide a dubious charter as Canadian Rangers.[8]

Given the lack of public information on the Rangers, Stevens may be excused for what seemed like uninformed, overzealous journalism.

This criticism, which appeared when the Ranger's future remained in doubt, demanded a response. Minister Claxton sent a letter to Stevens, clarifying that the Rangers did not serve as "spies and saboteurs," causing "alarm and despondency in the enemy's rear," but rather as guides, coast watchers, and supporters of civil authorities. The Rangers allowed the government to "make use of the special local knowledge and qualifications" of citizens in sparsely populated areas without Reserve units.[9] Stevens might have been correct in suggesting that the Rangers would be difficult to control, but he should have had no worries about their cost. Would they encourage the enemy to break the rules? Given the improbability of an enemy attack on the North, this scenario was highly unlikely.

Two days after Stevens's article appeared in the *Daily Star,* North Korea invaded South Korea, and Canadians shifted their focus even farther afield. The Americans promised to help defend the south and secured UN Security Council support for collective action. Canada sent an air transport squadron and three naval destroyers, and public opinion supported America's request to expand the country's contribution to help counter communist aggression. Because Canada could not furnish an expeditionary force and maintain other defence obligations with existing resources, Prime Minister Louis St. Laurent announced rearmament measures on 7 August. When China intervened in the war and set the UN's forces back on their heels, senior officials with External Affairs feared a major global war.[10] The centre of gravity shifted from continental defence to the containment of communism in Asia and Europe, and the Canadian Armed Forces could not be everywhere.

The Rangers represented the army in remote regions where the risk to national security was low, and defence officials could easily forget their modest contributions in this new global context. Consequently, the organization did not benefit directly from the dramatic increase in resources dedicated to defence. "We must keep these [Ranger] units active and interested but without spending any money," Colonel Roger Rowley, the director of military operations and plans, advised.[11] He reminded regional commands that the "go slow" policy remained in place, but he sought "bright and inexpensive ideas."[12] For instance, the armed forces would need military intelligence about northern settlements.[13] Western Command had distributed questionnaires about local conditions and infrastructure in the western Arctic, and army headquarters asked the other commands to undertake similar projects.[14] Over the next two years, local residents provided reports that described everything from transportation and communications to food and accommodations.[15]

The Royal Canadian Air Force (RCAF) saw particular benefit in this kind of support. Because bad weather often prevented aerial reconnaissance in the Arctic, ground patrols could supplement the air force's activities. The chief of the air staff requested that Ranger platoons report "through the most expeditious channels, any information on unusual activity which they might observe during exercises or patrols in the Arctic Archipelago and

Alec Tooktoo, one of three active Inuit Ground Observers at Great Whale River
(Kuujjuarapik), identifies an RCAF helicopter. Department of National Defence, Photo PC-2298

elsewhere in the Northwest Territories."[16] Along similar lines, the army arranged with the RCAF for Rangers to act as ground observers in relevant
areas. In late 1950, the *New York Times* reported that the RCAF was turning
"Canada's northland into a vast outlook post for potential enemy aircraft."[17]
The creation of the Ground Observer Corps – civilian volunteers who
manned observation posts throughout the country – lent this some credence.
Many Rangers also served as volunteers with the Ground Observer Corps,
and Major-General Matthew Penhale touted their role as "an adjunct to an
air-raid warning system in the manner of the old war-time [Royal Air Force]
Observer Corps."[18]

Watching over the breadth of Canada remained a daunting challenge,
particularly in the northern expanses of the prairie provinces and Ontario.

The army had established a basic Ranger footprint in northern Manitoba through its close relationship with the Hudson's Bay Company, but it still struggled to produce functional units. Prairie Command's constant reorganizing efforts reflected a limited grasp of realities on the ground. In early 1951, for example, Ottawa authorized four additional companies so that Prairie Command could reorganize its existing setup. "This new organization provides an interlocking band of posts across the north of Saskatchewan, Manitoba and Western Ontario," the regional commander touted. Yet staff officers changed their minds. A study of land, line, and wireless systems revealed that northern Manitoba had only one communication link, in Churchill, the site of a major military cold-weather testing station and airfield. Officials shifted the companies and platoons once again to centre on this military hub. They also relaxed national policies to accommodate Prairie Command's predicaments. Communications with prospective Ranger platoons in northwestern Ontario went through Moose Factory, which fell under Central Command's jurisdiction. The latter, still uninterested in assuming responsibility for the Rangers itself, supported Prairie Command in establishing a headquarters on southern James Bay to serve northern Ontario more generally.[19]

As was the case in other areas, Prairie Command devolved the task of organizing to the regional and local levels. The Hudson's Bay Company, the Canadian Pacific and Canadian National railways, Winnipeg Electric Company, Winnipeg Hydro Company, and the Department of Transport provided a pool of officers.[20] Given this strong reliance on the private sector, few official records remain that detail what transpired in the prairie North and Ontario. When the superintendent of the hydroelectric plant at Seven Sisters Falls in Manitoba became a lieutenant, he insisted on a platoon composed of "the proper type" of men. Because he planned to hold meetings and lectures in the plant, he wanted to ensure that no men of doubtful intentions were allowed in. The company harboured deep concerns about the safety of its facilities and had amassed thick files on communists who might sabotage them. Fears of subversion, ubiquitous in Cold War Canada, in this case centred on alleged communist efforts to stir up Native people. "The Indians in the district have been agitated by these people insofar as they have been telling them that half the water in the river belongs to them under the Charter by Queen Victoria," the Ranger liaison officer noted in January 1952. "Consequently they have been telling [them] that half the power plants and revenue are rightfully theirs." As a result, a transmission line running to

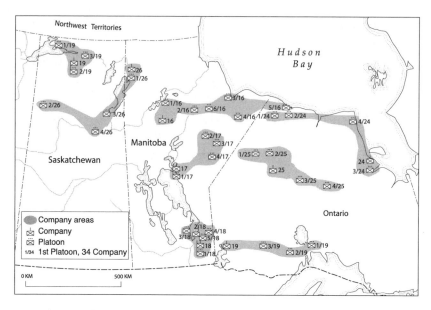

Prairie Command's reorganization plan for Ranger units, 1951

an Indian reserve "was constantly interfered with." Until it had ferreted out the communists, the company sought reassurances of the Rangers' loyalty and integrity.[21]

Gilbert George Faries epitomized the sort of man sought for Ranger service. Born in Fort Albany, an isolated Cree community on the coast of James Bay, to a Scottish father and mother of mixed European-Mushkegowuk ancestry in 1916, Faries attended residential school at Moose Factory. After he graduated, he asked to join the Moose band. He became an apprentice trader with the HBC in 1937 and ventured five hundred kilometres by dog team to assume his post on the Belcher Islands, where he learned Inuktitut. When war broke out, he returned to Moose Factory, married, and joined the army as a combat engineer. He trained British commandos in winter warfare and dog handling then fought with the 4th Canadian Armoured Division during the liberation of Europe. He suffered a wound to his leg when his jeep struck a land mine. When Faries returned home to his wife and children in 1946, he discovered that he did not have access to the same benefits as non-Indian veterans. "He was very proud of his country and of being a Cree," his wife Nellie recalled. "He went to fight for his country and for peace. And this was the way he was treated when he got home." After studying business in Toronto, he returned to Moose Factory and

Major David Scandrett presents Gilbert George Faries with the first Special Service Medal (Ranger Bar) issued in Canada, February 2000. At the time of his death, he also received a Canadian Forces Decoration (CD) with three bars, which recognized his service from the Second World War to his role as patrol elder in the Moose Cree First Nation patrol.
Courtesy of David Scandrett

worked with the Department of Indian Affairs for a short time before becoming elected chief of the Moose Cree band. Despite being frustrated about his treatment as a Native veteran (his wartime injuries eventually forced him into early retirement), Faries's loyalty was unquestionable. He joined the Canadian Rangers in 1952.[22]

Recruiting and retaining Rangers such as Faries required concerted local effort, but fitting the platoons and companies into a coherent regional structure required more than grassroots initiatives. To address its ongoing administrative challenges, Prairie Command wanted to promote Ranger Captain W.J. Cobb as a regional commanding officer at the rank of major. As an HBC executive in Winnipeg, Cobb had been slotted in as the commander of the company in Seven Sisters Falls. "[F]amiliar with the areas, personnel, problems and idiosyncrasies of the regions concerned," Prairie Command wanted to take advantage of Cobb's travel itinerary as manager of outlying HBC posts. Cobb's employment with the HBC precluded the army from calling him out on full-time service, but the promotion would allow him to give orders to company commanders.[23]

Senior military staff in Ottawa resisted this regional proposal but suggested another option that fit with developments in other commands. Prairie Command's plan for Cobb entailed grouping all companies under a single commander, which would create a larger Ranger unit. The deputy chief of the general staff wanted to avoid a top-heavy administration, which would set an unnecessary and undesirable precedent. Without an official command function, Cobb did not need to outrank the company commanders whom he instructed. In May 1951, the army authorized Prairie Command to make Captain Cobb a Ranger liaison officer at his present rank.[24] The appointment confirmed the organization's flexibility – and Ottawa's willingness to accommodate regional needs.

Eastern and Western Commands had already appointed Ranger liaison officers to supervise organization and activities in their areas. Western Command attributed its "disappointing" progress to inadequate liaison and infrequent instructional visits. Rangers, it argued, needed more contact than Reserve Force units because they did not "enjoy the same degree of recognition and support (financial and otherwise)." The minimalist approach had failed, Major-General Penhale insisted, and "the standard of organization and operational efficiency" had to improve to fit with "the increasing tempo of training due to the world situation." He suggested Captain Jake Woolgar, the Rangers' commander at Yellowknife. The army called him out in early 1951 to maintain personal contact with Rangers and sustain their interest.[25] Eastern Command likewise called out a Ranger liaison officer to prepare defence plans, give advice on communications and weapons, and provide other training. This appointment fit with expansion plans in Eastern Command. National authorities had reallocated Ranger strengths in the fall of 1950 to make space for new units in Newfoundland Area, a new military jurisdiction that coincided with the boundaries of Canada's newest province.[26]

Newfoundland and Labrador

Newfoundland and Labrador joined Confederation on 1 April 1949. Limited in resources and small in population, the province spanned the mouth of the Gulf of St. Lawrence and sat astride Quebec's northeastern boundary. Readers of the *Canadian Army Journal* learned that

[t]he general topography of the island is rough and broken. Fertile soil is limited, and the forested area, though extensive, in general bears only small trees. The coast is heavily indented with large bays and fiords. The area of the island is about 42,000 square miles: larger than Ireland, and about 84% of the combined area of Canada's three Maritime provinces. The sovereignty of Newfoundland also extends to some 110,000 square miles of Labrador on the mainland. In 1945 the population, which has been increasing relatively quickly, was about 320,000 (including 5,500 in Labrador). Close to 90% of Newfoundland's people live on the coast, in some 1,300 communities scattered along the 6,000 miles of shoreline ... With little immigration into Newfoundland during the past century, about 98.5% of the population are native-born and possess a distinctive national character.[27]

Newfoundland's distinctive national character included deep social and political divisions rooted in both memory and expectations for the future. Economic collapse had cost Newfoundland dominion status in 1933, when Britain imposed a commission government. During the Second World War, the colony's fortunes changed for the better because of its vital strategic location. Canadian soldiers began to relieve Britain of its defence obligations in 1939; Newfoundland was key to Canada's East Coast defences. When France fell, Canada sent more air and ground forces to the colony. The "friendly invasion" of Americans followed in early 1941. At one point, more than twenty-five thousand armed forces personnel manned major bases and repeater and radar stations as far north as Saglek on the Labrador coast.[28] "There were thousands of American and Canadian war personnel stationed in the area," Frank Mercer recalled, "and thousands of civilians, fellow Newfoundlanders, working feverishly, improving, expanding and upgrading runways; erecting barracks; fuelling planes and performing other tasks associated with the world-shaking events taking place all around us."[29]

When Hitler's campaign against Allied shipping brought German submarines to the Grand Banks in the spring of 1941, Canada's presence expanded, making Newfoundland "probably the most heavily defended area of North America during the war."[30] The Royal Canadian Navy based most of its fleet at St. John's to ply the North Atlantic run, and RCAF units based in Newfoundland covered convoys as far into the ocean as possible. Thousands of Newfoundlanders served overseas in British and Canadian ships and regiments, and nearly nine hundred did not return. The 570 members of the Newfoundland Militia provided full-time home defence as part of the five thousand-strong Canadian Army port and airfield defence forces. The Newfoundland Rangers, a constabulary force that policed outport areas on the island and in Labrador from 1935-49, patrolled the coastlines and watched for suspicious activities, as did 2,700 volunteers with the Aircraft Detection Corps.[31]

By war's end, Newfoundlanders faced an uncertain future. The average household income had doubled, and the colony's finances were solvent because of wartime military activity and the increased price of fishery exports. Yet there had been no structural transformation of the economy, and this uncertainty propelled the postwar confederate movement. While urban Newfoundlanders ("townies") on the Avalon Peninsula reminisced about a golden age and sought independent dominion status, residents of the outports ("baymen") and Labrador, who had no desire to see the "Water Street Merchants" of St. John's resume control, sought to confederate with Canada. After a bitter debate, the Canadian option squeaked through in a June 1948 referendum.[32]

The federal government inherited unambiguous defence responsibilities in its newest province. First and foremost, Newfoundland had military facilities vital to continental defence. The massive airbase at Goose Bay, Labrador, had obvious strategic significance during the Cold War, particularly to Strategic Air Command. The US Air Force asked to expand its presence at Goose Bay in 1950, resurrecting sovereignty concerns about US extraterritorial rights in the province. Bilateral negotiations produced a long-term lease agreement in 1952, which secured Canadian command of defensive forces in the northeast.[33] The establishment of Canadian Rangers would help to offset the United States' large footprint in the region. The Americans also welcomed the prospect of residents providing advanced warning of aircraft and helping with local defences.[34]

The Rangers presented an immediate solution to the question of outport defence, and they took preliminary form in isolated communities along the coast in 1950. In August, Major J.E. Roberts from Newfoundland Area Headquarters, aboard the RCMP ship *Irvine,* visited three settlements in northern Newfoundland and six in Labrador. "All the inhabitants with whom I came in contact were well motivated and patriotic," he reported, and he saw no evidence of "communistic [sic] activity." Most of the local residents (apart from wireless operators, missionaries, and traders) had little formal education – only a few had more than four years of schooling. He nevertheless identified suitable platoon commanders: W.H. Bennett, the superintendent of Bowater's in White Bay; St. Anthony's acting mayor, N.M. Penny; wireless operators A.W. Moores (Red Bay) and W.S. Moores (Cartwright); and W.J. Raymond, a representative of the Newfoundland Trading Company, in Hebron.

In Hopedale and Nain, predominantly Inuit communities associated with the Moravian mission, impending changes in resident merchants, wireless operators, and missionaries delayed formal appointments. In Hopedale, Major Roberts found Eli Nitsman, "an intelligent and well thought of Eskimo" who would "make an excellent sergeant" and temporary platoon commander until wireless operator J.R. Roberts arrived the following year. When Rev. Frederick C.P. Grubb, a former member of the British Home Guard who spoke both English and Inuktitut, arrived in Nain to act as assistant to the resident missionary, he immediately became a Ranger lieutenant.[35]

Collectively, these officers oversaw a diverse population. Roberts found that demographics north of Hamilton Inlet in Labrador differed from the south. In the northern reaches, Inuit and a "few Nascopie Indians" made up the bulk of population. The southern regions, by contrast, consisted mostly of White settlers. "Conversation with the Eskimos themselves and with white settlers who are familiar with them indicate that these people have a wide knowledge of the country and are very able at travelling both in Summer and Winter," Roberts noted, but he added the codicil that "they are lacking in fighting spirit. The Eskimo, therefore, in time of need will make excellent guides and advisers to our Armed Forces but will be of little or no use as combatants."[36]

Company and platoon locations depended on available communications. Wireless or landlines connected larger settlements, and missionaries or traders owned some private wireless stations in smaller outposts. From June to December, boats and the occasional seaplane provided the primary means of transportation. Apart from local fishing vessels and coasters, limited shipping occurred along the Labrador coast. In the winter, people could travel only by dog teams, sleds, or aircraft. "The apparently substantiated reports of enemy submarines, the completely unprotected state of the Newfoundland and Labrador Coast, and the sincere desire to assist on the part of the inhabitants would appear to combine to make the organization of the

Canadian Rangers in this area both necessary and practical," Major Roberts concluded. Limited education and isolation would make this a lengthy process, but Roberts believed the Rangers would succeed.[37]

In January 1951, the general officer commanding Eastern Command began planning for two companies. One would cover northern Newfoundland, including the Labrador side of the Strait of Belle Isle, and have headquarters in St. Anthony. The other would cover Labrador's "open coast" with headquarters in Cartwright.[38] A month later, No. 22 and 23 companies were officially established.[39] At the time, Eastern Command dedicated a staff officer to help organize the units on the ground. Although the company commanders possessed a solid knowledge of their own areas, they needed outside support to deal with the region's diverse population. The Ranger liaison officer would need to be an experienced soldier familiar with the entire region, and Captain Ambrose J. Shea fit the bill. The forty-two-year-old Newfoundlander had a wide circle of contacts and appropriate infantry and artillery experience.[40] He wanted to serve, approached the job with an open mind, and would prove remarkably adaptable and effective over the next decade.

Recruiters encountered practical problems. Newfoundland Area command noted that "weather conditions and almost total lack of road and rail communications make travel in the areas where the Rangers are being organized ... a slow and expensive procedure." The northern regions posed distinct challenges, particularly during the winter months, when "land and sea traffic is virtually at a standstill." Although the island lacked HBC posts to tap for local leadership, army officials found potential officers with civilian jobs that took them throughout the area. "In most cases we have had to content ourselves with patriotic citizens, who are more or less fixtures in one place" but who were willing to undertake organizational tours during the summer, an officer explained. "Few, if any, of the prospective Ranger Officers are in a position to spend their money on this project." If they did, the army would have to reimburse them. Otherwise, a Ranger liaison officer would have to do the work himself:

> The most cursery [sic] inspection of the map of the Newfoundland Area
> will indicate the magnitude of his task. Newfoundland alone has a coastline
> of 6000 miles even excluding the numerous inhabited islands of Notre
> Dame, Bonavista and Placentia Bays, to mention only the more obvious

ones. In addition, there is a further 1500 miles of coast to be dealt with in Labrador, making a total of some 7500 miles.

Assuming that 6 Ranger Coys are required to give this area an efficient coverage ... the RLO would have to visit, at a conservative estimate, approximately 600 different settlements spread over 7500 miles of coastline. In each he would have to find a suitable man or men, explain the organization of the Rangers, and persuade them (if possible), to enlist. It is estimated that this tour will take him at least two years to complete.

Unless the Ranger liaison officer had a plane at his disposal, he would have to charter a boat to visit most communities when weather permitted.[41]

Throughout 1951, Shea visited communities on the island of Newfoundland, from Port aux Basques to Lewisporte. He spoke with local authorities to set or adjust unit boundaries and commissioned suitable platoon commanders. When he arrived in communities, he visited the RCMP, the parish priest, and the local magistrate to obtain the names of residents who might make suitable Ranger officers and recruiters. If previously recruited officers had left town, he either tried to find replacements or relocated platoon headquarters to neighbouring communities. By June, the list of officers included traders, fish merchants, wireless operators, missionaries, railway workers, a town manager, a plant superintendent, a bank manager, a variety-store owner, and a schoolmaster. Many were war veterans, and most displayed considerable enthusiasm.[42] In the prosperous town of Clarenville, for example, Shea secured W.H. Adey, a fifty-eight-year-old Great War veteran and insurance agent "constantly on the move." Born in the Trinity Bay area, Adey had helped organize the Canadian Legion branch in Clarenville. Although Adey could not officially recruit until commissioned, by the time Shea returned in June, he had contacted prospective Rangers in Deer Harbour, Ivanhoe, Gooseberry, Southport, Caplin Cove, St. Jones Within, and Sunnyside. Records at army headquarters, which listed only numbers on the official rolls, failed to capture significant grassroots organizing.[43]

The Avalon Peninsula presented more of a challenge. Before leaving St. John's to establish Ranger platoons on the south shore, Shea called on Major Peter Cashin, the district's MPP, an ardent anticonfederate, and a former member of the Royal Newfoundland Regiment and the British Army. Although Cashin identified several potential recruits, most refused commissions. "The people of this area are friendly, extremely hospitable and elaborately courteous," Shea observed, "but they were also strongly opposed to Confederation and it is evident that the feeling still lingers on." On his first visit to Cape Broyle, Shea caused something of a panic when local residents mistook him for an RCMP constable checking dog licences. Several times along the route, he faced the question, "Are you a Canadian or a Newfoundlander?" Although Shea did not experience any open hostility towards the army, he found it difficult to recruit for an organization named the Canadian Rangers. Fortunately, W.M. "Mont" Winsor, an active sixty-year-old Great War veteran from the small village of Aquaforte, agreed to serve as platoon commander. Winsor had been a quartermaster sergeant with the Royal Newfoundland Regiment in France and Gallipoli. As a fish merchant, he was well known along the southern shore and among Grand Banks fishermen.[44] Shea entrusted him with recruiting on the Avalon.

In August 1951, Shea visited Labrador and the Northern Peninsula to complete the organizing initiated the year before. Hitching rides onboard SS *Kyle,* the Canadian National Railway's coastal boat, and HMCS *Revelstoke,* a navy training vessel, the Ranger liaison officer's resourcefulness paid off. Using this avowedly "inefficient" method of travel, he covered 1,700 miles (2,700 kilometres) in less than three weeks, seeing first-hand conditions along the Labrador coast and enjoying leisurely meetings with platoon commanders and other local contacts. He distributed 145 rifles and 16,992 rounds to the platoons. Shea highlighted in his post-trip report that "the Ranger armbands made quite a hit in Labrador. One of the [platoon] commanders told me that the Eskimoes would almost certainly wear them to church!"[45] Morale seemed high and the prospects for growth encouraging.

Even though officials had yet to finalize the new company layout for Labrador, Shea recruited company and platoon commanders along the route. He was pleased with the local progress. For example, Lieutenant A.W. Moores, the platoon commander at Red Bay on the Strait of Belle Isle, had not filed any reports, but in person he struck Shea as a capable, level-headed man of action. Moores had already completed an organizational tour of his platoon and, as justice of the peace, had attested twenty-seven Rangers along the coast. Shea knew that any effective organization depended on personal relationships, and the two men discussed Ranger prospects long into the night. The next morning, the platoon commander picked up 30 rifles, armbands, and 3,744 rounds of ammunition from the ship and distributed them to his men.[46]

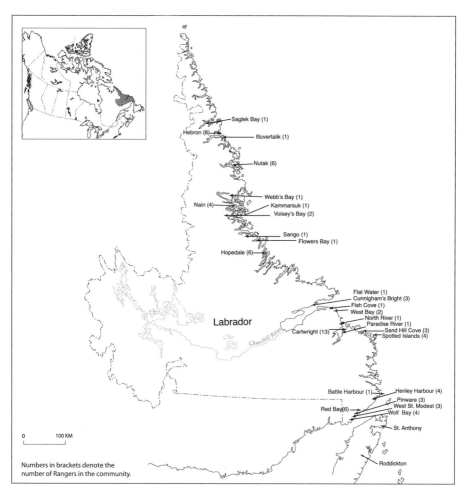

Dispersion of Rangers along the Labrador coast, August 1951

At the end of the trip, Shea declared the organizational stage in Labrador and northern Newfoundland complete. The Ranger liaison officer reported positively on "the interest and initiative shown by the Ranger Officers and the comparatively rapid development of the Force in this difficult area." By the end of the year, the two Labrador companies boasted six officers and ninety other ranks. The companies were well on their way to the 150 Rangers that Shea hoped to recruit. Experienced outdoorsmen such as Frederick Frieda of Hopedale, an Inuk who had served with the Royal Newfoundland Regiment in the Great War, gave the units local credibility. Reports from

Nutak and Gready also indicated "that the force has actually begun to function more or less coherently." A Ranger had already reported an unidentified submarine off the coast of Labrador.[47]

Eastern Command ran into the usual problems when it sought national approval to restructure the original two companies (eight platoons) in Newfoundland into a broader organization of nine companies and thirty platoons. A proposed company headquarters at St. John's violated policy because the city had two reserve units. Plans to locate two platoons at Lewisporte – a petroleum supply centre – also seemed to contradict the government's vital point policy because a private company owned the facility. Eastern Command explained that St. John's and Lewisporte had been singled out for headquarters, not platoons, because coastal towns and villages on the eastern coast and Southern Avalon had almost no communication network. These transportation hubs would serve as command-and-control centres for Rangers in isolated coastal locations. Army headquarters eventually accepted this logic. "This is an ambitious programme but one which leaves no loophole on the [Newfoundland]-Labrador coast," Colonel C.H. Cook commented. The area commander deemed the Rangers "a cheap form of defence insurance with advantageous political implications."[48]

Tommy Taylor's Failure to Rebuild His Empire

Although the situation in Eastern Command seemed to unfold according to plan, BC's Ranger force remained a disappointment as Tommy Taylor's crusade unravelled. In 1951, Taylor reported to Major-General W.H.S. Macklin, the vice chief of the general staff, "The Pacific Coast Militia Rangers ... are still very much alive in the minds and hearts of men and women throughout the length and breadth of British Columbia." He alleged that Claxton had not fulfilled his promise, made in 1946, to reactivate the PCMR once the Rangers were officially established. Former Rangers were clamouring to serve. To strengthen his case, Taylor mentioned the international situation and the need to appease the concerns of BC women:

> Reactivation of the P.C.M.R. would I feel be a very popular move. With
> the international situation as it is people here are becoming increasingly
> keen and anxious to see the old, well known P.C.M.R. "Vigilans" badge
> ... in use again.

In the event of any threat to this area the P.C.M.R. would be a very effective organization and certainly go a long way to prevent our good citizens from becoming "filled with alarm and despondency." It would also go a long way to relieving anxiety on the part of our women-folk and leave husbands and sons freer to join the Reserve Army.

Taylor stressed his personal commitment, particularly that he had created and commanded the PCMR "from start to finish" and had spent more than five thousand dollars since the war to maintain Ranger interest.[49] He had arranged a six months' leave from his business to survey former PCMR units and recruit individuals for the new force. In Taylor's view, it was essential to revive the Canadian Ranger organization in BC.[50]

The provincial army commander looked forward to the prospect of adding several thousand additional Rangers to the regional home defence structure, but other officers were wary of bringing Taylor onboard. Macklin noted that Taylor leaned towards empire building, which ran counter to the Rangers' postwar direction. Although Worthington acknowledged that "in his peculiar way" Taylor had "kept the P.C.M.R. very much alive and on 'its toes,'" he characterized him as "a very unorthodox man." Ironically, General Vokes, who had callously dismissed the Rangers' value in northern Ontario, vigorously supported the organization once he took over Western Command. He believed that Taylor's zeal and commitment would be instrumental to rejuvenating the neglected Ranger organization along the Pacific Coast. The new chief of the general staff, Lieutenant-General Guy Simonds, supported Western Command's plans, as long as new coastal units reflected the "forms and scale" of regional threat assessments, functioned under the same terms of reference and regulations as units across Canada, and took shape "in the normal manner." Like his predecessors, Vokes forbid establishing new units in areas with an Active or Reserve Force presence. He explained that Ranger units already existed on Vancouver Island and the Mainland's coast. In Vokes's view, Taylor should merely bring Rangers units up to an efficient state, not create new ones. Accordingly, Western Command called out Taylor as its liaison officer in May 1951.[51]

Taylor, however, set his own agenda. He marched throughout the province in July drumming up support from former wartime Rangers. When he reported back to headquarters in the fall, his empire-building proclivities were obvious. Representatives from 61 of the former 120 PCMR companies had replied to his overtures, and he had received 59 applications for new Ranger units and subunits. He believed his campaign would yield more than five thousand new Rangers – a number equal to the authorized Canadian Ranger strength for the entire country. When Taylor visited interested individuals, he gave the impression that they could go ahead and begin organizing companies. Taylor's wartime Ranger movement had outpaced normal planning procedures, and he anticipated the same momentum this time around. His detailed report, submitted in August, characterized the official vision and structure for the postwar Rangers as too constrained. He wanted more local units with clearer boundaries to better harness BC's geographic and demographic diversity.[52]

Taylor's criticisms had some validity. Existing unit boundaries did not adequately reflect the province's cultural and physical geography. He cited the case of No. 13 Company, commanded by Moise Dubeau at Terrace and platoon commander Edward Charles Valpy at Port Simpson. "Captain Dubeau is a railroad worker and represents one type of personnel," Taylor explained, "while Lieutenant Valpy is an Indian fisherman and represents an entirely different type." Under ordinary circumstances these two men would never meet, and the communication and transportation links between their communities made them "as far apart as Vancouver and Winnipeg, perhaps farther." His solution, however, ignored the Rangers' role and mission and sought instead to re-create the units as a home guard. Most of Taylor's proposed companies were based on former PCMR companies, and he drew a series of detailed maps outlining forty new units with an estimated strength of 4,210 Rangers. Even more revealing, he recommended that the units be reassigned the name "Pacific Coast Militia Rangers" and the old cap badge.[53]

Taylor had clearly overstepped his mandate. Although he managed to sell his vision to regional commanders, authorities in Ottawa did not buy it. The director of military operations and plans recognized that his reorganization plan violated and dismissed existing policy. Taylor's plans would more than double the prescribed limit for Western Command, and five of the proposed company locations already had Reserve Force units. Taylor had also ignored the remote and sparsely populated northern half of the province, focusing instead on the Okanagan and Fraser valleys, the Kootenay and Trail areas, and islands in the Strait of Georgia, all of which fell within the main population belt. Consequently, army headquarters rejected Taylor's recommendations. The director of military operations and plans reminded Western Command that the Canadian Rangers would serve a different purpose than the PCMR, stating unequivocally that "Canadian Rangers are not Home Guard units."[54]

Sounding the death knell for Taylor's bold plans, Brigadier W.J. Megill, the new BC area commander, accepted that the original plan for a modest nucleus of Rangers in strategic locations made more sense than a full-blown Ranger empire. Megill divided the province into priority areas, emphasizing the area north of the Yellowhead–Prince Rupert railway. Officers would recruit individual detachments along isolated parts of the coast, but they would not group the detachments into companies because doing so could "create a false impression ... and lead to considerable citizen agitation for a much larger organization." Instead, small groups of ten to fifteen men would "form a small community group that will retain its enthusiasm" and could quickly expand in case of emergency.[55] This approach excluded most of Taylor's disciples.

At a conference in November, Taylor complained that the 4,500 former PCMR members whom he had contacted that summer lived in the low-priority region, which, for planning purposes, had been capped at 420 Rangers. When he learned about the reduced plan, he warned of repercussions. In reply, senior staff officers simply told him the military would get to pick the cream of the crop.[56] In the clash of competing visions, the logic of a small, carefully selected force prevailed over Taylor's romantic dream of a revitalized citizen-guerrilla army watching over the length and breadth of BC.

Taylor predicted correctly that the more limited vision would provoke a backlash. Brooke Claxton received irate letters from individuals who had taken Taylor seriously enough to recruit potential companies of up to one hundred Rangers, only to discover that the military planned to enlist a mere five to ten men. Major Herbert Ashby, a former member of the PCMR who had organized ninety men in Bralorne and another sixty in surrounding areas, questioned why the military devoted significant resources to reserve army recruitment but refused the service of men in remote areas willing to devote their time and energies to national defence. A massive power project had recently been fast-tracked for completion in his area. The Rangers could help to prevent sabotage, but ten men could not protect a 3,600 square mile area.[57]

In reply, the minister stated that there had been some misunderstanding – a diplomatic way to correct the unrealistic expectations that Taylor's misinformation had created. Claxton pointed out that

> [t]here is considerable difference between the purpose and scale of organization of the Canadian Rangers and the former Pacific Coast Militia Rangers. The latter were organized on a fairly extensive basis and included in their terms of reference such roles as assisting to repel major attacks, employing guerrilla tactics against a possible invader and anti-sabotage measures. The Canadian Rangers are organized on a limited scale to provide assistance on an individual basis to formed bodies of troops which may be required to operate in coastal areas, to act as coast watchers, and to provide information on any unusual occurrences in their local areas. It is not intended to employ the Rangers as guerrillas, in organized defence tasks, in protection of vital points or in any role that is the assigned responsibility of other elements of the Army or of other government agencies.[58]

The minister quashed Taylor's empire-building aspirations. If companies or platoons ballooned to every location where citizens expressed interest, or if Rangers began to protect every civilian industrial installation across the country, then "the loose organization of the Canadian Rangers could develop into a more formal type with all the resulting financial, training and equipment implications."[59]

Taylor's ambitions exacerbated problems in Western Command. In March 1952, Brigadier Megill expressed his dissatisfaction with Taylor's organizational efforts. "The difficulty in Taylor's case most definitely is that he is very stubborn and set in his ways and is convinced that the Pacific Coast Militia Rangers was the only possible organization for BC Area."[60] Megill, the army commander in Vancouver, told his superiors that Taylor's "intimate knowledge of the geography and community life of the Coast and hinterland of British Columbia" would be difficult to replace. Nevertheless, Taylor had reached retirement age, and renewing his contract would require ministerial approval.[61] This was a convenient pretext to terminate his services. Taylor's time with the Rangers had come to an end. The visionary who had spearheaded the explosive growth of the PCMR had left the postwar Rangers in BC in dismal shape.

The Rangers and the North West Highway System

North of Taylor's gaze, the backbone of the western Canadian Ranger force was taking form in towns and camps along the "linear community" of the North West Highway System. The Alaska Highway had been hastily constructed during the war to secure the land connection between the southern US states and Alaska. As engineers smashed their way through the Canadian northwest, they changed the settlement pattern in the remote region beyond Fort St. John and ended its isolation. By 1945, new towns, warehouses, administrative headquarters, barracks, Quonset huts, and garages dotted the route from Dawson Creek to Fairbanks.[62] The highway crossed some of the most beautiful and rugged landscape in North America. From Dawson Creek, it wound its way north and west through the rich farmland of the Peace River Block, past the large RCAF airbase near Fort St. John, through dense forest, treacherous muskeg, and deep river valleys and on into the Rockies west of Fort Nelson.[63] Massive bridges spanned the majestic Peace, Muskwa, Liard, Teslin, and Yukon rivers. Beyond Whitehorse, the highway skirted the shore of Kluane Lake, along the St. Elias mountain range, to the main camp at Destruction Bay, named after the prospectors' rafts that washed up on shore during the Klondike gold rush era. North of Kluane, the highway crossed rivers that "do not behave like ordinary rivers ... They are wild, tricky and highly uncertain." Trickling creeks could "boom into bank-full torrents within a few hours as the glaciers melt or rain falls on the mountains nearby. They look innocent at times but can lash out with swollen tongues with devastating suddenness to treat man made bridges and roads with utter contempt."[64]

In April 1946, the Canadian Army assumed responsibility for the North West Highway System, the name for the Alaska Highway in peacetime. Although the general staff hardly saw the highway as a strategic supply route or gateway to invasion, it embraced the opportunity to maintain the route because it allowed military engineers to practise road and bridge building at minimal cost.[65] After military exercises exposed the army's limited capabilities to defend the highway, however, the army transferred an armoured car squadron and Reserve Force elements to the region. Western Command assumed responsibility for defending the North West Highway System in April 1950, and regional commanders pleaded for garrisons and mobile forces. Their appeals fell on deaf ears. Strategic planners deduced that Russia, having become a nuclear power, would not squander airborne troops on attacking the Canadian Arctic: an atomic bomb would have far more shock value than paratroopers. With the onset of the Korean War and the return of Canadian forces to western Europe in 1951, army headquarters refused to allocate the Mobile Striking Force to the highway's defence. The brigadier who commanded the road would have to make do with the limited, and declining, resources at his disposal.[66]

Placing Ranger units along the North West Highway System made sense. Civilian workers with the Highway Maintenance Establishment, the crews headed by officers of the Royal Canadian Engineers, lived and operated along the controlled highway on a daily basis.[67] In 1951, defence planners restructured No. 2 Company in Whitehorse to accommodate Ranger detachments of highway maintenance crews. The headquarters remained in Whitehorse, and a platoon protected vital installations in the town and would set up roadblocks if needed. Other platoons were based at Destruction Bay to defend Haines Junction, Brooks Brook to protect installations between Whitehorse and Mile 496, and Carmacks to protect the entry to the Alaska Highway from the Mayo-Whitehorse Road.[68] The army also hatched plans to extend the Rangers in northeastern BC.

At Dawson Creek, "Mile 0" on the highway, locals viewed their community as a strategic crossroads that connected southern Canada to the far reaches of northwestern North America. Major A. Glenn, the district Veterans' Land Act coordinator, asserted in January 1951 that if an enemy attacked from the northwest, "Dawson Creek would be a prime objective and that the country could well be penetrated, and probably overrun." He felt a Canadian Ranger unit would be of "great value."[69] Although he initially suggested that veterans would embrace Ranger service, he painted a different picture once he tried to form a reserve reconnaissance unit. Men would accept the Ranger rifle and ammunition, but "the people approached seemed to think that there was not enough organization, training, or planning for an emergency to make it worthwhile." Based on Glenn's sixteen years in the militia, he questioned the possibility of sustaining an unpaid, untrained volunteer force.[70]

When General Chris Vokes visited Dawson Creek in late May 1951, he convinced Glenn that a Ranger company was worth the effort. Kelly Haugen, a former RCAF officer and a Veterans' Land Act administrator in Fort St. John, assumed command of the proposed company. In June, he held meetings in the surrounding area. Contrary to Glenn's dismal predictions, locals responded with enthusiasm. Twenty-eight men from Hudson's Hope, a picturesque village on the banks of the Peace River in the Rocky Mountain foothills, met at the local poolroom on 23 June. The former PCMR commander in the community, Victor Peck, oversaw the gathering. The men nominated and elected by secret ballot a list of prospective lieutenants. The next month, K.B. Shaw, the secretary of the Dawson Creek branch of the Canadian Legion, applied for a company. By October, he had submitted attestation forms for individuals he had recruited before an announcement appeared in the local papers, a development he feared "might bring down the deluge." "So far we have got a very good bunch, some are veterans, some are trappers, and one or two are just young fellows whom I know," Shaw reported. "To the best of my knowledge they are all good shots and woodsmen and I believe they will all stick with the Rangers until they are no longer required." The Rangers wanted to know more about their status and role, and they wanted to receive their rifles.[71]

The local initiative hit a roadblock in Ottawa. Policy forbade locating Ranger and Reserve Force units together, and the carrier platoon of the Loyal Edmonton Regiment was already based in Dawson Creek. The acting chief of the general staff therefore rejected Western Command's proposal, as well as one to relocate the Ranger company from Prince George to Fort St. John. Defence planners in Ottawa considered Fort St. John a "comparatively populated area," and the Rangers' proposed home defence role allegedly violated policy.[72]

Vokes refused to back down. In an emergency, the Rangers would guard vital points, particularly bridges, along the highway until other troops arrived. Isolated areas required different strategies than those devised for "built-up areas." When the director of military operations and plans conceded that the Rangers were "a cheap form of insurance," he once again treated national policies as general guidelines rather than rules. In January 1952, the army moved 15 Company to Fort St. John and authorized 37 Company for Dawson Creek.[73]

The delay did not constrain interest or activities at the local level. During the summer of 1951, fifteen Rangers from Dawson Creek helped search for a civilian sportsman lost in the woods near the community. Although they acted as volunteers, without remuneration or official approval, they self-identified as Rangers.[74] Oblivious to debates among officers in Edmonton and Ottawa, Shaw had continued to enlist Rangers that fall. Joe Galibois, the Indian Agent at Fort St. John, likewise recruited "like a house on fire"

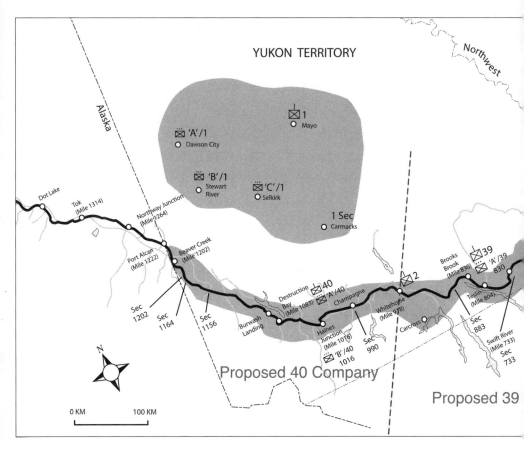

Ranger company and platoon locations along the Northwest Highway System, 1953

Sources: Data from Library and Archives Canada and Ken Coates, *North to Alaska* (Toronto: McClelland and Stewart, 1992)

and advocated raising the Dawson Creek company to two full platoons. Shaw nevertheless promised to stick to Western Command's plans. Considering his efforts a success, he boasted: "I have now got an ex-mortar Sgt and an ex-[Warrant Officer from the Royal Canadian Engineers] for explosives and booby traps." He had also recruited an electrician, who happened to be "a good man in the bush," and a projectionist who rigged up lights at the Peace River bridge. Careful organizing, rather than simply filling nominal rolls, would produce a "better company in the long run," Shaw insisted. "What a galaxy of talents we shall have!"[75]

This local optimism was mirrored along the expanse of the North West Highway System, which created problems for the company commander in

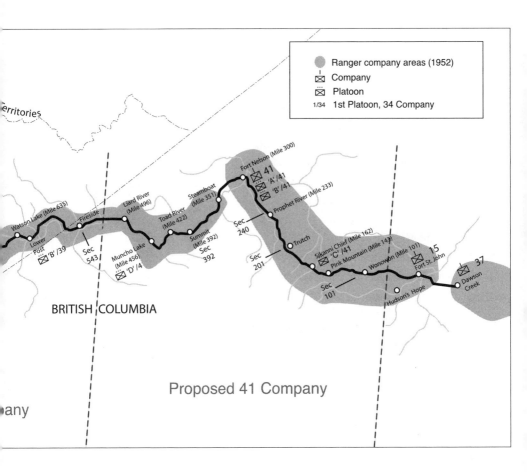

Ranger company areas (1952)

Company

Platoon

1/34 1st Platoon, 34 Company

Whitehorse. Civilian highway workers signed up in droves in 1951 and 1952, swelling the ranks of No.2 Company to 7 officers and 331 Rangers. Captain W.M. Emery, at least in theory, had control over all Rangers along the highway and an area that spanned 160,685 square miles (416,172 square kilometres). In practice, he frequently visited central Yukon but could not manage Rangers south of Whitehorse. Consequently, apart from receiving a rifle and their annual allotment of ammunition, Rangers along the highway had little knowledge about their role. Brigadier H.W. Love, North West Highway System commander, wrote in October 1952, "The present situation requires a remedy because those men who have volunteered for the Rangers in good faith are becoming increasingly disinterested and, to some extent, scornful of our efforts to organize them into a useful Reserve Militia unit." He suggested forming highway employees into a distinct Ranger company. Civilian employees who frequented the maintenance camps would serve as officers.[76]

Captain Emery in Whitehorse had no desire to maintain an untenable Ranger empire. How could the army expect a part-time, volunteer commander to coordinate activities and reports from such a large number of dispersed Rangers? The North West Highway System was a world unto itself. To "iron out existing discord" and make the Rangers useful, he advocated redrawing company boundaries to correspond with highway maintenance areas so that the superintendents of the Highway Maintenance Establishment could serve as officers.[77]

The following year, the army implemented his vision. It carved three new companies out of existing companies along the highway and located headquarters at Destruction Bay (Mile 1083), Brooks Brook (Mile 830), and Fort Nelson. It transferred employees of the Highway Maintenance Establishment, communications stations, and engineering detachments to these companies, which would now focus on defending their camps and equipment and reporting incidents in their area.[78] The original Ranger companies in Yukon also imagined taking on local defence tasks. In an emergency, No. 1 Company (the headquarters having moved with Captain Chapman to the booming silver-mining community of Mayo) would seal off the Keno mine and protect the local dam and power plant. No. 2 Company would help the Whitehorse Defence Force and Mobile Striking Force recapture the community following an invasion.[79] Reorganization gave the units focus and helped to cover a dispersed population.

North to Baffin Island

The Rangers now covered Canada's eastern and western flanks, but the Far North remained *terra incognita* to most defence officials. "The Eastern Arctic in winter has the appearance of a flat, cold, waste land relatively thinly covered with granular snow and in perpetual twilight or darkness," Lieutenant-Colonel G.J.H. Wattsford commented in 1948:

> During the few summer weeks, the land takes on a fen-like appearance due to the amount of water lying on the ground and to the profusion of wild flowers. The light precipitation in this area, and hence light snowfall,

permits the frost to get deep into the ground sometimes as much as 16 feet. In the northern part of the Territory the ground never thaws more than two feet down; consequently there is no drainage and surface water results. One can readily imagine the difficulties of moving vehicles through this type of terrain in either summer or winter but particularly during summer. The chief inhabitants of the area are the Eskimos. There are, however, a few hundred people of European descent, chiefly fur traders and trappers, miners, missionaries and government officials.[80]

Missions, HBC posts, and RCMP detachments dotted the North. The Arctic Islands drew modest attention during the war, when airfields and weather stations supporting the North East Staging (or Crimson) Route extended to Baffin and Padloping islands.[81] These developments affected local populations at sites such as Frobisher Bay (Iqaluit) but did not radically transform the Far North (as subsequent military megaprojects would).[82] They did, however, raise significant concern in the postwar period about Canadian sovereignty in the Arctic Archipelago.[83] Canada had acquired its High Arctic islands from Britain in 1880, and agreements with foreign countries confirmed its legal title in the interwar years.[84] Some government officials, however, still worried that Canada had not done enough to establish its *de facto* control. A few even mentioned the possibility of drawing the region's small population into some form of military service to help demonstrate Canada's sovereignty and contribute to continental security.

In the early postwar period, staff officers began to note the potential importance of Inuit to national defence. The Soviet Union had, ironically, given them the idea. The Russians had for decades devoted considerable attention to developing their Arctic areas and assimilating the inhabitants into their plans. The Soviet Institute for the Peoples of the North trained members of Soviet indigenous groups who returned to the Arctic as doctors, teachers, meteorologists, and aircraft technicians "thoroughly indoctrinated with the Red virus of future world domination." In contrast, a Canadian briefing paper observed that "both Canada and USA have been almost standing still where the Eskimo is concerned." Flight Lieutenant S.E. Alexander, who had visited the western Arctic in 1948, noted with regret that the armed forces had hired a few Inuit to do menial jobs. "Anyone who has knowledge of the Eskimos knows them to be most ingenious, of outstanding integrity, loyalty, patience and industrious far beyond the average whiteman in the arctic," Alexander explained. "Given half a chance the

Eskimos would prove beyond any doubt the ideal race for staffing Armed Service Units, meteorological stations, hospitals, schools, and scientific bases in the far North."[85]

Alexander envisaged a long-term project and many pitfalls. Government and mission schools had forced Inuit to "forsake their trapping grounds" and forget their "native ways." Alexander believed Inuit could be trained to perform most military duties in the Arctic and that those with promising ability could work "in a useful capacity in their own country after graduation." The military would not have to pay for "unclimatized personnel, who for the most part, are bitter and unhappy with their postings and consequently not too concerned in carrying out their duties." Alexander's plan would also contribute to Inuit acculturation. "This matter of utilizing the Eskimos to the fullest extent both for their own advancement and the good of their native land has been discussed many times with those who know the arctic," he noted. "There has never been a dissenting voice."[86]

The Americans had already fallen in with this line of thinking. After Pearl Harbor, army officers and territorial officials in Alaska organized Inuit (Inupiaq and Yup'ik) along the northern coastline into militia units. They hoped that, like the PCMR in BC, the territorial guard would provide an economy of force, freeing Regular Forces from civil defence obligations. The zealous leadership of Major Marvin "Muktuk" Marston won broad community support for the guard. He explained to the native residents that the Japanese wanted their villages and resources, and he provided them with free 1917 model Lee-Enfield rifles and ammunition. By the end of 1944, ten instructors – seven of whom were Inuit – were training Inuit companies. At war's end, Marston boasted that the "Tundra Army" had shot down and recovered Japanese balloons, built hundreds of miles of new trails, repaired sixty shelter cabins, put out tundra fires, and erected eighteen armouries – all on a shoestring budget. Although regular officers in Alaska and Washington viewed the units as superfluous in the postwar world, the Alaskan governor secured them permanent status as a National Guard organization.[87]

When Canadian officers contemplated the Rangers' expansion into the eastern Arctic, they looked to the Alaskan National Guard as a potential model. The Eskimo Scout Battalions in Alaska bore some similarities to the Canadian Rangers. Small units dotted Alaska's coastline from Bristol Bay to Point Barrow and islands in the Bering Sea, representing the only military presence in most of the region. They mainly gathered local intelligence, but they would also act as guerrilla forces if an enemy invaded western Alaska.

An American military officer swears in four Alaska Territorial Guardsman in Barrow, Alaska. University of Alaska Fairbanks, Elmer E. Rasmuson Library, Ernest H. Groening Papers, UAF-1976-21-587

In this regard, the Alaskan battalions were better trained, equipped, and organized than the Rangers. They received the same duty pay as National Guardsmen of similar rank, carried the same infantry rifle (the M1) used by the regular army, and were equipped with snowshoes, skis, mountain tents, binoculars, telescopes, and modern radio equipment. Despite challenges, the United States had managed to distribute equipment and conduct field training in the region without incurring unreasonable costs – at least by US standards.[88]

The US experience suggested that Inuit would be well suited to military service. "The enthusiasm with which the National Guard program has been accepted by the Alaskan natives is very high," Colonel Ned Norris, a US Army foreign liaison officer, observed. "Recruiting has been no problem. The extent to which the units have been organized has been limited only by the ability of the Army to supply needed equipment and administrative support." American officers, unlike their Canadian counterparts, supported the investment. "The native characteristics of the Eskimo lend themselves to the development of the intelligent mission," Norris elaborated. Military observers noted a typical Inuk's "keen ability to traverse Alaskan regions better than other people, his keen eyesight, hearing and powers of observation, his extremely keen memory, and his ability to sketch what he has seen in relation to his location." These traits allowed small units to cover a vast area and submit useful reports. In turn, military training and service helped "to develop qualities of citizenship, loyalty and patriotism among the Alaskan natives."[89] An article on the Tundra Army, published in late 1952, emphasized that Inuit loyalty was unimpeachable and that "the arming of these people paid intrinsic dividends in basic Americanism."[90]

At the time, the Canadian government was in the process of recognizing Inuit as citizens and extending to them the basic services of the state. It began distributing family allowances in the Arctic in 1945, and communities such as Coral Harbour, Lake Harbour, and Cape Dorset boasted federal schools.[91] Although government officials hoped that the "civilizing" influence of education would bring stability to Inuit of the eastern Arctic, the late 1940s brought a collapse of the fox fur trade instead. The Inuit economy and way of life changed irrevocably.[92] Income fell by four-fifths while the price of essential goods increased. The federal government made the situation more difficult when it imposed a 15 percent tax on rifles and ammunition throughout Canada in 1950. Northern administrators failed to secure an exemption for Inuit.[93] Considering that Inuit also had to absorb exorbitant transportation costs on consumer goods, Rangers and their families benefitted directly from a .303 and an annual allotment of ammunition.

In 1951, Eastern Command recommended creating two companies on Baffin Island. The companies would cover the north and south, and the army would draw officers from the HBC who, in turn, would recruit Inuit. Because no single person could act as an effective company commander, given the challenges of travel and communication, the chief of the general staff looked to his government colleagues. General Simonds noted that responsibility for Inuit fell to Department of Resources and Development officials. Although they had no desire to dictate how the military would use the local population, they wanted "to be kept informed and ... to provide any assistance possible." Before Eastern Command proceeded, Simonds instructed officers to meet with public servants who had spent much of their lives in the region and could suggest platoon and company headquarters locations and suitable leaders.[94]

In July, Captain Ambrose Shea and Major J.R. McLaughlin from Eastern Command, Major F.B. Perrott from army headquarters, and Alex Stevenson from Resources and Development met in Ottawa to discuss how best to organize Rangers in the Far North. As the officer in charge of the Eastern Arctic Patrol, a former HBC clerk in the eastern Arctic, and a former member of the RCAF, Stevenson had a wealth of knowledge. He suggested that Lake Harbour, Cape Dorset, Pangnirtung, Clyde River, Pond Inlet, and Arctic Bay could support Ranger platoons and Frobisher Bay could serve as a communication hub. Inuit, he explained, were "reliable, honest and intelligent and would make good Rangers." His department "was trying to induce the Eskimos to make their own way in life and not to expect everything for nothing." In particular, he wanted to make sure that they did not receive rifles as "free handouts." A rifle was "a major asset to an Eskimo and something he had to earn by hard work," and bullets for hunting cost significant money. The underlying message – the federal government had to inculcate Inuit with proper capitalist values. To support this vision, Stevenson recommended giving Inuit ammunition for their personal weapons or paying them a small annual honorarium rather than handing them a service rifle.[95]

Stevenson's recommendations touched off a minor debate. Major Perrott paid heed to Stevenson's comment that there was "little or no way of stopping the Eskimos from modifying issue weapons to meet their own particular requirements or ideas." They had always done so with material goods. In Perrott's view, however, distributing service rifles and ammunition to all Rangers was worth the risk. Colonel Cook, the director of military operations and plans, agreed that distributing .303 rifles would cause fewer problems, but he saw the move as neither "economical nor business-like." Inuit already had rifles, and "as an incentive to join the Rangers and do a good job, it is more practical to establish a credit with the platoon commander (a Hudson's Bay factor). This credit can be used by the Eskimos to draw ammunition to fit their own rifles in compensation for their Ranger activity."[96] The deputy chief of the general staff refused to make an exception, however. Inuit Rangers received their .303s like everyone else.

When the military authorized 28 Company and 29 Company for south and north Baffin Island, effective 21 August 1951, it acknowledged that the actual recruiting process would take time. It began with seven platoons and deferred the selection of company headquarters and commanders.[97] R.H. Chesshire, the general manager of the HBC's fur trade department, pledged his full cooperation and radioed posts on Baffin Island about the Rangers. As a result, all of the island's platoon commanders were HBC employees.

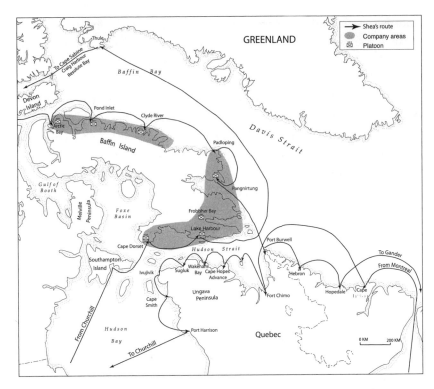

Ranger platoon locations on Baffin Island and the route of Captain Ambrose Shea's 1952 liaison trip to the Arctic

The factors promptly filled out their forms, but it took a while for the mail to travel to Eastern Command.[98] The army anticipated that the commanders would "recruit to full strength from the Eskimo population" before the end of 1952.[99]

Only direct military contact would make the Baffin Island organization more than a paper list of HBC factors authorized to hand out free rifles and ammunition. The army, following Alex Stevenson's suggestion, sent Captain Shea on the *C.D. Howe,* the new ice-strengthened Eastern Arctic Patrol ship, during the summer of 1952. The voyage took more than three months as the ship stopped at points on Baffin Island and in northern Quebec. The army did not have to pay for Shea's transportation, which fit its meagre Ranger budget, and the trip went off as planned. The Ranger liaison officer organized platoons, issued rifles and ammunition, advised platoon commanders, and planned communication exercises. He passed out a double

Ranger Peter Kuniliusie, who joined the Clyde River platoon in 1952, received a Special Service Medal (Ranger Bar) from the governor general in Ottawa in 2000. Courtesy of 1 Canadian Ranger Patrol Group

allotment of ammunition to the Rangers in northern Quebec, who had not been visited the previous year, and enlisted new members.[100]

The new recruits included Peter Kuniliusie (*Peterloosie* on the form), a twenty-two-year-old hunter and trapper who officially joined the Clyde River Platoon on 8 September 1952. He had been recruited, along with six

TABLE 2
Canadian Rangers, strength return, 31 December 1952

Company	Headquarters	Officers	Rangers	Total	Command
No. 1	Dawson City, YT	4	35	39	Western
No. 2	Whitehorse, YT	7	331	338	Western
No. 3	Longue Pointe, PQ	3	37	40	Quebec
No. 4	Baie-Comeau, PQ	2	26	28	Quebec
No. 5	La Tuque, PQ	–	–	–	Quebec
No. 6	Fort Chimo, PQ	6	113	119	Quebec
No. 7	Yellowknife, NWT	10	55	65	Western
No. 8	Fort Smith, NWT	1	5	6	Western
No. 9	Tofino, BC	3	20	23	Western
No. 10	Alert Bay, BC	2	12	14	Western
No. 11	Bella Coola, BC	1	30	31	Western
No. 12	Ocean Falls, BC	3	56	59	Western
No. 13	Terrace, BC	2	41	43	Western
No. 14	Smithers, BC	1	–	1	Western
No. 15	Fort St. John, BC	1	5	6	Western
No. 16	Flin Flon, MB	4	10	14	Prairie
No. 17	Norway House, MB	6	26	32	Prairie
No. 18	Seven Sisters Falls, MB	5	9	14	Prairie
No. 19	Kenora, ON	2	–	2	Prairie
No. 20	Aklavik, NWT	3	15	18	Western
No. 21	Norman Wells, NWT	4	34	38	Western
No. 22	Cartwright, Labrador	4	75	79	Eastern
No. 23	St. Anthony, Nfld.	1	–	1	Eastern
No. 24	Churchill, MB	4	36	40	Prairie
No. 25	Red Lake, ON	6	29	35	Prairie
No. 26	Moose Factory, ON	5	54	59	Prairie
No. 27	Fond du Lac, SK	1	–	1	Prairie
No. 28	Frobisher Bay, NWT	4	30	34	Eastern
No. 29	Clyde Inlet, NWT	2	–	2	Eastern
No. 30	Lewisporte, Nfld.	3	–	3	Eastern
No. 31	Bonavista, Nfld.	4	48	52	Eastern
No. 32	New Perlican, Nfld.	1	24	25	Eastern
No. 33	Grand Bank, Nfld.	2	–	2	Eastern
No. 34	Channel, Nfld.	2	18	20	Eastern
No. 35	Port Saunders, Nfld.	–	–	–	Eastern
No. 36	Hopedale, Labrador	4	52	56	Eastern
No. 37	Island Lake, ON	–	–	–	Prairie
TOTAL		121	1,392	1,513	

Source: Library and Archives Canada, RG 24, acc.1983-84/215, box 321, f. S-2001-1999/0, pt. 4.
The totals do not add up in the original document.

other hunters, three years earlier when a ship arrived to test for tuberculosis. Each received a .303 rifle, and an officer told them they were Rangers. Kuniliusie's status became official when Shea and Doug Wilkinson (a film-maker and author who agreed to serve as the north Baffin Island company commander during a long-term research trip) formally established the platoons and filled out enrolment forms. Kuniliusie served with the Rangers for more than five decades, observing dramatic changes in the organization and in Inuit society more generally.[101]

✤ THE CANADIAN RANGERS AS A national force took shape in the early 1950s. Brooke Claxton proudly boasted to the House of Commons in May 1951 that the Rangers now covered "fairly well the whole area of the Northwest Territories, the Arctic, the coast of British Columbia" and were "extending over the Hudson Bay area and the north Atlantic coast."[102] The Rangers had achieved remarkable geographical coverage given the paltry resources devoted to their organizing efforts. From fewer than five hundred men in February 1950, the Rangers nearly doubled in size by the end of 1951 and again by the end of 1952, when more than fifteen hundred Rangers had signed up across the country. More than half belonged to Western Command, but Prairie and Eastern Commands were expanding too (see the table on the previous page).[103]

The Rangers remained a paper army despite these advances. A few critics, such as a Conservative parliamentarian who applauded the Ranger concept in April 1952 but dismissed it as flawed and unworkable, insisted that the military either retool or disband the force.[104] The government and the military were more positive. Regional commanders persisted with their organizing efforts in the years ahead, responding to demographic and economic shifts in northern and coastal areas. The Rangers' role remained fundamentally unchanged,[105] but it remained to be seen how regional and local commanders would interpret this role in the future. As for the Rangers themselves, official paperwork in Ottawa mattered little to them. They wanted to actually do something.

5

Exercising the Rangers, 1952-56

❋ *YELLOWKNIFE, FEBRUARY 1955.* Ranger Captain John Anderson-Thomson, the commander of No. 7 Company in Yellowknife, had first learned about Exercise Bull Dog III in the fall of 1954. The army would assess new northern equipment and Arctic warfare, and professional soldiers would test his Rangers' capabilities. "If we could not contain them at the airport or prevent them from getting into town," he reminisced, "we were to break into small parties of scouts, and, avoiding any direct engagements[,] to know at all times where the enemy was and his strength, and how best to launch an attack when the [friendly] paratroopers came in. Most importantly we were to have guiding parties to lead them as secretively as possible to the most favourable point for attack." He likened the exercise to "playing cowboys and Indians all over again, with the added bonus that nobody was likely to get shot."[1]

The Yellowknife Rangers had met to prepare and formulate a strategy for the exercise. They reasoned that the troop-carrying planes would not land downwind, so they built machine-gun nests on both sides of each runway. This way, they could determine the wind direction and choose which locations to man come the morning of the actual event. As the snow deepened, the Rangers continued to improve their fortifications "to the point where on the last morning we would add fresh snow in copious dollops." They knew that a bullet would go through hard snow but that it would barely penetrate newly packed snow. They planned defence and retreat lines based on their familiarity with the local geography, set up false snowshoe

Soldiers with the Royal 22nd Regiment (Van Doos) land at Yellowknife airport, February 1955. Prince of Wales Northern Heritage Centre, NWT Archives, N-1992-254-0037

trails through the bush to lead the enemy in circles or straight into a strategically placed Sten gun, and laced cotton twine across the trails leading to their camp to signal an approaching enemy. "We therefore set up three lines," Anderson-Thomson explained, "each tent being equipped with spruce bed boughs, airtight heater, gasoline lantern, cut wood rations and kindling wood already to go, so that if we were beaten out of one position, all that we had to move were the sleeping bags and the rum."[2] The local Ranger captain prayed for cold weather on the day of the mock invasion so that the vehicles and men could get a real test of subzero operations.

When "D-Day" arrived on 23 February 1955, it was fifty-two below zero Fahrenheit (and remained consistently frigid throughout the three-day exercise). The enemy aircraft landed as anticipated. As the troops began to unload their supplies, they received a surprise. Unbeknownst to the Ranger liaison officer, Major Casimir Van Straubenzee, the local Rangers had formed what they called the Royal Yellowknife Air Force, composed of three planes flown by former Second World War pilots. The Rangers had made bombs using paper bags with a "pound or two of lamp black" from the Giant Mine.

When "the time was ripe," the three aircraft, which had been "cruising aimlessly and innocently in the vicinity," flew in line formation and dropped their mock bombs in the middle of the Royal 22nd Regiment – the vaunted Van Doos. The umpires agreed that the Rangers "destroyed the invasion force utterly."[3]

The Rangers proved relentless. "When they had given us this decision," Anderson-Thomson explained, "we then opened up with the machine gun and ... the umpires again gave us another total victory, called a halt to the hostilities, and we had to withdraw ... What a mess the poor devils were in, lamp-black all over them and on everything they touched!" The soot-covered invaders could hardly conceal themselves against the snow. In the hours ahead, the Rangers' air force took out the Van Doos's commanding officer and their communications equipment. The ground attack troops fell into the Rangers' snow-shoe trail trap, and the umpires gave the Rangers their "third victory in a matter of three hours." The Rangers withdrew to their second line of defences so that the Van Doos could attack them that night. After another rout, the invaders found themselves "no nearer to capturing the city than when they first landed." Demoralized by the cold weather and "continually being either shot or taken prisoner," the Van Doos nonetheless expressed their admiration for the Rangers' fortitude and persistence. The local Ranger captain boasted that a colonel with the Princess Patricia's Canadian Light Infantry who led his paratroops into Yellowknife the next morning was "quite miffed because there was nothing much for his troops to do." The Rangers had mapped out a trail that allowed the Princess Pats to reach the airport undetected and "put in a short and successful attack."[4]

Bull Dog III proved the Rangers' tactical value. When he congratulated the Yellowknife company, exercise director Major-General Chris Vokes, a former Ranger skeptic, called the exercise the "greatest upset the Cdn Army had ever had in war or peace."[5] Anderson-Thomson acknowledged that it all sounded "like a bit of school-boy pranks," but he recalled that "a few ski-equipped Finnish troops with the guts to fight for their homes and families, with nothing but their rifles, held up and completely demoralized a whole division of Russian troops" in the winter of 1940.[6] Could it really happen in the Canadian North? Unlikely. But in the Cold War, no one knew for certain, and the Rangers offered cheap insurance.

🍁 CANADA'S ARMED FORCES GREW from 47,000 to 104,000 personnel between 1950 and 1953, when the defence budget escalated to $1.9 billion

Soldiers on Exercise Bull Dog III, 1955. Prince of Wales Northern Heritage Centre,
NWT Archives, N-1979-052-2038

(more than ten times the budget of 1947).[7] Rather than heightening the
perceived threat to Canada's remote regions, Cold War developments reduced the likelihood of direct attack. A northern invasion would not impair
the North American allies' ability to wage a war. Although the Mobile Striking
Force "provided a financially inexpensive means of mollifying the Americans and calming the public in regard to the 'vulnerable' North," it would
not likely have to repel a ground invasion.[8] Nevertheless, the Rangers had
taken shape throughout much of northern Canada, so Mobile Striking Force
exercises provided the Rangers with opportunities to test their skills.

Journalists heaped praise on this "shadowy band of defenders."[9] They lauded their potential value as guerrillas who could use local knowledge to stymie invading forces.

Tactical training exercises with southern soldiers exacerbated ongoing debates about what Canadians could and should expect from the Rangers. While Western Command pushed its vision for a home guard, official army press releases emphasized the Rangers' more modest role as observers and aids to civil authority. Ranger liaison officers in Quebec and Eastern Command insisted that the Rangers' original role remained appropriate. The improbability of a foreign invasion helped their case. In this context, the Rangers offered a low-cost, self-equipped volunteer force that meshed well with the government's general unwillingness to invest in ground forces to defend remote areas. The Rangers also fit with the federal government's broader desire to re-Canadianize the North,[10] and units began to play more active roles in communities across the country.

A Community-Based Force

John Anderson-Thomson assumed command of No. 7 Company in the spring of 1951. Born in Scotland in 1900, he served during the First World War as a sniper and fighter pilot before moving to Saskatchewan in 1920 and earning a degree in geological engineering. In the late 1930s, he moved to northern Ontario to work as an engineer, geologist, and mine superintendent, and he served as a navigation instructor for the Royal Canadian Air Force (RCAF) at Rivers, Manitoba, for two years during the Second World War. In April 1944, he relocated to Yellowknife, where he wore many hats as a field engineer, geologist, surveyor, magistrate, and justice of the peace. Having served as a commissioned officer "off and on" since he was sixteen years old, the community knew him well, and he knew several of the Rangers when he became captain on 9 May.[11]

Anderson-Thomson believed that "a little shake up in personnel" would improve the Yellowknife company. The Rangers, "supposedly recruited from trappers, prospectors and bush men," had, in actuality, been recruited locally "from drunks and dead beats around the town."[12] He accepted command with the proviso that he would have "a free hand to get rid of any or all that I considered to be dead wood," and he immediately struck off the names of Rangers who he "felt would not pull a very stout oar, in an emergency." He wrote in his memoirs, "I kept on strength the genuine trappers

John Anderson-Thomson.
Prince of Wales Northern Heritage Centre,
John Anderson-Thomson fonds, N-1986-002

out in the bush; they would have their ears to the ground and would observe anything that was not normal in the area. The ones I wanted to get rid of were the rank and file in and around Yellowknife, the ones who would let you down if they were part of the defence force. There were a fair number of army veterans from both wars, so I picked men with battle experience, especially machine gunners or infantry men who could shoot and I found all the able men that I needed." He hand-picked Donald Macleod Morrison, an ex-infantry sergeant, as his second-in-command. "A fighting man from the Western Isles," Morrison "would have tackled the whole Russian army, single handed if necessary."[13]

The new commander worked closely with other military units in the area. His connections with the 24th Field Squadron of the Royal Canadian Engineers secured access to an old schoolhouse for lectures and meetings. Working together, the local officers produced what Anderson-Thomson described as "a rough strategy for the defence of Yellowknife in case of the cold war becoming a hot war." Russia, if it attacked, would target the airfield, which it then could use to harass allied bombers flying the old staging route from the United States to Siberia. In Anderson-Thomson's coordinated response, the 24th Field would handle administration and supplies, local army cadets would focus their training on communications, and his Ranger company would protect the airfield until outside reinforcements arrived. His Rangers would neither drill nor parade, nor would they don uniforms – "there was no point advertising our strength or weakness to the enemy or to subversive agents in Yellowknife, and indeed we had one or two persons whose loyalty was in question."[14]

Local defence plans generated enthusiasm and gave Rangers a clear sense of purpose. During the summer months in the land of midnight sun, they concentrated on shooting their Lee-Enfields and Bren Guns at the Department of National Defence range near the airport. Their practice in the evenings and on Sunday afternoons paid off, if Anderson-Thomson's assessment can be taken at face value. Of the sixty-five men in the Yellowknife platoon, at least forty were "really first class shots," he boasted, "any of whom was far above average regular army sniper ability."[15]

The Yellowknife Rangers directly benefitted from their close integration in the local military and civilian communities. They invited representatives from the local Royal Canadian Signals detachment to observe Ranger training so they too would be familiar with local defence plans. In turn, Rangers enjoyed mess privileges. They assisted an Army-RCAF reconnaissance team in May 1953 and took them to a ladies handicraft dance. They also served ceremonial functions when dignitaries visited. "We had one very special meeting with Governor General Vincent Massey ... on a Rangers-only basis," Anderson-Thomson recalled, "which was a howling success both literally and figuratively, because I had picked my 'other ranks' for their ability as bush men and fighting-men and all the rough edges were still rough on many of them. Mrs. Lionel Massey heard Bible stories that she had never heard before."[16]

Rangers participated in special events across the country. W.S. Moores, the acting company commander at Cartwright, Labrador, wrote in February 1952: "Yesterday morning I had a fairly good representation of No 1 Platoon out, at least parts of three sections, to take part in the firing of a 56 Gun Salute as a mark of respect to our late Sovereign King George VI ... It served manifold purposes; it gave me a chance to call them out, awakened them to a sense of duty, brought back old times for some of the veterans that love it, besides showing a mark of respect."[17] In communities farther north, Rangers turned out en masse to greet military representatives aboard the *C.D. Howe* when it showed up on its annual Eastern Arctic Patrol. "When the Ranger officer comes ashore," R.A.J. Phillips, an expert on northern affairs, explained, "any convenient piece of flat ground becomes a parade square, and though there is not much drill, the annual inspection of men and equipment is both solemn and impressive."[18]

For the most part, communities embraced the Rangers. After all, Ranger officers, as insiders, had close connections to local government and business leaders.[19] The lack of funding and supporting infrastructure for the Rangers made these relationships particularly important for sustaining their units. For example, in Ocean Falls, a flourishing pulp-mill town northwest of Bella Coola on the BC Coast, the Crown Zellerbach Corporation granted 12 Company the use of the community hall free of charge. It also gave the Rangers salvage lumber for a rifle range. The Rangers showed their appreciation to the community by throwing a wiener roast for 250 children. Officially, the Rangers had a military role, but they also had local value, which they demonstrated beyond a doubt during two successful searches for hunters missing from the community in October 1955.[20]

Search and rescue was the most frequent Ranger volunteer activity across Canada. Along the North West Highway System, for example, during Exercise Sweetbriar in February 1950, two Canadian Rangers helped rescue an airplane crew who had crashed off the highway near Haines Junction. In the summer of 1951, approximately fifteen Rangers from No. 37 Company searched for a civilian sportsman lost in the woods near Dawson Creek. That fall, Highway Maintenance Establishment personnel from the camp at Mile 1,202, employed as Rangers, searched for a soldier lost in the bush. During the summer of 1952, Rangers from No. 2 Company, Whitehorse, served as spotters on RCAF aircraft in the search for a Mitchell aircraft lost south of Mayo, while Rangers of No. 15 Company conducted a rescue operation near Fort Nelson. "It is significant that all these operations were successful mainly due to the local knowledge and ability of the Rangers to make their way through the bush," Brigadier H.W. Love, the commander of the North West Highway System, noted. Unfortunately, regulations prohibited Rangers from receiving remuneration for search and rescue if they had not been called up on active service to do so beforehand. "Such a procedure obviously would take too long to meet the circumstances pictured in the experiences quoted above," he explained. He wanted special authority to compensate them, which would "do a lot to strengthen their interest and morale."[21] Although senior defence officials never rectified this problem, Rangers continued to conduct search-and-rescue missions as unpaid volunteers, proving to their communities that they represented more than a symbolic military asset.

Rangers also volunteered to assist police. In April 1953, Rangers from No. 40 Company helped the Royal Canadian Mounted Police (RCMP) apprehend three bandits who had stolen a car in Alaska and were heading south on the North West Highway. When the fugitives' car broke down at Mile 1,165, they held up and stole a second vehicle. Ranger Captain Don Bakke, the officer commanding at Destruction Bay, Yukon, alerted his company. The Rangers, armed with their service rifles, followed the car and reported its progress to the RCMP detachment at Haines Junction. Three Rangers went to the Airport Lodge at Mile 1,095 to protect the family living there. When the criminals entered the lodge peaceably, the Rangers remained concealed, held their fire as instructed, and allowed them to proceed down the highway. The local RCMP commander requested further assistance to apprehend the bandits, and Ranger platoon commander Lieutenant Wally Wandga (who was also camp foreman at Mile 1,016) mustered ten Rangers to block the route with two road graders and a third vehicle to illuminate the highway. The Rangers took up a defensive position. "The bandits approached the block and looking down the business end of ten 303's realized that the game was up," a Ranger newsletter noted. With the Rangers covering his back, the RCMP constable stepped forward and made the arrest. Assisting the RCMP was part of their role, Van Straubenzee reminded the Rangers, "and in this case the action was firmly and sensibly carried out, forcibly illustrating the Rangers are suitable and available in this type of an emergency."[22]

Rangers also provided intelligence about their local areas on a routine basis and reported unusual occurrences, particularly in Eastern Command. They sighted submarines and surface ships as well as suspicious aircraft flying low or circling overhead. In August 1952, Lieutenant Fred Cox of 34 Company, 3 Platoon, reported what looked like a naval ship heading into the Gulf of St. Lawrence. Although he could not identify the ship, he recorded its speed and sketched its silhouette on a report to headquarters. Around the same time, Lieutenant W.S. Moores made an "extraordinarily acute" description of a suspicious character in Cartwright, and he provided a dossier "almost as complete as [the] R.C.M.P.'s." Although the man proved to be a religious fanatic not "subversively inclined," the Rangers' intelligence impressed the area commander.[23] A few months later, Moores reported what sounded like a naval engagement while visiting members of his Ranger company near West Bay, at the entrance to Hamilton Inlet. It turned out that Canada and the United States were conducting a joint naval exercise off the Labrador coast featuring lots of live ammunition. If defence planners did not leave enough time for their warnings to reach the more isolated settlements, Shea warned, the Rangers may "regard the attack as genuine and inject a wholly unexpected note of realism into proceedings by shooting back."[24] In these and other examples, Rangers expressed frustration when the military did not provide them with detailed responses to their reports.[25] Shea told them not to be dismayed. He explained that the Russians were likely operating in Canadian waters. Once reports of enemy activity passed up the chain of command, officials "often kept quiet for reasons of security. In fact, the more genuine the report the less likely you are to hear more of it."[26]

"Latter-Day Versions of the Flying Dutchman": Ranger Liaison Officers

The Ranger liaison officer, the glue that held the Rangers together as a military formation, kept in touch with company commanders, helped them with planning, and urged them to train "the boys for action in their areas."[27] It was no easy feat. Each command had one liaison officer, who could visit Ranger units only sporadically given their inaccessibility. In Eastern Command, Captain Ambrose Shea described himself as a "latter-day version of the 'Flying Dutchman,'" covering Newfoundland, Labrador, and Baffin Island. He also completed all of the considerable "desk work" associated with the Rangers.[28]

If the Ranger liaison officer had a thankless job, Shea recognized that the Rangers might feel the same. A January 1953 circular to Rangers encouraged them not to interpret limited visits and paltry financial support as evidence that they were no longer needed:

Rangers get no pay, no publicity and little thanks.

The liaison situation is not going to get any better and it may get worse. DON'T LET IT GET YOU DOWN.

The Canadian Rangers in this Command are doing a useful job simply by being in existence. But it is never possible to stand still. Any organization that tries that surely must go backward.

Don't let this happen. The Rangers have great possibilities. They could be the finest and most genuinely useful military organization either in peace or war that this Newfoundland Area has ever seen.

Use your own initiative and push ahead. If you don't know how then worry this Headquarters until you find out ...

One last word. The proudest motto ever borne by proud men was "I Serve." And now in the various languages that you speak –So long! au revoir! tabautisi! auksunai!

Perhaps "auksunai" is the best: "Be strong!"[29]

Shea knew that bureaucracy and centralized control would inhibit the creativity and flexibility that the Rangers needed to function. Even the simplest of considerations – such as reimbursing Ranger platoon commanders for sending out messages by telegraph or mail within their areas – seemed to create endless paperwork and few cheques.[30] The Rangers had neither the support nor the training available to other military units. Shea cringed at strict procedures; he knew that informal methods were more appropriate. "There appears to be growing tendency to regard detail as something which has value in itself regardless of whether it helps or hinders the working of the plan concerned," Shea explained to his superiors. He found needless complexity "symptomatic of an era and a mentality which believes that soap is improved when it is called a 'mild detergent' and that a garbage can is less odiferous when referred to as a 'disposal unit.'"[31] He preferred to keep things straightforward so that the Rangers could understand.

Quebec Command took a similar approach. The regional commander resumed responsibility for Ranger units in September 1952 and appointed Major Pat Templeton as Ranger liaison officer.[32] Templeton spent much of his time administering and organizing platoons, but he stressed the importance of "constant and consistent personal liaison" to maintain interest. In fact, the army had never visited some of the units, and some Rangers did not receive an annual allotment of ammunition. Templeton remedied this situation.[33] From October 1955 to September 1956, for example, he travelled more than 16,000 miles (25,750 kilometres) to visit Rangers in his command: 12,724 miles by air, 2,756 by boat, 146 by dog team, and 74 by snowshoe. "Despite the apparent general belief that the command Ranger officer spends his time on boat and air trips for the purpose of fishing and hunting," Templeton wrote, "it must be noted that considerable improvement in the Ranger situation has taken place."[34]

Creating and maintaining viable Ranger units meant sustaining contacts and fostering ongoing local relationships. Rangers signed on for three years and had to be re-engaged after that term elapsed. Only company and platoon commanders could reach individual Rangers spread across the country to do so. "It is apparent that the organizational period never ceases," the director of military operations and plans noted. "The Ranger officers can undertake these tours in their own time but not at their own expense." Ranger officers' civilian jobs put them in contact with their men in theory. In practice, "[s]ome Rangers are trappers and woodsmen but the officers do not, as a body, get very far afield in their day to day work, neither do they have the financial means to undertake such travel," a regional commander reported in 1954. "Weather conditions and the uncertainty of road and rail communications make travel conditions slow and expensive." The army authorized modest travel allowances so that company and platoon commanders could tour their areas and visit Rangers.[35] The dispersion of units and the lack of communication between Ranger platoons and company headquarters, however, seemed to inhibit command and control.

To solve this structural problem, Templeton recommended that the platoon replace the company as the basic Ranger subunit. Platoon officers could communicate directly with Quebec Command Headquarters in Montreal, obviating the need for an additional layer of complexity.[36] The army, however, was not ready to make this change in the 1950s. It preferred a more typical command structure, one that, on paper at least, provided fewer points of contact for liaison officers. Regional commanders would have to decentralize responsibilities within the existing framework and within the miniscule budget allotted to Ranger matters.

Templeton found ways to make this work in Quebec. Along the North Shore, for example, the company commanders, who were "capable and prominent citizens," could not visit their platoons (never mind individual sections) because of their civilian business obligations. To maintain contact, Templeton paid Ranger Lieutenant D.A. Rowsell, the platoon commander in Harrington Harbour, to inspect his unit's detachments each summer in the mid-1950s. He covered 600 miles (966 kilometres) over twelve days, visiting platoon members deployed up and down the coast in groups of three and four. In spite of the challenge, he gained renown for running one of the best-administered Ranger units.[37]

By late September 1956, Templeton could report that the Rangers in Quebec had been fully organized. Each platoon now had an officer, and

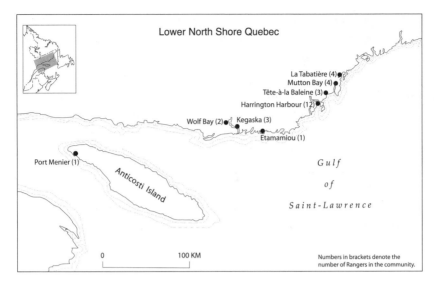

La Tabatière (4)
Mutton Bay (4)
Tête-à-la-Baleine (3)
Harrington Harbour (12)
Wolf Bay (2)   Kegaska (3)
Etamamiou (1)
Port Menier (1)

Gulf

of

Saint-Lawrence

Anticosti Island

0   100 KM

Numbers in brackets denote the
number of Rangers in the community.

Map of No. 3 Company, No. 2 Platoon at Harrington Harbour, July 1953

the Rangers covered the North Shore and the Quebec shores of James Bay, Hudson Bay, Hudson Strait, and western Ungava Bay. The Rangers could have up to 550 men in Quebec, but the liaison officer saw no need to try to reach that figure. The 13 officers and 364 Rangers in his command did the job.[38]

Western Command likewise depended on a dedicated liaison officer. The departure of Tommy Taylor opened up space for Major Casimir Bowen Van Straubenzee, a rancher and well-known outdoorsman from Enderby in the Okanagan Valley.[39] A military liaison job had already taken him throughout Yukon and Northwest Territories, where he had met "many Ranger characters."[40] As the command Canadian Ranger officer (CCRO, or "crow," as Western Command called its liaison officer), he visited each unit in western Canada annually for resupply and basic training and to confirm the suitability of the local leadership. The far-ranging dispersal of Ranger units and the difficulty of communications made this an ambitious task.[41]

Liaison letters helped maintain contact with Rangers. In Quebec, Templeton issued informal training bulletins twice annually. Written in English and translated into French and Inuktitut, they discussed rifle stores, safety, and equipment and offered updates on local Ranger commanders.[42] Western Command originally planned to send out its letters every six weeks, but averaged two issues per year in the early 1950s. In contrast to *The Ranger* – a glossy, professional wartime magazine – it printed the postwar circular on foolscap paper, all that the CCRO's budget allowed.

The circular provided Rangers with basic guidance and training tips. The occasional "foolishness," such as a poem penned by Van Straubenzee in 1954, kept the tenor light:

> A Ranger patrol can be mighty rough,
> When the wind chills high and the going is tough,
> With old joints a'creak and lungs like to bust –
> You would think these fellows had had enough!
> BUT
> The CCRO states he'll back a hunch
> That the Ranger gang is still a stout bunch,
> And that men who went through Vimy Ridge,
> Can patrol, bead a sight – guard a bridge,
> And still beat the teen agers to the punch![43]

What the poetry lacked in sophistication, the liaison letters made up for in providing updates on developments in Ranger companies across British Columbia, Yukon, and Northwest Territories.

Van Straubenzee concentrated primarily on companies in the territories, reflecting the army's preoccupation with the North.[44] There was also ample room for expansion in remote parts of BC, where previous organizing efforts had faltered. The army commander in the province warned against overly ambitious plans, given the false start that Taylor had created by promising more than the army intended to deliver.[45] Van Straubenzee more accurately discerned the differences between the old and new Ranger concepts. Approximately one-third of the Pacific Coast Militia Rangers' companies had been located along the Coast – 55 percent in the southernmost part of the province. Taylor had tried in vain to convince defence officials to replicate this pattern, but the national trajectory headed north. By 1954, 90 percent of Canadian Ranger units in the country fell above fifty degrees latitude. Accordingly, the BC army commander instructed the CCRO to focus his energies on isolated coastal regions and thinly populated areas in the northern Interior.[46] Like Taylor, Van Straubenzee capitalized on relationships initially forged during the war, but he was much better at following directions. Rangers in Western Command benefitted.

TABLE 3
Comparison of Ranger locations in BC, by latitude, 1945 and 1954

Company locations	PCMR (1945) (%)	Canadian Rangers (1954) (%)
Below 50° latitude	50	10
Between 50° and 55° latitude	47	55
Between 55° and 60 ° latitude	3	35

Source: Based on "Canadian Rangers – Pacific Region, 29 February 1988," Esquimalt Military Museum, f. "Canadian Rangers," 8-9.

The CCRO made modest headway expanding the Rangers' footprint in BC and consolidating it throughout Western Command. Annual liaison visits allowed him to build strong relationships, and he applauded veteran Rangers such as one-legged Captain Moise Dubeau, who had commanded 13 Company since the days of the PCMR and had "kept the Ranger ball rolling around the Terrace area with very little help." New company commanders such as Smithers resident Les Cox – a game warden, retired paratrooper, and commando who had fought throughout Italy and northwestern Europe – promised to revitalize moribund units such as 14 Company. Van Straubenzee recruited Marcel Jutkas and Ralph Andross, Indian Agents for the Hazelton and Vanderhoof districts, and C.V. Harrison, a "geologist, prospector, guide, and veteran of the First World War" at Burns Lake, to

TABLE 4
Canadian Ranger strength, by command, 1951-58

Year	National	Western	Prairie	Quebec	Eastern
1951	894	586	65	146	97
1952	1,513	855	197	187	274
1953	2,154	982	395	334	443
1954	2,490	1,211	404	315	560
1955	2,694	1,353	405	370	559
1956	2,725	1,376	404	392	550
1957	2,682	1,304	403	406	566
1958	2,374	1,316	80	413	562

Source: Library and Archives Canada, RG 24, acc.1983-84/215, box 321, f. S-2001-1999/0, pts. 4-9. National numbers also include officers on strength not assigned to active units.

organize platoons in their areas.[47] Although the number of Rangers in BC and the Northwest Territories remained far below authorized levels, the CCRO claimed Western Command would meet them by fall 1954, an impressive achievement that mirrored strong growth across the country. Since he believed that he could now recruit to maximum strength within a week if necessary, he set common training goals so that each section, patrol, platoon and company would be "FIT TO TAKE THE FIELD IN ANY EMERGENCY."[48]

Training and Exercises

Being fit to perform in an emergency required more training than the original concept for the Rangers allowed. The 1947 policy statement provided for training in elementary topography, message writing, the use of the wireless, and other "basic essentials." In 1951, Major Stan Waters in Ottawa placed a high priority on communications. About twice a year, he proposed, officers could set up "unusual activities" in Ranger areas to test the alertness, organization, and communication skills of each company. Rangers, he argued, should participate in all military training in areas covered by their units, particularly Mobile Striking Force activities. This way, the army could assess their usefulness as guides. How could the Rangers detect unusual activities unless they received pamphlets on enemy aircraft, shipping, equipment, and clothing? If a training officer met with Rangers in each area at least once a year, Waters predicted that the military would convince Rangers that it valued and wanted them.[49]

Waters's suggestions informed training policy in the early 1950s. It emphasized individual instruction in patrolling and reporting, aircraft recognition, navigating, and field sketching, as well as collective training in disseminating information, surveying vital points in their area, and participating in active force exercises.[50]

Translating policies into action was another matter. What could the Rangers actually do with a shoestring budget and few soldiers dedicated to train them? Eastern Command believed the national training directives were unrealistic:

> Canadian Rangers are scattered over an area 2100 miles long by 1400 miles wide. These units are located mostly on the perimeter of this area and can only be reached by sea or air. With the exception of Newfoundland,

transportation difficulties prevent their being visited more than once a year. On the other hand, it would not be possible to bring Ranger officers into a central point for instruction because of the difficulties of travel and the fact that few of these officers could leave their employment to attend. The Platoons themselves extend in some cases 100 miles or more along the coast and individual members are seen by their COs periodically when normal business interests bring them together. It will therefore be apparent that the only method by which instruction in military subjects can be given to these Rangers is by individual and personal tutelage.

Eastern Command had one Ranger liaison officer and could spare no one else for training. Understandably, the regional commander recommended dropping formal military subjects and confining instruction to practical exercises and communications.[51]

National Defence Headquarters did not want to centralize Ranger training or to send Regular Force instructors out to individual platoons. Instead, it recommended distributing regional liaison letters and training précis to Ranger officers. The Ranger liaison officer, out in the field all summer distributing arms and ammunition, could write these communiqués during the winter and pass them out during community visits. Western and Prairie Commands had successfully implemented this training directive, and with a little bit of imagination and initiative Eastern Command could also make it work.[52]

Eastern Command focused on passing messages rather than on field exercises. In Exercise Ambrose, the liaison officer sent telegraph messages to the platoons in Newfoundland, Labrador, and Baffin Island in November 1952 to see how long it took them to reply. He hoped for a response time of twenty-four hours, but many replies took much longer. For example, Captain Shea waited 107 hours and 22 minutes to hear back from the platoon commander at Cape Dorset, who had been frozen in for a month. Overall, however, the Rangers responded with surprising accuracy. In Exercise Seagull, conducted the following year in Labrador and Baffin Island, the platoons showed notable improvement in their response times. The exercise also allowed Shea to pass along Christmas greetings to Inuit Rangers and their families whom he had met during his travels.[53]

By contrast, Exercise Gabriel, which tested Ranger communications in the northwest in June 1952, yielded disappointing results. Many of the Rangers' reports to Edmonton contained mistakes.[54] Major Van Straubenzee, undeterred, filed the results under "lessons learned." He advised the Rangers to continue gathering information in case of an attack. "How will you get the information? I can't tell Rangers how to stalk the enemy, you are the experts in stalking, hunting and fieldcraft," he noted. "Follow the enemy, shadow him, hinder him if you can, shoot at him if you are sure you can kill him and get away. We do NOT want you chaps to fight a set piece battle, we want you to pass information to us and then act as guides and assistants when we come to beat up the enemy with our heavier weapons and trained troops."[55] Van Straubenzee would test these roles in the years ahead.

Paper exercises were one thing, practical field training with the Regular Force another. In the early 1950s, intelligence estimated that Soviet paratroops could, at most, mount company-size attacks on northern Canada and sea-borne attacks of up to ten men against coastal targets. Atomic weapons made these attacks unlikely, but the enemy could possibly sabotage vital points, such as bridges on the Alaska Highway, remote weather stations, and early-warning lines. In these cases, Canada would need some capacity to deal with small, isolated lodgements. The RCAF argued that aircraft could take out an enemy using high explosives and napalm, but the army insisted that special forces would also play essential roles. This raised the question: how much was enough? If the enemy did launch attacks, they would probably be diversionary. The chairman of the joint planning committee, as well as the chief of the general staff, insisted that Canada still needed paratroopers.[56] It also insisted that the government needed a contingency plan to protect the North.[57]

The Rangers, in theory, went to war during Exercise Bull Dog, which took place near Fort Norman, Northwest Territories. On 10 February 1953, Captain Kenneth Murray Mackenzie ordered Rangers from 21 Company to go to the local airstrip and transmitter station to report unidentified aircraft. Just before noon five days later, the enemy (the Royal 22nd Regiment or Van Doos) struck with airborne troops. Rangers Hodson and Godbold made it to the Royal Canadian Signals Station ahead of the enemy patrol and dispatched a warning to Western Command. For the next three days, the Rangers shadowed the Van Doos, stalked their positions, determined their strength, and identified snow forts, trenches, and machine-gun posts. When friendly paratroops, the Princess Patricia's Canadian Light Infantry, landed on the frozen lake near the transmitter station on 19 February, the Rangers used their rifles to neutralize enemy machine-gun fire. "This assault completely surprised the enemy," a Ranger noted. Ranger Lieutenant Russell

Rangers *(right)* meet soldiers of the Princess Patricia's Canadian Light Infantry on Exercise Bull Dog at Norman Wells, Northwest Territories, February 1953. Courtesy of Canadian Rangers National Authority

Wilfred Hanson briefed the friendly force's commander about the local situation. "All that night and the next the Rangers led friendly patrols upon the enemy positions seeking out information and taking prisoners in preparation for the big assault on the enemy lodgement," the post-exercise report documented. The soldiers and Rangers recaptured the airport, and "Norman Wells was liberated. The Rangers returned to their own camp hungry, tired, and unshaven but happy and this they felt was not too much to pay for the defence of their country."[58]

Newspapers played up the Rangers' guerrilla tactics,[59] but these grassroots units still had much to learn if they wanted to be interoperable with outside forces. The Rangers got confused when the enemy attacked their settlement. Consequently, immediately after the initial parachute drop, the Rangers started a fire fight with the friendly force. Officials stated that the Rangers needed to communicate clear plans and pass along "early and accurate warning" of enemy activities. The Rangers had guided friendly patrols, but they had provided poor advice because they did not anticipate how difficult it would be for troops to move at night while hauling heavy sleds. The Rangers, in their snowshoes, had "outdistanced and outpaced the enemy" – as well as their allies. Finally, officials stated that the Rangers needed training in small-scale raiding and ambushing.[60] If the Rangers wanted to play a useful combat role, they needed more experience.

The Rangers' interactions with well-trained southern soldiers during these exercises bolstered their enthusiasm and confidence, and Western Command sought more skill-enhancing opportunities, including formal training, for its men.[61] During Hot Dog II, which took place in 1954, the Princess Patricia's Canadian Light Infantry ran a course for eleven Rangers from eight different companies along the North West Highway System. Major P.J. Carson noted that the Rangers had embraced the idea and "wanted even more time on the course."[62] When other Rangers requested similar activities, Western Command offered indoctrination or refresher courses featuring lectures and tactical exercises.[63] These gatherings, held at central locations such as Yellowknife, Whitehorse, and Wainwright (Alberta), gave Rangers an opportunity to meet one another and receive basic military training. They provided a sense of "scope, and buil[t] a mutual respect and esprit de corps."[64]

Training exercises also fostered close relationships between Ranger units and Regular Forces. Along the North West Highway System, for example, Rangers watched army-training films and devised local activities with the Mobile Striking Force, the RCAF, and militia units.[65] Rangers participated in the North West Highway System's annual service rifle competition and often distinguished themselves in team and individual events against their military counterparts. Rangers also rivalled members of the Regular Force during the annual shoot in Northwest Territories.[66] In the Champagne area of Yukon, Major Van Straubenzee worked out a winter training program with the North West Highway System in which the Rangers conducted field firing, demolition, and reconnaissance exercises. Four Rangers were called out as sergeants to act as guides and assistant instructors alongside two regular army instructors.[67] They executed the CCRO's creative plans, emphasizing the tactical roles that Rangers might play in a military emergency.

Exercises such as Bull Dog also demonstrated the Rangers' allure to the media. When William Stephenson, a scriptwriter with the National Film Board, asked if he could produce a film reel about the Rangers, the director of military operations in Ottawa refused his request because he feared publicity would heighten pressure to extend the Rangers into southern regions.[68]

Despite his reservations, the Rangers crept into the public spotlight through media coverage of army exercises. In a report from Silver Creek, Yukon, a journalist with the *Montreal Gazette* told readers on 13 February 1954 about "unsung Ranger Arctic warfare defenders" engaging in "guerrilla warfare" for the army. This article and others like it helped promote the idea that the Rangers were a combat-orientated force. The reporter explained that during Hot Dog II this "little-known militia unit," which represented "North America's first line for Arctic defence," had demonstrated "the guerrilla tactics they would use if an enemy ever invaded sub-Arctic Canada from the north." The Rangers, a diverse lot, included "ex-RCMP officers who have settled in the north, trappers, guides, prospectors, Hudson's Bay Co. trading personnel, and a few Eskimos and Indians." Every Ranger, the author declared, "is a crack shot." Canadians could rest assured. "Should an enemy ever advance over the Arctic barrens," he reported, "the Ranger role would be hit-and-run operations to stall the invading force until Canada's mobile striking force could be transported or parachuted into the area."[69]

Later that same month, an *Ottawa Citizen* headline proclaimed that during an "Arctic Exercise: Indians Point the Way." Near Sept-Îles, Quebec, Rangers with No. 4 Company had acted as a local defence force during the Mobile Striking Force exercise Loup Garou. "Indians, woodsmen and trappers ... are emerging as the heroes of this fast-paced Arctic exercise," the newspaper reported. "For days before the paratroopers hurtled into the Sept Iles salient to box in the northern attacking force, Rangers scoured the ground, dodging the invaders but closely watching their movements as they set up defence positions." When the mock invasion force took over the airport, the Rangers, described as "a civilian commando outfit, faded in the surrounding woods," where they patiently bided their time and harassed the enemy until an airborne assault force arrived. "The Rangers knocked out one of the enemy's two medium machine-gun posts, shot up a light machine-gun outfit and captured a mortar position with the loss of only one man." Although the loss was theoretical, the excitement was palpable. The Rangers, who lacked radio facilities to communicate with air and ground forces, still emerged on cue from their bush hideouts and donned their red armbands when the airborne troops arrived. The official after-action report made no specific mention of the Rangers. The press, by contrast, homed in on them as unorthodox military heroes.[70]

These joint exercises drew favourable media attention to the Rangers, but they also highlighted the Mobile Striking Force's shortcomings. A vicious

Ranger TooToo, an Inuk from Churchill, Manitoba, relays information to Mobile Striking Force personnel in a Penguin during Exercise Bull Dog II in 1954. Department of National Defence, Photo PC-7066

article that appeared in the *Hamilton Spectator* on 8 December 1954 declared, "For years now, Canadians have been lulled into a false sense of security and have been completely misled on the capabilities of Canada's defence forces to defend this country against aggression from the North." Rather than highlighting problems with equipment and too many irreconcilable assignments, the media and officials questioned the paratroops' effectiveness and rationalized the Mobile Striking Force's dissolution.[71] Although the Rangers were spared national criticism, their participation in these exercises revived debates about their role – and the military's expectations for them.

Competing Visions: Home Defence or Minimal Expense?

The exercises fit with Western Command's view that the Rangers should be prepared for combat roles. Brigadier Megill at BC Headquarters argued that observation and reporting belonged to the RCAF's Ground Observer Corps, and he lobbied for the Rangers to transfer these duties to the corps and become a proper home guard.[72] Accordingly, the 1953 regional plans called for reconceiving the Rangers as a highly trained guerrilla force capable of "immediate retaliation" against an attacking force. Given the rapid growth of important industrial installations in isolated parts of the provincial norths, Western Command envisaged a new organization with a regular army organization at the helm.[73] This idea departed from the Rangers' role, mission, and tasks as outlined in army orders.[74]

Various local interests, particularly in BC, concurred that the Coast needed a proper home guard. James Flynn, the head of a self-appointed militia organization on Vancouver Island known as the Cowichan Commandos, and Brendan Kennelly, a former instructor with the Pacific Coast Militia Rangers in Princeton, were the most vocal. Defence officials rejected their suggestions because their proposed units overlapped with the militia.[75] Senior officers received other BC scenarios more favourably. In late 1954, the Aluminum Company of Canada asked Western Command to form a Ranger company at Kitimat – a bustling port, smelter, and townsite it had developed at the head of Douglas Channel – and station platoons at Kildale and Kemano. Company officials pushed for a military presence to "show the flag" to "New Canadians" working in the area. They preferred the Ranger concept over a traditional militia unit because the men would not be deployed overseas or forced to attend summer training. The Ranger "home guard" units at Port Radium and Norman Wells, equipped with machine guns and "appropriate environmental clothing," encouraged local defence without draining local resources.[76]

Once again, Western Command argued that special circumstances warranted special treatment. Senior officials in Ottawa rejected requests for battle dress and mortars, but they authorized the proposed Ranger company because of the aluminum plant's "national importance." To accommodate regional flexibility, national headquarters left it to the general officer commanding's discretion to assign the Rangers' local defence roles and issue weapons.[77] A revised Canadian Army order issued earlier that year removed the distinction between the Rangers' wartime and peacetime roles (a reflection of the Cold War itself) and allowed certain Ranger units to take on special defence tasks.[78]

The role of the Canadian Rangers is:

(a) to report to the appropriate army headquarters any suspicious activities occurring in their respective areas;

(b) provision of guides to organized troops within the area assigned to the unit; to assist in immediate local defence against sabotage by small enemy detachments or saboteurs. This does not include the responsibility for planning or directing local defence;

(c) air observation duties within their own localities, as required to supplement the RCAF Ground Observer Corps;

(d) coast watching;

(e) reporting, locating, and rescue work in connection with distressed aircraft and the provision of rescue parties for civilian or military purposes, where required;

(f) assistance to the RCMP and/or Provincial Police in the discovery, reporting, and apprehension of enemy agents or saboteurs;

(g) collection of detailed information concerning their local area likely to be of assistance to them in carrying out their role or of value to the armed forces.[79]

This flexibility pleased Western Command, but it frustrated other stakeholders who believed that it undermined the Rangers' original intent and violated practical realities on the ground.

The proposal to reconceptualize the Rangers as a home defence force, coupled with highly publicized exercises in the northwest, prompted Quebec Command to reiterate its distinct view of the Rangers. "A recent visit to Western Command has disclosed that Ranger Forces in that area are much more highly organized than is the case in this Command," Major Templeton noted in March 1955. In his view, activities out West contravened official terms of reference. Whitehorse, Fort Nelson, Dawson Creek, and Yellowknife already had Regular Force and militia units, and the Rangers' participation in training exercises set up unrealistic expectations:

The part played by Rangers in recent MSF exercises were beyond their actual capabilities and not in accord with their terms of reference. Aggressive fighting patrols such as were carried out during LOUP GAROU and BULLDOG III were rated to be successful, whereas it does not seem reasonable that a heavily armed, well trained enemy in superior strength would have been as effectively contained as happened on these exercises. Rangers were given tasks during the past two BULLDOG exercises which were far in excess of their normal abilities and in fact were treated as an integral fighting part of the Friendly Force. This is very unrealistic and only serves to give a false impression of the capabilities of the Ranger organization.[80]

Most army officers did not appreciate the Rangers' limitations, Major Templeton insisted. He attributed their much-touted successes in recent Mobile Striking Force exercises "to pre-exercise coaching and to the use of equipment and facilities which would not normally be available." Officials had expected the Rangers to attack and defend as if they were formal soldiers rather than guides and scouts. To achieve these fighting standards in reality, however, the army would need to organize the Rangers along militia lines and provide modern infantry weapons, equipment, uniforms, and formal training. Templeton himself had conducted a Ranger training course in Western Command, and he found it neither necessary nor desirable to adopt a similar national program. In his view, most Rangers could not absorb the information he presented, could not afford the time away from work to train, and would not receive enough professional instruction to train their own platoons. Finally, most Ranger platoons would not gather often enough to conduct the formal training required to play the role envisaged by Western Command.[81]

By overselling the Rangers, the military ran the risk of overlooking the Rangers' modest but clear contributions to national defence. Templeton reaffirmed that Rangers in Quebec Command should develop according to established Canadian Army orders, not Western Command's example. "In this way," he explained, "the Rangers afford a [potentially] valuable source of information and assistance to the [Mobile Striking Force] with a *minimum of expense.*"[82] Just because the concept was simple, he wrote to Captain Ambrose Shea, did not mean "it can't be any good!"[83]

Templeton and Shea were kindred spirits. Shea sent out an information bulletin to Rangers in Newfoundland, Labrador, and the eastern Arctic in June 1955 that offered a succinct overview of the Rangers' role – to provide the army with precise information and guide it when necessary. The Rangers "are a special part of the Army who serve freely to defend their home ... if Canada's Army must go to fight in this country in a place where there are no other soldiers, it is the Ranger's job to help them. He lives there and knows the country better than anyone else."[84] Actual combat was not their primary contribution, regardless of what Western Command suggested.

Instead, Templeton recommended that the military base its understanding of the Rangers' role on their attributes:

(a) They are permanent residents of their locality and district.
(b) They are familiar with the local terrain.
(c) They are most experienced hunters, trappers, fishermen and guides.
(d) They are capable of living "off the country" for considerable periods without a fixed base.
(e) They are experienced, all-weather travellers on land and water, ice and snow.
(f) They are keen and interested, and particularly responsive to any suggestions from higher authority.

The army should retain the Rangers, Templeton insisted, because they were cheap "insurance against surprise air or sea landing nuisance raids in isolated areas" and a way to indoctrinate residents "against docile or even helpful action to a potential enemy during an emergency."[85] Whether this last consideration hinted at concerns about the loyalty of Canadians living in remote regions is open to debate. Regardless, the Rangers were a direct link between communities, the military, and the Canadian state.

Templeton also recognized the danger of tying the Rangers too closely to the Mobile Striking Force. If the perceived value of a northern airborne capability plummeted, the Rangers would go down with it. Indeed, as political and military leaders in the mid-1950s downgraded the idea of the North as a gateway for an enemy invasion, Templeton's concerns seemed prophetic. In the 1954 *Defence Program,* the minister of national defence emphasized that "in the final analysis the task of Canadian defence is defence against aerial attack over the north pole. We have to discard from any realistic thinking any possibility of an attack by ground force on the area of Canada either by air or by sea." The Department of National Defence's annual reports confirmed this shift. Early postwar narratives had defined the military's efforts to defend Canada from direct attack. By the late 1950s, defence efforts simply provided for "the security of Canada." Because the manned bomber posed the most serious threat, the military placed less emphasis on the nebulous risk of an enemy lodgement and the forces expected to respond to ground incursions.[86] Fortunately, the Rangers' still had a role to play watching the seas and skies.

Looking Northward and Skyward

Defence planners had acknowledged the Rangers' potential as observers in a long-range warning system since the late 1940s. Strategic bombers posed the primary military threat to North America's peace and freedom, and many considered the Rangers an inexpensive asset for detecting possible enemy encroachments, particularly in the Far North. Colonel Rueben Kyle Jr., vice commander of United States Air Force Northeast Command, applauded the Canadian Rangers in the Foxe Basin area in June 1954. During a recent air force exercise, the intelligence officer at Goose Bay had reported that the RCMP at Lake Harbour on Baffin Island had relayed an airplane sighting by local Rangers. The report's information "could be correlated almost perfectly as to time, altitude, number and type of aircraft, and direction of flight with the scheduled operational flight." The base commander at Frobisher Bay had received the report a mere one hour and seven minutes after the event. "All reports were checked with mission plan and local air defense agencies," Kyle explained, "and the accuracy was amazing." He considered this an outstanding example of the Rangers' value in remote regions.[87]

The era when this sort of local reporting might suffice had almost passed. Strategic consensus now held that the Soviets would target the heavy bomber wings in the American heartland. If the Soviets destroyed the United States' ability to retaliate, they could dictate terms to the Western Allies. Infantry would play no role in a surprise attack on North America: radar arrays would detect enemy activities in Canada's airspace, and air defences would counter them. The lion's share of Canada's defence budget therefore went to the RCAF.

The United States had explored the possibility of creating a northern radar system after the Second World War, but implementing it required technological advances. The Pinetree Line, a radar line that stretched across Canada's western provinces near the forty-ninth parallel and across the Sub-arctic east from Manitoba, became operational in 1949 but did not offer adequate warning. The polar-orientation concept dictated that defences should expand northward.[88] Following Canada-United States Military Study Group reports outlining the feasibility of more northern defences, Canadian military engineers studied contour maps of a strip (fifteen miles or twenty-four kilometres wide) along the fifty-fifth parallel and plotted a radar line across the provincial norths in 1953. The Mid-Canada Line or "McGill Fence," named after the university where the technology was developed, became

Ranger Kadluk looking for aircraft through binoculars, 1953. Prince of Wales Northern Heritage Centre, NWT Archives, N-1979-051-0286

operational five years later. Manned stations in communities such as Dawson Creek, Winisk, Great Whale River (Whapmagoostui/Kuujjuarapik), Knob Lake, and Hopedale overlapped Ranger company and platoon areas. Ninety unmanned Doppler detection stations occupied a double-staggered line between them.[89] Canada alone paid for, built, and operated the line, thus avoiding sovereignty questions and establishing a more permanent military footprint.

The radar fence caused some officials to question whether Canada still needed the Rangers' eyes and ears to watch over the Middle North. Lieutenant-Colonel R.E. Nourse, writing in early 1954, commented: "There is no doubt as to the efficacy of Rangers on our coasts and in the far north but it is questionable if the Rangers in Ontario, Manitoba and Saskatchewan are serving a useful purpose ... There is a possibility, not yet explored, that the Rangers in the immediate vicinity may be of use in connection with the Southern Canada Line ... Other than the possible use of Rangers in this role, their usefulness is quite limited."[90] In the end, the radar stations had their

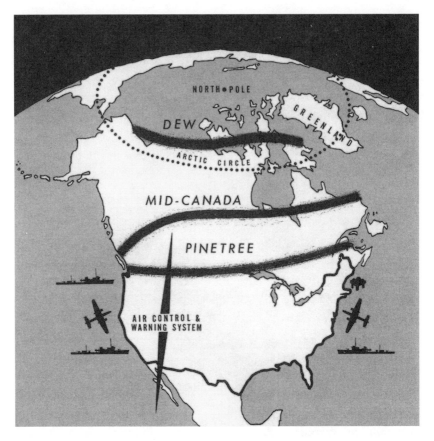

Radar systems in Canada in the 1950s
Source: Federal Electric Company, 1960

own security forces, removing even this possible responsibility. By 1954, Prairie Command stopped calling out its own liaison officer and instead asked Van Straubenzee to visit units periodically.[91] Command headquarters continued with routine Ranger staff work, and strength returns recorded sizeable companies headquartered in Manitoba (Norway House and Churchill) and Ontario (Red Lake, Moose Factory, and Island Lake). Although official records hold little information about the Rangers' activities on the ground, the Hudson's Bay Company's manager in Nelson House noted that the local Ranger company had lapsed in 1953.[92] The Ranger organization was tied to the HBC, and local interest rose and fell with that of local commanders. When Mid-Canada stations became operational, Ranger units in Manitoba and Ontario lost their raison d'être, and commitment waned.

In parts of eastern Canada, the Rangers coexisted with the modern military. At Great Whale River (Kuujjuarapik/Whapmagoostui), an Inuit-Cree-White community on the southeastern coast of Hudson Bay, local hunters and trappers sought jobs constructing the airstrip and radar station. When anthropologist John Honigmann visited the community in 1949, its permanent facilities consisted of a church, store, warehouse, small wharf, and five houses.[93] In 1956, Major Templeton recorded major changes, including a new townsite that accommodated the RCMP, the Department of Transport, the Hudson's Bay Company, and Native people. Lieutenant D. Woodrow, the local platoon commander and transport official, had enrolled twenty Rangers to provide security for military development. "When the RCAF project is complete there will, no doubt, be a general exodus of natives as hunting and fishing is very poor in the whole general area," Templeton anticipated. He greatly underestimated the effect of a sedentary lifestyle on Aboriginal residents, now split between hunters and labourers. Those who settled at Great Whale River found it difficult to leave, and this reality had affected Ranger planning. Templeton had to abandon his vision of creating a detachment on the Baker Islands that would complete coverage along the Richmond Gulf after nearly all the families moved to Great Whale River and the HBC post closed.[94] When the local hunting-and-trapping economy collapsed, a Northern Service Officer arrived to distribute relief and welfare allowances.[95] The spiral into dependency had begun.

Military modernization had a greater effect on the Far North.[96] Stretching about 3,000 miles (5,000 kilometres) from Alaska to Baffin Island along the seventieth parallel, the Distant Early Warning (DEW) Line offered even more advanced warning than the Mid-Canada Line. Early plans, hatched at the Massachusetts Institute of Technology and at Bell Telephone Laboratories, demonstrated the theoretical possibility of a High Arctic radar network, but local information would determine its actual feasibility. Decision makers had access to essential topographical data for Alaska, but survey and siting teams found the map coverage of Arctic Canada too imprecise.[97] Maps lacked terrain and contour detail, and incomplete or antiquated hydrographic charts complicated navigation in Canadian Arctic waters. The teams pieced together maps from aerial photographs, but these maps only solved part of the puzzle.[98] They needed intelligence from the people who actually lived and worked in the region.

Rangers played a modest role in the military's preparations for the DEW Line. In the early 1950s, the federal government possessed limited knowledge about the region above the northern-most transcontinental railway line, and defence officials turned to the Joint Intelligence Bureau in Ottawa for military geography data to plan the radar network. For general summaries of the terrain and climate, the bureau turned to the Rangers, who prepared indispensable reports on local topography, demography, infrastructure, communications, and weather patterns.[99] Individual Rangers also helped situate and survey the radar stations. Following Exercise Bull Dog III, Ranger Ernie Boffa recommended Captain Anderson-Thomson of Yellowknife to the officer leading the DEW Line survey. Boffa "had been advised to pick up his surveyors in Quebec and Ontario with the result that he wound up with all the out-of-work and not too competent engineers from those two provinces," Anderson-Thomson reminisced. "On top of this they had no suitable clothes nor suitable equipment, nor an adequate knowledge of surveying." The Ranger captain had lots of relevant experience. Starting at the BAR-1 site at Komakuk Beach in Yukon in March, he worked through to Cambridge Bay by June and in the process laid out seventeen airstrips ranging from 3,000 to 9,000 feet (900 to 2,700 metres) in length. "I wouldn't have missed it for a million, but I wouldn't do it again for two," he noted. "It was like a young war as far as the Americans were concerned and we worked in all weathers, except fog ... Thank heavens for double Caribou parkas and mukluks."[100]

The DEW Line fundamentally reshaped the Canadian Arctic. Filmmaker Kevin McMahon later observed: "Historians chronically speak of the military opening up the Arctic, as if it had been a kind of locked and mysterious room before some clever army engineers happened by with the keys. Really, the military swept over the Arctic – first during World War II and more so during the Cold War – like an iron cloud, carpet bombing the place with boxes. Their job was the assertion of sovereignty. Every place a box landed became a beach-head for industrialized society."[101] The DEW Line stations were sites of wage employment, new housing, and Western technologies and sources of disruption to northern ecosystems and traditional patterns of life. The sheer weight of the military assault, as journalists liked to call it, boggles the mind. More than 200,000 tons of cargo landed at DEW Line sites during the summer of 1955. Lining up the oil drums delivered that first summer end to end would have extended nearly three hundred kilometres, and the gravel used to build the landing strips could have made a two-lane highway from New York to San Francisco.[102] Unsurprisingly, journalists proclaimed that the Arctic had transitioned from the Stone Age to the Atomic Age practically overnight.

The Distant Early Warning (DEW) Line transformed logistics and life in the North.
Prince of Wales Northern Heritage Centre, NWT Archives, N-1979-051-1531

Although the federal government sought to protect Inuit and other northern peoples from any fundamental disruption to their traditional ways of life, the impact of the DEW Line reached far beyond individual stations. The young anthropologist Jack Ferguson, who visited the western sections of the line in the mid-1950s, observed that wage employment associated with military projects imposed a "radically different kind of living pattern" on Inuit. "The European has created desires for material goods among those people, and these desires can only be resolved by the Eskimos taking every opportunity to earn money." Ferguson noted in his final report that the DEW

Line's projection of "modern industrial life on Canada's last frontier" restructured Inuit time, movement, gender roles, and subsistence.[103] It changed what anthropologist Charles Hughes called the behavioural environment – the environment *as it is* and *as it is conceived to be*. Ferguson presciently predicted that the flood of southern workers into the Inuit homeland would lead to irreversible change.[104]

In January 1955, Captain Ambrose Shea left for Baffin Island onboard the Eastern Arctic Patrol vessel the *C.D. Howe*. He referred to the trip as his "Arctic indoctrination course," and he was prepared to learn. He first met with the Ranger officer at Frobisher Bay, HBC post manager Bob Griffiths, over a card table with local RCMP officers. He then ventured out on dog-team patrols with Constable Deer to visit camps along the bay. He carefully observed Inuit dress, travel techniques, and the setup of their camps, and he compared the Moravian missionary F.W. Peacock's Labrador Eskimo vocabulary to the local dialect. At Eethaloopia's camp, thirty miles (forty-eight kilometres) from the base, Shea discerned a difference between the Inuit living in settlements such as Frobisher and those living in outpost camps:

> We were accompanied on this trip by a relative of Eethaloopia's, who is an Eskimo version of a "Zoot-Suiter" or City Slicker. He parrots a few English phrases with a pseudo-Brooklyn accent and has an air of sleazy sophistication most unusual amongst Eskimoes, who generally have a simple dignity which is both impressive and appealing. Eethaloopia, on the other hand, is the exact opposite of his cousin and looks like something left over from the Paleolithic Age. I am certain that if he ever fell into the hands of an anthropologist he would be stuffed and mounted in no time![105]

In town, Shea had met with the local Ranger sergeant, Sageakdok, "a short, thick-set man of about thirty," who also surprised him. Not only did he have "an energetic, almost aggressive manner, rather unusual in an Eskimo," but Sageakdok had also become remarkably proficient in English for a person who had known little of the language a year earlier. "He takes an obvious pride in his efficiency both as a truck-driver and Ranger-Sergeant," Shea noted. "Well he might. These things represent a tremendous and rapid change in outlook."[106]

Shea respected Inuit and the Rangers in particular. He did not believe he had to civilize them. Instead, he attempted to learn what he could of

Sageakdok in Frobisher Bay, 1955. Prince of Wales Northern Heritage Centre, NWT Archives, N-1979-051-0221S

Inuktitut and Inuit culture and tested his knowledge in correspondence with Rev. Peacock (who had lived among the Inuit of Labrador for decades) and in liaison letters with Rangers. His travels had humbled him, and he did not pretend that his army training or sporadic visits gave him special authority on Arctic matters. "If you ever again refer to me as 'an expert,'" Shea replied to his counterpart in Quebec, Major Pat Templeton, "I shall definitely shoot to kill! In my opinion, there are far too many alleged experts around as it is, especially 'Arctic Experts,' and I have no intention of joining their ranks!" Shea recognized that "the only real Arctic experts are the Eskimoes, who have forgotten more about living in the North than most white men ever learn. That is why I am so anxious to hang on to them and encourage them where the Rangers are concerned, but it is not easy to make people see this point and take them seriously."[107]

Shea took Inuit participation in the Rangers seriously, but he saw their world changing before his eyes. The expansion of the military footprint in the eastern Arctic was drawing Inuit from southern Baffin into the web of modern settlement life. Canadian journalist and popular historian Pierre Berton found that the Frobisher Bay airbase, left "to rot and decay as another postwar ghost town," resembled "a confused mosaic of men and machinery" by April 1955.[108] When Shea returned to Frobisher a year later, he saw a community in a different state of flux. "Because of work connected with the D.E.W. Line and the setting-up of an 'Eskimo Centre' by the Dept. of Northern Affairs, there is much activity here just now and a good deal of coming and going." He witnessed abundant ironies and contradictions as southerners tried to impose the amenities of modern life on the North. For example, the building in which he stayed, owned by the Foundation Company of Canada, was heated to eighty degrees Fahrenheit (twenty-seven degrees Celsius), while the outside temperature fell below zero. He commented in particular on a film shown at the schoolhouse for a large, enthusiastic Eskimo audience. "Rather more shooting took place in this film than during the last World War," Shea observed, "and when the actors were not shooting they were hitting one another on the jaw with loud reports but with little effect." He mused that the film's violence, its "Western-type smooching," and the thirteen rounds of the Marciano-Walcott boxing match they also watched must make for surreal impressions of North American society. "If the Eskimos regard these films as representative of our normal way of life on the Outside," Shea reflected, "then I can easily understand why they prefer to remain in the Arctic."[109]

A few days later, the local Rangers were pressed into service to greet visiting dignitaries. The commanding officers of the US and Canadian air forces at Frobisher Bay "ganged up" on Shea and requested a guard of honour for a group of VIPs arriving the next day. The group included Charles Wilson, the US secretary of defense; Ralph Campney, Canada's minister of national defence; and C.D. Howe, Canada's minister of trade and commerce. Shea had little time to prepare. With the assistance of Northern Service Officer Doug Wilkinson, Bob Griffiths, and Sergeant Sageakdok, he assembled fourteen Rangers in the town garage. Ranger section Sergeant Simonee interpreted as Shea explained basic drill, "sized them," and taught them to stand at ease and come to attention. Shea planned a "purely Eskimo show," with Sageakdok as guard commander and Simonee as sergeant. When the first planeload of dignitaries arrived and the Rangers performed this novel duty, Shea watched with fascination, a sentiment shared by the VIPs themselves: "None of the men concerned had ever heard of a Guard of Honour or done any drill until last night. They were dressed in their best clothes and for the sake of uniformity wore the hoods of their parkas up. Normally, Eskimos tend to slouch, but I had told them that soldiers were important

Hon. Ralph Campney and Mr. Charles Wilson, the US secretary of defence, inspect a guard of honour at Frobisher Bay, 1956. Ranger Sergeant Sageakdok is on the left accompanying Campney. Courtesy of Canadian Rangers National Authority

people and that they should hold their heads high and not move a muscle while they were being inspected. They did this and were amazingly steady. As long as they didn't move anyone would have thought they had had months of training."[110]

Neither Sageakdok nor Simonee spoke much English and were visibly nervous, but they performed admirably. Sageakdok carried himself "with all the aplomb of a veteran NCO," Shea proudly noted, "and I was both amused and amazed to see him stop and adjust one man's arm-band as he walked behind the inspecting party, looking each man over from head to foot as though he had been doing it for years!" Shea felt surprised until he remembered the powerful observation and imitation skills of the Inuit: Sageakdok simply mimicked his own demonstration from the previous evening. Simonee, the section sergeant, proved similarly indispensable. "A young man, tall for an Eskimo, good looking, and very intelligent," Simonee worked as an interpreter, carpenter, and mechanic. Shea watched from behind a hangar door as the guard stood at attention through Howe's inspection and then through Wilson's. They did not move as "much as an eyeball" for thirty minutes. When Shea told them to stand down, he "congratulated them heartily and meant every word of it."[111] This event established the Rangers' custom of wearing their parka hoods up while on parade in the Arctic.[112]

When Chris Vokes received a photograph of the Frobisher Bay Ranger platoon from the vice chief of the general staff in May 1956, he lamented their uneven appearance. "The only thing uniform about the group, which can be recognized at a distance, is the rifle," Vokes observed. "In all other respects the group, if it were standing easy or just mooching along in the normal accustomed style of the citizenry, would look just like all the rest of the inhabitants and would not be recognized as any form of Militia or defence force." The commander thought they should have proper uniforms. The winter clothing issued for exercises and training made the Rangers look like soldiers. At the very least, he argued, they should receive black or khaki coveralls with a waist belt and cap. This would certainly not bankrupt the department. He ended with a compliment:

> I think that when we are concerned about the expense we might also remember the service which we are able to get from the Canadian Militia Rangers [sic] at practically no expense. They draw no pay ... yet in almost every case the effective strength of the Ranger companies make the effective strengths of Militia units in the more densely populated areas seem extremely poor by comparison. Furthermore you simply cannot beat the Canadian Militia Ranger units for their enthusiasm and public spiritedness, which is completely divorced from any idea of pay. I believe that if we expect these chaps to continue to get out and train on their own the least we can do is ... provide them with something to protect their own clothing from the wear and tear involved ... I am sure that administrative difficulties ... could be overcome once the principle were accepted.[113]

The Rangers' contributions notwithstanding, the army had already set policy regarding uniforms: the accounting would be too onerous and the expense unwarranted. The Rangers would not receive uniforms, even if they presented "a most untidy and polyglot appearance to their own intense dislike."[114] Their armbands, .303 rifles, and annual ammunition allotment would have to suffice. Maintaining even these paltry scales of issue proved challenging in the lean years ahead.

❋ As SOLDIERS GO, the Canadian Ranger isn't much to look at.

He may be a trapper, a prospector or an Indian cowboy.

He doesn't get paid, doesn't wear a uniform, his only issue is a .303 calibre rifle and an annual supply of 100 rounds of ammunition, and he probably needs a shave.

His territory is the backwoods country of British Columbia, the endless swamps of the north, the rugged, wind-swept coast, the forests and the mountains. His job is to report unusual movements of any kind in a wilderness large enough to hide a single enemy agent or swallow a small country.

– "Eagle-Eyed Rangers Roam Canada Wilds"[115]

The Rangers were not much to look at in the mid-1950s, but they had proven themselves as inexpensive, useful military assets. Broad and diverse, their strength as a national corps peaked in December 1956 when they comprised 2,725 active Rangers in forty-two companies.[116] Although little more than half the authorized limit, this establishment was an impressive achievement given the paltry resources dedicated to the organization. Rangers provided intelligence reports on strange ships and aircraft, participated in training exercises with the Mobile Striking Force and other army units, conducted search-and-rescue missions, and even captured bandits on the North West Highway System. Reporter Robert Taylor painted a reassuring portrait of the Rangers on their lonely polar watch in 1956. "Some of [the Rangers] can't read their own names but they are the real scholars of this country when it comes to reading signs on the trails of the north," he explained. "Eskimos, Indians, whites and all the mixtures of these races, they are united in one task: Guarding a country that doesn't even know of their existence." They were not only "the least expensive military force any nation has today" but also a useful source of reports on suspicious activities.[117]

In the next two decades, military modernization brought drastic change to the Rangers. Advances in aerial reconnaissance, communications, and electronic surveillance seemed to obviate the need for citizen-soldiers in isolated regions of the country. Ranger Alex van Bibber recalled that the

TABLE 5
Canadian Rangers, strength return, 31 December 1956

Company	Headquarters	Officers	Rangers	Total	Command
No. 1	Mayo, YT	4	62	66	Western
No. 2	Whitehorse, YT	5	246	251	Western
No. 3	Havre-Sainte-Pierre, PQ	5	132	137	Quebec
No. 4	Sept-Îles, PQ	3	56	59	Quebec
No. 5	Port Harrison, PQ	4	108	112	Quebec
No. 6	Fort Chimo, PQ	2	82	84	Quebec
No. 7	Yellowknife, NT	15	108	123	Western
No. 8	Fort Smith, NT	4	52	56	Western
No. 9	Tofino, BC	2	23	25	Western
No. 10	Alert Bay, BC	1	12	13	Western
No. 11	Bella Coola, BC	1	39	40	Western
No. 12	Ocean Falls, BC	4	70	74	Western
No. 13	Terrace, BC	4	101	105	Western
No. 14	Smithers, BC	4	57	61	Western
No. 15	Fort St. John, BC	7	180	187	Western
No. 16	Island Falls, SK	–	9	9	Prairie
No. 17	Norway House, MB	6	44	50	Prairie
No. 18	Seven Sisters Falls, MB	4	9	13	Prairie
No. 19	Kenora, ON	1	–	1	Prairie
No. 20	Aklavik, NT	4	35	39	Western
No. 21	Norman Wells, NT	3	22	25	Western
No. 22	Cartwright, Lab.	4	76	80	Eastern
No. 23	St Anthony, Nfld.	1	2	3	Eastern
No. 24	Churchill, MB	5	79	84	Prairie
No. 25	Red Lake, ON	6	76	82	Prairie
No. 26	Moose Factory, ON	5	56	61	Prairie
No. 27	Beaver Lake, SK	–	–	0	Prairie
No. 28	Frobisher Bay, Baffin Isle.	4	111	115	Eastern
No. 29	Pond Inlet, Baffin Isle.	3	85	88	Eastern
No. 30	Lewisporte, Nfld.	1	8	9	Eastern
No. 31	Bonavista, Nfld.	4	51	55	Eastern
No. 32	Heart's Content, Nfld.	2	45	47	Eastern
No. 33	Burin, Nfld.	–	–	0	Eastern
No. 34	Channel Islands, Nfld.	3	42	45	Eastern
No. 35	Port Saunders, Nfld.	1	49	50	Eastern
No. 36	Hopedale, Lab.	3	55	58	Eastern
No. 37	Dawson Creek, BC	4	110	114	Western
No. 38	Island Lake, MB	6	98	104	Prairie
No. 39	Brooks Brook, YT	2	34	36	Western
No. 40	Destruction Bay, YT	–	43	43	Western
No. 41	Fort Nelson, BC	2	116	118	Western
TOTAL		142	2,583	2,725	

Source: Library and Archives Canada, RG 24, acc. 1983-84/215, box 322, f. S-2001-1999/0, pt. 9.
The officer total includes three officers on strength but not in active localities.

DEW Line offered protection from Russia. Consequently, many Rangers felt they were no longer required and lost interest.[118] George Pearkes, a retired major-general and Victoria Cross recipient who later became minister of national defence, said to the House of Commons in 1955 that "it is fantastic to think that large armies could be landed on the Arctic shores of Canada and advanced through the barren lands of the great north."[119] Once Soviet long-range jet bombers could be refuelled in the air, the enemy had no need to secure forward bases in the North. No longer a probable invasion route or staging area, the Arctic simply offered strategic depth – a void that technology could exploit to provide advanced detection of incoming bombers in the thermonuclear age.[120] Support for the Rangers dwindled along with the threat of a ground incursion.

Radar networks and other technical marvels, predicated on deterrence and continental defence, transformed some of the remotest regions of North America. When the DEW Line system became operational in 1957, the new defenders of the continent ate steak and viewed first-run movies from the comfort of cat trains as they watched for an enemy invasion on consoles that relayed data from the giant geodesic domes that dotted the Arctic landscape. Where the Rangers fit in this new era remained unclear. One staff officer later summed up the prevailing belief that "as modern (southern) society began to roll back the frontiers, the Canadian Rangers became obsolete."[121]

6
Shadow Army,
1957-70

✣ CAPTAIN AMBROSE SHEA, the long-standing Ranger liaison officer in Eastern Command, became disillusioned with the military's disregard for the 550 Rangers in Newfoundland, Labrador, and Baffin Island. After expanding into communities throughout the northland in the 1950s, he lamented, "the Army seemed to stand aghast at its own temerity and from then on, and in an increasing degree, the attitude of Higher Command towards the Rangers can be best summed up in the words of the old ballad":

> "Mother, may I go out to swim?"
> "Yes, my darling daughter,
> Hang your clothes on a hickory limb
> But don't go near the water."

Shea had repeatedly received one simple message from Ottawa: "the Rangers may exist but under no circumstances must they do anything." This stance reflected a broader devaluation of part-time soldiering and highlighted the senior establishment's predisposition towards fully assimilated, professional forces. Army headquarters vetoed even the most minor requests. Shea found it "downright ludicrous" that officials refused lapel pins for the Rangers, which would allow them to identify one another, because they considered them an excessive public expense. The military's ignorance and neglect was obvious.[1]

Shea found the organization in his area unwieldy and ineffective. As the only liaison officer in Eastern Command, he was responsible for organizing and maintaining eleven Ranger companies scattered over 8,000 miles (13,000 kilometres) of coastline. Liaising with the Baffin Island Rangers alone consumed three months of his year, and although he enjoyed positive relationships with individual Rangers, he had limited influence. Itineraries that looked fine on paper proved impractical in the field. As matters stood, the Rangers relied on the telegraph and the postal system, and their paltry combat training and scattered presence rendered them ineffective when it came to local defence. Shea explained:

> It is doubtful if some of the Rangers really understand what the whole business is about and for various reasons it is difficult to explain it to them. The Eskimoes, in particular, have no real word for "soldier" ("Unataktik," that is, "one who fights," is as near as they get) and look upon warfare as a species of insanity peculiar to the white man. "I hear that the white men are fighting like dogs again," was one man's comment on the Suez affair. Furthermore, it is the RLOs [Ranger liaison officer's] belief that some of the Eskimoes think that he is the entire Canadian Army and that, as such, he is an eccentric but benevolent dispenser of free rifles and ammunition. The name given the RLO in certain localities, "Kokiutit angayak'ok," "Rifle Chief" or "Boss of the Rifles," is sufficient indication of this.

Bridging the cultural divide would require not only sustained contact but also greater clarification of the Rangers' role.[2]

Shea still envisaged a place for the Rangers. "The idea of arming a local population and asking them to take a hand in defending their own locality is an ancient one and eminently sensible," he argued. "It does not become out-dated, even in this atomic age." The Rangers' contributions had been modest but significant. They had amassed considerable military intelligence over the previous decade, including topographical detail, submarine and ship sightings, and reports of suspicious individuals. They had reported unexplained bomb drops on northern Baffin Island, verified their landing by collecting bits of the bombs, and provided evidence of guided missile activity. A fisherman near the Strait of Belle Isle had even picked a US Coast Guard manual for wireless communications out of the water and handed it over to a local Ranger. Intercontinental ballistic missiles had made the

An Inuk searches the sky for planes, performing the role of ground observer.
Department of National Defence, Photo PL-86656

"highly-organized and extensively staffed" Ground Observer Corps – a purely civilian group – obsolete, Shea conceded, but the Rangers would remain useful as "'friends on the ground' as long as the Canadian Army existed."[3]

Perhaps most importantly, the Rangers remained keenly interested. Although Baffin Island's Inuit Rangers had what Shea considered a distorted idea of their role, they self-identified as soldiers: "An extreme example of this occurred three years ago when a Ranger in North Baffin Island began, but fortunately did not complete, a single-handed attempt to capture the US Coast Guard Cutter 'Staten Island.' He realized that she was not a Canadian ship, jumped to the conclusion that she was a Russian, and felt that it was his duty as a soldier to take some action. This man's enthusiasm may have been misdirected but there is no doubt that he took his position as a Ranger seriously and realistically." Although isolated, Shea observed that the Rangers were "vividly aware of the Russian threat; so much so that the RLO has sometimes wondered whether they may not have had some personal contact with the Russians with which they are afraid to reveal." He found Inuit Rangers "intelligent, adaptable and intensely practical" – like the legendary Gurkhas of the British Army – and noted that they took naturally to military training given their hunting lifestyles. "If trained in arms," the officer added, they could prove "extremely effective guerrillas. It is a pity that there are not more of them." Indeed, few White men could navigate the Arctic without their assistance, making Inuit "good people to have on *our* side." With a final flourish, Shea reminded the military that this relationship needed to be respected. "A small quantity of obsolescent equipment is issued to them in the same spirit that an engagement ring is issued to a prospective bride: as a token of engagement," he noted. These "friends on the ground" married the virtues of civic engagement with voluntary military service at negligible cost to the public purse. They deserved encouragement.[4]

IN THE FALL OF 1958, THE CANADIAN government publicly revealed the strength of the "shadowy band of volunteers who patrol Canada's remotest areas on the lookout for any enemy landings." It equated the force of 2,690 men with trappers, woodsmen, prospectors, miners, and farmers quietly defending northern and isolated coastal areas. Inquiring journalists learned about the Rangers' general role, including their careful watch for enemy agents who might parachute "into remote areas to set up beacons to guide bombers or submarines." With less than forty-two dollars in issued equipment, these sturdy outdoorsmen – their identities "largely unknown" – could "operate alone for weeks at a time and can, for the most part, live off the land." On other Ranger details, the army remained "extremely close-mouthed," the *Toronto Star* noted on 10 September 1958. It did not mention them in public documents, and their activities were "known only to the commanders of their various commands."[5]

Even Worthy Worthington, renewed as the honorary colonel commandant of the Rangers in 1957, had difficulty securing access. When he asked to visit a few Ranger companies, the chief of the general staff refused on the grounds that the army did not sponsor visits by colonel commandants of militia corps to their units.[6] Undeterred, Worthington sent a letter to each Ranger company commander in August 1958:

My experience with the Pacific Coast Militia Rangers during the latter part of the Second World War convinced me of their value and that the organization should be extended across all of Canada in peace as well as war, and this has been done.

Sometimes you and your fellow Rangers must wonder just what good you are doing and why you should keep the Ranger Organization alive. My answer to this is sincere, simple and real:

First, your Company covers a hard, large and sparsely populated bit of country. In a time of emergency information will be required on any unusual happenings and about the area itself. The best information will come from men who know the country and what to look for and are able to put this together for military purposes. We know of no one better for this job than the Rangers.

The second point comes down to actual fighting – a few men who know the country and could live in it both winter and summer could do far more than large numbers of city bred soldiers with no experience in the bush. You know this fact as well as I do, and so the answer again is the Rangers.

The last point would be in a situation where soldiers must be used for operations in your territory. To get full value these soldiers must have guides and men to show them how to survive in the country. In my opinion this is a real job for the Rangers.

As I see it, the main thing is to be ready if and where an emergency comes, because afterwards it is too late.

I would like you to know that many of us on the outside appreciate the service that you are giving to Canada.

Although Worthington promised to visit a few Ranger companies "before too long,"[7] he never managed to do so.

The Rangers were fated to remain intensely localized units isolated from the rest of the military. When strategic interest in remote regions declined in the late 1950s and 1960s, the Rangers were left primarily to their own devices. In areas with strong local leadership, units flourished. Where it was weak, they deteriorated. No. 12 Company on British Columbia's isolated mid-coast, about 300 miles (480 kilometres) north of Vancouver and accessible only by sea, offers a case in point. When Lieutenant C.N.L. Westover visited the area in April 1958, he found the coast-watching units in mixed shape. The headquarters and platoon in Ocean Falls, consisting of four officers and forty-six Rangers, were in first-class condition. Determined local leadership kept the Rangers active in the pulp-mill town. "Interest is kept stimulated by a varied programme of theoretical and practical training," Westover observed. "Instruction is progressive and well conducted." The Rangers got together for weekend training, spent considerable time at the range, and held regular monthly meetings. They maintained all of the stores and equipment in good order, and local officers administered the platoon well. Rangers conducted search and rescue, assisted the RCMP, and participated in local civil activities. The platoon also financed a team to compete in the 1958 Dominion of Canada Rifle Association competition in Vancouver. Westover concluded that "through a well coordinated effort," it had "become a fine example of what can be accomplished by a Ranger unit."[8]

A less positive situation prevailed in the outlying patrols, which reflected the effects of isolation and distance on command and control. Westover could not visit the platoon at Skidegate Mission and Sandspit on the Queen Charlotte Islands (Haida Gwaii), but he learned that its nine Rangers had not undertaken any training, that it could not account for eighteen weapons, and that no one had found a replacement for the platoon commander when he left the area. Westover discovered another nine untrained Rangers at Butedale, where the platoon commander had been struck off strength "having reached the age limit." (Unlike other regions, BC Area imposed a mandatory age limit.) The officer recommended that the platoon, isolated from its parent unit and without a suitable commander, remain inactive.

At Bella Bella, which boasted one officer and ten Rangers, the situation seemed marginally better. The platoon could account for all of its equipment and stores (in good condition in a dry warehouse), but the local leadership was lacking. Lieutenant O. Bainbridge, an elderly man who had served as platoon commander since 1942, had lost interest. The population of the settlement, which revolved around a fish-packing plant, was transient apart from a few old-timers whom Lieutenant Westover considered "past being useful as Rangers." The company commander in Ocean Falls nevertheless hoped to replace Bainbridge with a younger man who could sustain the interest of a nucleus of Rangers through weekend rifle competitions and other activities.[9] Only local initiative could revitalize units in isolated communities.

In the Arctic, local leadership proved similarly essential. Coppermine (Kugluktuk) sits on the shore of the Arctic Ocean at the mouth of the Coppermine River. In 1950, this tiny "embryo of a settlement" consisted of two churches, a typical red-and-white Hudson's Bay Company (HBC) trading post, a government radio and weather station, and an RCMP detachment.[10] A Canadian Ranger platoon had been established the previous year under the command of Harold Webster, a missionary canon and "a veteran of many years experience in the Arctic, a great traveler, and a keen observer."[11] Jack Alonak, around thirty years old at the time, recalled representatives of the Canadian Army arriving with a "pile of rifles left over from the Second World War." They handed him one and told him to shoot at a couple of targets. When his aim proved to be "not too bad," they signed him on as a Ranger.[12]

When Rev. John R. (Jack) Sperry, a newly ordained Anglican missionary, disembarked from a floatplane at Coppermine in 1950, he had never heard of the Rangers. Born in Leicester, England, in 1924, Sperry volunteered for the Royal Navy in 1943 and served as an ASDIC (sonar) operator on a destroyer that plied the dangerous convoy routes of the North Sea. He ended the war on a minesweeper heading to the Pacific theatre, all of which constituted a "powerful missionary experience." Carrying his mission to the Arctic, however, seemed like entering an entirely "different world." Sperry spoke no Inuinnaqtun (the regional dialect of Inuktitut), depended completely on others for survival, and described the experience as being "like a baby" again. "You have so much more to learn than to teach" in the North, he explained. Yet Sperry immediately found himself in a leadership role. Two years later, he became the Ranger lieutenant at Coppermine, a position he held until 1969. He did not remember how he was asked to lead the Rangers, nor what steps his predecessor, Canon Webster, took regarding the force. He simply inherited command of the platoon and received his commission – a "fancy document" from the King – in the mail.[13]

As the platoon commander, Sperry was responsible for Rangers dispersed throughout the central Arctic. His administration was informal. Sperry held no meetings, provided no specific instructions or training, and received no visits from a liaison officer. No one ever asked him to report on the number of Rangers in the platoon. His regular activities as Ranger commander consisted of distributing ammunition and, less frequently, rifles. When the annual supply ship arrived at Coppermine in late July or August, it contained boxes of ammunition from Edmonton addressed simply to "the Ranger platoon." Sperry stored the boxes in his mission's warehouse and handed ammunition out to the Rangers in a casual way. Western Command Headquarters never asked for an accounting. Hunters found the Ranger-issue rifles "pretty good" at best, but they maintained them because they welcomed

Ranger Lieutenant John R. (Jack) Sperry commanded the Coppermine platoon
from 1950 to 1969. Courtesy of the Sperry family

the annual allocation of .303 ammunition for hunting caribou and seal.[14] The ammunition boxes also held two primus stoves perfectly.

Most Inuit still followed a seasonal, nomadic cycle and did not take these modest material perks lightly. John Matthiasson, an anthropologist who lived on Baffin Island in the early 1960s, observed that "land peoples" such as the 289 Tununermiut near Pond Inlet still depended on hunting for food, spoke Inuktitut almost exclusively, maintained "a fairly conventional Inuit family structure," and "respected traditional patterns of hospitality and sharing." Their psychological identity remained Inuit, even when they drove outboard motors instead of kayaks, cooked food on a primus stove rather than over an open fire, and hunted with rifles rather than harpoons. "Rifles were the most valued possession of Tununermiut men," Matthiasson observed, and all the men living at the Aullativik camp had Ranger .303s, "heavy, high-powered rifles designed to kill people," which they used "to hunt everything from ducks to polar bears." They had to buy bullets for their .22s, which could only be done after trading furs, so their free annual allotment of Ranger ammunition came in handy. "In return, they were expected to watch the Arctic skies for sightings of foreign aircraft and to report any sightings," Matthiasson wrote. "In moments of depression my spirits soared at the sight of men, faithful to their duty, watching high-flying jets streaking across the sky, then running into their houses to look up the markings in their English code books, and finally throwing up their hands and laughing. Even if they identified the markings of a low-flying aircraft, they could not afford to interrupt their hunting to take the trip to Pond Inlet to report it." Their transistor radios, after all, could not send signals.[15]

Matthiasson's observations about the absurdity of reporting from remote parts of Baffin Island do not detract from the Rangers' valuable contributions. "We just knew that if an aircraft went down we should look for it," Sperry reminisced about his responsibilities in Coppermine. If people were lost, the RCMP passed along the information, and community members went out to look for them. "All the men were going out anyway," he explained, so they did not necessarily view search and rescue as a "Ranger" activity. On one occasion, when a boat containing two Oblate priests and their Aboriginal guides went missing, Sperry and the local Ranger sergeant set out with community members (some but not all of whom were Rangers) to find them. They also took part in the search for Johnny Bourassa, a veteran wartime and postwar bush pilot who went missing after departing Coppermine. "We never dreamed of asking for recompense in the very early days," he recounted. "It was just what was done."[16]

The Rangers also provided military intelligence. Few Inuit lived permanently in settlements in the early 1950s; most congregated only after the ice formed in the winter. Indeed, *qallunaat* (White) agents in Coppermine actively encouraged them to continue their nomadic hunting and fishing patterns. As a result, their coverage extended down the coast to southern Victoria Island and inland to east of the treeline. One day, Bobby Klengenberg, a Ranger who lived with his family at Rymer Point near Reid Island, heard a strange noise as he hunted seals off the coast of Victoria Island. When he turned around, he saw a big black box emerge from the water. The box contained a man who looked at him through binoculars. "It took my mind off the seals," Klengenberg later told Sperry. The Ranger relayed the information to Billy Joss, the HBC manager at Holman who also happened to be a Ranger sergeant, and then on to Cambridge Bay, where officials confirmed that no US Navy submarines were operating in the area. Klengenberg had likely seen a Russian submarine observing one of the intermediate or auxiliary DEW Line stations on southwest Victoria Island.[17]

While on watch, a Ranger's only contact with the military came through liaison officers. They had little institutional support in the late 1950s. Captain Ambrose Shea's journal of his voyage on the 1958 Eastern Arctic Patrol, his seventh, provides an intimate perspective on the state of the Rangers and on the changes transpiring in the Arctic during the era. Shea embarked from Montreal on the *C.D. Howe* in late June, hitching a ride with administrators and medical personnel who annually braved the Arctic ice, storms, and fog to call in at isolated settlements. He approached the trip with his usual enthusiasm. He checked his Inuktitut phrases with the ship's interpreter, and was delighted to meet two Rangers on board returning from hospital stays in the south (a common occurrence given the high rate of tuberculosis in the Arctic and the large number of Inuit in southern sanatoriums).[18]

At each port, Shea met with Rangers and other members of the community. Circumstances dictated that he develop a flexible approach to doing "Ranger business." When his ship arrived at Lake Harbour (Kimmirut), he discovered the *Rupertsland*, a HBC ship, unloading. Shea therefore had trouble contacting the platoon commander, Don Baird, who was also the

HBC post manager. When Shea tracked him down, he learned that half of the men in the platoon had left or were leaving Lake Harbour for Frobisher, the new, bustling hub for Arctic weather and radar stations.[19] "The rapid growth of Frobisher is sucking the life out of the nearby posts," Shea noted, "and Baird thinks that Lake [Harbour] may cease to exist in a few years." The liaison officer off-loaded the ammunition and met some local Rangers, but he did not perform a formal inspection because they were all working. Although a chickenpox epidemic curtailed onshore excursions at Pangnirtung, he managed to meet with the local sergeants and hand over their ammunition. Along the northern Quebec coast, he met more Rangers, some of whom sported old army battledress with sundry flashes and badges. Resolute, founded in 1947 as the site of a military airfield and weather station, had been populated with Inuit relocated from Port Harrison (Inukjuak) and Pond Inlet six years later. Here, three Rangers met Shea aboard the ship. The liaison officer had few concerns about the platoon. He found that most local Inuit were prosperous and had access to adequate game and employment at the local weather station.[20]

Shea's down-to-earth demeanour allowed him to connect with Rangers. When he visited the Inuit camp near Resolute, he played "polar bears" with a young boy, all the while learning which Ranger had moved where, assessing the state of their rifles, and handing out military identification cards. He witnessed how the modern world had collided with traditional life. On 12 August, for example, he visited Ranger Sudlavinek in his tent. "To say that he is 'well-fixed' for an Eskimo would be putting it mildly," Shea wrote. Sudlavinek had an old military chesterfield (minus one cushion, which he used in his outboard canoe), an expensive radio, and a telephone to the RCMP constable.

Shea had taken photographs of Rangers the previous year and handed them out to the Rangers he encountered. Given Baffin Island's small population and the Inuit habit of visiting other camps, the men got "a big kick" out of recognizing one another. Shea also showed them pictures of Rangers in Labrador, army photographs of troops serving with the UN in the Middle East, and winter training at Churchill. "Labrador they had heard of as a legendary Eskimo country in the far South," he noted, "and Churchill they knew as 'Kokjuak' (Big River), but I don't know what they made of soldiers in an armoured car, stripped to the waist under a hot desert sun." Through this informal process, Shea connected the Rangers to other members of the force and to their military comrades around the world.[21]

Each annual trip was a voyage of intense crosscultural contact, and Shea forged strong relationships over the years. Grise Fiord on Ellesmere Island had only one Ranger, relocated from Pond Inlet, but he obviously appreciated Shea and his annual allotment of ammunition:

> When I met Const Bob Pilot, RCMP, who handles Ranger affairs, such as they are, in this lonely place, he told me that Ranger Akpaliapik had made a carving for me during the year which he proposed to give me on the grounds that I was "his boss." Later when I was issuing Akpaliapik with his ammunition he produced the carving from under his parka and with characteristic Eskimo detachment offered it to me "piumavit" – "if I wanted it?" Naturally, I did want it, gave him a clasp-knife in exchange and with the help of Alec Spalding [the interpreter], praised it and thanked him. It is a small ivory carving of a walking polar-bear, carefully carved and highly polished ... He said then that he was giving it to me because I was "always giving him things." When I pointed out that it was the Canadian Army that gave him the ammunition, not me, he said, "Well, anyway, I was easy to get along with." Although Eskimoes are intelligent they are often lacking good judgement.

Given Shea's demeanour and obvious respect for the Rangers, he directed this sarcasm more at himself than at Inuit.

The annual allotment of ammunition represented the only remuneration that the Rangers received for their service, and they welcomed it. When Shea called in at Inuit camps in the Pond Inlet area, he issued forty-eight rounds of ammunition to each Ranger he met and informed them that they could pick up the remainder from the Ranger officer in the community. When the *C.D. Howe* arrived in Eglinton Fiord, the ship's commander asked Shea if he had any .30-30 or .300 ammunition because the camp was short of it. He did not, but he explained that he could issue .303 ammunition to Rangers. Ranger Ashevak collected ninety-six rounds and explained that something had fallen off the side of his rifle but that it still worked. Functionality, not aesthetics, mattered to Shea.

Other equipment did need replacing. Shea learned, for instance, that Peeyameenee, a Ranger from Clyde River, needed a new rifle. Peeyameenee and his wife had been travelling by dog team that spring when he spotted a seal on the ice. Running ahead of the team, he asked his wife to bring his rifle. She responded immediately but dipped the muzzle in a snowdrift along

A military photographer noted that "typical of Eskimo hunters found along the DEW line, the traditional spear has been replaced by the gun, evidence of white man's influence in the region." Department of National Defence, Photo PC-1194

the way. Without taking his eyes off the seal, Peeyameenee simply aimed and fired. "How the seal fared I don't know," Shea reported, "but I should think that Peeymeenee must have got an awful jolt, and the muzzle of the rifle opened up like a piece of wet card-board." Shea exchanged the rifle for another left by a deceased member of the patrol. There were no reprimands and no hassle.

Shea's trip ended at Frobisher Bay (Iqaluit), the burgeoning administrative centre of the eastern Arctic and a hotbed of military and government activity. The community's rapid growth and the influx of Inuit (including Rangers) from the outlying posts had complicated the local situation. Frobisher originally had thirty Rangers, but officers recruited more in 1955 in anticipation that the army would assign the platoon a home defence role. Although this scheme did not materialize, local organizers had already enlisted twenty additional Rangers. The Hudson's Bay Company, which had always furnished the platoon commanders on Baffin Island, had converted their one-man trading post into a retail store with a manager and four clerks. Consequently, Captain G.M. Rennie, officer commanding No. 28 Company and the local platoon commander, found it difficult to juggle Ranger affairs and his civilian responsibilities, particularly when he knew that in addition to the fifty Rangers known to be at Frobisher, an unspecified number of others had arrived from outlying posts.[22]

Shea typically used his time in Frobisher to meet with as many Rangers as he could and to strengthen alliances for the local unit. In particular, he reconnected with Sageakdok, whom he had met during his first trip to Baffin Island. This time, Shea wrote that the five-foot-tall man looked like an "Eskimo gangster" but was demonstrably military-minded. He saluted correctly; wore a parka with a large, handsome beaded Ranger badge on the front; and startled Shea "by springing smartly to attention when I entered a room in which he was seated." His behaviour struck Shea as all the more surprising because Henry Larsen – an RCMP superintendent, venerable Arctic navigator, and Shea's "senior in rank, years, and experience" – was also in the room.

It pleased Shea that the RCMP were taking a greater interest in the Rangers. "They feel that in a place like Frobisher an organized and trained body of men, as the Rangers here might be, would be a source of moral and social strength in the Eskimo community, and would give direction to the efforts being made to turn the Eskimo into a responsible Canadian citizen." Shea had been touting this line for years. "If the Army could have the unofficial help of the RCMP with the Rangers, it would be mutually beneficial." Superintendent Larsen promised to take the matter up with the commissioner. Locally, at least, Shea had done all that he could to generate interest in the Rangers. If the military establishment failed to support the force in future, it would not be because of shortcomings at the liaison level. With his 1958 tour of duty complete, Shea boarded a US Air Force plane and flew back to Torbay airport.

A New Strategic Focus

By the late 1950s, strategists recognized that any enemy attack on North America would come from the air. The concepts of massive retaliation, deterrence, and mutually assured destruction entered the continental defence lexicon. Defence planners abandoned their early postwar interest in land and sea-based activities for high-tech solutions that conceptualized the Arctic as part of a broader continental space or grid, monitored and managed by modern technologies.[23] The Mid-Canada and DEW lines, designed to deal with the manned bomber threat, were operational by 1957. The Soviets responded by launching the *Sputnik* satellite, which demonstrated that they could hurl missiles at the North American heartland over the polar ice cap. "It did not take long for the message of this delphic communication to be interpreted," political scientist James Eayrs quipped. "Henceforth the missile was the message."[24] The United States' and Canada's existing detection and communication systems, from the technological marvel of the DEW Line to human assets such as the Rangers, could not counter this new challenge.

Ballistic missile technology meant that "the northern defence structure could not only be outflanked but could be literally hopped over," strategic analysts noted. "For all intents and purposes the Canadian north, in terms of a remote and safe battlefield, was obsolete."[25] In the second Cold War, as the period after the *Sputnik* flight became known, the global prize would go to the country with the most sophisticated weapons systems. Nuclear submarines avoided the age-old problem of trying to break through the Arctic ice by simply going under it. The ice canopy offered an added bonus of making submerged vessels difficult to detect.[26] In response, the United States developed new forms of deterrence that relegated Canada's Arctic territory (but not its waters) to the sidelines.

Because localized ground forces would not likely detect or prevent this new menace, Ottawa revisited its approach to domestic defence. One high-level proposal advocated integrating the Ground Observer Corps and the Rangers. The former organization, composed of civilians, differed from the

Nietook, an Inuit ground observer at Churchill, Manitoba, reports his observations to RCAF personnel. *Left to right:* Don J. Moyce, Nietook, and Flight Officer B.J. Hopkins.
Department of National Defence, Photo PL-86657

Rangers in that they did not have military status. If the Rangers were obsolete as an armed force, why not roll them into the Ground Observer Corps where they could fulfill their reporting functions as civilians? The navy found both organizations useful as coast watchers and saw no reason why they could not be joined together. After all, strategists argued that human detection systems would be outmoded once the Semi-Automatic Ground Environment, a computerized aircraft control and warning system, became operational, and the Royal Canadian Air Force planned to abolish the southern division of the Ground Observer Corps. Officials handed over the corps' secondary function – nuclear bomb and radiation fallout reporting – to Civil Defence, and its overall strength fell from 54,000 to 5,000 men. The RCAF retained the northern division to cover the area without radar coverage between the DEW and Mid-Canada lines. Why not simply integrate the Rangers into the northern observer corps? The civilian observers would not bear arms, but was there any rationale for retaining the Rangers as an armed force?[27]

The commands continued to hold different opinions about the future of the Rangers. Western Command, the most enthusiastic proponent of the concept in the 1940s, no longer saw any need to maintain an armed Ranger force. Quebec Command disagreed. First, as long as the Rangers had a place in the Defence of Canada Force (as the restructured and re-organized Mobile Striking Force was known after 1958), they would have a mandate to establish contact with an enemy to gather intelligence. They would not be able to do this as civilians. Second, the Rangers would continue to have a viable military role as guides for professional forces operating in northern regions. Eastern Command believed the Rangers needed weapons not only for operational tasks but also for morale. "As they are not paid," it reminded Ottawa, "their rifles and an armband constitute the only tangible mark of their connection with the armed services and if their rifles and a small allotment of ammunition were withdrawn, their interest might be considerably diminished." Above all, "the cost of retaining Canadian Rangers as a military force is negligible."[28]

Although the Joint Planning Committee told the chiefs of staff that the Rangers and Ground Observer Corps were already integrated as much as possible, George Pearkes, minister of national defence, and the service chiefs pushed to combine them. Would abolishing the Rangers cut costs? The 2,371 Rangers drew no pay, annual inspections cost only $3,000, and their ammunition – 240,000 rounds at seven cents – amounted to only $16,800 ($8.35 per Ranger) a year. By contrast, the Ground Observer Corps, 54,000 strong, cost about $1.3 million ($23.61 per observer) a year. Despite these figures, on February 1959, the director of military operations and plans recommended a gradual disbandment of the Rangers over three years and their enrolment in the civilian observer corps. Until the extent of the Ground Observer Corps reduction was clear, however, the Chiefs of Staff Committee put the integration on hold.[29] In the end, they did nothing. The Rangers' low cost led the committee to abandon the plan.

But what use were the Rangers when part-time soldiers in general seemed anachronistic in the thermonuclear age? After inspecting Ranger companies in BC in mid-1958, Major Van Straubenzee (the liaison officer in Western Command) observed that the dismal state of most companies and platoons reflected a "LACK OF LEADERSHIP ... caused by LACK OF INCEN-TIVE due to the lack of THREAT OF AN ENEMY LODGEMENT." Without a clear purpose, local commanders had lost interest and were "becoming more involved in local civilian affairs which prejudice Ranger training and activity."[30] The Rangers needed a cause, and the threat of an enemy air attack or "random bomb incidents" seemed a more logical pretext than the lodgement scenarios that had once framed Ranger training. Army officials suggested revising the Rangers' tasks to include civil defence – having Rangers "report on and trace nuclear incidents and fall-out patterns in remote areas." This role, they argued, could provide local leaders with the raison d'être they needed to rejuvenate their units.[31]

That this did not come to pass reflected the failure of civil defence efforts across the country.[32] In 1957, officials tasked the militia with assisting the Civil Defence Organization to deal with a nuclear attack and withdrew the reserves from the active defence of Canada.[33] As went the army, so too went the Rangers. "You are probably aware that the Army is now responsible for passing warning of air attack, nuclear fallout, etc, to the public," Major A. Osland, Van Straubenzee's replacement as liaison officer in Western Command, reported to the Yellowknife company in September 1959. "This has kept us hopping in order to get the system into effect."[34] Osland visited the Ranger units in Northwest Territories the following year to brief them on national survival. Rangers learned about locating and reporting nuclear explosions, as well as the effects of fallout, in anticipation that they would form part of the Civil Defence Organization in larger communities.[35] The liaison officers provided some Ranger officers with radiac meters (to detect radiation) and protective clothing. The Rangers, however, received little training on how to use either.[36]

Despite the new civil defence focus, Rangers quietly continued to be the military's eyes and ears in isolated areas. Along the Atlantic coast, they watched for submarine and trawler activities, passed along transcripts of bizarre communications from foreign fishing boats that interfered with weather forecasts off the Labrador coast, and reported the discovery of a strange, conical object found on a beach in Cape Ray that turned out to be a US Air Force target practice projectile.[37] Eight Aboriginal men in Sugluk (Salluit), Quebec, likewise spotted a large glowing object "shaped like a long bullet" in the sky south of their community in early October 1959. After ten minutes, it "exploded and made hea[v]y rumbling noise like thunder which shook ground at post." Quebec Command sent its Ranger liaison officer, Major Guy d'Artois, to investigate the remains – probably a radio device. "There is a dog team available for hire (part of the Hertz service)," the command intelligence officer teased him. "If you do not return by 1 Apr 60 rest assured we will take steps to find out what has happened."[38] Following up on Ranger leads had become a joke.

Northern Canada was changing, and federal initiatives promised to end the isolation that made it so distinct. Prime Minister John Diefenbaker's Northern Vision of 1958 proclaimed a new national policy, one that emphasized improved transportation and communication facilities to open up the North for development. There was no place for the Canadian Armed Forces as either defenders of the North or nation builders. Instead, the three *N*s – NATO, NORAD, and nuclear weapons – dominated defence.[39] When critics harped on about Canada's loss of sovereignty vis-à-vis the DEW Line, Canada took over operational control of the system's Canadian sections in 1959. As Americans lost interest, so too did Canadian officials. "The Rangers were not disbanded," historian Kenneth Eyre explains, "but they were left to wither on the vine." When Rangers left the North or passed away, the army did not recruit replacements. Nor did it replace lost or damaged rifles, and the annual resupply of ammunition "became sketchy" as liaison officers made fewer northern visits.[40]

The Rangers garnered little attention and paltry financial or political support during the late 1950s and early 1960s. They continued to perform their duties but existed in the shadows rather than in the public eye. From time to time, a journalist would pen an article noting their existence. In 1959, Larry Dignum wrote in *The Beaver:* "What are the chances of an enemy agent or a fugitive from justice hiding out in Canada's North? Pretty slim, for actually it's easier to hide in a crowd than in these great vacant spaces. Here the stranger may meet only prospectors, miners, or trappers, who may be Indian, Eskimo or white, but sooner or later word of his presence will reach the authorities through the Canadian Rangers, and his progress may be unaccountably delayed till he's been investigated." The article, titled "Shadow Army of the North," finished with a romantic tribute: "When on duty they wear a scarlet armband with the three maple leaves of the Canadian Army superimposed on a crossed rifle and axe. They have no uniforms, receive no pay, seek no glory, but these men of known loyalty, Indian, Eskimo and white, take pride in standing on guard in the empty and remote parts of Canada with vigilance and integrity, and in silence."[41]

The Rangers in Decline

The Rangers became more silent in the years ahead. The decline of army activity in the North in the late 1950s directly affected them. The lack of interest hurt morale, and the abolishment of other military units had spillover effects. For example, when the 24th Field Regiment in Yellowknife disbanded in 1958, the local Rangers had no place to meet as a group and no place to store their equipment, weapons, and ammunition. All of the military gear that they had drawn on for winter exercises was shipped out. Captain John Anderson-Thomson, the local Ranger commander, pleaded for rations, tents, and clothing to remain available in case of emergency. "I could not field more than six men who could go in the bush in the winter," he explained. Most Rangers in his unit were miners, not trappers or woodsmen. He lobbied to secure the old army officers and sergeants' mess in the hope that he could draw in "some excellent men" from the disbanded 24th.[42] The local commander's priorities did not align with those of the army.

The few military officials who remained committed to the Rangers tried to improve their efficiency through reorganization. Units in Prairie Command were the first casualties. In 1957 and early 1958, the army reassigned half of the platoons from No. 26 Company in northern Ontario to Quebec Command and the remainder to No. 24 Company under the command of the commandant, Fort Churchill. Only the Churchill platoon remained active, and staff officers were told not to form any additional subunits.[43] The remaining company and platoon locations in the command, considered too remote to control or train, were reduced to nil strength.[44]

Limited resources rendered proper liaison and support unrealistic. The regions had to fund Ranger activities out of the thin budgets committed to Regular and Reserve Force training. Captain Ambrose Shea recommended reducing the Ranger organization to a more workable size because, if the number of companies were reduced, a liaison officer could actually visit each one annually. He also felt that the military had, from the beginning, expected too much of the Rangers. Their organization into companies and platoons had led to distorted notions that the Rangers could function in a conventional manner. "Nothing could be further from the truth," Shea explained. "A 'Company' of Rangers is a collection of rugged individualists who may be scattered over a hundred miles of coastline and in twenty different settlements." The Rangers constituted "units" only on paper.[45]

Ranger Pierre Tootoo of Churchill receives a medal from Captain H.C. Miller while RCMP Staff Sergeant Smythe looks on. Diocese of Churchill Hudson Bay

The Newfoundland area commander agreed that a new structure, rooted in localized patrols and organized into geographical districts, would better reflect the Rangers' unique nature. If patrols could be organized in the areas of greatest operational need, and their structure left "extremely flexible so that a patrol can consist of two Rangers (as some platoons do now) or up to 30 or 40," then the units would be more sustainable. The army could simplify and improve the existing liaison system if the Ranger liaison officer did not try to visit everywhere but instead focused on district headquarters and the most accessible patrols.[46]

The military would implement this patrol model decades later, but Major Ed Carron, who took over as Eastern Command's liaison officer in 1961, decided to retain the existing company-platoon organization. Nevertheless, the regional commander transferred responsibility for the Baffin Island patrols to Quebec Command that year based on Shea's assessment that communication with those units had proven impossible. Thanks to this change, Carron devoted his considerable energies to Newfoundland and Labrador.[47] He travelled more than 3,000 miles (around 5,000 kilometres) a year by road in Newfoundland. "Anyone who has had any experience of the local road network, and particularly in the more remote areas, will know that the standard staff car or station wagon cannot cope," he explained before requesting a jeep or Land Rover like those used by officials with the RCMP or the Department of Fisheries. There would, however, be no liaison vehicle or radio sets for Rangers who lived in the outports.[48] Carron, like his predecessors, learned that the army would only support proposals that did not entail additional public expense.

After taking stock of the situation, Carron pointed out the limitations of Shea's approach. First, he believed that his predecessor had been overly ambitious in locating units in communities without reliable communications. Because liaison officers had a hard time contacting company and platoon commanders, they had little control or influence. Second, Shea had selected officers because of their local standing, with merchants the purported ideal. Some of these commanders proved "too old and tied up with personal affairs to be productive," so Carron tried to "ginger up" the Rangers by replacing a few of the old gentlemen with "younger, more able personnel." The St. Anthony platoon, for example, quickly filled to strength after Lieutenant Wesley Biles became platoon commander. In 1964, Carron appraised it as one of the best platoons in Eastern Command. Other leaders – such as Lieutenant F.M. Cox, who had kept his platoon alert with letters and periodic visits on weekends and holidays, alongside his work as town manager of Channel-Port aux Basques – received promotions (in Cox's case, to captain, in 1962). "In some cases the Rangers are difficult to stir up, at least you certainly can't hurry them," Carron noted, "but they *are* improving."[49]

Braving rough seas and frigid temperatures, the liaison officer worked diligently and creatively to sustain relationships with platoon commanders and individual Rangers, deliver rifles and ammunition, recruit new personnel, activate new platoons, and close moribund units. To visit the platoons each year, he hitched rides by boat, plane, and dog team with the RCMP, the US Air Force, the Royal Canadian Navy, other government departments, and commercial parties.[50] Carron (like Shea) knew that, at its core, command and control was about human relationships. Eastern Command still reimbursed Ranger platoon commanders for modest travel expenses when they met with Rangers and distributed ammunition.[51] The liaison officer also arranged for company and platoon commanders to receive copies of the *Canadian Army Journal* to help them "think in terms of service." Even if many Rangers were illiterate, they were far from ignorant, Carron learned. "Personnel in isolated areas normally follow geopolitical news to a greater extent and in more detail (from every source) than do we in the 'asphalt jungle' of our more settled areas."[52]

The situation in No. 33 Company, which was largely inactive along the isolated southwest corner of Newfoundland, is illustrative. By 1961, the company had not received a visit from a liaison officer for a decade. In February, Carron hitched an airplane ride with a fisheries inspector to Burgeo, a fishing and fish-processing town of about fifteen hundred people. He met with Sergeant Philip Matthews and other members of the platoon for a meal. Carron got "the impression that the Rangers in many cases are 'hungry' for a little recognition; they feel that they are the forgotten one; my immediate intention is to dispell [sic] this thinking and arouse enthusiasm by more frequent visits, and by newsletters which will serve to keep them abreast of current Ranger activities."[53] When he returned in June, hitching a ride on a yacht chartered by the Department of Veterans Affairs, he recruited new Rangers along the south coast and moved dormant platoons to Ramea and Gaultois, where Hector Reid and Cyril Jack Windsor, fishery plant managers, brought them up to excellent condition. The units benefitted from the changes, and Carron noted that he wanted to see all the Rangers in Newfoundland up to their level.[54]

Owing largely to Carron's efforts to reinvigorate inactive units, the Rangers in Eastern Command expanded modestly in the early 1960s. In 1958, Newfoundland and Labrador had 17 officers and 330 Rangers. In 1965, the province had 29 officers and 472 Rangers in platoons varying in size from thirty men at Clarenville to nine men in both Gambo and Fortune.[55] Modest growth continued in new areas such as the east side of the Burin Peninsula, and Carron anticipated the establishment of companies in

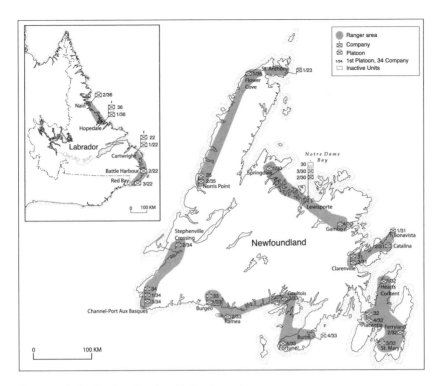

Ranger units in Newfoundland and Labrador, 1964

emerging communities such as Labrador City, where workers were taking up jobs in the Iron Ore Canada mine, which had opened in 1962. Although numbers in the province remained well below the authorized establishment of 850, when Carron was posted out in 1964 he took solace in having made progress. His colleagues in other commands had fewer grounds for optimism.[56]

The Rangers in Western Command were in sharp decline. Major Van Straubenzee noted in early 1958 that "[t]he current economy drive has curtailed my swans, therefore I have been delegated to various other projects which will keep me employed until April."[57] He did not plan a liaison trip north in 1959 or for "the foreseeable future." Western Command also tightened its grip on reimbursements for those few company commanders who bothered to visit outlying Ranger platoons.[58] Captain Chapman, the first Ranger officer appointed in 1947, recalled having no money for stationary or postage, never mind transportation or rent for a meeting hall, in the years before the Dawson company disbanded and he took his release in 1958.[59]

In the years that followed, most units failed to provide annual status reports or updated nominal rolls, and administration and accounting fell into disarray.[60] When local commanders resigned, the liaison officer struggled to find replacements. By June 1964, only 140 Rangers remained on the rolls in BC Area, and they were concentrated in platoons in Ocean Falls, Vanderhoof, Smithers, and Alexis Creek–Tatlyoko Lake. A board of officers, convened to look into the Rangers' future earlier that year, noted: "most of the units complained that they had not been in contact with a Regular Army Representative for some years." Western Command transferred control of its units to the provincial areas; however, without resources or a liaison officer to maintain contact with company commanders, the Rangers languished after 1965.[61]

A few stalwart company and section commanders did remain committed in the face of Ottawa's indifference. In Ocean Falls, Captain Richard John Frazer, a thirty-six-year-old millwright, kept his platoon active with weekly parades and search-and-rescue operations with the RCMP. The unit also enjoyed free accommodations from Crown Zellerbach, which employed local Rangers.[62] The Rangers at Alexis Creek had not fared as well. In the late 1950s, the platoon held quarterly meetings and conducted rifle competitions on the weekends. Van Straubenzee had noted in 1958 that "[t]his is a good platoon which includes some excellent Rangers in the persons of Ranchers, Big Game Guides and outdoor men." By 1964, however, Lieutenant P.J. Yells had resigned as platoon commander. He left the stores and records with the Highway Department. When a board of officers from Vancouver met with Ranger W.A.G. Telford, a highway foreman, he still had the stores in his office but no information on what had been issued to individuals. No one had resupplied the unit in years, and the board learned that the platoon had split in two. The investigators travelled sixty miles by dirt logging road to Tatlayoko Lake, where they interviewed Sergeant K.W. Haynes, a forty-one-year-old rancher and postmaster who oversaw a subunit of eighteen Rangers. His group, remarkably well maintained and active, had equipment in good repair and the best accounting anywhere. Thirty-nine Rangers remained on the nominal rolls, and the board appointed Telford and Haynes lieutenants.[63] In an era of apathy and disinterest, they faced an uphill battle to rebuild the platoons and sustain interest.

Dramatic changes along the North West Highway System, coupled with neglect and waning command and control, took their toll. Bereft of support, individuals such as Bill Emery, the commander at Whitehorse, lost interest in the Rangers, failed to return nominal rolls, and spent little time maintaining control of stores and equipment. No one inspected rifles in outlying detachments after Rangers received them, and through poor maintenance and carelessness many were lost or beyond repair.[64] In 1963, H.V. George reported No. 39 Company at Brooks Brook, Yukon (Mile 830), at nil strength. "All camp personnel now have own rifles and do not appear interested in being recruited for the Rangers," he explained. Apart from the annual North West Highway System rifle shoot, the Rangers had not held any activities for five years.[65]

The North West Highway System had also declined in strategic importance. The United States could reinforce Alaska by air, historian Steven Harris explains, and "the shock value and threat of either a Russian lodgement or of a Soviet march down the Northwest Highway System had dwindled to almost nothing in comparison with an all-out nuclear attack." As civilian traffic increased and as campgrounds, service stations, and rustic hotels popped up along the route, complaints about the condition of the highway escalated. National Defence, anxious to rid itself of an unwanted burden on its resources, arranged to transfer control of the Alaska Highway to the Department of Public Works in 1964.[66] The North West Highway System staff had administered the Ranger companies along the route, so Western Command proposed taking them over. Army headquarters denied its request.[67] The Rangers would have to fend for themselves, and in most cases units along the highway simply disbanded.[68]

A Quiet Vigil in a Changing Country

Military support for the Rangers had clearly dissipated by the mid-1960s, but at least one reporter held out hope for the force. In March 1964, readers of *Canada Month* magazine learned that the Rangers remained "ready for almost *any* emergency." Jack Worsell's description was colourful: "In the North, down the bleak coast of British Columbia, and scattered in scores of out-of-the-way spots from one end of Canada to the other are little groups of civilians who, by natural bent or by particular experience, are a little better prepared to deal with emergencies than their fellows. They are the unsung men of the Canadian Rangers. If the country goes to war, they will report to local military commanders as scouts. If Canada is ever invaded without warning, they are ready to take to the hills as guerrillas." This story perpetuated the Ranger mystique and focused on units in Yukon. Kit

Ranger Squirechuk at the ready.

Ranger Captain Kit Squirechuck, Whitehouse company, "at the ready."
Canada Monthly, March 1964

Squirechuck, the ranking officer at Whitehorse, worked as a civilian armourer in the army's local ordinance shops and was a crack shot. "In an emergency," Worsell continued, "Squirechuck, could summon 35 men – civil servants from Whitehorse offices, truck drivers from the Alaska Highway, construction workers, Indian trappers (a third of Squirechuck's group are Indians)." Many were veterans, and the rest led lives that equipped them for unconventional fighting. Don Shailer, who worked at the Department of Transport's office in Dawson City, led the fourteen Rangers in his community. He expected the military to call on his group for scouting and for advice on living and travelling in the area.[69]

The army, however, seemed at a loss to clarify the Rangers' role. National Defence Headquarters admitted that the units were "fairly autonomous, put up their own commanders, and simply asked for approval." They had been created when the threat of invasion did not seem far-fetched, "and no one has seen any reason to stand them down." The Rangers cost little while offering a military presence in convenient locations. A defence spokesman intimated that they remained "just as much a requirement today as they ever were." The army did not explain the military nature of this requirement, but it did point out that the Rangers helped the police in emergencies. In any case, Worsell found "good reason to encourage the Rangers" at a time when the military was withdrawing from the Arctic and Subarctic for economic reasons.[70]

Garrison towns such as Whitehorse and Churchill recoiled from particularly hard hits. In Whitehorse, for example, the transfer of the North West Highway System to civilian control, coupled with the closure of RCAF and radio stations, had a multiplier effect that reduced the size of the population, hurt the economy, and weakened cultural, social, and recreational organizations. The defence department's pre-eminent strategist, R.J. Sutherland, stressed that a military presence would be the key to confirming Canada's questionable legal claims to the Far North. "That is something the Rangers can do," Worsell concluded perceptively. In the vacuum left by the army, some Rangers still held out hope for funding and training.[71] The military withdrawal occurred, but support for the Rangers did not.

Two years later, Sutherland explained how technology had altered the Arctic's strategic significance. "Coincident with the arrival of the ICBM era there has been a general withdrawal by the Department of National Defence from several northern activities and programmes," he reported. This withdrawal left a gap that other departments and civilian agencies would have to fill.[72] The federal government focused elsewhere. After all, the 1964 white paper on defence did not make a single reference to the North. "It is, for the foreseeable future, impossible to conceive of any significant external threat to Canada which is not also a threat to North America as a whole," the policy statement asserted. Although the military would be responsible for surveying Canada's territory, waters, and airspace and countering any "military incidents" on its soil, the latter possibility seemed remote.[73] By the mid-1960s, there was "no military incentive to urge the Canadian Forces to be active in the North," strategist Colin Gray noted. "Reference to 'foreign incursions,' let alone 'lodgements,' should be treated with the contempt they deserve."[74]

Politicians and senior defence officials fixated on debates about Canada's stance on nuclear weapons and Minister Paul Hellyer's efforts to unify the Canadian Forces. The Canadian Forces Reorganization Act combined the Royal Canadian Navy, the Royal Canadian Army, and the Royal Canadian

Air Force under a single chief of the defence staff in 1968. In this new structure, responsibility for the Rangers fell to the land reserves section at Canadian Forces Headquarters. The staff officer responsible for force requirements could find little information on the Rangers and asked Force Mobile Command – the integrated headquarters now responsible for land and tactical air forces – to decide whether the Rangers were still needed and, if so, how they could be altered in light of the "changing times." Initial reports suggested that the organization needed overhauling and more liaison officers and noncommissioned officers (with at least an annual visit to each unit). With the Canadian Forces in a state of perpetual reorganization and with few conventional military threats to remote regions, however, the Rangers got lost in the shuffle.[75]

Some dedicated Rangers continued to serve despite the military's indifference and neglect. Their northern and coastal communities were also in a state of flux in the 1960s, reshaped by relocation and resettlement as Canadians congregated in fewer communities. Although the federal government did not encourage Inuit to adopt a sedentary lifestyle (it clung instead to a policy of dispersal, which it hoped would encourage self-sufficiency), the last camp groups had migrated into settlements by the decade's end, attracted by housing, health facilities, schooling, and the welfare state more generally.[76] In Newfoundland and Labrador, the province's centralization programs led to the abandonment of 110 communities between 1954 and 1965 and the establishment of the joint federal-provincial Fisheries Household Resettlement Programme. Relocating people from small, isolated sites to larger centres would, in theory, facilitate access to amenities and government services, help to modernize the fishery, and attract new industries.[77] Population growth along the Lower North Shore of Quebec also slowed during the 1960s, and winter settlements throughout the region decreased in number as residents congregated in larger villages.[78]

Oral histories from Labrador reveal that although life still focused on the fishery, the human geography changed. The decentralized settler lifestyle – in which families moved seasonally from summer fishing stations to smaller, dispersed family-based winter homesteads – gave way to year-round settlement in centres such as Cartwright with more promising economic prospects. Between 1967 and 1970, when the government resettled one quarter of the population of southeastern Labrador, traditional harvesting areas decreased, the rate of state dependence increased, and society became more divided.[79] The Rangers persisted along the Labrador coast, but their dispersion reflected demographic centralization and the military's lack of interest in their fate. When Captain W.S. Moores of Cartwright retired, Lieutenant Billy Walsh, a fisherman who ran the local cinema, took over as platoon commander. Hayward Holwell brought in the bullets by boat, and although Sam Morris's uncle shot at icebergs to keep up his marksmanship, no one discussed the Rangers publicly. The units held no meetings and no field training exercises. "They were almost invisible in the community," Lieutenant Oswald Dyson reminisced years later. The Rangers were simply individuals expected to keep watch for anything unusual during their everyday life.[80]

The army had abandoned any formal recruitment process. When a Ranger retired, he either simply handed his rifle to someone else (often a relative) or his position remained vacant. Gordon Foreman of Harrington Harbour joined in 1967 because he "just sort of liked the idea." The military offered few opportunities for involvement after the war, particularly in remote communities, and he saw the Rangers as a way to serve his country.[81] Others had less idealistic reasons. Ron Knight, a resident of Smith's Harbour in central Newfoundland, joined the Rangers in 1965 and served with the Springdale section for thirty-five years. He was out on a boat with his cousin Cyril Pelley who "was talking about the Rangers one day and told me I should join," Knight reminisced. "He said they would give me a rifle and all the ammunition I wanted to fire. This is what made me think of joining." Only in time would Knight come to think of his service as more than "extended use of a .303 rifle."[82]

The Rangers at Harrington Harbour continued to serve quietly along the coastline. Snowmobiles replaced dog teams, and government employment and assistance programs changed local economies. The introduction of medical and education services and modernized fishing methods to fewer winter settlements reshaped life on the Lower North Shore.[83] Gordon Jones knew all the Rangers in the region – "old men" such as Wilfred Kippen, his uncle Frank, and Great War veteran Gilbert Jones. Jones always kept his Ranger rifle in the bottom of his boat when he was out on the water in his civilian job as game warden or with the auxiliary coast guard. Although wardens were prohibited from carrying other firearms, he had special permission to carry his .303 during daily activities. Still, no one conducted training, and the platoon never met. For Jones, like others, the "perk" of being a Ranger was putting food on the table. He always used up his annual allotment of hard-point ammunition, which the company commander replaced whenever he visited communities along the coast.[84] David Reginald Anderson – a carpenter, mechanic, and jack of all trades – received no military instruction whatsoever, but "living off the land" was a way of life for him and his friends.[85] Hunting seals not only allowed Rangers to "feed their families," Gordon Foreman explained, it also helped many became "very good shots." This was "*real* practice," he insisted, not like going to a range and shooting at stationary targets.[86]

The Rangers in a few communities rejuvenated themselves even as other military operations shut down. Abraham Metatawabin, a Mushkegowuk (Cree) born into a trapping family in 1921, joined the Rangers when the Fort Albany platoon re-formed in the early 1960s. Although Canada had built and manned a Mid-Canada Line radar station in the community, the military decided to close it in 1965. Metatawabin, with his son serving as translator, recounted that the military "still needed some kind of security, and they formed the Rangers." The local chief, who enjoyed positive relations with the base personnel and knew every community member, verbally invited certain people to join. No one refused, Metatawabin explained, because Mushkegowuk had been aware of security concerns in the area since the days of pre-contact tribal warfare and French-English battles. "So they were used to looking out after themselves, looking out after the community, and when the Rangers were instituted, they saw it as a continuation of a pattern that they were used to and the stories that they heard from their grandfathers." Metatawabin's father had served in the trenches during the First World War and taught his son "to value, as a weapon, a rifle, and to keep it in good shape, to clean it, and to take care of it as if it was a very important piece of your life ... Your life depends on your rifle, and you never know when you're going to need it." Metatawabin took this wisdom to heart and saw the Rangers as "a continuation of what his father did."[87]

Each of Fort Albany's initial seven recruits received a new rifle and a promise that he would receive an annual supply of ammunition. Metatawabin stored his in his shack. The Rangers were encouraged to use their guns for hunting so that they could practise and become "skilful in handling these rifles as soon as possible." They received basic instruction in weapons handling and maintenance, as well as map reading, from the base personnel, who assured them that their role was strictly defensive. They provided simple instructions: "keep your eyes open," report any encroachments, and protect your area. Metatawabin recalled:

Ranger Abraham Metatawabin receives his Special Service Medal (Ranger Bar) in 2000. Courtesy of Canadian Rangers National Authority

We were not given any telephone number or addresses or names or anything like that, to call anybody, if there was something major that happened in the area. It was for us to monitor, to listen and be aware of events that happened in our own territory. We maintained our equipment, the rifle, the ammunition, always to be ready for use. We checked it, we took them out when we went out for ... hunting purposes which we had to do anyway. We used those [army] rifles, their weight, their behaviour, the mechanism, very different ... from the rifles we used to go hunting here ... so ... we practiced with them, and we made sure that we were ready to use them at any time ... No money [was] paid to us, nobody ever received any ... remuneration, or any kind of reward, for doing this, and we just did this.

Rangers were expected "to figure it out" and "use their own initiative." Metatawabin applied his father's advice from the war, his own experiences, and "word from his elders" to guide his work. As he boiled it down – "it was 'do it yourself,' and good luck."[88]

Situating the Rangers in Defence Policy

By the late 1960s, the Rangers were left to their own devices. "The DND has, primarily for financial reasons, withdrawn from most of its activities in the Canadian Arctic during the past 10 years," a November 1968 policy paper noted. Nevertheless, a massive hydrocarbon discovery on the Alaska North Slope and the prospect of similar resource development in northern Canada renewed interest. National defence policies had to be synchronized with broader national policy and objectives. These policies also had to fit within the military's basic priorities, namely, maintaining sovereignty and territorial integrity through surveillance and "active defence capability to prohibit free access into the North by land, sea or air."[89] The DEW Line provided air surveillance capabilities, but no naval ships operated in Arctic waters, only a few maritime patrol aircraft carried out routine patrols, and the army no longer conducted major land operations in the North.[90] Could the Rangers help the military resuscitate its northern capabilities?

"One of the unfortunate aspects of the Rangers, in our experience, is the lack of understanding of the limited capabilities of this force," Colonel Roland A. Reid, the commander of Quebec region, noted in early 1968. Proposals to train the Rangers to a high degree of military effectiveness to defend industrial installations misrepresented and were based on a misunderstanding of the Rangers' unique traits and limitations. The Rangers were deliberately chosen from among people who would not be mobilized for active service. They brought a modest suite of attributes to the defence of Canada: they were permanent residents of their locality and district who lived and worked on the land and who could thus survive on it without a

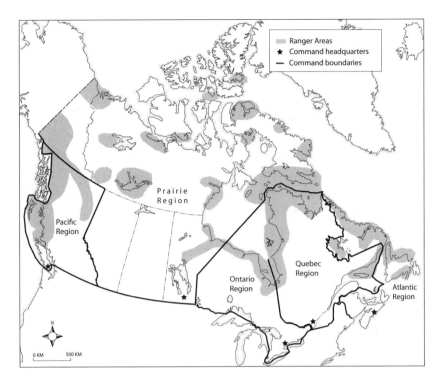

Legend:
- Ranger Areas
- ★ Command headquarters
- — Command boundaries

Pacific Region

Prairie Region

Ontario Region

Quebec Region

Atlantic Region

N

0 KM   500 KM

Ranger boundaries, July 1968

fixed base. As "experienced all-weather travellers on land and water, ice and snow," Rangers offered continuous surveillance while hunting or "making excursions." Reid emphasized that, despite their minimal training, the Rangers offered a cheap form of insurance against nuisance raids. Echoing earlier commentators, and equally important in Reid's mind, the Rangers helped to indoctrinate residents of remote regions "against docile or even helpful action to a potential enemy."[91]

So began nearly a decade of continuous discussion about the Rangers' future and their role. Under the auspices of a new Steering Committee on the Canadian North, the director general of operations formed an inter-departmental study group with representatives from Indian Affairs, the Department of Justice, the Department of Transport, Mobile Command, and other military headquarters. With one exception, the participants concluded that the Rangers should continue to exist. (Representatives from Pacific Region suggested that the RCMP and provincial employees should take over the Rangers' tasks.) Although active Rangers fulfilled a useful military function, the study group suggested that the force had to be re-vitalized if the Rangers were to play a meaningful defensive role. Even then, they could not meet the nation's need for an effective military presence in the North. The group envisaged a new military command structure, one that extended the militia to Arctic communities and effectively controlled the Rangers. Anticipating broader social benefits, the group proclaimed that "military assistance to our native Indians and Eskimos would enhance the position of individuals and groups, develop an awareness of citizenship and be of value to other government and commercial agencies."[92]

The army's director of operational readiness and sovereignty planning agreed with the study group's assessment. Population growth and the rapid concentration of people into permanent settlements meant northern communities could potentially sustain primary reserve units. Lieutenant-Colonel W.B.S. Sutherland, turning to history to support this view, argued that the militia had flourished for a time in Whitehorse, Yellowknife, Flin Flon, and Noranda but that economic factors had brought about their downfall. "Most of the official interest and support of the Rangers died with the dissolution of the former Canadian Army Command Structure," he explained. Ranger units only remained "viable and effective" in areas where "support and interest were continued as a matter of policy." Although this quirky, "para military, widely dispersed" force did not itself constitute an effective military presence, the Rangers remained the only organization capable of filling the gaps between northern settlements. In short, Sutherland concluded that the North needed both militia and Ranger units – a consensus that he claimed was shared by local authorities, representatives of the territorial governments, and "many citizens of the North."[93]

Despite the lack of a clear military role in Diefenbaker's "Northern Vision," the former prime minister, now sitting in the Opposition benches, criticized Canada's paltry Arctic presence. He demanded that the government clarify its position on sovereignty, alleging that the United States had maps disputing Canada's ownership of the Arctic Islands (a spurious assertion given that no US administration had questioned Canada's sovereignty).[94] Diefenbaker asserted that Canada had only four hundred military personnel in a territory the size of Europe and only two Arctic military bases, at Inuvik and Alert. He proposed a new northern armed force to safeguard national interests. In a speech in Whitehorse, he proclaimed that Canada should establish an Arctic unit composed initially of five hundred Inuit. This force, divided into platoons of twenty to thirty men, "would emphasize Canada's physical presence on a permanent basis" in what he described as Canada's least secure areas: "Mackenzie Bay, Cape Bathurst, Amundsen Gulf, Banks, Borden, Meighen and Mackenzie King Islands." It would achieve four objectives:

1 Preserve for Canada the greatest undeveloped frontier.
2 It would expand and emphasize the Canadian presence and show that Canadians are determined to keep what we have.
3 It would provide new vistas of opportunity for the Eskimo.
4 It would provide for youth a new challenge to a worthwhile life.

"Personally, if I were younger I would be in on this Crusade for National greatness," Diefenbaker told the audience. "When I was a boy the call was 'go West, young man.' That will be changed to 'go North, young man,' and be a builder in the greatest adventure ever. The day of the Pioneer is not over."[95]

Diefenbaker's proposal bore a striking resemblance to the Canadian Ranger organization.[96] Journalist Scott Young reminded Canadians that the military had had "a force precisely of this nature for nearly 22 years." When Young visited defence headquarters in Ottawa to gather information about the Rangers, officials had little to share. "One thing you have to give [the military] credit for is stealth," he reported. "Not many people know about them. Even Mr. Diefenbaker, one of the most North-conscious of all prime ministers, either wasn't aware of them" or was confused.[97] It is unlikely that defence officials wilfully withheld information; they too were merely ignorant of the Rangers at this point. One colonel, admitting the limitations of his knowledge, explained: "They don't get any training – but then they're born with most of the training they need. I think we give them a few rounds of ammunition, but that is about all I know about them." On a more optimistic note, Young learned that some "recommendations have been made to the Cabinet that more work, training, pay and attention be given to the Canadian Rangers." He speculated that Pierre Trudeau's revisions to defence policy may include a "tiny item" announcing "expansion of this almost-unknown force."[98]

A few Ranger companies remained active, particularly along the East Coast. The Atlantic region commander, Colonel M. Turner, praised the Rangers after they completed Exercise Northern Ranger on the Burin Peninsula in Newfoundland in July 1969. "During the course of the exercise they gave invaluable assistance to Mobile Command and Maritime Command forces in providing enemy intelligence, and information about local waters, weather and terrain," Turner lauded. Their time, energy, and re-sourcefulness had made the exercise a success and brought compliments from both the army and the navy. Given their broader functions in remote coastal areas, Turner used this occasion to recommend additional equipment and support. He believed the Rangers should be given binoculars, for ex-ample. "Fishermen Rangers" in Labrador had noted but could not confirm sightings of foreign ships because the ships moved off before they could get close enough to identify their place of origin. Turner also suggested forming a Ranger auxiliary composed of the women who ran the Bell radio telephone network in Newfoundland and Labrador.[99] Senior officials ignored his sug-gestions and instead commissioned more studies.

Lieutenant-Colonel William B.S. Sutherland, the director of operational readiness land and director of sovereignty planning, visited Frobisher Bay in September 1969. The local platoon commander, Lieutenant J.A.C. Nuyens, wrote afterwards about how reassured he was "that someone in the Can-adian Armed Forces was sincerely interested in the efforts being made by local people ... to further the continuity of The Canadian Rangers in the Canadian Arctic." Nuyens had found it frustrating trying to communicate with headquarters and offered various suggestions to make the Rangers "a closer knit and viable force." First and foremost, Rangers needed basic rifle-cleaning kits and replacement weapons. "Two thirds of the rifles currently on issue are unsafe; obsolete and dangerous to use as the moving parts are worn and corroded beyond repair." He urged officials to translate a basic policy statement into Inuit syllabics and to issue platoon commanders teaching aids and silhouette cards so they could instruct Rangers on their duties. In addition, his platoon had never been contacted when military units carried out exercises in the area. He felt the military should use the Rangers "in any capacity" to show his platoon members that the military considered them "a vital part of the Canadian Armed Forces." Nuyens also wanted to make decision makers in the south more "aware of the import-ance of the Canadian Rangers in the Arctic." These volunteers, who freed up regular troops to serve elsewhere, had to "continue in their part to preserve the Sovereignty of the North for all Canadians."[100]

The Ranger organization ultimately suffered from a fundamental weak-ness: it lacked focus. After more than a decade of neglect, informal and ineffective arrangements governed what remained of the organization, and national defence headquarters provided no clear direction. Nevertheless, the

Steering Committee on the Canadian North recommended retaining the Rangers in November 1969. Noting that "an organization of this type fulfills a legitimate Defence requirement and makes a direct and positive sociological contribution," it suggested immediate revitalization with no fixed ceiling on the size of the force.[101] Lieutenant-Colonel Sutherland disagreed. He declared the Rangers moribund and insisted on a fundamental retooling because the Rangers' original role and concept were "no longer entirely valid due to changes within [the] North."[102] When Mobile Command (the army) begrudgingly assumed command of the Rangers early the next year, it immediately asked Major W.K. (Bill) Stirling to undertake a more in-depth study of the force to determine what should be done "to reorganize the Canadian Rangers to perform their prescribed functions."[103]

The Stirling Report and the Proposal to Disband

When Stirling set out to study the Rangers in early 1970, he found the force in disarray. In an era when the military sought technological answers to northern defence problems, the Ranger organization had withered, seemingly confirming the arguments of early postwar skeptics who suggested that interest would wane in peacetime. Stirling mobilized these arguments to justify disbanding the force. "It would appear that some considerable doubt existed in the earliest days as to the military value and possible roles of the Canadian Rangers," he observed after reviewing the army's files from 1946-47. "When one considers the dramatic changes that have taken place with regard to communications, transportation and social and economic conditions in the remote areas of Canada in the past quarter century there is even more reason now to believe that these doubts were well founded."[104] In his eyes, the Ranger experiment had failed.

Stirling visited seventeen of the sixty-one communities alleged to have active Ranger units in the summer of 1970. The Rangers still had 1,647 active members on paper but "for all practical purposes no activity." Stirling reported that "members of the Rangers, RCMP, Government officials and other citizens were at a loss to describe any requirement or role for an organization of this type other than in the most nebulous terms based on self interest." He saw no reason to revitalize such a force.

Individual communities across the country told their own stories. St. Anthony, Newfoundland, for instance, had twenty-eight Rangers, but when

Major Bill Stirling
investigated the
Rangers in 1970.
Library and Archives Canada/
The Sentinel/Nov-Dec 1970, Vol.
6. No. 10/AMICUS 34810/P. 38

Stirling met with six current and former members, they conceded that they had never had a gathering, had never been told what to do, and "were unable to define a purpose [for continuing the Rangers] other than to hold rifle practices and report conditions on the coast." At Cartwright, Labrador, Stirling met with W.S. Moores, a representative of the Department of Labrador Affairs and the senior Ranger. He maintained that the Rangers had a role to play reporting incidents and that the issue of rifles and ammunition remained important to the local inhabitants. At Port Menier on Anticosti Island, Stirling discovered that there had been no Ranger activity since 1964. The district superintendent of Consolidated Bathurst Limited – which, Stirling wrote, owned "the island lock, stock and barrel" – told Stirling that "there was no need for the Rangers as the Company had excellent communication with the mainland and would report any unusual activity as a matter of course." At Harrington Harbour, Stirling discovered a total of five Rangers. A meeting with three of them revealed that they too had never gotten together, had never been told what to do, and "were unable to describe any role they could perform other than report unusual incidents at sea which they would do anyway." The local Anglican priest and pilot, Reverend John Blake, informed Stirling that DOT radio operators, lighthouse keepers, fishing patrol vessels, and commercial pilots were more familiar than the Rangers with activities in the area and reported items as a matter of course.

Further west, the situation was even worse. Stirling met with the RCMP constable at Moose Factory. He saw no need for the Rangers along either James or Hudson Bay. The RCMP was responsible for submarine reporting, and radio telephone now connected the entire coast, allowing ordinary civilians to report unusual incidents. Furthermore, in Stirling's view, the radar site at Moosonee made the unit at Moose Factory redundant. In British Columbia, Stirling found an active unit with seven Rangers at Ocean Falls. The local commander, A.A. Peters, wanted the organization to continue but could only muster shooting practices and assistance with search-and-rescue missions as viable reasons to retain the Rangers. Stirling learned that the RCMP used the Rangers as a town patrol on Halloween but that police boats had negated the need for coastal patrols. Dawson Creek had been reported as an active unit of 107 men, but Stirling could not locate a single Ranger. The local RCMP knew nothing about them and saw little need for the force. He reported twenty-one auxiliary police capable of carrying out Ranger-type tasks. Fort St. John, Stirling discovered, had the only truly "active" unit with a paper strength of ninety men. Commander E.J. Galibois explained that thirty local Rangers had acted as enemies and guides for the army during Exercise Top Hat in 1969. He believed that "the Rangers could still serve a useful purpose as guides and for traffic control on the Alaska highway," but they needed uniforms, radios, standard issue military rifles, identification cards, and considerable training. Andy Graychuk, the senior Ranger at Fort Nelson, stated that he had thirty-seven names on his books, men who could be useful guides and guards at critical points on the Alaska Highway. He too requested support.

Stirling found the Rangers in the Territorial North in an equally sorry state. He could find only three of the twenty active members in Whitehorse. The two he met did not know what they could actually do, but they requested uniforms and ammunition for an annual rifle competition. At Dawson City, Stirling located one former member of the Pacific Coast Militia Rangers who saw no interest in or need for the Rangers. He encountered the same assessment at Fort Simpson. At Inuvik, he discussed the

Major Bill Stirling noted, "Wise in the ways of life in the north, these are some of the Canadian Rangers who serve at Inuvik, Tuktoyaktuk and Harrington Harbour."
Library and Archives Canada/The Sentinel/Nov-Dec 1970, Vol. 6. No. 10/AMICUS 34810/P. 38-39

situation with Ranger Dave Jones, with the RCMP, and with Mayor Dick Hill. They explained that the platoon had been formed in 1952 but had never been called out for any reason.[105] Although Aklavik had twenty-nine active members on paper, Stirling could not find one. He spoke with Rev. H.G. Cook, the Anglican bishop of Northwest Territories. Cook had travelled extensively in the Arctic but knew nothing of the Rangers' existence. Regardless, Cook felt the force "would be of little value today considering the majority of the natives live on welfare in fewer and larger communities and no longer hunt or fish to any extent."[106]

Only a generation earlier, at the end of the Second World War, most northern indigenous communities consisted of extended family groups that lived together and hunted for most of the year. The situation had changed by 1970. The collapse of the fur trade market, the availability of unskilled wage labour, and Inuit migration from camps to permanent settlements undermined traditional community leadership. *Qallunaat* (non-Inuit) representatives of commercial interests, religious institutions, or the federal government held dominant positions. The influence of family groups weakened, and northern Native peoples got caught up in the vortex of welfare colonialism.[107] Stirling concurred with Rev. Cook that northern Canada was no longer a place where the Ranger organization would find solid ground:

> Perhaps the most important piece of general advice I received was that southern Canadians should rid themselves of their romantic concept of the North. The Arctic has become a rather sophisticated social environment. Hunting and trapping, although still carried on[,] are not the main

pursuits of the indigenous people. Eskimos are being collected into permanent settlements ... where they are provided with houses and to a large extent live on welfare. The young Indian and Eskimo is being well educated in modern schools ... When they complete their education they will be trained to take their place in modern society and not on the Arctic ice or the trap line.

Individuals who lived most of their lives on the land now represented the exception, not the rule. "The people who know the North best are the RCMP, bush pilots, certain members of the Territorial Government, some prospectors and the missionaries," Stirling asserted. Unfortunately, these were not the people defence planners had originally envisaged as Rangers.[108]

When Stirling reported to his superiors in Ottawa in August 1970, he got straight to the point: "The Canadian Rangers as presently constituted both in form and concept should be disbanded." The North had changed, the Rangers were obsolete, and the military should preserve its reputation by avoiding commitments in the region:

> There are a considerable number of people in the North who have dedi-
> cated their lives to the development of this vast estate and to the welfare
> of the native peoples. These people are to be found amongst the RCMP,
> Federal and Territorial governments and the various church organizations.
> They are unlike the majority of Northerners who are there simply for the
> "fast buck" or because they could not fit into southern society. These
> people feel somewhat protective of the North and particularly resent what

they call "do-gooders" making a brief tour of the Arctic and then deciding what is best for the poor natives. There are too many instances of this to be recorded, however, [and] the effects of these well intentioned programmes are still felt and resented in the North. The Canadian Armed Forces have an extremely good reputation in this part of the country and we must ensure that this is maintained. No programme should be conceived or initiated until such time as we once again have an intimate knowledge of current social and economic conditions in Northern society. In addition we must work very closely with the people in the various agencies of the North to make sure that our objective[s] reinforce and not disrupt the pattern of development.[109]

In Stirling's opinion, the era of the Ranger had passed.

7

Sovereignty and Symbolism,
1970-84

❧ *MARCH 1974, CAMP ANTLER, thirty-seven miles (sixty kilometres) west of Yellowknife.* One officer and seven noncommissioned officers from third battalion, Princess Patricia's Canadian Light Infantry in Victoria, spent a month training five Inuit from Arctic Bay, six from Holman Island (Ulukhaktok), and four Dogrib (Tłı̨chǫ) from Lac La Martre. The Rangers were a diverse group. John Avilingak, from Holman Island, was sixteen years old, and Isaac Attagutsiak, from Arctic Bay, was fifty-six years old and had twenty-five years of Ranger service. Because only one of the Rangers spoke English, communications required simultaneous interpretation – and patience. Exercise Nanook Ranger II proved to be a learning experience for everyone. "None of the instructors had ever worked with Rangers," Captain Craig Mills explained. Inuit rarely operated that far south of the treeline, and the Tłı̨chǫ – who had spent five days travelling by dog team to the camp – found the shacks "too hot and confining."[1]

Nanook Ranger II trained Aboriginal people from below and above the treeline together for the first time. Mills remarked, "but it worked ... Indian and Eskimo Rangers proved they are able to work with each other and with a military force successfully." Food provided common ground for co-operation. When everyone complained about the freeze-dried rations, one Ranger proposed a solution:

> Bannock just may have been the thread that tied [the team] all together.
> Early in the training, one Ranger, tired of chewing the spongy glob most

"Bannock Builds a Better Team," Nanook Ranger II, Lac La Martre, Northwest Territories, March 1974. Library and Archives Canada/The Sentinel /1975, Vol. 2. No. 7/AMICUS 34810

Canadians call bread, took matters literally into his own hands. Using gestures sparingly, and no words at all, he demonstrated the ancient art of making bread, Northern style, to [the] course cook ... It would be understating somewhat to say that the cook's first efforts did not quite reach epicurean heights – but time, determination and practice finally brought forth a product closely resembling bannock.

It proved an instant morale booster. A common ground had been found – everyone liked it. Military rations became more palatable with it, game and fish tasted better than ever, and it proved especially delightful for tea dunking.[2]

The idea of finding common ground offered a metaphor for the entire exercise – and the northern Rangers more generally. Rangers learned basic military skills and mastered the snowmobile, and they in turn taught the instructors trapping and fishing techniques. Mills concluded that Canadian Forces personnel had learned to appreciate the "Rangers' unsurpassed bush skills and how to live harmonious with Northerners ... Nanook Ranger II proved that different Canadian life styles can be compatible and can help to build a better country. Isn't that a worthwhile objective?"[3]

❦ AN AMERICAN, NOT SOVIET, challenge had shattered the federal government's complacency about the Arctic in 1969. In August of that year, the oil tanker *Manhattan* pushed through the Northwest Passage, leaving anxieties about Canadian sovereignty in its wake. When Prime Minister Trudeau unveiled his government's new defence priorities that April, he assigned primary importance to the surveillance of Canada's territory and coastlines and the protection of sovereignty. Indeed, the latter consideration became a cause célèbre in Parliament, where the Opposition pressured the government to strengthen Canada's presence in the High Arctic. The Steering Committee on the Canadian North concluded in December 1969 that

> [l]arge scale military activity in the Canadian North would not be justified on the basis of the direct military threat alone, nor would it be valid to permanently station large military establishments in the North. Nevertheless, it is imperative that the capability to conduct operations against a hostile enemy ... be developed and maintained. By so doing the Canadian Forces would substantially contribute to the defence against the indirect threat to Canadian sovereignty ... In order to make its contribution both to economic and social development, and the maintenance of sovereignty, the Canadian Forces must establish a presence in the Canadian North. This presence can be established largely by operational and exercise activity however, some permanent presence is considered essential.[4]

This new, rather perplexing sovereignty mission made it difficult for the military – and the public – to grasp the Canadian Forces' role. The Trudeau government insisted that no one had legally challenged Canada's sovereignty over its northern lands, territorial waters, or Arctic seabed. The only issue was the status of the Northwest Passage, which the United States insisted was an international strait used for commercial navigation. The Canadian government therefore equated "sovereignty protection" with surveillance and establishing a presence in the North, not with preparing for war against

Canada's foremost ally and trading partner.[5] Vice-Admiral J.C. O'Brien, the chief of the maritime staff, proclaimed in March 1970 that "if Canada is serious about asserting its sovereignty in the Arctic, it must be prepared to pay a fantastically high price ... There's only one nation we need to worry about encroaching on our sovereignty. The only way to combat it is to be there and prove you care."[6]

Canada had limited choices. Argus long-range patrol aircraft, designed for submarine hunting, were limited by seasonal darkness, harsh weather, and the lack of northern bases from which to operate. Canadian naval vessels could patrol only certain waters in ice-free months, and the geographical expanse of the North limited ground surveillance. The relatively minimal US threat to Canadian sovereignty hardly warranted a major investment of military personnel and resources. Therefore, the best option remained a symbolic presence – akin to the arrival of the Royal Canadian Mounted Police (RCMP) in the North in the early twentieth century.[7]

Despite grand plans for the Canadian Forces in the Arctic, money never matched rhetoric. In early 1970, however, soldiers resumed training in the northern territories, Maritime Command sent naval ships on their first northern deployment since 1962, and the military established Northern Region headquarters in Yellowknife as the regional administrative, liaison, and support unit. Although responsible for the largest military region in the world, Northern Region had almost no operational units under its direct command. The Rangers were the exception: seven hundred members in thirty-six northern communities, at least on paper. Having been left to atrophy, these Rangers offered a bedraggled symbol of Canadian sovereignty.[8]

Reorganization or Disbandment?

On 1 April 1970, Canadian Forces Headquarters passed command and control of the Rangers to the Commander of Mobile Command (the army), who directed Major Bill Stirling to study what should be done.[9] Potential options included upgrading the Rangers to militia (Primary Reserve) status or to a paramilitary force akin to the Alaskan National Guard. In Stirling's view, however, the militia had few prospects. The army had disbanded units in Whitehorse and Yellowknife because of limited local support, and nothing suggested the situation would change. To be viable, militia units needed a large, stable population base, something even the largest northern centres could not provide. Stirling viewed many northern residents as transient "new

Canadians." Furthermore, militia units required staff, accommodations, and training facilities, all of which isolation and distance rendered prohibitively expensive. As for a paramilitary organization composed of Native peoples, Stirling suggested investigating the possibility with the Department of Indian Affairs and Northern Development and the territorial governments. He disliked special treatment, however, and asserted that "equal treatment" should remain "equal opportunity" for ethnic groups to enlist in the Regular Forces.[10]

Stirling recommended disbanding the Rangers, but his position contradicted previous reports that saw utility in an active Ranger force. Lieutenant-Colonel W.B.S. Sutherland, the director general of land operations in Ottawa, encouraged the military to revitalize the Rangers *and* to extend the Primary Reserve to northern communities to supplement the force. "Canadian national objectives in the North dictate a requirement for a military presence in that area which is beyond the scope of the Rangers," Sutherland asserted. In his view, a formal militia establishment would bring the Rangers under more effective command and control and would have ancillary benefits for the northern population. "Military assistance to our native Indians and Eskimos would enhance the position of individuals and groups, develop an awareness of citizenship and be of value to other government and commercial agencies."[11]

The commander of Maritime Command (MARCOM) in Halifax also identified a need for the Rangers in the Atlantic region.[12] When the military reorganized the reserves, administering and training the militia fell to the new Newfoundland Headquarters in April 1970. Official documents made no mention of the Rangers whatsoever. Maritime Command assumed responsibility for the regional plans and operations section, which controlled the Rangers through the commanding officer of Canadian Forces Station St. John's, where the Ranger liaison officer was co-located. Although the Rangers had supported both army and navy exercises, their primary role remained coast watching. "The [Newfoundland] and Labrador coasts are of prime importance to MARCOM," Vice-Admiral J.C. O'Brien reminded the vice chief of the defence staff in Ottawa, "and timely information is required on all activities in this area. Rangers can and do provide some of this information." Increased maritime activities along the Atlantic Coast, coupled with the government's heightened interest in pollution detection and control, made the Rangers a valuable asset to the navy.[13]

Military officials had mixed opinions. Stirling's recommendation to disband the Rangers enjoyed the support of all the senior army staff officers

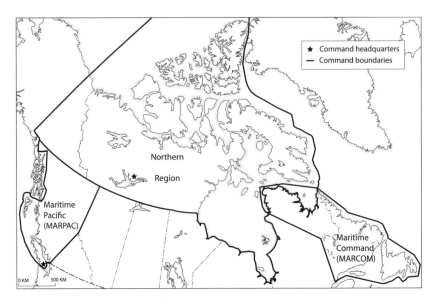

Division of Northern Region and Maritime Command

in Ottawa, including the commander of Mobile Command, who could not justify their continuation "on military principles."[14] Voices from the North, however, insisted that the region needed a Ranger organization, particularly one retooled to fit Canada's new sovereignty and security imperatives. Defence planners, like the politicians, believed the military's presence and surveillance activities would affirm Canada's legal claims in the Arctic.[15] Who could do this better than Rangers serving in their home communities? Stirling's recommendation – not the Ranger concept – was abandoned in the end.

In November 1970, the chief of the defence staff decided to "spare" the Rangers "for the foreseeable future" but split command and control into two parts. As of 22 February 1971, operational responsibility for Ranger units north of the sixtieth parallel fell to Northern Region Headquarters and those on the Pacific and Atlantic coasts to Maritime Command. The army no longer controlled the Rangers, and each command assumed responsibility for assessing the Rangers' unique requirements in their area. In theory, the commanders of the two headquarters would coordinate activities for a common Ranger force.[16] In practice, the Atlantic Rangers and the northern Rangers developed distinct operational concepts and evolved independently of each other. The remaining Ranger units in Alberta,

Brigadier Ramsey Withers. Library and Archives Canada/The Sentinel / Nov-Dec 1970, Vol. 6. No. 10/ AMICUS 34810/P. 26

Saskatchewan, Ontario, and Quebec south of Povungnituk (Puvirnituq) fell dormant,[17] and the Rangers in BC did not survive the decade.

A New Northern Ranger Concept?

Thirty-nine-year-old Brigadier General Ramsey Withers was ready to make his mark when he took command of the new Northern Region Headquarters in April 1970. As former director of policy control and coordination at Canadian Forces Headquarters, he knew bureaucratic politics.[18] Although military analysts believed that the only real threat to the Arctic would come in the context of a general nuclear war, the departmental Steering Committee on the Canadian North insisted that the Canadian Forces had a role to play "in furthering government objectives in the North."[19] They did not specify, however, what that role would be or where the Rangers would fit. Withers and his staff, who operated out of a building in Ottawa until their head-quarters moved to Yellowknife, therefore headed north to visit communities and talk with Rangers about the future.[20]

Colonel Sutherland, in confidence, tipped off Withers in early May 1970 that Stirling's report might recommend removing the Rangers "from their parish." The northern commander developed alternative plans.[21] Within Northern Region's concept of operations, which it outlined in June, Rangers would assist with surveillance, act as guides during large-scale operations, and contribute a sustained military presence in the area.[22] The Canadian Forces' northern detachments supported Withers. Major F.L. Berry wrote from Yellowknife, "The isolated and remote areas of Northern Canada make it essential that as many Northern residents as possible be made aware of the problems of preserving Canadian Sovereignty in the High Arctic and Eastern Arctic." His counterpart in Whitehorse, Major W.S. Deacon, inter-viewed Yukoners and discovered "an active interest in an organization such as the Canadian Rangers." He anticipated that ex-Rangers ranging in age from forty-five to sixty, as well as younger recruits, would help reconstitute the force. Berry and Deacon both wanted the Rangers to remain a volunteer force organized along military lines with "evolved" roles, including search and rescue, air observation, riot and traffic control, surveillance, sovereignty assertion, and service as game wardens and fire rangers. To accomplish this, the officers advocated more formal training.[23]

The detachment commanders' research indicated that northerners did not trust the Canadian Forces. Over the years, the military had made plans and then cancelled them when national interest waned. With an "Arctic revolution" in governance and development in progress, the military would have to be more cautious managing its relationships with Aboriginal peoples and would have to consult with experts familiar with the North's social and community issues.[24] Major Berry argued, "A radical approach to a revitalized Ranger Programme must be developed in view of present communication, travel and social development of the North ... Our plan must be based on the most simple and straightforward approach. No plan is workable unless we are in a position to give it complete follow-up support." If National Defence failed to deliver on promises because of costs or timing, he warned, its reputation would deteriorate further.[25]

In the past, the army had found it convenient to appoint the token "white" resident as the Ranger company or platoon commander. Emerging trends in northern governance, however, gave Aboriginal communities more say in their own affairs. "What we are doing wherever possible," the commissioner of the Northwest Territories had explained in 1969, "is electing people from and by the community to the various forms of local government."[26] The first Inuk joined the Northwest Territories Council in 1965, the territorial government took over the federal government's northern bureaucracy two years later, and a system of local governance that encouraged Native people's participation developed in the early 1970s. A revitalized Ranger force would need to acknowledge and reflect these new realities. Major Berry stressed that command and control had to be vested in communities: "The Eskimo is not one to be easily regimented. He does not accept imposed leadership, in fact his communities are more akin to a gathering of closely knit family groups banded together for social and welfare advantages. He respects intelligence and skill rather than imposed authority ... The old Ranger concept of appointing the HBC factor or the DOT engineer as Ranger Officers is not considered the answer. The active white resident in some communities should be encouraged to participate but not as automatic leaders."[27] An effective – and more representative – Ranger organization in the "new North" would depend on devolving responsibility to Aboriginal Canadians who could and would form a strong leadership cadre.

The Canadian Forces Northern Activities Task Group on Rangers, Reserves and Cadets, which had conducted its own independent study into the future of the Rangers, concurred. In the task group's September 1970 report, the members observed that command and control had been hampered by national and regional headquarters moving in different directions. The overall organization lacked coherence, and the company-platoon structure had never worked effectively in the North. Ranger liaison officers had not visited Rangers often enough to sustain interest, and company commanders only saw their platoons "on the very rare occasions when they were travelling on their employer's business." As a result, the Rangers had few links to the military. Distances between settlements were too large, and resources too few, to sustain an organization "above the small post level." Similar to detachment commanders in Yellowknife and Whitehorse, the task group advised that "natural leaders selected by the Rangers themselves would have a much better chance of success."[28] Moving away from the army's conventional, hierarchical structure would make the organization leaner, more effective, and more representative of local communities.

Stirling suggested that the Ranger concept was obsolete. The Northern Activities Task Group, by contrast, insisted that Rangers *could* perform a useful military function – provided they had better training. The creation of Northern Region Headquarters made it possible for the Canadian Forces to "regularly visit or contact the Rangers and thus instil a high degree of interest and effectiveness." A team of instructors based in Yellowknife could give Inuit and Indians formal training in their communities, allowing the Rangers to provide Northern Region with important local information, report "anomalies," and participate in Regular Force exercises. Although defence officials associated a permanent military presence with Canadian sovereignty, they would have to determine precisely what they expected, or did not expect, of the Rangers. For example, Rangers would not receive sufficient training to defend vital points, so the task group concluded that they should be confined to observing and reporting.[29]

General Withers convinced senior decision makers in Ottawa that the Rangers should survive.[30] The practical implications, however, remained unknown. Field studies would help to determine locations that needed Rangers and the jobs they could do, as would conversations with other federal departments and agencies. Times had changed, and the ad hoc approach to organizing that had taken place in the early postwar period no longer sufficed. Instead, the military would have to define the Rangers' role within the broader context of the government's objectives for the North at a time of surging political interest in the region. The Arctic received unprecedented attention in the government's 1971 white paper, *Defence in the '70s*, which reaffirmed that sovereignty – "the protection of Canada and Canadian national interests" – would be the Canadian Forces' primary role. The new policy statement promised to increase Arctic surveillance and training, and it directed the military to explore "the desirability of reconstituting the Canadian Rangers."[31] The Ranger concept fit with Withers's belief that humans provided a "flexible, relatively unsophisticated, inexpensive surveillance and reconnaissance system," one well suited to challenges faced in the modern North. Strategists no longer emphasized "alliance-type" operations and potential enemy lodgements. Instead, they warned that threats of a nonmilitary nature endangered Canada's interests and that *northerners* could best approach, investigate, and even converse with these "new northern targets." Military training would provide local residents with money and skills, and Withers emphasized the simple "fact that essential Defence tasks ... would instil pride of accomplishment and dignity in an area where these qualities have perhaps suffered from the invasion of southern ways of life."[32] Placing national interests above narrowly defined

TABLE 6
Northern surveillance and reconnaissance: Differences between a
traditional target and a new northern target, 1971

Traditional target	New northern target
Evasive	Not evasive and often co-operating
High ability to conceal and deceive	Overt and possibly co-operating
Hostile and responsive	Not hostile and probably not dangerous
Mobile	No or low mobility
Limited in variability	Complex and variable
Easily recognized and identified	Difficult to recognize, often requiring sampling and data analysis
Countered mainly by fire power	Rarely if ever countered by fire power or force

Source: Northern Region Headquarters, "Canadian Arctic Rangers: Operational Concept," 1 October 1971.

military ones contributed to the federal government's broader development objectives.[33]

Ironically, the task of discerning the Rangers' future again fell to Major Bill Stirling, who was posted as staff officer for operations at Northern Region Headquarters in late 1970. Although he remained skeptical about the Rangers' potential effectiveness, he listed various possible roles to justify the creation of a full-time "Northern Service Unit" based on the Rangers. He supplemented the traditional Ranger roles (surveillance, reporting anomalies, and providing a military presence) with search and rescue, assisting other government departments with communications, supporting community development, surveying flora and fauna, reporting damage to the ecosystem, maintaining weather stations and navigational aids, and monitoring ships and aircraft through snowmobile and boat patrols. Yet, in his view, Canada still needed a more effective and consistent presence: part-time reservists would not suffice.[34]

Stirling's proposal departed radically from the original Ranger concept. He envisaged the Northern Service Unit as a Regular Force formation composed entirely of northerners and employed full-time in four companies overseeing "a designated portion of Canadian territory, territorial waters and airspace." This year-round military presence would also create 415 well-paying jobs in remote communities. "The relief to the welfare system, contribution to the economy of the communities and the development of pride in the

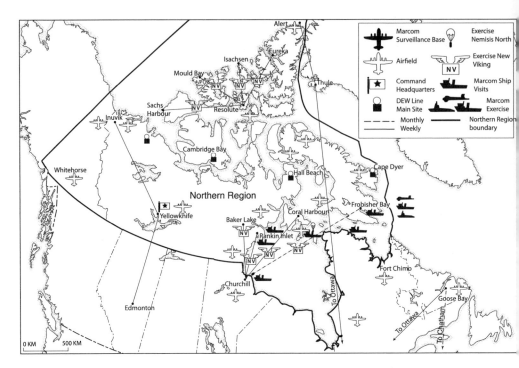

Northern Region, 1971

individual employed in renumerative [sic] and essential employment [will be] incalculable," Stirling touted.[35] He never explained how a full-time military force would strengthen Canada's sovereignty; he merely equated boots on the ground and improved surveillance with enhanced sovereignty, as did many military analysts.[36] Stirling's vision also seemed to support using the military as a form of northern workfare, an idea that he might have developed based on observations west of the Yukon-Alaska border.

Stirling visited the Alaska National Guard in February 1971 to examine how it had incorporated Alaskans into defence plans. He developed a particular interest in the two Scout Battalions of Eskimos, whom he found "well trained and motivated, capable of performing their assigned mission and without doubt full fledged Americans." In his view, the guardsmen were more effective than Canadian Rangers because they were better trained and equipped, better paid (something he found "particularly important in the Eskimo villages where unemployment is very high"), and better motivated. American men could fulfill their draft obligation by serving in the National Guard, thus avoiding active duty in Vietnam. Stirling was most impressed "that the Eskimo members of the Guard are treated as normal American soldiers. He receives no special treatment other than he is allowed to wear his mukluks (which he prefers) rather than the Vapour Barrier ... boots." Eskimo servicemen qualified to Regular Force standards and were expected to perform, in their particular environment, like every other state National Guard. Stirling lauded this as a viable model for the Ranger organization in the Canadian North.[37] Nowhere did he mention that the US Army spent millions maintaining the Alaskan units.[38]

Stirling's ideas enticed General Withers, who agreed on the need for a full-time, professional Ranger force. The Northern Region commander pitched the idea of a battalion of Rangers – composed of 350 Regular Force personnel and more than 450 Ranger reservists – to his superiors in Ottawa. As the unit evolved, Withers argued, leaders from within the Ranger force would take over Regular Force training and administrative responsibilities. Northern Region's grandiose concept also included an Arctic Air Squadron, which would operate out of Yellowknife, and communications and control personnel at regional headquarters.[39]

The plan came with a massive price tag. Although a dispersed Northern Service Unit would obviate the need for a large and costly Canadian Forces base in the North, it would entail major new construction (hangars, communications systems, and housing), expensive new equipment (aircraft, snow vehicles, and boats), and elaborate support services – for a total estimated cost of $60 million over five years, a staggering sum considering how little had been spent on the Rangers in the past. Withers had discussed his ideas with "a great many people of experience in the North," from the commissioner of the Northwest Territories, to Department of Indian Affairs and Northern Development officials, to educators and businessmen. "All have considered it to be an excellent concept which they hope will be implemented," he boasted. Informal discussions with the minister of national defence, deputy minister, and chief of the defence staff also suggested "great interest."[40] Would the money follow?

Groundwork

While senior defence officials continued to ponder the Rangers' future form and role, politicians and local officers demanded action. Paper planning was no substitute for practical trials, and regional staff stressed the importance of having northerners actually doing something.[41] Major Berry noted

An Inuk instructor leads soldiers on an advanced winter warfare course on a march across tundra, March 1971. Library and Archives Canada/Department of National Defence collection/ R112-536-X-E/Accession 2008-377/e010767162

in April 1971 that none of Northern Region's plans, "based on observations and studies," offered a "*proven workable* programme ... The Canadian Arctic and the people who live in it, the potential Rangers, present problems in recruiting and training that *no one* can foretell." Regardless of whether Northern Region secured the funding for its grand plans, Berry advised it to set up trial training programs in a few communities, paying Rangers for up to ten days' training as reservists.[42] This way, Northern Region could take the initiative and build momentum to revitalize – or re-create – its Ranger organization.

In May 1971, Captain David Jones visited the community of Holman (Ulukhaktok) on Victoria Island to determine the feasibility of restoring the Rangers. A few weeks later, Northern Region conducted its first field training in more than a decade. The diverse training team – a Cape Breton–born infantry captain with seventeen years' service, a Welsh infantry master warrant officer with twenty-nine years' service, and a Saulteaux Indian with twenty-years' service who had been "deeply involved" in Manitoba Native organizations – shared a "common respect for and interest in the North and northern people." Well-suited to the job, the instructors visited prospective Rangers, and with the help of Simon Kataoyak, the president of the community council, they planned a meeting at the school. About forty people (mostly women and children) gathered to watch army films. Unfortunately, an unexpected delay unloading the barge in town kept the men from attending. The following evening, however, a dozen men gathered at the instructor's tent on the edge of town. Eight Inuit from Holman and one from Sachs Harbour decided to participate in the training. They brought their boats, motors, and fuel drums to the camp; the instructors purchased fuel and food; and the group left on 3 August for a campsite suggested by one of the locals.[43]

The two-week pilot project would determine whether experienced hunters and trappers were interested in receiving military training and employment with a "surveillance, reconnaissance force." Captain Jones, impressed with the trainees' map recognition, remarked that the younger participants even gave correct latitude and longitude references. Although high winds hindered marksmanship training, the recruits still managed to hold a short shooting competition and hunted for seal, for which the military's "hard nose" ammunition proved excellent. Taking care of a military rifle, however, did not come as naturally. Jones reprimanded one Ranger for leaving his rifle in the bottom of his water-filled canoe. "His reaction was truculent," the instructor noted in his after-action report. "Once again I spoke with him privately and pointed out that his actions and attitude would never be tolerated in a military force. He was not impressed and I dropped the subject." Jones knew not to push the point, or he would risk undermining the positive spirit that had developed.[44]

When the group returned to Holman, Inuit trainees enthusiastically frequented the instructors' camp, and "there was much friendly discussion over tea and bannock." They asked for a local Ranger unit and wanted to know when the instructors would return. Other community members expressed interest in joining. The residents explained that the soldiers had special appeal because most visiting government workers simply sent a long telegram stipulating who they wanted to meet. Their official visits consisted of a brief discussion with the local priest and HBC manager, a shopping trip at the co-op, and an early departure to a community with better accommodations. By contrast, military personal were self-sufficient, spoke with everyone, and treated local people with respect. The Northern Region staff officer responsible for the Rangers considered the training exercise a success, and he appointed three more noncommissioned officers as Ranger instructors that fall.[45] The instructors arranged training in other communities.

These modest efforts complemented the Canadian Forces' Arctic operations in the early seventies. Platoon-size groups of soldiers from southern Canadian units flew from Churchill and Resolute to remote locations in the archipelago as part of New Viking exercises, which exposed troops to the difficulties of living, moving, and fighting in the Arctic. By the end of 1972, four thousand Regular Force officers and men had taken part in the exercises. The Canadian Airborne Regiment also undertook elaborate paratroop assault exercises in the Far North.[46] NORPLOYs brought Canadian Forces ships into Arctic waters during the ice-free season, and Canadian Coast Guard icebreakers took on naval personnel to give them some experience working in the Arctic. Long-range Argus aircraft flew periodic surveillance patrols over the archipelago, and military engineers built northern airfields and bridges across the Ogilvie and Eagle rivers. By the middle of the decade, all three services had rekindled their northern expertise – even though the military had fewer personnel permanently stationed there than it had in the 1950s.[47]

The army's training activities also allowed Northern Region to test the interface between prospective Rangers and other military units. The first opportunity came with exercise Patrouille Nocturne, launched near Frobisher Bay (Iqaluit) in early 1972. Northern Region staff had conducted preliminary training with fourteen men from the community and from Lake Harbour (Kimmirut) the previous November, and two months later the military transported skidoos and *komatiks* to a training area laid out carefully to not disrupt caribou herds.[48] When the exercise began, the Rangers played a key role guiding small groups of lightly equipped soldiers. On 28 January, one hundred paratroopers with 1er Commando aéroporté of the Canadian Airborne Regiment dove into the cold air and cascaded through bitter wind and driving snow. On the ground, two Inuit Rangers greeted them and helped establish an airfield defence. The Rangers carried reports that the enemy had established a position about ten miles northwest of Frobisher. The terrain – hilly, rocky, and deeply crevassed – would render wheeled vehicles useless, and the snow, which blanketed all discernible landmarks, made navigation difficult. The wind chill brought the temperature down to minus eighty degrees Fahrenheit, and distance forced the combat group to advance in stages to avoid overextending critical supply lines. Equipment

A Ranger in front of the 3rd Battalion, Royal 22nd Regiment Headquarters on Patrouille Nocturne, February 1972. Library and Archives Canada/Department of National Defence collection/R112-536-X-E/Accession 2008-377/Box 136, Photo ISC-72-1001-17

and communications failed in the cold. The Rangers offered valuable advice to help the men cope. They shared their knowledge about trails and topography, taught the soldiers how to build igloos, and offered them vehicles and komatiks (Inuit sleds with wooden runners). The soldiers uniformly applauded their expert guidance and appreciated the fresh caribou meat they supplied.[49]

The exercise revealed cultural challenges. Four of the original Ranger trainees had not shown up to the exercise: two had obtained full-time work, one was in hospital, and another considered himself too old. After navigation and movement training at the camp, two more Ranger recruits left, one for work and another because of abdominal pains. The remaining Rangers had no choice but to work with every subunit and head out on every patrol. One trainee working with 1er Commando returned to his home at Lake Harbour abruptly on 28 January. When a staff officer flew there to confirm his safe arrival and investigate the incident, the Ranger told him that a soldier had shouted at him and that he had been "afraid of a certain very large man." The Ranger agreed that he should not have left without an explanation but declined to return to the exercise. Considering the cultural differences, Captain Jones worried that "the average regular solider is too inflexible for achieving the maximum from irregulars such as the Canadian Rangers."[50] For the partnership to work, soldiers would have to learn that loud, intimidating behaviour, part of regimental culture in the South, had no place among Inuit.

As expected, lessons learned on the ground reaffirmed that interactions between Rangers and soldiers demanded mutual learning and cultural sensitivity. The Rangers had their limitations, but the military had to recognize and trust in the northerners' unique capabilities borne from experience and traditional knowledge. Furthermore, Rangers benefitted from military training because it encouraged them to go out on the land and share their skills. The older Rangers from Frobisher Bay knew the area well, but the younger members of the community and the Rangers from Lake Harbour did not. The after-action report noted that the younger Rangers appreciated learning from both elders and military instructors.[51] Analysts could have concluded from this experience that the Rangers should remain flexible and grassroots – that they should continue to encourage northerners to exercise their traditional knowledge and skills without imposing orthodox military expectations on them. Staff officers at Northern Region, however, wanted something more grandiose and conventional.

Grand Plans, Financial Constraints

In December 1971, from their new headquarters in Yellowknife, a building that consisted of seventeen ATCO trailers bolted together and painted to form a "yellow submarine," Withers and his staff unveiled a revised but ambitious proposal to recast the "Canadian Arctic Rangers" as a Primary Reserve unit.[52] Complete with elaborate equipment tables, communication plans, designs for regimental colours, plans and locations for permanent married quarters, and a draft organizational order, the proposed program would, if implemented, cost more than 26 million dollars over its first three years.[53]

Once again, Ottawa stood firmly in Withers's way. Although the chief of the defence staff's advisory committee approved Northern Region's pilot project in early 1972, the Defence Management Committee revoked the authorization. The project's enormous financial and manpower costs alarmed both Mobile Command and the director general land forces. Neither authority wanted any part of their budgets redirected towards the North.[54] "Consequently all Ranger activities are in limbo," the northern commander noted in his annual review, "and approximately one year has been lost." His staff went back to the drawing board and produced a scaled-down version of the plan in September 1972.[55]

Withers, clearly frustrated with Ottawa's unwillingness to invest substantial resources in the Rangers' future, wrote in the fall, "Long neglected due to shifting command and control structures, our Rangers have been in limbo patiently awaiting word of their fate ... Some two and one half years ago they were told of the reconstitution study. They have kept the faith and continued to wait. Equally, our other supporters in the North have been standing by us accepting our word that a course would finally be set. We have stretched their patience to the limit." If the military did not make an announcement regarding the Rangers soon, Withers warned, it "will have failed in [northerners'] eyes and the damage done will be great." The government's credibility was at stake:

> Government policy has been such as to dispel the notion that Northerners are second class citizens; the Northerner deserves the same consideration as all other Canadians. It follows that a Northern reserve unit must have the same consideration as any other reserve unit in Canada. Northerners, and in particular those devoted very publicly to the cause of native rights, will be looking to see that Canadian Forces reservists here receive comparable and equitable treatment, keeping in mind of course the very different and demanding conditions which exist, to that of their southern counterparts. We cannot afford to do less.[56]

National Defence Headquarters remained fixated on the cost. Withers could not implement his plans without Ottawa's support, and without an official response to the revised proposal, Northern Region had to put its recruiting and training efforts on hold.[57]

Maritime Command's Operational Concept

The Rangers in Maritime Command constituted an entirely different force than their counterparts in Northern Region. Although the Ranger liaison officer in St. John's had sustained modest contact with the Rangers in Newfoundland, Labrador, and the Lower North Shore, those units along Hudson Strait, Ungava Bay, and the east coast of Hudson Bay were thoroughly neglected throughout the 1960s. They finally received liaison visits in the summer of 1970, when a three-ship naval task group deployed to eastern Subarctic waters. Three Sea King helicopters flew officers to coastal posts in Labrador and northern Quebec, where they resupplied Ranger "outposts" and discussed communications, organization, and training. These visits restored the connection between the Regular Forces and the Rangers. Re-supply activities also had broader community benefits. For example, remote Payne Bay enjoyed a visit from a military dentist, movies, treats, and a makeshift playground for children, as well as income when military personnel bought local furs and handicrafts. At Nain in northern Labrador, fresh provisions "graced the tables of the orphanage" thanks to the naval ships. Northerners roundly welcomed this new military interest, celebrating rather than fearing the return of the navy to their home waters.[58]

The Rangers under the control of Maritime Command faced different pressures and had different priorities than Northern Region. Naval planners struggled to reconcile competing demands for a simple "naval presence" and "a more versatile general purpose capability" in their fleet modernization and renewal plans.[59] They had little time and few resources to dedicate to the Rangers.[60] Maritime Command nevertheless acknowledged the theoretical usefulness of having a modest Ranger presence along the coastline to support operational surveillance. In 1971, Captain A.L. Collier described the Rangers as "a vital source of intelligence in the wilderness ... either in war or in the role of protection of sovereignty."[61] That stated, the navy had no desire to enlarge or expand units. Although the Rangers in Newfoundland and Labrador had not deteriorated to the same extent as had the northern and western companies, Maritime Command constrained its initial planning to fit with the existing organization given the prevailing budgetary climate.[62]

When Maritime Command officers saw Northern Region's bold plans, however, they decided to review their needs and put forward a more ambitious proposal for what they called the Canadian Coastal Rangers in December 1971. Like Northern Region, Maritime Command recognized that the Canadian Forces were responsible for surveillance and control of Canadian territory, territorial waters, and airspace, as well as search and rescue and aid to civil authority in an emergency. The variables of time, space, terrain, weather, resources, and people made coastal areas "a special and most demanding challenge." With little threat of a Soviet invasion, the best means to investigate and counter new "regional targets" would be inexpensive, "on-the-ground and on-the-water" sensors – people. Maritime Command emphasized that the sovereignty issue was "not a question of combat, or force or contesting land": it was about upholding Canadian law and regulations in territorial waters and pollution-control zones. Considering that the navy had more than 60,000 miles (97,000 kilometres) of sparsely populated coastline to watch, the Rangers certainly could help with small-boat reconnaissance. In addition to their traditional tasks, the Rangers could assist civil authorities and agencies in emergency situations, support "environmental preservation" and community and social development activities, report on meteorological and ice conditions, maintain navigational aids, control resource exploitation, and monitor individuals or groups operating in coastal areas. The Rangers would also help establish an "all-Canadian capability" to defend northern North America.[63]

Maritime Command emphasized that the Rangers could contribute to regional development. Ottawa was committed to maximizing the participation of permanent residents in regional economies, but staff officers worried that members of remote coastal areas did not have adequate education to participate in Canada's modern economy. "The adult heads of family still retain ancestral skills which can be harnessed in the interests not only of defence objectives but also of national policy and priorities for the regions," Maritime Command's report noted. The Rangers were a natural fit:

> Through the Maritime Command regions, settlements exist which are inhabited by men who have lived for generations by their skill as hunters,

fishermen and seamen. Although urbanization on a small scale and the introduction of wage economy have dulled the sharpness of the skill in some localities, it is still true to say that there is an extensive resource of manpower proficient in observation and travel with minimum resources in a most demanding environment. Given the necessary organization and appropriate training they are the natural selection for our human sensor system. That these men would be prepared to undertake such tasks has been proven by over twenty years of Canadian Ranger experience.

A revitalized Ranger force could provide job opportunities, technical experience, and training to "assist in the inevitable adaptation to new ways." Direct spending would invigorate local economies, and military service would bring the intangible benefit of "pride of accomplishment and dignity." Young men under the age of twenty-five with "rather bleak employment prospects" would have the opportunity to serve for pay, which would also encourage a sense of leadership and community responsibility.[64] For an underfunded and overstretched military, filling vacancies with local residents rather than Regular Force personnel offered a cheap solution.

Maritime Command envisaged a new Ranger unit within the Primary Reserves – similar to Northern Region's revised concept. If implemented, Ranger officers and men would no longer form a distinct subcomponent of the reserves and would assimilate into the mainstream structure. The proposal also included special provisions for standards of education, age, and medical fitness to ensure that "if a man is able to work outdoors and support himself and is trustworthy and reliable, he is suitable for enrolment." Training would "develop leaders who are acceptable by regional community standards." Regular Force personnel would provide command-and-control and logistics support from St. John's and Victoria. Planners promised to keep equipment and procedures simple while cutting the existing ceiling of 3,000 Rangers in half. They would restrict the new force to 1,000 Rangers in Ungava, Newfoundland, Labrador, and the North Shore of the St. Lawrence. Another five hundred would watch the Pacific Coast. Despite these reduced numbers, the price tag would go up dramatically. Basing their estimates on ninety days of training for each Ranger, Maritime Command estimated that the Canadian Coastal Rangers would cost $4,695,592 in the first year.[65] This estimate was hundreds of times more than had been spent on the Rangers in previous years, but it was still a fraction of what would be spent if senior officials adopted Northern Region's proposal.

In charting a course for the future, the military needed to keep the Rangers themselves in mind. "Twenty years of promises, 300 rounds of ammunition, and no action," was one Ranger's sardonic summary of his experience. This reality hardly inspired faith in the Canadian Forces' commitment. Some Rangers had served up to twenty-four years without pay or recognition, Maritime Command noted, and one way to keep the faith would be to reward loyal service with the Canadian Forces Decoration. Records of service were incomplete and unreliable, and Inuit names had changed thanks to the government's insistence on surnames, so officers would have to accept a Ranger's length of service based on sworn statements. Nevertheless, issuing medals would boost morale.[66] Yet even this inexpensive initiative was not acted upon until the 1980s. For all their high-level military talk and requests for ideas, senior officials' priorities lay elsewhere.

National Decisions

The proposals from Northern Region and Maritime Command generated prolonged policy deliberations in Ottawa. Senior staff officers considered four options: the Ranger concept then in operation, a Regular Force Ranger battalion as proposed by Northern Region, a reserves-based unit as proposed by Maritime Command, or a limited adaptation of the existing concept. Although the first option would cost little and would not disrupt the Rangers' lifestyles or normal routines, it lacked coordination and would not contribute to broader national goals. Northern Region's elaborate program would improve military capabilities and civilian skills in remote areas, but it was far beyond the scope of military requirements and was prohibitively expensive. In addition to disrupting "the normal pursuits of the local residents," the program would also produce economic benefits for Regular Force personnel and the defence industry rather than community members. A reserves-oriented Ranger force would be more flexible and sustainable for local residents, at a more moderate expense.[67]

Continuing this logic, the vice chief of the defence staff recommended adapting the existing Ranger organizational concept in a limited way. His main focus was the North rather than the Atlantic Coast. Based on Northern Region's advice, he recommended a basic subunit of community-based patrols instead of conventional company-platoon structures. Unlike Northern Region, he imagined a small full-time staff of twelve Regular Force personnel, stationed in Yellowknife, who would provide administration, training, and periodic liaison visits to up to seventeen hundred Rangers. On the ground, Rangers would continue to provide surveillance and reconnaissance alongside their civilian jobs – perpetuating the Rangers' traditional focus on individual initiative and independent action. They would be paid at militia rates when they participated in training, military exercises and local ceremonies.[68] This plan, while less formal and much cheaper than the one proposed by Northern Region, would still promote a modest – and positive – military presence in remote communities.

The Department of National Defence's latest white paper had indicated that the government expected the Canadian Forces to help in the "social and economic development of Canada."[69] Senior officers used this goal to defend Ranger revitalization. In November 1973, the deputy chief of the defence staff explained to the Defence Management Committee:

> Generally, the Native Indian and Eskimo populations of the North are now living in larger communities and it is in these areas that military training and assistance will be concentrated. Training in a variety of special skills would enable the Ranger who ventures out on trap lines or annual hunts, to make a more significant contribution to the defence of his country. He will be made to feel that he is making a worthwhile contribution that is being recognized. A new Ranger identity, the provision of functional training and equipment, along with pay on a similar basis to that of Reserves in other parts of Canada, will provide enhanced recruiting incentives.

In theory, this option would cost $6 million over five years – a significant increase over previous budgets but far less than the alternative options. If future developments warranted a more robust Ranger force, this investment would provide a foundation upon which to implement either the Northern Region's or Maritime Command's plans.[70]

Just when National Defence seemed prepared to proceed, shifting priorities and budget pressures blocked the implementation of even this modest plan. In the early 1970s, the Trudeau government fixed the military's $1.8-billion budget in current dollars and rapid inflation reduced actual spending power. Military priorities took a backseat to broader fiscal austerity programs, and defence planners had no additional funds to fulfil the new sovereignty and national development tasks that the government imposed on them.[71] Although the deputy minister proposed a detailed submission to cabinet supporting the vice chief of the defence staff's proposal for the Rangers, the changes were delayed several times.[72] In August 1973, the deputy chief of the defence staff placed the matter on hold until the assistant deputy minister (policy) could table a policy paper. In turn, the Defence Management Committee decided that the military should invest nothing more in the Rangers until the Land Forces Review ended in May 1974. By this time, Brigadier-General J.A. Fulton had replaced Withers. The new northern commander requested funding for three Ranger training exercises in 1975-76 and justified them partly as social-development assistance to Indians and Inuit, which would "help them to become better integrated into the Canadian social mosaic." The deputy chief of the defence staff replied that the plans cost too much and authorized a paltry $44,000 for the fiscal year – despite his earlier acknowledgment that the existing Ranger concept required more than five times this level of support.[73]

Financial constraints stymied Northern Region's plans for the remainder of the decade. In the end, the much anticipated 1974 Land Force Policy Review found no military reason to retain the Rangers, prompting yet another study on their future. The ensuing results contradicted the policy review by reiterating that the Rangers could fulfill the requirement for a militia presence in the North and along the East and West Coasts if they were refashioned into primary reservists. The seesawing continued when the DCDS again disagreed. It would cost too much money to convert the Rangers to full militia status, and it would require too many Regular Force personnel to train them to an effective level.[74]

Northern Region and Its Rangers

Without clear direction or funding from Ottawa, Northern Region Headquarters staff could do little but despair of the failure of their grand schemes. They insisted that regular forces who visited the North did not constitute a continuous presence – only Rangers could claim a sustained footprint in remote areas. It therefore fell to regional staff to implement small changes to improve the organization in northern communities. "The Rangers didn't get many resources and they were an oddity to staff" in Ottawa, explained Major David Sproule. Sproule had married Ranger Jake Woolgar's daughter and replaced Major Stirling at Northern Region Headquarters when the latter died suddenly in December 1973. "They continued to exist in spite of seeming disinterest by the army." Sproule credited Bob Lemaire, other staff

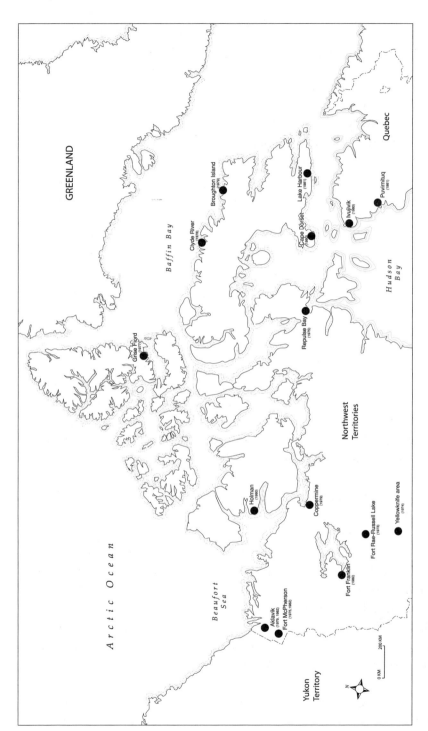

Nanook Ranger exercises in the North, 1973-82

Source: Annual reports of the Department of National Defence and Northern Region Headquarters, 1972-83

officers, and noncommissioned members for the Rangers' survival and success.[75]

In the mid-1970s, Major Lemaire, the senior staff officer (SSO) Rangers and Cadets in Yellowknife, and Command Sergeant Major Bob Clarke planned a series of trial training exercises to prepare Inuit and Dene Rangers for service with the Canadian Arctic Rangers. They had a modest goal: to see how trainees in northern indigenous communities would respond to a basic Canadian Ranger course, which included weapons handling, map reading, patrolling, information reporting, first aid, and ground search methods. The small staff at Northern Region Headquarters conducted the fourteen-day Nanook Ranger exercises in two communities each year. The exercises re-established isolated patrols in the Arctic Archipelago, along the Arctic Coast, and in communities along the Mackenzie River, which in several cases had never received any formal instruction. By 1982, most northern Rangers had received at least basic military training.[76]

Staff officers and Ranger instructors from Yellowknife rebuilt moribund units from the ground up, allowing for innovation and improvement. First and foremost, Northern Region followed through on its plans to replace the old company-platoon structure with localized patrols named after their communities. Patrols, rather than complicated company organizations spanning a broad area, reflected the Arctic's demographic and geographic realities following the nucleation of Aboriginal peoples into permanent settlements. This reorientation affirmed the Rangers' primarily role: to support "sovereignty policies and programmes."[77] In 1948, the army had deleted any territorial identification in company or platoon names "in the interests of security." Numeric designations made sense for combat-oriented units but not for ones demonstrating sovereignty. Community names emphasized the military's presence across the Arctic, which was the primary goal.[78]

The emergence of new forms of community-based leadership provided a stronger basis for Ranger training. Command and control in the North had proven notoriously difficult in earlier years, particularly in regions where the platoon commanders lived in fixed locations, and most of the Rangers followed a seasonal cycle of living on the land. Community-based patrols of ten to twenty Rangers, however, no longer needed Ranger captains and lieutenants. Ranger sergeants commanded patrols, with master corporals as seconds-in-command. Patrol members now elected Rangers to these positions, and Ranger leadership became more reflective of northern communities.[79] "In true Spartan style, squad commanders are appointed

Master Corporal Ted Luscombe *(right)* talks with two members of his patrol, Rangers Simmionie Olayuk and Issac Attaqutsiak from Arctic Bay, during Exercise Nanook Ranger II, 1974. Library and Archives Canada/Department of National Defence collection/R112-536-X-E/Accession 2008-377/Box 114, Photo IEC 74-34-3

according to proxy of rank and file," the Ranger staff in Yellowknife explained to a journalist. "Inevitably, patrol chain of command parallels the community's pecking order."[80] These changes proved "highly popular in small Arctic communities."[81]

Reorganization efforts at the grassroots level laid a viable foundation for future growth. There were only 212 Rangers in Northern Region in July 1976 (compared to 1,006 in Maritime Command),[82] but the organization's northern dimension aligned with national policy, and the federal government's relationship with northern residents assumed a higher profile in the 1970s. Jean Chrétien, the minister of Indian affairs and northern development, announced an integrated northern policy that prioritized the maintenance of Canadian sovereignty and security, the protection of the northern environment, and economic and social development.[83] Defence policy followed suit, recognizing that the North had intrinsic value to Canada as a place rather than simply as a remote space.[84] Northern Region Headquarters' mandate to "serve as a link between [the Canadian Forces] and the northern settlements in which they operate and exercise" obliged military authorities to balance traditional security needs with socially and environmentally responsible programs.[85]

Even commentators who saw little military value in the Rangers acknowledged the positive connection that the group had with northern communities. John Gellner, the editor of *Canadian Defence Quarterly*, asserted that these "native hunters and trapsmen" could "hardly [be called] ... a military organization" but noted the sociopolitical relevance of their presence: "Even if it were not for the regrettable gradual urbanization of the Eskimo (in the sense that they are becoming increasingly dependent on the services provided in industrial society), the military value of the Canadian Rangers would be minimal. The main benefit lies in the ties that membership in the organization forges between the native population and the apparatus of the state, still somewhat foreign to them."[86] At most, he begrudgingly accepted the Rangers' basic usefulness as a nation-building measure.

As the internal complexities of Canadian sovereignty became more apparent, positive relationships with Northern communities grew in importance. Discussions about the proposed Mackenzie Valley Pipeline revealed that the future of the northern frontier would no longer be decided solely in government or corporate boardrooms. When the Indian Brotherhood of the Northwest Territories rallied against the proposed pipeline development because they believed it would harm their homeland and disrupt their livelihoods, the federal government appointed Thomas Berger, a civil and Native rights lawyer, to investigate.[87] The Berger Inquiry heard impassioned speeches from Native witnesses. Frank T'Seleie, the young chief of the Fort Good Hope Band, likened southern oilmen to the Pentagon and General Custer and asserted that he and his people (like the Sioux who had faced off against the Seventh Cavalry in the American West) were prepared to die to defend their lands. Native leaders believed the most immediate danger was not a Soviet nuclear attack or American encroachment: it was southern Canadian businessmen. Berger's final report, *Northern Frontier, Northern Homeland*, recommended that all pipeline development be delayed for ten years until Native land claims were settled.[88]

Deliberations about the future of the Canadian North raised core political questions relating to civilian development, for which the military had little responsibility. When the oil industry decided that the Northwest Passage had no commercial value at that time, the likelihood of a sovereignty challenge declined. The military's practical responsibilities in a region facing nonmilitary threats had been unclear even when sovereignty concerns raged; now that the threat had receded, the rationale for anything more than a symbolic presence weakened. Although planners had indicated earlier in the decade that studies would clarify military needs, in 1978 Major Ron McConnell explained that the Rangers in the North still faced one main problem: "the lack of a clearly defined role and tasks not adapted to the realities of Canada in the 1970's." Nearly everyone said the Rangers could perform a useful military function, but few identified precise tasks:

> During [Ranger] training sessions, a constantly recurring question is "what are we to do? what is our purpose?" The book roles do not go far in convincing the native northerner that he is indeed a valuable member of the Canadian Forces. Though he is dedicated, and immensely loyal to the Crown, he is somewhat suspicious that we come and give him two weeks training, for which he is paid, and then walk away and leave him with a rifle and 300 rounds of ammunition, which we promise to replenish annually.[89]

Why could no one come up with a more formal, practical role?

McConnell suggested ground search and rescue. "The point is constantly made that if a light aircraft is missing, even if only one person is aboard, no expense is spared in trying to locate it, whereas a party of hunters who are overdue from a trip get no attention at all. This, to the natives, is inexplicable and to some degree tied to their perception of 'the white man looks after his own and to hell with the natives.'" McConnell pointed out that formalizing a local supporting role could provide the Rangers with a real purpose: "With the training given to the Rangers, they feel they are ideally suited to taking on the role of search and rescue on the land. We have taught them to read maps and to navigate, to use [high frequency] manpack radios for communication, to select, lay out, and mark a rough airfield for Twin Otter aircraft. If we do not let them use this training, why do we give it to them?" With a minimal budget increase, the Rangers could perform this role in places with few alternatives. If the military simply offered the Ranger the same benefits he had during annual training – fuel, rations, daily pay, rent for his snow machine and komatik, and protection against undue damage to his machine – "this would eliminate the individual's worry over

Rangers standing in front of a military plane, 1970s. Library and Archives Canada/Department of National Defence collection/R112-536-X-E/Accession 2008-377/Box 131, Photo REC 74-378

his family, equipment and well-being if he volunteered to go on a search." The RCMP believed the plan would draw many volunteers. From a government standpoint, the plan would also ensure that indigenous people played a role in northern operations.[90]

McConnell's suggestion seemed eminently sensible, but legalities complicated matters. Although the Rangers, trained to operate as a unit, were indispensable assets for ground search and rescue, the RCMP had primary responsibility to coordinate and undertake these activities.[91] Every year, citizens living in remote communities remained lost because the police lacked sufficient resources to mount sustained searches. Rangers seemed a natural solution: they lived on the land and received navigation and basic first-aid training. Many Rangers also belonged to hunters and trappers associations, which assisted in local ground searches in the North. Local RCMP constables were not authorized to call out the Rangers directly, however, and had to secure official approval from National Defence prior to doing so. In practice, few experienced community members waited around for an official tasking before setting out to find someone who was lost, even if they had to pay for their own gasoline and supplies. Rangers therefore routinely participated in searches, rescues, and recoveries, but they generally did so as unpaid, civilian volunteers rather than as Rangers on official duty. This distinction confused (and continues to confuse) many Rangers, but in emergencies they acted first and foremost as community members, regardless of discrepancies between their practical contributions and official policies.[92]

In general, national policy development moved at a glacial pace. As the decade neared its end, McConnell accepted that Northern Region's earlier revitalization plans were bolder than the department's pockets were deep. It was futile lobbying Ottawa to upgrade the Rangers to full-fledged militia status, given that senior officials would reject any proposal involving additional money. With funds for Regular Force and militia programs in southern Canada severely stretched, Ottawa had nothing extra to devote to the North.[93]

The assistant deputy minister (policy) and the deputy chief of the defence staff group also opposed structural changes on principle. First, a Ranger force would seldom participate in Canadian Forces tasks, making it a low operational priority. Second, individual Rangers already possessed "ample skills for the tasks which the CF wishes them to perform." Third, a more elaborate organization would conflict with northern values and customs. Without a perceived threat, they could not justify investing more resources in the Rangers and redefining or expanding their tasks.[94] The Rangers symbolized Canada's presence in the Arctic, and that sufficed in Ottawa.

Reporters occasionally conjured up scenarios to perpetuate the idea that the Rangers could play a pivotal combat role in defending Canada from foreign aggression. "What if a grim historical pattern repeats itself, global conflict breaks out and the North is threatened by over-the-pole invasion?

Who would stand on guard for us until the arrival of reinforcements from the South?" David Miller asked readers of *News of the North* on 7 November 1979. "The Canadian Rangers, that's who – a rough-and-ready bunch of unsung latter-day heroes, our shadow army of the North and, according to DND military strategists, probably the most cost-effective armed forces in the Canadian military." His overly dramatic depiction raised basic questions. Had the enemy ever threatened Canada with an over-the-pole invasion? Were the Rangers really still expected to "emerge from hamlet and settlement to confront the enemy guerrilla-style until a Canadian vanguard of regulars could mobilize and deploy"?[95]

Overzealous journalism that cast the Rangers as a combat force always missed the mark, but Miller's descriptions of their cost-effectiveness and quiet contribution to sovereignty were more accurate. Readers learned that in twenty-three settlements "scattered thinly across tundra and taiga, a total of 450 Ranger reserves stand as our northern sentinels, maintaining a vigilant eye over our nation's Arctic approaches." Miller perpetuated the Ranger mystique when he described "rugged hunters and trappers" – 90 percent Inuit, Dene, or Metis – all patriotic Canadians and "humble servants of the Queen." Given their background, the military adjusted its behaviour. "You don't order the Rangers out; instead you ask them – and kindly," Captain Sandy McDonald, the operations officer at Northern Region Headquarters, explained to Miller. "And then, you still don't know how many will show up. If it's in the middle of hunting season, they may just say 'bugger-off.' On the other hand, if it's a slow time of the year you may have to beat 'em off with a stick." This dynamic did not worry officers such as McDonald who knew they had no other option to "get troops of that potential – very handy militarily – for the cost of an old .303 rifle and 300 rounds of ammo a year." The Rangers, "a bit of an anachronism," resembled the pre-Confederation militia more than modern reservists, but Captain McDonald's view intended no criticism. He saw the Rangers as patriotic northerners unencumbered by the popular "cynicism" that dominated southern Canadian society. "They believe they're defending their homeland," he insisted. "They're sincerely loyal, like to be associated with the armed forces, and are very proud of it."[96]

Captain McDonald applauded the success of the Rangers' grassroots organization, however unorthodox by military standards. The Alaska Scouts had resembled the Rangers, but McDonald suggested that when American

Cartoonist Edd Uluschak's depiction of a Canadian Ranger, 1979.
Courtesy Edd Uluschak

military authorities decided to convert them into a national guard, "they destroyed them because all they had time for was polishing boots and sending memos." He perceived a similar threat in Canada: over-organization undermining Ranger effectiveness. On the other hand, the erosion of traditional skills in the modern North – "those special talents which make the Rangers so valuable" – also endangered the effectiveness of the organization. Training encouraged the Rangers to exercise their skills. In deciding which direction to take, Miller concluded that Northern Region would have "to juggle this dilemma of organization versus extinction."[97]

By the end of the decade, defence planners had little incentive to do anything because politicians and the public had few concerns about northern sovereignty and security. In March 1979, the minister of national defence noted that "neither the military threat nor the non-military threat to Canada's sovereignty in the North is considered to be significant" and that "Canada's presence in the North seems now to be well established."[98] Ongoing proposals to redefine, restructure, and better equip the Rangers in the North fell on deaf ears.[99] Freezes, squeezes, and cutbacks left National Defence with little room to manoeuvre.[100] The North was out of sight – and out of mind.

Although sovereignty concerns and overall support for most Canadian Forces activities had dissipated, the Ranger support staff in Yellowknife actually benefitted from a modest increase in personnel in the early 1980s. Major John Tattersal, the senior staff officer for Rangers and Cadets, assumed overall responsibility for the Rangers in Northern Region from 1979-82. He built a convincing case for more resources by avoiding grand designs to reconstitute the Rangers as something new. As a result, Ottawa approved the additional support of a master warrant officer and four combat arms sergeants who, as Ranger instructors, conducted liaison resupply and training and maintained records for each patrol.[101]

With additional staff and funding, Northern Region redesigned its Ranger Training Plan to follow a three-year cycle. Each patrol would receive an annual ammunition resupply and liaison visit, and every third year it would participate in a Nanook Ranger field exercise conducted in and around the patrol community. In-town Ranger training included basic drill, first aid, map use, surveillance, and reconnaissance. Advanced training included five days of refresher training and a four- or five-day field-training exercise, which usually involved a long-range patrol. In March 1981, for example, fifteen Rangers went on a 100-mile snowmobile patrol out of Lake Harbour, and in October the Puvirnituq patrol travelled 150-miles by freighter canoe. The Ranger staff devised formal course-training standards on subjects such as first aid, radio messaging, patrolling techniques, basic drill, rifle safety, and map use. The staff in Yellowknife had formerly only been able to conduct two Ranger exercises per year, which meant that it would have taken fifteen years to train each patrol in the region.[102]

The media liked what it saw, particularly when the Rangers worked with the Regular Forces. In September 1981, thirty members of "C" Company, 2nd Battalion Princess Patricia's Canadian Light Infantry (2 PPCLI) underwent four days of survival training with two Inuit Rangers from Resolute Bay. Levi Nungaq, a hunter and carver, and Ludy Pudluk, the local member of the territorial legislation for the High Arctic, dazzled the soldiers with their "amazing Arctic skills." The southern troops overcame their initial horror at the prospect of eating raw seal meat, learned how to build igloos, and watched the Rangers pull "Arctic char out of 12-Mile Lake with ease." As part of the larger Operation Sovereign Viking, these activities (as touted by press reports) helped to establish "a firm military presence of Canadian sovereignty in the Arctic islands."[103] The words *sovereignty* and *presence* became synonymous with the Rangers – even if Canada's legal sovereignty did not depend on a military presence in the Far North.[104]

Sovereignty and symbolism aside, the Rangers increasingly cooperated with the other military units training and operating in the North. In 1983, Ranger activities included the following: support for a Regular Force company during Exercise Kovik Punch in Eskimo Point (Arviat); aid to Canadian Forces Station Inuvik, along with winter survival training in that community and in Fort McPherson; and assistance to the RCMP in the search for a missing person near Cambridge Bay. The Resolute patrol helped Air Command recover fuel drums in Polar Bear Pass, Bathurst Island, while the Pangnirtung and Broughton Island (Qikiqtarjuaq) patrols supported an army cadet Arctic indoctrination course and an adventure-training exercise.[105] "These native men of the land possess special knowledge that cannot be obtained from books or briefings," the annual report on defence noted in 1982. "Most rangers know the land intimately up to 500 kilometres from their homes. They have excellent hunting and fishing skills that can be utilized for survival training. Their uncanny ability to improvise can assist troops in coping with a harsh land."[106]

The Rangers' navigation skills in arduous conditions earned them accolades. In April 1984, northern commander Brigadier Mark Dodd presented Rangers Peter and Johnny Mamgark of Eskimo Point (Arviat) with the Chief of the Defence Staff Commendation for their actions during Exercise Kovick the previous year. "While their deed may not seem extraordinary

The commander of Northern Region presents the Chief of the Defence Staff
Commendation to Rangers Peter and Johnny Mamgark of Eskimo Point (Arviat), NWT,
for guiding a seven-man patrol of soldiers to safety through a blinding blizzard, 1984.
Library and Archives Canada/*Defence 1984*/AMICUS 124800/P.82

by Inuit standards," *News/North* reporter Brian Mitchell noted, "the Canadian military believe the Mamgarks' actions saved the life of one soldier
and contributed to the safe return of an entire patrol." The two Rangers
had guided a seven-soldier patrol to a lake about twelve miles (twenty kilometres) from the main company position when a blizzard stranded the
group. Suffering from the cold and short on rations and food, they decided
to return by skidoo to Eskimo Lake on the sixth day. On the journey, a
soldier was thrown from a sled and struck by a trailing komatik. After administering first aid, the men placed him in a sleeping bag, strapped him
to Peter Mamgark's sled, and took him to the community-nursing station
at high speed. At the same time, Johnny Mamgark's snowmobile broke
down, and he had to guide the rest of the patrol home on foot, in total
darkness. "Their courageous action undoubtedly saved the patrol from
extreme hardship and possible serious injury as weather conditions worsened
the next day," the commendation read. Local residents who filled the community hall for the formal award ceremony saw first-hand how much the
military appreciated northerners' survival skills.[107]

The Rangers' interest could not be taken for granted, however. The number of active patrols remained steady at thirty-six through to 1983, when there were 729 Rangers under the command of Northern Region. The following year, the numbers fell to 627 Rangers in thirty-two patrols. The numbers declined for two reasons. First, some patrols exceeded the thirty-member limit and "had to be brought into line." Second, and perhaps more ominously, Northern Region declared patrols in Aklavik, Inuvik, Iqaluit, and Fort Franklin inactive because of a lack of local interest. The three-year training cycle was not frequent enough; in 1983, more than half of the patrols did not receive training.[108] The Rangers in Northern Region would soon rebound, prompted by new concerns about sovereignty and an activist federal government.

Maritime Command

Like Northern Region's grandiose plans, Maritime Command's 1971 proposal to revitalize Ranger units along the Atlantic and Pacific coasts never came to fruition. Major Bob Bridgeman, responsible for the Rangers in Atlantic Canada, expected to visit Rangers in northern Quebec and Labrador twice annually and those in Newfoundland even more frequently. After his first liaison visits in the early 1970s, he forecast that "in a couple of years the Ranger organization will prove to be a viable force."[109] Maritime Command, however, found itself in a severe budget crisis for the rest of the decade. It cut back on naval and air operations to save fuel, thereby reducing sovereignty and surveillance operations off the Atlantic Coast. Force reductions and morale issues reduced the navy's strength from 17,000 in 1969 to 9,500 in 1978. Operational and budget pressures precluded the commander from refitting or replacing ships, never mind investing in an expanded Canadian Ranger force.[110]

The several hundred Rangers who continued to serve along the Atlantic Coast cost so little that they survived the general cutbacks, but in an era of austerity no new resources emerged for training and operations. Maritime Command listed their coast-watching role low on its priority list. "When the 1971 study resulted in no visible effect on the Rangers," an officer recalled, "the interest generated during the study evaporated to be replaced by acute scepticism ... on the part of the Rangers."[111] Their small budget explained their dilapidated state. Ranger liaison officers, who sometimes carried addi-

Canadian Rangers with the Nain platoon on boat patrol in the 1970s.
Courtesy of 5 Canadian Ranger Patrol Group

tional roles such as provincial warning officer or used the posting as an opportunity to take career courses or attend university, did little to improve the situation. Individual Rangers and platoons still watched over areas not covered by radar station personnel or militia units in Newfoundland and Labrador, but the Atlantic group was nearly dormant from an organizational perspective.[112]

Activity continued only at the community level, fuelled solely by local initiative.[113] Long-serving Rangers maintained direction in some areas. For example, Captain Fred Cox, the officer commanding No. 34 Company in Channel-Port aux Basques, had served continuously since 1950. He had three platoons scattered over 3,000 square kilometres from Stephenville to Rose Blanche, yet he managed to hold frequent meetings with his platoon commanders. At his own expense, he also produced a newsletter for company members and acted as the de facto liaison officer along Newfoundland's west coast. A pillar of the community, Cox achieved the rank of major on

1 September 1979.[114] The first and only Ranger promoted to this rank, Cox served as a rare testament to the continued relevance of those serving along the East Coast.

Former Rangers recall quiet recruitment and local service sustaining the Rangers in this period. Jack Berry, born in Marystown on the south coast of Newfoundland, served with the Royal Canadian Air Force from 1951 to 1965 before he became a public health inspector in Clarenville. Captain Rueben T. Vardy recruited him into the Rangers during an inspection tour in the Random Islands in 1971. "There was not much training at that time," Berry explained. The captain "always promised meetings, but they never took place." Over the next few years, Berry was promoted to corporal and then to sergeant, but he had few duties. This was a common story. Lieutenant Chesley Lilly approached Junior Roberts and eight other men at the Legion in Milltown in 1979 and pushed enlistment papers in front of them. "Stick the rifle in your closet," he told Roberts. "We'll be in touch with you if we need you." No one offered the recruits training or guidance. Austin Adams, a provincial forestry and wildlife enforcement officer, joined because his father-in-law had served with the Rangers from 1962 to 1980. When Vardy signed his papers, he gave Adams "a .303, three boxes of bullets (fifty rounds each), and a box of capelin." They met maybe once a year to discuss promotions and to distribute ammunition. The Rangers felt that the navy, based in distant Halifax, had little interest in or support for what they did.[115]

In contrast to low-keyed persistence in the East, the Rangers along the West Coast atrophied. The Maritime Command plan had not laid out a firm direction for the organization in Pacific Region. Indeed, Pacific Headquarters itself had dissented in 1968 when National Defence Headquarters recommended revitalizing the Rangers. Although regional staff continued to visit Ranger companies on a haphazard basis in the early 1970s, Maritime Command eliminated the BC Ranger liaison officer position in 1973. After that time, planners simply abandoned the Pacific units, with predictable results. By July 1976, Ranger strength in British Columbia had dwindled to thirty-six members. Only the Ocean Falls company met on a regular basis and "perform[ed] community functions along the lines of a service club." The Vanderhoof unit met annually for a social gathering and rifle competition. The commander Pacific region pleaded to Maritime Command to take some action and suggested that "the lack of a viable role, the absence of a full time Ranger LO and the consequent lack of purpose and direction is an embarrassment to the Forces." He recommended reducing the Rangers strength in BC to nil.[116]

Maritime Command took no official action for two years. By May 1978, all Ranger companies in BC lay dormant. This time, when asked to disband them, Ottawa complied. Staff noted that the Rangers had been "studied to death." They agreed with Maritime Command's position, citing an "obvious doubt about the validity of the Rangers – particularly those in the populated areas of the West Coast."[117] No formal announcement eliminated the companies and platoons, but as a gesture of good faith, the former Rangers in BC kept their rifles "as a gift from DND for their personal use."[118] In the province where the Ranger concept had been born during the Second World War, the Rangers were no more.

Maritime Command still retained responsibility for the Rangers in Ungava (northern Quebec), which proved a source of persistent concern for logistical, economic, and political reasons. The relative isolation of the communities made liaison visits difficult, and the military offered little support, even for community-based activities such as search and rescue.[119] When the community-development director in Fort Chimo (Kuujjuaq) suggested that the Ranger sergeants from each northern Quebec community should get together to meet with Department of National Defence representatives to discuss "what they feel they should be doing," Maritime Command rejected the proposal for financial reasons.[120] Inuit who had served with Ranger units south of Puvirnituq grew frustrated when Ranger operations expanded in Northern Region but did not resume in their own area. In 1977, for example, twenty-three former Rangers at Inukjuak requested that an officer visit their community to re-establish their platoon. Maritime Command replied that it had no plans to reactivate dormant units.[121]

Political considerations actually led Maritime Command to scale back its annual resupply to Rangers in northern Quebec that year. In the wake of the Parti Québécois' announcement of Bill 101 (the French Language Charter), tensions built between Inuit residents in the Fort Chimo (Kuujjuaq) area and provincial government officials. When Maritime Command staff expressed concerns about a Ranger liaison officer distributing ammunition to Aboriginal units during a potentially volatile situation, staff officers in Ottawa recommended that he quietly hold off his annual resupply of ammunition until tensions abated.[122] This recommendation did not depart significantly from existing practice because there had been little liaison or

Captain Les Palhazi *(far right)* with Rangers and a military officer in the early 1980s.
Courtesy of 5 Canadian Ranger Patrol Group

resupply in the region. When Maritime Command wanted to relinquish responsibility for the Rangers in northern Quebec, Northern Region agreed to assume control of the units in 1979.[123] The transfer lessened the administrative burden on the Ranger liaison officer in St. John's, who could now focus entirely on Rangers along the Lower North Shore and in Newfoundland and Labrador.[124]

The situation in Atlantic Region improved modestly in the early 1980s, and the growing sense of identity and rising esprit de corps was largely due to the new Ranger liaison officer, Captain Les Palhazi. This young, single infantry officer took over in 1980 and enthusiastically embraced his mandate to revitalize the organization.[125] In 1982-83, for example, he spent 168 days on the road visiting Rangers. He put 21,000 miles (nearly 34,000 kilometres) on his military vehicle and flew to remote areas. He hosted meetings with each platoon every year, often in central areas but also in the homes of section and platoon commanders. They discussed training options, planned local activities, and watched films on the Canadian Forces. Palhazi recognized the Rangers as an informal, grassroots organization, and he focused on social gatherings that maintained local connections.[126]

The Rangers had "official" tasks and those that they performed in reality. Rangers in groups could serve as guides and rescue parties. They also served as "unofficial CF recruiters" because isolated communities had no militia.[127]

They received little to no field training and no pay except during the occasional training seminar. Palhazi explained to a Newfoundland newspaper that the Rangers were not combat soldiers – they were simply points of military contact. "They get together for target shooting and marksmanship as an activity that each of them can take part in, which keeps the unit intact," he explained. "Certainly it's a low-key organization in that they're not perceived as defenders of the country. The Canadian Armed Forces doesn't revolve around the Rangers, but they do perform and serve a useful function."[128]

The training program reflected the Rangers' modest role and mission. Because Palhazi only had a budget of $30,000 to sustain all Ranger activity in Atlantic Canada, he had to be resourceful. He turned to Canadian and US military bases, rod and gun clubs, Legions, fire halls, and hotels to provide meeting rooms and rifle ranges free of charge.[129] Rather than conducting individual platoon training, every two or three years each platoon selected a handful of Rangers to attend group seminars. They had to raise their own money to attend two-to-three-day sessions, during which they acquired general service knowledge. Junior Roberts, recalling one seminar in Argentia, stated, "It ended with a bit of machine gun shooting on the range until an older Ranger lost control [of the gun] and almost killed everyone. So we put an end to that." Because some Rangers appreciated the cheap draft beer on the American base a little too much, the military dealt out the twenty-five dollars for travel and meals at the end of the exercise.[130] The seminars not only served an important instructional function but also "afforded the Canadian Rangers from various areas an excellent opportunity to meet one another," Palhazi explained. "These training seminars in no small way contribute to a rising sense of identity and esprit de corps amongst members of the Canadian Rangers."[131] He did not host a lot of seminars – for example, 110 Rangers from 19 platoon locations attended 4 training seminars in 1982 – but Rangers such as Jack Berry in Clarenville recall happily receiving some direct training for the first time.[132]

The Rangers particularly embraced the rifle-range practice introduced in the early 1980s. In October 1985, Lieutenant John Fennemore Sr. of the St. Anthony platoon told a reporter that although "the act of observing comes natural" to men who live close to the sea, "weapons training is not something that happens every day."[133] The military took marksmanship skills for granted in the North, given the subsistence lifestyle of Inuit and settlers. In Newfoundland, however, it discouraged Rangers from using their rifles

Canadian Rangers in Newfoundland practising their marksmanship skills with the Lee-Enfield .303 rifle on an improvised range in the early 1980s. Photo by Lieutenant Junior Roberts, courtesy of 5 Canadian Ranger Patrol Group

for hunting. "There has been some problem with people using 303s as hunting weapons" a Maritime Command briefing note stated in 1983. "We emphasize that the weapon is used as a training aid – not a hunting weapon – to be fired at organized range practices." Platoon and section commanders instead controlled the ammunition and distributed it only for formal shooting exercises.[134] Junior Roberts reminisced that rifle training in Milltown consisted of stringing balloons along the backstop of the range at the local rod and gun club. "We stopped when we ran out of bullets or balloons." Although Palhazi stated that he wanted to generate friendly competition and teach basic range safety, Rangers received little of the latter. "We don't issue rifles so they can roam the countryside, rifle on their shoulder, defending their communities like some irregular militia," the liaison officer explained to a reporter. Rifle shooting promoted "esprit de corps and is a visible sign that they belong to something."[135]

Although the Rangers in Atlantic Canada invested personal resources in Canada's defence, they received little recognition. When they complained,

Palhazi convinced military authorities to amend the regulations. In May 1982, Rangers became eligible to receive decorations for their military service. Over the next year, officers presented 367 Canadian Forces Decorations (CDs) to Rangers in Maritime Command to recognize at least twelve years of service, 161 First Clasps for at least twenty-two years of service, and 6 Second Clasps for more than thirty-two years of service. They handed out the awards at community gatherings, during group-training activities, or in individual Rangers' homes, events which "helped foster a greater sense of recognition and pride within the organization."[136]

By late 1983, 740 Rangers belonged to 4 companies and 30 platoons in Atlantic region. Because they ranged in age from twenty-five to seventy and from fishermen to trappers to high-paid executives, Palhazi felt that his training regime had to be "more flexible and varied" than North of 60. First, the Rangers were dispersed in groups of three or four per village or outpost. Second, they hailed from three distinct cultures. "The Canadian Rangers of Northern Region are composed almost entirely of native peoples, the Dene and the Inuit, whereas in Maritime Command's area of responsibility there is a far greater diversity of cultural backgrounds within the programme.

A group of Rangers gather at Cartwright, Newfoundland, to receive their Canadian Forces Decorations and clasps. Courtesy of 5 Canadian Ranger Patrol Group

TABLE 7
Comparison of Canadian Rangers in Northern Region and Maritime Command, 1984

	Northern Region	Maritime Command
Canadian Rangers, all ranks (7 March 1984)	661	730
Canadian Rangers support staff		
Officers	1	1
Senior non-commissioned officers	5	0
Budget in support of (1984-85)	$160,000	$31,200
Aircraft available for transport of staff	Yes	No

Source: Capt. L. Palhazi to Staff Officer Regional Operations (SORO), Maritime Command HQ, 16 April 1984, LAC, H-2003-00872-1, box 6, file 1775-1 (Visits).

From the primarily Francophone population of the Lower North Shore of Quebec, to the Inuit of the Labrador Coast, to the Anglophone New-foundlanders, this great divergence of cultures presents great challenges."[137] Although blending the Aboriginal population of the Territorial North into a single category was reductionist, Palhazi's larger point was clear: training had to take into account the culture of individual units.[138]

To find out how the Atlantic Rangers compared to their Arctic counter-parts, Palhazi visited staff in Yellowknife in March 1984, where he discovered striking disparities. Northern Region had a major and five NCOs to support its 661 Rangers, while Palhazi alone administered the entire organization along the East Coast. The Ranger budget in Northern Region was more than five times that of Maritime Command, even though it had fewer Rangers. Furthermore, the Ranger staff in Yellowknife had access to two CC-138 Twin Otter aircraft based in Edmonton, while Captain Palhazi had none what-soever. Unlike the closely co-located units of a typical battalion, Ranger sub-units were dispersed throughout Newfoundland, along the entire Labrador Coast, and Quebec's Lower North Shore. Despite budget and personnel pressures, Palhazi argued, more staff was essential to revitalize and increase the effectiveness of the Rangers in Maritime Command.[139] They had been neglected long enough.

✤ "The vastness of the Arctic makes it impossible for the Armed Forces to do more there than show the Canadian presence," an editorial in the *Globe and Mail* asserted on 23 September 1971.[140] The Rangers might have been a token response to this newfound recognition, but they fit with the growing belief that military activities had to be visible to support sovereignty – or at least to generate public awareness that politicians were doing something in remote regions.[141] The national preoccupation with linking sovereignty to a military presence helped justify the Rangers' revitalization rather than disbandment in the North. As an officially constituted element of the Canadian Forces, the Rangers provided a low-cost military footprint.[142] Whether they (or any other element of the Canadian Forces) offered a reliable operational capability in remote regions did not seem to be particularly important to the federal government or the Canadian public.[143]

The government's focus on symbolism rather than substance throughout the decade ensured that the Rangers remained an informal military organization. Both Northern Region Headquarters and Maritime Command articulated plans to restructure the Rangers into more conventional Regular or Reserve Force units, which they argued would provide more opportunities for residents in remote regions and promote economic and social development. Neither component received the support of officials in Ottawa when it came time to cut cheques. In an era of austerity, the concept of the Rangers as unpaid and lightly equipped volunteers held more appeal than funding something new. The onus to revitalize and sustain Ranger units therefore fell to the regional headquarters. Like the Trudeau administration's whole approach to sovereignty protection, promises to enhance the Rangers proved fleeting.

"Until Canadian sovereignty in the North was an issue, believe you me there was no money for the Rangers," Captain Gordon Foreman of Harrington Harbour later reminisced.[144] The Rangers in Maritime Command enjoyed a modest increase of activity in the early 1980s, but the absence of a clear sovereignty mission along the Atlantic and Pacific coasts meant little public profile for Rangers in Newfoundland and Labrador and led to the demise of the organization in BC during the 1970s. Demographics and politics also conspired against the Rangers South of 60. Inuit occupied northern Quebec and Labrador, but there were no concerns about external threats to Canadian sovereignty in those areas. Non-Native Rangers along the Lower North Shore and the coasts of Newfoundland did not have the same exotic appeal as their northern counterparts and consequently garnered no national media attention.

Ironically, when the Naval Officers Associations of Canada recommended in 1984 that the federal government use the Rangers to bolster Canada's sovereignty claims, it acknowledged the existence of Rangers in the High Arctic but not Maritime Command. This group of mainly Inuit volunteers, the association explained, gave National Defence "a 'friendly' presence in the North among the native people that is the envy of other Government departments" – and at very little cost. The benefits, it suggested, went both ways. The Ranger organization supported positive federal-Inuit relations, and Ranger membership was "looked upon as a status symbol in the community."[145]

By this point, Ranger patrols spanned the breadth of the Arctic, from the most easterly patrol at Broughton Island (Qikiqtarjuaq) to the most westerly patrol at Aklavik. A Northern Region briefing book from the early 1980s trumpeted the Rangers' involvement: "It is significant also that the Ranger concept capitalizes on those attributes of native northerners that they themselves espouse as their traditional way of life – their knowledge of their environment, their ability to live and survive on the land, their hunting instinct. In sharing an important defence commitment, the Canadian Rangers fulfil a role no less important than any other component of the Canadian Armed Forces, and have a justifiable pride in doing so." The new language revealed a new focus: northerners making a contribution to their country. The mystique surrounding their inherent knowledge of the land and natural instincts made them useful participants in the Canadian Forces. New staff at Northern Region learned that the military establishment had only a dim understanding of the Rangers' role within the armed forces, and that role was understood "far less by the populace as a whole. Nevertheless, their contribution to the defence of Canada and maintenance of sovereignty should not be underestimated. Given the circumstances and environment, it is a role that could only be filled by other components of the Forces with very much difficulty and more expense."[146]

The message was positive and hopeful, but it confirmed that the Rangers still suffered from a poorly defined role. Commentators suggested that an active Ranger force could fulfill an important military function, but no one could readily define what that function was. "Over the years, there have been many ideas, concepts and proposals regarding the training, employment and development of the Canadian Rangers," Major S.J. Joudry noted in 1986. "Most of these ideas have attempted to answer the very fundamental question, 'What do we do with the Rangers?'"[147]

Perhaps the question, posed to senior officers, was directed at the wrong level. Soldiers who trained and operated with the Rangers realized the value of their contributions. Following an exercise at Cambridge Bay in January 1984, Captain E.F. Reumiller of the Princess Patricia's Canadian Light Infantry wrote:

> We must remember that the Rangers have a different culture, have worked under arctic conditions for many generations and in order to survive, we must be prepared to accept their advice and assistance.
>
> The Ranger's sense of loyalty is very high and we found that they watched over our well-being. We also learned a great deal from the Rangers by watching them do maintenance on stoves, lanterns, and skidoos. Their methods are quite unorthodox; however, no one blew themselves up and the end result was that the piece of equipment was normally fixed in half the time it would have taken us.
>
> The Eskimos were willing to share their food while on the trail. Several members of the course tried eating pieces of raw frozen caribou covered with hair. It was different, filling and not unlike beef jerky. Eating raw char however, did not sit well with any of the personnel. The Eskimo version of bread (banik) was excellent. We ate over 50 pounds of it in five days. Several people even took some loaves home along with the recipe. The purpose of existing on the native diet was to prove to everyone that we could survive on what was available in the North.[148]

Once again, bannock helped bind the Rangers and the Regular Force, just as it had on Nanook Ranger II a decade before. For soldiers, winter warfare training offered a form of contact with different peoples in what they saw as a hostile environment. "Training in the North is as close to war as we can get," Reumiller reported. "If one doesn't follow the rules then he might not survive – what better incentive for learning than this?" Soldiers found that the Rangers could teach them a great deal about how to survive in their own country, and the army officer insisted that their knowledge should be "'exploited' as much as possible."[149]

8

"The Most Cost-Efficient Program in the Canadian Forces," 1985-93

✤ WHEN MONTREAL *GAZETTE* REPORTER William Marsden visited Resolute Bay and Grise Fiord in the fall of 1985, he painted a disturbing portrait of "essentially artificial communities kept alive by federal government welfare." The region faced deep troubles. Environmentalists had quashed the fur trade, alcohol disrupted social and family life, and "incidents of wife beating and child molesting are so frequent and harsh that a Northwest Territories task force recently stated their numbers are of 'grave proportions.'" Southerners could point to dots on a map and rest well knowing that Canada had a presence in the Far North, but they knew nothing about the isolation and the desperation that existed there.[1]

Against this dismal backdrop, Marsden introduced readers to the Canadian Rangers:

> On the shores of Resolute Bay, beyond a graveyard of rusting snowmobiles, Walter Audla crouches low behind his Honda three-wheeler. His rifle rests against the seat, pointing down a shallow gravel gully toward the figure of a man outlined in black against a white target.
>
> Behind Audla is Barrow Strait, where the U.S. icebreaker Polar Sea passed one month earlier without Canadian consent, sparking renewed political cries to protect Canada's sovereignty ... Audia, bracing against a sub-zero wind sweeping inland off the Northwest Passage, aims, fires and hits the target figure squarely in the chest. He's getting ready for the enemy.

In his uniform, a scarlet baseball cap and armband, Audla stands on guard for thee. Should the Red Army suddenly dash over the ice packs, he and his men – a military reserve unit of 15 Inuit called the Rangers – would probably fire the first shots in anger, if the world wasn't already nuked.

The Rangers, with their .303 rifles, served as "Canada's only permanent military presence in the High Arctic" – a significant consideration in the wake of the *Polar Sea* incident. Although the reporter evoked the image of Rangers battling the Soviets, he perceptively noted that "interest in the Rangers seems to rise and fall according to the latest U.S. ship going through the Northwest Passage." Sixteen years after the *Manhattan* voyages, the *Polar Sea* "initiated a new flurry of recruiting and training sessions." In Resolute Bay, for example, Marsden found that four recruits had joined the Rangers in the previous month alone.[2]

SOON AFTER BRIAN MULRONEY's Conservatives took office, Canadians cried out for a bolder presence in the North. The voyage of the US Coast Guard icebreaker *Polar Sea* through the Northwest Passage in August 1985 was not intended to undermine Canadian sovereignty claims, but it generated such a flurry of media interest that the new government in Ottawa had to re-evaluate Canada's Arctic policies.[3] In September, it announced steps to assert Canada's legal claim by establishing straight baselines around the entire Arctic Archipelago. To show the flag, the Canadian Forces would increase their northern patrol flights and naval activities, thus repackaging military activities that had been ongoing since the 1970s. The government's intention to build a Polar 8 class icebreaker to operate in Arctic waters indicated a definite commitment to asserting Canadian sovereignty.[4]

Joe Clark, the minister of external affairs, made an oft-quoted statement to the House of Commons on 10 September 1985 that directly linked Canadian sovereignty to northern peoples: "Canada is an Arctic nation ... Canada's sovereignty in the Arctic is indivisible. It embraces land, sea and ice ... From time immemorial Canada's Inuit people have used and occupied the ice as they have used and occupied the land ... Full sovereignty is vital to Canada's security. It is vital to the Inuit people. And it is vital to Canada's national identity."[5] The federal government's mobilization of use and historical occupancy to justify its position raised legal, moral, and practical reasons to encourage Inuit participation in defence activities. After all, highly publicized self-government negotiations and statements by Aboriginal leaders received significant exposure in the political arena.[6]

During this era, security and sovereignty discussions became intertwined with the broader themes of militarization and indigenous survival. Low-level flying controversies, persistent environmental concerns, and public appeals by Aboriginal leaders to demilitarize the polar region pushed conventional definitions of national security. George Erasmus, the national chief of the Assembly of First Nations, saw "no *military* threat in the Canadian North," only a threat to the cultural survival of Aboriginal peoples posed by a military buildup. Mary Simon, president of the Inuit Circumpolar Conference, also stressed that military activities "justified by the government on the basis of defence and military considerations ... often serve to promote our *insecurity*." Inuit ties to the environment and a collective social order meant that, for them, "Arctic security includes environmental, economic and cultural, as well as defence, aspects."[7] In short, a holistic strategy would accommodate and accept indigenous peoples' physical welfare, their homeland, and their cultural survival.

What did northern Aboriginal people think about military activities? Kevin McMahon, a Toronto-based writer and filmmaker, spent several months visiting Inuit communities and northern military bases in 1987. His book *Arctic Twilight* emphasized that militarization and its corollaries – technology and bureaucracy – had fundamentally transformed Arctic society. Southern "virtues and vices, machines and organizations, ideals, morals, values and goals" had moved north, overwhelming Inuit. This transnational people had traditionally eschewed conflict. Now, however, they repeated "national propaganda" about the Russians, even though they had trouble distinguishing friend from foe (some Inuit lived in the Soviet Union, after all).[8] McMahon viewed this discourse as painful evidence of their assimilation. Rather than as an expression of patriotism and traditional knowledge, he saw it as evidence of their fading way of life.[9]

McMahon did acknowledge that Aboriginal people who felt uncertain about most military activities unequivocally supported the Rangers. Nonetheless, he remained skeptical about these "cousins to the khaki-clad misfits who gather Saturday mornings in southern cities." What did they actually do? Once annually, "the army came to the village for an exercise and then the men earned $400 for a few easy days on the land teaching soldiers how to build an iglu or skin a seal." Although federal ministers and

Ranger Raymond Mercredi fires his .303 Lee-Enfield rifle during the on-land phase of Exercise Nanook Ranger, November 1988. Library and Archives Canada/Department of National Defence collection/R112-536-X-E/Accession 2008-377, Box 147, Photo ISC88-367

reporters labelled them "sovereignty soldiers," McMahon insisted the Rangers had little understanding of their practical role. "When I asked Rangers what they did, the initial response was always a slightly puzzled look," he reported. A man in Resolute stated that the military "told us at the meeting that if the Queen is asking for help that we are supposed to be involved in that. I'm not too sure." A Ranger in Cambridge Bay suggested that the Rangers were to report "strange people" (Russians) and to protect sovereignty. Even if war was unlikely, the Ranger explained, he and his colleagues took their role "very seriously.... We look after our country here for Canada. And I guess that's what the Rangers are mainly for, for sovereignty." McMahon asked why sovereignty was important to Inuit. "I don't know," the Ranger replied. "Maybe because the Americans are coming into Canada as well and we have to set it up so that we keep it for Canada rather than any other country."[10]

McMahon returned to southern Canada struck by what he considered the nonsensical paradox of the Rangers' perceived role. On the surface, the author had no problem with the government sending money and rifles to the North to "keep up an Arctic brigade of Keystone Kops." He found the broader implications more troubling. "The Inuit are rather more sophisticated than the military would believe," he observed. "They know their creaky old Lee Enfield rifles are really pointed at the Americans. They know, too, that in the interests of patriotism they are bound to support the rhetoric of enemies and war. They are not being paid to actually do anything, but to simply say something which none of them believes."[11] If the logic behind the Rangers conflicted with core Inuit beliefs, as McMahon believed, then participation was inherently destructive.

Inuit spokespersons, politicians, and military officials offered a fundamentally different interpretation of Ranger service. Mark Gordon of Inuit Tapirisat of Canada believed that Inuit had "a valuable contribution to give" to northern security and praised the Canadian Rangers for acting as "the eyes for the Armed Forces." Testifying before a parliamentary committee, he highlighted that the Rangers provided "valuable services to our communities, such as search and rescue." They also "help our communities a great deal in providing us with food." Within the new discourse of Aboriginal autonomy and self-government, Rangers offered the most viable answer to the security paradox: although Inuit needed the military to protect their interests, they could not withstand massive influxes of outsiders and had to be able to "feed [them]selves."[12] In essence, Gordon framed an Inuit version of *defence against help*. In his eyes, the Rangers, "who in most instances are the most experienced and the best hunters of the communities and the most knowledgeable of the area surrounding their communities," facilitated constructive dialogue between the military and local populations.[13]

Other Inuit representatives saw security as a concept that transcended the military and civilian realms. Rhoda Innuksuk, president of the Inuit Tapirisat of Canada, advocated a more inclusive policy-making process, one that would allow for Inuit participation "to minimize the disadvantages and negative impacts of [defence] activity and to maximize the benefits and opportunities it may present." She envisaged a partnership in which the Rangers would offer Inuit an appropriate vehicle to contribute to national defence: "Inuit understand Arctic conditions. National Defence has demonstrated the importance of this fact to Arctic operations by training Canadian troops in Inuit survival techniques and through the Canadian

Ranger program, a program we would like to see expanded. We feel Inuit have more to contribute ... Northerners are different, and different from an operations perspective. This is itself an opportunity for innovation." As active participants and not simply as observers, Inuit could assist the military in protecting Canada's sovereignty and security.[14]

Hearing these enthusiastic appraisals, members of the parliamentary committee on national defence lauded the Rangers in September 1985. The Rangers, they argued, provided a cost-effective military presence and allowed northern residents to play a direct role in defending their country. Dan Heap, social activist and New Democrat, articulated the logic that would guide the future expansion of the Ranger organization. "It is not a matter of the people accommodating the old way of life to the military necessity ... It is a matter of accommodating the military necessity, not to the old way of life but to the people who are here now with some old knowledge and some new knowledge."[15]

Northerners' outspoken support for the Canadian Rangers stood in stark contrast to failed attempts to recruit northern indigenous peoples into the Regular and Primary Reserve Forces. This failure reflected a particular sense of homeland. Community leaders explained to Brigadier-General J.E.L. (Larry) Gollner, the northern commander, that parents and elders simply did not want their youth to go south. "The view they hold of Southern Canada is a cross between Sodom and Detroit, drugs, alcohol problems, social problems, and turmoil being the norm," Gollner observed. "In the native leaders' eyes the youth recruited in the North simply are incapable of coping with the cultural shock associated not only with the CF but with Southern society as such." Retention statistics bore this out – few northerners who signed up for the Regular Force actually served.[16]

By contrast, the Rangers accommodated and reflected the diversity of the North. By 1986, the organization in Northern Region (with a total strength of 642) was 87 percent Inuit and 12 percent Indian. The average age was forty, and the average length of service was twelve years. Only 41 percent spoke some English, while 87 percent spoke Inuktitut and 12 percent spoke an Indian language. "Native leaders and the Rangers themselves have expressed a renewed interest in the program," Major S.J. Joudry commented. "While their motivation and enthusiasm may not be entirely military oriented, it is genuine." Now that Northern Region had amassed "several years of detailed knowledge and extensive exposure" to the Rangers, it could explore options:

Rangers on patrol in Northwest Territories, 1985. Library and Archives Canada/*Defence 1986/* AMICUS 124800/P.76

Moreover, the Ranger staff have established an excellent rapport with the Rangers and are respected visitors to their Native communities. This relationship is only possible because we have distinguished ourselves apart from other "government" agencies in the North. That is not to say that Ranger staff are experts on the North, but the experience and knowledge that they have gained cannot be achieved by brief stops on a [whirl]wind tour of the North. In order to maintain our credibility we must[,] therefore, avoid making judgments and far reaching decisions on such an extremely superficial perception of the North and its aboriginal people.[17]

Northern spokespeople, staff officers, instructors, and the Rangers internalized his message of respect and distinctiveness. Instructors did not enforce orders and rules about punctuality (a central pillar of military life) rigidly because "the hours of the day are not always relevant in the land of the midnight sun. Children play in the streets at two o'clock in the morning, meetings rarely start on time and watches have no place on the traplines." The military tried "to gradually acquaint them with basic military rules," but it had modest expectations. Captain Bob Gauthier, the officer in charge of the Rangers at Northern Region Headquarters, explained that the chief threat to the Rangers was Aboriginal people's abandoning hunting and trapping for wage employment. The military encouraged traditional pursuits because "as the traditional native lifestyle dies out, the usefulness of the Rangers diminishes."[18]

Serving as eyes and ears in and around their home communities allowed the Rangers to provide military intelligence. But did they provide relevant information? "For detection of cruise missiles, I don't think the Inuit Rangers would be that effective," a Yellowknife businessman told the parliamentary committee.[19] He missed the point, but offered a typical description of Rangers facing off against a modern military foe. Commentators continued to describe the Rangers as home defence forces ready to take on Russian paratroopers. Christopher Wren wrote in the *Globe and Mail,* "If an enemy ever sweeps down to invade North America, it will have to contend with the Ikkidluak brothers and their bolt-action rifles." He reassured readers that Lake Harbour (Kimmirut) residents Iola and Lucassie Ikkidluak, with their Ranger armbands and ball caps, were well suited to their role. Although Wren admitted that the Rangers would not likely have to repel a Soviet invasion, he recognized the need for a continuous military presence. After all, just six months before, the Kangiqsujuaq Rangers had reported a submarine in Hudson Strait.[20]

Rangers actually reported several submarine sightings in the mid-1980s. On 26 July 1983, two "Native girls" from Broughton Island spotted two men wearing orange toques and brown uniforms on the deck of a submarine before it submerged and moved out into Davis Strait. In September 1985, Ranger Master Corporal Lukasie Naapaluk reported the sighting of a large wake, "as large as the icebreaker which serves that area," and bubbles moving into Wakeham Bay. One year later, two Inuit fishers passed on separate sightings of a vessel "larger than a whale" with a large mast and "mirrors" near Arctic Bay. During the summer of 1987, a group of hunters watched a submarine surface in Akimski Strait (James Bay) and called out to the men on its deck, while Rangers at Coppermine (Kugluktuk) identified two submarines.[21] Sergeant Clarence Rufus of Tuktoyaktuk recounted how, upon seeing a strange object in water, "one Ranger asked if it was a whale. The other guy said, 'if that's a whale it's got a guy walking down its back.'"[22] Without Canadian submarines or subsurface sensors to detect foreign incursions into the country's Arctic waters, the Rangers fulfilled an important surveillance role in the North.

By the mid-1980s, the Rangers had also established their value to Regular and Reserve Force field operations. "We don't permit any army training north of 60 without Ranger involvement," Brigadier John Hayter explained.[23] In 1985, for example, Rangers supported twelve military exercises as guides, advisers, and instructors in northern survival skills. In February, they participated in a company-level field-training exercise with B Company, 1 Royal Canadian Regiment, in Baker Lake. That summer, Rangers supported a cadet indoctrination course in Pangnirtung and adventure-training exercises with members of the regiment on King William Island and on the Mackenzie River from Norman Wells to Tuktoyaktuk.[24] The following year, eight Rangers from Lake Harbour supported a French Army winter-training exercise near Frobisher Bay; sixteen Rangers from Broughton Island taught Arctic survival to members of the regiment near their community; and ten Rangers from Holman Island supported more than one hundred militia personnel from Nova Scotia on a northern sovereignty exercise.[25]

Southern troops who ventured north remarked on the Rangers' capabilities. When "G" Company, Second Battalion, Royal Canadian Regiment (based in Gagetown, New Brunswick), went to north Baffin Island with members of the Arctic Bay patrol on Royal Hiker '87, they raved about their local guides and teachers. Corporal John Thompson was impressed with the Rangers' ability to operate when it was minus thirty-five degrees Celsius or lower with the wind chill. Soldiers camped in tents, but the Rangers found them too cold and preferred "traditional technology" – their own igloo. The Rangers did not allow the troops to shoot game, but they taught them techniques and allowed them to butcher and eat the meat. Southerners found the Rangers friendly and learned a lot from them. "They're very intelligent – they definitely know how to survive," twenty-one-year-old Private Nick Corbett commented, "and they're teaching us the tricks of the trade."[26]

To enhance its competency in the Arctic, the military hatched training scenarios that saw the Rangers contribute to large-scale exercises. Exercise Lightning Strike '87 involved more than three hundred troops, airmen, and Rangers. The sixteen-day exercise involved hundreds of flying missions, airborne assaults at Cape Dyer and Cape Dorset, and the "fortification" of Iqaluit (Frobisher Bay) as a forward operating base. Northerners did not view the exercise as intrusive because local Rangers participated. "Sovereignty is a matter of deep concern to us," Iqaluit mayor Andy Theriault explained. "We've been wondering when people 'south of 60' are going to wake up." Jim Bell, the editor of *Nunatsiaq News,* stressed that Inuit believed that their presence protected sovereignty and therefore needed to be recognized. The military agreed and encouraged the army to integrate communities into

Rangers from Cape Dorset pose with Regular Force soldiers during Exercise Lightning Strike, 1987. Courtesy of 1 Canadian Rangers Patrol Group

their activities. "It used to be that we would just show up, disappear in the bush for our exercises and then when we were finished, fly out," Brigadier Kent Foster explained. "Now, a major objective is to see how well we integrate; we want our presence felt but we don't want to disrupt the lifestyle."[27] The armed forces did not simply have an outsider-insider relationship with northerners because the Rangers bridged the military and civilian worlds.

These exercises supported the government's promise to affirm Canadian sovereignty with an increased military presence in the Arctic. How exactly the Rangers fit within this strategic agenda, which emphasized air and naval capabilities, remained unclear. Vice Admiral Nigel Brodeur, the deputy chief of the defence staff, commended the 638 Canadian Rangers in the Territorial North when he appeared before the Standing Committee on National Defence:

> Having observed them first-hand, it is remarkable: the talents they have for survival on the land, the ability they have to transmit this knowledge and information to our military people, and the very close co-operation that exists between them, the pride the Canadian Rangers take in their

job. I believe we are really using them in a most effective manner. As you are probably aware, it is the communities whose advice is sought as to whether they wish to establish a Ranger unit, and it is the community whose advice is sought as to who should be the leader of that unit. It is not a decision we impose in the north, nor a decision that the Commander, Northern Region Headquarters, imposes on them.

The chair of the committee remained skeptical about whether these "peace-time militiamen" could play more than a limited role given their small numbers and wide dispersal, but Brodeur dismissed his proposal to incorporate the Rangers into the Regular Force. The military used the Rangers "to the maximum limit of the effectiveness they have at this time," Brodeur insisted, and he had no intention of recasting them into typical soldiers. The separate question of whether the military should create militia units (Primary Reservists) in the North unnecessarily confused discussions about the Rangers and their role in remote regions.[28]

The 1987 white paper on defence, *Challenge and Commitment*, exuded Cold War rhetoric. Although Mikhail Gorbachev, in his Murmansk Speech that same year, called for making the Arctic a "zone of peace," the Canadian government's defence policy statement stressed the Soviet Union's military buildup over the previous decade and its intent to weaken Western democracies. The white paper identified a military "commitment-capability gap" that required extensive funds to modernize equipment and obtain new weapons, including long-range patrol aircraft, nuclear-powered attack submarines capable of operating under the polar ice, and fixed sonar arrays to detect submarines. The government pledged to upgrade airfields at forward operating locations in the North and to contribute $760 million to modernize the North American Aerospace Defence Command (NORAD) and construct the North Warning System to replace the antiquated DEW Line. Sovereignty and territorial defence required "appropriate land forces to demonstrate presence, authority, and effective defence within Canada in peace time and to defend against incursions and sabotage in war." The Primary Reserves and the Rangers had to grow. The white paper stated that the Rangers' "significance as a surveillance force and as a visible expression of Canadian sovereignty in the North requires its expansion and an improvement in the equipment, training and support it receives."[29]

Bolstered by Aboriginal support and national defence policy, politicians and senior officers touted the Rangers' contributions. "In a part of the country where the federal government spends $1.5 billion a year, the Ranger program has a $210,000 budget," a reporter noted in 1987.[30] Brigadier John Hayter, the commander of Northern Region, referred to the Rangers as the "most cost-efficient program in the Canadian Armed Forces."[31] Perrin Beatty, the minister of national defence, also committed to improving the force. He not only deemed the Rangers "an important expression of sovereignty," he also anticipated an increased role for them as military activities expanded in the region.[32] The standing committee on national defence concurred and reported in 1988 that Rangers would receive new rifles and communications equipment. It expected the number of Rangers in the region to rise to one thousand by 1995 with new patrols in several communities.[33] Political support paved the way for this growth.

The Rangers expanded more rapidly than expected. In the late 1980s, Igloolik, Baker Lake (Qamani'tuaq), Behchoko (Rae-Edzo), Tuktoyaktuk, Paulatuk, Sachs Harbour (Ikaahuk), Sanikiluaq, Chesterfield Inlet (Igluligaarjuk), Whale Cove (Tikiraqjuaq), and Pelly Bay (Kugaaruk) gained new patrols.[34] Tellingly, the standing committee report did not mention the Rangers in Atlantic Region, even though they were more numerous and

TABLE 8
Ranger strengths, 1981-90

Year	Northern Region		Atlantic Region	
	Patrols	Rangers	Platoons	Rangers
1981	29	600	30	750
1982	32	658	30	750
1983	36	729	30	750
1984	32	627	31	730
1985	32	620	31	730
1986	33	632	31	810
1987	37	707	31	950
1988	40	758	31	950
1989	43	846	31	990
1990	45	987	31	950

Sources: Department of National Defence annual report *Defence* 1981, 34, 84, 86; *Defence* 1982, 21, 57; *Defence* 1983, 29; *Defence* 1984, 37; Defence 1985, 37, 83; *Defence* 1986, 26; *Defence* 1987, 37; *Defence* 1988, 37, 76; *Defence* 1989, 34; *Defence* 90, 27, 65; Northern Region headquarters (NRHQ) annual reports, 1982, 4; 1983, 4; 1984, 5; 1985, 6; 1986, 7; 1987, 5; 1988, 5; 1989, 5. NRHQ annual report statistics are used for the Northern Rangers from 1982 to 1993 and Atlantic Rangers numbers from 1981 to 1990 are based upon DND annual reports as Maritime Command reports are not available for this period.

operated on a budget less than one-third that of Northern Region. There were no sovereignty concerns along the Eastern Seaboard and thus no national attention.

The Rangers in Atlantic Region

In the 1980s, Rangers continued to be spread throughout outport Newfoundland, Labrador, and the Lower North Shore and boasted higher numbers than the organization in the Territorial North. When Captain Palhazi handed over liaison officer responsibilities to Captain Jan Kwasniewski in mid-August 1985, he left the Rangers in much better shape than they had been a decade before. In 1985-86, for example, 134 new members joined, and places such as Terra Nova National Park, Churchill Falls, and Wabush gained platoons.[35] Platoons recruited and supported cadet activities in Newfoundland, and they sought more training in practical subjects such as map and compass reading, communications, first aid, marksmanship, and naval vessel identification.[36] Kwasniewski believed that more staff and an increased budget would help to improve the Maritime Command training program, which in his assessment stood about three years behind the Northern Rangers' program.[37]

In May 1986, Major-General R.W. Lewis, the chief of reserves, visited ten of the thirty-one Ranger patrols in Newfoundland and Labrador to elicit their advice on how to improve the organization. He applauded the close integration of the Rangers, Cadets, and Legion in the outports and how the Rangers injected "a highly visible military presence in the life of the communities," keeping alive an "appreciation of things military." He also found that the Rangers had an impressive skill set:

> While it is true that the popular image of Rangers as rugged and silent fishermen, trappers and hunters is correct in some areas visited, these Rangers also count highly qualified technicians and professional people in their ranks. Examples of this talent include ten pilots, twenty-one longliner operators, twelve radio operators (ham), doctors and heavy equipment operators, most long-standing residents with extensive bush experience. There are usually several members in each platoon with former CF experience. Waiting lists for enrolment are high, particularly in the more built-up areas where no Militia exists and general dedication within the ranks is extremely good.

The Bonavista platoon, circa 1990. Photo by Sergeant Cyril Abbott, courtesy of 5 Canadian
Ranger Patrol Group

Lewis noted that most Ranger platoons met voluntarily twice a month – an
obvious show of enthusiasm. The public, however, remained unaware of
the force's quiet dedication along the Atlantic Coast, and he urged a proactive
publicity campaign to enhance their image as the "perfect example of the
citizen soldier."[38]

Finances limited what regional officials could reasonably accomplish.
The Atlantic Region in 1986-87 had a meagre Ranger budget of $75,000.
General Lewis recommended that the Department of National Defence
double or triple this amount. Although the Rangers remained quite content
with their baseball cap, armband, and lapel pin, they told Lewis that they
wanted rank badges and plastic nametags for social gatherings and seminars.
Similarly, "with the exception of some very articulate and enthusiastic
weapons collectors," most seemed to be satisfied with the .303 Lee-Enfield
rifle. Lewis's final appraisal was glowing: "in their character, qualifications
and enthusiasm, I consider them to represent the best of our Reserve Force
in Canada."[39] The chief of reserves harboured no doubts about their value.

It was a time of transition in Atlantic Region. Long-standing Rangers such as Major Frederick M. Cox, awarded the Order of Military Merit for thirty-five years continuous Ranger service in 1985, were retiring.[40] As members of the new generation took their place, they injected companies and platoons with fresh ideas and energy.[41] When Cyril Abbott – who had served with the Regular Force in Germany and Cyprus and then as a training adviser for the Royal Newfoundland Regiment – retired to his hometown of Bonavista, Captain Burt Dunn asked him to become a Ranger section commander. Because Abbott enjoyed outdoor activities and felt he could contribute to training, he joined in 1985. He commanded up to a dozen men, some of whom had been Rangers for a long time (Phil Dunham, for instance, retired at age eighty). The Rangers received no annual training – just occasional day shoots at the local range. Ranger instructors visited only sporadically, so Abbott took it upon himself to train the men. The Rangers still did not receive any pay (only money for bulk meals), he explained, but they did not care – they simply enjoyed the training.[42] About three-quarters of the men attended on average, and Abbott's monthly training plan, the first of its kind, drew accolades from regional military staff.[43]

By 1989, the department's annual report boasted that "each unit seems to have reached the ideal balance of youthful vigor and mature experience."[44] While local leaders such as Abbott showed initiative and kept their units active, Captain Kwasniewski overhauled the training regimen. He changed the traditional liaison visit to more closely resemble Northern Region's approach to community-based training. Kwasniewski expected the local commanders to hold monthly platoon meetings that followed regional-training directives and course standards developed by himself. Instead of cost-intensive seminars that gathered Rangers in a centralized location, the liaison officer or another instructor would visit and conduct classroom training at a motel in local communities. Map and compass lessons led to brief trips onto the land to test skills.[45] Each company also held a paid, two-day training exercise each year; this was the first pay that Rangers in Maritime Command received. These exercises exposed roughly one-quarter of the Rangers in Atlantic Area each year to military equipment, modular tents, field kitchens, communications, and army patrolling techniques.[46] As liaison officer, Kwasniewski sought to organize Atlantic region into functional subunits. His successor, Captain Anthony Lynch, followed the same strategy.

In many units, the new training program and concentrated field training "led to an upswing in unit morale and efficiency."[47] In other cases, Ranger

A Ranger loading caribou along the trail, Postville, Labrador. Photo by Sergeant Cyril Abbott, courtesy of 5 Canadian Ranger Patrol Group

leaders expressed concern about the new approach. Although local commanders had dispensed guns and ammunition to platoon members over the years, the new structure placed more responsibility on their shoulders. The Rangers "feel like recruits," Captain Garland (Harry) Martin, the officer commanding No. 22 Company (South Labrador), complained in 1989. He threatened to resign if officials forced the Rangers to clean and present their twenty-year-old weapons for formal inspection. He also worried about rising expectations associated with classroom training. Illiteracy was an issue for many of his Rangers who had dedicated a lot of time to their units and were proven assets. A written test would not reflect their practical abilities. The liaison officer explained that the delivery of course content remained flexible, and Rangers could take an oral examination instead.[48]

The new Ranger training program allowed local leaders to take the initiative. Platoon commanders submitted annual training plans to their company commander, who in turn forwarded them to the liaison officer for approval.[49] As long as budgets remained modest, he usually approved local plans for field training and patrolling. In March 1988, for example, six Rangers from the Churchill Falls platoon planned a trip by snowmobile to Lobstick Lake about thirty kilometres outside the community. They set up a range, fired four hundred rounds of ammunition, and supplemented military rations with midnight snacks of ptarmigan stew and caribou steaks.[50] Grassroots exercises such as this built morale and also provided Rangers with a stronger sense of purpose.

Training outside units also became more common in the mid-1980s, particularly when the renewed Cold War sparked national and international interest in the airbase at Goose Bay. Although the vigorous debate between Innu and the military over low-level flight training divided Labradorians (and Canadians more generally),[51] local Rangers benefitted from the increased activity. Five members of the newly created Goose Bay platoon assisted the Special Service Force during Exercise Lightning Strike, conducted in southern Labrador in January 1986. The force expected the Rangers to act simply as guides, but when the commander recognized their skills, he used one as his adviser and the others in tasks that ranged from security in platoon and section areas to conducting an ice reconnaissance for helicopter landings. During the exercise debriefing, Special Service Force officers, obviously impressed, noted that the Rangers could provide excellent winter survival training to Regular Force members.[52]

From this point onward, the Rangers in Goose Bay found regular employment as guides and scouts for Canadian and allied fighter pilots who needed survival training in case they crashed in a remote northern area. Joe Anderson, who joined the platoon in January 1987, was well-established in the community: his family had moved there in 1958, and he worked as a kitchen-equipment mechanic at the base. In winter, the Rangers would take airmen or soldiers out on the land to teach them how to build snow houses and lean-tos, how to hunt and fish, and how to determine when it was safe to travel. In summer, they showed them how to make temporary shelters, select berries safe to eat, and snare and prepare game. "The soldiers came back year after year," Anderson recalled. British paratroopers would employ twenty-five Rangers for three to four weeks to meet them on the ground after they dropped from the planes. Over the years, the Rangers taught survival training to American, British, German, and Dutch special forces, and they always received high praise for their assistance and expertise. Indeed, by the mid-1990s, the base commander decreed that any foreign personnel leaving the base needed a Ranger escort to go out onto the land.[53]

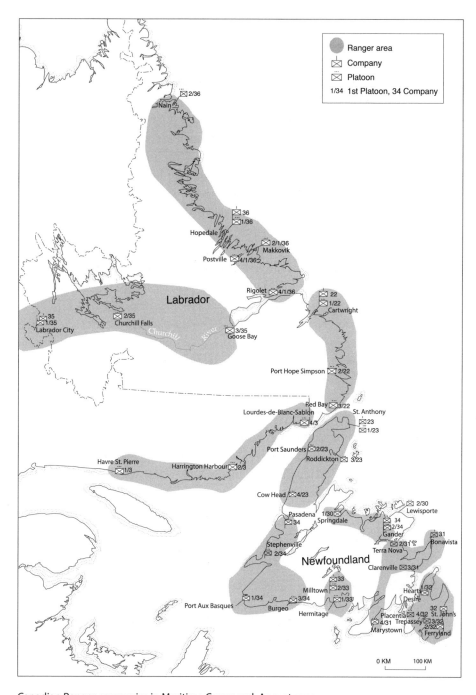

Canadian Ranger companies in Maritime Command, August 1991

The Rangers applied their expertise to new operational tasks such as security patrols of unmanned North Warning System sites. When Canada and the United States modernized the continental radar network in the 1980s, they commissioned new long-range radar stations at Cartwright and Saglek along the Labrador coast. Once completed, Maritime Command turned to the Rangers to monitor each site. Lieutenant Harry Martin of the Cartwright patrol, a full-time wildlife officer, explained that the LAB-6 station was located twenty-six kilometres from town in a prime hunting area. The new access road attracted hunters and trappers as well as people gathering firewood and winter picnickers. To deter local scavengers, Rangers from the Cartwright platoon kept watch on weekends and random weekdays. Saglek, located 270 kilometres north of Nain, was less accessible, but Rangers from the Nain platoon conducted winter exercises in the area to watch over the site.[54] These activities gave Rangers opportunities to test their land skills while reducing the need for expensive Canadian Forces overflights and contracted surveillance of the North Warning System.

In contrast to Northern Region, Atlantic Region favoured training and effectiveness over expansion.[55] Instead of lobbying for more units, officials relocated platoon headquarters to provide more comprehensive coverage of coastal areas and "important interior locations."[56] Training prepared Rangers for situations they would likely encounter. The platoon in Terra Nova National Park, for example, would likely assist in search and rescue, so it received training in first aid, CPR, and search and rescue. The Rangers in Gander and Placentia could be called on to help defend Canadian Forces and US naval bases, and the platoons in Milltown and Churchill Falls could play a similar role securing the safety of their local power plants. Dealing with these combat scenarios would require tactical military training.[57]

Revisiting the Rangers' Role, Mission, and Tasks

The idea of employing Rangers in local defence schemes intersected with the persistent question of whether the Rangers should have a stronger combat orientation. In the late 1980s, the Regular Force and Reserve Force had too many commitments abroad, and the Rangers had proven themselves as a popular and inexpensive resource at home. Major David Iley, a strong supporter of the Rangers in Atlantic Area working on the reserve staff in Ottawa, recommended a spate of new roles to augment the Rangers' military

On guard for Canada. Canadian Rangers Gary Kukilukk, Calvin Pedersen, and Eric Hitkolok from the Kugluktuk patrol at Lake Aptalok, Nunavut, 2001. Canadian Forces Combat Camera, Photo ISD01-6302a

The many faces of the Canadian Rangers.
Left to right: Rangers Katherine Wesley, George Edwards, and Maggie Sutherland during Exercise Trillium Response 12 in northern Ontario, March 2012. Photo by Sergeant Peter Moon, courtesy of 3 Canadian Ranger Patrol Group

Rangers on a multi-patrol exercise on Mount Moresby, June 2002.
Front row, left to right: Warrant Officer Dan Hryhoryshen (instructor), Ranger Laurel MacNeil, Warrant Officer Pete Malcolm (instructor). *Back row, left to right:* Rangers Peter Grundman, Dave Blanchette, Larry Hamilton, and Monty Cobbs. Courtesy of 4 Canadian Ranger Patrol Group

Unity in diversity.
Canadian Rangers on
Exercise Northern Bison
near Churchill, Manitoba,
2011. Courtesy of 4 Canadian
Ranger Patrol Group

Ranger Quara Amamatuaq,
Puvirnituq patrol, 2011.
Photo by Captain Francis
Arsenault, courtesy of
2 Canadian Ranger Patrol Group

◄ **Subject matter experts in their homelands.**

Top: Ranger Caleb Sangoya of the Pond Inlet patrol discusses local terrain with Corporal Amy Taylor on Bylot Island during Operation Nanook, August 2010. Photo by P. Whitney Lackenbauer

Bottom: Ranger Ronald Minoza of the Fort Simpson patrol shows Corporal Devon Kidd how to set a snare during Operation Narwhal, 19 April 2007. Canadian Forces Combat Camera, Photo IS2007-0095

Left to right: Sergeant James Vogl of the Algonquin Regiment and Master Warrant Officer Mitchell Hepburn of Princess of Wales' Own Regiment learn how to filet freshly caught cod from Canadian Ranger Louie Qimirpik near Kimmirut, Nunavut, August 2008. Department of National Defence, Photo ISX2008-0015

Navigating local land and seascapes.

Top: Rangers Hendley Angel, Marvin Rogers, and Kevin Chaulk from the Cape Freels patrol on tracker training along the Newfoundland coast, November 2008.   Photo by P. Whitney Lackenbauer

Bottom: Rangers from the Nain patrol *(right to left)* Levi Nochasak, Kristopher Shiwak, and Joe Atsatata trace map routes in northern Labrador with Ranger instructor Sergeant Mike Rude, September 2012.   Photo by P. Whitney Lackenbauer

A reflective moment on the trail in British Columbia. Courtesy of 4 Canadian Ranger Patrol Group

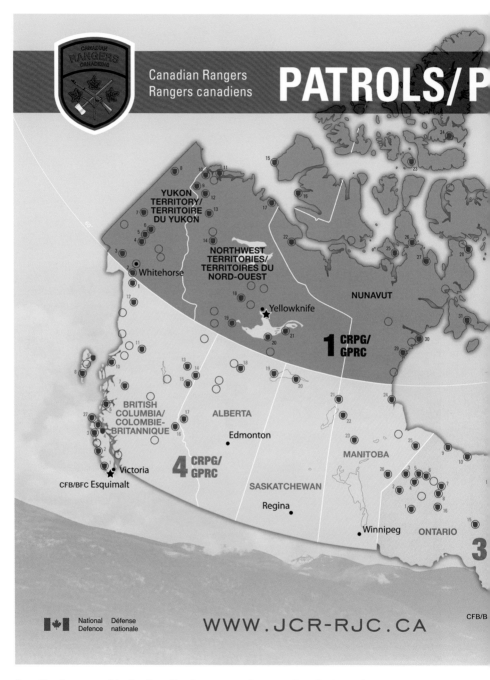

Canadian Ranger and Junior Canadian Ranger patrols across Canada, December 2010.
Courtesy of Canadian Rangers National Authority

ROUILLES

Junior Canadian Rangers
Rangers juniors canadiens

★ CRPG HQ/NDHQ – GPRC QG/QG DN

● Capital / Capitale

○ **170** Canadian Rangers Patrols /
Patrouille de Rangers canadiens

4,394 Canadian Rangers /
Rangers canadiens

▮ **123** Junior Canadian Rangers Patrols /
Patrouille de Rangers juniors canadiens

3,463 Junior Canadian Rangers /
Rangers juniors canadiens

CRPG/GPRC	1	2	3	4	5
patrols JCR/patrouilles RJC	37	29	16	27	14
JCR/RJC	971	778	642	622	450

Iqaluit

5 CRPG/GPRC
NEWFOUNDLAND
& LABRADOR/
TERRE-NEUVE-
ET-LABRADOR

CFB/BFC Gander

Saint John's

2 CRPG/GPRC

QUEBEC/
QUÉBEC

PEI/Î.-P.-É.
● Charlottetown

N.B./N.-B.
● Fredericton

Québec ●
● Halifax
N.S./N.-É.

★ Ottawa
St-Jean-
sur-Richelieu

★
● Toronto

Canadä

Dec 2016-12-01 1:36 p.m.   ADM(PA) DPAPS CS08-0500

Sharing traditional knowledge.

Ranger Sergeant Mark Haongak *(foreground)* and Ranger Andy Kaotalok *(background)* from the Cambridge Bay patrol build a snow-house (igloo) during a sovereignty operation in the Augustus Hills, Nunavut, March 2006.
Canadian Forces Combat Camera, Photo AS2006-0201a

Ranger David Nasogaluak (right) teaches Ranger Kevin St. Amand traditional Inuit string games, January 2009.
Photo by P. Whitney Lackenbauer

Canadian Rangers from across northern Ontario, joined by other military personnel, form a giant circle around a fire during a sunrise ceremony observing Aboriginal Veterans Day in November 2012. Photo by Sergeant Peter Moon

Junior Ranger David Kawapit at Camp Okpiapik, 2011. Photo by Captain Francis Arsenault, courtesy of 2 Canadian Ranger Patrol Group

Showing the flag for Canada.

Right: Operation Nunalivut, April 2012. Canadian Forces Combat Camera, Photo IS2012-3006-04

Bottom: On the Labrador Sea ice between Postville and Hopedale, Labrador, February 2005. Photo by Captain Terry Stead, author's collection

The voice of Canada's remote regions. ▶

Top: Rangers Alexandria Elanik *(left)* and John Jerome *(centre)* meet with Danish Rear Admiral Hendrik Kudsk during Operation Nanook in Inuvik, August 2012. Canadian Forces Combat Camera, Photo CC-2012-0815-001

Bottom: Mourning the tragedy of First Air flight 6560, which crashed in Resolute Bay, Nunavut, in August 2011. Rangers carry a memorial wreath with the Rt. Hon. Stephen Harper, prime minister of Canada. Courtesy of Office of the Prime Minister

Providing predator control against polar bears during Operation Nanook 2010. *Left to right:*
Ranger Pauloosie (Paul) Atagootak, Uluriak (Star) Amarualik, and Caleb Sangoya. Canadian
Forces Combat Camera, Photo 10-0542

Master Corporal Albert George Duncan of Muskrat Dam First Nation in northern Ontario shows Junior Canadian Rangers how to snare a snowshoe rabbit, February 2010. Photo by Sergeant Peter Moon, courtesy of 3 Canadian Ranger Patrol Group

Ranger Pierre Bernier and Junior Ranger Kyle Dettanikeaze of the Lac Brochet patrol during Exercise Western Spirit in northern Manitoba, March 2009. Photo by P. Whitney Lackenbauer

Canadian Ranger George Munick from Tasiujaq navigates through difficult ice during an annual twelve-day training exercise in Nunavik on 28 February 2012. Photo by Captain Francis Arsenault, courtesy of 2 Canadian Ranger Patrol Group

capabilities. He modelled the proposed Territorial Defence Regiments on Australia's North-West Mobile Force (NORFORCE), an infantry reserve regiment formed in 1981 and drawn from local indigenous communities throughout northern Australia. Iley argued that a more formal military organization, one with army-oriented training, would befit the Rangers who saw themselves as a "quasi-military, guerrilla force" employed in home-land defence that freed up other soldiers for international deployments. Rather than supporting a separate program to "accommodate the natives in the form of a flag waving and sovereignty exercise," he outlined a nation-wide organization that would extend into nearly every small, isolated community, beginning with British Columbia.[58]

Iley's proposal, which resembled ideas that had circulated in Northern Region in the 1970s, was passed over in Ottawa.[59] Lieutenant-Colonel John Tattersal, who had been the senior staff officer responsible for the Rangers in Northern Region from 1979 to 1982, argued that the draft strategy would perpetuate misconceptions about the Rangers' purpose and their capabilities. He believed that the Rangers' relevancy had waned as enemy incursions into remote regions became less likely and as technology allowed soldiers to navigate with greater ease. Furthermore, the Canadian Forces' long-standing ambivalence towards the Rangers had left them with no national standards or guiding policy. Regional headquarters determined "what local traffic will bear," and Tattersal cautioned that a broad territorial defence concept could never accommodate their diversity.[60] In his assessment, bold enhancement plans exceeded the Rangers' mandate, which was neither desirable nor plausible.

Other defence planners were receptive to simply expanding the existing organization into new areas. This prompted questions about where the Rangers should concentrate their efforts: the North, the east and west coasts, or the interiors of the provinces?[61] Did plans to expand south contravene the 1987 white paper, which emphasized the Rangers' significance "as a visible expression of Canadian sovereignty in the North"?[62] Planners also raised the classic debate about whether Ranger expansion in the provinces would overlap or compete with the Primary Reserve and wondered whether the public would react negatively to the military issuing "rifles and ammunition to additional special segments of society."[63] These concerns notwithstanding, sparsely populated areas along the West Coast represented an obvious gap in domestic defence.

The Rangers Return to British Columbia

A decade after the last Ranger unit had disbanded in BC, Lieutenant-Colonel Mike Gentles, the director of regional operations in Pacific Region, proposed their re-establishment. "The Canadian Ranger programme in both Atlantic and Northern Region is prospering," he observed in February 1988. Although each region had adopted different organizational and training philosophies, planners could draw upon their successes to re-create a viable Ranger organization along the West Coast.[64] "The greater part of Pacific Region is devoid of any military presence," a staff report from Maritime Forces Pacific noted. Primary Reserve units were confined to larger, southern cities, and the closure of the Canadian Forces stations at Baldy Hughes and Kamloops had removed all Regular Force personnel from the Mainland "North of 50." Rangers could, consequently, play a vital role. "The popular image of the Ranger as the rugged, silent fisherman, trapper or hunter is applicable in some of the more isolated regions," the report suggested. Aboriginal peoples would form the bulk of the Ranger force in northern areas, and "highly qualified technicians and professionals" would likely enlist in southern communities along the Coast. Pacific Region suggested reactivating twelve Ranger companies, each with three platoons.[65]

After two years of uncertain budgets and structure reviews,[66] the deputy chief of the defence staff authorized a revival of the Rangers in BC in 1990.[67] The commander of Maritime Command fully supported the initiative, foreseeing maritime coastal defence roles, territorial defence operations, antidrug operations, environmental protection, and emergency or disaster assistance in the case of an earthquake or oil spill – an expansive list of tasks that far exceeded the original "eyes and ears" concept. The Rangers would have a modest start, but if all went according to the five-year plan, they would expand to one thousand personnel, equalling the establishments in Atlantic and Northern Regions by 1995.[68]

Major Ian Hay, the operations and training officer with the Victoria Militia District, had free rein to get the Rangers back up and running. Reactivating the Rangers meant long hours and lots of travel, but Hay jumped at the chance. Having visited both Yellowknife and St. John's, Hay "took the best of both and made it his own."[69] He decided that the Northern Region's community-based patrols would better accommodate the cultural and political traditions of West Coast Aboriginal peoples and emphasize the Rangers' "unique character."[70] Hay sent a letter to band and village

Major Ian Hay.
Courtesy of 4 Canadian
Ranger Patrol Group

councils in prospective communities and then waited for invitations to come and make a formal proposal. During visits, Hay and Master Warrant Officer D.C. Haines, his non-commissioned officer responsible for training, stressed the Rangers' value as long-time residents of their areas.[71]

Hay followed a five-year re-establishment plan. During the first year, his staff recruited, trained, and exercised two Ranger patrols. The first patrol, in the non-Aboriginal community of Port Hardy on Vancouver Island, attracted thirty-three Rangers. The second, the Lax Kw'alaams patrol in the Coast Tsimshian community of Port Simpson on the North Central Coast, had an initial strength of twenty-seven. A mixed Nuu-cha-nulth and non-Aboriginal patrol followed at Ucluelet on Vancouver Island in April 1991. The Rangers proved their value immediately when a Japanese tanker went aground near Ucluelet and about fifty government agencies descended on the small community. The after-action report crucified many of these agencies for being ill prepared. Only the Rangers received a glowing report. They knew the coast and were "walking encyclopaedias of local knowledge."[72] The communities of Kitkatla, Bella, Kincolith (Gingolx), New Aiyansh, Tahsis, Tumbler Ridge, and Masset also requested patrols. "Response to the reactivation of the Canadian Ranger program in BC has been well beyond our expectations," Major A.K. Hamilton noted from Pacific Command Headquarters in June 1991. "In order to capitalize on the present level of interest ... the number of patrols should be expanded to the greatest extent possible."[73]

Warrant Officer Dan Hryhoryshen became a Ranger instructor in October 1991. Hay had called Hryhoryshen, a medic at the reserve battle school, to inform him of the reactivation. Although Hryhoryshen had never heard of the Rangers, he leapt at the opportunity. As an instructor, he faced a tremendous learning curve. He described the culture shock he experienced when he set up the Kitkatla patrol. The air force offered to fly him into the community after the civilian airline with which he planned to fly went bankrupt. When a huge Labrador helicopter dropped Hryhoryshen and his large load of equipment on the community ball diamond, he felt isolated. "All of a sudden, the tables were turned on me," Hryhoryshen later reflected. "I am the White guy in town, in a combat uniform, representing the federal government." All of the soon-to-be Rangers, who stood behind the backstop, simply told him about a community dinner that evening and that they expected him to attend. Over time, he learned to relax, to be informal, and to focus on building trust. "Ignore the timetable – you will eventually get there," he observed. The key was to "throw your beret in the corner and roll up your sleeves." Seeking advice about culture and appropriate behaviour was essential. "It is all about developing relationships," Hryhoryshen explained. "You cannot behave like a bureaucrat ... The Rangers is not policy and strategy and directives. It is a grassroots connection to the people and the land."[74]

Frequent visits to patrols for weekend training allowed people to balance full-time jobs with Ranger service and helped instructors build strong local connections.[75] Mutual learning remained key. Patrol members knew one another, so they knew one another's potential. They also recognized that they would have to educate instructors on the limits of their military capabilities. "We as civilians adapt to military protocol," Ranger Bill Leighton of Gold River explained, "but the military also adapts somewhat to ours." He recalled that Hryhoryshen was "really militant" when he first showed

A Ranger in BC holding a C-7 rifle. Courtesy of 4 Canadian Ranger Patrol Group

up. "We told him to lighten up. We were a bunch of fucking welders, loggers, and millworkers." Hryhoryshen proved a good student, a good instructor, and grew alongside the patrols.[76]

The organizers, however, still had to address critics who questioned the logic of establishing and arming Rangers in their province. Some antigovernment and antiauthority activists in remote BC communities tried to disrupt Ranger organizing in places such as Zeballos and Port Clements.[77] Circulating free .303 rifles also caused concern. The Ranger organizers explained that people already had guns and that Ranger training would teach them safe use of their weapons.[78] Not everyone believed them. *British Columbia Report,* a right-wing newsmagazine, printed a story in August 1991 under the headline "Happiness Is a Free Gun: The Federal Government Hands Out Rifles to Indians." Just weeks after the Oka crisis in Quebec, journalist Tim Gallagher reported that the military had handed out guns to volunteer "militia" units in remote and coastal areas of the province. Residents of northern BC, he alleged, "fearing a repeat of the violence at Oka ... believe the Canadian Rangers policy, which issues rifles to units on native reserves, is both ill-advised and ill-timed." In Prince Rupert, for example, the military had supposedly handed out sixty-three rifles to Aboriginal people. Native roadblocks had disrupted BC residents the previous year. Was the government now arming these same people? This article sensationalized the situation, of course, but it also questioned the very need for Rangers. "In the absence of any wartime enemy and the end of the Cold War," Peter Lester, Prince Rupert's mayor, told the reporter, "I can't see it."[79]

The Northern Growth Spurt Continues

The changing geostrategic context raised questions about Canada's domestic defence posture. The Department of National Defence's annual report in 1989 noted that "no one seriously believes that the current Soviet leadership has any intention of attacking Western Europe or North America."[80] As the Cold War evaporated, Canada cancelled its nuclear submarine program – the centrepiece of its 1987 white paper.[81] The government scuttled its ambitious icebreaker project less than a year later, partly in response to Canada's successful negotiation of the 1988 Arctic Cooperation Agreement in which the United States and Canada "agreed to disagree" about the status of the Northwest Passage.[82] The government's 1991 defence policy update conspicuously lacked the nationalist language of the mid-1980s, and Defence Minister

Marcel Masse pointed out that "the best way to defend the sovereignty of Canada is within a coalition" with the United States and the European members of NATO.[83] More generally, the military retrenchment reflected the government's desire to cash in on a "peace dividend" so that it could cut federal deficits and the massive national debt.

Fortunately, the Canadian Ranger budget remained too inconsequential to attract the federal government's knife. Indeed, their low cost, coupled with favourable media coverage, made them particularly attractive compared to other military organizations and activities. "The Ranger budget continues to grow despite major cutbacks in other areas of defence spending," Lieutenant-Colonel E.L. Schrader told the Ranger commanding officers who gathered in St. John's in March 1991. "When Maj[or] Iley was working with the Canadian Rangers (Atlantic) the budget was $37,000.00; it now amounts to over $500,000.00."[84] The total Ranger budget for the following fiscal year was $2.27 million, split roughly between Northern Region and Maritime Command.[85] This influx of money facilitated expansion at a time when most Canadian Forces activities faced deep cuts.

The Rangers had enjoyed steady growth in the Territorial North through the 1980s, and Brigadier Gollner continued "to press growth with *vigour*"[86] in the early post–Cold War period. "While I fully understand our current resource problems within the CF and the natural tendency to look on anything involving expansion with a somewhat jaundiced eye," he wrote, "I would like to put things in context. There are not very many places in Canada amongst the native population where the CF and our activities are welcomed these days. In the North, the Rangers are welcome as a vital and integral part of the native communities. We have a chance to expand, using very few resources ... our influence and at the same time our ability to enhance our national sovereignty and security." A full-time support staff of sixty personnel oversaw five hundred primary reservists in Northern Alberta Militia District, while seven personnel in Northern Region looked after "almost 1000 Rangers spread over an area larger than continental Europe." By June 1990, Northern Region had forty-four patrols and 935 Rangers: thirty-eight patrols were predominantly Inuit, five were Dene, and one was non-Aboriginal. In "basic military skills, musketry, field craft, robustness and survival knowledge," Gollner argued, "the Rangers are every bit as proficient as their Primary Reserve counterparts at a fraction of the cost." While in Yellowknife, the chief of the defence staff, General John de Chastelain, voiced his support for expansion and directed the commander of Northern

Region to recommend new patrol locations.[87] The Rangers in the North fit both the spartan military budget and political imperatives.

Given the strained relationship between Aboriginal people and the military in other parts of Canada, politicians and defence officials highlighted the importance of "wide positive public and territorial support" for the Rangers. Aboriginal people's frustrations with the state surfaced during the "Indian summer" of 1990, when Elijah Harper's stoic stand defeated the Meech Lake Accord and when camouflaged Mohawk warriors faced off against the Canadian Forces in Quebec. In the North, however, the Rangers embodied cooperation. Inuit, for example, actively supported the Rangers because elders saw the organization as a way to take young men "out on the land or ice to learn and master the old way of life and skills." These elders were often community leaders, so the military had friends in places of influence. The Rangers' other activities helped Aboriginal communities and drew attention to northerners' contributions. "The pivotal role played by the Rangers in [securing the town of] Old Crow last summer during the forest fire driven evacuation and several successfully concluded searches for missing people have received excellent coverage in the Northern media," Brigadier Gollner explained. Samisa Passauraluk and Alasua Tamusi Nutaraalu, two Rangers from Puvirnituq to whom the chief of the defence staff had personally presented commendations, became local folk heroes when they retired after forty-one years of continuous service. "All of this public acceptance and positive feeling about our Rangers did a great deal to ameliorate the post Oka anti-military feeling amongst the military in the North," Gellner noted, particularly among Inuit and Inuvialuit. One Ranger in Old Crow quit in protest of government and military actions against the Mohawks, but one out of 975 Rangers (98 percent of whom were Aboriginal) was "not a bad figure!"[88]

The Ranger patrols in most northern communities benefitted from relatively stable membership. Numbers continued to grow modestly, and new recruits quickly replaced Rangers who retired. Motivations for enlistment varied. Some Rangers wanted access to a "free" rifle and ammunition for hunting, others were curious about the military, and still others wanted to serve their community. Rangers Charlie Evaglok and Bruce Hikhaitok of Coppermine (Kugluktuk) enjoyed travelling on the land.[89] Others viewed the Rangers as a family legacy. When Kuujjuaq Ranger Sergeant Vallee Saunders joined in 1988, he followed in the footsteps of his uncle who had been a Ranger since the early 1960s. Saunders had tremendous respect for one member of the patrol in particular. "There was this elder [who taught] me the techniques of hunting and trapping, and methods, and seasons, and he was a Ranger," Saunders recalled. "That's when I decided to join."[90]

Although Northern Region believed that major growth was neither expected nor necessary within the existing patrols, Brigadier Gollner received full support for his plan to expand to fifty patrols and then to add two or three patrols per year in the early 1990s.[91] His headquarters raised and trained new patrols in Inukjuak, Inuvik,[92] and Hall Beach in 1991.[93] At this point, practically every Inuit community capable of supporting a Ranger patrol boasted one. The northwestern Subarctic offered room for expansion, however, and Yukon became Northern Region's highest priority.

The Yukon Territory had changed dramatically since the Rangers' footprint had faded away in the late 1960s.[94] "The once closely connected string of maintenance yards, service stations, hotels and regional centres" along the Alaska Highway became less connected over time, historian William Morrison observed. "As the highway settlements became communities in their own right, oriented largely toward the First Nations peoples, the highway community itself diminished in importance, connectivity and social coherence."[95] Most Yukoners lived in a few settlements (with more than two-thirds of the population concentrated in Whitehorse), and the First Nations population had moved out of the bush to seek wage employment and access to services.[96] The military, in general, had little presence: one Ranger patrol in the remote community of Old Crow, along with five Regular Force officers and four cadet units in the entire territory.[97] Although the NDP had adopted a "military-free Yukon" platform, the premier, the commissioner, and leading business and Aboriginal leaders publicly supported resurrecting the Rangers.[98]

When the military stood up new patrols in the hamlets of Mayo, Haines Junction, Ross River, and Dawson City in early 1991, the enthusiastic response caught Northern Region off guard. "We optimistically estimated that approximately 50 Rangers would volunteer for service," Brigadier Gollner observed. "Instead we had more than triple that number ... Thus we had the bittersweet experience of having to turn good applications away simply because we could not, given our present asset base, cater to the numbers and their needs." By July, 117 Rangers had enlisted, and regional

Rangers in Dawson in the early 1990s. Photo by Roy Johnson, courtesy of Sergeant John Mitchell, Dawson patrol

planners grappled with how to accommodate even more diversity in their organization.[99]

With the exception of the remote Old Crow patrol, Northern Region anticipated that Rangers in Yukon would be more like their counterparts in the Atlantic region than patrols in Northwest Territories (NWT) because 75 percent of Yukoners were non-Aboriginal. Although most residents engaged in outdoor pursuits, they did not derive their primary livelihood off the land and owned less equipment – such as skidoos – than Rangers in NWT. Furthermore, regular employment meant evening and weekend training.[100] Their ranks included influential businessmen, airplane and helicopter pilots, a lawyer, a doctor, and several registered nurses.[101] Although their counterparts in NWT seemed quite content to follow scheduled and often repetitive training, instructors learned that in Yukon recruits "both expect and have the capability for a progressively challenging programme, incl[uding] a significant military flavour to their activities." These activities were more akin to reserve-unit training than to traditional Ranger activities.[102]

Seizing the opportunity, Northern Region appointed a dedicated instructor in Whitehorse to train and liaise with the Yukon Ranger Company.[103]

Although the Yukon's population was largely non-Aboriginal, Northern Region contacted the fourteen Yukon tribal councils to see if any had an interest in the Rangers. Their initial responses were "guarded but positive."[104] Unsettled land claims translated into a delicate, uncertain political climate. For example, a series of "minor but quite violent confrontations between developers, local whites and natives" over land ownership near Carcross Landing put initial plans for a patrol on hold. When the military finally set up the Carcross patrol in September 1991, its diverse membership included Rangers from Carcross, Tagish, and the Alaska Highway between Whitehorse and Teslin. The patrol's presence actually mitigated crosscultural tensions by providing common ground for interactions, and the Rangers' quiet progress in Yukon attracted positive attention. A representative in the territorial legislature exclaimed, after watching patrol training in his hamlet, that "this is the first time I've seen white and native people ever doing something together other than argue here in Ross River."[105]

Rangers in Yukon embraced service zealously and quickly established a name for themselves in the territory. In 1992-93, they broke eight hundred kilometres of trail for the Yukon Quest International Sled Dog Race between Fairbanks, Alaska, and Whitehorse and attracted international media attention. Rangers assisted the RCMP in locating the coordinates of the famous Lost Patrol of 1934, participated in re-enactments, provided honour guards during the fiftieth anniversary of the Alaska Highway, and resupplied fuel caches for a military aerial survey. Most also belonged to Emergency Management Organization (EMO) volunteer societies, and many took EMO-sponsored training for basic search and rescues, search management, emergency planning, and water rescue. The Haines Junction patrol specialized in avalanche rescue and cliff rescue. As a consequence, the Rangers participated regularly in ground search and rescues, and their popularity soared. "All of our existing [patrols] have waiting lists of applicants wanting to join," the detachment commander boasted in early 1993.[106]

More modest expansion along the Mackenzie River and in the Great Slave area of Northwest Territories increased First Nations and Metis representation. Communities in this region initially expressed little interest, so Brigadier Gollner tried to raise two patrols in the South Mackenzie region in 1992 to better gauge popular interest.[107] Fort Smith produced a small but well-motivated patrol, while efforts in Fort Resolution floundered

Rangers in Fort McPherson, March 1987. Courtesy of 1 Canadian Ranger Patrol Group

because of internal, "family-related" problems.[108] Despite the mixed results, new patrols formed the following year in the Gwich'in communities of Tsiigehtchic (Arctic Red River) and Fort McPherson (Teet'lit Zhen), as well as in the Dene and Metis community of Fort Simpson in the Dehcho region. This laid the groundwork for continued expansion along the Mackenzie River.

The Rangers' growing footprint across the North ensured the military's integration into local and regional political networks. Many Rangers held respected positions within their communities as band chiefs, hamlet mayors, deputies, members of the legislative assembly, and past members of Parliament. They had a vested interest in using Ranger training as bulwarks against skill fade. Instructors concurred with elders that "the younger generation of northern natives is gradually losing its knowledge of traditional skills." Accordingly, Ranger exercises specifically included time "for the older members to teach and reinforce this knowledge to younger members of the patrol."[109] The Ranger concept was predicated on local knowledge, so passing along traditional skills such as igloo building, ice fishing, and special hunting techniques remained essential to sustaining the organization.

The realities of life in the North required special accommodation and adaptation. General military policy dictated that reservists not have criminal records, but northern officials recognized that "most of the best candidates wishing to become Rangers" had a record. Rather than rejecting these would-be Rangers, the staff in Yellowknife worked with the RCMP and the Sûreté de Québec to screen all new applications. They arrived at a working principle: if individuals could qualify for a firearms acquisition certificate, they could become Rangers.[110] Instructors also noted the prevalence of alcohol abuse in the North. "Those patrols who have relatively easy access to booze are deeply affected by tardiness, unreliability, indifference and all the other misfortunes that alcohol abuse causes," one report observed. "Somewhat related is the high incidence of gambling for money, TV sets, snowmobiles, rifles or almost anything else of value." Ranger instructors specifically discussed and discouraged alcohol abuse and did not pay Rangers until they finished training or an exercise.[111]

To adapt to northern realities, all new military personnel posted to Yellowknife attended a week-long cultural awareness course. They learned that during char and halibut fishing season, for example, Inuit would pursue subsistence activities rather than Ranger training. Opportunities to hunt caribou, muskox, or narwhal took priority over Ranger duties. The Ranger staff emphasized tolerance, patience, and humour, along with the importance of keeping the Ranger "organization as far away from peace time bureaucracy as much as possible." They also noted a growing sense among Rangers of "what's in it for us?" "For at least two generations now, natives have been at the receiving end of seemingly endless gov[ernment] handouts," a 1993 briefing commented. To some northerners, the Canadian Forces represented another form of welfare – easy money for little effort. Sometimes residents couched this sentiment in diplomatic language; at other times, it was "unashamedly overt." Ranger instructors needed to demonstrate sensitivity to ensure that the Rangers did not become simply another program perpetuating Aboriginal dependency.[112]

Northern Region's expansionist efforts paid off. In January 1992, it oversaw 1,160 Rangers in fifty-two patrols that represented nearly half of the national strength. This membership eclipsed that of Atlantic Region, which had boasted larger numbers than its northern counterpart since the 1970s. More than half of the total Ranger establishment still lived south of the sixtieth parallel, where pressures continued to build for Ranger growth along the Pacific Coast and in the provincial norths.

Canadian Rangers from the Grise Fiord patrol reading a map with a Ranger instructor, **1988.** Library and Archives Canada/Department of National Defence collection/R112-536-X-E/Accession 2008-377, Box 147, Photo ISC88-314

Restructuring South of 60

Restructuring Land Force Command (the army) in the early 1990s had significant implications for Ranger units South of 60 and in northern Quebec. In 1992, Rangers who had been assigned to Maritime Command returned to army control and the commanders of the newly created land force areas.[113] Would the transfer change the organizational culture of the

TABLE 9
Ranger strengths by province and territory, January 1992

Region	Province/territory	Platoons/patrols	Strength	Percentage
Atlantic		30	1,017	43.0
	Newfoundland	20	664	28.1
	Labrador	7	270	11.4
	Quebec (Lower North Shore)	3	83	3.5
Northern		52	1,160	49.0
	Quebec (Ungava)	12	246	10.4
	Manitoba	1	18	0.8
	Northwest Territories	34	779	32.9
	Yukon Territory	5	117	4.9
Pacific		7	190	8.0
	British Columbia	7	190	8.0
NATIONAL TOTALS		89	2,367	100

Source: Department of National Defence, file 1901-260/4, 9 January 1992.

Rangers? Company and platoon commanders in Atlantic Region stressed that the Rangers needed to remain distinct from militia organizations. Additionally, the regional commander insisted that "any attempt to cast all Canadian Rangers in a National mould should be resisted. Western, Northern and Atlantic Rangers must maintain their differences to be effective."[114] Seeking to minimize the disruption to the Rangers themselves, regional commanders across Canada retained ample latitude to shape their units to suit regional priorities. The geographical boundaries of the new land force areas, however, did not correspond neatly with the existing Ranger organization. Northern Region was responsible for units in northern Quebec and Maritime Command for those along the Lower North Shore – both of which fell within Quebec Area.[115]

Land Force Quebec Area (Secteur Québec de la force terrestre) pushed to align the Ranger and land force area systems so that regional operations had clearer command responsibilities. When formed, the area commander immediately sought operational command of the nearly 250 Rangers in northern Quebec. A year later, area headquarters assumed control of the twelve patrols in Nunavik[116] as well as three platoons on the Lower North Shore between Havre-Sainte-Pierre and Blanc-Sablon (transferred from Land Force Atlantic Area).[117] The Domestic Operations branch initially

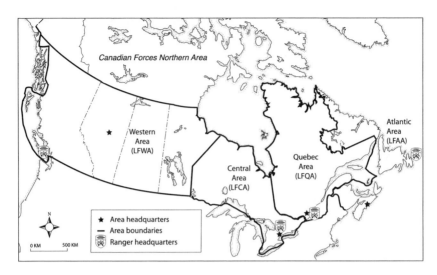

Land Force Areas, 1981

oversaw the Rangers cell. Captain Marc Morin, the Ranger liaison officer, supervised a training cadre composed of Sergeant Mario Aubin (transferred from Northern Region) and Sergeant Pasqualino (Pat) Rizzo. They set to work managing two different cultures: the former Northern Region patrols and the company along the Lower North Shore previously maintained by Maritime Command. Major-General J.A. Roy understandably promoted harmonization rather than standardization.[118]

After conducting training in eight communities, Morin, Aubin, and Rizzo judged the Lower North Shore difficult to administer. A single platoon encompassed several small coastal communities rather than being concentrated in a single settlement as in Nunavik. Furthermore, most of the Lower North Shore residents had regular wage employment and were not hunters and trappers. Ironically, training a platoon along the Lower North Shore cost thousands more than training a patrol in Nunavik.[119] In the North, Rizzo recalled, the approach had been "beans and bullets" – an instructor came in, and the patrol headed out on the land for training. The Lower North Shore units had followed the Atlantic Region model of classroom meetings, shooting at a rifle range, and a big "boil up."[120]

Liaison staff had always found it difficult to maintain the Ranger units along the Lower North Shore. Atlantic Region had struggled to deliver a training program commensurate with that offered in Newfoundland and Labrador. To justify infrequent visits to the area, liaison officers' reports often cited budget restrictions, staff constraints, and the difficulty of co-ordinating schedules with fishers living in the region. Training the franco-phone platoon at Havre-Sainte-Pierre posed another challenge, given that the liaison officers were not proficient in French.[121] The instructors were enthusiastic and did what they could with limited resources, Ranger Ernie Waye of Chevery remembered, but they simply did not have enough time to train the Rangers to an acceptable standard in one weekend each year. "The Rangers was the Rangers – just a rifle and some ammo," Gordon Anderson recalled. "If you could shoot straight, you could get supper out of it," Waye added.[122] Training improved after the Lower North Shore units transferred to Quebec Area. Rizzo and Aubin "came in with armed forces style training," Waye explained, and started teaching weapons drill, map and compass, and search and rescue. "Things just started happening. We were actually doing something ... not just sitting in the house with a rifle."[123]

The old company-platoon structure did not survive. Quebec Area replaced it with patrols, standardizing the organization within the province. It also abolished Ranger officer positions: Ranger sergeants now served as patrol commanders. Given that Ranger instructors were noncommissioned mem-bers and not officers, and that the traditional "liaison" role of handing out bullets had given way to annual training, the old hierarchy no longer made sense. "A sergeant does not give a captain orders," Rizzo explained. As a concession, existing Ranger officers could retain their commission, but the army would not replace them when they retired.[124] The new regulations also invoked mandatory retirement for Rangers along the Lower North Shore when they reached the age of sixty-five. An army officer would come up and take their rifle – a move that some Rangers found difficult to accept, particularly because Inuit elders in the North were not subjected to the same age limits.[125]

Quebec Area focused primarily on the northern reaches of the province, where Inuit had a long-standing relationship with the military through the Rangers. In Puvirnituq, some members had served continuously since 1948. Their communities writ large, however, had had no direct connection with the army in Quebec since the 1960s. Sergeant Aubin provided continuity after the transfer, and his pre-existing relationships ensured that new in-structors working with Inuit acknowledged and respected cultural differ-ences. "It was not just an 8-4 job," Pat Rizzo reminisced. "Aubin explained that you needed to build relationships with the community." When changes in leadership were needed to revitalize patrols, instructors gave Rangers the

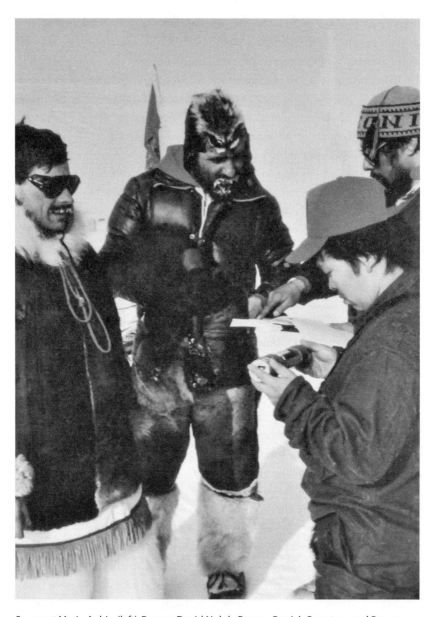

Sergeant Mario Aubin *(left)*, Ranger David Nuluk, Ranger Patrick Qaqutaq, and Ranger Sergeant Simeoni Natsek meet at Cape Lady Pelly on Committee Bay, Northwest Territories, during Exercise Baton Ranger in 1992. Library and Archives Canada/Department of National Defence collection/R112-536-X-E/NRS0392-018

option of resigning rather than being fired. "This allowed them to save face in their community," Rizzo explained. "You could not be pushy like you would be firing someone in the army down south."[126] In the end, it came down to embracing pluralism, being sensitive to cultural difference, and retaining flexibility in the organization so that instructors could connect military goals with local practices and priorities.

Taking Stock at Fifty

By 1992, the Rangers had much to celebrate. In addition to Canada's 125th birthday activities, the Department of National Defence officially celebrated the Rangers' fiftieth anniversary. The date was contrived, based as it was on the formation of the Pacific Coast Militia Rangers in 1942 rather than the formation of the Canadian Rangers five years later. Nonetheless, this convenient pretext justified Exercise Baton Ranger. Starting in Victoria, Rangers relayed a twelve-sided wooden baton from coast to coast to coast. For six months, the baton travelled more than twelve thousand kilometres – by dog sled, canoe, snowmobile, small boat, light aircraft, and by foot. Temperatures dropped to minus ninety degrees Celsius with the wind chill. Planners treated the Northwest Territories leg, also called the "Trans Arctic Expedition," as a route reconnaissance exercise that covered the short-range radar sites of the North Warning System. The trek confirmed that the Ranger units could successfully carry out security checks at various unmanned stations in extreme conditions. Furthermore, local Ranger patrols along the route marked and timed the winter trails, acted as guides between communities, and resupplied the two continuous travellers: Sergeant Mario Aubin and Ranger Sergeant Simeoni Natsek from Repulse Bay (Naujaat). A military aircraft flew the baton from Lake Harbour (Kimmirut) to Kangiqsujuaq on the northern tip of Ungava then Rangers carried it down the coast of Labrador. It arrived in St. John's on Canada Day. "This relay reminds us of the important role played by Canadian Rangers in our more remote regions," extolled the chief of reserves and cadets. "It is symbolic of people's hands coming together all across this country, to pass along a message of unity."[127]

Outside commentators praised the Rangers for their unique contributions to security and to their communities. When scholar Richard Langlais visited Grise Fiord on Ellesmere Island in 1992 to look at how residents understood concepts of security, he confirmed the existence of a disconnect between the conventional security discourse, which simply equated security with

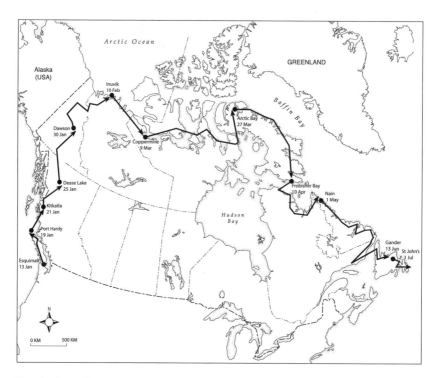

Exercise Baton Ranger, 1992

military threats to the state, and a more local and unconventional frame-work, which included ecological and environmental security. While other military initiatives in the North – such as NORAD forward operating loca-tions, the DEW Line cleanup, and the proposed system of underwater acoustic sensors – had generated friction and frustration between the military and local residents, the Rangers generated universally positive regard. Not only were the Rangers "sensitive to the relations between people and the Arctic environment," they also allowed local residents to share responsibility for Canadian security. The mayor of Iqaluit, a former Ranger, felt that the Rangers helped ensure that the military respected the land. "The military ... learns a lot from the Canadian Rangers, who learn a lot from the military," the mayor explained, "so ... the Canadian Rangers ... aren't going to allow the land to be too polluted by the other military, the full-time, or permanent military. So there is a working relationship there."[128]

Rangers accepted their role as custodians of their homeland. Patrol mem-bers in Grise Fiord happily served as eyes, ears, and trainers for the military,

A Canadian Ranger on a snowmobile pulls a komatik over a frozen fiord in southern Ellesmere Island. Library and Archives Canada/Department of National Defence collection/R112-536-X-E/ Accession 2008-377, Box 147, Photo ISC88-332

the local RCMP officer explained, but they would never participate in missions overseas. It was "just not their lifestyle," he told Langlais. "Someone once told me that ... in the Inuktitut language [there are] ten different ways to say kayak, just depending on the breakdown of the language ... but they don't have a word for war ... They see themselves as Rangers, not as soldiers." The local Parks Canada superintendent situated the Rangers in a local and circumpolar context, emphasizing their continuous presence and their importance to community life. "You see Ranger baseball caps everywhere you go, and sweatshirts," he observed. If anything made Inuit pro-military, a major in Yellowknife explained, it was the Rangers. They received little direction, elected their own leaders, and reported environmental pollution. "That's the only thing that we do up in the North, army-wise, with the military, and it'll probably remain so," the military's regional training officer explained.[129]

In Grise Fiord, every young male that the RCMP officer could think of between the ages of twenty-two and thirty-five was a Ranger. They were proud of their membership. "It's something that they feel they're contributing to the Canadian way of life," he explained. Langlais hypothesized that high Inuit participation rates might reflect "the supply of a certain amount of free ammunition as well as modest monetary income," the novelty of outside activity and contact with outsiders, and "a certain amount of pride and status in contributing and participating as Canadian citizens in a federal program that emphasizes an impression of the valuable contributions of aboriginal and local people." Regardless of cause, the Rangers were undeniably popular. Indeed, given their self-management, Langlais suggested that the Rangers offered a "clue to what future Inuit-style government might be."[130]

Aboriginal groups were realizing self-government through the painstaking process of settling comprehensive land claims, which culminated in modern treaties with the government of Canada. The agreements were complex and the negotiations nuanced. For example, when Inuvialuit of the western Arctic completed their agreement in 1984 and when the Tungavik Federation of Nunavut, which represented Inuit of the eastern Arctic, signed the Nunavut Agreement nine years later, Inuvialuit and Inuit accepted outright ownership of 91,000 and 353,610 square kilometres of land, respectively.[131] After nearly a decade of negotiations, Dene and Metis leaders in the Mackenzie Valley reached a settlement agreement with the government in April 1990, which was defeated in a ratification vote that July. Two of the five original groups, the Gwich'in and Sahtu, promptly entered into negotiations for separate agreements, which were reached in 1992 and 1994.[132] In Yukon, the federal government reached an umbrella agreement with the Council of Yukon First Nations (an association of fourteen groups) on points of common interest in 1990 and then began negotiating specifics

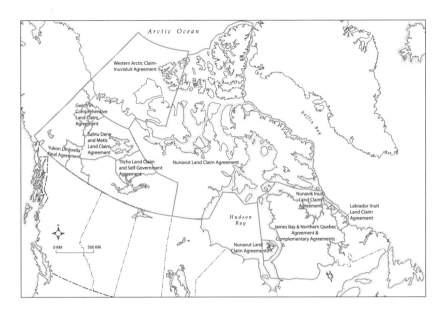

Modern land claim agreements in the Canadian North

with each group.[133] This new form of treaty federalism transformed northern governance and significantly enhanced Aboriginal peoples' influence over land, wildlife, and resource decisions.[134]

Land claim agreements also generated friction as the federal government and Aboriginal groups sorted out the practical implications of their new relationships. In the western Arctic, the Inuvialuit Final Agreement empowered the Inuvialuit Land Administration to regulate activities, including military training, in their settlement area. Accordingly, the Inuvialuit Regional Corporation now demanded land access fees for Ranger training. Senior military officers agreed in principle that the Department of National Defence had to abide by the rules and procedures laid out in the agreement, but they questioned whether fees were appropriate given that Ranger training directly benefitted residents and that a typical exercise infused up to twenty-five thousand dollars in a community. The military threatened to stop exercising on settlement lands unless the Inuvialuit reduced or waived the fees. While individual community leaders supported the department's position, regional Inuvialuit representatives opposed giving special consideration for Ranger training. That almost all of the Rangers were Inuvialuit and would earn money from the training exercises had little sway with Roger

Gruben, the chairman of the Inuvialuit Regional Corporation. He would not allow the department to "dictate terms of access to the IRC," particularly when the settlement agreement laid out the process.[135] Inuvialuit had to establish relationships from the ground up, and Gruben feared that allowing Ranger activities on settlement lands without pay would set a precedent for other groups, particularly those in the oil-and-gas sector.

The matter came to a head in January 1991 when National Defence made plans with patrols and local governments in Inuvik and Sachs Harbour to conduct Ranger training, informed the Gwich'in Tribal Council, and then applied to the Inuvialuit Land Administration for permission. Although Gruben appreciated the consultation, he argued that the military had violated the Inuvialuit Final Agreement, which stipulated that the Inuvialuit Regional Corporation "must be the first point of contact." Although Gruben met with military officials "on a short time frame to allow the exercises to proceed," he explained that unauthorized activities on their lands were "an item for arbitration or a court case."[136] Defence officials in Ottawa seemed to grasp the new decision-making regime, but officers in Yellowknife needed to adjust their approach to consultation.

In Inuvik, the Rangers decided to train on Crown land to avoid a legal showdown. In Sachs Harbour, however, they went out on Inuvialuit-controlled lands. When the Ranger instructor arrived "with little or no advanced notice" and took the Rangers onto the land without a permit, a former mayor asked the RCMP to arrest them. When the police refused to intervene, the Inuvialuit protested to the department that the land claim agreement "superseded the National Defence Act." Northern Region Headquarters apologized for the "unintentional" misunderstanding and promised to seek approval from the Inuvialuit Land Administration before seeking community consent in the future. The added complexity had direct repercussions. The department cancelled the winter warfare training it had planned for Inuvialuit lands. When the Inuvialuit Land Administration would not grant it a "one-time waiver," the military confined its training to Crown lands around Inuvik, and the Tuktoyaktuk Ranger patrol did not participate.[137]

The Canadian Forces avoided exercising in the Inuvialuit area for several years. Faced with tightened purse strings in the early 1990s, National Defence would not concede to paying land-use fees.[138] The parties eventually reached a cooperation agreement in 1996. The Inuvialuit Regional Corporation agreed to waive charges for land use in exchange for the Canadian Forces' promise to abide by the land administration's rules and to contract with Inuvialuit businesses.[139] The military had no problem accessing other land claim settlement areas in Northwest Territories and otherwise enjoyed a good rapport with all First Nations on issues related to accessing their lands for military exercises.[140]

In most cases, the military, the Rangers, and remote communities had a relaxed relationship. The Dawson Ranger patrol, stood up in 1991, enjoyed easy relations with both the military and its host community. In August 1993, two representatives from Third Battalion, Princess Patricia's Canadian Light Infantry (3 PPCLI), met with representatives of the Dawson (Trondëk Hwëch'in) First Nation, the city, and the Rangers to plan a November training exercise. During the first phase, soldiers would learn winter survival skills from the Rangers. "They'll teach us all those lessons we won't have to learn ourselves the hard way," Major Shane Fisher told a local reporter. During the second phase, the army would train the Rangers in tactics and weaponry. When a local resident worried that the exercises might affect the 40 Mile caribou herd, she received reassurances from the local Ranger sergeant and army representatives that they would not disrupt the animals and would adjust their locations if necessary.[141] The community threw its full support behind the exercise.

Exercise Reliant Nordic did not have an auspicious start. Inclement weather delayed the arrival of Bravo Company, 3 PPCLI. The last of the soldiers arrived shortly after midnight on 11 November. Later that morning, the Dawson Ranger patrol led the soldiers through town to the Remembrance Day ceremonies at the elementary school, the local cenotaph, and the Anglican church. Afterwards, the troops met locals over lunch at the Dawson First Nation Band Centre before heading into the wilderness. The frozen Yukon River prevented access to the training area, forcing adjustments to the plan. Nevertheless, the Rangers shared their knowledge and experience in winter transportation, survival, tracking, and trapping. "The training was excellent, and the standard and professionalism of the Dawson City Patrol was outstanding," an after-action report exclaimed. Afterwards, a section of Rangers attached themselves to each platoon to participate in ambush or raid tasks and target practice.[142] Despite delays and deviations, the soldiers and Rangers came away pleased with the experience.

In this case, and throughout the remote northern and coastal regions of Canada, Rangers provided the essential link between outside military units and the local community. The soldiers returned to Dawson on 20 November to demonstrate mock attacks, display their equipment, and play touch

The Dawson patrol at the local cenotaph, Remembrance Day, 1993. Photo by Roy Johnson, courtesy of Sergeant John Mitchell, Dawson patrol

football and ball hockey with locals in "thirty-five below" weather. The day ended with a potlatch supper hosted by the Dawson First Nation. "This was quite a feast, with plenty of Moose and Caribou, and was rumoured to have been the largest community supper in recent history," 3 PPCLI's after-action report noted. "All ranks of the company left Dawson City and the Yukon with good memories of excellent training, the Ranger Patrol, and a town that received them with open arms."[143] Experiences such as this sowed the seeds of positive relationships, reinforcing the idea that military activities and community life were compatible.

🍁 WHEN *GLOBE AND MAIL* REPORTER Miro Cernetig visited Grise Fiord for Canada Day in 1993, he commented on the "patriotism among the icebergs." When the crowded finished the national anthem, seven Rangers fired off rounds towards Jones Sound, "giving the wind a hint of cordite and sparking a round of applause and laughter." Despite the community's tragic history – Inuit families from northern Quebec had been relocated to the southern tip of Ellesmere Island in 1955 – Cernetig found the hamlet "the most patriotic collection of people in the nation." Amon Akeeagok, a twenty-three-year-old Ranger, told him: "there's no tension up here ... I'll be Canadian all my life, until I ... die."[144]

In the late 1980s, political scientist Franklyn Griffiths suggested that the Arctic states had to decide whether they wanted the circumpolar region to be one of enhanced civil cooperation (civility) or of military competition. In his view, accepting "an integrated concept of security – one in which military requirements are combined with an awareness of the need to act for ecological, economic, cultural, and social security" – would allow northerners to play a more direct role in setting agendas and fostering cooperation and dialogue.[145] Through the Rangers, residents of remote regions contributed directly to sovereignty and security. "The Ranger program is without a doubt the most respected military activity in Northern Canada," Major Marcel Beztilny explained, "and the public support it fosters is of extreme benefit to the Canadian Forces."[146] Daniel Norris, the commissioner of the Northwest Territories, whom General de Chastelain inducted as an Honorary Ranger in 1990, mentioned to the chief of the defence staff that he would "be held in greater respect as he tours the villages of the NWT now that he is a Ranger and can wear the hat and arm-band."[147] In this unique force, civility and military service went hand in hand.

In contrast with the image of military-Aboriginal tension captured in photographs from the Oka Crisis of 1990, the Rangers offered a positive portrait of cooperation. Northern leaders from the Dene Nation and the Inuit Tapirisat of Canada singled out the Rangers as a positive contribution to the defence of Canada and expressed a desire to see the force expanded. The government paid heed to their advice. Officials viewed enhancing the Rangers and publicizing their activities as the keys to furthering relationships with northern communities and Native organizations.[148] When Rosemary Kuptana, president of the Inuit Tapirisat of Canada, was asked to lay a wreath at the National War Memorial on Remembrance Day 1993, she felt it "only appropriate" that an Inuk serving with the Rangers carry the wreath for her.[149] Even Audrey McLaughlin, the leader of the federal New Democratic Party who was perennially critical of all things military,

Passing the baton in northern Labrador, 1992. Sarah Webb *(centre)* of the Nain platoon was one of the first three women to join the Rangers four years earlier. Courtesy of Sarah Webb, Nain patrol

wrote to the chief of the defence staff in 1992 asking him to expand the Rangers in Yukon, her home territory. "Can't have it both ways," a Canadian Forces Northern Area internal briefing noted pithily.[150] But with the Rangers, it seemed that people could.

Unfortunately, popular attention to the defence of remote regions followed a typical cycle of alarmism followed by apathy in the late 1980s. Six years after the *Polar Sea*'s voyage had triggered a diplomatic row between Canada and the United States, the Conservative government cancelled or scaled back nearly all of its promised investments to consolidate control over the Northwest Passage. The sovereignty crisis had passed – as had the Cold War itself. Growing deficits and constitutional discussions dominated the federal agenda. Yet the Canadian Rangers fared remarkably well, and indeed grew.[151] The military did little to publicize the Rangers, but the media remained positive. "As 'Twice the Citizens' and true volunteers they have a good message to put out," Brigadier-General Ernest Beno commented in 1991.[152] The Rangers were cheap and inclusive: a winning recipe.

Officers who worked with the Rangers recognized that the political climate was hospitable for expansion and enhancement. Rising interest in the organization (at a time when the government was slashing other elements of the Canadian Forces) presented a unique window of opportunity. Although the media directed nearly all of their attention to the Rangers in the Arctic, the popularity of the organization flourished throughout Canada, and Ranger units in Newfoundland, British Columbia, and Yukon had waiting lists of potential recruits.[153]

Despite their high profile within territorial governments and local communities, only a few "specifically involved senior officers and staffs" at National Defence Headquarters seemed to know much about the Rangers.[154] Indeed, the Rangers' low profile within the military establishment helps account for their steady growth in the North and their return to British Columbia. In 1993, the director of reserves emphasized "the importance of the anonymity of the rangers within the system." The less senior decision makers knew, the less they would meddle in Ranger matters. Captain Paul Chura, the staff officer responsible for the Rangers in Northern Region, was advised to avoid "rock[ing] the boat which will cause questions to be asked."[155] The Ranger organization was not broken, but if senior officials looked closely, they might still try to fix it – without fully understanding why the relationship worked so well on the ground.

The absence of a national, strategic plan for the Rangers did raise questions about the informal arrangements that governed the highly unorthodox organization.[156] In early 1994, Colonel J.R.P. Daigle argued that planners had to "be cautious when advocating a role and tasks" based upon documents produced during the Cold War. The demise of the Soviet Bloc "substantially reduced" the threat to the North, and the Rangers' role had to take "today's realities – diminishing funding, restructuring of the CF, defence priorities, operational requirements and national goals" – into consideration. In his assessment, no one had justified the Rangers' tasks through substantive analysis of their contributions to the army. "They are neither training tactically nor are they equipped to carry out tactical missions, be it to contain an enemy lodgement or fix it," Daigle noted. "Their sole and only tasks are to observe and guide. We must also balance these tasks against cost and other priorities."[157]

Questions about the Rangers' role, mission, and dispersion persisted. Daigle cautioned against continuous expansion:

> Canada needs to ascertain its sovereignty in the Arctic, and the Rangers provide a "de facto" presence, thus justifying their raison d'être. The same

cannot be claimed for Ranger detachments South of 60, considering that the RCMP and other Government Departments have increased their activities in these regions, thus relegating the Rangers to a lesser role. Expanding the Rangers' tasks in these areas to include fighting forest fires, search and rescue and support to local agencies will result in DND footing the bill for a force for which we will have no military use, and for tasks which are clearly other department's [sic] responsibilities. In fact there is little[,] if any, justification for the Rangers South of 60.

The Rangers had neither the capability to conduct more military-oriented missions nor an operational requirement to do so. As a defence resource, they had to perform practical, feasible, and credible military tasks. Assisting other government agencies in civil emergencies remained a secondary consideration. "We must be able to justify their requirements from a military point of view," Daigle insisted. "Rangers detachments [sic] must not become social organizations for grown ups looking for a bit of adventure, nor must they become para-reserve organizations."[158] Before the decade ended, however, developments in the provincial norths – particularly in Ontario and Quebec – pushed the organization down the socio-political path that Daigle cautioned against.

9

Enhancement and the Junior Canadian Rangers, 1994-99

❧ CAPTAIN DAVID SCANDRETT, the officer responsible for re-establishing the Canadian Rangers in northern Ontario, arrived in Fort Albany to organize a patrol in January 1995. He knew that Ranger service would continue a long history of Aboriginal contributions to the Canadian Forces: Ojibway (Anishnabek), Oji-Cree, and Cree (Omushkegowuk) soldiers from northern Ontario had enlisted in high numbers during both world wars. Scandrett learned that one chief, Gilbert Faries of Moose Cree First Nation, had actually served under his own grandfather in the Royal Canadian Engineers during the Second World War. Yet he still expressed surprise when he met Abraham Metatawabin, who had joined the Rangers in 1965 and "was still here, doing his work." As far as the elder was concerned, "he was still on duty, and he had received no other instructions to stop doing his work," despite having received no communication or support from the military for nearly three decades.[1]

Things changed in the years ahead. Metatawabin later recalled that the training he received in the 1990s had been "very, very full" compared to his earlier experiences. The instructors taught community members how to work together "for a common purpose," true to the spirit of the force and proportionate to the Rangers' expected roles and way of life. "In this area, the kind of life that we follow ... the land is free, no fences, our area is to sustain ourselves, to obtain our food and to obtain other goods for ... our homes and our communities," Metatawabin explained. "So nothing happens, usually. There's no danger of something falling from the sky or something

Major David Scandrett in front of 3 Canadian Ranger Patrol Group headquarters, Camp Borden. Courtesy of David Scandrett

breaking, or something exploding ... We don't have those kinds of accidents" like they do in the cities. Instead, we "just have to keep looking out for the small things that can happen" – like airplanes flying overhead at night.[2] The idea of being the military's "eyes and ears," ready to respond to any emergency, remained after two decades. "We don't train these guys to take their .303s and charge across the ice floes of Hudson Bay to shoot at [Russian] Whiskey-class submarines," Scandrett told reporter Peter Moon in 1994. Instead, Ranger training exercises taught them how to organize to respond to community emergencies, plane crashes, or searches for missing people.[3]

The Rangers also connected Aboriginal communities to the Canadian state. A few years later, Scandrett elaborated on how changes in Aboriginal governance would affect Canadian sovereignty:

> With the moves towards self government amongst First Nations ..., training and operating in northern Ontario may become very sensitive in the coming years. Sovereignty issues may well arise from internal rather than external sources. Land claim problems and land use negotiations are rapidly becoming contentious particularly in the resource areas related to hydro, timber and mineral exploitation. By establishing the Ranger presence we demonstrate good faith, we take a dynamic, contributory interest

in the affairs of the north and we are pro-active in our approach. Native people are extremely patient and they take a long term view in their dealings. Trust is a highly regarded commodity and gone are the days when First Nations can be shouldered aside. That is why we need to be in the north now, so that we can go there in twenty or thirty years and not be strangers in our own land.[4]

Linking the Rangers to nation-building objectives was a common thread in the late 1990s. Even with Arctic sovereignty concerns out of the political spotlight, the Rangers still represented a positive government presence in remote communities, a bridge between the Canadian Forces and Aboriginal peoples, and a new instrument for internal cohesion and capacity building through the Junior Canadian Rangers program.

THE 1990S WERE NOT KIND to the Canadian Forces. The Cold War had ended, the Conservatives' 1987 defence policy became obsolete, and national debt and constitutional issues dominated the political agenda. During the 1993 election campaign, all federal parties promised to cut military spending and personnel. The 1994 budget axed the Department of National Defence's budget by $7 billion and announced widespread base closures. The white paper on defence, released later that year, foreshadowed even deeper cuts.[5] In the years ahead, scandals tarnished the military's reputation: the Somalia Affair exposed a systematic cover-up, and the government found it easier to eliminate the Canadian Airborne Regiment than to weed out culpable individuals. The military seemed more a political liability than a source of national inspiration.[6]

By contrast, constitutional debates and Aboriginal activism continued to push Aboriginal issues to the forefront of the nation's political agenda. Still reeling from the 1990 Oka Crisis and evidence of high rates of poverty, poor health, family distress, and suicide in Aboriginal communities, the government appointed the Royal Commission on Aboriginal Peoples – the largest and most expensive royal commission in the country's history – to examine the relationship between Aboriginal peoples, the government, and Canadian society. The commission's reports emphasized the destructive legacy of colonialism, misguided attempts to assimilate Aboriginal people into mainstream society by eradicating their distinct cultures and identities, and the resiliency of Canada's "First Peoples," who retained "the secret of cultural survival." Nation served as the central concept of the commission's reports; not simply the nation-state but also the hundreds of Aboriginal communities that now self-identified as nations. According to the commissioners, to repair historical damage, the state needed to acknowledge Aboriginal peoples' status as "political and cultural groups with values and lifeways distinct from those of other Canadians." *Status* did not necessarily imply "nation-states seeking independence from Canada" but rather "collectivities with a long shared history, a right to govern themselves and, in general, a strong desire to do so in partnership with Canada." The Two Row Wampum belt (Gus-Wen-Tah), which commemorated the treaty between the Haudenosaunee and the Dutch in 1613, served as the commission's model for an appropriate relationship based on peace and friendship: "The two rows of purple are two vessels travelling down the same river together. One, a birch bark canoe, is for the Indian people, their laws, their customs and their ways. The other, a ship, is for the white people and their laws, their customs and their ways. We shall travel the river together, side by side, but in our own boat. Neither of us will try to steer the other's vessel."[7] Not everyone accepted the concept of parallelism as a realistic or desirable vision, and the government never fully implemented the commission's recommendations.[8] Nevertheless, the main principles of recognition, respect, sharing, and responsibility resonated in political and public discourses on Aboriginal rights.

Given its predominantly Aboriginal membership, the Canadian Rangers remained highly relevant, and the organization continued to expand in an era of military austerity. Most political and national media attention continued to fixate on Inuit participation in the Far North, where the Rangers retained their appeal as an inexpensive, culturally inclusive, and visible means of demonstrating Canadian sovereignty. Although concern about Arctic sovereignty receded (along with military activity), the Rangers saw enhanced budgets and efforts to expand their presence and capabilities North of 60. The organization also enjoyed modest growth throughout the rest of Canada, consolidating its footprint in Quebec and along the Atlantic and Pacific coasts and returning to northern Ontario. Most new growth came in Aboriginal communities, reflecting the political saliency of building and reinforcing Aboriginal-military partnerships. Observers applauded the Rangers' role not only in teaching the military but also in facilitating the transfer of traditional knowledge within communities. The creation of the Junior Canadian Rangers represented a clear move in this direction. The relative weight given to sociopolitical and operational requirements, however, coupled with pressure for accelerated growth, had the unintended consequence of exacerbating divisions between the various regional commanders.

Re-creating the Rangers in Ontario

The Rangers' distinctly regional flavour became evident in Ontario. The organization had been dormant in the province's north for a quarter century. Neither concerns about sovereignty nor concerns about national security justified its resuscitation. Instead, Captain David Scandrett, a Regular Force officer from Toronto (who had paddled the Albany River from Hearst, Ontario, to Fort Albany as a university student in 1970), took a keen interest in the state of First Nations communities and saw the Rangers as a constructive solution to an array of social problems. He realized that the typical government-Aboriginal relationship was flawed. In early 1990, Scandrett was deployed as part of a Canadian Forces aid to the civil power operation at Akwesasne, a Mohawk reserve along the Canada-US border rife with violence related to gambling, drug running, and smuggling. His epiphany came when he decided to leave the police barricade in the community centre, cross the street, and visit a home with a "Crafts for Sale" sign posted outside. "This isn't Lebanon," he replied to those who said he could not go. Wearing combat fatigues, he spoke with an elderly Mohawk woman (a community matriarch) for several hours. She was "very articulate, highly intelligent, well informed, very pleasant to be with and made an excellent cup of tea," Scandrett told a reporter. "When I got back, the police across the road said: 'Another 15 minutes, and we were coming in to get you.' I guess it was one of those profound moments. It was a very tense time. People were on edge, and here was this Mohawk lady who was elegant and gracious and pleasant, who had a sense of calm in this storm. You look out of window, and here's this recreation hall with sandbags in the window, soldiers, police – the antithesis of my concept of Canada." He suddenly got it: "We were strangers in our own land."[9]

After that experience, Scandrett decided to revive the Rangers as a way to reach out to First Nations "north of 50" in Ontario. On 30 May 1991, he presented his proposal to Land Force Central Area. He outlined why the Rangers would not only contribute to defence but also improve the Canadian Forces' "relations with, and understanding of, the native peoples of this country." His long-term threat assessment included sovereignty, pollution,

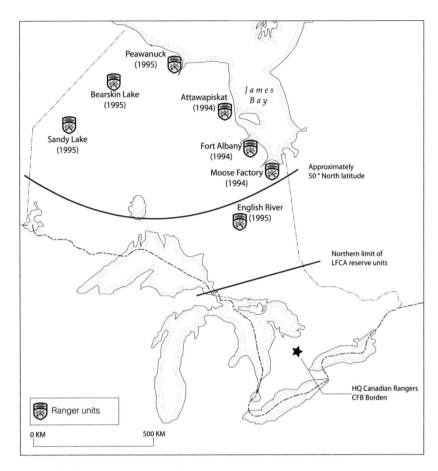

Re-establishing the Rangers in northern Ontario, 1994-95

the environment, forest fires, and transportation disasters. Scandrett thought the Rangers could build leadership skills in ailing communities, act as local search-and-rescue teams, and serve the military as a territorial surveillance, reconnaissance, and early-warning system. In his view, Rangers could provide "the local wisdom and skills that we in the south do not possess," while the military would offer "socio-economic, citizenship and cultural" benefits. His initial five-year plan included opening thirty patrols with about one thousand Rangers in the province.[10]

After the area commander endorsed the proposal, Scandrett met with Ranger staff across the country, visited a few coastal communities in northern Ontario that were keen on the Ranger idea, and clarified his plans. Concurrently, he attended meetings of the Royal Commission on Aboriginal

Peoples and met with Madame Justice Bertha Wilson at Rama First Nation, where he heard stories about Aboriginal war veterans who had been denied benefits because of their Indian status. Scandrett acknowledged the importance of learning as much as possible about the North, its peoples, and their traditions, customs, languages, and value systems. To succeed, the Rangers could not be "yet another six-month federal government program" – he had to ensure a long-term commitment to the host communities and the Canadian Army, a commitment rooted in mutual benefit for the military and northern communities. Scandrett took the "fifty-year view," acknowledging that the Rangers could not be "a military Jesus" – that is, they could not serve as a panacea for all northern problems. He encountered limited military support for his ideas. "The mainstream army saw the Rangers as a perceived threat as they would be siphoning off resources that were better spent on Regular Force and Militia capabilities," Scandrett recalled. "Just following Oka, there was still a hefty dose of suspicion about arming Native people." On the other hand, the military "could not recruit enough Aboriginal or female personnel due to context and culture. The Canadian Rangers made the numbers look good," and this helped Scandrett make his business case.[11]

In February 1993, the Canadian Ranger Working Group approved his plans,[12] and Headquarters Canadian Rangers (5 Company, James Bay) was stood up at Canadian Forces Base Borden later that year. Above all, Scandrett wanted to avoid perpetuating a history of colonialism and assimilation. "There is considerable sensitivity required in this training process," he noted, "and all staff must demonstrate a positive attitude towards native people and be mindful of their customs and ways."[13] The following January, he ran a cultural awareness training course led by Anishinabe elder Bill Sault from Thunder Bay (who Scandrett enlisted as a chief warrant officer). The course challenged his new staff to see the world through First Nations' eyes. "This is a radical departure from any military course you've ever been on," Scandrett warned the participants.[14]

Scandrett approached Ranger organizing in northern Ontario with the same zeal and creativity that Tommy Taylor applied during the heyday of the Pacific Coast Militia Rangers. "Trust was the critical component" to success, Scandrett emphasized. His staff visited First Nations, tribal councils, and federal, provincial, and municipal groups and agencies. "Patience and good 'cultivation'" were prerequisites to establishing patrols, and military representatives had to overcome preconceived notions of what a military unit should be. They had to adjust their usual patterns of behaviour.[15] During his first visits to northern villages, Scandrett acknowledged that he "kinda blundered" by using "crushing handshakes, loud expansive gestures." These conventions worked in the "big" army but not with First Nations people wary of men in uniform. Elders in particular backed away, worried that "uniforms" were coming to take away their children yet again. Scandrett and his staff learned to leave their combat fatigues at Borden and instead donned fleece jackets, gortex boots, blue jeans, and Ranger sweatshirts when they went north. They stayed overnight to indicate that they were not simply another group of transient civil servants, and they went into the bush with local residents "to fish and hunt and listen to stories under the stars."[16]

When the organizers faced tough questions, they answered them with humour and honesty. At Sandy Lake, for example, Chief Warrant Officer Harry Austen requested an interview with the chief and council. Near the end of his presentation, one of the councillors asked him, "What did you think of Oka?" Austen paused for a few minutes – something that Aboriginal people did – and then replied, "I come into your community, give you ammo, .303s, teach you search and rescue. What do you think I think about Oka?" After a few moments of silence, the room erupted in laughter, and the chief and council gave him permission to open up the patrol.[17]

First Nations wanted to know what they would get out of a Ranger patrol, and Austen recalled the importance of disclosing both the benefits and drawbacks. "We knew that if we were ever caught in a lie we would immediately be thrown out," he explained. The residents liked the guns and ammunition, but they wanted more.[18] "The lack of activities in our community have resulted in many tragedies, including suicides, vandalism, drug and solvent abuse," the Attawapiskat First Nation explained to the Canadian Forces. "Our people need hope: something to help them learn self-discipline and community involvement."[19] Chief Ignace Gull welcomed the opportunity that the Rangers would give to young people in remote communities, where boredom was acknowledged as the main cause of a disturbingly high suicide rate. "It's good for the young people to do this," Gull told a reporter. "Both cultures can feed off the talents of each other." Captain Scandrett affirmed that he had "no illusions we're going to produce proficient soldiers here," but sharing skills was certainly worthwhile.[20]

Scandrett's team formed the first Ontario patrols at Moose Factory First Nation in February 1994 and at Attawapiskat First Nation the following month. The Rangers responded to regional emergencies almost immediately. On 12 May, six hundred people had to be relocated from Kashechewan to

Rangers meet with a Ranger instructor in northern Ontario. Courtesy of Canadian Rangers
National Authority

Moosonee when the Albany River flooded. A few days later, the overflowing
Attawapiskat River forced an evacuation at Attawapiskat. The army activated
both Ranger patrols for the operations. They patrolled the streets, provided
security in the evacuee centres, monitored flood levels, helped 1,375 residents
settle in at Moosonee, and then helped them return home with their belong-
ings. The acting coordinator of emergency planning for Ontario, in his
letter of appreciation, noted that the Rangers had "performed a very important service to all of the communities involved and should be listed as a
resource in the local community emergency plans." He noted that "their
smart red accoutrements made them highly visible, but it was their enthusiasm and sincerity that made them stand out!"[21]

Once the communities recognized that Captain Scandrett had no ulterior
motives and that the Rangers were not a veiled attempt at military indoctrination, they eagerly supported his efforts. The Weenusk (Peawanuck)
First Nation patrol received its initial training in November 1994, followed

by the Fort Albany, Sandy Lake, English River (Constance Lake), and Bearskin Lake First Nations in early 1995. By 1 April 1995, there were 150 Rangers in 7 patrols. Nearly all of the Rangers were Aboriginal. In their first year, they participated in four funerals for veterans, the recovery of three bodies from fires (earning police commendations), six search and rescues, and Canada Day and Remembrance Day celebrations. First Nations communities, tribal organizations, and the local and national media all applauded their contributions.[22] When the Bearskin Lake population was evacuated to Geraldton because of a forest fire, the Rangers patrolled the pubs and took anyone "acting out" to the "penalty box" at the local arena, which housed the evacuees. One elder exclaimed to Austen, "I like my Rangers really good!" It was a ringing endorsement, given how wary elders had been about the military coming to northern Ontario.[23] The comment fit the growing success story of the Rangers nationally.

The Ranger Enhancement Program

Although the Rangers grew in the late 1980s and '90s, they remained a highly regionalized organization.[24] Representatives of National Defence Headquarters and the various regional headquarters met annually for Canadian Ranger Working Groups where they shared status reports and coordinated future planning, but their exchanges also highlighted the regions' different priorities. "We want the best for the Rangers," explained Major David Iley from the directorate of reserves at the inaugural meeting in February 1993 in Whitehorse, "but because of the diversity of each Ranger area – the Ranger staff are not always in agreement with each other." As a result, they adopted a guiding philosophy of "harmonization not standardization."[25] Some participants expressed concern that this logic had gone too far. Regional officers felt that the absence of national policy inhibited their efforts to acquire new equipment, set compensation rates, and standardize training. Captain Paul Chura concluded that the "likelihood of getting any firm direction from NDHQ is slim to nil. Our present tactic of doing our own thing here at [Canadian Forces Northern Area (CFNA), as Northern Region Headquarters was renamed in 1992] and in the other areas seems to be the only means of progress."[26]

Although the Rangers had no national policy, support came in the form of budget increases. Ironically, the 1994 federal budget and defence white paper – which foreshadowed the Liberal government's declining commitment to national defence – marked the beginning of the Rangers' formal, nation-wide revitalization.[27] A joint parliamentary committee on defence contemplated how to utilize resources effectively and recommended augmenting the Rangers, especially North of 60. It deemed other sovereignty operations either unrealistic or too expensive. Arcturus air patrols cost $9,083 per hour and produced "ephemeral" results. The navy could not operate in ice-covered waters and thus could not sustain Arctic operations for most of the year. Ranger patrols offered greater flexibility, a permanent and visual presence, and social benefits.[28] Most importantly, modest increases in Ranger budgets still represented a miniscule percentage of total national defence expenditures, and high rates of Aboriginal participation made the Rangers politically attractive. The 1994 white paper stated that "the Canadian Rangers reflect an important dimension of Canada's national identity and the Government will improve their capability to conduct Arctic and coastal land patrols."[29] The white paper clearly emphasized the importance of the North, where the Regular Forces had little presence, despite the previous governments' promises.

For its part, the military brass had not sought to enhance the Rangers. The Canadian Forces' new post–Cold War strategic outlook placed little priority on northern security and sovereignty matters.[30] In fact, the army did not want to devote more resources (instructors, weapons, and ammunition) to an element that could not address the growing "commitment-ca-pability" gap overseas.[31] Nevertheless, Colonel Pierre Leblanc, the director general reserves and cadets from July 1994 to July 1995, recognized that the Rangers remained "a unique and in some ways romantic force" and that officials had a political interest in promoting Aboriginal involvement.[32] The language that Leblanc used to sell the Rangers Enhancement Program in 1995 told its own story: "low risk, cost effective ... a tangible improvement that will meet the letter and the spirit contained in the White Paper ... while remaining within a reasonable funding envelope."[33] The modest cost was key: $5.1 million over five years, a significant investment compared to historical spending but a modest sum in an $11-billion annual defence budget. The vice chief of the defence staff supported a "common sense" solution, and the Ranger Enhancement Program fit the bill. The minister of national defence approved it in July 1995,[34] and so opened, in Leblanc's words, "a new era for the Canadian Rangers."[35]

In early 1995, enhancement planning began in earnest. Major-General Rick Linden, the chief of reserves and cadets, wanted to uphold "the

Colonel Pierre
Leblanc at the
Canadian Forces
Northern Area
change
of command
ceremony, July
1995. Courtesy of
Pierre Leblanc

characteristics of voluntarism, austerity, simplicity and intimate local knowledge" that had governed the Rangers. He did not intend, as Northern
Region officers had earlier, to bring the Rangers' terms of service closer to
that of the Primary Reserve or the Regular Force.[36] The Rangers' role would
remain unchanged: "to provide a military presence in those sparsely settled
northern, coastal and isolated areas of Canada which cannot conveniently
or economically be provided by other components of the Canadian Forces."
The task list confirmed the Rangers' historical focus on basic observation,
reconnaissance, and reporting, but it made no mention of guerrilla-type
action to delay an enemy. The director general of reserves and cadets explained that "the essential requirement to exercise sovereignty over Canadian territory" underpinned the Rangers' role, mission, and tasks. "In all
areas except the Arctic, this legal requirement is met by other means."[37]

Leblanc equated the "remote and isolated" part of the Rangers' mandate with "North of 60" and focused the enhancement program on that region. The first component of his plan entailed opening patrols in nine communities in the territories that had the demographic potential to sustain them. National Defence Headquarters agreed and argued that two more communities in northern Quebec on the shores of Hudson Bay should also receive patrols. The rationale for these new patrols was not to address "the new strategic environment," Leblanc argued; rather, they could improve "the social fabric" of the communities. His assessment reflected the reality of a limited budget as well as forward thinking. The military could not cover the entire North given the region's low population density and the issue of restricted mobility. "Fiscal and practical realities have always limited the Rangers coverage to the immediate areas around the main communities," Leblanc explained, "leaving ample room for expansion as new communities were formed or established communities grew in size." Enhancement would simply reduce these gaps while allowing for future expansion if the strategic environment changed for the worse.[38]

Senior defence officials knew the patrols would need significant training, at a considerable expense, if they expected the Rangers to use the military's sophisticated assets. They told Leblanc to avoid equipment with high capital, training, or maintenance costs; modest material contributions would have to suffice. Local knowledge of landforms, weather patterns, and the stars allowed Rangers to navigate in a difficult environment, but it did not allow them to communicate specific locations to others. Northern patrols would now receive global positioning system (GPS) units to support land navigation, but military personnel who worked with the Rangers often lamented that the Rangers had no way of reporting events – centralized communications meant day- or week-long delays. Patrols that visited North Warning System sites had been issued high-frequency radios to communicate back to their home base. The equipment withstood the rigours of the northern climate, so each northern patrol would receive two SBX-11A radios.[39]

The Ranger Enhancement Program also addressed the long-standing issue of uniforms. Leblanc understood that "recognition as a member of a Ranger patrol is extremely important to the morale of the Rangers and their standing in their community." On their own initiative, Rangers had designed and purchased sweatshirts and t-shirts.[40] A national organization needed more. Standard-issue combat uniforms, however, cost a lot and could not accommodate climatic and seasonal differences across the country. They also

Canadian Rangers
Rangers canadiens

Inspector of Canadian Forces
Colours and Badges
Inspecteur des drapeaux et insignes
des Forces canadiennes

National Defence Headquarters
Quartier général de la Défense nationale
June/juin 1996

The official Canadian Ranger badge, signed by Governor General Roméo Leblanc in June 1996. Canadian Rangers National Authority

violated the principle that Rangers would use their own kit. The Rangers needed something simple but distinctive and symbolic, so officials decided to issue standardized red sweatshirts with hoods, t-shirts, and toques adorned with the Ranger crest to all members. Although of questionable quality, the clothing provided a huge boost to morale. The red "hoodies" quickly became the hallmark of the Rangers in their communities and in the media.[41]

New funding for sovereignty patrols also enhanced the Rangers' community profile, encouraging them to go farther from their communities to exercise a "northern capability." During these "SOVPATs," four Rangers travelled to designated locations, within range of their home communities, to show the flag.[42] A Ranger instructor from Yellowknife would normally brief the local patrol leader on expectations, but the Rangers operated independently on the three- or four-day excursions. These patrols proved a resounding success. The first SOVPAT was held in Sachs Harbour on 13 November 1996, and nine more were completed before the end of the fiscal year. The patrols allowed the Rangers to exercise sovereignty visibly over lands and waters and the military to delegate responsibility for maintaining a northern "presence" to northerners themselves. Even if this patrolling did little to bolster Canada's legal sovereignty position,[43] it gave the Rangers of the Territorial North an operational role that differentiated them from their counterparts in the provinces.

Rangers in the provincial norths and along the Atlantic and Pacific coasts provided a military presence in these regions, but they lacked an obvious sovereignty role, and their operational purpose was never clearly defined.[44] Consequently, Colonel Leblanc did not understand where and how they fit within the military. In early 1995, he commissioned a "South of 60" study. The results paired operational roles with a strong social mission. Although the Ranger Enhancement Program drew an arbitrary line at sixty degrees north, the Rangers provided the only military presence in the provincial norths, where the army's official responsibilities included land surveillance and helping civil authorities in emergencies. By extension, the Rangers represented an operational asset across the country. Equally important, the Rangers provided broad social benefits:

> Their presence is very worthwhile both from the perspectives of the communities themselves and for the Canadian Forces and the Canadian government. Frequently the Rangers represent the only identifiable and formed group that is readily available to the community in time of need. Furthermore, because of the present fiscal environment all government levels are in the process of reducing expenditures. This will result in a further reduction in services and the presence of government agencies in isolated areas. Therefore, the Canadian Rangers either are, or will be, the only permanent federal presence in many isolated communities ... In pure business terms, which seems necessary these days to justify any military

endeavour, the Ranger program is analogous to a "Goodwill" class of asset. Its value is above and beyond the meagre budget that sustains it, yet that difference in value could only be realized once another means had to be funded to replace those services that the Rangers provide.[45]

The main report of the Special Commission on the Restructuring of the Reserves, released in October 1995, reinforced the Rangers' value by highlighting their cost-effectiveness and "significance in enriching the social fabric in remote areas." It also recommended southward expansion to incorporate more Aboriginal people in the Subarctic.[46]

These supportive reports ensured that the military brass did not shut down or scale back the Rangers in the provincial norths, but the main focus continued to be North of 60. "Although the threat scenario to our nation is now very low," Vice-Admiral Larry Murray explained in September 1995, "there is still a requirement to maintain a deployed observation capability and a military presence to demonstrate sovereignty." His direction for the "way ahead" emphasized the Rangers' role in the Territorial North and offered only conditional support for patrols "in the central part of Canada," which primarily supported national development. Consequently, regional Land Force commanders had to fund any new patrols South of 60 out of existing budgets, without drawing money from Primary Reserve or cadet allotments to subsidize them.[47] In short, regional army commanders would have to restructure and reallocate Ranger resources to create opportunities rather than counting on more money from central coffers.[48]

Reorganizing Atlantic Area

Divergent patterns of regional growth had historically precluded the Rangers from developing a uniform national structure. Patrols had replaced the cumbersome company-and-platoon structure in Canadian Forces Northern Area in the 1970s. Atlantic Canada, however, retained the original structure, and commissioned officers continued to liaise between Ranger units and regional headquarters. "If form is to follow function," staff officer Major Brian Sutherland noted in 1995, "it would appear that since Rangers work individually or in small groups, then they should be organized at a very low level, commensurate with their dispersion." He recommended converting the company structure into patrols. He also suggested that liaison officer functions should change so that they assumed formal command over Ranger units in each regional headquarters. In short, Sutherland believed that the organizational structure designed a half century earlier needed a complete overhaul.[49]

Reorganizing the Rangers in Atlantic Area into patrols significantly changed the regional culture. Captain Eugene Squires, posted to St. John's as the liaison officer in the fall of 1994, set out to rationalize the force in Newfoundland and Labrador.[50] He concurred with Sutherland that the company-platoon structure unnecessarily consumed scarce resources. Squires wanted most of the budget to flow directly to the Rangers for pay and personal equipment. This meant creating a "lean and effective" organization: reducing numbers in some areas and increasing them in sparsely populated coastal areas that fit the Rangers' mandate. He recommended disbanding companies in places that had other military units: the Avalon Peninsula, Gander, Stephenville, and Goose Bay. He also knew that substantive change would come only if both instructors and Rangers bought into his plan.[51]

The push to disband well-established units on the Avalon Peninsula met with strident opposition from a vocal and confrontational company commander. The Avalon, one of the most densely populated parts of Newfoundland, had a sizeable military presence at Canadian Forces Station St. John's, a well-developed road network and coastal watch program on the peninsula, and ample police and other emergency services. Furthermore, Squires observed, many Rangers on the Avalon actually lived in the provincial capital, which went against the spirit of the force.[52] This rationale for disbandment made sense to military decision makers but not to company commander Nelson Sherren, who described the decision as a "kick in the face" to his 120 Rangers. "The Rangers have been around a long time and have really provided an awful lot of useful service, to the reserve and to the regular force and to the general population," Sherren told a reporter. The Rangers had allowed locals to express "some civic pride and some sense of responsibility."[53] They bombarded the minister of national defence with appeals to retain the Avalon company, but to no avail. The military officially stood down the company, established in 1951, in November 1995.[54]

Units beyond the Avalon also felt the effects of Squires's reorganization efforts. The military closed down platoons at Gander and Stephenville (cities with military bases) and released those Rangers who lived in town. Rangers who lived outside of these urban areas were retained and reassigned to renamed coastal patrols: Kippens and Musgrave Harbour–Cape Freels.[55] The base commander at Goose Bay, who lobbied on behalf of the Rangers in

Her Excellency the Right Honourable Michaëlle Jean, governor general and commander-in-chief of Canada, presents the Order of Military Merit to Lieutenant W.J. Anderson on 24 February 2009. Sergeant Serge Gouin, Rideau Hall, Office of the Secretary to the Governor General, Photo GG-2009-0051-050

his community to prevent disbandment, argued that they remained an essential asset. They often trained Allied pilots in survival techniques, compensated for a limited security presence in Goose Bay, and would be a valuable ground security force if a plane crashed in central Labrador. The Rangers, he argued, were active, well trained, and versatile, and the new local commander was dependable and resourceful. Unlike its Avalon counterparts, the Goose Bay platoon survived the cuts.[56]

Joe Anderson was the last individual commissioned as a Ranger lieutenant when he became platoon commander in Goose Bay in 1995. It was a difficult time to take charge. The following year, Land Force Atlantic Area re-designated all of its Ranger platoons as patrols and stood down the company headquarters. "Quite a few people quit when we changed from platoons to patrols," he recalled.[57] With the transition to a patrol structure, existing platoon commanders retained their commissions and command of the patrols. From this point onward, however, new patrol leaders would be sergeants not officers, and section commanders would be master corporals, not sergeants. Company commanders and their seconds-in-command no longer had a place in the organization. Most resigned rather than face a reduction in status to patrol commander or Ranger.[58]

While officers responsible for the Rangers in the rest of Canada pushed for growth, Squires recommended a 20-percent *reduction* in strength in Atlantic Area in 1995. People in Newfoundland and Labrador faced an uncertain future. When the East Coast ground fishery collapsed in 1992, the subsequent moratorium on cod fishing put thirty thousand people out of work, devastating small fishing communities along the coast.[59] Was the Ranger organization fated to follow a similar course? Headquarters had already reduced the part-time staff support to the Rangers from ten to eight personnel and put recruiting on hold.[60] The authorized strength for Rangers in the area decreased from 1,000 in twenty platoons to 778 in twenty-four patrols.[61] Establishing patrols in the predominantly Inuit communities of Postville, Makkovik, and Rigolet along the Labrador Coast (areas that were formerly part of the Hopedale platoon) as well as the lumbering town of Buchans in central Newfoundland still left regional numbers well within authorized limits.[62] The Atlantic establishment would remain content to focus on selective recruiting and replacing retiring Rangers rather than expanding its footprint.[63]

As part of his general overhaul, Captain Squires made training more effective and stimulating. The seminar system, implemented in the 1980s, had Rangers gather in a central location for two to three days "to do map and compass" in a hotel meeting room about once every five years. Squires reoriented training to focus on outdoor field work and designed a twelve-day annual training program for each patrol: four weekends with an instructor and two without one. The Rangers would cover a range of subjects and focus on practical applications. In addition to refresher courses on basic skills, Rangers would concentrate on patrolling, marksmanship, and other outdoor activities. They would have one key objective: to conduct patrols along the coastline and within the interior of their respective patrol areas.[64]

Rangers in Newfoundland and Labrador received comparatively little fanfare for their contributions. Yet like their northern counterparts, they frequently volunteered to assist the RCMP in missing person searches and occasionally worked in conjunction with the Coast Guard auxiliary.[65] They helped with various community events, from Remembrance Day services, to dogsled races in Labrador West and Port Hope Simpson, to the Labatt twenty-four-hour relay in Clarenville. In 1994-95, Rangers in Labrador conducted three North Warning System site visits and instructed Canadian Forces and Allied units on Arctic survival in Goose Bay and Churchill Falls. The Red Bay patrol helped with efforts to clean up unexploded ordnance in the Strait of Belle Isle.[66] The Rangers also showcased their skills for provincial residents during the Cabot 500 Relay. From January to June 1997, they carried a ceremonial chrome axe on a four-thousand-kilometre trek to mark the five hundredth anniversary of John Cabot's voyage to the New World. By dog team, snowmobile, saddle-pack pony, longliner, car, truck, or on foot, they travelled from Labrador City to Churchill Falls, north to Hebron, south along the Labrador Coast, across the Strait of Belle Isle, and around the island of Newfoundland to Bonavista.[67] Every Ranger patrol in the province took part. The exercise tested the Rangers by having them use "navigation and survival skills under arduous conditions that are fundamental to their military jobs."[68] Rangers displayed the axe in schools and took it around to communities, they put on displays at local Legions and community centres, and they visited veterans and former Rangers.[69] Each of these activities raised their local profile significantly.

Growing Pains in Land Force Western Area

While Captain Squires and his staff in Atlantic Area were content to shrink their Ranger establishment, officers in other areas grew frustrated with the slow pace of expansion. Without clear central direction and with a major defence review ongoing in Ottawa, some regional commanders hesitated to expand. This hesitation had direct implications in Land Force Western Area. Major Ian Hay needed full funding to stand up new patrols that he had promised to various communities. The area commander, however, had halted his expansion plan. This no-growth policy upset not only communities slated for new patrols but also existing patrols, which were refused permission to recruit or even replace retirees. Hay understandably feared that these developments would once again damage the Rangers' credibility.[70] One local resident wrote to the minister of national defence to explain that "[i]n the Tofino Ucluelet area there is a need for an active, responsive, and knowledgeable Ranger patrol." Despite this need, he was not allowed to join and replace a Ranger who had dropped out.[71] He and other frustrated local residents had to wait, "in this period of severe budgetary constraints," until the military clarified the Rangers' roles.[72]

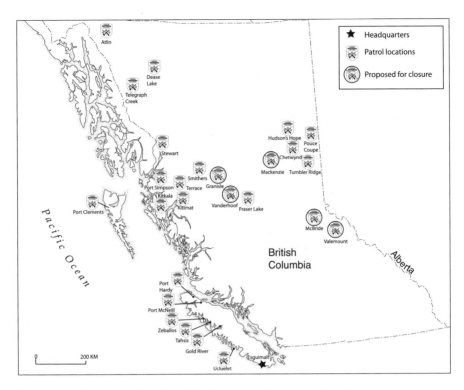

Ranger patrol locations in Land Force Western Area and proposed closures,
September 1996

Western Area had built a solid foundation for growth in the early 1990s,
but it struggled with restructuring because of inconsistent direction from
National Defence Headquarters. When Ottawa officials rejected the area
commander's initial proposal for not being "cost neutral," he went back to
the drawing board. Because coastal and isolated communities not serviced
by other government agencies were a national priority, officers identified
fourteen patrols that fell outside of these parameters. In 1996, Western Area
proposed closing five locations in the interior of the province: Granlisle (a
ghost town since the closure of the local copper mine in 1994), Valemount,
McBride, Vanderhoof, and Mackenzie. In their place, Western Area proposed establishing five new coastal patrols in Hartley Bay (a Tsimshian
fishing community), Kincolith (a Nisga'a community on the Nass River
system close to the Pacific), Ocean Falls or Bella Coola, Powell River (strategically located on the Sunshine Coast), and Sandspit on Haida Gwaii

(Queen Charlotte Islands). These new patrols would boost Aboriginal representation in the BC organization.[73]

The proposal fit with the national criteria set in Ottawa but still ran into insurmountable political obstacles. The minister of national defence felt the closures would elicit a backlash from Rangers and community leaders. Considering the reaction to platoon closures on the Avalon Peninsula, Land Force Command vetoed Western Area's plan.[74] Despite a waiting list of eager recruits, expansion had to await authorization and new funding.

Lacking support for his plans, Major Hay maintained the status quo and, like his counterparts in Atlantic Region, focused on enhanced training. He invited Captain Jim Miller, who had retired from the Regular Force after a long career with the Black Watch and the Princess Patricia's Canadian Light Infantry, to prepare a leadership program. Miller was soon hired full-time to take the course on the road. He set up in a BC community, rented a hotel, and brought in Rangers from surrounding patrols. He taught drill, public speaking, and the basic military orders process, and he ran mini exercises in which Rangers would write up orders, make plans, and execute them. Weekend training ensured that no one had to take time off work or leave his or her family for an extended period, but it never offered enough time to cover the material.[75] As the training program evolved, Major Hay decided to centralize the leadership courses at Camp Albert Head near Victoria. These "RVs" blended classroom and field training and included two components: a basic recruit course for Rangers and a course for patrol leaders. The two groups worked independently until the last couple of days, when all the Rangers implemented their classroom training in the field.[76]

Captain Miller and Major Hay formed a solid team. Hay, approachable and laissez-faire, did not micromanage his instructors like officers in some regions.[77] Miller passed on this philosophy to the Rangers. "Getting the job done through motivation, cooperation and personal example has been found to be a much better method of leadership than that of using force or fear," Miller explained to course participants. "This is especially true in the Rangers, because you are neither fish nor fowl, neither civilian nor military, but some of each, some of the time."[78]

Survival and Sovereignty: Quebec

If anyone embodied the hybrid nature of Ranger culture it was Sergeant Mario Aubin, a Ranger instructor in Quebec Area. Journalist Monique

A relaxed moment at an "RV" in Albert Head. Courtesy of 4 Canadian Ranger Patrol Group

Giguère described him as the Davy Crockett of Quebec's Grand Nord, the "super-Ranger" who was away from home 250 days out of the year on Ranger activities. "I have one foot in the army and one foot in Inuit life," Aubin explained. He never barked out orders in Nunavik but instead thought and acted like an Inuk, seeking consensus wherever possible. He was patient, even during half-hour debates over which type of tea or coffee the Rangers should purchase. In his nine years as an instructor, he learned two dialects of Inuktitut and the importance of maintaining a sense of humour. He had a paternal relationship with some villages and a more equal one in others. In all cases, he noted that Inuit were not "primitive," they were doctors and pilots and ran committees and cooperatives while maintaining their trad-itional hunting and fishing pursuits. "They are not onboard with the [mil-itary] system," Aubin commented. "It is freedom that they love."[79] As a Ranger instructor, Aubin enjoyed a similar freedom.

Ranger training and activities in Quebec lacked structure and account-ability. Master Warrant Officer François Duchesneau recalled that every instructor did his own thing. Some saw annual training as a big hunting and fishing trip, with fishing contests and rifle shoots, and offered little to

Long-standing Rangers in Quebec. Courtesy of François Duchesneau, 2 Canadian Ranger Patrol Group

no practical training. Another sat in a hotel room with a radio while the Rangers did exercises on the land.[80] Quebec Area had no standard operating procedures, and the deputy chief of staff cadets provided minimal oversight. The liaison officer, Captain Marc Morin, managed the Ranger cell and its budget, but he did not have the authority of a commanding officer.[81] The lack of accountability and the large sums of cash that instructors carried to communities to cover Ranger pay and equipment use presented opportunities for abuse. These serious shortcomings in training and financial controls reflected the downside of institutional flexibility.

Although the Ranger cell did not have formal unit status, its personnel brought patrols together to build capacity and reinforce broader regional identities. For example, in late March and early April 1996, Quebec Area launched Défi Nunavik (Nunavik Challenge) to evaluate its ability to deploy Ranger patrols in Nunavik. For the first time, more than one hundred Rangers from the thirteen Inuit patrols in Nunavik and one from Northwest Territories met up in a joint training exercise. Rangers from every patrol in Nunavik left their villages by snow machine and travelled at least four hundred kilometres to Klotz Lake, a remote location in the heart of northern

Quebec. Upon arrival, they built a survival village – including igloos – and studied how to identify and build a runway to support a Twin Otter on skis. On 3 April, an aircraft filled with journalists landed on the strip. Major Carlo de Ciccio observed, "The reporters appreciated the Rangers' help and guidance in eating the uncooked, frozen meat and fish and in sleeping in igloos while the outside temperature was − 30° ... The journalists confirmed why southerners associate the Inuit Rangers' way of life with the term 'survival.'"[82]

Québécois journalists noted a sovereignty subtext to this exercise – one that did not relate to potential external threats to Canada's Arctic. The divisive referendum debate on Quebec sovereignty the previous October, which the federalist forces had won by the narrowest of margins, served as a reminder of ethnolinguistic cleavages in Canada and Quebec. In their own referendum, for example, 96 percent of Nunavimmiut (Inuit of Quebec) had voted against Quebec independence.[83] Mayors and other influential community leaders filled the Inuit ranks in Ranger patrols, Morin explained, and "they act out of love for their country." Indeed, Inuit residents told journalist André Noël that the decision to hold the military exercise had been tied to the debate over Quebec separation. They saw Défi Nunavik as a means of reinforcing "Inuit pride and their sense of belonging in Canada, via the Canadian army."[84] When Major-General Alain Forand visited Inukjuak in 1996, Ranger Marroosie Patsauq asked him the following question: If Quebec decided to separate and Nunavimmiut wanted to remain part of Canada, could Nunavimmiut call upon the Canadian Army to protect their territory?[85] The Canadian Rangers in Nunavik wore their red sweat-shirts with great pride and provided a clear example that Inuit attachment to Canada was sincere.[86]

Major Claude Archambault, an energetic Regular Force officer who assumed responsibility for the Rangers in Quebec in 1997, wanted to foster a similar connection with the Cree, the most outspoken Aboriginal group in the province. He saw the Rangers as a viable expression of the province's regional ethnocultural identities and encouraged relevant training plans that balanced local priorities and needs while promoting intercultural dialogue.[87] To implement his plans, Archambault had to find common ground in a delicate political environment. Cree declared their right to self-determination under international law. Like Inuit, the Grand Council of the Cree insisted that this meant they had the right to remain in Canada if Quebec chose to secede, and 96 percent of Cree voters agreed. Despite this common ground, Cree and Inuit had a long history of enmity.[88] They lived in the adjacent villages of Kuujjuarapik-Whapmagoosui at the mouth of the Great Whale River, for example, but only Inuit participated in the Ranger patrol. The two did not mix until 1996, when the Cree band chief allowed his members to become Rangers. Quebec Area welcomed this "foot in the door"[89] and recruited seven Cree and seventeen Inuit to form a mixed Cree-Inuit patrol in Kuujjuarapik.[90]

Within the Rangers, the military accepted Aboriginal territorial identities, and overlapping or enmeshed notions of sovereignty did not conflict. Although media attention continued to fixate on Nunavimmiut participation, Quebec Area had a diverse membership: by November 1997, it consisted of 362 Inuit, 86 "Whites" (both anglophones and francophones, predominantly along the Lower North Shore), and 26 First Nations (Cree and Innu [Montagnais-Naskapi]).[91]

This diversity challenged instructors, who had to adjust their teaching to suit distinct cultural and linguistic groups. To succeed as a Ranger instructor, Aubin explained, an individual needed to possess patience, a strong will, an open spirit, and a positive attitude. Northerners had different notions of time than city dwellers; they lived day to day, from one moment to the next. When travelling on snowmobile, they stopped frequently along the route to look at animal tracks or chat with people they met on the trail. Aubin appreciated their sense of democracy, which they applied much better than southerners. In northern communities, both Aboriginal and non-Aboriginal, people never raised their voices, he explained. Everyone listened to one another, and youth respected the judgment and experience of their elders. Accordingly, the Rangers learned from the instructors and taught one another. "It is an opportunity for older Inuit to transfer their traditional knowledge to younger ones," Aubin emphasized. The military respected their culture; it never behaved like a conqueror, lording it over them.[92]

David Scandrett and the Rangers of Ontario

In Ontario, Scandrett did not want to conquer or indoctrinate the Aboriginal population with traditional military values; he wanted to adapt the military to the Rangers' world. "It took nearly three years for Scandrett to convince the army that it had to change to accommodate natives," journalist Sarah Scott reported. Scandrett told her that the military's reaction had been "curious, interesting." He laughed and said that he had to choose his words carefully. "We've taken the army and really bent it, cranked it around. It's based on the premise that you guys [Native peoples] have been here for 10,000 years, you've learned a thing or two, so let's not reinvent the wheel. Let's use some of the devices and techniques you have."[93] Political realities dictated that new patrols be "placed in communities that will actively support the Rangers – and not necessarily where the Canadian Forces require them to be." Nevertheless, they provided a positive "interface" between members of the CF and First Nations.[94] The contrast between Scandrett's opinion and General Vokes's 1948 comments dismissing the value of Aboriginal people in northern Ontario as potential Rangers could not be more striking.

Although outsiders accused Scandrett of "going Native" or of being a "wannabe Indian," Major Guy Ingram (who worked with Scandrett in the 1990s and eventually became commanding officer of the Rangers in northern Ontario in 2007) disagreed. Scandrett was entranced by Aboriginal ceremonies, ethos, and traditions and read voraciously about Native culture, but he did so to understand and foster the military's awareness.[95] He also had a personal mission to change things. Described by his former staff as an "ideas man" and a "doer," Scandrett's philosophy was "rules are a guide and meant to be adapted if common sense prevails. What works in Toronto may not work in the North." Understanding and accommodating Aboriginal culture took priority over typical military practices. This frustrated some members of the Canadian Forces, but Scandrett had a clear philosophy: friendly human interaction, not military activities, would build the respect and trust needed for a constructive relationship.[96] Scandrett's unorthodox methods achieved results. The Nishnawbe Aski Nation, which represented fifty First Nations in northern Ontario, faced a youth suicide crisis. They applauded the Rangers for contributing to "long-term suicide prevention strategies by providing youth in [high-risk] communities with meaningful tasks and training, and providing them with a way of gaining pride and self-esteem." The Rangers also helped "to dispel some of the distrust of military type organizations" that prevailed in the region.[97]

Scandrett's Rangers also helped maintain Canadian sovereignty, albeit in an unconventional way:

> The matter of sovereignty ... is a concern for all Canadians, whether they
> live in Toronto, Fort Severn or Resolute Bay. The political realities of the
> north are that First Nations are rapidly gaining autonomy under the

devolution to self government. The principle political structure [in north-ern Ontario] is based on the Treaty Nine native communities who are now called the Nishnawbe-Aski Nation or NAN. NAN is ostensibly Ontario north of the 50th parallel. Last year [1994] NAN assumed policing duties on James and Hudson Bay coasts and will expand to the entire area by 1997. NAN is assuming forest fire responsibilities as of this summer. The devolution process is moving quickly into schooling, child welfare and a variety of other areas. If the DND wishes to train or operate in the north in the future the time to establish the links to NAN is now. The Ranger presence is being recognized and we are gaining in credibility. The con-sequences of withdrawal at this time would be a loss of credibility for the CF, a loss of access for the future, a lack of presence, increased costs for assistance operations, [search and rescue], [the danger of a major air dis-aster], and the social consequences. The essence of cessation would be "bridge burning" rather than "bridge building" to an alienated portion of Canadian society.[98]

First Nations people could serve Canada and their communities simul-taneously, providing the military "with local knowledge and coverage and at the same time empowering communities to be self reliant, all at a very low cost."[99]

Ottawa's definition of sovereignty differed. When Colonel Leblanc ex-plained that Ranger enhancement plans would focus on the Arctic, particu-larly "sovereignty and international laws dealing with legal entitlement to land," Major Russ Smye of Land Force Central Area took up Scandrett's argument. In the provincial norths, the Rangers could also "be viewed as improving the 'sovereignty' of native communities, by increasing the public awareness of aboriginal issues in Canada."[100] To counter criticisms that the Rangers were merely "a group of adults seeking a bit of adventure," Scandrett rejoined that the same held true for the Primary Reserve and Regular Force. "If it were not the case," he observed, "then no one would join any compon-ent of the forces."[101]

As a result of Scandrett's energy and initiative, Ranger headquarters in Central Area was distinctive, proactive, and innovative in forging relations with Aboriginal Ontario. When the Stoney Point faction took over Camp Ipperwash in the summer of 1995, the military police searched for ways to maintain the peace in a confrontational situation. Captain Scandrett acted as a facilitator to help diffuse the situation. (The tragic events that followed

Rifle-range training in northern Ontario. Courtesy of Canadian Rangers National Authority

the clash between the Ontario Provincial Police and the Stoney Pointers at Ipperwash Provincial Park a few months later proved the volatility of the situation.) His unit ran Native awareness seminars for other military units. Instructors taught Aboriginal history, culture, and values in an effort to prevent the kind of showdown that had occurred at Oka. Headquarters staff and instructors displayed care by going into northern communities to help with the healing after suicides or when a respected elder passed away. Following a series of deadly house fires on the James and Hudson Bay coasts, Scandrett's staff arranged and supported training for volunteer fire fighters through the Canadian Forces Fire Academy.[102] Local authorities appreciated these efforts, expressing their confidence that, with the Rangers around, the military would be able to respond more quickly to emergencies.[103]

The Rangers' evolving raison d'être required carefully balancing operational requirements and community interests. Critics accused Scandrett of diluting the Rangers' military identity and role. Did he stretch military policy beyond its reasonable limits, or did his approach represent the sort of creative interpretation of the Rangers' mission necessary to serve broader national policy goals and nation-building efforts? Even his critics could not deny the helpful relationships he had built in northern Ontario. There, like elsewhere across the country, community members and the media celebrated the Rangers for their positive connection to the Canadian state and their important contributions to cultural survival in Aboriginal communities.

Creating the Junior Canadian Rangers

Sustainable community development in remote regions was not just about economics – it was about human capital. Elders who deplored the loss of traditional knowledge among younger generations applauded the Rangers as a mechanism for community members to exercise and share their skills on the land. Ranger service reinforced ties of sentiment, knowledge, and responsibility to homeland and community. Aboriginal spokespersons and scholars emphasized the important link between country space, community healing, and cultural renewal, which helps explain why Northern communities embraced the Rangers so strongly.[104] While attending school, young people had less time and fewer opportunities to acquire knowledge about hunting, fishing, trapping, and gathering. These practices are not anachronistic in a modern world; they are "an integral part of present-day reality" that "represent[s] a specific way of being in the world."[105] They offer tools for survival – both out on the land and in communities.

Community members, scholars, journalists, and civil servants all recognized the overwhelming pressures that modern ideals and expectations placed on youth in remote regions. Anthropologist Richard Condon observed that the diversification of youth recreational activities reflected a broader process of social change, where increasing contact with southern culture altered behaviour and attitudes. Northern communities increasingly looked like southern settlements. They had schools, street grids, Western-style homes, and all the amenities of the South: Internet, TV, cable, video games, pop, and candy. Young Inuit were not only playing hockey, basketball, baseball, and volleyball, they were watching television and simply "hanging out ... in a remarkably un-Inuit manner." Their activities included overt competition, ranking, and physical confrontation – behavioural changes that were connected to economic acculturation processes and challenged traditional values.[106] The Royal Commission on Aboriginal Peoples' final report concurred that the "majority of Aboriginal youth spend much of their lives immersed in non-Aboriginal culture. Many get little encouragement from the world around them to celebrate who they are, who their forebears were, who they could become as Aboriginal people." Studies emphasized that government-funded, community-based initiatives represented the only viable solution to the multidimensional problems of suicide, alcohol, drug and solvent abuse, criminal activity, and other self-destructive behaviour.[107]

The National Cadet League, a fixture in several northern and coastal communities, offered opportunities for youth between the ages of twelve and eighteen to develop leadership skills. "Cadets themselves are invariably enthusiastic; indeed, in some of the units, it is only the leadership exerted by senior cadets which keeps the units going," Captains J.N. Gri and S.A. Cameron explained in 1992. "Parents, teachers, principals, community leaders and RCMP officers all note regularly that communities with active cadet units are less likely to suffer youth related crime, substance abuse, and suicide than those without. Cadets ... perform better in school and have more drive to succeed in other areas as well." Unfortunately, organizational problems offset these positive attributes. By the early 1990s, staff officers in Northern Area concluded that the national cadet program was "not meeting the needs of all Northern communities in its current guise." Nineteen out of the twenty cadet units in the territories had failed to meet normal training standards and would be on probation if authorities decided to apply national standards to them. Most northerners – particularly in Aboriginal communities – found the bureaucratic requirements of cadet leadership too onerous and failed to see how national training goals applied to their youth.[108]

Given that Northern Area had already relaxed the rules of the cadet program more than regulations allowed, it contemplated a new youth program built around the Canadian Rangers. Officials applauded the Rangers as a "success story insofar as adapting Canadian Forces regulations and procedures to other cultures are concerned." This adaption had taken place with minimal paperwork. Could this experience be applied to cadet units led by Rangers? Activities could focus on traditional skills and values and provide opportunities for youth to spend time on the land. In addition, the program would not burden community leaders with formal requirements. The military could implement the new youth program, aimed primarily at Aboriginal northerners, in communities without functioning cadet units.[109]

(This attempt to complement the cadet program rather than compete with it mirrored the long-standing logic that situated the Canadian Rangers vis-à-vis the Primary Reserve.)

In early 1994, Northern Area formally proposed a two-year pilot project to test a Junior Canadian Ranger program for twelve to seventeen year olds. Major Rick Bell, the senior staff officer for the Rangers and cadets in Northern Area, explained that, "as many of the Native people of the far north in particular move towards independence and self-government, they continually stress two basic requirements for their youth: (a) a good education; and (b) the need to be educated in traditional values and skills." This posed a problem because some elders believed the cadet program threatened indigenous values. Local Ranger leadership would dispel similar concerns about the Junior Rangers. The core curriculum would focus on three areas: Ranger skills, traditional skills, and life skills. Only the Ranger skill component, which complemented Canadian Ranger training, would be fixed. The other areas were designed to reflect the uniqueness of the program and its adaptability. Traditional skills, determined in partnership with a community-based committee and taught by local subject-matter experts, would vary. This ensured that a participating community continued to shape its own identity. The community would also have considerable latitude to address issues affecting local youth within the life skills portion of the program. In short, the Junior Rangers would offer a community-based youth program supported by the military, not a defence program designed to assimilate youth into military modes of thinking.[110] The chief of the defence staff approved the proposal in June, and the chief of reserves and cadets funded a pilot program.

Local and territorial politicians supported the concept and approved a trial in Paulatuk, Northwest Territories, in November 1994. Predominantly Inuvialuit, the hamlet of about three hundred people on Amundsen Gulf relied heavily on a traditional economy of fishing and harvesting game and had an unemployment rate of over 30 percent. Forty percent of households had six or more people, and more than one-third of households were in "core need."[111] Official documentation described the Ranger patrol in Paulatuk as "above average ... but certainly not one of the best in CFNA." Officials suggested that "if the trial succeeded there, it would have a good chance anywhere in the North." The Ranger sergeant and mayor responded with enthusiasm, and the hamlet approved the military's proposal. According to the plan, regular Canadian Forces staff would visit the community about once every three months to conduct field and classroom training. Ideally, the community would run the program, with little external direction and at minimal cost.[112]

By this measure, the Paulatuk trial failed. A dozen youth, "desperately searching for meaningful activities to occupy themselves within the community," signed up with high expectations. Activities, however, were sporadic and run primarily by the staff officer from Yellowknife. The local Ranger sergeant responsible for organizing and conducting training seemed uncomfortable with and confused by his responsibility for the Junior Rangers. Being an efficient and competent patrol commander did not necessarily translate into the leadership skills required to run a youth organization. Community members who had offered verbal support for the concept proved unwilling to commit to actual activities. As part of the trial, military officials established an adult committee, chaired by a community member, to establish a training timetable, select local instructors, and supervise activities. No parents or other community members met for discussions or volunteered to help. "As nearly every activity in the community offers some form of payment to participants," an appraisal concluded, "there is little interest in the coffee and cookies presently offered at meetings to discuss the Junior Rangers." Money would ensure community participation and pay for equipment, which "few if any" community members would supply or loan without compensation.[113]

As excitement about the Junior Ranger idea spread, failure became politically unacceptable. When Canadian Forces Northern Area briefed the national working group on its pilot project in May 1994, Quebec Area noted that it was already developing a similar program in Ungava (Nunavik), which had the highest youth suicide rates in the country.[114] Lieutenant-Colonel Robert Chartrand, the officer responsible for cadets and Rangers in Quebec, had first recognized the urgent need for a youth program following a spate of suicides in Puvirnituq at the start of the decade. Premier Robert Bourassa and the deputy minister of Aboriginal Affairs raised similar points when they met with the newly appointed commander of Quebec Area, Major-General Armand Roy. The idea for the Junior Rangers hatched soon after. In June 1994, Roy called Chartrand into his office after meeting with Jean Dupuis, the president of the Kativik Regional Government, and told him: "The Junior Rangers, you're going to carry that forward!" When Chartrand explained that he did not have the money to proceed, Roy replied, "Thou shalt not!"[115]

Thanks to support from regional organizations, the Junior Canadian Rangers did proceed. That fall, Quebec Area signed a statement of principle with the provincial government and the Kativik Regional Government. Cadet officials presented a proposal to the regional health authority and met with the thirteen Ranger patrol leaders in February 1995 to discuss the concept. Unlike the pilot in Northern Area, Quebec Area received no additional defence funding for its "unauthorized" trial. The Kativik Regional Government, demonstrating its clear determination to see the project succeed, offered $5,000 in start-up funds to each patrol and another $45,000 for equipment such as tents and sleeping bags.[116] In July 1995, twelve Junior Rangers and Rangers participated in a ten-day cadet camp at Valcartier (their home communities paid for travel), and in September the first annual training exercise was held in Nunavik. By December, Quebec Area had established Junior Ranger patrols in Puvirnituq, Salluit, and Kuujjuaq comprising nearly ninety youth. The Kativik Regional Government wanted to expand the Junior Rangers throughout Nunavik, so Quebec Area devised a plan to extend the program to fourteen Inuit communities over the following three years.[117]

Although Quebec Area officials believed their efforts validated the Junior Ranger concept and justified official military support, Northern Area officials acknowledged that their trial in Paulatuk had "failed spectacularly."[118] Some departmental officials in Ottawa also expressed hesitancy to invest in the program in a time of fiscal austerity. Rem Westland, the director general of Aboriginal affairs, feared that the Junior Rangers represented "a dilution of the seriousness of the Ranger business." Creating a social service that fell outside of the military's primary mandate might misrepresent the Rangers as "grown-up kids, playing at the defence of sovereignty." If the program failed to function as planned, there would be no escape: local community leaders – and the Department of Indian Affairs and Northern Development – would not allow the Department of National Defence to step away. Furthermore, Westland worried, unless Junior Rangers had the opportunity to join the Canadian Rangers when they reached the age of eighteen, they would end up frustrated. In his assessment, the department had been "encouraged by political pressures and by [politically] correct thinking to take the important idea and activity of the Rangers and add to it a social services tail."[119]

Westland's assessment of the political context was prescient. Ministerial statements proclaimed that the pilot program in Paulatuk had yielded impressive results. Despite the acknowledged problems with the trial, the commander in Yellowknife still recommended the establishment of a national program – as long as it came with new support positions.[120] The office of the vice chief of the defence staff concurred. "All the disadvantages prevalent in small isolated communities in the Territories can also be found 'South of 60,'" Major Brian Sutherland noted in February 1996, "and it is assumed that, sooner rather than later, political pressures will be brought to bear and the Forces will be required to institute the Junior Ranger programme in Labrador, the Ungava peninsula of Quebec, north-western Ontario, across the Prairies, and throughout the interior of British Columbia and along the Pacific coastline."[121] He was correct. The Rangers in Ontario submitted a business plan to establish a "Young Ranger" program in their area the following month. The plan cited appalling social conditions among Aboriginal youth, who were seeking "to escape boredom and hopelessness through petty crime, alcohol, narcotics, gasoline sniffing," and suicide.[122]

Military officials correctly anticipated positive public reactions. Communities attached value to the Junior Rangers, not only because of the Ranger organization's popularity but also because of the youth program's merits. Teachers noticed increased attendance and improvements in schoolwork among Junior Rangers, along with decreased levels of vandalism and destructive behaviour. Journalists, inundated with government reports about endemic Aboriginal youth suicide rates, began to discuss the program as part of the solution. Monique Giguère labelled the Junior Rangers "an antidote to suicide" in *Le Soleil*, citing local sources in Puvirnituq who believed that the program had contributed to the absence of suicides in the community that year. "Our youth behave better, they are better citizens, and they learned to respond effectively in a crisis," Akulivik mayor Adamie Alayco confirmed. Junior Ranger activities helped Inuit youth live in two cultures – one modern, one traditional – at the same time.[123]

These positive social indicators, anecdotal as they were, generated even more enthusiasm. Given that eight mayors in the Nunavik region were Rangers, Quebec Area had little difficulty selling the idea to local councils.[124] When Major-General Alain Forand visited four villages in Nunavik to officially open new Junior Ranger patrols in September 1996, two hundred of the four hundred residents of Akulivik showed up at the opening ceremony to applaud their youth. In Kangiqsujuaq, 120 people crowded into the school gymnasium. Practically the whole community of Tasiujaq (150 people) showed up. Communities without patrols waited impatiently and

Junior Canadian Ranger Anna Ningiuk from Inukjuak, Quebec, during Camp Okpiapik, July 2002. Courtesy of 2 Canadian Ranger Patrol Group

pushed for more rapid expansion. "Last year, I wanted to begin the program with two patrols," Chartrand explained. "We finally agreed on three. Kuujjuaq, Salluit, and Puvirnituq were created. This year, I was considering three. There are four: Tasiujaq, Kangiqsujuaq, Akulivik, and Inukjuak. I do not like strict timetables that leave no wiggle room." In two years, he predicted, each of the fourteen communities in Nunavik would boast a Junior Rangers patrol. Despite tremendous demand, however, questions of budget and instructors remained.[125]

When the minister of national defence officially announced the creation of the Junior Canadian Rangers in November 1996, the implementation plan called for fifteen patrols: seven each in Northern Area and Quebec Area and one in Central Area.[126] Managing expectations and building the program in a sustainable manner became more difficult as political momentum increased. In February 1998, the Kativik Regional Government unanimously adopted a resolution requesting additional Junior Ranger funding and training resources. Chairman Jean Dupuis noted that "the Canadian Rangers have always been role model[s] for many Inuit youth who for a long time have been looking forward to the day that they will be old enough to becom[e] a Canadian Ranger. The creation of Junior Ranger units piloted by the Canadian Rangers now provides for a structured framework in preparing the youth for the future." Rangers taught life skills to youth, skills that would help reduce suicide rates and serve them throughout their lives. "The elected representatives of Nunavik ... want to see a sustained development program on a permanent basis in order to ensure continuity," Dupuis asserted. In the past, successful programs had died because of cutbacks "without giving any consideration to the social impacts."[127]

The threat of retrenchment loomed. Finance minister Paul Martin cut federal budgets deeply in the late 1990s. When Ethel Blondin-Andrew – a Dene from Tulita, Northwest Territories, and the secretary of state for youth – announced three years of federal funding for the Junior Rangers in July 1998, she eased fears. "It's a success story the government wants to see grow," she explained. The funding supported plans to double the number of patrols by 2001.[128] The Department of National Defence would share costs with other federal, provincial, and territorial departments. The question of consistent funding to sustain long-term growth lingered. "Unfortunately, there is a very bad track record of youth programmes that have started off as joint ventures and ended with the Department of National Defence footing the entire bill," Major Sutherland reflected.[129] The government made no promises of ongoing support, and planners warned that a sudden funding cut would surely destroy local relationships.

The additional workload associated with the Junior Rangers certainly caused concern at some regional headquarters. Rapid expansion meant that Ranger instructors had to conduct Junior Ranger patrol training in addition to their existing responsibilities.[130] At the local level, this could include caribou, goose, or buffalo hunting, fishing excursions, basket making, or learning about traditional medicine from elders. Instructors struggled to secure sustained commitment from community support groups. "As forewarned last year the Adult Committees in most communities quickly disappeared once JCR patrols were formed," Northern Area Headquarters reported in 1998. The Ranger patrols and instructors picked up the slack.[131] The introduction of Junior Ranger advanced summer training sessions taxed regional resources even further. Colonel Tom Geburt, the director general reserves and cadets, agreed to Quebec Area's proposal for a camp in 1998, even though it did not mesh with Junior Ranger policy.[132] These annual

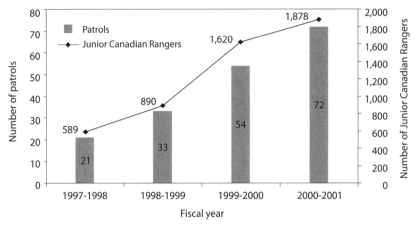

Junior Canadian Rangers expansion, 1997-2001

Source: Director of Reserves, Annual Report No.1 for FY 00-01 CAN RAN 2000, 1 June 2001

events offered opportunities for cultural exchange and gave youth from remote communities a chance to experience new environments.[133] The summer training sessions had no baseline funding, but Geburt agreed to support them as long he could.[134] Once expectations had been built up, it was difficult to backtrack. With resources stretched to the limits, both Northern Area and Quebec Area requested additional instructors and a supply technician to manage Junior Ranger stores. In Northern Area, which had no local source of primary reservists, human resources were particularly expensive and difficult to secure.

When Colonel Geburt approved Quebec Area's summer camp proposal, he urged the other regional commanders "to remain open minded so that the programme could evolve." Everyone believed that the program should have national standards that could accommodate each area's particular needs, but practical interpretations remained contentious. When Major Claude Archambault insisted that he needed more equipment and "an approved program of progressive training" to retain interest among youth, Geburt recommended the cadet program as a model.[135] Staff in Northern Area protested because the recommendation contravened the original idea of a modest, community-based initiative, one "capable of being operated by a very small staff" until it proved viable.[136] The program's strength lay in its grassroots origins: Junior Rangers could identify with local Rangers, which is why initial recruitment had been so successful in Northwest Territories and Yukon.[137] The communities themselves – not the Canadian Forces – should be the primary "shareholders." Were accelerated development plans diverging from the initial vision?[138]

All told, the ad hoc approach to building the Junior Rangers facilitated rapid growth but opened deep regional rifts. The program had forty-one patrols by the end of 1999 (seventeen in the Territorial North, eighteen in Quebec, and six in Ontario) but no general consensus on what the future should or would look like. What happened in one region had implications for the rest of the country. For instance, when the initial plans conceived in Ottawa failed to include additional funding for area commanders, Land Force Western Area and Land Force Atlantic Area opted out. With existing cadet corps in many coastal communities, they had a ready excuse.[139] Their tune changed, however, when the program garnered support from the highest echelons of National Defence and when outside funds sweetened the pot. The deputy minister wanted the "good news story" of the Junior Canadian Rangers to grow across Canada.[140] Although the director general reserves and cadets had told Northern Area to base the opening of new patrols on available personnel,[141] the department's announcements projected seventy-one patrols by 2001. Confusion reigned: nationals officials expected the regions to develop the program but did not provide them with the resources or direction to do so.

Establishing Canadian Ranger Patrol Groups

Development problems within the Junior Ranger program mirrored those that had plagued the Rangers for decades. The regional nature of the organization meant it had the flexibility to accommodate diversity, but it also meant that each region interpreted national directives differently. Command-and-control issues confused matters further.[142] In theory, the direct chain of command for a Ranger patrol sergeant in Northern Area led straight to the vice chief of the defence staff in Ottawa.[143] In practice, this was ludicrous. Given the growing responsibilities and the expanding size of regional Ranger staff, it made sense to organize the patrols into a formal "patrol group" in Canadian Forces Northern Area and in each of the Land Force areas.[144] This happened in early 1998 with the creation of five new patrol groups. 1 CRPG, based in Yellowknife, was responsible for patrols in Yukon, Northwest Territories, Nunavut, Alberta, Saskatchewan, northern British Columbia, and northern Manitoba. 2 CRPG was responsible for Quebec, 3 CRPG for

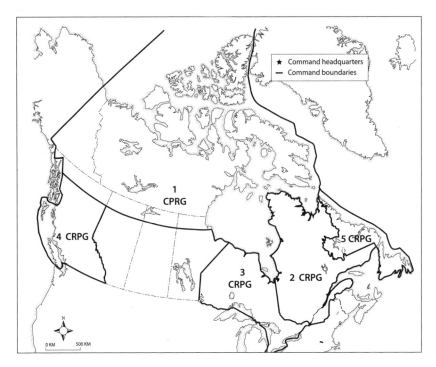

Canadian Ranger Patrol Groups, 1998
Source: Department of National Defence

Ontario, 4 CRPG for the West Coast and Interior of BC, and 5 CRPG for Newfoundland and Labrador.[145]

The establishment of patrol groups created total force units. The military personnel who supported training and administration came under the command of a major (as commanding officer) and a captain (as deputy commanding officer). Officer and Ranger instructor cadre positions became full-time command positions, and the Ranger liaison officer designation in Atlantic Area was disbanded. Patrol commanders now reported to the commanding officer of their patrol group, who in turn reported to his or her area commander.[146]

These changes only partially answered the question of who owned the Rangers. The area commanders controlled the patrol groups and directed operations, but the overall chain of command remained divided: Canadian Forces Northern Area reported to the vice chief of the defence staff, and the land force area commanders reported to the chief of the land staff. Although the director of reserves monitored Ranger issues at National

Defence Headquarters, it was not empowered to set training standards or establishment levels or to guide the areas on policy or organization. Without a central authority asserting some measure of control over the Rangers, ambiguity about overarching roles and expectations continued. Conflicting interpretations of directives and of the Rangers' raison d'être complicated decision making and generated disagreements as patrol groups competed for resources.[147]

Major Claude Archambault, newly appointed as the deputy commanding officer of 2 CRPG when it was established in April 1998, had a bold vision for patrols in Quebec. Although his unit did not garner the same national attention as its territorial counterpart (1 CRPG), it enjoyed strong regional support, which Archambault wanted to translate into a much larger presence. He first had to deal with deep-rooted administrative problems. Revelations of loose financial practices and fraud in the Ranger cell in 1997 eventually led to courts martial against three soldiers. The lack of formal Ranger policy or governing documents, however, complicated the proceedings. The Quebec Area commander sought out Archambault to establish better financial and training controls and to bring the unit up to an acceptable state. To do so, Archambault needed to professionalize 2 CRPG Headquarters, which at that time simply consisted of a couple of instructors without adequate oversight.[148] To formalize operations, he established all the elements of a proper unit: administration, a quartermaster, operations, and finance. He invoked standard operating procedures for booking tickets, administering money, enrolling and releasing Rangers, and controlling stores. Given his excellent relationships with Quebec Area and all of the generals, he could restructure the patrol group as he saw fit. When he ran into obstacles, he intimidated anyone who opposed him with "his boxes and boxes of knowledge," Warrant Officer Pat Rizzo observed. "He was the godfather. He had the connections to get things through."[149]

Archambault refused to distinguish between units "north and south of 60," the criterion that had framed the Ranger Enhancement Project. He believed that everyone should have access to the same military "kit,"[150] and in the absence of clear national policy he distributed Canadian Forces parkas and wind pants to the Rangers in Quebec. Archambault pushed for more used combat clothing so that Rangers would have a more complete uniform for summer training and ceremonies. Representatives from the other areas and National Defence Headquarters opposed issuing combat clothing on principle: even if the Rangers wanted it, they did not require

Major Claude
Archambault.
Courtesy of
2 Canadian Ranger
Patrol Group

it for operations.[151] On occasion, each region had issued items to their Rangers for training and then withdrawn them at the end of the event. This practice fit with the original premise of the Rangers: "that they come as they are and DND provides what is needed for operations."[152] Issuing combat clothing undermined this philosophy.[153] In the end, Quebec Area only succeeded partially – the director general reserves and cadets conceded to a one-time issue of boots and combat pants.[154] The cart, it seemed, was pushing the horse.

By the spring of 1999, the Rangers' footprint in Quebec had grown to nineteen Ranger patrols and sixteen Junior Ranger patrols. Archambault wanted more and requested additional Ranger patrols to accommodate a more expansive youth program. Quebec Area committed to expanding to twenty-nine Junior Canadian Ranger patrols, which first required an additional ten Ranger patrols: five in Ungava and five in the central interior of the province.[155] The area commander requested additional funding from the vice chief of the defence staff. Brigadier Robin Gagnon touted that at minimal cost the program was having a clear social impact in remote Aboriginal communities and that the Rangers' image continued "to rub off favourably on the Canadian Forces."[156] This proposal – the first formal request to expand the Rangers for nonoperational, social-development reasons – raised core questions about future direction of both the Canadian Rangers and Junior Canadian Rangers.

Other commanders raised concerns about the pace of the Junior Rangers' expansion and about 2 CRPG's use of national development as a rationale for new Ranger patrols. Colonel Pierre Leblanc, who had assumed command of Canadian Forces Northern Area in 1995, believed that 2 CRPG had sacrificed the Rangers' operational dimension to serve a social development agenda. Although both the Rangers and Junior Rangers continued to expand modestly in the Territorial North,[157] Leblanc and his staff would not allow the youth program to dictate the pace of Ranger expansion. The Ranger Enhancement Project, which Leblanc had directed as director general reserves and cadets, limited expansion South of 60 to coastal areas, but some patrol group commanders flagrantly disregarded this principle to advance their personal and regional agendas. Major R.D. (Bob) Knight, the commanding officer of 1 CRPG, agreed. The Junior Ranger program had not stalled, as 2 CRPG alleged – the problem was implementation; 2 CRPG pushed for unauthorized expansion before the completion of the first phase. Why were communities in the Territorial North, which actually met valid criteria for Junior Ranger patrols, short-changed by empire building in central Canada? Why not reallocate some of the resources from 2 CRPG to 1 CRPG, which could stand up additional Junior Ranger patrols without increasing its Ranger ceiling? Growth for the sake of growth was dangerous. "There is no rush," Knight insisted. "There must be a pause to consolidate and contemplate before proceeding in a new direction. Without a solid base to work from the entire programme could be jeopardized later."[158]

While voices from Yellowknife urged restraint, Major David Scandrett (who had assumed command of 3 CRPG in 1998) developed bold expansion plans that pushed policy boundaries. Captain Guy Ingram, his operations officer, forecast the creation of twenty Ranger patrols and twenty-five Junior Ranger patrols or satellites in Ontario, the latter to be created in communities with resident Rangers but no official Ranger patrol. Decoupling Ranger and Junior Ranger patrols contravened policy, as did the patrol group's proposal to establish Junior Ranger centres in urban areas where Aboriginal youth from remote northern Ontario communities attended high school (such as Sioux Lookout, Thunder Bay, and Timmins). The patrol group wanted to co-locate these centres with reserve units, cadet corps, Native friendship centres, or First Nations communities and run them with Ranger volunteers. Consequently, these Rangers would leave their communities to serve a youth program. "We have responsibilities to the Ranger and Junior Canadian members including a trust relationship and a fiduciary responsibility established by the treaties," Ingram noted. In his view, cultural and social agendas, the political relationship between the federal government and Aboriginal communities, and the criterion of operational effectiveness should all influence Ranger expansion plans.[159]

The competing messages from Quebec, Ontario, and the Territorial North, and the lack of any firm national direction, placed the director general reserves and cadets in a difficult position. Colonel Tom Geburt believed the program was "moving in the right direction," but he cautioned that "vigilance is required to ensure that it stays on track and that objectives remain obtainable." Under the federal government's Youth Initiatives Program, the department aimed to support 2,130 Junior Rangers by 2001. Geburt wanted to attain this goal and stabilize the program before growing it further.[160] Vice-Admiral Gary Garnett, the vice chief of the defence staff, conceded that the approach had been ad hoc and recommended a fundamental review of both the Ranger and Junior Ranger organizations. "There must be a national and Departmental focus to any Ranger expansion," he insisted, "and that has not been applied in this case." The chief of the defence staff and deputy minister concurred and instructed Quebec's area commander – who was in charge of the region with the strongest expansionist pressures – not to create any new Ranger patrols until the review was completed.[161]

The Rangers themselves remained largely insulated from debates about their strategic direction. *Vigilans* (meaning "watchful") became their official motto in 1997.[162] The adoption simply confirmed what the Rangers had always done. Apart from new responsibilities associated with the Junior Rangers and sovereignty patrols, there had been little change in the general activities since the organization's inception. Like other Rangers, Solomon Curley, a Ranger raised along the DEW Line who joined the Hall Beach patrol in 1993, recalled that he had found the annual training exercises particularly enjoyable. The first four or five days of classroom training included first aid, map reading, using GPS, and rifle assembly and cleaning.

Hélène Girard's painting of Rangers on patrol near Hall Beach was featured on the cover of the Northwest Territories 1998 telephone book. A copy also hung behind Governor General Roméo Leblanc's desk at Rideau Hall. Reproduced with permission of the artist

On the four-day field exercise that followed, Rangers had a chance to fire the Colt Canada C7 rifle and a 9mm pistol, and they learned how to build igloos, "make a runway out of nowhere," conduct search-and-rescue exercises, and do some traditional hunting. Curley exercised skills that he already had and developed new ones. As patrol sergeant, he received "a lot of phone calls from headquarters in Yellowknife saying whatever they need us to do." For example, the Hall Beach Rangers met with radar inspectors visiting from Yellowknife, and every few months four members of the patrol went out to inspect the unmanned North Warning Sites near the community. Polar bears sometimes stepped on the lights surrounding the helicopter pads, which then needed to be replaced. "I have learned a lot of things" through the Rangers, he explained. "It's pretty much a big part of my life right now. Because being a Sergeant I have to be a contact person for this community and it's keeping me busy and it's quite fun."[163]

Curley enjoyed having the opportunity to meet Rangers and other Canadian Forces personnel. "Top shots" from various patrol groups met one another at the Canadian Forces Small Arms Competition held every summer at Connaught Ranges. Being selected for the competition "was like making the Olympic team," Captain Squires explained, and it gave the Rangers something to work towards.[164] Curley, a regular participant in the late 1990s, said it was wonderful to meet members of the military from different places: "They were pretty much from all over the place, all the way from Yukon to Eastern Baffin Island ... We met people from all across Canada and ... from the United States and the British Army, Army MPs who participate in shooting. Also private shooters and I've met some people from Australia and Netherlands." The trips had a downside, however – the heat. "Sometimes we have to be outside most of the day in sun and we are not used to that. We are sweating a lot and drinking water and all that."[165]

Curley and the other Rangers did well at the competition, but they were really in their element in their home communities. The proof came during times of tragedy such as during the 1999 avalanche in Kangiqsualujjuaq. For the Hall Beach patrol, their training paid off when a helicopter went down about sixty-five kilometres west of the settlement during the annual Victoria Day fishing derby in May 1998. According to Curley, "We were called up through the radio that there had been a crash and who ever is around near this area could report to the area to do what ever was necessary, if there were any injured persons." Rangers carried six of the seven casualties back to the Hall Beach health centre by snowmobile, a two-hour drive in whiteout conditions. (Only one person, whose leg had been broken in the crash, suffered injures severe enough to require transport by air ambulance.) In recognition of its part, Curley explained that the patrol received "a nice little flag that we would carry around every time we were on duty."[166] General

Junior Rangers hold the Nunavut flag during the territorial creation ceremonies in 1999.
Courtesy of 1 Canadian Ranger Patrol Group

Maurice Baril personally presented a Chief of the Defence Staff Unit Commendation to the Hall Beach patrol during the national ceremonies celebrating the creation of Nunavut.

The birth of Canada's newest territory on 1 April 1999 reflected Canada's sense of northern identity and inclusivity. The prominence of Canadian Rangers and Junior Rangers during the creation ceremonies affirmed the Rangers' place as a nationally recognized and respected symbol of Inuit patriotism and participation in state building. "What was fascinating about the creation of Nunavut was the extent to which it captured attention around the country," philosopher John Ralston Saul reflected. "Why were our imaginations so engaged? Because the formalization of a big slice of our North into a new, clearly Arctic body to be run by Northerners was a very positive expression of Canada as a whole. Of Canada as a northern nation."[167] Fifty Rangers representing twenty-four of the twenty-five patrols in Nunavut (bad weather prevented the Repulse Bay patrol from participating) formed an honour guard during ceremonies in Iqaluit. A colour party of fourteen Junior Rangers also played a high-profile role. Junior Rangers Ryan

Nivingalok of Kugluktuk and Daryl Tee of Coral Harbour had the honour of unveiling the territorial flag and coat of arms. The Canadian Rangers embodied the old and the new in the North: Sergeant Tony Manerluk of Rankin Inlet, the oldest Ranger on parade, and Tommy Naglingniq of Iqaluit, the youngest, lowered the Northwest Territories flag and hoisted the new Nunavut flag for the first time. With a new millennium dawning, the Rangers had clearly come of age.[168]

✤ IN *A GENEALOGY OF SOVEREIGNTY*, Jens Bartelson explains that sovereignty has external and internal dimensions.[169] Aboriginal self-government, embodied in the creation of Nunavut, certainly blurred such lines in Canada. The Canadian Rangers had evolved by the end of the twentieth century to accommodate this complexity. When Rangers set out on exercises, they did so both as members of their communities and as representatives of the Canadian Forces. Their very existence as largely self-administering, autonomous patrols allowed them to represent both the local and the national simultaneously.

The Canadian Rangers in November 1999 comprised 3,446 Rangers in 140 patrols. Their physical footprint had expanded and so had their raison d'être. Over the preceding decades, the Rangers went from being the informal eyes and ears of the military to become Canada's sovereignty soldiers.[170] In the process, they assumed more sociocultural and political roles within their communities, roles that matched the priorities of Aboriginal self-government. Lieutenant-Colonel Rory Kilburn, the chief of staff at Canadian Forces Northern Area, observed that some elders had played a

TABLE 10
Canadian Rangers, November 1999

		Rangers	Patrols
1	CRPG	1,340	58
2	CRPG	505	19
3	CRPG	187	8
4	CRPG	640	27
5	CRPG	774	38
TOTAL		3,446	140

Source: Minutes of 29 November–1 December 1999, Canadian Ranger/Junior Canadian Ranger Working Group, 6 March 2000, DND, f.1901-260/4 (D Rgr-JCR 2), Appendix C.

direct role in identifying Rangers with leadership potential and encouraging them to become sergeants and master corporals so they could develop skills to lead their communities and territorial governments. The Rangers also groomed future leaders by facilitating the transfer of knowledge and land skills to younger members. It presented a "win-win" situation for communities and for the military, which is what made it so popular.[171]

The concept of mutual benefit underpinned the entire organization. The Rangers aligned perfectly with the spirit of political cooperation and national support that Ottawa hoped to foster with Aboriginal communities. The connection between encouraging traditional land skills, teaching traditional knowledge, and sustaining military operations in remote regions over the long-term became increasingly clear. In late 1998, 1 CRPG anticipated that

> [t]he Canadian Ranger profile will start to change dramatically in the next few years. Currently Ranger training places a priority on development/ integration of technological skills and the demonstration of land skills. The land skills are for the most part traditional skills learned from elders. Retention of these skills is disappearing. Most Rangers over 40 years of age have them, but few under thirty have the same capability. Despite a resurgence of traditional values through the North the common complaint in communities is that the young are becoming town bound and exhibit little interest in seriously pursuing traditional skills. These young people are, however, better educated than their parents and retain information such as GPS and map reading better than their elders. To maintain our current deployable capability more emphasis will have to be placed on exercising on the land.[172]

These ideas were not new, but the political environment of the 1990s was more receptive to this emphasis on knowledge transfer. Commentators recognized that the Rangers' vitality depended on healthy communities. The line between what was of military value and what was of national value had blurred.

The creation of the Junior Canadian Rangers formalized a nation-building role, but the form and pace of the program's expansion raised core questions about the Rangers' overall direction. On the one hand, the Junior Rangers had obvious community benefits and served as an unofficial form of succession planning for the Canadian Rangers. The youth program sent a strong signal that the military accepted the importance of Aboriginal cultures and that Aboriginal communities trusted the military to teach their youth. On the other hand, long-standing questions about the Rangers' legitimate operational roles (particularly South of 60) muddied the waters. As a component of the Canadian Forces, policy makers had not designed the Rangers to be an Aboriginal program. The positive relations that the Rangers fostered between the military and Aboriginal peoples were an ancillary benefit. Expanding south to engage more First Nations communities for sociopolitical rather than operational reasons – as Majors Archambault and Scandrett proposed – departed radically from the organization's original intent. Were the Rangers becoming a conduit for federal social support to Inuit and First Nations rather than a military asset designed to contribute to the Canadian Forces?

Whether Rangers pondered these questions is unknown. It is clear, however, that they quietly trained and prepared to serve their country – and their communities – when called upon. The Rangers' response to the avalanche in Kangiqsualujjuaq on New Year's Eve 1999 demonstrated their "real value."[173] When Sergeant Jean-François Gauthier, an instructor from Saint-Jean who flew up a week after the event, offered to postpone the opening of the Junior Rangers patrol scheduled for that winter, the community insisted on going ahead without delay. It considered the Junior Rangers a part of the healing process.[174] Jane Stewart, the minister of Indian affairs and northern development, singled out "the tremendous recent contribution made by the Canadian Rangers here in the North in providing relief services." She pledged fifty thousand dollars in new funding to the Junior Rangers as part of the government's action plan to offer "practical, hands-on support to the Northern communities."[175] The high-profile gesture clearly demonstrated the Rangers' tremendous political value.

The Rangers' low cost continued to be their most politically attractive attribute. To withstand the austere fiscal climate in Ottawa and retain their military relevance, Canadian Forces Northern Area and 1 CRPG were adamant that the Rangers had to stay focused on their military role: sovereignty, security, and surveillance activities. If the youth program expanded without restraint because regional commanders South of 60 found it politically marketable, officials in Yellowknife worried that the organization as a whole could collapse under its own weight. Creating Ranger patrols simply to support Junior Rangers would drive costs through the roof and tax overburdened instructors and headquarters staff even further. 1 CRPG urged restraint before ambitious regional commanders carried the Rangers in new – and dangerous – directions.[176]

The federal government embarked on a new direction when it reappraised Arctic sovereignty and security issues in the late 1990s. The growing emphasis on the Rangers' contributions to the social fabric of remote communities seemed to fit with the government's emerging circumpolar emphasis. The parliamentary committee report *Canada and the Circumpolar World,* released in 1997, explained that the "new agenda for security cooperation is inextricably linked to the aims of environmentally sustainable human development." Promoting international Arctic cooperation through multilateral governance (particularly the Arctic Council) offered a long-term foundation for circumpolar security, as long as safeguards protected Arctic peoples "from intrusions which have impinged aggressively on them."[177] The Liberal government dismissed the committee's calls to demilitarize the Arctic, citing the Canadian Forces' mandate to defend all parts of the country. Its official response emphasized that crosscultural exchanges between the military and northerners (particularly Aboriginal people who seized the "opportunity to serve their country and community through participation in the Canadian Rangers") strengthened national awareness on all sides.[178]

The government's focus on diplomacy and international cooperation meant that traditional preoccupations with "defending" sovereignty slid to the back burner. No emerging Arctic security crisis warranted an increased military presence. *The Northern Dimension of Canada's Foreign Policy,* released in 2000, confirmed that environmental and "human security" considerations were paramount. The new politics of globalization, inclusion, and cooperation had replaced the old strategies of exclusion and confrontation that had marked the Cold War Arctic.[179] The government anticipated that constructive engagement and sustainable development, not confrontation, would mark the twenty-first century.

Colonel Pierre Leblanc, the commander in Northern Area, noted a disturbing trend away from maintaining a military presence in the Arctic. In 1998, for example, the army decided to reduce the number of annual sovereignty operations from five to three. The change further eroded the Canadian Forces' already weak capabilities in the North and, in Leblanc's view, also eroded Canada's sovereignty. Many unoccupied islands in the Far North received "very little military coverage," and he asserted that international law provided a basis for foreign powers to claim unoccupied territories if Canada was "perceived as losing interest in the Arctic."[180] Although the Canadian Rangers provided an extensive and visible military presence, as well as constructive and intimate connections with northern communities,[181] Leblanc warned that Rangers were not enough.

Arctic security issues were becoming more complex at a time when the government allowed military capabilities to atrophy.[182] Increasing maritime activity in the Arctic, in particular, demanded more surveillance. In 1999, Rangers reported a submarine sighting in Cumberland Sound as well as the unannounced arrival of a Chinese research ship in Tuktoyaktuk. Cruise ship visits increased exponentially after the end of the Cold War. Global warming, which made Canadian waters more accessible, amplified the risks. Reductions in ice cover on the Northwest Passage increased the possibility of international traffic exploiting extended ice-free periods to run cargoes between Asia and Europe. Leblanc cited pessimistic reports warning that Canada's Arctic resources – from fish to freshwater – would be plundered because of the government's weak regional presence. In the new millennium, concerned journalists paid heed when Leblanc warned that sovereignty threats prompted by global warming could eventually consume most of the military's budget.[183]

How should the government balance a sociopolitical agenda that prioritized human security and nation building with the military's evolving operational needs? The Canadian Ranger Patrol Groups could not agree on an answer. Pressures for expansion, the widening mandate associated with the Junior Ranger program, and competition for scarce military resources required coordination (or even arbitration) between the patrol groups, but they had no central authority to bring them to agreement.

While teaching a leadership course at 4 CRPG, Captain Jim Miller described "free-rein" leaders as informal and observed that the approach had a drawback: "it is often harder for the leader to get back into control once free-rein has been instituted."[184] Bringing national coherence to an organization that was already well established locally and regionally would be a major challenge in the new millennium.

10
"Very Special Forces,"
2000-06

There's a lot riding on the shoulders of a few Rangers. It's ironic these days when the mighty American military is talking about continental defence. They will rely on satellites, high-flying planes and other high-tech sensors to keep terrorists and others from infiltrating our shores – from Mexico to the Arctic.

All well and good. But that doesn't diminish the importance of the women and men in red who have been the guardians of the North for the last 60 years. If anything, it makes the Rangers' role more essential to Canadian sovereignty in the Arctic.

With their .303 rifles, ball caps and sweat shirts these "citizen soldiers" have been Canada's eyes and ears in the North, patrolling on snow machines for decades.

And for the past two weeks, 29 Rangers from around the NWT, Nunavut and Yukon have been taking part in one of the most ambitious sovereignty patrols in Canadian history, making their way from Resolute to the Magnetic North Pole and back. A publicity stunt?

Perhaps.

But such a trek to uninhabited territory – and publicity that comes with it – does help establish Canadian ownership to the Arctic and reinforces the Rangers' importance.

> – Editorial, "The Heavy Responsibility of Sovereignty,"
> *Northern News Services,* 22 April 2002

❋ Throughout the 1990s, various defence studies and expansion plans acknowledged the Rangers as a worthy national investment that contributed to the social fabric of communities. The main tension lay in trying to retain operational focus while the Rangers' social and political profile grew throughout Canada. When Land Force Quebec Area proposed expanding its Ranger operations to facilitate the expansion of the Junior Rangers in 1999, it was the first time that a commander had explicitly sought growth for nonoperational reasons. While some patrol groups pushed for rapid development of the youth program, others expressed reservations. The Ranger organization remained divided. Senior military decision makers in Ottawa worried about the lack of central coordination and directives, which allowed each CRPG to develop initiatives "tinted with personal preferences." Major Daniel Gilbert of the directorate of land reserves warned National Defence Headquarters to "be vigilant to make sure that the Ranger program keeps its operational focus."[1]

Senior decision makers insisted on a sober strategic assessment. CAN RAN 2000, the name of the national review, confirmed the Rangers' status as a valuable, inexpensive operational resource. The original concept remained

TABLE 11

CAN RAN 2000 expansion plan for the Canadian Rangers and Junior Rangers

Location	Current			Proposed			
	Ceiling	Patrols	Ranger instructors	Augment	Ceiling	Patrols	Ranger instructors
CFNA							
1 CRPG	1,340	58	8	460	1,770	59	10
LFC							
2 CRPG	525 (520)	19	3	345	870	29	5
3 CRPG	205	9	2	395	450	15	3
4 CRPG	650	27	4	100	920	34	5
5 CRPG	790 (778)	27	4	–	790	28	5
Sub-total LFC	2,170 (2,153)	81	12	840	3,230	106	18
TOTAL	3,500	140	21	1,300	4,800	165	28

Source: DGRC, "CAN RAN 2000: A Review of the Canadian Rangers and of the Junior Canadian Rangers," 27 January 2000, 24; adjusted figures from Director of Reserves, Annual Report Number 5 for FY 04-05 CAN RAN 2000, September 2005.

valid, the study observed, but the representational and functional roles that the Rangers played in their communities went beyond simply being the military's eyes and ears. These roles, however, were poorly defined. In general, communities turned to the Rangers in times of need, and the Rangers' presence helped the government achieve its national objectives. "The minimal amounts of pay, training funds and equipment that are provided to Rangers are inversely proportional to their impact in our vast, underpopulated areas," the report stated.[2] It recommended increasing the Rangers from 3,500 to 4,800 members and the Junior Rangers from 2,130 to 3,900 members over seven years. This expansion would require more resources (pay, training, instructors, staff, and equipment) but would "positively influence social behavior at the community level ... particularly with respect to a growing youth population who is deemed to be 'at risk.'"[3]

The CAN RAN 2000 report respected the Rangers as community role models. Aboriginal communities had suicide rates up to seven times higher than in the Canadian population at large and higher-than-average rates of illness, family violence, alcohol abuse, and incarceration. They also had lower-than-average life expectancy, education, and employment rates, and they suffered from poor housing and sanitation conditions. The Rangers offered a ray of hope in an otherwise dreary picture:

> By their nature, the Canadian Rangers are having a tremendous impact on the lives of the people and communities in which they are located ... They are active community members who are in a position to have a positive influence on their local environment. Rangers, in those communities where there is no other federal presence, are often perceived to be the elite of the community and are held up as role models for others. Frequently the Rangers represent the only identifiable and formed group that is readily available to the community in times of need ... The Rangers have now taken on a new role – they are educators and role models for over a thousand youth that participate in the JCR Programme. Consequently, there is beneficial value in the presence of Rangers in a community both from the perspective of enhancing the community environment as well as adding to the image of the federal government and the Canadian Forces.[4]

The Rangers served as a consistent, visible link to the state and were worthy of expansion.

Had the overall philosophy behind the Rangers changed? Some officers argued that CAN RAN 2000 revealed a priority shift from operational to social objectives.[5] "The creation of a Canadian Ranger patrol for national/social fabric reasons should be considered to be legitimate," the report suggested. "The overall guiding principle for establishment of a patrol should be the benefit to the country as a whole."[6] Area commanders would have the power to choose patrol locations based on social and political reasons, including support for the Junior Canadian Ranger program. The new directive reversed the well-established process of creating Ranger patrols for operational reasons and then investigating whether that community wanted a Junior Ranger patrol.

This new strategic direction yielded a dramatic increase in funding. In March 2000, the Defence Management Committee approved a seven-year plan to implement the report's forty-nine recommendations. Staff and Ranger instructors in several patrol groups expressed concern that Major Claudia Ferland, a cadet instructor cadre officer heading a new Canadian Ranger–Junior Canadian Ranger coordination cell in the directorate of reserves in Ottawa, was looking at priorities from a distinctly cadet-focused viewpoint, skewing Ottawa's perception of where National Defence should direct its resources. Nevertheless, CAN RAN 2000 had an immediate impact: the number of instructors and headquarters staff grew in the patrol groups, and the Rangers began to receive modest allotments of new equipment.[7]

The strategic review ushered in the second phase of the Ranger Enhancement Project, a phase that included Rangers South of 60. Echoing decades of studies, the report confirmed that Rangers should be self-sufficient and lightly equipped. Officials had always expected Rangers to use their own equipment and supplies, but some patrol groups had already received binoculars, stoves, lanterns, tents, and even strobe lights to set up runways or helipads. While some commanders pushed vigorously for a more extensive scale of issue,[8] the national project settled on common navigation and communication issues. Observing and reporting anomalies required binoculars and communications devices, so each patrol would receive radios and two GPS units.[9] Each patrol group also received satellite telephones for use during exercises.[10] Nonetheless, discussions about equipment raised questions about broader expectations. What did *self-sufficient* and *lightly equipped* actually mean? The Canadian Forces provided each Ranger with a basic uniform and the equipment needed for the safe conduct of his or her assigned task. But should this equipment include lifejackets or safety helmets? Answers varied from region to region.[11]

The Rangers received red sweatshirts and ad hoc distributions of surplus pieces of army uniforms, but some patrol groups lobbied for more. The Rangers wanted to appear more uniform, particularly when they acted as colour parties for visitors to their communities. The latest enhancement program promised standardized combat pants and boots. Rather than unifying the organization, the delivery of these uniforms generated more frustration. Only after the Regular Force and Primary Reserve received their new Canadian Disruptive Pattern (CADPAT) uniforms did the Rangers receive the old olive-green pants.[12] The delay upset the Rangers, as did disparities between when patrol groups received the surplus army clothing. When commanding officers warned that unfulfilled promises damaged the military's credibility in communities, Ottawa simply discontinued the practice of issuing surplus military clothing. It could no longer be said that the Rangers received obsolete uniforms.[13] The Rangers did receive new combat pants and boots, but they were issued as a one-time offer. The director of reserves maintained that "simpler was better," but expectations proved more difficult to manage.[14]

As the Rangers' profile expanded and politicians became more aware of their value, national recognition followed. Governor General Roméo Leblanc (1995-99) had been a strong supporter of the Rangers: a painting of them hung behind his desk at Rideau Hall, and he lobbied for special recognition of Ranger service. As one of his final acts as Canada's viceroy, he approved the Ranger Bar to the Special Service Medal, presented to Rangers who had served for at least four years and participated in at least three patrol exercises.[15] On 14 February 2000, his successor, Adrienne Clarkson, hosted a special ceremony at Rideau Hall to hand out the first Special Service Medals to seventeen Rangers from across Canada.[16] "You are the eyes and ears of the military in remote communities in the Territories and the northern parts of the provinces," Clarkson proclaimed. "You support the military and help to protect our sovereignty. You also serve as guides and advisors, and participate in search and rescue. Your skills, your knowledge, your know-how, are unparalleled ... You, the Canadian Rangers, have made great contributions to the north – and you continue to do so – and to our journey as your fellow Canadians. I thank you."[17] Like her predecessor, Clarkson supported the Rangers. She toured the North and remote coastal communities, where

Ranger Master Corporal Lily Kerr of Telegraph Creek, British Columbia, receiving the Special Service Medal (Ranger Bar) from Governor General Adrienne Clarkson at Rideau Hall in Ottawa, 2000. Courtesy of Canadian Rangers National Authority

she presented the medals and even camped overnight with Rangers on occasion.[18] Rangers became a regular feature of her northern visits as governor general.

For the Rangers, the Special Service Medal indicated that they were no longer a forgotten element of the Canadian Forces. When Sergeant Markusie Quinuajuak of Akulivik, Quebec, received his medal in Ottawa, he appreciated the official recognition.[19] Individual Rangers had won Canadian Forces decorations before, but the Ranger Bar represented national acceptance of the Rangers' unique contribution. For individuals, the medals carried a multitude of meanings. They were certainly a mark of recognition for their service to the country, as Quinuajuak explained. For others, the Ranger Bar represented appreciation of their traditional ways of life and an affirmation of the connection between community life and active citizenship.[20]

The need for connectivity between communities and the national security apparatus took on heightened significance after 11 September 2001. The shock of the terrorist attacks in New York and Washington led the Canadian and US governments to make public safety and national security their highest priorities. Canada had not been attacked directly, but the threat of foreign aggression reaffirmed the importance of the military's home game – the defence of North America.[21] When authorities grounded civil aviation throughout North America following 9/11, twelve Rangers from Newfoundland assisted with humanitarian and security aid at Gander airport during Operation Support, as Canada's first response became known.[22] The Rangers did not participate directly in Operation Apollo, Canada's military contribution to the international campaign against terrorism, but military officials stated that they had a essential, ongoing domestic role. "Our primary goal is to maintain and protect sovereignty and security in the North," public affairs officer Captain Brian Martin explained shortly after 9/11. "The Rangers report anything unusual immediately and we respond to that."[23]

Footprints in the Snow: 1 CRPG and the New Northern Threat

Heightened awareness of security issues in the new millennium drew attention to a region on the precipice of massive change. "The Arctic Region is a huge, vast treasure chest for Canada and her future generations," Colonel Kevin McLeod, Colonel Pierre Leblanc's successor, asserted in his cover letter for the *Arctic Capabilities Study* released in December 2000. "The increased threat to both the people and the resources of this area should be a concern to all of us. This threat and the increase in vulnerability must be countered."[24] Canadian Forces Northern Area's detailed study linked Canada's Arctic sovereignty and security challenges to the issues of environmental protection, climate change and the opening of new northern shipping routes, the opening of Russia's airspace and heightened commercial airline activity, and the transnational criminal activity that accompanies resource development such as diamond mining. To meet its obligations, Northern Area argued for improved capabilities to monitor and respond to emergencies.[25] Although the study triggered significant media attention, the Department of National Defence decided that its scarce resources should go to more pressing priorities. Northern Area would have to fulfil its surveillance responsibilities with what it already had.[26]

Patrol areas in 1 Canadian Ranger Patrol Group: The Ranger concept in this group was based on the principle that patrol members would know their local area – theoretically a three-hundred-kilometre radius around their community that corresponded with normal hunting and fishing areas

The majority of the Canadian Forces' activities in the Territorial North revolved around the Rangers, which remained a cost-effective and high-profile way to let northerners show the flag. National Defence Headquarters consequently doubled 1 CRPG's annual budget in 2001 to more than $5 million and authorized it to increase its Ranger strength to 1,800 members by 2008.[27] "My goal is to have a Ranger patrol in every community in the North," Major Yves Laroche, the commanding officer, told a reporter. In reality, however, he had few opportunities to expand the Rangers' footprint. Only eight communities without an existing patrol had the demographic potential to support one.[28] (There were no communities in the Arctic Archipelago in which to establish new patrols.) Northern Area had funding to conduct thirty sovereignty patrols (SOVPATs), its main flag-planting activity, each year. Combined with the Rangers' existing footprint in communities across the territories, the coverage looked impressive on paper, but it remained modest in terms of Canada's perceived need to demonstrate a continuous military presence in the remotest reaches of the archipelago.

McLeod focused first on increasing the Rangers' capabilities and activity level.[29] For its part, 1 CRPG prided itself on being the only patrol group that accomplished operational tasks on direct orders from Ottawa, and it insisted that sovereignty and security patrols took priority. Increased funding permitted a wider variety of activities. All Rangers in 1 CRPG received annual training, and various patrols inspected forty-seven North Warning System sites periodically throughout the year. Mass exercises allowed multiple patrols to meet and train at a predetermined location. These exercises challenged Rangers not only to operate in unfamiliar terrain but also to build esprit de corps as a patrol group.[30] Alongside sovereignty patrols, joint training with other Canadian Forces units, and tasks such as confirming reports of submarines or "suspicious movement in Canadian territorial waters or airspace," Major Laroche estimated that Rangers conducted about 350 activities each year in the Territorial North.[31] The area commander, Colonel McLeod, explained that the military expected the Rangers "to know their backyards very well," and this would not change.[32] Their "backyard," however, was growing in the minds of both military officials and the Canadian public.

Rangers had always gone on patrols but never far from their home communities. With the renewed emphasis on Arctic sovereignty, Northern Area recommended that Rangers conduct regular enhanced sovereignty patrols over vast, uninhabited stretches of the High Arctic. "What they will do is

Types of Ranger patrols in 1 CRPG		
Type 1	Ranger training patrol	Annual standard training for each patrol, consisting of classroom and field exercises.
Type 2	Ranger North Warning System (NWS) patrol	Inspections of NWS installations by individual patrols.
Type 3	Ranger mass exercise	Collective training exercises conducted by two or more patrols.
Type 4	Ranger sovereignty patrol	Patrols tasked by northern headquarters as part of the area's surveillance plan.
Type 5	Ranger enhanced sovereignty patrol	A long-range patrol sent to a remote part of the area of responsibility. One enhanced sovereignty patrol is conducted each year. It involves 1 CRPG headquarters personnel and representatives from various patrols.

Source: Commander's briefing, Canadian Forces Northern Area Headquarters, 27 February 2004.

cover some area, and they will show the flag and report any unusual activity," Major Laroche told reporters. Major Bob Knight, the former commanding officer at 1 CRPG, used the maxim "possession is nine-tenths of the law" to rationalize these activities. "In purely legal terms, they're proving Canada's sovereignty over the territory they're travelling through simply through their presence," he asserted. "If you claim that you have sovereignty over a certain area, yet you have never been there, then someone else could turn around and say, 'Is that really your sovereign territory?'"[33] Other media, political, and academic commentators framed similar arguments for Ranger patrols based on the idea that Canada's legal sovereignty depended upon effective occupation. Although many of their interpretations did not correctly reflect international law, they fired up the imaginations of politicians, academics, and journalists alike.[34] These highly publicized patrols also served to increase awareness of the Rangers' existence and solidified their role as sovereignty soldiers.[35]

The connection between sovereignty issues, security threats, and land-based surveillance took tangible form at the dawn of the new millennium. Rumours of polar bear hunters crossing from Greenland to Ellesmere Island led 1 CRPG to participate in Operation Ulu, a fifteen-man assignment with the RCMP, in April 2000. In an unprecedented move, the military airlifted Rangers from their communities to the uninhabited Alexandria Fiord region of Ellesmere Island, 300 kilometres above Canada's northernmost settlement of Grise Fiord, to show the flag and deter illegal hunters from violating Canadian laws. Whether the primary goal was to enhance Ranger skills or deterrence, the operation took the Rangers beyond their typical area of responsibility. Although a more covert operation might have caught "Greenlandic hunters red-handed," a Northern newspaper editorial noted that "the whole point of sovereignty patrols is to fly the flag and let the world know the borders of Canadian soil and tundra."[36]

The scale of the enhanced sovereignty patrols quickly grew as Northern Area conceived plans to both demonstrate sovereignty and bolster the Rangers' national profile. To mark the Rangers' sixtieth anniversary celebrations in 2002, thirty-three Rangers from patrols in 1 CRPG met in Resolute Bay to launch Operation Kigiliqaqvik Ranger – a 1,700 kilometre expedition to the Magnetic North Pole. The extensive media coverage of the patrol reflected a growing interest in Arctic sovereignty and the Rangers' activities in support of it. Applauding this "heroic and historic accomplishment," Lieutenant-General George Macdonald wrote: "This courageous expedition in support of our country's sovereignty was not only a clear demonstration of the importance of the mandate and roles of the Canadian Rangers, but is also a testament to the special breed of person it takes to fulfill this most important duty. The sheer magnitude of the journey leaves one breathless and the daily media releases ... could only provide us with a small glimpse of this grand adventure. This initiative can only serve to reflect positively on the Canadian Rangers organization and the Canadian Forces."[37] For the Rangers, a sense of personal accomplishment was matched by political accolades. The governor general awarded the Queen's Golden Jubilee Medal to each of the participants the following year and thanked each one in a letter "for the support you have given me as Commander-in-Chief and for the loyal and dedicated service you provide Canada."[38] She also applauded the Rangers for the operation in her Canada Day message on Parliament Hill.[39]

Media coverage of the conclusion of Operation Kigiliqaqvik Ranger was overshadowed by the tragic news that an American F-16 fighter had accidently dropped a bomb on Canadian troops in Afghanistan, killing four and injuring eight others. Canadian Rangers mourned the loss, which placed their sovereignty operation in sober perspective.[40] One could not forget that the war in Afghanistan was the Canadian Forces' foremost priority. Nevertheless, as climate change and Arctic sovereignty questions commanded attention, the Rangers' perceived importance grew apace. "These enhanced

"Showing the flag" during Operation Kigiliqaqvik Ranger at Cape Isachsen, April 2002. *Courtesy of 1 Canadian Ranger Patrol Group*

sovereignty patrols made Canadians more conscious of the need for a Canadian military presence in the North, and particularly that of the Rangers," observed Ranger Sergeant Peter Moon, a retired *Globe and Mail* reporter who worked diligently to raise the Rangers' profile during these operations. By creating events to give reporters something to write about, Moon explained, these patrols served as a catalyst for growing media interest in northern security issues.[41]

Canada's concerns about sovereignty revolved primarily around the issues of global warming and the potential opening of new international transit routes through the Northwest Passage.[42] This focus on the maritime domain raised serious questions about Canada's military capabilities as well as the Rangers' proper role in supporting naval operations. The navy had not undertaken an Arctic mission for thirteen years prior to participating in Exercise Narwhal Ranger in July 2002. During this joint sovereignty operation, two coastal patrol vessels rendezvoused with twenty-five Rangers and army officers in Iqaluit who then led them to Resolution Island off the southwest tip of Baffin Island.[43] Not everyone was impressed. Former diplomat Harry Sterling asked whether it was "high Arctic drama or high Arctic farce?" Sending Rangers to a remote area on two small naval vessels and flying them out on Twin Otters verged "on theatre of the absurd, a feeble and belated attempt by the Chrétien government to reiterate Canadian sovereignty over Arctic waterways on a shoestring budget." In Stirling's eyes, the operation's small scale reflected the dismal state of Canada's military preparedness, particularly "on the heels of the Bush administration's proposed North American Defence Command."[44] Other criticial commentators thought the Rangers symbolized Canada's limited presence and paltry capabilities and dismissed them as "a motley band of Inuit reservists"[45] equipped with "museum-piece Lee Enfield rifles."[46]

Careful observers recognized that the Rangers served as force multipliers: when they joined combat forces, they significantly increased those forces' operational effectiveness.[47] Rangers gathered local intelligence, provided ground-based surveillance, and played a supporting role in exercises such as Narwhal Ranger. Training activities helped to improve interoperability between land, maritime, and air forces, and the Rangers' experiences reinforced the long-standing theme of mutual learning. Pitseolak Alainga, a thirty-five-year-old Ranger from Iqaluit who travelled aboard HMCS *Goose Bay,* enjoyed the experience of working with the soldiers and preventing polar bears from intruding on their camp on Resolution Island. The trip produced less cultural shock than one would expect. The camp reminded Alainga of home. He saw rifles outside the tent and men socializing. "When you grow up with your dad and all the other brothers that travel down here for walrus hunting, it's just like any other trip," he told a reporter. His Ranger responsibilities – helping others and keeping them safe – were simply an extension of his everyday life. He had learned this role from his grandfather and father, both former Rangers. The learning continued during the exercise. "When we're out on the land, it's usually us being the teachers and the army being the students, but sometimes it turns around," Alainga explained.[48]

In the years ahead, Rangers had even more opportunities to participate in enhanced sovereignty patrols. The Kigiliqaqvik series of patrols occurred annually and included increasingly ambitious plans to trace lines over Canada's remotest islands. Costs escalated accordingly, but capturing national media attention made the patrols worthwhile.[49] "Canada is launching

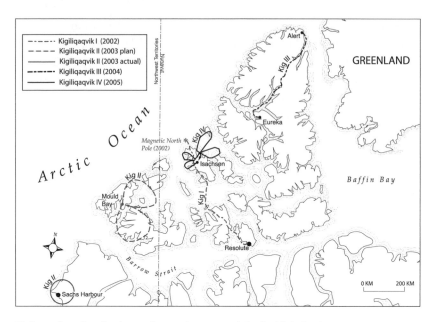

Legend:
- ·-·-·- Kigiliqaqvik I (2002)
- - - - - Kigiliqaqvik II (2003 plan)
- ———— Kigiliqaqvik II (2003 actual)
- -·-·-· Kigiliqaqvik III (2004)
- ———— Kigiliqaqvik IV (2005)

GREENLAND

Alert

Kig III

Eureka

Arctic Ocean

Magnetic North Pole (2002)

Kig IV

Isachsen

Kig II

Mould Bay

Kig I

Baffin Bay

Northwest Territories / Nunavut

N

Barrow Strait

Resolute

Kig II

0 KM   200 KM

Sachs Harbour

Kigliqaqvik series of enhanced sovereignty patrols in the High Arctic, 2002-05

an extensive five-year plan to march soldiers through all of its uninhabited Arctic territory in the largest bid yet to exert sovereignty over its northern domain, an area drawing increasing international attention and conflicting territorial claims," journalist Adrian Humphreys reported in 2004. "We're putting footprints in the snow where they are not normally put," Colonel Norris Pettis, commander of Canadian Forces Northern Area, told him.[50] Even when operations did not go as planned, the media emphasized the durability of the Rangers and their essential contributions to sovereignty.[51]

Losing Operational Focus? Expansionism South of 60

While 1 CRPG emphasized the Rangers' operational focus in support of Arctic sovereignty, Majors Archambault, Scandrett, and Hay – the commanding officers in Quebec, Ontario, and British Columbia, respectively – pushed in other directions. They had built up their units with minimal constraints and interpreted the Rangers' mission liberally. Their willingness to push boundaries and exploit the lack of national direction meant that they broke rules. Because these three "godfathers," as they were commonly described in interviews, were not rotated out of their positions like the

Regular Force commanders in Northern Area and Atlantic Area, they ran their units as "personal fiefdoms."[52] They knew there was no national policy to constrain them, and they resisted attempts to impose national controls that might box them in.[53] Their different visions for the Rangers and competing expansion plans raised difficult questions about the lack of national direction and overall sustainability.

Major Claude Archambault's personality certainly shaped 2 CRPG. Several of the Ranger instructors who worked under Archambault described him as a Tasmanian devil, as a short, stout whirlwind within the military establishment and in his interactions with communities. Described as a doer, a mover, and a shaker, the commander would rattle any chain to get what he wanted. "Change was constant," Warrant Officer Pat Rizzo recalled. "You never knew what was coming down the pipe."[54] Archambault pushed his instructors and staff until he exhausted them, which helps explain the high rate of instructor turnover in the patrol group during his tenure. He was there around the clock, another instructor explained, "like a father watching over everyone."[55] Financial issues related to theft and fraud that predated his command partially explain his micromanagement, but it also reflected his zealous personality.

Major Archambault exploited political and popular interest in the Junior Rangers to justify aggressive Ranger expansion in Quebec. His three-phase plan sought to expand both organizations into more Aboriginal communities, including the Cree nation east of Hudson and James bays. This growth would depend on strong regional support, and his tireless promotion of the Junior Rangers struck a chord with audiences throughout the province. Archambault's understanding of power relations in northern Quebec and his jovial personality allowed him to forge strong relationships in each community. Adept at politicking, he met with mayors, regional politicians, Aboriginal organizations, and corporations to marshal support.[56] He trumpeted the Junior Rangers' contributions for youth, particularly the summer camp, and convinced stakeholders that they would receive positive publicity for supporting the program financially. "He would talk so fast that heads were spinning," Rizzo recalled, "but the cheques were written."[57]

Archambault's restructuring efforts yielded an innovative approach to training. When he lacked core funding to support both Ranger and Junior Ranger visits, he merged the training programs to reduce costs. Under this system, two instructors visited each of the five patrols under their purview up to five times a year. Unified training forced instructors to focus on both programs, but trying to run three field trips in each community and complete all the administration associated with each visit proved overwhelming. Instructors in 2 CRPG travelled an average of twelve days per month.[58] The staff who stayed with the patrol group believed that the Rangers benefitted from standardized training: everyone worked from the same curriculum, which was focused on practical abilities such as building austere airstrips. As a result, the Rangers were better organized and better prepared, and 2 CRPG considered its youth program to be highly professional and successful.[59] The patrol group's disproportionate emphasis on the Junior Rangers, however, prompted debate about sustainability. Outside critics accused the group of placing the proverbial cart before the horse, taking everyone else in unintended (and unwanted) directions.

Funding and staffing the expanding Junior Ranger program generated concern in several patrol groups. Rangers, with considerable validity, began to complain to instructors about resources that should have gone to them being redirected to the Junior Rangers.[60] Youth-training activities were resource-intensive, particularly in remote communities where instructors flew in to compensate for inactive volunteer committees.[61] Advanced summer training took a particular toll on patrol group resources and led to staff burnout.[62] These activities had no core program funding; the patrol groups funded them annually by reallocating money from operations and maintenance budgets.[63] A few cautious observers warned that this practice was setting up unreasonable expectations. In the moment, these concerns were pushed aside.

Consequently, the line between discretionary Junior Ranger activities and core Ranger priorities became increasingly blurred. When 1 CRPG advised members of the national working group that the emphasis of the Ranger and Junior Ranger organizations should return to community visits and patrol-based training rather than advanced summer training, 2 CRPG insisted on the centrality of its summer camp. Equally important, regional stakeholders now expected the camps each year and argued that a halt would have political repercussions for the Junior Ranger program.[64] This was indeed the case in 2003, when the Department of National Defence faced a funding shortfall and announced that it would not fund the summer camps. Members of Parliament, community leaders, and Aboriginal groups bombarded the minister with protest letters.[65] The department backed down and ran Junior Ranger camps rather than face the political fallout. Rizzo later recalled that Archambault's relentless energy and unwillingness to take

Brigadier-General Marc Caron, commander Land Force Quebec Area, inspecting
Junior Rangers in northern Quebec during the Nunavik 2000 Expedition.
Library and Archives Canada/Department of National Defence collection/R112-536-X-E/Accession 2008-377,
Box 153, Photo ISD00-1905

no for an answer ended up "creating a monster that we could not harness
anymore: the Junior Canadian Rangers."[66] Others took note. Pita Aatami,
president of the Makivik Corporation, recognized that the Rangers were
suffering from their own success. "When a kid has something to look forward
to, their self-esteem is much higher. We believe in it, but we can only do
so much with the funding," Aatami told General Marc Caron, the commander of Land Force Quebec Area. Even Caron, who described himself
as a true believer in the Rangers and Junior Rangers, conceded that 2 CRPG
was already "operating at the edge of our military mandate."[67]

Major David Scandrett, the commanding officer of 3 CRPG, also interpreted the Rangers' mandate broadly. Rather than creating an organization
that conformed to military rules and culture, he did the opposite: he sought
to bend the army to fit with Aboriginal culture. In 2000, the military still
suffered from an image problem in northern Ontario; memories of confrontations at Oka, Gustafsen Lake, and Ipperwash lingered. Scandrett
sought creative ways to sell the Ranger message to promote nation building

Ranger Sergeant Peter Moon in Resolute, 2002. Photo by P. Whitney Lackenbauer

and cultural survival. He purchased three large teepees painted with the 3 CRPG crest that became a regular feature at annual Junior Ranger camps, powwows, the Canadian National Exhibition in Toronto, and Winterlude in Ottawa.[68]

The real identity boost came after reporter Peter Moon met David Scandrett in Fort Albany and published several favourable stories about the Rangers. The two men became friends: Moon appreciated Scandrett's frankness about conflicts between the military and Aboriginal communities. When Moon retired from the *Globe and Mail*, Scandrett invited him to attend and publicize his patrol group's first Junior Ranger summer camp, which was being held at Constance Lake. Moon refused a short contract but said Scandrett could make him a Ranger and pay him the normal sixty-five dollars a day. Moon, sweetgrass in hand, was sworn in and officially placed on the Moose Factory patrol roll – even though he had never been to the community. In turn, Moon offered a simple, positive message: Junior Ranger camps trained kids to be safe on the land, water, and in their personal lifestyles. The message resonated with the northern media and community newspapers. Moon originally agreed to help 3 CRPG for a year, and Scandrett made him a Ranger sergeant in recognition that this rank would give him more status with the military.[69]

Moon's zealous approach to publicizing the Rangers had resounding success. He met with public relations experts that he knew from his days as a reporter, and they advised him to portray the Rangers as heroes. The frame of Aboriginal-military cooperation allowed him to write up every Ranger activity as a success story. A tri-annual newsletter, pamphlets, and website followed in 2001. The Rangers in northern Ontario began to appear frequently in local, regional, and national media coverage. *The Maple Leaf*, the national military newspaper, also contained a regular feature on the Rangers that often bore Moon's byline. Moon did not step down after a year but instead continued to produce a torrent of stories for the print media, CBC radio, and regional and provincial television. These stories generated a huge amount of publicity for 3 CRPG, Moon explained, and were successful beyond his "wildest dreams ... We gave them a legitimate story ... on a slice of Canadian life."[70]

Whereas national coverage of Ranger activities in the Arctic gravitated towards sovereignty and security themes, Moon emphasized human interest and community building, which resonated in northern Ontario. When 3 CRPG launched a recruiting drive to establish a patrol in Kashechewan in 2001, the turnout was overwhelming. "We ended up with 44 Canadian Rangers and 54 Junior Canadian Rangers and we had to turn people away," Captain Guy Ingram explained. He attributed the response to the surging popularity of the Junior Rangers and a heightened awareness of the Rangers' positive role.[71] The Red Whistle program, introduced by 3 CRPG in collaboration with the Nishnawbe-Aski Police Service and a private-sector sponsor, was another key factor. By early 2002, headquarters staff – particularly Warrant Office Bruce Dunn – had distributed more than thirty thousand red whistles to children in Grades 1 through 6 in forty Anishinabek and Cree communities. These soldiers trained the children (who did not have easy access to emergency systems commonplace in the south) to carry the whistles at all times and use them whenever they were in distress: on the land, on the water, when they encountered physical or sexual abuse, or any other emergencies. "If the whistle helps one kid who gets lost on the land or ends up in trouble, because a snowmobile breaks down or goes through the ice," Dunn explained, "then it's worth giving them out. A whistle is a cheap way to save a life."[72] It also represented a relatively inexpensive way to promote the Rangers and their contributions to isolated communities.

Positive relationships with corporate and political leaders further enhanced the Rangers' profile. For instance, Moon developed a close relationship with James Bartleman, the first Aboriginal lieutenant-governor of Ontario and another strong proponent of the Rangers. When Bartleman launched a program in 2004 that encouraged Ontarians to donate books for children living in northern communities without public libraries, 3 CRPG led a convoy of army trucks with more than forty thousand books across frozen muskeg roads to sixteen northern communities. This support, labelled Operation Wawatay Express (*Wawatay* being the Cree word for "northern lights"), piggybacked on the annual Ranger resupply trip. A "feel good" story in all respects, it elicited favourable media attention.[73]

By refocusing its training on community distress or disorder operations, 3 CRPG ensured that patrols had a local raison d'être and "not just a CF purpose."[74] Scandrett seized unorthodox opportunities to showcase the Rangers, foster Canadian soldiers' awareness of them, and enhance Ranger leadership skills. For example, even though Rangers were not expeditionary forces, Land Force Central Area funded eight Rangers to fly to the US Army's urban combat facility at Fort Knox, Kentucky, for a week of advanced training in 2002. The Rangers rode on M1 Abrams tanks, fired automatic weapons, crawled under barbed wire during a live-fire exercise at night, and practised land assaults from freighter canoes.[75] They also played the role of partisans assisting Canadian troops and developed a system of goose calls to identify and communicate with one another over the crackle of bullets and explosions. Sporting combat clothing as well as red sweatshirts, the

Canadian Rangers from northern Ontario at Fort Knox, Kentucky, 2002.

Photo by Sergeant Peter Moon, courtesy of 3 Canadian Ranger Patrol Group

Rangers received a lot of attention. "Wearing traditional braids instead of the military buzz cut, the Canadian Rangers are the only soldiers on base that know how to tie together a teepee, hunt caribou and skin a polar bear," one television reporter observed.[76] The commanding officer at the base asked the Rangers to set up their teepee at the main entrance, and they "became headline stars when the media learned about their presence." They received a full-page report in the *National Post,* appeared on CTV's main newscast as well as on CNN, and were featured in special reports by CBC-Radio in both Ontario and Quebec.[77] "The objective here is not to turn them into combat soldiers," Scandrett explained. "It's to give them experience, have them participate so that when they train with regular reserve army units in the north that they have an understanding of what those soldiers go through."[78] As one Canadian officer quipped, "The American Rangers are Special Forces. Our Rangers are very special forces."[79]

To support his "very special forces," Scandrett continued to push the proverbial envelope. He filed few reports, one of his staff officers recalled, because "this would have signalled how they were doing things" – and because Land Force Central Area ignored the reports in any case.[80] The connection between the patrol group and Central Area Headquarters grew tenuous. On his own initiative, Scandrett enlisted prominent figures and elders such as Stella Blackbird, a Cree medicine woman from Keeseekoowenin First Nation in Manitoba, to promote his patrol group. The organizational plans for 3 CRPG had always included a civilian Aboriginal adviser, but Central Area Headquarters told Scandrett "that getting soldiers was hard, [and] getting civilians impossible. So the position morphed into that of a Canadian Ranger Chief Warrant Officer who served as the Group Elder." Beloved by all as "the quintessential grandmother," Blackbird's Manitoba roots did not dissuade Scandrett, who claimed that 3 CRPG's cultural watershed ran across the provincial boundary. Given the strong familial ties between Cree and Oji-Cree communities in northwestern Ontario and northeastern Manitoba, he hoped to extend his patrol group's area of operations west to the Nelson River, where interior patrols would support a robust search-and-rescue network. In general, 3 CRPG hoped to expand its number of patrols from nine to twenty. Despite Scandrett's cultural rationale, which saw no "pink lines in the snow dividing the Muskegowuk Cree people," the proposal also dismissed existing military lines of communication, an important consideration for both defence planners and 4 CRPG.[81]

Manitoba and the other prairie provinces fell within Land Force Western Area, where Major Ian Hay envisaged expansion of his own making. In the 1990s, National Defence Headquarters had stymied Hay's efforts to redistribute the Ranger patrols in British Columbia, so he shelved his plans. When CAN RAN 2000 justified Ranger expansion for nonoperational reasons and promoted a broader nation-building role, Hay (who was appointed the commanding officer of 4 CRPG in August of that year) resuscitated those plans.[82] The area commander supported extending the Rangers into the prairie provinces and authorized Hay to restructure the patrol group to support and sustain this growth. Hay turned command of the BC detachment over to Captain Jim Miller and started a detachment in Manitoba later in the year. Supported by two instructors and a clerk, Master Warrant Officer Doug Colton oversaw the creation of patrols in Tadoule Lake, Gillam, Lac Brochet, and Shamattawa in 2002.[83] That same year, the Alberta detachment commanded by Captain Tim Byers opened new patrols in Peace River, Grande Cache, and Fort Vermilion.[84] Establishing Ranger patrols in the prairie North "magnifie[d] the CF's visibility, especially in the smaller, more remote communities," Hay explained.[85] It also added to the diversity of

Using the map and compass during a field-training exercise.
Courtesy of 4 Canadian Ranger Patrol Group

the patrol group. Citizens living in the provincial norths had different skill sets, so Ranger instructors once again confronted the challenge of how to manage and use this diversity to local advantage.[86]

The establishment of a new patrol in Lac Brochet, a Dene Sųłiné community of eight hundred people about 1,050 kilometres northwest of Winnipeg, followed a trajectory experienced by other Manitoba communities. Fourteen residents enrolled during the first two briefings. By the end of the first night of actual basic recruit training in April 2002, the numbers had grown to sixteen men and thirteen women. "Shooting went well considering a lot of the Rangers had never fired a rifle before," instructor Master Warrant Officer Wade Jones noted. This lack of experience was not due to a lack of bush skills. Although Lizette Denechezhe "had never shot a big gun before," Jones reported, "she was [definitely] a bush woman." These seasoned travellers could "make the coldest and worst day feel like a friend rather than an enemy."[87] A Junior Ranger patrol followed soon after, led by Rangers Modest Antsanen and Pierre Bernier, adult committee members, and many young people from Lac Brochet.[88]

The explosive growth of 4 CRPG – which grew to forty patrols and more than eight hundred Rangers by 2003 – pushed well ahead of the expansion plan authorized by CAN RAN 2000. Although the chief of the land staff approved this growth,[89] the situation revealed that no one was policing the patrol groups' expansion more generally. Was the strategic plan for the Rangers still valid? The patrol groups had developed five distinct training plans, and some commanders were equipping their Rangers far beyond self-sufficiency with minimal justification. The domestic security climate had changed dramatically since 9/11, but had the area commanders taken the Rangers down a path "out of focus with reality and the new world and national priorities"? Senior officials, either oblivious to the roadmap laid out in the strategic document or simply acknowledging the changed military and political context, now worried that effusive sociopolitical aspirations had supplanted the organization's military focus. How did the Rangers fit with national priorities, Canadian Forces requirements, and available resources?[90]

To resolve core issues, the vice chief of the defence staff and the chief of the land staff commissioned yet another review. The department's chief of review services confirmed that the patrol groups differed in organization, funding, training, and command and control. Over the preceding six decades, the report observed, "the Rangers spent longer as a number of regional entities than as a national program." Each of the patrol groups reflected the "natural environment, cultural makeup, operational needs, and political situation" of their areas at the time of their formation. Other differences had emerged since the late 1990s as commanding officers pursued "different paths to achieve an end or ... interpreted guidelines or even directives differently." Strong national oversight, which could have corrected the problem, did not exist, placing the Rangers in a precarious, even untenable, situation.[91]

The vice chief of the defence staff imposed Operation Pause in July 2003 until the military sorted out command-and-control issues and produced a new strategic plan.[92] Statistics revealed that expansion was slightly below target when it came to the number of individual Rangers but above target when it came to the number of Canadian Ranger patrols.[93] Colonel Tom Tarrant, the director of reserves, informed the area commanders that they could apply to open a new patrol only if they had a compelling reason to do so. National Defence Headquarters would consider each case on its own

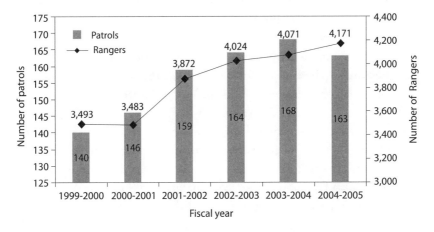

Canadian Rangers, growth, 2000-05

Source: Director General Reserves, "Annual Reports on CAN RAN 2000: A Review of the Canadian Rangers and of the Junior Canadian Rangers," 2001-05

merits in light of the Rangers' role, mission, and tasks. In a clear rebuke of CAN RAN 2000, he insisted that operational reasons would again take precedence over a social agenda.[94] Critics such as Archambault, who wanted to open seven new patrols in central Quebec and had given his word to communities, argued that the strategic pause jeopardized their credibility.[95] The halt had also drawn cries of "broken promises" from communities, 4 CRPG complained.[96] Nonetheless, the long-term view in Ottawa prevailed. A coherent and sustainable Ranger organization required consolidating the growth that had already occurred, clarifying the national direction, and reining in practices that deviated from national goals.

Professionalizing the Patrol Groups

Some of the issues facing the organization were personality driven. Change came after long-standing commanding officers left their positions. When Major Keith Lawrence took over command of 3 CRPG in March 2004, Land Force Central Area instructed him to "operationalize" the patrol group and make it an "army" unit that conformed to military regulations. He immediately ordered all instructors and staff to wear their uniforms, rewrote standard operating procedures, and insisted on proper authorization before anyone went on leave. The unit sorted out major problems related to the control of military equipment and soon "re-engaged" with Land Forces Central Area.[97] Major Ingram observed that "3 CRPG became a professional military unit under Lawrence," and more money flowed into the group. Whereas Scandrett had earned the trust of the Aboriginal community but had alienated his superiors in Central Area (where staff nicknamed him "Lawrence of the Albany" or "Colonel Kurtz"), Lawrence enjoyed the trust of the regional Land Force establishment and high regard in the army reserves. By extension, he sought to re-create 3 CRPG in an infantry mould to make the Rangers more interoperable with other elements of the Canadian Forces. If Scandrett's approach had been "too Aboriginal," some of Lawrence's subordinates believed that he was "too military." He insisted on strict timings and, lacking knowledge of Aboriginal culture, he sent inappropriate communications to chiefs and councils. He ran three Junior Ranger summer camps with record participation in the year he assumed command, but the Ranger staff considered it the "summer from hell." Although some patrols complained that the infrequent visits undermined existing trust relationships, and some Rangers who did not "fit the military mould" felt alienated, Ingram believed that the patrol group had "come of age" under Lawrence's command.[98]

Aligning the other patrol groups was less dramatic; 5 CRPG, which had more continuity than other groups, pursued a much quieter path along the Atlantic Coast. The commanding officer was based in Halifax, ensuring a continuous connection with the military hierarchy, while detachment commander Captain Gord George and the Ranger staff dealt with day-to-day operations in Gander. After restructuring in the 1990s, the Rangers in Newfoundland and Labrador achieved a steady state of thirty patrols. Instead of pushing for new ones, George focused on using additional funding to better equip the Rangers and instructors.[99] At the headquarters level, however, the patrol group had to change its employment practices. Until December 2003, full-time positions in Gander were classified as Ranger positions. To become instructors, primary reservists who had joined the detachment headquarters had to take their release from their unit and re-enrol as Rangers. Because this violated Canadian Forces administrative orders, the patrol group leadership had to convert instructors back to primary reservist status. This corrective also allowed the detachment commander to get rid of ex-military personnel with red sweatshirts who had been appointed by previous commanding officers but no longer fit with the unit training program.[100]

With the departure of a few long-serving personnel, 4 CRPG also underwent structural changes. When Captain Jim Miller neared the end of his time as BC's detachment commander in the summer of 2003, he recognized that the Ranger organization in the West had become "a bit static." Declining Ranger numbers in BC reflected a growing complacency within patrols and at the detachment itself. It also revealed the simple reality of many small communities: as coastal and northern resource economies declined, young people left town. Patrols had a limited population base from which to recruit.[101] The problems also extended to hiring practices at headquarters. The commander and his senior staff did not chose instructors based on merit; they simply went to people that they already knew and appointed them directly. As a result, critics accused headquarters of cronyism, with the instructor cadre resembling a retirement club for ex-members of the Princess Patricia's Canadian Light Infantry. In Miller's view, the full-scale turnover of the staff after he stepped down brought in "new, fresh ideas" and improved the unit.[102]

In March 2004, when Major Tim Byers took over from the "long-time and much-loved" commanding officer Ian Hay, he used the change of command to reconstitute the patrol group. He closed the Saskatchewan detachment, reorganized the structure of his headquarters, and realigned training objectives and procedures to bring the group more in line with Land Force Western Area directives. He introduced new hiring practices, ensured that new detachment commanders and instructors were "outdoorsmen," and sought out more opportunities for Rangers to work with the Primary Reserve and Regular Forces by increasing the profile of 4 CRPG within Western Area.[103] Efforts to coordinate interunit training injected the patrols with a new sense of purpose, as did joint exercises involving multiple patrols. Planning and participating in large-scale exercises generated enthusiasm and helped patrols "develop the tools necessary to handle anything which might arise on a smaller level."[104] To prove his point, Byers held up the example of Exercise Northern Run, held in the winter of 2005. On roughly a twenty-thousand-dollar budget, five Ranger patrols planned and coordinated an expedition that covered 1,451 kilometres by snowmobile in eight days, supported only by a quarter-ton truck.[105] The exercise was the brainchild of Ranger instructor Warrant Officer Darryl Bazin, who continued to keep the Rangers in Alberta engaged and inspired.

Ranger Instructors: The Essential Connection

Regardless of the changes occurring in the patrol groups, the importance of having dedicated Ranger instructors continued unabated. The organization's credibility was vested in these soldiers, who remained the primary interface between the military establishment, the Rangers, and local populations. Instructors assumed the heavy burden of logistical and administrative responsibilities so that potential recruits would not be dissuaded from volunteering because of paperwork and bureaucracy. Instructors liaised with communities before training exercises; budgeted for ammunition, weapons, equipment, and rations; and planned field-training exercises with Ranger patrol leaders. Once they arrived in a community, they worked non-stop purchasing fuel, sorting out rations, and teaching up to thirty Rangers for ten days. By comparison, a sergeant in the south was typically responsible for an eight-to-ten person section. Ranger instructors were expected to be everything in one: paymaster, quartermaster, and "padre when a guy is not feeling so well."[106]

Most instructors specialized in combat arms. They brought skills gained from military training and experience and had to transmit them in a manner that accommodated the ways and needs of diverse communities. No two patrols were alike, nor were the Rangers homogenous within a patrol. "The diversity is always there," Warrant Officer David Gill explained.[107] In Yukon, for example, patrols with a largely non-Aboriginal membership enjoyed army hierarchy and direct command, met on a regular basis even without an instructor present, and provided periodic reports to headquarters. By contrast, Nunavut patrols composed almost entirely of Inuit did not respond favourably to authoritarian leadership and rarely met in groups unless they had a clear incentive to do so.[108]

Successful instructors learned that the standard approach to army training did not work with most Rangers. Decision making often involved lengthy discussions in which participants looked at an issue from multiple perspectives and subtlety emphasized particular facts rather than making clear statements of opinion. They reached conclusions only after a prolonged distillation process.[109] Sergeant Joe Gonneau emphasized that a rigid schedule did not work: "we run it at their pace."[110] The best way to approach any challenge with the Rangers, Warrant Officer Kevin Mulhern explained, was to sit down and discuss it with them. He suggested reversing the army's top-down "mission focus" mentality when dealing with the Rangers by

Ranger instructor Sergeant Jeff Gottschalk *(right)* meets with Ranger Corporal Richard Akana and Master Corporal Baba Pedersen in Kugluktuk, Nunavut, 2001. Library and Archives Canada/Department of National Defence collection/R112-536-X-E/Accession 2008-377, Box 550, Photo ISD01-6187

describing what the military wanted to accomplish and then devising the actual mission with patrol members.[111]

The Canadian Forces' acceptance of these unorthodox practices – which diverged from the military's rigid and hierarchical culture – revealed a capacity for flexibility, inclusivity, and acceptance seldom recognized by scholars.[112] Most Ranger instructors found that egalitarianism was a fundamental principle in Aboriginal communities and communal approaches to decision making the norm. Although Ranger command appeared hierarchical on paper, in practice it more often mirrored local power dynamics. For example, when an instructor asked a Ranger sergeant a question in some communities, the patrol commander would turn to the elders in the patrol for guidance before responding. In Igloolik, the patrol commander had power and influence on paper, but in practice the elder led most aspects of the patrol. The distinction between formal and informal leadership structures was particularly salient, so instructors learned to present their plans to the entire patrol.[113] These unique dynamics fit with the organization's explicit emphasis on self-sufficiency and grassroots leadership as well as on traditional skills "uniquely defined according to the cultural and historical practices in the local community."[114]

A spirit of cooperation ensured mutual intelligibility and facilitated reciprocal learning. Ranger instructors accepted compromise as a source of strength, not a display of weakness. Rangers also accepted that meshing army culture with local culture required compromise. Although Rangers brought a wealth of skills to their patrols, they also enjoyed working with Ranger instructors because they learned from the military. For example, many older Rangers still used memory to navigate. They knew certain lands and seas through rock piles, snowdrifts, and ice patterns, but they did not possess the techniques necessary to navigate outside of their traditional territories. Instructors taught them how to use maps, compasses, and GPS and, more generally, communication skills that expanded the area in which they could comfortably operate. Rangers possessed individual skills suited to their local areas, but instructors taught patrols how to work as a group.[115] This training increased the patrols' ability to fulfill their duties and benefit their communities.

Revisiting the Rangers' Role, Mission, and Tasks

When the chief of review services highlighted the need for more national coherence in the Canadian Rangers in 2003, he noted that understandings of the Rangers' mission and tasks differed across Canada. The Rangers' general mandate had not changed significantly over the years, but commanding officers had certainly interpreted it broadly, leading to mission creep. Several documents identified the Rangers' tasks, but the official version was not definitive. Some patrol groups had unilaterally added or deleted tasks to suit their area without national authorization. The review concluded that the Rangers needed a "nationally approved task list" to ensure that training, equipment, and support were well managed, national, and within the Rangers' mandate.[116] This task list would be the key to securing a sustained investment plan.

During national working-group discussions, representatives from the patrol groups agreed that the Rangers served two central elements of Canada's defence mission: surveillance and control of Canada's territory, airspace, and maritime areas; and helping the federal government achieve national goals. The Rangers' revised role, mission, and task list reflected this consensus. The original role, first outlined in 1947, still resonated. Despite demographic changes over the previous half century, the Rangers remained the only military presence in some of the least populated parts of the country. Their mission statement emphasized that they were expected "to provide lightly equipped, self sufficient, mobile forces in support of the CF's sovereignty and domestic operation tasks," and that future decision making should take into account that Rangers would use personal equipment and supplies.[117]

Some things, however, had changed since 1947. The Rangers no longer factored into Canadian defence plans as a potential combat force. Tasks with a tactical military connotation (providing local defence by containing or observing small enemy detachments, or assisting police in reporting or apprehending enemy agents or saboteurs) required a level of training and liability far beyond the Rangers' mandate. The chief of review services therefore recommended the official removal of these duties from their approved tasks. The Rangers also lacked the training needed to assist with government activities that required the application of force, such as aid to the civil power or riot control.[118] These duties fell within the purview of the Regular Force and Primary Reserve. Did removing these tasks affect the Rangers' credibility as a component of the Canadian Forces? According to 2 CRPG, these tasks had been the basis for the Rangers' creation and justified their military training and possession of rifles. Furthermore, military status conferred prestige that Rangers enjoyed in their communities.[119] These arguments downplayed simple realities. Ranger rifles were equally justifiable as survival tools necessary to perform their surveillance, operational support, and training tasks in remote regions.[120] The Rangers also had military status regardless of whether they engaged enemies with force.

The revised national task list reiterated that the Rangers would do the following:

a. *Conduct and Provide Support to Sovereignty Operations:*
   - conduct surveillance and sovereignty patrols as tasked
   - participate in CF operations, exercises and training
   - report suspicious and unusual activities
   - conduct North Warning Site patrols as tasked
   - collect local data of military significance

b. *Conduct and Provide Assistance to CF Domestic Operations:*

- conduct territorial, coastal and inland water surveillance as required/tasked
- provide local knowledge and Canadian Ranger expertise (guides and advice)
- provide assistance to Other Government Departments
- provide local assistance and advice to Ground Search and Rescue operations
- provide support in response to natural disasters and humanitarian operations

c. *Maintain a CF Presence in the Local Community:*
- instruct and supervise the Junior Canadian Rangers Program.[121]

The exercise of producing this list encouraged sober reflection about what the Rangers were actually doing across the country. As chaotic as expansion had been, the Rangers still had many things in common. The revised task list provided a frame to discern what their service meant in the twenty-first century.

To Conduct and Provide Support to Sovereignty Operations

The Rangers would first and foremost conduct and provide support to sovereignty operations. Patrolling, which had grown in scale and tempo, constituted the most basic element of this role. 1 CRPG's epic and enhanced sovereignty patrols in the Far North certainly dominated political discussions and media coverage, but Rangers across the country completed more modest, regular patrols by snowmobile, all-terrain vehicle, and boat. In August 2001, nine members of the Fort Simpson Rangers undertook a five-day sovereignty patrol up the Mackenzie River during which they honed their map-reading skills and harvested a moose to feed the community.[122] In 2 CRPG, the well-trained patrols had the opportunity to undertake more ambitious training exercises. In some cases, Hercules aircraft picked up sections along with their skidoos and komatiks, carried them to a distant point, and then left the Rangers to travel back home.[123] In addition to the local coastal and inland patrols conducted by each unit in Newfoundland and Labrador, 5 CRPG conducted annual patrols on the sea ice up the coast of Labrador.[124] Rangers also liaised with naval ships conducting annual sovereignty patrols along the Pacific Coast.[125] These activities demonstrated a national presence, familiarized Rangers with new areas, and encouraged them to refine their capabilities.

The Rangers had always worked with other military units, but as their national profile grew, so did their participation in Canadian Forces exercises and training. In 2002, for example, thirteen Rangers from 5 CRPG served as local security and guides, reported environmental observations, and collected fish killed by explosions during Operation Test Shot, which destroyed ordinance on HMS *Raleigh* off the coast of Forteau, Labrador. Other Rangers provided cold weather survival and snowmobile training to soldiers of the Royal Newfoundland Regiment prior to a sovereignty patrol at Arctic Bay in Nunavut as well as basic winter indoctrination and first aid training during other field exercises. Goose Bay Rangers continued to support foreign forces at 5 Wing, serving as guides and survival instructors to the German, British, and Dutch air forces during ground-training exercises.[126]

During military operations, Rangers acted as local ambassadors to both the Canadian military and to foreign units. In 2005, for example, two Rangers from Constance Lake First Nation, Sergeant Albert Sutherland and Master Corporal Stanley Stephens, assisted a twenty-one-member team from the British forces as they spent three weeks cold-weather testing new communications equipment. "In its own small way, Exercise *Bowman Ranger* exemplifies the need for interoperability between allied forces," said Major Lawrence, commanding officer of 3 CRPG. "The joint experiences of my staff, my Rangers and the Royal Marine commandos and trial team were a microcosm of Canada's participation in its various alliances and operations. Both sides have benefitted greatly from this interaction and, on the personal level, many strong friendships were made." Sergeant Heath Blewitt, a Royal Marine expert in survival and winter warfare, applauded the Rangers' bush skills. "They were fantastic. They are experts; they are unique," he extolled. "They use skills taught them by their fathers and grandfathers and they passed some of that down to us."[127] Allied soldiers who received survival training from Rangers across the country echoed these same themes.[128]

Although the Rangers themselves could not be deployed overseas, the training they offered to soldiers who visited their communities proved useful in international taskings.[129] Rangers in 4 CRPG participated in civil-military relations exercises with Regular Force and Primary Reserve units preparing to deploy overseas. Senior officers applauded the Rangers for convincingly playing villagers and civilian forces in coastal mountain settings that resembled what soldiers would encounter in Bosnia or Afghanistan.[130] These

Rangers advise 2nd Battalion Royal Canadian Regiment soldiers during Exercise Narwhal in Panniqtuuq (Pangnirtung), Nunavut, 2004. Canadian Forces Combat Camera, Photo IS2004-2128

contributions grew in scale. Over a two-month period in 2005, for example, 136 Rangers from British Columbia, Alberta, and Manitoba participated in the brigade-level field exercise Phoenix Ram, which prepared five thousand soldiers for deployment to Afghanistan. The Rangers performed admirably, and 4 CRPG received a Land Force Western Area commander's commendation for its efforts. Wolf Christiansen, 4 CRPG's newsletter editor, reported that the Rangers came away with a strong feeling of "individual and group accomplishment ... Every Ranger was acutely aware of where these soldiers were going."[131]

There was no need to generate awareness about the Rangers in the Far North, where a growing emphasis on resuscitating the Canadian Forces' Arctic capabilities ensured that the Rangers were a regular fixture in joint exercises with the army, navy, and air force. Exercise Narwhal – held off the coast of Baffin Island in August 2004 – involved 200 infantry soldiers, the frigate HMCS *Montreal* with its complement of 220 sailors, five helicopters, and the Twin Otter fleet.[132] Thirty Rangers, including the mayor of Pangnirtung and the local MLA, helped train soldiers in general land skills and acted as predator control when the army went out on expeditions. When two unaccompanied soldiers got lost during the exercise, the Rangers who were forced to search for them scolded the military. "You shouldn't be going out there without us," Sergeant Simeonie Keenainak of Pangnirtung told a reporter. With Ranger escorts, "this never would have happened."[133]

Rangers served as subject-matter experts in their local areas. Their traditional role reporting suspicious and unusual activities – their raison d'être since 1947 – remained relevant.[134] Ranger reports of submarine sightings generated particular interest given worries about Canadian maritime sovereignty in the Arctic. On 24 August 2000, Pond Inlet Ranger Sergeant Norman Simonie telephoned the patrol group headquarters in Yellowknife to report three separate sightings of potential submarine activities around Bylot Island that summer. The information had come to him from an experienced local Inuit hunter (who insisted that the speed and size of the wake generated could not have come from an organic life form), a photojournalist kayaking in the region, and a party of ten Inuit (including two Rangers) out hunting bow whale who observed "a strange and unusual but consistent (mechanical) wake with no visible source."[135] When Lieutenant-Commander S.C. Bloom met with the local patrol, he advised the Rangers on how to spot a submarine. "The Rangers listened intently to every word," the naval officer observed. They asked how aircraft such as the Aurora detected submarines, which led to a discussion about sonobuoys. Their questions revealed sophisticated knowledge about modern military technology (suggesting that they had watched the film *The Hunt for Red October*), the naval officer noted. "There were no quizzical looks when it was explained that a hydrophone was deployed from a sonobuoy and that sound was then transmitted to an aircraft by radio and interpreted aboard."[136] Twenty-first-century Rangers were technologically adept and far from naive.

The Rangers' function as the military's eyes and ears gained renewed emphasis after 9/11. When the Moose Factory, Webequay, and Peawanuck patrols reported to 3 CRPG Headquarters that six fighter aircraft and two larger aircraft had flown over their communities, it turned out that Russian Bear bombers (accompanied by Canadian escorts) had crossed overhead. This unusual event, undertaken through the international Open Skies Treaty,

Vigilans – Ranger Mike Taylor on watch during Operation Beaufort at Shingle Point, Northwest Territories, 10 August 2006. Canadian Forces Combat Camera, Photo AS2006-0480

proved benign, but it confirmed the Rangers' value. "They provided an amazing amount of detail about the aircraft and the direction they were heading," recalled Captain Mark Rittwage, the deputy commanding officer of 3 CRPG.[137] Other Rangers reported sightings of unidentified flying objects, illegal Chinese migrants off the coast of BC, and suspicious activities in areas frequented by smugglers off the East Coast.[138]

Although terrorists were less likely to attack a remote location than a metropolitan area, commentators emphasized the need to guard against terrorist and criminal infiltrations. In 2004, Colonel Norm Couturier, commander of Canadian Forces Northern Area, suggested Canada's northern territories could prove a tempting target because they represented the "soft underbelly of the continent."[139] His chief of staff reassured Canadians that northerners would report any suspicious people or activities through the Rangers.[140] When a Romanian tried to sneak into Canada by taking an eighteen-foot fibreglass boat from Greenland to Grise Fiord two years later, Ranger Sergeant Jeffrey Qaunaq met him on the beach. "It could have been anybody who was a terrorist, and he could have just bombed us right away, so it kind of our opened our eyes," the local patrol commander told a reporter. Instead, the RCMP apprehended the illegal visitor and had him deported.[141] The Rangers' tasks in support of sovereignty continued to be both symbolic and practical.[142]

To Conduct and Provide Assistance to Canadian Forces Domestic Operations

The Rangers' second major grouping of tasks related to their contributions to the Canadian Forces' domestic operations. The phrase "to conduct and provide assistance" emphasized that this was a supporting role. Rangers could help out their communities during a domestic emergency, but they could not be treated as the "force of first resort." First responders such as police, fire, or medical specialists had primary responsibility for most emergencies.[143] The Rangers regularly supported other federal departments and agencies in activities as diverse as flood watches for the RCMP to search-and-rescue training exercises with the Canadian Coast Guard.[144]

Ranger support for law enforcement activities was a touchier subject. Although the Rangers were often the only trained organization in the community who could take on a legitimate enforcement role,[145] legal constraints precluded their official involvement. In practice, however, Rangers often assumed responsibility when alternatives did not exist or broke down.[146] In various Nunavik communities, for example, Rangers protected the scenes of violent crimes until investigators arrived. In one case, when a prisoner escaped from jail, three Rangers helped the Kativik Regional Police track and eventually apprehend the individual. According to a confidential source, "the Rangers provided vital assistance to keep the pressure on him."[147] Similarly, Rangers in northern Ontario assisted the Nishnawbe-Aski Police Service with anti-substance abuse patrols, evidence preservation, site guarding, and "peacekeeper operations."[148] Various community leaders called for direct Ranger involvement to help deal with crime waves in communities.[149] Although these activities were never formalized, common sense dictated that the Rangers – the best organized, trained, and trusted group in many communities – could be relied upon to uphold the law and protect community members.

The Rangers' response capabilities in remote regions were routinely linked to search and rescue. Officially, their task list stated they would "provide local assistance and advice to Ground Search and Rescue operations." Although police retained primary responsibility for ground searches, in many locations Rangers represented the only trained, equipped, and knowledgeable group available. Rangers often led rescue missions into the bush, onto the tundra, over and in rivers, and out on the sea ice in brutal weather conditions and to great media fanfare. "While Rangers continue to reinforce Canadian sovereignty, their most important role has been found in search and rescue operations," Daniel MacIsaac, editor of the *Inuvik Drum,* extolled in 2000. "Just as the Canadian army has evolved into a peace-keeping force so, too, do the Rangers act as a source of support in the Arctic."[150] In addition to the hundreds of recorded cases they participated in each year, Rangers conducted searches that went unreported because they did not fill out paperwork describing their actions or did not want to embarrass the people who got lost.[151] The RCMP, community leaders, and people rescued by Rangers regularly applauded their professionalism, knowledge, and leadership.[152]

In recognition of their leadership roles and unique capacity in many remote communities, Rangers received specialized training so they could respond to natural disasters and humanitarian operations. The lack of government capacity in many communities made Rangers the de facto lead in any community-based crisis response, and this role has been integrated into regional emergency plans.[153] Training scenarios that replicated a major air disaster or a cruise liner running aground encouraged Rangers to practise building improvised airstrips or helicopter landing pads. They also prepared for region-specific disasters such as tsunami relief operations on Vancouver Island.[154]

In northern Ontario, Rangers conducted frequent flood and forest fire evacuations in concert with the Provincial Emergency Measures Act.[155] In 2002, for example, the Sandy Lake patrol won accolades for its "invaluable and exemplary" assistance when a forest fire forced the evacuation of more than four hundred residents of their First Nation community.[156] After local residents were flown to Geraldton, the Rangers provided security for the evacuees, acted as interpreters and intermediaries, and worked with the local fire department to prevent house fires.[157] Two years later, when the overflowing Attawapiskat River threatened to wash away its namesake village, local Rangers played a central role coordinating evacuation efforts and remained behind to monitor water levels and conduct around-the-clock security-and-safety patrols. They even organized a Sunday church service for residents who remained in the community. Five Junior Rangers answered phones and radios, in both English and Cree, at the operations centre.[158]

Major Keith Lawrence during Operation Canopy, Kashechewan, Ontario, 2005.
Canadian Forces Combat Camera, Photo IS2005-6110

Rangers also provided emergency support when an *E. coli* outbreak in Kashechewan's drinking water threatened the health of residents and forced an evacuation in 2005. Within thirty minutes of receiving a telephone call from 3 CRPG Headquarters, about two dozen Rangers stood ready in front of the local patrol commander's house. Rangers delivered bottled water to residents, acted as interpreters, completed manifests, and transported evacuees to planes. In the end, more than one thousand residents were airlifted out of the community. Rangers travelled by freighter canoe from nearby Fort Albany and by air from Webequie to assist their beleaguered comrades. "In the first three days I'd have to say we all worked 20-hour days," Ranger Sergeant Philip Stephen told a reporter. "When help came from other Rangers we really appreciated them coming. It gave us relief. The Rangers have done a really good job." Canadian Forces aircraft delivered military engineers and a reverse-osmosis water-purification unit to provide safe drinking water to the community. "This is a tremendous story about the ability of the Canadian Forces to respond to the needs of a First Nation in difficulty," explained

Major Keith Lawrence, commanding officer of 3 CRPG. "I'm very proud of the Canadian Rangers and of the composite military team we've put together. We've shown that the Canadian Forces can assemble disparate members of the Canadian Forces on short notice in a time of crisis, put together a good plan, and execute it well. It's a story about Canadians helping Canadians."[159] The Rangers' response to the crisis in Kashechewan not only made for good press, it also revealed their burgeoning leadership capabilities. "This was the first time that a Ranger unit was the lead agency in a domestic operation," Peter Moon explained. It was also the first domestic operation conducted under the newly formed Canada Command.[160]

Other domestic operations, while not as well publicized, served to reaffirm the Rangers' contributions in times of crisis. When a fire shut down the power plant in Sanikiluaq in May 2000, forcing Nunavut to declare its first state of emergency, local Rangers and Junior Rangers "came to the rescue."[161] The following year, when a similar fire cut off power in Kuujjuarapik for four days, Canadian Rangers mitigated a precarious situation as the temperature plummeted. Rangers such as Sergeant Alex Tuckatuck went from house to house to ensure that everyone was safe and provided information about food and alternative shelter.[162] When a massive snowstorm drove people from their homes in Pangnirtung in February 2003, Canadian Rangers worked with the RCMP and volunteer firefighters to shuttle people to school gymnasiums.[163] On Canada Day 2003, Rangers from the Peace River patrol assisted the town of Grimshaw after a tornado struck.[164] The examples could go on and on. "We're like the fire department, we're there in case you need us," Major Lawrence explained. "If we do get the call then we're one step ahead, we have eyes and ears on the ground."[165]

To Maintain a Canadian Forces Presence in the Local Community

The third pillar of the revised task list – maintaining a Canadian Forces presence in the local community – recognized the prominent position that the Rangers played at home. By formalizing these grassroots contributions, officials highlighted the Rangers' unique knowledge of local needs and community expectations. "When they perform these tasks the Rangers may be wearing the Ranger 'uniform' but they are performing the task [as private citizens] on behalf of the community and not as Canadian Rangers," Colonel Tom Tarrant, the director general reserves and cadets, explained in April 2004.[166] The line between civilian and Ranger was easily blurred but made little difference in practice. "Perhaps more than any other branch of the Canadian armed services ... Rangers bring their military status and training directly to bear on their own communities," one journalist commented. Their training and "an elevated sense of social responsibility" meant that Rangers were held up as community leaders.[167] They embodied the values of voluntary service.

The Rangers' varied forms of service earned them reputations as the "doers" of their communities.[168] In Churchill, patrol members protected trick-or-treaters from polar bears on Halloween,[169] while the Vanderhoof patrol provided security for the annual Halloween dance, a local craft show, and the annual snowmobile poker ride.[170] The Port Hardy patrol maintained the Tex Lyon hiking trail, a popular tourist destination,[171] while Rangers in Iqaluit delivered Christmas hampers to needy families.[172] Rangers from Goose Bay and Labrador City supported Cain's Quest, an international snowmobile race.[173] Rangers in Yukon blazed a trail for the Yukon Quest International Dogsled Race, packing down the race route with their snow machines and placing thousands of reflective markers through "forest and brush, over frozen rivers and streams, and up and down steep and sometimes dangerous terrain."[174] The Carcross patrol also put in the trail for the annual Carcross-to-Atlin Commemorative Mail Run, while the Dawson patrol did the same for the Percy DeWolfe Mail Race.[175] Rangers served as safety crews for the Yukon River Quest, supported the launch of the northern branch of the Trans Canada Trail through the Arctic, and assisted with the Hudson Bay Quest (a sled race from Churchill to Arviat).[176]

As one of the most recognizable symbols of Canadian patriotism in remote regions, Rangers often represented the human face of the North to prominent visitors. Clad in their red sweatshirts, they appeared regularly in media photographs documenting visits by senior military officials, politicians, and foreign defence attachés. They formed dozens of ceremonial guards of honour for the governor general on her visits to remote northern and coastal communities – so many that some Rangers jovially referred to themselves as "Adrienne Clarkson's Army."[177] When Prince Charles visited Whitehorse in April 2001, he inspected a guard of honour mounted by fifty Rangers. The Yukon River in the foreground and snow-capped mountains in the background offered imagery befitting royal visitors. The following year, Rangers greeted Queen Elizabeth II and Prince Philip when they arrived in Iqaluit to begin their Golden Jubilee visit. The Queen made particular note of the Rangers' presence and told them how much she liked their uniforms.[178]

Ranger Sergeant Nick Mantla of Lac La Martre, Northwest Territories, lays a wreath at a Remembrance Day ceremony in 2003. Courtesy of 1 Canadian Ranger Patrol Group

The Canadian Ranger sweatshirt, however modest a uniform, was a source of pride that connected the Rangers to the rest of the Canadian Forces. Rangers became a regular fixture at Remembrance Day ceremonies in their communities across the country and in Ottawa.[179] They also played a prominent role at national gatherings celebrating Aboriginal peoples' military contributions more generally. For example, Rangers and Junior Rangers from the Constance Lake patrol formed part of the honour guard at the inauguration of the National Aboriginal Veterans Monument in Ottawa in 2001. "The veterans got very emotional when they saw our Junior Canadian

Rangers in the parade," Master Corporal Florrie Sutherland observed.[180] Commentators celebrated this connection to youth – particularly through the Junior Rangers – as one of the Rangers' most important contributions to nation building and sustainable, healthy communities.

The meteoric growth of the Junior Canadian Rangers testified to their widespread acceptance in communities across Canada. All patrol groups had introduced the youth program by the early 2000s, and all considered it a resounding success.[181] Like the Rangers, the Junior Rangers were representative of their communities, and they were even more balanced in terms of gender.[182] The emphasis on community direction and traditional skills continued to make the program particularly appealing.[183] Archambault referred to the Junior Rangers as a necessity; to him, they represented "the only programme in the north and remote areas that gives youth in the communities a sense of responsibility, honesty, loyalty, and uniformity."[184]

Local voices echoed praise. The Junior Rangers provided youth with a sense of identity, purpose, and civic awareness that community leaders saw as a way to prevent juvenile delinquency.[185] "Junior Rangers gives kids a sense of responsibility for each other and the environment," Sergeant Mike Swanson, commander of the Port McNeill Ranger patrol, told a reporter in 2002. "It instils values that keep kids from engaging in destructive activities such as vandalism and substance abuse."[186] Elders accepted the program

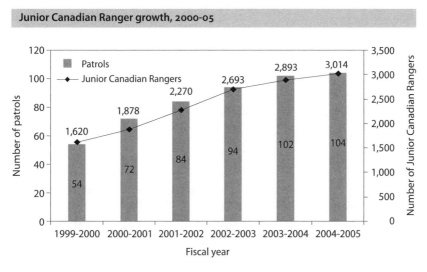

Junior Canadian Ranger growth, 2000-05

Source: Director of Reserves, Annual Report Number 5 for FY 04-05 CAN RAN 2000, September 2005

because Rangers, some of the most well-respected people in their communities, ran it.[187] Not one commentator accused the program of attempting to colonize or assimilate indigenous youth. While the cadet program had a mixed reputation in remote regions, the Junior Rangers' blend of self-direction and military structure struck people as relevant, interesting, and culturally appropriate.

As the youth program became more entrenched, pressures to formalize it required planners to carefully balance national, regional and local priorities. Rangers taught standardized Ranger skills, but each patrol group designed the other aspects of Junior Ranger training with little guidance or accountability. When the coordinating cell at National Defence Headquarters proposed a formal training package, staff in some patrol groups felt that it wanted to make the Junior Rangers into cadets. 1 CRPG saw itself as a "fence" protecting the program from increased regimentation and bureaucratization from Ottawa. "For the last fifty years, we imposed programs on the North: all failed," Captain Christian Bergeron explained. Each community and each culture had different needs, and the Junior Ranger program worked because it was flexible enough to meet the specific needs of each patrol.[188] When responsibility for the Junior Rangers shifted from the director of reserves to the director of cadets in 2004,[189] some stakeholders worried that the transfer would erode the connection between the Rangers and the Junior Rangers. If the program assimilated into the cadet system with its bureaucratic structure and rigid national standards, local support for the Rangers could dissipate.[190]

Communities did not seek military intervention to teach their youth and address social issues. When Rangers assumed mentorship roles, they self-identified as citizen-servers in their communities as much as citizen-soldiers defending Canadian sovereignty. Indeed, these roles and identities were mutually supporting. Journalist Bob Weber, the sharpest observer of Arctic issues in the national media, revealed that military officers and the Rangers themselves shared a growing concern about skill fade, the erosion of those traditional skills that allowed people to safely and confidently operate on the land and waters. As elders retired from Ranger service, the Canadian Forces lost access to their knowledge of the land, the seas, and the skies, and each successive generation had fewer basic survival skills. "I've had people that didn't know how to make a snow block, didn't even know how to try to start an igloo," Ranger Sergeant Solomon Voisey from Whale

Ranger Simeonie Elijassiapik carving with a Junior Ranger in Inukjuak.
Courtesy of 2 Canadian Ranger Patrol Group

Cove (Tikiraqjuaq) explained. He estimated that less than 5 percent of Rangers younger than twenty-five had a solid grasp of traditional knowledge. Even older people used their skills less frequently; without more resources dedicated to facilitating the sharing of knowledge, Voisey predicted that traditional land skills would gradually die out. These developments amplified the value of having elders involved in training younger Rangers and the importance of a more aggressive patrol program.[191] After all, these skills were vital to the long-term viability of the Canadian Rangers and, by extension, the Canadian Forces in remote regions.

Because skill fade was occurring throughout the country, commentators trumpeted the Rangers' integral role in promoting cultural values and skills across Canada. In 2005, fifty-seven Rangers from thirteen patrols in northern Ontario travelled by freighter canoe to Cheepay Island on the Albany River. Media coverage of Exercise Cheepay highlighted the knowledge transfer aspect more than it did the military skills being taught to the Rangers. *Toronto Star* reporter Joseph Hall described the exercise:

There'll be skeet-shooting, first-aid, map-reading, compass navigation and the art of knots and pulleys. But the bulk of the drills [will] focus on the hunting, fishing and survival skills that the Indians themselves bring to the Rangers table. They will build goose blinds – and fashion instant flocks of wooden geese decoys to go with them. They'll compete in geese-calling contests, with some gratuitous moose calls thrown in. They'll fish – how they'll fish! – build lean-tos and conjure roaring fires in seconds. They'll prepare bannock – a bread-like concoction introduced by Scottish trappers during the Hudson's Bay Company days – over open flames. And they'll try – in what is likely one of the most important forums left for preserving the culture of Northern Ontario's Indians – to stem the steady erosion of these traditional skills.[192]

In general, the media extolled the Rangers' social and cultural benefits alongside their role as sovereignty soldiers. On 22 April 2002, a *Northern News Service* editorial concluded: "Overflights and satellite surveillance are important, but nothing beats a person on the ground for accurate intelligence gathering. Rangers are perfect for the job. They live in the North and understand the land and the climate. When full-time soldiers come to the Arctic, they turn to Rangers for advice. They mean as much, and more to their communities. The Canadian military understands this and has been working to expand Ranger ranks. It's building upon a fine tradition for which all Northerners should be grateful."

✤ HANS ISLAND, NUNAVUT, LONGITUDE 80°50' N, latitude 66°37' W, 12 July 2005. At 10:45 A.M., two CH-146 Griffon helicopters swooped down over a windswept rock in the middle of Kennedy Sound between Ellesmere Island and Greenland. Onboard were three Rangers from the Grise Fiord patrol – Sergeant Jeffrey Quanaq, Corporal Manasie Kaunak, and Ranger Jimmie Nungaq – along with Ranger instructor Sergeant Denis Lalonde. Their mission – Operation Sovereign Inukshuk – would demonstrate Canadian sovereignty over a barren, uninhabited 1.3-square-kilometre rock in the middle of Nares Strait that had become the subject of intense political scrutiny.

When Canada and Denmark signed a continental shelf boundary agreement in 1973, the negotiators could not agree on the status of Hans Island. The island did not contain any exploitable resources, so neither country

Rangers help hoist the flag on Hans Island, 13 July 2005. Canadian Forces Combat Camera, Photo RE2005-0114-37

placed a high priority on settling the issue for the next three decades. In 2005, however, political and media attention suddenly made the island an acid test of the Canadian government's resolve to protect its Arctic. "The Vikings are back. A thousand years after the Norse colonized Vinland, they're again staking a claim to Canadian territory," warned political scientist Rob Huebert. "This time, they have not come in traditional longboats but in a modern, ice-strengthened frigate." Huebert, whose alarmist predictions that Canada's sovereignty would melt away with the sea ice grabbed media headlines in the mid-2000s, inaccurately asserted that the status of Hans Island affected the maritime boundary between Canada and Greenland and thus could affect fishing or hunting rights. "The issue ... demonstrates our almost total inability to defend our interests in the Canadian north," Huebert asserted. "Our boundaries in the region are already contested and under pressure, a trend that is likely to continue as a warming Arctic gives increasing access to previously ice-bound coastlines."[193]

When the first helicopter landed on Hans Island, the Rangers reconnoitred the ground. They found evidence of past visits by foreign nationals: a cairn and two Danish flags, one on a flagpole and the other in a barrel. After unloading the equipment, two of the Rangers gathered rocks and built an *inukshuk* (an archetypal symbol of human presence in the Arctic). In the meantime, an engineer from Canadian Forces Northern Area and the third Ranger prepared a base for a flagpole. They affixed a trilingual brass plate to memorialize their visit and finished the ceremony with a rendition of "O Canada, We Stand on Guard for Thee." They raised the Canadian flag at noon. Thirty minutes later, the team departed from the island. The Rangers had done their job. The national media broadcast their presence, and the Rangers left the diplomatic fallout to the politicians and the Department of Foreign Affairs.[194]

Growing concerns about climate change, the opening of the Northwest Passage, and global demands for Arctic resources and security in the post-9/11 world conspired to put the Arctic back on the national and international agenda. The Rangers, Canada's "boots on the ground," played a major role in the unfolding drama. The perception that countries such as the United States and Denmark were challenging Canada's ownership of remote regions gave renewed meaning to sovereignty operations. In the early twentieth century, the RCMP had planted cairns to establish Canadian ownership. In the post-9/11 world, Canadian Rangers served as Canada's sovereignty soldiers. "You have to have government activity to establish ownership,"

Ranger sergeant Peter Moon asserted. "If we don't own it now, it could be taken from us in the future."[195] This popular idea perpetuated misconceptions about sovereignty and ownership, but this symbolism offered a common-sense solution that would satiate public and political appetites for action. The Rangers ended each enhanced sovereignty patrol in the Far North by erecting a fibreglass pyramid inscribed with the date the exercise had taken place.

In the military's eyes, the Canadian Rangers had one main role: to assert Canadian sovereignty.[196] Their activities as guides, scouts, and patrol members conducting surveillance and demonstrating a military presence around their home communities fit within the organization's traditional mandate. The growing expectation that Rangers should demonstrate Canadian sovereignty over the most remote stretches of coastline in the Far North applied in particular to 1 CRPG. "The significant amount of equipment needed to conduct a patrol of several days duration several hundred kilometres away from established communities" was "still more economical than a series of Aurora flights or naval patrols," the chief of review services noted in 2003. Nonetheless, these enhanced sovereignty operations cost significantly more than "a ball cap, .303 rifle and a couple of hundred rounds of ammunition."[197]

The investments were certainly worthwhile from a public relations standpoint. The Canadian Ranger mystique gained new lustre in the national spotlight, and assumed almost mythic proportions in media stories. "They're the MacGyvers of the Canadian Arctic," reporter Stephanie Rubec exclaimed in 2002. "Strand any Canadian Ranger on an ice floe north of 60 with their military issued .303 rifle and they can live off the land indefinitely. Throw in a needle and some dental floss – which no Ranger would be caught dead without – and they'll sew up a fur outfit to ward off the most chilling arctic wind."[198] Caricatures such as these hardly represented all Rangers, who had varied skill sets, yet they reveal their exalted status in the popular imagination. Stories about the Rangers appeared regularly in regional and national newspapers, and a postage stamp released in 2003 depicted a Ranger peering through binoculars that reflected a snow-crusted mountain peak. The Rangers exemplified the military's positive cooperation with all Canadians in remote areas, particularly Aboriginal communities. Furthermore, the organization proved that the military could successfully integrate national security and sovereignty agendas with community-based activities and local priorities.

The Canadian Rangers postage stamp, issued 3 March 2003. Canada Post

Rising concerns about climate change and its implications for sovereignty, security, and safety brought the connections between local management, national preparedness, and transnational forces into sharper focus. Residents in remote regions faced daunting challenges. In 2004, the Arctic Climate Impact Assessment report showed that the impacts of global warming were already felt locally (rising temperatures, melting ice caps and glaciers, and changes in flora and fauna) but that the root causes were global.[199] Security and sovereignty threats had to be considered alongside food security, cultural survival, physical health, coastal erosion, permafrost degradation, and the vulnerability of critical infrastructure in a changing world.[200]

Fortunately, the Rangers' expertise contributed to the defence of North America and to the protection of local communities. The Rangers' updated role, mission, and tasks incorporated the broad notion that protecting Canadians included helping relatives and community members in emergencies or disasters.[201] Although the military's national focus remained North of 60, the Rangers' northern mission applied to patrols in remote areas of the provinces as well. Expansion South of 60 reshaped expectations about the Rangers more generally. "The Rangers have become something of a social program," 3 CRPG commander Major Keith Lawrence stated in 2005.[202] Perhaps more important than the money or military instruction, the Rangers provided incentives and opportunities for people to get out on the land and share their knowledge with one another, an achievement perfectly compatible with their overall role.

In July 2005, Warrant Officer Dan Hryhoryshen, a Ranger instructor with 4 CRPG, explained to me that "the Canadian Rangers is not policy and strategies and directives – it is a grassroots connection to the people and the land."[203] The Rangers had found their role at the local level, and the patrol groups had begun to formalize their practices as regional entities. Consolidating a national task list represented a step forward, but the chief of reserves and cadets recognized the existence of a policy vacuum when it came to the Rangers' place in the grand scheme of things. Although the broader process of Canadian Forces Transformation (reorganizing the military's structure and culture to entrench a fully integrated and unified approach to domestic and international operations) halted more general plans to solve command-and-control issues by creating a formal national authority,[204] politicians began to build the Rangers into their expectations for a more robust military presence in the Canadian North.

When Prime Minister Paul Martin landed in Pond Inlet during a northern tour in August 2004 to reaffirm Canada's sovereignty over the Arctic, he applauded the Rangers. "These are the very men and women who are at the very forefront of the protection of our sovereignty and have been for generations." Martin told the audience at the airstrip, "I just want to say to those of you in this room who are Rangers, on behalf of all Canadians, how grateful we are to you."[205] The Rangers had a dual role in the media, as indigenous residents who contributed to Arctic sovereignty and as an example of Canada's limited defence capabilities in the North. Martin's government promised to address this shortcoming through a stronger military presence, something that Bill Graham, the defence minister, hoped to accomplish by "boosting" the Rangers patrols and conducting more military exercises.[206] The Liberals' *International Policy Statement,* released the following year, identified the Arctic as a priority area in light of "increased security threats, a changed distribution of global power, challenges to existing international institutions, and transformation of the global economy." It predicted commercial shipping in Canada's Arctic waters as early as 2015 and with it "the need for Canada to monitor and control events in its sovereign territory, through new funding and new tools."[207] Even Rob Huebert applauded the government's new direction. When the accompanying *Defence Policy Statement* highlighted the Rangers' role, Huebert remarked, "It's saying that the Rangers are important ... It elevates their status. I think it sends a positive signal that they're going to receive consideration as future funds are made available."[208] Paul Martin's government fell before it could deliver on its promises.

The campaign that led up to the federal election of 23 January 2006 featured the Rangers for the first time in national party platforms. When Conservative defence critic Gordon O'Connor visited Iqaluit in late 2005, he promised that his party would expand the Rangers as part of its plan to strengthen Canada's Arctic sovereignty position. "I look on the Rangers as one of the prime instruments in enforcing our sovereignty," O'Connor said. When he spoke with Rangers, they told him that they wanted better equipment, more training, and more work. "Patrols have to increase in frequency," the former brigadier-general told a northern reporter. "As I understand it, the current 4,000 Rangers are capable of doing more patrols, but there just isn't enough money." In O'Connor's assessment, Rangers "should be touching every island and every piece of land in the north on a regular basis." He would deliver GPS units, more cash to maintain personal equipment such as snowmobiles, camouflage uniforms to complement the red sweatshirts, and a new rifle. These promises meshed well with his party's "Canada first" approach to defence, which concentrated on sovereignty and security at home.[209] When Stephen Harper's Conservatives won a minority government in early 2006, they inherited a Ranger organization that had come of age.

11
Sovereignty, Security, and Stewardship

Rangers are our guiding light, our pathfinders, those eyes and ears and hearts and souls of the North that provide us the protection. To me, that role will never change, simply because it's been so successful.

– Brigadier-General David Millar, Commander Joint
Task Force (North) (2009)[1]

I do it for my community and my Canada.

– Ranger Paul Ikuallaq, Gjoa Haven, Nunavut (2007)[2]

✤ WHEN STEPHEN HARPER'S CONSERVATIVES swept into office in 2006, they resolved to make the defence of Arctic sovereignty a priority. The prime minister's "use it or lose it" refrain tapped into primordial national anxieties about sovereignty and resonated with southern Canadians who believed that increased military capabilities could shield their country from the so-called perfect storm brewing in the circumpolar North.[3] "We believe that Canadians are excited about the government asserting Canada's control and sovereignty in the Arctic," Harper told a *Toronto Sun* reporter on 23 February 2007. His plan strategically aligned with his broader agenda to rebuild the Canadian Forces, and he hoped that strengthening Canada's sovereignty over the Arctic would be a major legacy of his government.[4] Many of the Conservatives' military commitments, announced as sovereignty initiatives, bore striking resemblance to unfulfilled promises made by the Mulroney government in the 1980s: a High Arctic base, an icebreaker, surveillance systems, and a promise to expand "the size and capabilities of the Arctic Rangers," an unfortunate but revealing misnaming of the Canadian Rangers.[5]

The Rangers – habitually depicted as Canada's frontline sovereignty soldiers – have been highly visible in the recent spasm of attention paid to Arctic issues. Most commentators assert that Canada needs a continuous military presence to maintain Canadian sovereignty in remote reaches of the Arctic Archipelago and over the Northwest Passage – a contortion of legal realities that nevertheless has significant political and popular traction. "The Rangers are our eyes and ears, and there's no substitute for boots on the ground and people living in the communities," Brigadier-General David Millar explained during a tour of Arctic communities in March 2009. "Technology doesn't always work in the extreme conditions of the High Arctic. That's why nothing can replace the Rangers, and why I reassured them they are the vital link in the North for maintaining sovereignty, representing the forces and providing security for their communities." According to Millar, the Rangers' red sweatshirts and ball caps have become "as symbolic to Canadians as the Snowbirds or RCMP."[6]

Politicians, always keen to tap into symbolism, understood this. As political interest in Arctic sovereignty and security issues rose, pressure to expand the Rangers up to and beyond the forty-eight hundred members authorized by CAN RAN 2000 grew apace. "The Rangers are the sole military presence over large parts of the Canadian north," the Standing Senate Committee on National Security and Defence reported in 2006. "The Government has committed to a robust presence in the North to maintain Canadian sovereignty in the region. Announcements of icebreakers, deepwater ports, [and] training facilities are welcome news, but the implementation of these initiatives is still a long way off. Until that time, Canadian security is in the hands of our Rangers." The committee recommended expanding "this valuable resource for national security" to seventy-five hundred members by 2011.[7] It offered neither a clear rationale for this number nor an explanation of how an expanded force would provide Canada with greater security and sovereignty. The political calculus was simple: more Rangers would evoke an image of stronger security and sovereignty.

The need for action took on new urgency when a Russian expedition led by Artur Chilingarov, a bombastic Duma politician and explorer, planted a titanium flag at the North Pole in July 2007. Although Russia's foreign minister later dismissed the act as a publicity stunt undertaken without Kremlin approval, the world took notice. Many Canadian politicians and journalists held up Chilingarov's action as the quintessential example of Russian belligerence and an abject disregard for due process and international law.[8] Their response in turn spurred domestic and international fears of a "polar race" for frontier resources. Academics Rob Huebert, Michael Byers, and Suzanne Lalonde raised serious doubts about Canada's ability to uphold its sovereignty in the face of external challenges. Reports that the Arctic contained up to one quarter of the world's undiscovered oil and gas reserves amplified the alarm.[9]

Building on his earlier campaign promises and spurred by this external development, Prime Minister Harper announced measures to bolster Canada's sovereignty in the Arctic on 10 August 2007. He unveiled plans for a Canadian Forces Arctic Training Centre in Resolute, a deepwater docking and refueling facility at Nanisivik, and the expansion of the Canadian Rangers from 4,100 to 5,000 members. The Ranger expansion program had four objectives:

- to add new patrols and strengthen existing ones in the North and farther south where required
- to put in place the command-and-control systems necessary to manage the expanded force
- to formalize business plans for the Rangers' $29-million-annual budget
- to support the Ranger Modernization Project, designed to address all aspects of the Rangers' uniforms and equipment.

The plan would cost $12 million dollars more each year – a nearly quarter-billion-dollar investment over twenty years.[10] According to the Prime Minister's Office, the commitment would "significantly strengthen Canada's sovereignty ... [and] benefit communities throughout the region by creating jobs and opportunities and enhancing the safety and security of the people who live here."[11]

Media commentators uniformly applauded the prime minister's announcement.[12] "There's obvious potential to improve surveillance over a region claiming 75% of Canada's coastline using a force that's five times the size of our combat troop deployment in Kandahar yet costs less than

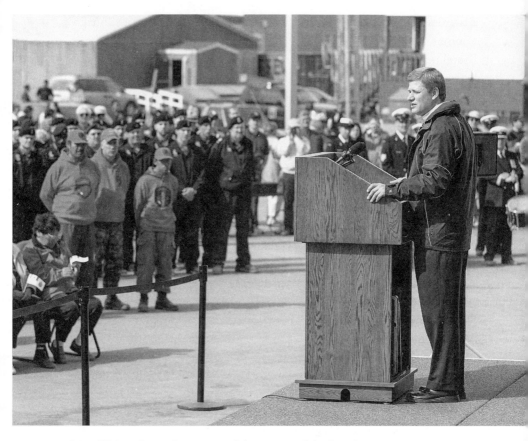

Prime Minister Steven Harper viewed the Arctic, and the Canadian Rangers, as a key component of his "Canada First" defence strategy. Canadian Forces Combat Camera, Photo AS2006-0491

the sticker price for three light-armoured vehicles," Don Martin wrote in the *National Post*.[13] The Rangers' cost-effectiveness had always been a key selling point, and so it remained.

Basic questions lingered. Why did Canada need more Rangers? Should the Rangers continue to expand along the East and West Coasts and in the Subarctic? What should grow: the number of patrols or the number of Rangers in existing patrols? Would new patrols be opened for sociopolitical or for operational reasons?[14] Canadians feared external threats to their sovereignty and security. Should the Rangers be trained for combat or interdiction roles? Did the Rangers need to be modernized to fit with the evolving security environment of the twenty-first century?

Stephen Harper's Inheritance

The Canadian Rangers that Harper inherited were an unquestioned success story, more numerous and well known than ever before. They had emerged from the shadows to occupy centre stage in the unfolding Arctic drama. After Operation Nunalivut in 2008, reporter Bruce Valpy wrote that "just as sturdy stone inuksuit mark the territory of Inuit hunters, [Rangers] David Issigaitok, Douglas Nakoolak and Pitisulaq Ukuqtunnuaq are living symbols and not so secret weapons in Canada's Arctic sovereignty strategy."[15] The Rangers had become icons of Canadian sovereignty.

Large-scale military patrols, those that extended to the remotest reaches of the Arctic, received the most attention from media and politicians. The Rangers' primary responsibility throughout the second half of the twentieth century had been to know their local areas. In the twenty-first century, however, their operational area extended far beyond their home communities. From 2007 onward, Rangers in 1 CRPG participated in three major exercises: Nunalivut in the High Arctic, Nunakput in the western Arctic, and Nanook in the eastern Arctic. The annual Nunalivut operations featured an "all star" team of Rangers.[16] The Rangers exercised their skills, showcased their unique contributions, and worked with other elements of the Canadian Forces (and foreign military representatives on occasion).[17]

Other patrol groups mounted their own enhanced sovereignty patrols or expeditions to showcase their Rangers and raise their profiles. To celebrate Quebec City's 400th anniversary in January 2008, three expeditions of Rangers from 2 CRPG ventured by snowmobile from Nunavik, James Bay, and the Lower North Shore to the provincial capital.[18] A year later, 4 CRPG launched Exercise Western Spirit, a 3,400-kilometre odyssey from Kitimat, British Columbia, to Churchill, Manitoba. Fifteen Rangers completed the entire journey, while others rotated in to complete the provincial legs of the route. The expedition finished on schedule, a remarkable achievement given the vast distances and harsh conditions.[19] Although these operations offered impressive displays of the Rangers' capabilities, the absence of a perceived sovereignty threat meant that they drew comparatively little national and international media attention.

The sovereignty frame and northern focus was typical of recent decades. The government's intermittent interest in Arctic sovereignty and security had generally dictated the military's attentiveness to the Rangers (in theory and in practice) since the Second World War. As Canada lurched from

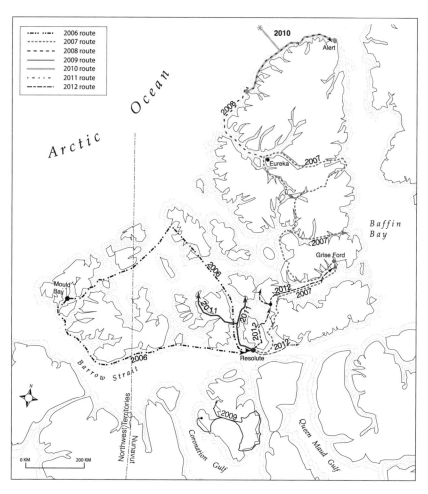

Operation Nunalivut coverage, 2006-12

sovereignty crisis to sovereignty crisis, military interest rose and fell accordingly. The improbable threat of an enemy incursion on Canadian soil, strained defence budgets, alliance obligations, and simple geography precluded the Canadian Forces from maintaining a conventional presence over the entire length and breadth of the country. Having a lightly equipped, self-sufficient group of local experts to act as Canada's eyes and ears in remote regions had always made sense – and the idea fit the budget when it came to meeting sovereignty and security agendas.

Rangers meet up with a CC-138 Twin Otter of 440 Squadron during Exercise Western Spirit, 27 February 2009. Photo by P. Whitney Lackenbauer

The Rangers survived waning interest in their activities mainly because of their tiny cost, modest material demands, and grounding in local communities. The low priority given to the defence of northern and isolated coastal regions meant, however, that the organization lacked a clear national policy and financial support for much of its history. By necessity, the Rangers developed a local and regional orientation. The unorthodox approach to recruiting and sustaining Rangers accommodated diversity. Commanders insisted that adopting national directives that failed to take into account their region's distinctive demographic, social, and cultural realities would undermine the positive relationships that grounded the Rangers.

This grassroots, regional approach had its own set of complications. For more than a decade, military studies suggested that the persistent confusion over command and control hindered the organization's growth. In operational terms, the Rangers fell under the command of their patrol group headquarters after 1997. (The "areas" owned the patrol groups and directed operations.) Less clear was who controlled the Canadian Rangers as a "national program providing a channel for governmental presence in remote communities, a bridge between the Canadian Forces and aboriginal peoples, and participating in a vital and successful youth program." The decentralized command structure worked on an operational level, but it lacked a central authority to coordinate and oversee enhancement and expansion on a national scale. The chief of review services cautioned in 2003 that "different interpretations of directives, different levels of oversight and even different views of the program's raison d'être, place what is generally accepted as a vital national program in some jeopardy, especially as the program becomes more complex as it inevitably will."[20]

To solve the problem, the chief of review services recommended the creation of the Canadian Ranger National Authority (CRNA), which would issue national directions on nonoperational elements but leave command of the units to the Land Force areas and Canadian Forces Northern Area. The Armed Forces Council approved the idea, but before the idea could be implemented the Canadian Forces announced that it would overhaul its entire command structure in June 2005. The new blueprint created Canada Command, which would be responsible for domestic and continental operations and oversee six regional joint task forces. This fundamentally changed how the military viewed Canada as an operational command – as well as the perceived operational value of the Rangers. Consequently, on 1 April 2007, the Canadian Rangers returned to the army. The chief of the land staff assumed responsibility for setting standards for Ranger readiness and employment (as the force generator) to meet Canada Command's operational needs (as the force employer). This development brought some cohesiveness to the organization and paved the way for consistent recruitment, training, equipping, and administrative support.[21] Although each patrol group remained under the command of its respective land force area or joint task force, the transfer to the army gave them a clearer identity within the military hierarchy.[22]

The Rangers' modest uniforms and equipment marked their unique place in the Canadian Forces. Their red sweatshirts were associated with honour and respect in their communities and across the country. Their .303 Lee-Enfield rifles – issued since 1947 and respected for their reliability in some circles and ridiculed as relics of a bygone era in others – likewise distinguished them. When journalists characterized the Rangers as "ragtag forces,"[23] they were really using them as a means to deride the military's weak Arctic capabilities. Some outside commentators misread the modest uniforms and kit as evidence that the military valued the Rangers less than other Reservists,

A Ranger on Exercise Frigid Wabusk near Moosonee teaching survival
skills to southern soldiers in 2008. His snowshoes, handmade, have
purple pompoms that muffle the sound of moving through the woods.
Canadian Forces Combat Camera, Photo LC2008-0314-85

but they could also interpret their lack of uniformity as an acceptance of
diversity. Journalists relished opportunities to depict Rangers in stereotypical
costumes: sealskin mukluks, fur-trimmed hoods, wolverine mitts, or weather-
beaten rainwear. The Rangers' self-sufficiency, borne of adaptation to unique
environments, was, and remains, a key part of their mystique. They serve as

a touchstone to a way of life unimaginable to most Canadians living in southern, urban centres.

Popular descriptions of the Rangers emphasized their Aboriginal composition and typically equated Rangers with Inuit defending their homeland.[24] In the spectacle of the media and in political discourse, the most appropriate boots on the ground were mukluks on the tundra, planted during regular hunting activities or sovereignty patrols. As Sheila Watt-Cloutier, the president of the Inuit Circumpolar Conference (Canada) in 2002, explained, "Inuit are proud Canadian citizens and our commitment to the country is enduring; and Inuit will hold up the Canadian flag." She in turn held up the Rangers as the primary example of how instrumental her people had been in Canada's demonstration of sovereignty in the Arctic. Inuit would not tolerate being seen or treated, and would certainly not act, "as powerless victims of external forces over which we have no control."[25]

Readers of the Inuit publication *Naniiliqpita* learned in early 2006 that the Rangers gave Inuit a critical and direct role: "I get a little tickle in the back of my neck when I think about [the Canadian Forces] depending on us," Ranger Abraham Kudlu of Pond Inlet explained. "This is important to Inuit because we've never had much military presence here. It makes us feel more like Canadians." The Rangers themselves had no question that their role, mission, and tasks remained appropriate. "We hunt here so I want to keep this as ours," explained Ranger Norm Simonie, also with the Pond Inlet patrol. "This is our hunting area for muskox, walrus, beluga, polar bear, [and] rabbits." Nunavut commissioner Ann Hanson described the Rangers' vital importance and how their knowledge of land, sea, and skies had inspired Nunavummiut. "Every time I go into a community," she observed, "I see the respect and admiration of their peers. They have the skills for survival."[26]

The Canadian Rangers represent both Canada's military presence in the North and a national strategy that engages northerners directly, accommodating both Prime Minister Harper's characterization of sovereignty as a simple matter of "use it or lose it" and Inuit leaders' appeals to the Canadian government to "use the Inuit."[27] Interest in their homelands is not transient, their commitment does not vacillate according the whims of the southern political agenda,[28] and their activities reflect the interests of both the military and their communities. The Rangers build capacity, embody the idea of stewardship as sovereignty, and are neither reactionary nor alarmist in their design or operations. Furthermore, the organization's established record of operations, extending back over more than half a century, affirms the

Ranger Wally Pauloosie of Taloyoak, Nunavut, provides predator control for the
1 Canadian Rangers Patrol Group tactical command post camp near Baring Bay, Nunavut,
during Operation Nunalivut 2012. Canadian Forces Combat Camera, Photo IS2012-1012-06

interconnectedness between Aboriginal knowledge, identities, and practices,
on the one hand, and the nation's interest in exercising its sovereignty on a
continuous basis, on the other.

The Rangers' practical contributions to their communities – not only in
the Far North but from coast to coast to coast – reflect roles and responsibilities that transcend the national, regional, and local scales. The benefits
of the community-military relationship flow both ways: the military receives
local expertise, traditional knowledge about lands and waters, and practical
support for activities in "extreme environments." Local people benefit from
modest pay, training and operational experience, leadership development,
and public recognition of their contributions to sovereignty and security.
"Both the Canadian Ranger and the Junior Canadian Ranger programs are
strong and effective in the North and make a real contribution to local
safety, national sovereignty and preservation of land skills," Jackie Jacobson,
the representative for Nunakput, told the Northwest Territories Legislative

Assembly in 2008.[29] As a long-standing member of the Rangers and the patrol sergeant in Tuktoyaktuk, he was well situated to make this case.

How do you improve upon a success story without changing the essential characteristics that made the organization a success in the first place?[30] To preserve trust, expectations that grow during an upswing must be sustained during a downswing. How do you balance the needs of a community-based organization with regional agendas and those of the nation? As political and popular interest in the Rangers grew – and as more resources flowed into expansion, operations, equipment, and training – decision makers had to confront questions debated since the early postwar period: What should the Rangers be expected to do? Where should they be located? Who should participate? How should they be organized? And how does Ranger service fit with Canada's evolving military and civic identities?

Expansion

The Harper government promised to expand the Canadian Rangers to an average paid strength of five thousand members by fiscal year 2011-12 for political reasons.[31] There is no evidence that increasing the Rangers' size would have any effect on the Canadian Forces' ability to fulfill its mission. Five thousand Rangers would not provide more security or more sovereignty than forty-two hundred Rangers. By championing Ranger expansion, however, the new government could claim an existing success story as its own.

The genesis for Ranger growth did not come from the Department of National Defence, where staff officers had little advance notice of the prime minister's announcement. In fact, some patrol groups thought numbers would only increase in 1 CRPG, given that the media and political announcements had trumpeted Ranger expansion as part of the government's Arctic sovereignty agenda. Central authorities quickly clarified that the military would expand the organization nationwide.[32] Based upon its operational requirements, Canada Command ranked the priorities for new patrols in British Columbia, Ontario, the Territorial North, and the prairie provinces.[33]

Despite the government's strong Arctic sovereignty focus, 1 CRPG would see the smallest percentage of change. This weighting reflected the Rangers' general evolution since the 1970s. Arctic sovereignty and security crises usually prompted Ranger growth, but the actual expansion extended beyond settlements along the Northwest Passage and in the Arctic Archipelago,

TABLE 12
Canadian Ranger expansion plans (adjusted), 2008-12

	Patrols			Rangers		
	2008	2012	% change	2008	2012	% change
National	161	178	1.09	3,941	5,000	1.27
1 CRPG	56	60	1.07	1,530	1,800	1.18
2 CRPG	23	25	1.09	601	740	1.23
3 CRPG	15	20	1.33	377	575	1.53
4 CRPG	37	41	1.11	730	975	1.34
5 CRPG	30	32	1.07	703	910	1.29

Source: Brig.-Gen. G.J.P. O'Brien, "Canadian Ranger Expansion Update," 20 April 2010, Department of National Defence, f. 1920-1 (CRNA).

where some commentators suggested that Canadian sovereignty remained precarious. The Rangers already had a permanent footprint in all of the High Arctic communities by the early 1990s. This footprint, coupled with simple demographics, limited expansion possibilities north of the treeline. Captain Conrad Schubert, the deputy commanding officer of 1 CRPG, reported in October 2007 that "Military membership in the North ... is already more than five times the national Canadian average with 1.44% of northerners serving as Canadian Rangers against 0.27% of Canadians serving in the Regular Force and all other reserve components."[34] Every community in Nunavut had a patrol except Bathurst Inlet – an Inuit outpost in the Kitikmeot Region with no population, according to the 2006 census.[35] Five communities south of the treeline in Northwest Territories and Yukon could, potentially, accommodate new patrols.[36] These patrols could hardly be justified on the grounds that they would bolster Canada's sovereignty against threats to its maritime domain in the Far North.

The Rangers could expand in the Arctic by recruiting more people into existing patrols. This approach would ensure (in theory at least) that each patrol would "make a credible presence if called on in an emergency or for training." Once again, local demographics constrained that possibility. The average strength of patrols in 1 CRPG was twenty-seven Rangers in late 2007. This meant that, in many communities, most able-bodied adult members had already participated. In patrols with a waiting list, raising the authorized limit from thirty to forty Rangers would open up new spaces.

Ranger Donna Geddes of Carcross, Yukon, building a *komatik* (wooden sled) in Resolute Bay, Nunavut, in preparation for Operation Nunalivut 2011. Canadian Forces Combat Camera, Photo IS2011-8250-02

Accordingly, Schubert produced a theoretical total of twenty-four hundred potential Rangers in the Territorial North.[37] 1 CRPG eventually settled on a more modest target of eighteen hundred Rangers in sixty patrols by 2012.[38]

This expansion plan met with a mixed response at the patrol level. When 1 CRPG cleaned up its administrative files and removed inactive personnel from its nominal roll in 2009, its Ranger strength actually decreased by three hundred members. Although this did not surprise local patrol commanders, they now faced pressure to make up "lost ground" in addition to expanding their membership more generally. Some long-serving Rangers expressed concern that increasing numbers for arbitrary political reasons could actually dilute the quality of recruits and destroy the fabric of their patrols. As self-administered units, many patrols managed to strike a healthy balance between youth and experience. A rapid influx of people without experience on the land or the right chemistry with existing Rangers could lessen the patrol's ability to respond confidently in an emergency.[39] The long-term implications remain unclear, but 1 CRPG is set to exceed its expansion quota, indicating (numerically at least) that the growth plan has proven successful.[40]

The national attention directed towards Rangers in the Territorial North conceals the simple reality that expansion plans after 2007 focused on Rangers "south of 60." Indeed, two-thirds of the expanded Ranger organization would be located in the provinces.[41] Defence planners had previously hesitated to authorize new patrols in the Subarctic, which faced no perceived sovereignty threat. National Defence Headquarters had invoked Operation Pause in 2003 precisely to ensure that regional sociopolitical agendas, developed by individual patrol group commanders, did not propel Ranger growth. The political imperative to reach a national target set by the prime minister himself trumped these concerns. The restraints were lifted.

2 CRPG led the way and established all of the patrols it was authorized to create. The patrol group had been the most strident in pushing for new Ranger and Junior Ranger patrols since the late 1990s. Major Guy Lang, the commanding officer from 2006 to 2010, continued to pursue growth. Like his predecessor, Claude Archambault, Lang was enthusiastic and engaging and related well to political officials throughout the province. He also proactively recruited Rangers in communities slated for new patrols. As a result, when the Chisasibi and Îles de la Madeleine patrols opened in July 2009, they were at full strength from the onset.[42] The patrol group's area of responsibility within the province of Quebec expanded farther south and east than ever before.[43]

By 2007, the Rangers had established themselves in fifteen communities in northern Ontario. Communities along the coasts of Hudson and James bays were well represented, and planners in 3 CRPG saw no benefit to increasing patrol sizes: thirty Rangers sufficed, given regional demographics.

Nevertheless, the Rangers could expand into First Nations communities in the interior. Joint Task Force (Central) proposed six new patrols to enhance its situational awareness, broaden its geographical footprint, and exploit the "excellent value added and cost effective training" that the Rangers afforded Regular Force and Primary Reserve units in Ontario. More boldly, 3 CRPG pushed for southern patrols ("south of fifty") on the national highway because it considered them ideal locations for cost-effective northern training exercises.[44]

Expansion efforts in 4 CRPG, which straddled two joint task force areas, took longer to produce results. By late 2006, Joint Task Force (Pacific) had noted "presence gaps" in coverage along the West Coast, "not because of a lack of capacity or planning, but because of uncertainty regarding the future of the Ranger programme for much of its existence." In a region that had seen its Rangers come, go, and come again, this hesitation was understandable. Now that the Rangers' had a clearer future, 4 CRPG proposed two new patrols in British Columbia.[45] Major Byers also identified three First Nations communities in Saskatchewan and two in Manitoba that would provide increased situational awareness for Joint Task Force (West).[46] Although the Rangers certainly had room for new patrols and expansion within existing patrols, 4 CRPG's numbers also dropped when it updated its nominal rolls.[47] After completing the resource-intensive Exercise Western Spirit, which raised the patrol group's profile across the northern Prairies in early 2009, Major Byers made a conscious effort to increase Ranger membership. Recruiting became his "number one priority," and he produced excellent results. At one point, Captain Russ Meades, the deputy commanding officer who took over as BC detachment commander in March 2010, swore in twenty-two Rangers in twenty-two days.[48] New patrols opened in Wollaston Lake and La Ronge,[49] and the patrol group's strength increased from 700 to 966 members by February 2011. There is little doubt that it will reach its expansion targets.[50]

5 CRPG remained the relatively quiet partner along the Atlantic Coast, attracting mainly regional and local media coverage. When approached about possible expansion in 2007, the patrol group did not forecast growth but stated that it would maintain its authorized limits of 30 patrols and 790 Rangers. Two years later, it approved modest plans to increase individual patrols to 34 Rangers and the patrol group to 920 Rangers. It also committed to opening two new patrols and to dividing the Port Saunders and Rocky Harbour patrols.[51] Individual Rangers in Newfoundland were still

TABLE 13
The Canadian Rangers organization, 14 November 2012

CRPG	Headquarters personnel	Patrols	Rangers
1 CRPG	53	59	1,617
2 CRPG	46	25	731
3 CRPG	41	20	610
4 CRPG	70	42	1,054
5 CRPG	42	32	896
TOTAL	252	178	4,908

Source: Canadian Rangers National Authority.

scattered along the coastline, so simply adjusting boundaries enabled the creation of new units.[52] The Ranger organization had more members to carry out its quiet vigil along the Atlantic Coast, but its spatial coverage stayed the same.

The overall impact of this latest round of Ranger expansion remains to be seen. Once the organization reaches an active strength of five thousand Rangers, it will have reached the authorized ceiling set in 1947 for the first time – a political triumph.[53] Nonetheless, one wonders if the old maxim from the early postwar period still rings true: having the right Rangers in the right locations, doing the right things, is more important than having more of them.[54]

The Rangers' Role

Are the Rangers doing the right things? Since the Second World War, military officials have debated the Rangers' role, mission, and tasks. History reveals a litany of enhancement proposals. Some officials wanted more Ranger training, others more equipment, and still others a more orthodox military structure. Bold plans to reconstitute the Rangers as a typical Regular or Reserve Force unit have never come to fruition. Typically, authorities in Ottawa cast aside ambitious plans because of their cost. For years, the patrol groups operated on subsistence funding augmented by money from their respective land force or joint task force headquarters.[55] With the federal government's commitment to dramatically increased funding and its promise to enhance the Rangers, is it time to update their responsibilities?

The Rangers evolved from simply being the military's eyes and ears to serving operational, sociopolitical, and representational functions. Patrol group commanders continue to debate whether the operational or the social dimension should take priority, and commentators from outside the military have joined the discussion. Seldom do their proposals display an appreciation for how and why the Rangers took their unique form or how the Rangers' role, mission, and tasks translate across national, regional, and local scales – for both military and civilian partners. Instead, various stakeholders have pushed to repackage the Rangers into a form that fits their agendas, without recognizing the broader implications for the organization.

First and foremost, Aboriginal advocacy groups hold strong opinions about what the Rangers are and what they should become. Their perceptions align with the four pillars of Canada's northern strategy as well as their calls for a deeper understanding of sovereignty than simply "use it or lose it."[56] Mary Simon, the leader of Inuit Tapiriit Kanatami, which represents the fifty-five thousand Inuit in Canada, insisted in 2007 that Canada needed more than new Arctic patrol ships to prove that "sovereignty begins at home." Suicide rates, respiratory diseases from overcrowded housing, unfulfilled land claims provisions, and global climate change all pose more serious challenges to Inuit communities than external military threats. "It is sometimes said that war is too important to be left to the generals," Simon wrote. "In Canada's case, Arctic sovereignty is too important to be treated as just an adjunct to foreign relations or as a stage for foreign investment. It must be built from the inside out. The bedrock of Canada's status as an Arctic nation is the history of use and occupation of Arctic lands and waters by Inuit for thousands of years." Simon's practical program of action suggested ways "to goose up Arctic surveillance at a fraction of the cost" of new naval vessels. She included within her list the dramatic expansion of the Canadian Rangers.[57]

Northern Aboriginal groups tout the Rangers as a key component of an integrated Arctic strategy that can contribute positively to isolated communities. The Rangers confirm how Aboriginal people "continue through use and occupancy to assert sovereignty in quiet ways."[58] Ranger service meshes well with messages of Aboriginal patriotism, cultural viability, capacity building, and community sustainability. As a result, spokespersons have promoted transforming the military-community partnership to create jobs and to effect sociopolitical change. Why not have the military hire full-time Rangers to alleviate unemployment in Arctic communities rather than paying transient southern troops to come north on sovereignty exercises?[59] Why not recast the Rangers as a work-training program? Nunavut Senator Willie Adams observed that "boosting the Rangers' abilities could lead to more jobs for Inuit, who could work on ships and in the Canadian Coast Guard."[60] In Pond Inlet, settlement manager Malachi Arreak argued that "we want our Rangers trained to be pilots, military specialists, search and rescue technicians, anything to create jobs."[61] Inuit Tapiriit Kanatami called for "a re-conceptualization and expansion of the Arctic Rangers program" so that the Rangers' official tasks would include environmental monitoring, supplying country food to communities, providing "work for those unqualified or unable to work in wage employment, particularly in small communities," and sustaining land-based skills, cultures, and languages.[62]

Rangers already perform many of these tasks. The net result of formalizing this vision, however, would be the transformation of the Rangers into a military workfare program directed at Aboriginal communities.[63] The Rangers are not an Aboriginal program, even if some military officers, journalists, and politicians have characterized them as such. The Rangers are a subcomponent of the Canadian Forces Reserves. Proposals to recast them as a socioeconomic program, however well intentioned, threatened to erode the Rangers' relationships with and within the Canadian Forces. Their credibility with the broader military community – one half of their identity – is at stake.

Rising expectations in regard to the Rangers' operational role may also pull them away from community activities and local service, the other half of their identity. By 2008, for example, 3 CRPG had reaped the benefits of its aggressive, ongoing public relations campaign to educate northern Ontario residents, the Canadian Forces, and Canadians more generally about its Rangers.[64] Army units in Ontario inundated headquarters with requests to conduct winter indoctrination training with the Rangers. Commanding officer Major Guy Ingram explained that Ranger instructors already spent two hundred days each year conducting Ranger and Junior Ranger training exercises. It became a burden "to be wanted by everyone," Ingram noted ironically. "What was 3 CRPG putting on hold to support other CF units?"[65]

Other patrol groups likewise risked overextending themselves. In 1 CRPG, the heightened tempo of activity, coupled with a shortage of clerks and Ranger instructors, began to have direct effects on the ground. Ranger instructors had managed to insulate the Rangers from staffing shortages in the past, but they could not contain the impact of a deluge of extra taskings in 2009. Rangers learned that 1 CRPG would not support the Yukon River Quest, the Yukon Quest, or territorial shoots in the upcoming year. These important regional and community events fell below sovereignty operations and implementing a new national training program on the list of priorities.[66] Rangers took offence. They had built and maintained the Yukon Quest trails as an official military exercise for seventeen years and considered the task an important way to exercise their skills, publicize their contributions, and support a Yukon tradition.[67] They questioned whether the third pillar of Ranger tasks – that of maintaining a Canadian Forces presence in the community – had become less important than politically motivated growth plans hatched in Ottawa? After a change in patrol group leadership, Ranger support for the Yukon Quest and similar community-based events resumed in 2011.[68]

These situations reinforced the need for a careful balance between operational and community roles, whereas concerns about Arctic sovereignty and security renewed debates about whether the Rangers should evolve into a more typical military unit and receive more conventional training. Photographs of Rangers in Zodiac skiffs participating alongside southern troops in beach landings during Operation Nanook in 2009 suggested a tactical role, but the Rangers officially served the exercise as guides and as "predator control."[69] Back in the 1950s, Ranger liaison officers in Newfoundland and Quebec had cautioned that Ranger activities during army exercises could set up unrealistic expectations and distort perceptions about roles. Was imagery of Rangers operating alongside combat-ready soldiers during high-profile sovereignty operations having the predicted effect a half century later?

In a world where perception often matters more than reality, some commentators believed that the military should better prepare the Rangers for combat. Unaware of previous proposals to improve the Rangers and oblivious as to why the Rangers' responsibilities and relationships had evolved to their present form, these pundits downplayed the Rangers' practical contributions while propagating the idea that without more formal training they would not, and could not, contribute to Canadian sovereignty or security. One former intelligence officer scolded the Canadian Forces for vesting its Arctic defence responsibilities in reservists, particularly the Rangers, who, despite "the flow of public affairs ink at National Defence," were "nowhere near being a serious military presence in the region."[70] This observation reflects historical debates about amateur versus professional soldiering as much as it is a critique of the Rangers themselves. Geographer and popular author James Raffan asserted that "the Rangers' sovereignty patrols on snow machines are something of legend, but for all their virtues, this willing band of some 4,000 part-time armed reservists in 163 communities across the North hasn't the training or the equipment to consider any kind of interdiction, in winter or summer, on the open sea, where the only real tests to Canadian sovereignty will occur."[71] In other words, unless they could enforce Canadian laws themselves, the Rangers had little value.

Other commentators went further in their calls to professionalize the Rangers. John Ralston Saul, renowned author and formerly Canada's vice-regal consort, told an audience in Montreal in 2010, "I think if you asked any Canadian officer in any one of the three services they would tell you that the defence of the Arctic must primarily be civil, although there is a real need for a military presence ... There is a very real need not simply to enlarge the Canadian Rangers – the one truly Northern force – but to formalize them as a Regiment with Inuit and other Northerners in its officer-level leadership."[72] Without explaining how or why formalization would improve the organization, Saul's solution sought to correct the "perfectly colonial" way in which Rangers reported to "southern commands."[73] He did not explain how command and control actually functioned or acknowledge the military hierarchy's respect for and unique relationship with the Rangers' patrol-level leadership. This well-intended corrective failed to grasp the logic of the organization as it had evolved.

Parliamentary committees provided similar lines of advice. In April 2009, the Standing Senate Committee on Fisheries and Oceans recommended that the military should make the Rangers "an integral part of the Canadian reserves" and provide them with a "marine capability."[74] Committee chair William Rompkey of Labrador explained that this would entail converting them into full reserve units with extensive formal training and more equipment. "It's a signal for us that they're not useful simply as guides," Rompkey explained to reporter Bob Weber. "They are fully capable of doing the job that needs to be done in the Arctic." Rompkey acknowledged that transforming the Rangers into primary reservists would change their terms of service, but he promised – like others before him – that a more formal maritime role and enhanced military status would bolster Canadian sovereignty over lands and seas. Who better to assert ownership and control over coastal and marine resources than a more muscular Ranger force?[75]

As the debate about Arctic sovereignty and security picked up tempo, northerners complained that their voices were being marginalized by so-called experts who had jumped on the bandwagon and had no qualms about offering recommendations on how to improve matters, without having spent actual time on the ground. Few of these southern pundits displayed the self-awareness of Captain Ambrose Shea, who, humbled by his travels north in the mid-1950s, studiously avoided claiming any special authority on Arctic matters. As he put it, "the only real Arctic experts are the Eskimoes, who have forgotten more about living in the North than most white men ever learn." Had anyone canvassed the Rangers (or the instructors who worked with them on a regular basis) about whether they thought their military status needed to change? Were commentators aware that their proposals to reconstitute, modernize, and professionalize the Rangers had been floated (and sunk) previously? Could they anticipate the real consequences for the Rangers, or could they only proffer answers to national sovereignty and security questions as they framed them from afar?

Local reactions to these calls for militarization varied, but the core debate revolved around training for combat and interdiction. "I didn't become a Canadian Ranger to go fight in combat," Master Corporal Warren Esau of Sachs Harbor explained. "I'd have a big problem if they decided to do something like this ... I'd rather be out shooting caribou and geese, not humans. It's not what I want to be doing as a Ranger." Sergeant Jonah Nakimayak of Paulatuk, a Ranger since 1988, said that he would quit if the military foisted combat training on the Rangers. "I'm getting up there in age and it wouldn't be something I'd be interested in doing," he said. "I can't speak for the younger rangers, it might be something they would want to do, but I don't really like the idea personally."[76] These voices (and others like them) clearly indicated that the Rangers had a strong sense of their personal contributions. Many imposed specific conditions on their service, and the vast majority of Rangers whom I interviewed over the last decade were pleased with their unique military status. Nevertheless, did treating and equipping the Rangers differently than other members of the Canadian Forces imply that they were lesser members?

"Let's hope there's never a Canadian Ranger put in a potential combat situation," Darrell Greer, a reporter in Nunavut, stated. "But it's asinine to suggest large numbers of Canadian Rangers would quit if the challenge to Canadian sovereignty in the North ever reached the point where they were called upon to do their share." The Rangers' origins lay with Pacific Coast

Ranger Corporal Free Mitchell Strid of Dawson, Yukon, rides past two CC-138 Twin Otter aircraft resupplying the Rangers' temporary camp in Viks Fiord, Nunavut, during Operation Nunalivut 2012. Canadian Forces Combat Camera, Photo IS2012-1011-08

Militia Rangers, which had been designed to repel a Japanese invasion. During the Cold War, the Rangers formed to defend northern communities from the Soviets. "Maybe it's just me," Greer stated, "but that doesn't sound like the lineage of a group of people who would cut and run at the first sign of trouble." Although he found it ridiculous to expect elders to prepare themselves for combat, he conceded that they would be among the first to sign up in an emergency. "Either way you cut it, they're indicative of most Nunavummiut in that they're a long way from being the undereducated and unpatriotic bunch some who don't know any better suggest they are."[77]

Greer, and others like him, missed the point. No one was questioning northerners' patriotism, their knowledge of lands and waters, or their capacity to learn from the military. The real issue was not whether the Rangers *could* be trained up to the Primary Reserve's standards but whether they *should* be. The Rangers had proven their value in recent decades, and they had achieved a balance between their military and community contributions. Their original combat role had been removed from the Ranger task list, but that did not mean that the Rangers had ceased to contribute to the Canadian Forces. The military still had to be able to "force project" into remote regions in case of emergency, and the Rangers remained a vital force multiplier – essential subject-matter experts in their home areas. Was there a probable threat of enemy invasion that required enhanced military status and rigorous combat training for citizen-soldiers who were never expected to deploy overseas? Journalists seldom explored the deeper question of *probable* risks; they preferred instead to cite potential scenarios that played to a basic (and largely fictional) storyline of volatility and uncertainty in the circumpolar Arctic.[78]

History should play a greater role in discussions about the Rangers' future. Lieutenant-Colonel Bob Keane wrote in 1947, "We don't want, and we don't need, further organized military bodies supplementing Active and Reserve Forces but what we need is that small groups of specially adapted people take an interest in the defence of their country in order that we may derive the greatest benefits from their knowledge and particular facilities and it is necessary that they be organized to some extent; but I am afraid that if we try to make them too military we will certainly stand to lose by it."[79] This line of argument is as valid today as it was when Keane wrote it more than six decades ago. The Ranger organization, managed on a local level, succeeds because it draws on the indigenous knowledge of its members rather than on conditioning them through regularized military training regimes. If the Rangers as an organization are not broken and actually accomplish their mission through an intimate connection between the military and their home communities, why do they need to be fixed?

Fortunately, the army has rejected the idea of turning the Rangers into combat-ready units.[80] Public statements by senior military officers suggest that the Canadian Forces are pleased with the Rangers' existing roles and contributions and do not intend to add new responsibilities.[81] The army already considers the Rangers a cornerstone of their emerging Arctic strategy, which relies heavily upon reservists: four newly created Arctic response company groups designed to respond to incidents in the Arctic as well as the Yellowknife Company of the Loyal Edmonton Regiment.[82] Building an effective response capability will take time, but the army considers the Rangers "a mature capability" and "the foundation of the CF's operational capability across the North for a range of domestic missions."[83] In a military emergency, the army would expect the Arctic response groups, not the Rangers, to conduct "combined arms kinetic manoeuvre operations" – military jargon for actual fighting.[84] Nevertheless, the Rangers could keep them abreast of local developments and would help to advise and act as guides. In preparing for this unlikely eventuality, the Rangers play an important role in teaching southern-based units how to survive on the land, a skill not included in training tailored for foreign missions such as Afghanistan.[85]

While official planning documents focused on 1 CRPG, the new Arctic mission also affected patrol groups South of 60. After all, the boundaries of what constitutes "northern" and "Arctic" remain flexible, and developing skills in northern operations does not necessarily require deployment to the High Arctic. In Alberta, for example, an innovative detachment commander designed a canned survival school, which Ranger patrols delivered to Regular and Reserve Force units. These low-cost activities proved to be tremendously popular and are now offered in the other prairie provinces.[86] Since February 2011, when Canada Command redefined "the North" as the area north of 55° N, units operating in the provincial norths are now considered to be on "northern deployments." This conceptual shift simply respects realities on the ground. Various patrol groups have long provided advanced winter warfare training to primary reservists.[87]

The patrol groups still have latitude within their areas of responsibility to undertake activities that reflect national, regional, and local priorities. Major Jeff Allen, who assumed command of 1 CRPG in mid-2010, insists that the Rangers' official role, mission, and tasks do not need amending.[88] Rangers have ample room to support nonconventional activities that meet military, community, and "whole of government" objectives. For example, during Nunavut's two-week mass vaccination program against swine flu (the H1N1 virus) in November 2009, Rangers played a pivotal role guiding Nunavummiut through the process and helping them fill out paperwork. *Nunatsiaq News* editor Jim Bell noted that, alongside health workers, the Rangers "achieved something that most other governments in the country have fumbled so far ... They managed to conduct a mass flu-shot clinic that worked."[89] On the scientific front, Rangers supported southern scientists working on an International Polar Year project on ice shelves during Operation Nunalivut in 2008 and set up huts for polar bear researchers along M'Clintock Channel in 2010. They also supported other government departments in identifying and verifying sites as part of the federal "legacy

Canadian Ranger Lieutenant Oswald (Ozzie) Dyson of Churchill Falls shows Private Ryan Scott of the 1st Battalion Royal New Brunswick Regiment how to start a fire on top of snow, March 2010. Canadian Forces Combat Camera, Photo LH2009-005-016d

sites" cleanup project, and they worked with Fisheries and Oceans Canada to install navigation buoys. Allen encourages these activities, which provide new opportunities for collaboration, serve broader national interests, and give his Rangers opportunities to "patrol with a purpose."[90]

The idea of purposeful activity informs many of the patrol groups' recent priorities. 2 CRPG has assumed formal domestic operations responsibilities within Joint Task Force (East) and introduced a new regional approach to training to prepare Rangers for land-based emergencies and search-and-rescue at sea.[91] Major Guy Ingram, who commanded 3 CRPG from 2007 to 2010, encouraged "operationalizing" Rangers so they could respond to emergencies themselves.[92] Ranger instructors in Ontario even started to receive formal suicide prevention training in 2011 so that they could intervene effectively in situations that they encountered in the field.[93] Maintaining the balance between operational and sociopolitical benefits continues to lie at the heart of sustaining the Rangers as both a military formation and as a community-based organization.

Enhancement

What does Ranger enhancement actually mean if the Rangers, and the military establishment more generally, consider their existing role and military status to be sound? After the chief of the land staff became the Canadian Rangers National Authority on 1 April 2007, he set up a dedicated cell of staff at National Defence Headquarters to provide "overall direction and clarity" to the army commander, the patrol groups, and the Rangers. This direction included establishing national policy, validating equipment and training needs, coordinating dress changes, standardizing human resources and financial management practices, and ensuring that patrol groups had a similar structure and organization across the country.[94] In short, the army would provide the Rangers with a stronger national framework without making that framework so restrictive that the Rangers could not do their job in their particular environments. In this context, *enhancement* meant improving the day-to-day operations and administration of the Rangers as a national organization while fostering the unique aspects of each patrol group and each patrol. The army would need to recognize and balance the Ranger's operational and representational value to the military with their roles in local communities and in Canada as a whole.

Striking the right balance between national direction and flexibility is challenging. The army could no longer use the Rangers' distinctiveness as an excuse to avoid devising and implementing national policies. New Land Force Command Orders standardized enrolment, set criteria to determine whether individual Rangers were "non-effective," and articulated a formal process for releasing them.[95] The orders abolished some unique regional practices. For example, 5 CRPG had forced its Rangers to retire at age sixty-five, but the orders quashed compulsory retirement.[96] Similarly, the patrol group's commanding officer in Halifax appointed patrol commanders until 2008, when the group introduced patrol elections to bring it in line with the rest of the country.[97] The national authority also simplified the claims process for damaged equipment,[98] and it raised and standardized compensation rates for equipment use.[99] The net result brought more coherence and greater protection for Rangers and patrol groups across the country. Master Warrant Officer Bruce Dunn, responsible for implementing national training standards, explained that the national authority got rid of the grey areas that used to get the commanding officers into trouble. Clearer policies meant that they were "no longer put out on a limb and acting in a dangerous zone."[100]

What about safeguarding the Rangers themselves? Staff officers had long complained about the lack of national policies to cover Rangers whose activities in harsh and unforgiving environments placed them in hazardous situations. The military expected Rangers to report unusual activities but did not pay them for this everyday task. What if Rangers had accidents that caused damage to themselves or their equipment en route to reporting a submarine or strange aircraft? What liability would the military incur for medical injuries and long-term disability benefits?[101] When Ranger Sergeant Jamesie Kootoo of Kimmirut broke his pelvis while providing support to a dog sled race across frozen Frobisher Bay, he was airlifted to hospital in Ottawa, where he remained for several months.[102] To apply due diligence, 1 CRPG began to conduct basic medical screening of Rangers who wanted to participate in sovereignty patrols.[103] And what if a Ranger died on duty? In April 2007, Pauloosie Paniloo, a sixty-four-year-old Ranger and highly respected elder from Clyde River, died during a routine patrol to the Fox-3 North Warning site. His family requested that he be buried in his Ranger uniform, a tremendous honour to the Rangers given his distinguished political career. He received a full military funeral akin to that of a soldier killed overseas.[104] Deceased Rangers are now recognized for their Canadian

Appa Josephee, Lysa Pitseolak, Jamesie Kootoo, and Louie Qimirpik *(left to right)* observe soldiers from eastern Ontario's 33 Canadian Brigade Group, which established an observation post near Kimmirut, Nunavut, during Operation Nanook in August 2008. Canadian Forces Combat Camera, Photo ISX2008-0018

Forces service with permanent grave markers on their headstones, physically marking their military status.[105]

While national policies made sense in many respects, the Ranger organization needed to retain enough latitude to manage regional diversity. Major Guy Ingram aptly described the Rangers as "a national unit with five distinct units underneath it."[106] The five patrol group establishments differed widely across the country. To bring them into alignment, the national authority proposed an "85% solution": 85 percent of the positions would be the same to ensure organizational uniformity and control, while the remaining 15 percent would be flexible to accommodate regional differences and tasks.[107] The ensuing changes to CRPG headquarters provided the personnel and flexibility to expand.[108] In 4 CRPG, for example, Major

Tim Byers complained in October 2007 that his budget had not changed significantly in seven years, even though his patrol group had expanded from twenty-eight to thirty-seven patrols. Without more resources, he could not cover even six days of training per patrol. "We are at our breaking point," Byers told the national working group, "and need National Authority to get things moving very soon."[109] The army increased funding so that patrol groups South of 60 could achieve the mandated twelve days of training.[110] Two years later, the chief of the land staff approved a new establishment for 4 CRPG that saw its permanent staff jump from forty-two to sixty personnel. The ensuing hiring frenzy meant new faces in each provincial detachment and the patrol group headquarters in Victoria, as well as promotions for the commanding officer and group sergeant major.[111] "I can honestly say that 4th Canadian Ranger Patrol Group has never been in a better position," the newly promoted Lieutenant-Colonel Byers told his Rangers in the summer of 2010.[112]

All of the Ranger patrol groups received similar boosts, and their distinctiveness has remained intact. The clearest example is 2 CRPG, where Major Lang appointed seven Ranger warrant officers: a rank that did not exist in the officially sanctioned patrol group structure. He envisaged the warrant officers as regional liaison officers who would look after patrols in their region, with patrol sergeants reporting directly to them. In this way, Rangers would lead Rangers.[113] Lang also broke with convention by sending Rangers to army leadership qualification courses, an obvious attempt to fit the Rangers into a Primary Reserve mould.[114] "My greatest challenge is to have the Rangers accepted as soldiers," Lang noted in 2009. Rangers were responsible and capable of autonomous action; they "know their territory, they comprehend their mission very well, and they are proud of their work ... I call them my 'Warriors.'"[115]

The Canadian Ranger National Authority had no interest in making Rangers into warriors through standardized and streamlined training. Although the original Ranger concept had not included formal military training, over time Rangers had received both basic and collective instruction. Each patrol group had developed its own training packages and standards with varying degrees of formality and success. Representatives from each patrol group and the director of reserves had met to discuss training policies, but the need to incorporate regional uniqueness stymied efforts to standardize the training regime. When the army commander assumed responsibility for the Rangers in 2007, he specifically tasked the directorate of army training and the national authority with developing a Canadian Ranger training package in line with the army training system.[116] The resulting program comprised two development phases: DP1 Ranger, designed to provide Canadian Rangers with the general military knowledge and skills necessary to operate as a patrol member and to interoperate with other Canadian Forces units; and DP2 Patrol Commander, designed to enhance Ranger leadership skills.[117]

During my visits to patrols across the country, long-serving Rangers expressed frustration that training had become boring and repetitive. Instructors trained recruits and experienced Rangers simultaneously; some Rangers had heard the same material on expectations and basic skills for decades. The new training system introduced in 2009 allowed Ranger recruits to take their DP1 course at a centralized location within their patrol group area. They received basic training in map and compass, GPS, first aid, weapons safety, and marksmanship. Much friendlier than "boot camp" in southern units, the course gave new Rangers an opportunity to receive focused attention from instructors (both patrol group staff and Canadian Rangers), meet new people, and build a sense of patrol group identity. When they returned to their patrols, they had basic qualifications that paved the way "for more advanced, formal training that would keep the Canadian Rangers interested, motivated and challenged."[118]

The method of delivering the new training system differed from patrol group to patrol group. Instructors continued to adapt training to suit their audiences. In 1 CRPG, for example, Major Luc Chang, the commanding officer from 2007 to 2010, centralized DP1 training in the territorial capitals and tied it to expansion as a form of recruit training. Individuals who wanted to become Rangers applied through the patrol in their community, but they had to pass the DP1 before they could function as a Ranger. This program succeeded in terms of expansion,[119] but it forced recruits to leave their community to become Rangers when the organization's goal was to foster service at home. Ranger instructors also worried that the process disempowered patrols when it came to selecting Rangers and made it more difficult to weed out recruits who did not have the skills to contribute safely to Ranger activities.[120]

When Major Jeff Allen replaced Chang as commanding officer in 2010, he changed direction. He decoupled the DP1 course from expansion and clarified that Ranger training would not "create" Rangers: Rangers were expected to *come* with skills to contribute to their patrol. Recruits once again trained in their home communities, where patrol members could observe them and determine whether individuals possessed the skills expected of a Ranger in that patrol. A new Ranger would then attend a DP1 course for indoctrination into the military context and culture.[121] This process reaffirmed 1 CRPG's long-standing emphasis on the patrol as a largely self-governing body, one responsible for determining and managing its membership.[122]

According to Canadian Rangers and Ranger instructors, developing and applying common training standards helps everyone, as long as the instructors can deliver the program in ways that can be adapted to the socio-economic and cultural diversity of the Rangers they visit. Whereas training lessons in the past had been inconsistent, the new national-training plan has both substance and structure. Alongside common courses, delivered to every Canadian Ranger, Rangers take supplementary courses customized for their patrol's tasks, terrain, population, location, and culture. For example, Rangers in British Columbia and Alberta take advanced mountain operations courses, while Rangers in Newfoundland and Labrador take boating and maritime safety courses.[123] While some patrol groups offer twelve days of training to each Ranger in a two-week span, others send instructors to patrols more frequently and offer training over six separate weekends. "Everybody brings something to the table," Captain Darryl Bazin, the Alberta detachment commander, explained. "The strength of the Rangers is the fact that, at my level, I have the flexibility to plan, create and execute the training."[124]

One of the most acute pressures facing the Ranger organization is the need for more Regular and Reserve Force instructors. Historically, these soldiers – from Captain Ambrose Shea to Sergeant Mario Aubin to Warrant Officer Dan Hryhoryshen – forged and sustained relationships based on trust even as high-level support for the Rangers ebbed and flowed. They often did (and do) so at personal expense, enduring much of the year "on the road" or "on the land," adapting their training to distinct communities and cultures, all the while learning from the Rangers.[125] When the government promised expansion and enhanced training in 2007, the patrol groups were already overstretched by the high tempo of training and the small number of instructors available. Some patrol groups found it difficult to fill instructor positions given the competition for experienced combat arms sergeants while Canada was at war abroad. For all the heightened political interest in the Rangers, instructors remain a Priority 6 posting – the lowest

Warrant Officer Dan Hryhoryshen *(centre)*, an instructor with 4 CRPG, watches Ranger Cheri Berlingette of the Zeballos patrol fire her .303 Lee-Enfield in 2006.

Canadian Forces Combat Camera, Photo ET2006-0166-09

in the military.[126] More money now flows into the Ranger organization than ever before, but instructors – the critical link between the patrols and the military establishment – remain the scarcest commodity of all.

If the chief constraint on the Rangers' growth has been their budget, this ceased to be the case when Prime Minister Harper made his announcement in August 2007. To facilitate expansion, his government promised sustained annual funding of $29 million, an incremental investment of $12 million annually that would amount to more than $240 million over twenty years.[127] Once the money started flowing, it more than doubled the operating budget of some patrol groups.[128] "To date, the money issue has dominated," Major Ingram explained in July 2008. "It has been 'This is how much money you have. What can you do with it?' But now that is changing to 'What do you want to do, and how much money do you need?'"[129]

The Rangers reaped material benefits. Equipment usage rates for "use, wear and tear" on their personal equipment during formal activities increased, as did their allotment of Ranger kit.[130] Since the initial Ranger

Enhancement Project in 1995, patrols and individual Rangers have received a growing array of military-issued equipment. The Canadian Rangers Equipment Modernization Project allotted $45 million to ensure that the Rangers have "light equipment of the best quality to allow them to perform their tasks effectively."[131] The new equipment list (scale of issue) includes duffel bags, ballistic eyewear, backpacks, and multi-tools.[132] Despite this investment, communications remain a persistent issue, just as Quebec Command anticipated in 1947. The modernization program has allocated satellite phones to patrols and will also deliver a new radio.[133] More equipment (still unspecified) will be prepositioned in communities so that Rangers can respond more quickly to emergencies.[134]

The Ranger uniform is also changing. The red sweatshirt, however modest a form of military dress, is distinctive and unique to the Canadian Rangers. It is also compatible with the original principle that the Rangers be self-equipped and wear their own environmentally appropriate clothing when operating on the land. For decades, Rangers have requested additional army clothing so they can look more uniform while on parade. Individual patrol groups issued pieces of clothing on their own initiative, but senior military authorities usually resisted increasing the official scale of issue on logistical and financial grounds. After the handover ceremony of the Ranger national authority in October 2007, however, the chief of the land staff committed to a "Clothe the Ranger" project so that all Rangers would receive tangible evidence that the army valued them.[135] Only a few years before, patrol groups were refused CADPAT combat pants for their Rangers. Once they joined the army, the rules changed. The military has begun to supplement the Rangers' ball cap, sweatshirt, and t-shirt with a red fleece, an ICE jacket, a rain suit, wet-weather boots, socks, wind pants, and combat gloves.[136] The army still expects the Rangers to wear personal clothing appropriate for local conditions, but this new ensemble has clearly expanded the "Ranger red" brand.

Although the red sweatshirt has become an icon of Canadian sovereignty and patriotism in remote regions, the .303 bolt-action rifle remains the most enduring symbol of the Rangers. "For more than half a century, the mostly Inuit patrols have roamed around the rugged region on snowmobiles and on foot, toting antique wooden rifles in defence of Canadian sovereignty," one journalist noted.[137] The depiction of the rifle as an obsolete relic of a bygone era is less a metaphor for the Rangers themselves than a means for media commentators to criticize the military for not supporting

Prime Minister Stephen Harper presents Ranger sweatshirts and ball caps to Prince Charles, the Prince of Wales, and his wife, Camilla, the Duchess of Cornwall, to honour the prince's appointment as honorary head of the Canadian Rangers, 10 November 2009.
Photo by Sergeant Serge Gouin, Rideau Hall, Office of the Secretary to the Governor General, Photo GG2009-0530-01

the organization sufficiently. A few Rangers complained about the rifle,[138] but most appreciated its reliability. Military officials had discussed replacing the rifle for decades, but without a clear deficiency they had trouble identifying and justifying a replacement. General Walt Natynczyk, the chief of defence staff, explained the problem during a brief stop in Yukon in January 2011: "Over the past five years, this is an issue that's come in and gone out so many times, because we have folks, mostly from the South, who want to give the Rangers a newer, more modern weapon ... But the feedback we get from many Rangers, depending on who you talk to, they want a simple weapon. And the Lee Enfield .303 rifle that the Rangers have, although it's old, it's one of the most reliable, simple and accurate weapons, that's ever been designed." He recalled a conversation at Rideau Hall with Ranger Sergeant Allan Pogotak of Ulukhaktok (Holman), who told him that "you can take this weapon, it can be dropped in the ocean, you pick it up and shoot and it fires and fires true. And when anyone in my patrol breaks this weapon, I can go on the Internet and order the parts, and it's delivered in a week."[139]

Time, however, has caught up with the Ranger rifle. In 2007, the military estimated that, with the planned expansion to five thousand Rangers, its existing stock of Lee-Enfield rifles would only last up to twelve years. The worldwide pool of used .303 rifles has shrunk steadily, and there is a high risk that the Canadian Forces will not be able to procure suitable replacements when its stock runs out. Finding a replacement will not be easy. "There is a good probability that the New Ranger Rifle would resemble the current rifle in fit, form and function," Major Jim Mills, the staff officer responsible for Ranger training and equipment, noted. "Only a very robust model, with a bolt-action would have the guaranteed reliability and service life to meet the Rangers' expectations."[140] Delivery of the new rifle is expected to start in 2014.[141] Time will tell if the replacements have the same endurance, reliability, and mystique as the vaunted .303.

A Living History: Citizen-Soldiers Plus in a Time of Change

The endurance, reliability, and mystique of the .303 Lee-Enfield reflect the same traits found in the Rangers themselves. Much has changed since Johnny Tookalook was first handed his rifle as a teenager in Sanikiljuaq in the late 1940s. He used the rifle faithfully and stood out as one of the best marksmen at a regional shooting competition on Baffin Island more than a half century later. In the early years, he received little training or contact from authorities, but he helped train soldiers to operate in extreme weather. "The army from the South didn't know how to survive on the land," Tookalook recalled, his observation translated by an interpreter. "I would teach them how to hunt and trap." The spirit of comradeship, as well as the importance of sharing knowledge, was noted and respected within his northern community. "It's good to see all these young people out here learning," Tookalook stressed, drawing attention to his role as an elder working with less experienced Rangers. "It's important for elders to pass on their knowledge to the younger generation."[142]

Other elders shared his sentiments. When eighty-seven-year old Ranger Ollie Ittinuar, the oldest active member of the Canadian Forces, learned at a local council meeting in February 2008 that he would be receiving the

Michaëlle Jean, governor general and commander-in-chief of Canada, presents the Order of Military Merit to Ranger Ollie Ittinuar of Rankin Inlet during an investiture ceremony at Rideau Hall, 30 January 2009. Master Corporal Jean-François Néron, Rideau Hall, Office of the Secretary to the Governor General, Photo GG-2009-0036-059

Order of Military Merit from the governor general later that year, he hoped that the community would be as "uplifted by this news" as he was. Rather than touting his own accomplishments, he seized the occasion to express concerns about the state of the Ranger patrol in Rankin Inlet. Fewer young people seemed interested in joining the Rangers, Ittinuar lamented, and many of those who did failed to take the obligation seriously. "I would be the first to say sometimes being a Ranger can be quite difficult ... But I would urge more young people to join because it's a very big responsibility for us here."[143] He reiterated this message when he received the award a year later, hoping that it showed what hard work and dedication could accomplish. His son, Harry, who was also a Ranger, noted that people such as his father, people who showed great loyalty and cultural leadership, were instrumental in sharing survival skills. "It has helped me to be successful in my life today," Harry explained, "and I will do my best to teach these same skills to future generations."[144]

Both the military and remote communities benefit from Rangers such as Tookalook and Ittinuar who share knowledge across generations. Although the Canadian Rangers is not an Aboriginal program, its future depends upon sustaining the vitality of diverse cultures and lifestyles. In this respect, it is in the military's best interest to support a continuing partnership with members of remote communities to facilitate the exercise of traditional skills on the land and sea. Rather than seeking to assimilate Aboriginal people, it promotes cooperation, mutual respect, and crosscultural awareness. Since the Rangers' inception, the military has recruited individuals for the skills that they already possess.[145] Ensuring that youth have access to local knowledge and skills – whether through the Junior Canadian Rangers or other experiences – is vital to sustaining the Rangers more generally.

The Junior Rangers exemplify the Rangers' ability to bridge generations to promote vibrant, healthy communities. An influx of money into the youth program in 2008 funded more expansion to ensure "that the culture, traditions and customs of our Arctic communities are preserved and will continue for future generations."[146] Although the Junior Rangers have never been subjected to a formal review, there are countless testimonials to the program's value.[147] The simplest examples are sometimes the most telling. In November 2010, ten Junior Rangers from 1 CRPG went to Ottawa to participate in Remembrance Day activities. They met with war veterans, personally connecting to Canada's long history of military service. They also attracted attention in their own right. Everywhere they went, Captain Sharon Low observed, current and former members of the Canadian Forces recognized their green Junior Ranger hoodies and the red sweatshirts of their Canadian Ranger escorts. "On Remembrance Day, as we marched past the veterans to honour them for their service and remember the sacrifice of their

Rangers David Nasogaluak and Kurtis Wolki of the Tukoyaktuk patrol cutting snow
blocks for an igloo alongside Husky Lakes, Northwest Territories, 19 January 2009.
Photo by P. Whitney Lackenbauer

comrades, there were shouts of, 'Here comes the Rangers,'" she observed.
"We all marched a little prouder, with heads held a little higher."[148]

Like pride and patriotism, self-esteem and confidence are difficult to
measure. They are also essential for remote communities navigating the
complex challenges of the twenty-first century. Responding and adapting
requires leadership by people who possess knowledge of local lands and
traditions, who have a strong commitment to community service, and who
can communicate effectively.[149] Community spokespersons so frequently
associate these traits with the Rangers that there is rarely a major northern
media event related to sovereignty, security, or safety issues without men
and women present in their red sweatshirts. "The Canadian Rangers embody
some of the best qualities of the North including self-sufficiency, on-the-
land knowledge, practical problem solving skills and a willingness to help
others," journalist Roxanna Thompson told readers of the *Deh Cho Drum*
in late 2007. "People join Canadian Ranger patrols for a number of reasons.
They might be looking for something fun to do to get them closer to the
land or they might see Rangers as one of the few activities available in their

communities. People also join so they can use their daily lifestyle to be part of something bigger. No matter what reason draws a person to the Rangers, their contributions are an important part of keeping our country strong and free."[150]

"If Canada's Arctic sovereignty has a brand, it's the red Rangers hoodie," journalist Tim Querengesser noted in *Up Here* magazine in 2010.[151] The military does not take this symbol lightly. Historically, commentators often associate military practices (and those of the state more generally) with physical dislocation, environmental degradation, political disruption, and culture shock.[152] In the case of the Canadian Rangers, however, the interconnectedness between the military, remote communities, and Canadian society is respected as a constructive force. "We're here to make sure Canada's North stays safe and sovereign," Ranger David Nivingalok explained. "Rangers patrol some of the most important hunting ground of the Inuit people."[153]

This comment encapsulates how Ranger service straddles community, nation, and country. During a decade of travel with Rangers across the country, I have been struck by the strong current of patriotism and loyalty that underpins their sense of service. One of the original benefits that defence planners emphasized when they conceived the Rangers was having "friends on the ground" when conducting operations in remote regions. This remains as true today as it was during and immediately after the Second World War. In Inukjuak, Ranger Eli Weetaluktuk told me that the Rangers bring "respect and integrity" to the military in Nunavik.[154] This is true from coast to coast to coast.

Although the Rangers hardly fit the typical army mould, these *citizen-soldiers plus* represent an important link between the military and its host society. "These people are everyday, normal citizens – teachers, bankers, fishermen, and loggers," 5 CRPG spokesperson Lieutenant George "Junior" Roberts explained. "Membership in a Canadian Ranger patrol is not military (personnel) – it's ordinary people in the community who can readily come together to help the area they're in."[155] In 2002, Major Ian Hay offered a nearly identical depiction of 4 CRPG. He characterized the Rangers as "ordinary people who are proud citizens ... jumping at the chance to serve the country they love so much." These men and women served as models of good citizenship, producing "a win-win situation for both the Canadian Forces and the communities in which they reside."[156] Major Guy Lang, the former commanding officer of 2 CRPG, described the Rangers as "a truly beautiful organization, the dream of any commander: 750 soldiers deployed in 25 municipalities and communities, a mixture of Cree, Inuit, Montagnais and Naskapi, of Whites, anglophones and francophones, a 'cauldron' of cultures from which we can learn a great deal."[157]

If Canada's essence lies in its plurality – the multitude of overlapping or multilayered identities that exist and thrive in a country that embraces diversity – the same holds true for the Rangers. The Rangers integrate the military into a broader (and more intimate) network of societal relations that produces a sense of social cohesion and connectedness in remote regions. The Rangers have evolved into an organization with the core attributes of the "linear communities" described by historian William Morrison: regular contact, shared values and ethos, familiarity, and interdependence, even across great distances and difficult terrain.[158]

Rangers in the eastern Arctic unilaterally added the word *voice* to their organization's official motto: they consider themselves the eyes, ears, and voice of the Canadian Forces in their communities and in the North more generally.[159] This grassroots addition reinforces the importance of meaningful communication at all levels. The Rangers represent an ongoing dialogue – about what is happening in remote regions, about how the military can best operate in the North, and about the importance of connecting considerations of sovereignty and national security to an intimate sense of place. Skeptics may dismiss the Rangers as another form of subordination, as token accommodation by the military to co-opt Aboriginal people into accepting state sovereignty, militarism, and liberal state hegemony,[160] but this view denies the Rangers' own sense of empowerment. Rangers recognize that they have power – the military depends upon them. During annual patrol training in 2007, Sergeant Simeonie Nalukturuk, the patrol commander in Inukjuak, described the Rangers as "the eyeglasses, hearing aids, and walking stick for the CF in the North."[161] His allusion to the Canadian Forces' inability to operate unassisted in Inuit Nunangat – the Canadian Inuit homeland – is unmistakable.

In the twenty-first century, questions about how to sustain the integrity of northern and coastal societies and ecosystems in the face of climate change and geostrategic uncertainty raise important ethical issues. "Climate change is the defining issue of our time that will ultimately impact on us all," insisted Sheila Watt-Cloutier, a leading voice in discussions about global warming, in 2007. "The Inuit are giving the world the gift of an early warning."[162] Political scientist Franklyn Griffiths took this idea one

Ranger Sergeant Simeonie Nalukturuk on Hudson Bay north of Inukjuak.
Photo by P. Whitney Lackenbauer

step further, emphasizing that the Inuit have come to constitute a new Distant Early Warning Line.[163] Those who are in the Rangers, an organization that predates the actual DEW Line, are our northern and coastal sentinels.

The Rangers' long tradition of monitoring, surveillance, and sharing of expertise also supports the health and vitality of remote communities. Concerns about skill fade are nothing new. Major Stirling noted it in his 1970 report recommending the disbanding of the Rangers. Ironically, the generation of people who Stirling believed were fated to "take their place in modern society and not on the Arctic ice or the trap line" are now elders worried about passing along their knowledge to younger people. Will industrialization and social pressures remove people from the land and subvert their special attachment with it? Will climate change irrevocably alter homelands and patterns of life? Will commercial vessel traffic through the Northwest Passage demand technological solutions that will push the Rangers back into the shadows? Considering historical trends, will heightened support for the Rangers withstand future cycles of interest and disinterest? Will the past repeat itself?

Rangers are raising these questions. I was embedded with an Arctic Response Company Group on Bylot Island during Operation Nanook in August 2010. After we established camp, Ranger Pauloosie (Paul) Atagootak from Resolute invited me for a walk. As we walked over the tundra and down lush valleys, I asked him questions about the land, and he told me stories and shared his thoughts on living in the North.[164]

After walking for about half an hour, Paul sat down on one of the downward slopes, just above a small stream, and lit a cigarette. When he finished smoking, he laid back. After a couple of minutes of silence, he said the simple words: "I'm home." It was at that moment, perhaps more than at any other time during my extensive travels with the Rangers, that I felt it: the connection to the land, his homeland, his identity. He had spent much of his childhood in camps along this stretch of coastline. This land was as familiar to him as it was exotic and remote to me.

As we sat on the soft ground, we talked about community life. He worried about the younger generation who spent all their time plugged into iPods and playing video games. Even some of the younger Rangers spent little time on the land, he observed, and did not have well-honed survival skills to pass along to soldiers from the south. Everyone from the outside assumed that they had an innate ability to live on the land just because they were Inuit. This, he argued, was a fallacy. Many had not learned a lot of land skills from their elders and were more preoccupied with trying to imitate the southern way of life than seeking guidance from experienced members of their communities. Children were the future, Paul, a father and a grandfather, reminded me, and Inuit were changing. The expression on his face, which always carried a smile, was more serious than I had seen before.

Paul pointed out that the clouds told of the weather coming in. How many children in Nunavut still looked to the skies each night, as his grandfather had taught him to do? Would climate change alter weather patterns so much that it would render such traditional knowledge moot? If resource development did spark a modern-day gold rush in Nunavut, how would the next generation of Nunavummiut fare? I dared not speculate. Nevertheless, Paul provided a reassuring message. Inuit had faced challenges in the past, and they had proven resilient. He advocated patience. He embodied it as he sat on the tundra, relaxed, quietly puffing on his cigarette. Confident. Soulful. Wise.

"I am home."

Ranger Pauloosie Attagootak of the Resolute patrol on Bylot Island, Nunavut, August 2010. Photo by P. Whitney Lackenbauer

Paul's words echoed those of Rangers whom I had met from coast to coast to coast. If there is a common thread that I have taken away from this diverse group of men and women, it is the intimate attachment of people to the environments in which they live. I saw it first-hand in smiling eyes as Rangers with the Gold River patrol on Nootka Island swapped stories during a seaside boil-up of shellfish, the Pacific washing up on the beach. I heard it murmured along the trail from Ross River to the frozen shores of Quiet Lake in southern Yukon and in youth cheering on their fellow Junior Rangers as they played sports at Camp Loon in northern Ontario. I learned of tenacity and challenges over the endless drone of snowmobile engines when we paused for short breaks on frozen lakes in northern Manitoba.

The strong voice of the elders was unmistakable on the shores of Hudson Bay at Witch Bay, where they explained the responsibilities of stewardship to younger Rangers in the Inukjuak patrol. The spirit of camaraderie in the face of adversity was readily apparent over pepperoni sticks warmed by snowmobile exhausts on the frozen Labrador Sea north of Hopedale and in jovial exchanges over fried moose meat in a canvas tent with the Cape Freels patrol in Newfoundland. However central nature and geography are to the Canadian imagination and identities, they assume a new poignancy when you move beyond the southern population belt and into remote regions where Rangers serve as Canada's eyes, ears, and voices.

Mutual dependency – one of the core characteristics of community – is not a thing of the past. It is alive in the present. So too is the Ranger concept. The Canadian Rangers are not an anachronism; nor are they broken and in need of retooling. Sometimes, in unexpected places, and in unexpected ways, the most successful of relationships take shape – at their own pace and in unique forms that both reflect and shape the world in which we live.

A Note on Sources

❧ UNCOVERING THE LONG HISTORY of the Canadian Rangers has been a wonderful adventure that required a mixed methodology. On the one hand, I was drawn into the archives and into the media record to uncover the development and logic of the organization. I have also had many opportunities to "ground truth" stories and ideas from the documentary record with Canadian Rangers, Ranger instructors, staff officers, and commanding officers from coast to coast to coast over the last decade.

The basic archival record on the Pacific Coast Militia Rangers and the Canadian Rangers through to the mid-1960s can be accessed through Library and Archives Canada (Record Group 24) and the Directorate of History and Heritage, Department of National Defence, in Ottawa. The documentary record since 1970 is more difficult to access. Some material on the Rangers under Maritime Command was acquired through formal access to information (ATIP) requests from Library and Archives Canada and the Department of National Defence. There is no similar collection of material on Rangers in the Territorial North. Without the support of Major Conrad Schubert, formerly of 1 Canadian Ranger Patrol Group, who shared a smattering of historical records in a dusty file cabinet, tracing policy developments through the 1970s would have been impossible. The Canadian Rangers National Authority also facilitated access to material on the 1990s, which was indispensable to filling out the recent history, and supplemented key documentation that I had acquired through formal ATIP requests. The

Department of National Defence published annual reports from 1949-1990 that often contained basic updates on the status of the Rangers. Researchers can best access House of Commons debates through their detailed indexes. Parliamentary material since January 1994, including committee proceedings and reports, is available online at http://www.parl.gc.ca/.

Newspapers and magazines also offer important anecdotes and frames to understand expectations and perceptions both of and from Rangers. Newspaper indexes at the BC Archives in Victoria helped me reconstruct the history of the Pacific Coast Militia Rangers and early postwar period in BC. The Centre for Newfoundland Studies at Memorial University of Newfoundland also has valuable clippings files with an extensive range of regional newspaper coverage since the 1990s. For the period since 1987, I consulted a wide range of databases, including the Canadian Periodical Index (CPI.Q), Factiva, Eureka.cc, and Lexis Nexis. I compiled my favourite articles in *Canada's Rangers: Selected Stories, 1942-2012,* a commemorate volume published in 2013.

For several reasons, I drew many of my insights into the Canadian Rangers and their relationships with the military from reports generated by or interviews conducted with Ranger liaison officers, Ranger instructors, and staff officers. First, the liaison officers and instructors were uniquely placed to document and archive Rangers' experiences in communities, on exercises, and on operations. These astute observers helped to discern local patterns and broader regional trends. They also identified what worked with the organization and which aspects needed improvement. Few Rangers, by virtue of language, livelihoods, and orientation towards practical action, are predisposed to record their experiences in writing. Instructors' first-hand observations and analyses therefore offer invaluable and accessible insight into relationships over time.

Oral histories and ongoing conversations with Rangers played an important role in this history. My direct participation in Ranger training exercises and operations (what anthropologists call participant observation) over the last decade, as well as shorter visits to various patrols, has yielded an intimate sense of "lived realities." I found it difficult to incorporate all of this fieldwork into this book, however, because most of the Rangers' stories need to be situated in specific contexts to do justice to their insights. Furthermore, many of my most memorable conversations and experiences with the Rangers fell beyond the scope of this particular book. Accordingly, I have decided to narrate what I learned through participant observation in a separate study. My conversations with Rangers nonetheless enriched this history in profound ways – even when they do not appear in the endnotes.

Specific information on the current state of the Canadian Rangers is available on their official website (http://www.army.dnd.ca/land-terre/cr-rc/index-eng.asp). An interactive map of patrol locations contains basic information about individual units (http://www.army.dnd.ca/land-terre/maps-cartes/crpg-gprc-eng.asp). Various patrol groups also maintain websites with newsletters, training schedules, and photographs:

1 CRPG: http://www.army.forces.gc.ca/1crpg/.
3 CRPG: http://www.army.forces.gc.ca/3crpg/.
4 CRPG: http://www.army.forces.gc.ca/4crpg/.
5 CRPG: http://www.army.forces.gc.ca/5cdn_rangers/.

2 CRPG plans to create a website but it is not yet online. It does produce a regular newsletter, *Bulletin Info Rangers*.

Notes

Abbreviations

ADC	Aircraft Detection Corps
ARHQ	Atlantic Region Headquarters
ATIP	Access to Information Policy
BGS	Brigadier General Staff
CAO	Canadian Army Order
CDA	Canadian Defence Academy
CDS	Chief of the Defence Staff
CFHQ	Canadian Forces Headquarters
CFNA	Canadian Forces Northern Area
CFNR	Canadian Forces Northern Region
CGS	Chief of the General Staff
COPFD	Chief Operational Planning and Force Development
COS	Chief of Staff
CRNA	Canadian Ranger National Authority
CRPG	Canadian Ranger Patrol Group
CRS	Chief of Review Services
DCDS	Deputy Chief of the Defence Staff
DCGS	Deputy Chief of the General Staff
DEXAF	Department of External Affairs
DGMPO	Director General Military Plans and Operations
DGOL	Director General Operations Land
DGRC	Director General Reserves and Cadets
DHH	Directorate of History and Heritage
DM	Deputy Minister
DMOP	Director of Military Operations and Plans
DMT	Director of Military Training
DND	Department of National Defence

DOC	District Officer Commanding
DORL	Director Operational Readiness Land
D RES	Director of Reserves
DSD	Directorate of Staff Duties
GOC	General Officer Commanding
GSO	General Staff Officer
HQ	Headquarters
JTFN	Joint Task Force (North)
LAC	Library and Archives Canada
LFCA	Land Force Central Area
LFQA	Land Force Quebec Area
LFWA	Land Force Western Area
MD	Military District
MND	Minister of National Defence
NARA	National Archives and Records Administration
NDHQ	National Defence Headquarters
NNSL	Northern News Services Ltd.
NRHQ	Northern Region Headquarters
PCMR	Pacific Coast Militia Rangers
PJBD	Permanent Joint Board on Defence
PPCLI	Princess Patricia's Canadian Light Infantry
PWNHC	Prince of Wales Northern Heritage Centre
SCND	House of Commons Standing Committee on National Defence
SO	Staff Officer
SORO	Staff Officer Regional Operations
SQFT	Secteur Québec de la Force terrestre (Land Force Quebec Area)
VCDS	Vice Chief of the Defence Staff
VCGS	Vice Chief of the General Staff
WG	Working Group

Introduction

1 For overviews of the operation, see Julian Tomlinson, "The Canadian Rangers and the North Magnetic Pole Sovereignty Operation: An Exhibition and Archiving Project" (NORS 698 project, University of Alaska's Department of Northern Studies Graduate Degree Program, July 2003), and Ian Hannah, "Operation Kigiliqaqvik Ranger," CBC News Sunday, 6 October 2002, http://www.cbc.ca/sunday/northpole/diary.html (last accessed 2 December 2002).

2 Sgt. Peter Moon, "Canadian Ranger Patrol Reaches the Magnetic Pole," *Maple Leaf* 5, 21 (2002): 6.

3 Guyot made a similar comment to a reporter soon afterwards. See Derek Neary, "Almost There," Northern News Services, 3 May 2002.

4 Margaret Atwood, *Survival* (Toronto: Anansi, 1972).

5 "Rangers Mark 60th Year with Polar Trek," *Montreal Gazette,* 9 April 2002.

6 Stephanie Waddell, "Polar Expedition Called a Boost to Sovereignty," *Whitehorse Star,* 26 April 2002.

7 "Canadian Rangers' Sovereignty Patrol Praised," *Klondike Sun,* 26 April 2002.

8 "Rangers Mark 60th Year with Polar Trek."

9 Editorial, "Vital Service," Northern News Services, 18 October 1999.

10 Eileen Travers, "Avalanche Kills 9 in Remote Inuit Town," *Ottawa Citizen,* 2 January 1999; Stewart Bell, "5 Young Children among 9 Killed by Avalanche," *National Post,* 2 January

1999; Ranger Sammy Unatweenuk's comments, "Canadian Rangers Honoured," Saturday Report, CBC television, Toronto, 20 November 1999, host Ben Chin.

11 Sgt. Vallee Saunders, as told to Buzz Bourdon, "The Experience Was Very Hard to Go Through," *Ottawa Citizen,* 15 February 2000.

12 Campbell Clark, "Grief Washes over a Northern Town," *National Post,* 4 January 1999; "Saying Goodbye to the Victims of a Northern Tragedy," *CTV National News,* CTV television (Scarborough), 6 January 1999, host Lloyd Robertson; Nelson Wyatt, "Funeral Delays Weigh on Town," *Calgary Herald,* 6 January 1999.

13 Department of National Defence (DND) Backgrounder, BG-00.005, "The Canadian Rangers," 8 February 2000.

14 See, for example, Franklyn Griffiths, Rob Huebert, and P. Whitney Lackenbauer, *Canada and the Changing Arctic: Sovereignty, Security, and Stewardship* (Waterloo, ON: Wilfrid Laurier University Press, 2011).

15 See Kenneth C. Eyre, "Forty Years of Defence Activity in the Canadian North, 1947-87," *Arctic* 40, 4 (1987): 292-99.

16 If most northern history is still written as a "romantic nationalist fairy tale," this story is not. See Kenneth Coates and William R. Morrison, "The New North in Canadian History and Historiography," *History Compass* 6, 2 (2008): 640.

17 Bill Waiser, "A Very Long Journey: Distance and Northern Canadian History," in *Northern Visions: New Perspectives on the North in Canadian History,* ed. Kerry M. Abel and Ken S. Coates (Peterborough, ON: Broadview, 2001), 38-39.

18 On this theme, see Richard White, *The Middle Ground: Indians, Empires, and Republics in the Great Lakes Region, 1650-1815* (Cambridge: Cambridge University Press, 1991).

19 Interview with Col. Pierre Leblanc, Yellowknife, NT, 20 March 2000. The Reserve Force is the component of the Canadian Forces "that consists of officers who are enrolled for other than continuing, full-time military service when not on active service." See *National Defence Act,* Section 15(3). Nevertheless, some primary reservists, including many Canadian Ranger Patrol Group staff and instructors, serve on a full-time basis.

20 Lt.-Col. W.H. Porter to Director General Reserves and Cadets (DGRC), "Canadian Rangers – CF Policy and Objectives," 28 May 1990, DND, f. 1901-260/4.

21 Chief of Review Services (CRS), "Review of the Canadian Rangers [Draft]," September 2003, amended 12 November 2003 (hereafter CRS Review); Canadian Ranger National Authority (CRNA), f. CRS and CRNA Report.

22 Bernd Horn, *Bastard Sons: An Examination of Canada's Airborne Experience, 1942-1995* (St. Catharines, ON: Vanwell, 2001), 16, 99.

23 See Andrew Burtch, *Give Me Shelter: The Failure of Canada's Cold War Civil Service* (Vancouver: UBC Press, 2012).

24 Commentators often misapply the legal concept of effective occupation (the right of a state to claim a territory not subject to the sovereignty of another state) to uninhabited islands of the Canadian Arctic Archipelago. See, for example, John Gellner, "The Military Task," in *The Arctic in Question,* ed. Edgar Dosman (Toronto: Oxford University Press, 1976), 95, and P. Whitney Lackenbauer and Peter Kikkert, eds., *The Canadian Forces and Arctic Sovereignty* (Waterloo, ON: Wilfrid Laurier University Press, 2010).

25 Barry Buzan, Ole Waever, and Jaap de Wilde, *Security* (London: Lynne Reinner, 1998).

26 Nils Ørvik, *Northern Development: Northern Security,* Centre for International Relations No. 1/83 (Kingston, ON: Queen's University, 1983), 18-19.

27 Rob Huebert, "Canadian Arctic Security Issues: Transformation in the Post-Cold War Era," *International Journal* 54, 2 (1999): 203-29.

28 Andrew F. Cooper, *Canadian Foreign Policy* (Scarborough: Prentice-Hall, 1997). See, for example, Canada, Parliament, House of Commons Standing Committee on Foreign Affairs and International Trade, *Canada and the Circumpolar World* (Ottawa: Publications Service, 1997), 100. This document reflects the recommendation made by parliamentarians from

Arctic states to "broaden Arctic security issues from a predominantly military focus to the development of collective environmental security that includes the values, life styles, and cultural identity of indigenous northern societies."

29 The Coasts Under Stress project – which looked at the impacts of socio-environmental restructuring on the health of coastal people, their communities, and the environment – defined community health as "the condition of a socio-economic-environmental system where the economic, social, and political components are organized and maintained in such a way as to promote well-being of both the human and the natural environment." This framework "suggests that healthy communities – those with high levels of trust, social engagement, equitable economic prosperity, for example – are more likely to nurture healthy people." Rosemary Ommer and Coasts Under Stress, *Coasts Under Stress: Understanding Restructuring and Social-Ecological Health* (Montreal/Kingston: McGill-Queen's University Press, 2007), 20.

30 CRS Review.

31 See, for example, the Speech from the Throne, 16 October 2007, http://www.parl.gc.ca/parlinfo/documents/thronespeech/39-2-e.html; Stephen Harper, House of Commons, *Debates (Hansard), 17* October 2007, 39; Maxime Bernier, *Hansard,* 18 October 2007, 106; and Peter MacKay, *Hansard,* 27 May 2010, 3039.

32 Kenneth Coates, "The Discovery of the North," *Northern Review* 12, 13 (1993-94): 18.

33 William Wonders, Introduction to *Canada's Changing North,* ed. William Wonders, rev. ed. (Montreal/Kingston: McGill-Queen's University Press, 2003), xii-xiii.

34 Louis-Edmond Hamelin, "An Attempt to Regionalize the Canadian North," *North* 11, 4 (1964): 16-19, and *Canadian Nordicity: It's Your North Too,* trans. W. Barr (Montreal: Harvest House, 1979).

35 On the territories as colonies, see Kenneth Coates, *Canada's Colonies: A History of the Yukon and Northwest Territories* (Toronto: Lorimer, 1985); Kenneth Coates and Judith Powell, *The Modern North* (Toronto: Lorimer, 1989); Kenneth Coates and William R. Morrison, *Land of the Midnight Sun: A History of the Yukon* (Montreal/Kingston: McGill-Queen's University Press, 2005), and William R. Morrison, *True North: The Yukon and Northwest Territories* (Oxford: Oxford University Press, 1998). On the forgotten norths, see Kenneth Coates and William R. Morrison, *The Forgotten North* (Toronto: Lorimer, 1992), and their edited work *The Historiography of the Provincial Norths* (Thunder Bay, ON: Centre for Northern Studies, Lakehead University, 1996). Morris Zaslow's pioneering study *The Northward Expansion of Canada, 1914-1967* (Toronto: McClelland and Stewart, 1988) remains indispensable.

36 Ommer and Coasts Under Stress, *Coasts Under Stress,* 23.

37 See Gabriel Dionne, *In a Breaking Wave: Living History of the Lower North Shore,* trans. H. Miller and T. Marion, rev. by W.E. O'Meara (Montreal: Les Missionaires Oblats de Marie Immaculée, 1988); Louise Abbott, *The Coast Way: A Portrait of the English on the Lower North Shore of the St. Lawrence* (Montreal/Kingston: McGill-Queen's University Press, 1988); Cleophas Belvin, *Forgotten Labrador: Kegashka to Blanc-Sablon* (Montreal/Kingston: McGill-Queen's University Press, 2006); Kevin Major, *As Near to Heaven by Sea: A History of Newfoundland and Labrador* (Toronto: Penguin, 2001); John Charles Kennedy, *People of the Bays and Headlands: Anthropological History and the Fate of Communities in the Unknown Labrador* (Toronto: University of Toronto Press, 1995); Bill Rompkey, *The Story of Labrador* (Montreal/Kingston: McGill-Queen's University Press, 2003); Margaret Ormsby, *British Columbia* (Toronto: Macmillan, 1976); Jean Barman, *The West beyond the West* (Toronto: University of Toronto Press, 1991); Brett McGillivray, *Geography of British Columbia* (Vancouver: UBC Press, 2000); and Hugh Brody, *Maps and Dreams* (Vancouver: Douglas and McIntyre, 1981).

38 Major D.I. Hay, "The Canadian Rangers," 8 February 1991, DND, f. MARP 1901-2 (RG RS).

39 For an introduction to the historiography, see P. Whitney Lackenbauer and Scott Sheffield, "Moving beyond 'Forgotten': The Historiography on Canadian Native Peoples and the World Wars," in *Aboriginal Peoples and Military Participation*, ed. P. Whitney Lackenbauer and Craig Mantle (Kingston, ON: CDA Press, 2007), 209-31.

40 Deborah Cowen, *Military Workfare: The Soldier and Social Citizenship in Canada* (Toronto: University of Toronto Press, 2008), 160-61. Cowen incorrectly identifies the Rangers as an "Aboriginal program" on p. 169.

41 US Joint Chiefs of Staff, *Department of Defense Dictionary of Military and Associated Terms* (Washington, DC: Department of Defense, 2005), 211.

42 On the distinction between schemes of acculturation, differentiation, accommodation, and acceptance in armed forces, see Brian Selmeski, "Aboriginal Soldiers: A Conceptual Framework," Centre for Security, Armed Forces and Society Occasional Paper Series No. 3, Royal Military College, Kingston, Ontario, 23 October 2007.

43 Coates and Morrison, "The New North," 643-44.

44 Ommer and Coasts Under Stress, *Coasts Under Stress*, 445, 447.

45 Coates, "Discovery of the North," 41.

46 Social power is the capacity to get someone to produce desired outcomes wilfully by working on the other's perceptions, dispositions, interests, and will (i.e., changing their incentive structure). By contrast, physical power seeks to achieve a desired effect without respect for the other's self. See R.J. Rummel, *Understanding Conflict and War*, vol. 2, *The Conflict Helix* (Beverly Hills: Sage, 1976), and Keith Dowding, *Power (Concepts in Social Thought)* (Minneapolis: University of Minnesota Press, 1996).

47 On the central role of the military in the modern bureaucratic state, see Max Weber's classic work *Theory of Social and Economic Organization*, trans. A.M. Henderson and Talcott Parsons (1922; repr., New York: Free Press, 1947).

48 CRS Review. On the dangers of commanders doing "whatever one likes," see Horn, *Bastard Sons*, 124-25.

49 A formal comparative study is beyond the scope of this book. On other military units around the world, see Desmond Ball, ed., *Aborigines in the Defence of Australia* (Sydney: Australian National University Press, 1991); Charles Hendricks, "The Eskimos and the Defense of Alaska," *Pacific Historical Review* 54, 3 (1985): 271-95; and Palle Norrit, "The Sirius Sledge Patrol," http://www.eastgreenland.com/database.asp?lang=eng&num=415.

50 Hedda Schuurman contrasts *community* with terms such as *town, village, or settlement*, which refer to geographic locations fixed in time. Community, in contrast, "embraces the intangible forces that unite people in a shared world of culture and experience"– a social meaning with regard to place. See "The Concept of Community and the Challenge for Self-Government," in *Aboriginal Autonomy and Development in Northern Quebec and Labrador*, ed. Colin H. Scott (Vancouver: UBC Press, 2001), 379. See also George Wenzel, "Clyde Inuit Settlement and Community," *Arctic Anthropology* 45, 1 (2008): 1-21.

51 Giuseppe Caforio, Introduction to *Handbook of the Sociology of the Military*, ed. Giuseppe Caforio (New York: Springer, 2006), 4.

52 Samuel Huntington, *The Soldier and the State* (Cambridge: Harvard University Press, 1957), viii, 80.

53 Morris Janowitz, *The Professional Soldier* (New York: Free Press, 1960).

54 See Charles Moskos's many studies, including *The American Enlisted Man* (New York: Sage, 1970); "The Emergent Military, Civil, Traditional or Plural?" *Pacific Sociological Revue* 16 (1973): 255-80; "The American Dilemma in Uniform: Race in the Armed Forces," *Annals* 406 (1973): 94-106; and "From Institution to Occupation: Trends in Military Organizations," *Armed Forces and Society* 4, 4 (1977): 41-50.

55 Rebecca L. Schiff, *The Military and Domestic Politics* (London: Routledge, 2009).

56 For a definition of professional soldiers, see D.L. Sills, ed., *International Encyclopedia of Social Science*, vol. 10 (New York: Macmillan, 1972), 305.

57 In Canada, see Desmond Morton, *Ministers and Generals: Politics and the Canadian Militia* (Toronto: University of Toronto Press, 1970); Stephen Harris, *Canadian Brass: The Making of a Professional Army, 1860-1939* (Toronto: University of Toronto Press, 1988); and Douglas Bland, *Chiefs of Defence* (Toronto: Canadian Institute for Strategic Studies, 1995).

58 James Wood, *Militia Myths: Ideas of the Canadian Citizen Soldier, 1896-1921* (Vancouver: UBC Press, 2010), 11.

59 Standing Committee on National Defence (SCND), *Proceedings*, 3 December 1987, 19:51-60. See also Terry C. Willett, *A Heritage at Risk: The Canadian Militia as a Social Institution* (Boulder, CO: Westview Press, 1987). Although Willett mentions the Rangers in passing, he provides no interpretation of their unique place in the Canadian military.

60 Special Commission on the Restructuring of the Reserves, *Report* (Ottawa: DND, 1995), 21.

61 Alan Cairns, "Afterword: International Dimensions of the Citizen Issue for Indigenous Peoples/Nations," *Citizenship Studies* 7, 4 (2003): 501.

62 On citizenship in Canada, see, for example, Jean Laponce and William Safran, *Ethnicity and Citizenship: The Canadian Case* (London: Routledge, 1996); William Kaplin, ed., *Belonging: The Meaning and Future of Canadian Citizenship* (Montreal/Kingston: McGill-Queen's University Press, 1993); Will Kymlicka, *Finding Our Way: Rethinking Ethnocultural Relations in Canada* (Toronto: Oxford University Press, 1998); and Alan C. Cairns, ed., *Citizenship, Diversity and Pluralism* (Montreal/Kingston: McGill-Queen's University Press, 1999). For international discussions about what this has meant for the military as an expression of national citizenship, see Morris Janowitz, *The Reconstruction of Patriotism: Education for Civic Consciousness* (Chicago: University of Chicago Press, 1983); David R. Segal, *Recruiting for Uncle Sam* (Lawrence: Kansas University Press, 1989); and Matthew J. Morgan, "The Reconstruction of Culture, Citizenship, and Military Service," *Armed Forces and Society* 29, 3 (2003): 373-91.

63 Bradford Booth, Meyer Kestnbaum, and David R. Segal, "Are Post-Cold War Militaries Postmodern?" *Armed Forces and Society* 27, 3 (2001): 330-31.

64 Charles C. Moskos, John Allen Williams, and David R. Segal "Armed Forces after the Cold War," in *The Postmodern Military*, ed. Charles C. Moskos, John Allen Williams, and David R. Segal (New York: Oxford University Press, 2000), 5.

65 Ibid., 6, 9.

66 Cowen, *Military Workfare*, 108.

67 Charles C. Moskos and James Burk, "The Postmodern Military," in *The Adaptive Military*, ed. James Burk (New Brunswick, NJ: Transaction Publishers, 1998), 179-80.

68 See, for example, Franklin Pinch, Allister MacIntyre, Phyllis Browne, and Alan Okros, *Challenge and Change in the Military: Gender and Diversity Issues* (Kingston, ON: Canadian Defence Academy Press, 2004).

69 Cowen, *Military Workfare*, 259

70 *Defence Strategy 2020*, quoted in DGRC, "CAN RAN 2000: A Review of the Canadian Rangers and of the Junior Canadian Rangers," 27 January 2000.

71 Bernard Boëne, "The Military as a Tribe among Tribes," in *Handbook of the Sociology of the Military*, ed. Giuseppe Caforio, 179.

72 Ramsay Cook, "Identities Are Not Like Hats," *Canadian Historical Review* 81, 2 (2000): 260-65.

73 This has been the motto of the European Union since 2000, but it has been applied to Canada for decades. See, for example, Adélard Godbout, "Canada: Unity in Diversity," *Foreign Affairs* 21, 3 (1943): 452-61, and Paul Cornell, Jean Hamelin, Fernand Ouellet, and Marcel Trudel, *Canada: Unity in Diversity* (Toronto: Holt Rinehart and Winston, 1967).

74 Jens Bartelson, *A Genealogy of Sovereignty* (Cambridge: Cambridge University Press, 1995), 30, 247.

75 Mary Simon, testimony before the Special Joint Committee of the Senate and the House of Commons on Reviewing Canadian Foreign Policy, *Minutes of Proceedings and Evidence,* 9 June 1994, 36:30.

76 Paul Nadasdy, *Hunters and Bureaucrats: Power, Knowledge, and Aboriginal-State Relations in the Southwest Yukon* (Vancouver: UBC Press, 2004), 9.

77 This model is introduced in Chapter 9.

78 Colin H. Scott, "On Autonomy and Development," in Scott, *Aboriginal Autonomy and Development,* 8.

79 Taiaiake Alfred and Lana Lowe, "Warrior Societies in Contemporary Indigenous Communities," report prepared for the Ipperwash Inquiry, May 2005, 13, 36, http://www. attorneygeneral.jus.gov.on.ca/inquiries/ipperwash/policy_part/research/pdf/Alfred_and _Lowe.pdf. See also Taiaiake Alfred, *Peace, Power, Righteousness* (Toronto: Oxford University Press, 1999).

80 Taiaiake Alfred and Jeff Corntassel, "Being Indigenous," *Government and Opposition* 40, 4 (2005): 597-614. For an elaboration, see Taiaiake Alfred, *Wasáse: Indigenous Pathways of Action and Freedom* (Peterborough, ON: Broadview Press, 2005).

81 Harry Hawthorn and Marc Adelard-Tremblay, *Survey of the Contemporary Indians of Canada,* vols. 1-2 (Ottawa: Department of Indian Affairs and Northern Development, Indian Affairs Branch, 1966-67). For recent proponents, see Alan Cairns, *Citizens Plus: Aboriginal Peoples and the Canadian State* (Vancouver: UBC Press, 2000), and J.R. Miller, *Lethal Legacy: Current Native Controversies in Canada* (Toronto: McClelland and Stewart, 2004).

82 Cairns, *Citizens Plus,* 8.

83 Ibid., 210.

84 Scott, "On Autonomy and Development," 3. In the American context, Tom Holm suggested that military service reflected the push of tangible rewards (economic, political, material) and the pull of cultural factors such as tradition, prestige, and cultural resurgence. Both motivations have led many Native people to see military service as a means to confront states' acculturation policies. See *Strong Hearts, Wounded Souls: Native American Veterans of the Vietnam War* (Austin: University of Texas Press, 1992).

85 Cynthia H. Enloe, *Ethnic Soldiers: State Security in Divided Societies* (Athens: University of Georgia Press, 1980), ix.

86 "True North Strong, Free Thanks to the Rangers," *Toronto Star,* 11 April 2002.

87 Inuit Tapiriit Kanatami (ITK) adopted the terminology *Inuit Nunangat* to refer to the Canadian Inuit homeland, including land, water, and ice. See "Maps of Inuit Nunangat (Inuit Regions of Canada)," http://www.itk.ca/publication/maps-inuit-nunangat-inuit -regions-canada.

88 See Canada Command Backgrounder no. 09.002a, "The Canadian Forces in the North," 17 April 2009.

89 *Oxford English Dictionary,* online edition, s.v. "Eskimo."

90 See, for example, Gilles Champoux, "Toponymy and the Canadian Arctic," *Frontline Defence* 8, 2 (2011): 17-20.

Chapter 1: The Pacific Coast Militia Rangers, 1942-45

1 William Strange, *Canada, the Pacific and War* (Toronto: Thomas Nelson and Sons, 1937), 212-13. On defences on the eve of war, see T. Murray Hunter, "Coast Defence in British Columbia, 1939-1941," *BC Studies* 28 (Winter 1975-76): 3-28.

2 For BC examples, see "Retired Men Want to Do Their Bit," *Victoria Times,* 30 January 1940; "Demand for Civilian Defence Corps Sweeps across Canada," *Vancouver Sun,* 17 May 1940;

"Defence Corps in Fraser Valley," *Victoria Times,* 18 May 1940; and "Band Sharpshooting Hunters into Units in Skeena Valley," *Vancouver Province,* 17 June 1940. On civil defence in British Columbia more generally, see Department of National Defence (DND), Directorate of History and Heritage (DHH), 322.019(D1), and BC Archives (BCA), British Columbia Legislative Assembly Sessional Clipping Books, Newspaper Accounts of the Debates, microfilm reel 15. A prime example is the Victoria Fish and Game Protective Association, formed in 1939 to secretly patrol watershed areas around Victoria. See "Hunters Enlist in Civilian Corps," *Victoria Times,* 4 April 1942.

3 See Ian Beckett, *The Amateur Military Tradition, 1558-1945* (Manchester: Manchester University Press, 1991).

4 On these units, see Peter Guy Silverman, "A History of the Militia and Defences of British Columbia, 1871-1914" (master's thesis, University of British Columbia, 1956); Reginald Roy, "The Early Militia and Defence of British Columbia, 1871-1885," *British Columbia Historical Quarterly* 18, 1-2 (1954): 1-28; and Peter N. Moogk, with Robert V. Stevenson, *Vancouver Defended: History of the Men and Guns of the Lower Mainland Defences, 1859-1949* (Surrey, BC: Antonson, 1978).

5 On fears of Asians in British Columbia, see Patricia Roy, *The Oriental Question: Consolidating a White Man's Province, 1914-41* (Vancouver: UBC Press, 2003) and *The Triumph of Citizenship: The Japanese and Chinese in Canada, 1941-67* (Vancouver: UBC Press, 2008).

6 "Defences at Pacific Command Well Prepared by Canada," *Globe and Mail,* 4 December 1941; C.P. Stacey, *Six Years of War* (Ottawa: Queen's Printer, 1957), 166-67; Terry Copp, "The Defence of Hong Kong," *Canadian Military History* 10, 4 (2001): 6. On earlier military assessments of the Japanese threat, see Gregory Johnson, "North Pacific Triangle? The Impact of the Far East on Canada and Its Relations with the United States and Great Britain, 1937-1948" (PhD diss., York University, 1989) and Timothy Wilford, *Canada's Road to the Pacific War: Intelligence, Strategy, and the Far East Crisis* (Vancouver: UBC Press, 2011).

7 See DHH, AHQ Report no.3, "The Employment of Infantry in the Pacific Coast Defences (Aug 39 to Dec 43)," 12. On coast defence artillery, see Hunter, "Coast Defence."

8 Desmond Morton, *Canada and War* (Toronto: Butterworths, 1981), 110.

9 On the Fishermen's Reserve Service, see Donald Peck, "The Gumboot Navy," *Raincoast Chronicles* 7 (1977): 12-19; Carol Popp, *The Gumboot Navy* (Lantzville: Oolichan Books, 1988); and W.A.B. Douglas, Roger Sarty, and Michael Whitby, *No Higher Purpose: The Official Operational History of the Royal Canadian Navy in the Second World War, 1939-1943, Vol. 2, Part 1* (St. Catharines, ON: Vanwell, 2002), 338. The navy outfitted their boats with guns and equipment.

10 Patricia Roy, J. L. Granatstein, Masako Lino, and Hiroko Takamura, *Mutual Hostages: Canadians and Japanese during the Second World War* (Toronto: University of Toronto Press, 1990), 75.

11 Ibid., 87-88; Canada, House of Commons, *Debates (Hansard),* 20 January 1942, 152.

12 "Birth of the PCMR," *The Ranger,* January 1944, 5; "History – Pacific Coast Militia Rangers," DHH, 322.009(D298). Copies of *The Ranger* are available at DHH, in Ottawa, and at the CFB Esquimalt Military and Naval Museum. There is a lot of anecdotal evidence on citizens' committees or individuals' taking unilateral action to establish local defences. For example, Grand Forks, Stewart, Courtenay, and Victoria organized unofficial home guard units before Pearl Harbor. See "History – Pacific Coast Militia Rangers," DHH, 322.009(D298), and Kerry Steeves, "The Pacific Coast Militia Rangers, 1942-1945" (master's thesis, University of British Columbia, 1990), 24; *Victoria Times,* 5 July 1978.

13 Both newspapers cited in Steeves, "Pacific Coast Militia Rangers," 15-19.

14 Parliamentary Secret Session, Notes on Canadian Defence Policy, 19 February 1942, DHH, 112.3M2(D495). See also C.P. Stacey, *Arms, Men and Governments: The War Policies of Canada, 1939-1945* (Ottawa: Queen's Printer, 1970), 131.

15 "History – Pacific Coast Militia Rangers," DHH, 322.009(D298). The government considered the most damning indictment the "The Derelict Defence," a series of *Vancouver Sun* editorials. See "Defence of Canada Forces," 16 May 1950, DHH, 112.3M2(D363).

16 Recent studies on the subject include Roy, *The Oriental Question,* and Stephanie Bangarth, *Voices Raised in Protest: Defending Citizens of Japanese Ancestry in North America, 1942-49* (Vancouver: UBC Press, 2008).

17 Chief of the General Staff (CGS) to Assistant CGS and Vice Chief of the General Staff (VCGS), 31 January 1942, DHH, 112.1(D35); Brigadier for Chief of the Defence Staff (CDS) to General Officer Command-in-Chief, Pacific Command, 31 January 1942, DHH, 322.009(D298).

18 CGS to Assistant CGS and VCGS, 31 January 1942.

19 S.P. Mackenzie, *The Home Guard: A Military and Political History* (Oxford: Oxford University Press, 1995), 32; D.K. Yelton, "British Public Opinion, the Home Guard, and the Defense of Great Britain, 1940-1944," *Journal of Military History* 58, 3 (1994): 461-80. BC journalists also made reference to guerrilla units around the world. See, for example, "The Guerrillas," *Vancouver Sun,* 9 April 1942.

20 Alexander to Secretary, DND, 7 February 1942, DHH, 159(D1).

21 Assistant CGS to CGS, 10 February 1942; CGS, "Note for file," 23 February 1942, DHH, 112.1(D35). On Canada and military law, see Chris Madsen, *Another Kind of Justice: Canadian Military Law from Confederation to Somalia* (Vancouver: UBC Press, 1999).

22 "Taylor, Thomas Alexander Hatch," Library and Archives Canada (LAC), RG 150, Ministry of the Overseas Military Forces of Canada, acc. 1992-93/166, box 9549; "Roll of Honour, British Columbia Land Surveyors," http://www.russiansinthecef.ca/; *London Gazette,* 29 March 1917, S3084; Lt.-Col. C.S. Grafton, *The Canadian "Emma Gees"* (London, ON: Canadian Machine Gun Corps Association, 1938), 43; "Various Authorities," *Canada in the Great World War,* vol. 6 (Toronto: United Publishers of Canada, 1921), 353.

23 Marion Angus, "The Rangers," *National Home Monthly,* July 1943, 28.

24 A.G. MacDonald, "Men of the PCMR Reviving Frontier Tactics," *British Columbia Lumberman,* November 1942, 54; Taylor, "Memorandum: Auxiliary Defence Corps – Organization," 18 March 1942; "History – Pacific Coast Militia Rangers," 2, DHH, 322.009(D298). On the British debate, see Mackenzie, *Home Guard,* 112-29.

25 For a recent treatment of la petite guerre, see Bernd Horn, "La Petite Guerre – A Strategy of Survival," in *The Canadian Way of War,* ed. Bernd Horn (Toronto: Dundurn, 2006), 21-55.

26 John Grenier, "The Public Identity of Early American Rangers and Its Impact on American Society," *War and Society* 21, 1 (2003): 2-5, 11; John Grenier, *The First Way of War: American War Making on the Frontier, 1607-1814* (Cambridge: Cambridge University Press, 2005); and James Wood, *Militia Myths: Ideas of the Canadian Citizen Soldier, 1896-1921* (Vancouver: UBC Press, 2010). Newspapers and literature on the PCMR made frequent reference to the Rangers' predecessors, labelling them "Roger's Rangers Mark 1942" or likening them to the Western Scouts for Custer. See, for example, MacDonald, "Men of the PCMR," 53-54; H. Straight, "Pacific Coast Rangers Planning 'Hornet's Nest' for Any Invader," *Vancouver Sun,* 22 April 1942.

27 Boyd to William, 20 March 1942, DHH, 159(D1).

28 Memorandum V-2-27-1, 18 March 1942, DHH, 159(D1).

29 "A Brief on the PCMR," 5-6, DHH, 159(D1).

30 The 5 March 1942 press release stated that the initial organization proceeded in Port Renfrew, Alberni, Tofino, Port Alice, Zeballos, Kelsey Bay, Alert Bay, Queen Charlotte City, Masset,

Bella Coola, Ocean Falls, Mill Bay, Kitimat, Port Essington, Port Simpson, Stewart, and Saanich North. See DHH, 112.1(D35).

31 "Historically Speaking," *The Ranger,* October 1945, 6; "A Brief on the PCMR," 4, DHH, 159(D1). On local organizing efforts, see, for example, J.E. Kingsley, *Did I Ever Tell You About ...* (Parksville: privately published, n.d.), 55-56, and his diary at BCA, MSS-2516.

32 "Stabilizing the New Corps," *The Ranger,* January 1944, 10.

33 Taylor to Col. R.S. Carey, 31 May 1944, DHH, 322.009(D24).

34 Kennelly to Minister of National Defence, 21 April 47, DHH, 112.1(D161), 1-2.

35 Taylor, 18 March 1942, DHH, 322.009(D298).

36 See, for example, "Rangers Appeal Directly to Ralston to Send Guns," *Victoria Daily Times,* 2 July 1942; "Island Rangers Keen to Train for Emergency," *Victoria Daily Times,* 11 August 1942. In due course, the Rangers were issued Sten submachine guns, .303 and .30-06 service rifles, and .30-.30 US sporting rifles on a general scale as well as khaki denim "Drybak" uniforms and distinctive armbands.

37 "10,000 Rangers in Four Months," *The Ranger,* January 1944, 6, 11.

38 See, for example, "BC's Rugged Defenders," *Vancouver Sun,* 15 September 1942; "Canada's Newest Western Army Shaping Up Rapidly," *Hamilton Spectator,* 14 April 1942; "BC Guerrilla Sharpshooters Guard Coast," *Hamilton Spectator,* 27 March 1943; and G. Magee, "Cariboo Commandos," *Vancouver Sun,* 27 June 1942.

39 See, for example, "Guerrilla Army to Guard BC Urged by Stevens," *Vancouver News-Herald,* 20 February 1942; "Army of Woodsmen and Miners Could Make BC Impregnable," *Vancouver Sun,* 6 March 1942; H. Straight, "Prowess in the Woods Their Chief Weapon," *Vancouver Sun,* 21 April 1942; "A Lease-Lend Army," *Vancouver Daily Province,* 22 May 1942; and "BC Has 6,000 Rangers Ready to Welcome Japs," *Globe and Mail,* 22 May 1942.

40 Macdonald, "Men of the PCMR," 54-55.

41 See, for example, Angus, "The Rangers," 30-31; and J. Strickland, "Vigilance Is Their Motto," *Vancouver Daily Province Saturday Magazine,* 7 April 1945, 1.

42 Tina Loo, "Making a Modern Wilderness: Conserving Wildlife in Twentieth-Century Canada," *Canadian Historical Review* 82, 1 (2001): 92.

43 See, for example, Adele Perry, *On the Edge of Empire: Gender, Race, and the Making of British Columbia, 1849-71* (Toronto: University of Toronto Press, 2001); and Christopher Dummitt, "Risk on the Rocks: Modernity, Manhood, and Mountaineering in British Columbia," *BC Studies* 141 (2004): 3-29.

44 Para. 3(1), General Staff Officer (GSO) 320, 12 August 1942.

45 Angus, "The Rangers," 28. Further evidence of its "democratic" nature included the ability of company members to dismiss and elect their own commanding officers. See, for example, "Defence Force Elects Heads," *Victoria Colonist,* 21 April 1942, 5.

46 Larry Worthington, *"Worthy": A Biography of Major-General F.F. Worthington* (Toronto: Macmillan, 1961), 205; Steeves, "Pacific Coast Militia Rangers," 37-41.

47 Jeffrey Keshen, *Saints, Sinners, and Soldiers: Canada's Second World War* (Vancouver: UBC Press, 2004), 22, 206, 214.

48 "A Brief on the PCMR," 15.

49 Steeves, "Pacific Coast Militia Rangers," 48.

50 Quoted in ibid., 78.

51 Maj. Gen. J.P. Mackenzie, Report on Chilliwack Rangers, 8 December 1943, LAC, RG 24, Department of National Defence, reel C-4992, f. 8328-1178.

52 "A Brief on the PCMR," 16.

53 "Veterans Keen on Plan for Civilian Corps," *Vancouver Sun,* 24 December 1941; "South African Vets Want Commando Units for Defense of Canada," *Vancouver Daily Province,*

28 February 1942; "Recruiting to Start 'At Once' for Guerrilla Forces to Protect BC Coastal Areas," *Province,* 28 February 1942; "Paardeburg Veterans Ready to Take Up Arms in Commando Groups throughout the Province," *Vancouver News-Herald,* 28 February 1942; and editorial, *Comox District Free Press,* 2 April 1942.

54 Kerry Steeves, interview with Lloyd Cornett, former member of No. 89 Company PCMR, Burnaby, BC, 29 November 1988. Transcript in the possession of Steeves, used with permission.

55 Angus, "The Rangers," 30. See also Sid Godber, "Disbanding Ranger Unit Acclaimed," *Vancouver Sun,* 1 October 1945.

56 "10,000 Recruits in Four Months," 7-8.

57 Members of Home Guard units who did not feel that the War Office had supplied them with sufficient weaponry ignored the order and manufactured "everything from armoured cars to soup-tin grenades." See Mackenzie, *Home Guard,* 66.

58 See, for example, "Rangers Snipe with Futuristic Ray Gun," Casey Wells's PCMR Scrapbook, and T.A.H. Taylor, "Pacific Coast Militia Rangers – Circular Letter No. 30," 20 October 1942. Both in CFB Esquimalt Naval and Military Museum, box 33. See also *The Ranger* magazine throughout the war.

59 "Historically Speaking," *The Ranger,* October 1945, 6.

60 "Guerilla: 'Yank' Levy Preaches the Art He Has Practiced," clipping in Casey Wells's PCMR Scrapbook. On Levy, see Michael Petrou, *Renegades: Canadians in the Spanish Civil War* (Vancouver: UBC Press, 2008), 18, 21, 62.

61 "Common Garden Horse-Sense," *The Ranger,* 15 November 1942, 6. See also "Rangers Publish Corps Magazine," *Victoria Daily Times,* 10 October 1942.

62 I.E. Phillips, "Salute to the Pacific Coast Militia Rangers," *Okanagan Historical Society 29th Annual Report* (1965), 149-50. To facilitate teaching at the community level, the army also trained instructors within the Pacific Coast Militia Rangers' own ranks. Company commanders selected individual Rangers to attend a two-week "Ranger Training School" at the Royal Canadian Engineer training centre at Sardis (Vedder Crossing) near Chilliwack.

63 G.W.L. Nicholson, "Interview with Lt.-Col. T.A.H. Taylor SO i/c PCMR," 26 January 1944, DHH, 322.009(D298).

64 Macdonald, "Men of the PCMR," 54-55.

65 "Formidable Units of Coast Rangers Being Organized on Island," *Victoria Daily Colonist,* 14 April 1942.

66 On hunting as a bourgeois distraction, see Tina Loo, "Of Moose and Men: Hunting for Masculinities in the Far West," *Western Historical Quarterly* 32, 3 (2001): 296-319.

67 "10,000 Recruits in Four Months," 9.

68 Quoted in Strickland, "Vigilance Is Their Motto," 1.

69 See Galen Perras, *Stepping Stones to Nowhere: The Aleutian Islands, Alaska, and American Military Strategy, 1867-1945* (Vancouver: UBC Press, 2003) and Stetson Conn, Rose C. Engelman, and Byron Fairchild, *Guarding the United States and Its Outposts* (Washington, DC: Centre of Military History, US Army, 1964), 92.

70 Angus, "The Rangers," 31.

71 See, for example, O.V. Maude Roxby, "The Caravan of Hope," *Okanagan Historical Society* 37 (November 1973): 62-63, and "Haney Wolf-Dog Hunt a Wow," *Vancouver Daily Province,* 22 February 1943.

72 "War Dance," *Dawson News,* 23 January 1945; "Moosehide Benefit Affair Successful," *Dawson News,* 27 January 1945. See also "Militia Rangers Sponsor Successful Dance at Chase," *Kamloops Sentinel,* 27 October 1943.

73 Strickland, "Vigilance Is Their Motto," 1.

74 "General Public Meeting Draws Big Attendance," *Dawson News,* 16 January 1942.

75 C.H. Chapman, "Pacific Coast Militia Rangers: 135 Company Yukon Rangers," manuscript in possession of John Mitchell, Dawson, YT.

76 Maj.-Gen. J.P. Mackenzie, Report on No.135 Coy, PCMR, Dawson, YT, 4 May 1944, LAC, RG 24, reel C-4992, f. 8328-1309.

77 Ibid.

78 J.J. van Bibber, interview with author, Dawson City, YT, 11 August 2007.

79 "Historically Speaking," *The Ranger,* October 1945, 7.

80 "These Are Our Friends," *The Ranger,* October 1945, 16. See also James Edward Kingsley, Pacific Coast Militia Rangers Diary, 1942-46, BCA, MSS 2516, v. 2.

81 See, for example, "'Rangerettes' Likely in Courtenay District," *Victoria Daily Times,* 24 April 1942.

82 Patricia E. Roy, "British Columbia's Fear of Asians, 1900-1950," *Social History* 13, 25 (1980): 161-72; *The Oriental Question;* and *The Triumph of Citizenship.* Of course, few Japanese resided on the Coast after the spring of 1942, and Ranger units in the BC Interior had the additional task of monitoring Japanese Canadian internment camps in their regions. See "The Japanese Menace" in Steeves, "Pacific Coast Militia Rangers," 79-99.

83 "And Their Work," *The Ranger,* April 1945, 9. For another example of a Chinese shopkeeper in Yale, see Steeves, "Pacific Coast Militia Rangers," 58-59. For discussions on the acceptability of Hindus with previous British army service in the PCMR, see DHH, 112.21009 (D204).

84 On this subject, see Scott Sheffield, *The Red Man's on the Warpath: The Image of the "Indian" and the Second World War* (Vancouver: UBC Press, 2003).

85 Angus, "The Rangers," 30. Contrast these depictions of Aboriginal Rangers with Loo's characterization of Native imagery in "Of Moose and Men."

86 See, for example, "Veterans" in Royal Commission on Aboriginal Peoples, *For Seven Generations: Final Report of the RCAP,* vol. 1, *Looking Forward, Looking Back* (Ottawa: Canada Communication Group, 1996), 523-76; Fred Gaffen, *Forgotten Soldiers* (Penticton: Theytus Books, 1985); Janice Summerby, *Native Soldiers, Foreign Battlefields* (Ottawa: Minister of Supply and Services, 1993). Michael Stevenson disputes this notion of high enlistment in *Canada's Greatest Wartime Muddle: National Selective Service and the Mobilization of Human Resources during World War II* (Montreal/Kingston: McGill-Queen's University Press, 2001), 38.

87 See Michael Stevenson, "The Mobilisation of Native Canadians during the Second World War," *Journal of the Canadian Historical Association* 7 (1996): 205-26. On BC responses, see LAC, RG 10, v. 11289, f. 214-4.

88 See Lt.-Col. T.A.H. Taylor to Indian Commissioner for BC, 26 February 1943, LAC, RG 10, v. 11289, f. 214-4.

89 Kennelly to Taylor, 28 February 1943, DHH, 169.009(D94).

90 Thomas Boston, *From Time before Memory* (New Aiyansh, BC: School District No. 92 (Nisga'a), 1996), 240; O'Grady to Staff Officer (SO) Rangers, 19 July 1942, and Gillett to Taylor, 8 April 1943, DHH, 169.009(D77).

91 See, for example, P.J.C. Ball, Report on Vancouver Indian Agency, December 1942, and P.B. Ross to H.W. McGill, 10 February 1944, LAC, RG 10, v. 6769, f. 452-20-3.

92 On Brendan Kennelly's visit to Kincolith, see his memorandum to SO Rangers, 28 February 1943, DHH, 169.009(D94).

93 When six Nisga'a Rangers attended the training school at Sardis, reports of their exceptional performance so impressed the commander of the army's Mountain and Jungle Warfare School that he requested they serve as instructors for soldiers who came through to train. Hendrie to HQ 6 Canadian Division, 30 October 1944, DHH, 169.009(D94), also quoted in Steeves, "Pacific Coast Militia Rangers," 57.

94 O'Grady to SO Rangers, 1 November 1942, DHH, 169.009(D94); D'Arcy to SO Rangers, 30 June 1943, DHH, 169.009(D77).

95 Steeves, "Pacific Coast Militia Rangers," 34-50, 81-2, 120.

96 "Historically Speaking," *The Ranger,* October 1945, 7.

97 "10,000 Recruits in Four Months," 8.

98 Ranger "Andy" Rigors, "Past Two Meetings Devoted to Sten Gun and Compass," *Kamloops Sentinel,* 23 June 1943, 3.

99 "BC Rangers Trap 28 Paratroopers," *Vancouver Sun,* 14 October 1944; Steeves, "Pacific Coast Militia Rangers," 85; and "Canadian Ranger Organization," ca. August-September 1947, DHH, 324.009(D542).

100 The Pacific Coast Militia Rangers' strength returns from DHH, 322.009(D99); Director Military Operations and Plans to General Officer Commanding in Chief Pacific Command, 13 November 1943, DHH, 322.009(D592). On reductions in Pacific Command more generally, see Army Headquarters Report No. 3, "The Employment of Infantry in the Coast Defences (August 39 to December 1943)," 94-109, DHH library.

101 Arthur Mayse, "Ranger Units to Be Cut," *Vancouver Sun,* 18 October 1943.

102 Taylor to Brigadier, General Staff, Pacific Command, 12 October 1944, DHH, 322.009(D24).

103 "The Japanese Balloon Enterprise against North America," Army HQ Historical Section Report No. 28, 15 October 1949, 1-10. Pacific Command's balloon incident log disclosed that "the activities of the PCMR perhaps exceeded the combined activities of all other organizations used for counter-measures against balloons." See "A Brief on the PCMR," 13. The balloons did not lead to rampant forest fires, and media silence about the bombs deprived the Japanese of intelligence on their initiative, leading them to stop releasing balloons in April 1945. See Worthington, *"Worthy,"* 206. Although there were no deaths in BC, six people were killed when a child triggered a balloon bomb found hanging from a tree in Oregon. See Bert Webber, *Retaliation: Japanese Attacks and Allied Countermeasures on the Pacific Coast in World War II* (Corvallis: Oregon State University Press, 1975).

104 "Interior Rangers 'Stand Down' in Colourful Pr. George Rites," *Vancouver Daily Province,* 15 October 1945.

105 Worthington, *"Worthy,"* 205, 207. See also Sid Godber, "Disbanding Ranger Unit Acclaimed," *Vancouver Sun,* 1 October 1945.

106 PCMR Circular Letter No. 103, 5 October 1945, DHH, 112.3S2009(D232); General Officer Commanding in Chief Pacific Command to Secretary, DND, 11 September 1945, DHH, 322.009(D24).

107 Stacey, *Arms, Men and Governments,* 133.

108 Emily Carr, *Hundreds and Thousands,* quoted in Jean Barman, *The West beyond the West,* rev. ed. (Toronto: University of Toronto Press, 1996), 261.

109 "Notes on the Pacific Coast Militia Rangers," DHH, 145.2P(D1).

110 "Stabilizing the New Corps," 10.

111 "Pacific Coast Militia Rangers," n.d., DHH, 322.009(D24).

112 Taylor to Col. A. Duguid, 4 April 1945, DHH, 322.009(D24).

113 "Historically Speaking," *The Ranger,* October 1945, 7.

Chapter 2: Setting the Stage, 1946-47

1 Department of National Defence (DND), Directorate of History and Heritage (DHH), 112.3M2(D49).

2 Robert Bothwell, "The Cold War and the Curate's Egg: When Did Canada's Cold War Really Begin? Later Than You Might Think," *International Journal* 53, 3 (1998): 407-18.

3 Richard Duibaldo, "The Role of the Arctic Islands in Defence," in *A Century of Canada's Arctic Islands, 1880-1980,* ed. Morris Zaslow (Ottawa: Royal Society of Canada, 1981), 94.

4 C.P. Stacey, *The Military Problems of Canada: A Survey of Defence Policies and Strategic Conditions, Past and Present* (Toronto: Ryerson Press, 1940), 5.

5 On the northern defence projects, see Stanley Dziuban, *Military Relations between the United States and Canada, 1939-1945* (Washington, DC: Department of the Army, 1959), as well as several books by Kenneth Coates and William R. Morrison, including *The Alaska Highway in World War II* (Norman: University of Oklahoma Press, 1992) and *Working the North: Labor and the Northwest Defence Projects, 1942-1946* (Anchorage: University of Alaska Press, 1994).

6 See Shelagh Grant, "Northern Nationalists: Visions of 'A New North,' 1940-1950," in *For Purposes of Dominion: Essays in Honour of Morris Zaslow*, ed. Kenneth Coates and William R. Morrison (North York: Captus, 1989), 47-70.

7 Vincent Massey, *What's Past Is Prologue: The Memoirs of the Right Honourable Vincent Massey, C.H.* (Toronto: Macmillan, 1963), 371, 396.

8 On wartime concerns, see Shelagh Grant, *Sovereignty or Security? Government Policy in the Canadian North, 1936-1950* (Vancouver: UBC Press, 1988), and Bernd Horn, *Bastard Sons: An Examination of Canada's Airborne Experience, 1942-1995* (St. Catharines, ON: Vanwell, 2001), 43-58.

9 Quoted in Richard J. Diubaldo and S.J. Scheinberg, *A Study of Canadian-American Defence Policy, 1945-1975: Northern Issues and Strategic Resources* (Ottawa: Department of National Defence, 1978), 19.

10 See Donald Page and Donald Munton, "Canadian Images of the Cold War, 1946-1947," *International Journal* 32 (1977): 577-604, and Denis Stairs, "Realists at Work," in *Canada and the Early Cold War, 1943-1957*, ed. Greg Donaghy (Ottawa: Department of Foreign Affairs and International Trade, 1998), 91-116.

11 David Bercuson, "Continental Defense and Arctic Security, 1945-50," in *The Cold War and Defense*, ed. Keith Neilson and Ronald Haycock (New York: Praeger, 1990), 154.

12 See Final Report of the Advisory Committee on Post-Hostility Problems, January-February 1945, in *Documents on Canadian External Relations*, vol. 11, *1944-45*, ed. John F. Hilliker, part 2 (Ottawa: Department of External Affairs, 1990), 1567-73; and Group Captain W.W. Bean, "An Appreciation of the Requirements for Canada-U.S. Security," 8 November 1946, Library and Archives Canada (LAC), RG 2, Privy Council Office Records, vol. 74, f. D-19-2 (1946 Sept.-Dec.). For context, see Peter Kikkert, "1946," in *Canada and Arctic Sovereignty and Security: Historical Perspectives*, ed. P. Whitney Lackenbauer (Calgary: Centre for Military and Strategic Studies, 2011), 69-109.

13 Stephen Harris, "Really a Defile throughout Its Length," in *The Alaska Highway: Papers of the 40th Anniversary Symposium*, ed. Kenneth Coates (Vancouver: UBC Press, 1985), 121-22. See also "An Appreciation of the Requirements for Canadian-U.S. Security," 23 May 1946, National Archives and Records Administration (NARA), RG 59, State Department, Permanent Joint Board on Defence (PJBD), box 2, f. "Basic Security Plan II"; Joint Working Committee of the American Embassy, Moscow, "Analysis of Soviet Strength and Weakness," 1 September 1946, and Memorandum, "Political Appreciation of the Objectives of Soviet Foreign Policy," 30 November 1946, NARA, RG 59, PJBD, box 2, f. "Basic Papers, 1946-47."

14 Director of Military Operations and Plans (DMOP) to Chief of the General Staff (CGS), 12 March 1946, DHH, 112.3M2(D382).

15 David Bercuson, *True Patriot: The Life of Brooke Claxton, 1898-1960* (Toronto: University of Toronto Press, 1993), 159, 164-65.

16 Exercise Eskimo, held in north-central Saskatchewan in winter 1945, showed that defence planners needed to increase their geographical and operational knowledge if soldiers were to survive, move, and "fight against both the enemy and winter" in northern areas. "Exercise 'Eskimo': Lessons Learned," DHH, 81/675. Exercise Polar Bear in northern British Columbia and Exercise Lemming on the Barren Grounds and sea ice exposed problems of

endurance and survival. Hugh Halliday, "Recapturing the North: Exercises 'Eskimo,' 'Polar Bear' and 'Lemming,' 1945," *Canadian Military History* 6, 2 (1997): 29-38. Quote on "Lemming" from Diubaldo and Scheinberg, *Study of Canadian-American Defence Policy*, 17.

17 See, for example, "No Canadian Law Compels Eskimos to Take Up Arms," *Ottawa Citizen,* 22 June 1943.

18 Alan Harvey, "Eskimo – Watch the Skies!" *Winnipeg Free Press,* 30 January 1946.

19 Matthew Farish, "Frontier Engineering," *Canadian Geographer* 50, 2 (2006): 192.

20 For more details, see Kevin Thrasher, "Exercise Musk Ox: Lost Opportunities" (master's thesis, Carleton University, 1998).

21 "Joint Canadian–United States Basic Security Plan, 5 June 1946," NARA, RG 59, PJBD, box 2, f. "Basic Security Plan II."

22 "Minutes of the Cabinet Defence Committee, 13 Nov. 1946," DHH, 112.3M2(D125).

23 See Larry Worthington, *"Worthy": A Biography of Major-General F.F. Worthington* (Toronto: Macmillan, 1961), 213, 216. The army's reorganization program of 1946 renamed the Non-Permanent Active Militia the "Reserve Army."

24 J.M. Hitsman, "The Canadian Rangers," Army Historical Section Report No. 92, 1 December 1960, 3. See also Worthington to GSO I, 10 March 1947, DHH, 327.009(D205).

25 "Societies Act": Pacific Coast Militia Association – Declaration, 5 April 1946; Pacific Coast Militia Rangers Association Bulletin No. 1, 1 May 1946; Taylor to Jenkins, 18 June 1946, DHH, 112.3M2(D49), vol. 1; General Officer Commanding (GOC), Western Command to Secretary, National Defence Headquarters (NDHQ), 15 July 1946, LAC, RG 24, Department of National Defence, acc. 1983-84/215, vol. 321, f. 2001-1999/0, vol. 1.

26 See DHH, 112.3M2(D48) and DHH, 112.1(D161); CGS to Minister, 12 September 1946, DHH, 112.3M2(D49), vol. 1; "Historical Background of PCMR and Cdn Rgrs," 3 July 1947, LAC, RG 24, reel C-8266, f. 603-18.

27 Worthington to District Officer Commanding (DOC) Military District (MD) 11 and DOCMD 13, 24 June 1946, DHH, 327.009(D205).

28 See, for example, Macklin to All GOCs, 20 August 1946, DHH, 112.3M2(D49), vol. 1.

29 CGS to General Officers Commanding, 17 June 1946, LAC, RG 24, acc. 83-84/215, vol. 321, f. 2001-1999/0, vol. 1.

30 Appendix A to HQS 24-1 FD 81 (DMOP) (Ops 268), 17 June 1946, LAC, RG 24, reel C-8266, f. 603-18.

31 Worthington to DOCMD 11 and DOCMD 13, 24 June 1946, DHH, 327.009(D205).

32 Macklin to Adjutant General, 28 June 1946, LAC, RG 24, acc. 1983-84/215, vol. 321, f. 2001-1999/0, vol. 1.

33 Macklin to Adjutant General, 28 June 1946.

34 "Canadian Rangers Questionnaire" and Appendix, 3 October 1946, LAC, RG 24, vol. 2440, f. 604-18.

35 Maj.-Gen. F.F. Worthington to Secretary, Army HQ, 12 October 1946, LAC, RG 24, acc. 1983-84/215, box 321, f. 2001-1999/0, vol. 1.

36 Maj.-Gen. E.J. Renaud to Secretary, Army HQ, 16 October 1946, and Brig. M.H.S. Penhale to Secretary, DND, 17 October 1946, LAC, RG 24, acc. 1983-84/215, box 321, f. 2001-1999/0, vol. 1.

37 Maj.-Gen. H. Foster to CGS, 12 October 1946, LAC, RG 24, acc. 1983-84/215, box 321, f. 2001-1999/0, vol. 1.

38 See "Canadian Rangers Questionnaire" and Appendix, 3 October 1946.

39 Worthington to Secretary, Army HQ, 12 October 1946.

40 Prairie Command agreed that the Rangers should be unpaid, except when they successfully completed work such as compiling reports or participated in exercises or courses with the Active and Reserve Forces. Central and Quebec Commands recommended paying expenses only to unit commands and not to individual personnel. See LAC, RG 24, acc. 1983-84/215,

box 321, f. 2001-1999/0, vol. 1, and "Canadian Rangers Questionnaire" and Appendix, 3 October 1946.

41 Worthington to Secretary, Army HQ, 12 October 1946.

42 "Canadian Rangers Questionnaire" and Appendix, 3 October 1946.

43 "Canadian Rangers," Appendix B to HQS 601-18 (DMOP) (Ops 328), 30 October 1946; CGS to Adjutant General, 30 October 1946, LAC, RG 24, acc. 1983-84/215, box 321, f. 2001-1999/0, vol. 1. Senior defence officials were asked to comment on this framework within twenty-four hours.

44 Macklin to Adjutant General and marginalia, 31 October 1946, and Adjutant General to DMOP, 2 November 1946, LAC, RG 24, acc. 1983-84/215, box 321, f. 2001-1999/0, vol. 1.

45 Deputy Chief of the General Staff (B) to DMOP, 1 November 1946, LAC, RG 24, acc. 1983-84/215, box 321, f. 2001-1999/0, vol. 1.

46 Director of Military Training (DMT) to DMOP, 31 October 1946; Master General of the Ordnance (MGO) to CGS (through DMOP), 1 November 1946; Quartermaster General (QMG) to DMOP, 31 October 1946, ibid.

47 "2nd CGS Conference with Commanders," Ottawa, 2-7 December 1946, DHH, 112.3M2 (D49), vol. 1; Foulkes to Minister, 22 January 1947, and Foulkes to Tees, 4 February 1947, LAC, RG 24, acc. 1983-84/215, box 321, f. 2001-1999/0, vol. 1.

48 "Rangers Added to Reserve Army," *Globe and Mail,* 10 April 1947.

49 Quoted in Hitsman, "Canadian Rangers," 4-5.

50 "Canadian Rangers" (Ops 463), 20 July 1947; Lt.-Col. B. Keane to Col. L.M. Chesley, 9 July 1947, DHH, 112.3M2(D49), vol. 1. The General Staff Officer I in Western Command also opposed any medical restrictions: "For functions envisaged, a trapper may have lost an arm to a bear, but still be ideal for our purposes." GSO I to GSO II (Int), 7 July 1947, DHH, 324.009(D542). On Keane, see George Kitching, *Mud and Green Field: The Memoirs of Major-General George Kitching* (St. Catharines, ON: Vanwell, 1992), 249-50.

51 Keane to Chesley, 9 July 1947.

52 Although original proposals recommended issuing sporting or .30-30 rifles to the Rangers, similar to the PCMR, the military had fewer than fifteen hundred on hand. The acting director of weapons and development suggested giving them standard army-type rifles to ease procurement and control. The obsolescent .30-06 Lee-Enfield rifle fit the bill. Johnston to DMOP, 1 November 1946, LAC, RG 24, acc. 1983-84/215, box 321, f. 2001-1999/0, vol. 1.

53 Canadian Army Policy Statement No. 26 (DMOP), Canadian Rangers, 12 August 1947, LAC, RG 24, acc. 1983-84/167, box 4975, f. 3201-1999/0. See also Hitsman, "Canadian Rangers," 2-3.

54 "Canadian Army Policy Statement No. 26." Amendments to this statement can be found in DHH, 112.3M2(D49), vol. 2. The strength allocations were based on the percentage of the population living within Ranger territory as delineated by Ottawa. A/DMOP to Directorate of Staff Duties (DSD), 27 June 1947, DHH, 112.3M2(D49) vol. 1.

55 Lester Pearson, "Canada Looks 'Down North,'" *Foreign Affairs* 24, 4 (1946): 647.

56 "Memorandum of Canadian–United States Defense Conversations held in Ottawa," 16-17 December 1946, NARA, RG 59, PJBD, box 2, f. "Basic Papers 1946-47," emphasis in original.

57 Kenneth Eyre, "Forty Years of Military Activity in the Canadian North, 1947-87," *Arctic* 40, 4 (1987): 294.

58 Kikkert, "1946."

59 Bercuson, *True Patriot,* 164, 171; Adam Lajeunesse, "The True North As Long As It's Free: The Canadian Policy Deficit 1945-1985" (master's thesis, University of Calgary, 2007), 25.

60 See Tamara Sherwin, "From Total War to Total Force: Civil-Military Relations and the Canadian Army Reserve (Militia), 1945-1995" (master's thesis, University of New Brunswick, 1995) and G.M. Urquhart, "The Changing Role of the Canadian Militia, 1945-1975" (master's thesis, University of Victoria, 1977).

Chapter 3: "Teething Troubles," 1947-49

1   Col. L.M. Chesley to Lt.-Col. R.A. Keane, 24 July 1947, Department of National Defence (DND), Directorate of History and Heritage (DHH), 112.3M2(D49), vol. 1.

2   Keane to Chesley, 9 July 1947; reply, 24 July 1947; Acting Director Military Operations and Plans (DMOP) to Directorate of Staff Duties (DSD), 27 June 1947; Assistant DSD to DMOP, 27 July 1947, DHH, 112.3M2(D49), vol. 1; Acting DMOP to Deputy Chief of the General Staff (DCGS)(A), 5 August 1947, DHH, 112.3M2(D49), vol. 2.

3   General Staff to Western Command, 6 March 1947, DHH, 112.3M2(D48); Western Command to Army HQ, 6 March 1947, Library and Archives Canada (LAC), RG 24, Department of National Defence, acc. 1983-84/215, box 321, f. 2001-1999/0, vol. 1. See also Worthington to General Staff Officer (GSO) I, 10 March 1947; Worthington, "Canadian Rangers Organization," 3 April 1947, DHH, 327.009(D205).

4   T.A.H. Taylor to R.W. Mayhew, 14 February 1947, DHH, 112.3M2(D48); Chief of the General Staff (CGS) to Minister of National Defence (MND), 24 March 1947, LAC, RG 24, acc. 1983-84/215, box 321, f. 2001-1999/0, vol. 1. See also correspondence in LAC, MG 27, III B5, Ian Mackenzie fonds.

5   Similar civilian groups had requested rifles and ammunition from the military, Brooke Claxton explained, but the military had also "carefully considered" and rejected these appeals. Claxton to Mackenzie, 5 February 1947, DHH, 112.3M2(D48).

6   Taylor to Lt.-Gen. C. Foulkes, 26 March 1947, DHH, 112.3M2(D49) vol. 1.

7   Maj.-Gen. F.F. Worthington to Foulkes, 22 May 1947, DHH, 327.009(D205).

8   Worthington to Army HQ, 22 May 1947, DHH, 112.3M2(D49), vol. 1. BC's provincial police commissioner promised to help screen and recruit prospective leaders, and Worthington advocated similar cooperation with the RCMP.

9   "Canadian Ranger Organization" (ca. August-September 1947); GSO I to GSO II (Int), 7 July 1947, DHH, 324.009(D542).

10 Kenneth Coates and William Morrison, "The Federal Government and Urban Development in Northern Canada after World War II," *BC Studies* 104 (1994): 27-29; Morris Zaslow, *The Northward Expansion of Canada, 1914-1967* (Toronto: McClelland and Stewart, 1988), 175; and Richard Stuart, "The Impact of the Alaska Highway on Dawson City," in *The Alaska Highway: Papers of the 40th Anniversary Symposium,* ed. Kenneth Coates (Vancouver: UBC Press, 1985), 188-204.

11 Brig.-Gen. Walsh to General Officer Commanding (GOC), Western Command, 16 September 1947, DHH, 327.009(D205).

12 GOC, Western Command to Army, Dawson City, 22 September 1947, DHH, 327.009(D205).

13 Walsh to GOC, Western Command, 16 September 1947. For context, see Kenneth Coates, "Best Left as Indians: Native-White Relations in the Yukon Territory, 1840-1973," *Canadian Journal of Native Studies* 4, 2 (1984): 179-204.

14 Walsh to GOC, Western Command, 16 September 1947; Worthington to Army HQ, 5 September 1947, DHH, 327.009(D205). For a military perspective on the Alaska Highway, see Lt.-Col. F.LeP.T. Clifford, "Report on a Visit to Northwest Highway System, 25 August-9 September 1946," 16 September 1946, DHH, 112.3M2(D276).

15 Alex van Bibber, interview with author, Beaver Creek, YT, 17 June 2009. Van Bibber was joined by others such as Paul Berchel and Dave Hume (a crack shot who was issued a sniper rifle) whose sons are Rangers today. Ranger Chuck Hume, interview with author, Haines Junction, YT, 16 June 2009.

16 Worthington, Memo no. 56, 12 August 1947, DHH, 327.04(D1) vol. 1.

17 Maj.-Gen. C. Mann to GOC, Western Command, 4 October 1947, DHH, 112.3M2(D49), vol. 2.

18 Worthington, Memo no. 56.

19 Lt.-Col. W.A. Todd to Major C.R. Douthwaite, 25 October 1947, DHH, 327.009(D205). The RCMP also justified their hesitation on the basis of growing government requests for security vetting.

20 Douthwaite to Todd, 3 November 1947, DHH, 327.009(D205), emphasis in original.

21 See Officers Commanding RCMP divisions across Canada, 22 October 1947, Prince of Wales Northern Heritage Centre (PWNHC), NWT Archives, RCMP fonds, G-1979-043, f. "Arctic Red River–Army–Miscellaneous, 1947-1948." The commissioner later reassured the military that the RCMP supported the Ranger concept and were "glad to assist in any way that is feasible," but this support was clearly contained. See S.T. Wood to Foulkes, 19 February 1948, LAC, RG 24, vol. 2440, f. 604-28, vol. 1.

22 Cooper also conveyed disappointment to his old friend Col. A.F. Duguid. When the chief of the general staff followed up with an official request, Cooper and Philip A. Chester, the company's managing director in Winnipeg, promised their full cooperation and assistance. Correspondence on DHH, 327.04(D1), vol. 1; Maj.-Gen. N.E. Rodger to Vice Chief of the General Staff (VCGS), 22 October 1947, DHH, 112.3M2(D49), vol. 1.

23 See, for example, R.A.J. Phillips, *Canada's North* (Toronto: Macmillan, 1967), 78-79. The HBC's factors had already contributed to a northern guard when the RCAF Aircraft Detection Corps organized civilian volunteers along Canada's coasts during the Second World War. See S.G.L. Horner, "The North on Guard," *The Beaver* 20, 4, outfit 271 (March 1941): 6-7, and W.A.B. Douglas, *The Creation of a National Air Force* (Toronto: University of Toronto Press, 1986), 380, 426.

24 Acting Brigadier, General Staff (BGS) (Plans) to VCGS, 24 October 1947, DHH, 112.3M2(D49), vol. 1; Acting DMOP to BGS (Plans), 27 October 1947; "Appreciation – Organization Canadian Rangers," Winnipeg, Manitoba, 13 December 1948, DHH, 112.3M2(D49), vol. 2.

25 "Appreciation – Organization Canadian Rangers," Winnipeg, Manitoba, 13 December 1948, DHH, 112.3M2(D49), vol. 2; BGS (Plans) to CGS, 7 February 1949; "Summary of Gen. Worthington's Letter," enclosure 6 to HQC 604-18TD 15, 31 January 1949, DHH, 112.3M2(D49), vol. 3. The other main concern was boundary maintenance. Ranger companies that followed HBC zones and transcended Military Command boundaries created command-and-control issues. It was preferable to observe these military boundaries as much as possible.

26 Brig. R.O.G. Morton to CGS, 29 January 1948, LAC, RG 24, vol. 2440, f. 604-28, vol. 1; Maj.-Gen. E.J. Renaud to DMOP, 15 November 1947, DHH, 324.009(D461).

27 Michael L. Hadley, *U-Boats against Canada: German Submarines in Canadian Waters* (Montreal/Kingston: McGill-Queen's University Press, 1985); W.A.B. Douglas, Roger Sarty, and Michael Whitby, *No Higher Purpose: Official Operational History of the Royal Canadian Navy in the Second World War, 1939-1943, Vol. 2, Part 1* (St. Catharines, ON: Vanwell, 2002), 429-76; "Defence of Canada Forces," 16 May 1950, DHH, 112.3M2(D363); J.M. Hitsman, "The Canadian Rangers," Army Historical Section Report No. 92, 1 December 1960, 1; C.P. Stacey, *Six Years of War: The Army in Canada, Britain, and the Pacific* (Ottawa: Queen's Printer, 1957), 176-77.

28 On this organization, see "Aircraft Detection Corps" (1944), Air Force HQ History, vol. 2, DHH, 80/395, A-12.

29 DMOP to DGS (Plans), 24 January 1948, DHH, 112.3M2(D49), vol. 2.

30 Lt.-Col. M.E.P. Garneau, "General Staff Letter No. 1: Canadian Rangers," n.d. (ca. October 1948), DHH, 324.009(D461).

31 For a regional overview, see Benoît Brouillette, "La côte nord du Saint-Laurent," *Revue canadienne de géographie* 1, 1-4 (1947): 3-37.

32 Anne Carney, *Harrington Harbour ... Back Then* (Montreal: Self-published, 1991), 63.

502 NOTES TO PAGES 88-91

33 Louise Abbott, *The Coast Way: A Portrait of the English on the Lower North Shore of the St. Lawrence* (Montreal/Kingston: McGill-Queen's University Press, 1988), 3-4, 20, 47. See also Cleophas Belvin, *The Forgotten Labrador: Kegashka to Blanc-Sablon* (Montreal/Kingston: McGill-Queen's University Press, 2006).

34 Capt. A. Gaumond, "Report on Visit by Area Intelligence Officer HQ; Eastern Quebec Area to the Area Known as the North Shore of the St. Lawrence River," 12 August 1948, DHH, 324.009(D 461).

35 Carney, *Harrington Harbour*, 11-12; Gabriel Dionne, *In a Breaking Wave: Living History of the Lower North Shore*, trans. H. Miller and T. Marion, rev. by W.E. O'Meara (Montreal: Les Missionaires Oblats de Marie Immaculée, 1988), 39, 89. See also Louis Garnier, *Dog Sled to Airplane* (Quebec: 1949), and Albert S. Whiteley, "Communications on the Lower North Shore," *Canadian Geographic* 95, 1 (1977): 42-3.

36 GOC, Quebec Command to DMOP, Army HQ, 30 September 1955, LAC, RG 24, acc. 1983-84/215, box 322, f. S-2001-1999/0, vol. 8.

37 Gordon Jones, interview with author, Chevery, QC, 12 April 2007. See also Major Pat Templeton, report on liaison visit to Canadian Ranger Units, 10 August 1953, DHH, 324.009(D 512). Rowsell's job as postmaster put him in regular contact with the coastal villages. He spent the evenings in the settlements along his route but bivouacked if caught in a storm. See Whiteley, "Communications," 45.

38 Gaumond, Report, 12 August 1948. On H.A. Sewell, see Robert Sewell, "The Family of Dr. James Arthur Sewell," 7 May 2003, http://www.robertsewell.ca/drjasewell.html.

39 James Cantley, *Economic Report on Eskimo Affairs* (Ottawa: Department of Resources and Development, 1950), 16. Copy available at the Aboriginal Affairs and Northern Development Canada Library in Gatineau, Quebec.

40 Paraphrased message, 2 August 1948; Morton to DMOP, 7 December 1948, LAC, RG 24, vol. 2441, f. 604-18, vol. 2.

41 Jane George, "Top Gun Has Lots of Experience," *Nunatsiaq News*, 21 November 2003. Tookalook claims that the visit occurred in 1947, but this is mistaken. There is no record of his official enrolment.

42 Gaumond, Report, 12 August 1948; Gaumond to Rangers, Company Commanders, Platoon Commanders, 7 October 1948, DHH, 324.009(D461).

43 Telegram, D. Rowsell to Gaumont, 31 October 1948; reply, 13 November 1948, DHH, 324.009(D461). Information on Rowsell from interview with Gordon Jones.

44 "Canada Forms Ranger Units to Defend North," *Globe and Mail*, 20 March 1948; "Canada North Defence Is Set," *Montreal Gazette*, 20 March 1948.

45 "Canadian Ranger Organization" (ca. August-September 1947), DHH, 324.009(D542). These points were along the Mackenzie River and the North West Highway System, at exposed locations along the coast where operational troops had been posted during the war and at vulnerable points along interior communication lines. The acting director of military operations and plans noted, "The location of units at these points would provide some measure of protection to localities where, in the majority of cases, it would not be desirable or economical to station operational troops in the event of an emergency." Acting DMOP to DCGS(A), 15 September 1947, DHH, 112.3M2(D49), vol. 2. For proposed locations, see "Brief: The Canadian Rangers," n.d., DHH, 324.009(D542).

46 CGS to H.L. Keenleyside, 14 January 1948, DHH, 112.3M2(D49), vol. 2.

47 "Brief: The Canadian Rangers," n.d., DHH, 324.009(D542). The city already had a reserve unit (24 Field Squadron of the Royal Canadian Engineers), and officials sought to avoid locating Ranger and reserve units together. Officials rationalized that the Rangers would tend to be older and "not generally acceptable" to reserve units, that their presence may even stimulate greater interest in the reserves among residents. Hitsman, "Canadian Rangers,"

7-8; Penhale to Army Headquarters, 10 March 1948, LAC, RG 24, vol. 2440, f. 604-18, vol. 1.

48 G.R. Ingram to Maj Douthwaite, 15 October 1947; Army Vancouver to Army Edmonton, 5 November 1947; Western Command to Army Vancouver, 5 November 1947, DHH, 327.009(D205). Information on Woolgar's war record from David Sproule, email to author, 31 May 2008.

49 Douthwaite to J. Prescott and J. Woolgar, 15 May 1948; Maj.-Gen. E.G. Weeks to Western Command, 18 May 1948; Prescott to Douthwaite, 22 May 1948, DHH, 144.6(D1). For security reasons, the military decided to remove territorial references from unit designations in May 1948 and to number companies consecutively across the country in order of their formation. Hitsman, "Canadian Rangers," 8-9; SD 1, Letter no. 3685, 29 May 1948, DHH, 327.009(D205). When the military introduced a Ranger patrol structure (rather than companies and platoons) beginning in the 1970s, Ranger units were designated by their community names once again. For clarity's sake, however, I use community names to identify companies and platoons in this book, but the postwar secrecy reinforced that the Rangers were intended for a combat role (rather than a symbolic presence for sovereignty purposes).

50 Woolgar to Douthwaite, 11 June 1948, DHH, 327.009(D205).

51 Worthington, Memo no. 56, 12 August 1947, DHH, 327.04(D1), vol. 1; Lt.-Col. M.R. to HQ Western Command, 24 September 1947, DHH, 324.009(D542). Worthington had stressed the need for interservice cooperation from the onset. See Worthington, "Canadian Ranger Organization," 3 April 1947, DHH, 324.009(D542).

52 Capt. J.A. Gray to Commander, BC Area, 1 December 1947, DHH, 327.04(D1), vol. 1; Col. T.E.D'O. Snow to GSO 11 Intelligence, Western Command, 17 May 1948; Douthwaite to Commander, BC Area, 27 July 1948, DHH, 327.009(D205); Col. A.G. Chevrier to DSD, 28 April 1948, LAC, RG 24, vol. 2440, f. 604-18, vol. 1. Cross-referenced with list of PCMR company commanders in CFB Esquimalt Naval and Military Museum, "PCMR Companies."

53 Col. J.E.C. Pangman, DMOP to BGS (Plans), 28 May 1948, LAC, RG 24, vol. 2440, f. 604-18, vol. 1.

54 DMOP to BGS (Plans), 29 June 1948, DHH, 112.3M2(D49), vol. 2; Adjutant General, Order: Formation Reserve Militia Units, 21 July 1948, LAC, RG 24, vol. 2441, f. 604-18, vol. 2. Again, the army ignored official policy. A company of the Rocky Mountain Rangers, a reserve unit, already existed in Prince George, but officials authorized the Rangers because Prince George represented an important communications centre, and the reserves would be withdrawn on mobilization for war.

55 Hitsman, "Canadian Rangers," 8. Branches of the Canadian Legion in Muskoka lobbied for Ranger units in their area, but National Defence Headquarters refused their request. See LAC, RG 24, acc. 1983-84/215, box 321, f. 2001-1999/0, vol. 1.

56 Robert Nielsen, "Canada Like Alert Athlete in Her Defence – U.S. Paper," *Toronto Daily Star,* 22 October 1948.

57 DMOP to BGS (Plans), 23 November 1948; Foulkes to Maj.-Gen. C. Vokes, 3 December 1948, DHH, 112.3M2(D49), vol. 2.

58 David Bercuson, *True Patriot: The Life of Brooke Claxton, 1898-1960* (Toronto: University of Toronto Press, 1993), 177.

59 DMOP to BGS (Plans), 22 September 1948, DHH, 112.3M2(D49), vol. 2.

60 Lt.-Col. J.F. Lemieux to DMOP, 15 November 1948, DHH, 112.3M2(D49), vol. 2.

61 Megill to BGS (Plans), 17 November 1948, DHH, 112.3M2(D49), vol. 2.

62 Peter Wright to Claxton, 27 October 1948; BGS (Plans) to DMOP, 3 November 1948; CGS to Minister, 5 November 1948, LAC, RG 24, acc. 1983-84/215, box 321, f. S-2001-1999/0, vol. 1.

63 Bernd Horn, *Bastard Sons: An Examination of Canada's Airborne Experience, 1942-1995* (St. Catharines, ON: Vanwell, 2001), 76-77. See also Stephen Harris, "'Really a Defile throughout

Its Length': The Defence of the Alaska Highway in Peacetime," in *Alaska Highway: Papers of the 40th Anniversary Symposium,* ed. Kenneth Coates, 122-23, and Sean Maloney, "The Mobile Striking Force and Continental Defence, 1948-1955," *Canadian Military History* 2, 2 (1993): 75-88.

64 Horn, *Bastard Sons,* 77.

65 "Defence of Canada Interim Emergency Plan: Canadian Rangers," Appendix H, 30 June 1948, and "Defence of Canada Emergency Plan," Appendix A, 11 August 1948, DHH, 112.3M2(D10). On Ranger reconnaissance support for the Mobile Striking Force, see "Appreciation on the Employment of the Active Force Brigade Group in the Defence of Canada," 7 November 1949, DHH, 112.3M2(D400).

66 Foulkes to Minister, 5 November 1948, LAC, RG 24, acc. 1983-84/215, box 321, f. S-2001-1999/0, vol. 1.

67 Vokes to Foulkes, 9 December 1948, LAC, RG 24, vol. 2441, f. 604-18, vol. 2. This thinking was not unique. When "Anglos" arrived in the James Bay region to deliver education, health, and welfare programs in the early 1950s, anthropologist Willard Walker observed that they tended to be of two minds when it came to Aboriginal people: they were either "good men in the bush" but "dirty, lousy, lazy and cruel to animals" or "innocent children, deserving the spiritual and material patronage of whites." See "Acculturation of the Great Whale River Cree" (master's thesis, University of Arizona, 1953), 17. See also Toby Morantz, *The White Man's Gonna Getcha: The Colonial Challenge to the Crees in Quebec* (Montreal/Kingston: McGill-Queen's University Press, 2002), 246-47.

68 Vokes to Foulkes, 9 December 1948. In marginalia dated 13 December 1948, the vice chief of the general staff concurred with Vokes that the Rangers should not be organized in Central Command. For an introduction to Aboriginal service during the world wars, see Fred Gaffen, *Forgotten Soldiers* (Penticton, BC: Theytus Books, 1985); Janice Summerby, *Native Soldiers, Foreign Battlefields* (Ottawa: Veterans Affairs Canada, 1993); and P. Whitney Lackenbauer, James Moses, Scott Sheffield, and Maxime Gohier, *A Commemorative History of Aboriginal People in the Canadian Military* (Ottawa: Department of National Defence, 2010). Planners worried that Central Command's lack of interest would leave a major gap in the "intelligence screen" along southern James Bay, but they decided that the army could form a company in the area later, placing it under Prairie or Quebec Command and taking advantage of the lessons learned elsewhere. Accordingly, Central Command passed along offers of Ranger service to the other commands. See, for example, Major G.B. Green to Directorate of Military Intelligence, 7 May 1948, LAC, RG 24, vol. 2441, f. 604-18, vol. 2.

69 Morton to CGS, 17 December 1948, LAC, RG 24, vol. 2441, f. 604-18, vol. 2.

70 J.J. Honigmann, "An Episode in the Administration of the Great Whale River Eskimo," *Human Organization* 10, 2 (1951): 5-14.

71 Morton to CGS, 17 December 1948. In this letter, Morton proposed inviting missionaries of various denominations to serve as honorary chaplains, given their travel throughout Ranger country. Morton believed that "most missionaries would look forward to service in the Rangers and ... their experience in the North country and their knowledge of various native languages would be an asset." National Defence headquarters shot down this proposal without explaining why. Brig.-Gen. Kitching to Quebec Command, 13 May 1949, LAC, RG 24, vol. 2441, f. 604-18, vol. 2.

72 Morton to DMOP, 7 December 1948, LAC, RG 24, vol. 2441, f. 604-18, vol. 2.

73 BGS (Plans) to CGS, 7 February 1949; "Summary of Quebec Command Submission," Enclosure 2 to HQC 604-18TD 15, 31 January 1949, DHH, 112.3M2(D49), vol. 3.

74 Foster to Army HQ, 23 November 1948, LAC, RG 24, vol. 2441, f. 604-18, vol. 2. There was no thought of establishing Rangers on Prince Edward Island. The island was thoroughly cultivated and did not possess any industrial targets to entice saboteurs.

75 BGS (Plans) to CGS, 7 February 1949, DHH, 112.3M2(D49), vol. 3.

76 Dare to GOC, 15 December 1948, DHH, 327.009(D205).

77 Maj.-Gen. M.H.S. Penhale to Foulkes, 30 December 1948, DHH, 327.009(D205).

78 Ibid. When the Canadian Rangers armband finally appeared in March 1949, Penhale sent "the first exhibit off the press, so to speak," to his friend Worthington. Penhale to Worthington, 24 March 1949, LAC, MG 31-G21, M.H.S. Penhale fonds, vol. 1, f. "Correspondence – Western Command and Personal, 1947-1949."

79 Penhale to Worthington, 8 March 1949, LAC, MG 31-G21, vol. 1, f. "Correspondence – Western Command and Personal, 1947-1949."

80 Penhale to GSO I, n.d. (ca. December 1948 to January 1949), DHH, 327.009(D205).

81 Ibid.

82 Woolgar to Penhale, 22 April 1949, and reply, 25 April 1949; Douthwaite to Penhale, 9 May 1949, DHH, 327.009(D205).

83 Douthwaite, "Survey of Western Arctic: Establishing Cdn Rangers, 14 Apr–1 May 49," 25 October 1950, LAC, RG 24, acc. 1983-84/215, box 399, f. S-9105-25/0; Penhale to Army HQ, 18 June 1949; Douthwaite to Chief of Staff, 16 August 1949, DHH, 327.009(D96). Working with Canon J.W. Webster at Coppermine, Maj. Douthwaite also produced topographical intelligence reports, which the Joint Intelligence Bureau used. Col. R. Rowley to Joint Intelligence Bureau, 24 June 1950, DHH, 112.3M2(D49), vol. 3.

84 Penhale to F.A. McCall, 18 June 1949, DHH, 327.009(D96).

85 Douthwaite to GOC, 14 May 1949, DHH, 327.009(D205); Penhale to Frank Willock, 20 June 1949, DHH, 327.009(D96). Imperial Oil's Toronto office pledged to help establish a Ranger company. K.M. Mackenzie to Douthwaite, 10 May 1949, DHH, 327.009(D96). On Port Radium and Eldorado, see Robert Bothwell, *Eldorado: Canada's National Uranium Company* (Toronto: University of Toronto Press, 1984). The primary documents also refer to *Fort Radium*, but I have adopted *Port Radium* for consistency.

86 DMOP to BGS (Plans), 16 April 1951; DMOP to DCGS, 29 May 1951, DHH, 112.3M2(D49), vol. 3. Previous policy had limited the Rangers' equipment to rifles. Similar to Port Radium, the Department of Transport installations at Yellowknife made that community "a vital forward base," and the thirty-five Rangers in the local platoon received training to defend the area in case of emergency. They made arrangements to store their Bren and Sten guns in the local Reserve Force armoury. Hitsman, "Canadian Rangers," 16.

87 GOC, Western Command to DMOP, 7 April 1951, 7 June 1951; CGS to GOC, Western Command, 29 May 1951, 21 June 1951, LAC, RG 24, acc. 1983-84/215, vol. 321, f. 2001-1999/0, vol. 2.

88 G.W. Rowley to Maj. H.E.C. Price, 5 November 1949, DHH, 112.3M2(D49), vol. 3.

89 Lt.-Col. A.H. Lowe to Price, 24 November 1949, 13 December 1949; reply, 30 November 1949, DHH, 112.3M2(D49), vol. 3.

90 MO 2, G 2 to DMOP, 29 December 1949, DHH, 112.3M2(D49), vol. 3.

91 Rowsell to Records Officer, Montreal, 20 February 1950, DHH, 324.009(D461).

92 Brig.-Gen. Walsh to GOC, Western Command, 16 September 1947, DHH, 327.009(D205).

93 Dare to Capt. C.H. Chapman, 8 February 1949, DHH, 327.04(D1), vol. 1.

94 Two Rangers (together with military personnel with the North West Highway System) were involved in rescuing the crew of an aircraft which crashed off the highway north and east of Haines Junction. Both were North West Highway System employees and their normal pay continued during this activity. Brig H.W. Love to Western Command HQ, 22 September 1953, DHH, 327.049(D2).

95 Lt.-Col. L.A. Gagnon to DMOP, 3 April 1950, RG 24, acc. 1983-84/215, vol. 321, f. 2001-1999/0, vol. 2.

96 Simonds to Maj.-Gen. C.B. Price, 5 April 1948, DHH, 112.3M2(D49), vol. 2.

97 Reserve Militia–Canadian Rangers, 2 February 1950, DHH, 112.3M2(D49), vol. 3.

98 Bercuson, *True Patriot,* 177.

99 Penhale to Worthington, 3 May 1948, LAC, MG 31-G21, vol. 1, f. "Correspondence – Western Command and Personal, 1947-1949"; Weeks to GOC, Western Command, 30 April 1948; Worthington to GOC, Western Command, 10 May 1948, DHH, 000.9(D125); "Worthington Heads Canadian Rangers," *Toronto Daily Star,* 21 May 1948, 2. Worthington's association with the Rangers also contributed to his selection as the minister's civil defence coordinator in October 1948. See Andrew Burtch, *Give Me Shelter: The Failure of Canada's Cold War Civil Defence* (Vancouver: UBC Press, 2012).

100 Worthington received two responses. Captain Chapman in Dawson recommended that the army should liaise with US military officials in Alaska. His unit, still waiting for rifles, hoped to acquire radios. Captain Woolgar in Yellowknife remained completely in the dark about what to do. Worthington to Claxton, January 1949, quoted in Hitsman, "Canadian Rangers," 14. Worthy still held the appointment of honorary colonel commandant of the Canadian Rangers when his biography appeared in 1961. "Much to his regret, the remoteness of their posts has prevented him from visiting them." Worthington, *"Worthy,"* 207.

101 BGS (Plans) to CGS, 7 February 1949, DHH, 112.3M2(D49), vol. 3.

102 George Kitching, *Mud and Green Fields: The Memoirs of General George Kitching* (St. Catharines, ON: Vanwell, 1986), 248-49.

103 BGS (Plans) to VCGS, 29 June 1949, DHH, 112.3M2(D49), vol. 3.

104 Col. J.E.C. Pangman to BGC (Plans), 19 May 1949, DHH, 112.3M2(D49), vol. 3.

105 By June, the VCGS had conceded that he would consider specific requests on their respective merits. See CGS to GOC, Quebec Command, 20 May 1949, LAC, RG 24, acc. 1983-84/215, vol. 321, f. 2001-1999/0 vol. 2; Hitsman, "Canadian Rangers," 14.

Chapter 4: The Formative Years, 1950-52

1 House of Commons, *Debates (Hansard),* 9 June 1950, 3416-20.

2 George Kitching, *Mud and Green Fields: The Memoirs of General George Kitching* (St. Catharines, ON: Vanwell, 1986), 249.

3 David Bercuson, *True Patriot: The Life of Brooke Claxton, 1898-1960* (Toronto: University of Toronto Press, 1993), 195.

4 David Bercuson, "'A People So Ruthless as the Soviets': Canadian Images of the Cold War and the Soviet Union, 1946-1950," in *Canada and the Soviet Experiment: Essays on Canadian Encounters with Russia and the Soviet Union, 1900-1991,* ed. David Davies (Waterloo, ON: Centre on Foreign Policy and Federalism, 1991), 98.

5 David Bercuson, "Canada, NATO, and Rearmament, 1950-1954," in *Making a Difference? Canada's Foreign Policy in a Changing World Order,* ed. John English and Norman Hillmer (Toronto: Lester Publishing, 1992), 106-7; James Eayrs, *In Defence of Canada,* vol. 3, *Peacemaking and Deterrence* (Toronto: University of Toronto Press, 1972) and vol. 4, *Growing Up Allied* (Toronto: University of Toronto Press, 1980); and Bercuson, *True Patriot,* 206, 227.

6 "Defence of Canada Forces," 16 May 1950, 6, 9, Department of National Defence (DND), Directorate of History and Heritage (DHH), 112.3M2(D363).

7 Military Operations (MO) 2 to Director of Military Operations and Plans (DMOP), 4 January 1950; extract from Minutes of CGS Conference with General Officers Commanding (GOC), 9 January 1950, DHH, 112.3M2(D49), vol. 3.

8 G.R. Stevens, "Mr. Claxton's Rangers," *Montreal Daily Star,* 23 June 1950.

9 Draft letter, Minister of National Defence to G.R. Stevens, July 1950, Library and Archives Canada (LAC), RG 24, Department of National Defence, acc. 1983-84/215, vol. 321, f. 2001-1999/0, vol. 2.

10 Bercuson, "A People So Ruthless," 98-99.

11 Col. R. Rowley to Col. E.C. Brown, 9 February 1950, LAC, RG 24, acc. 1983-84/215, box 399, f. S-9105-25/0.

12 Rowley to Col. M.L. DeRome, 9 February 1950, LAC, RG 24, acc. 1983-84/215, box 399, f. S-9105-25/0.

13 Director, Joint Intelligence Bureau to Director Military Intelligence, 20 December 1949, LAC, RG 24, acc. 1983-84/215, box 399, f. S-9105-25/0.

14 Defence coordinator, 6 February 1950, LAC, RG 24, acc. 1983-84/215, box 399, f. S-9105-25/0.

15 On Worthington's excitement about the Rangers' contributions, see F.F. Worthington to Maj.-Gen. M.H.S. Penhale, 8 February 1950, LAC, MG 31-G21, M.H.S. Penhale fonds, vol. 1, f. "Correspondence – Western Command Military Exercises, 1950."

16 Air Vice Marshall F.R. Millar to Chief of the General Staff (CGS), 16 October 1951, LAC, RG 24, acc. 1983-84/215, box 399, f. S-9105-25/0.

17 Clipping in National Archives and Record Administration, RG 59, State Department, Permanent Joint Board on Defence, box 5, f. "Observer Corps – Warning System PJBD 1950."

18 Maj.-Gen. M.H.S. Penhale to Worthy, 14 February 1950, LAC, MG 31-G21, vol. 1, f. "Correspondence – Western Command Military Exercises, 1950." See also G.R. Pearkes to CCOS, 17 November 1958, DHH, 86/29. Penhale emphasized that this role would require reliable communications (radios), and Claxton intimated "some degree of financial support," but it was never delivered.

19 Lt.-Col. R.L. Houston to Chief of Staff, Prairie Command, 6 December 1950, DHH, 326.042(D3); General Officer Commanding Western Command to Army HQ, 18 October 1950, 26 December 1950; DMOP to Brigadier, General Staff (Plans) and marginalia, 26 January 1951, LAC, RG 24, acc. 1983-84/215, vol. 321, f. 2001-1999/0, vol. 2; DMOP to Vice Chief of the General Staff (VCGS), 24 July 1951, 112.3M2(D49), vol. 3. On authorizations and restructuring efforts through 1951, see J.M. Hitsman, "The Canadian Rangers," Army Historical Section Report No. 92, 1 December 1960, 12-13.

20 The Winnipeg Electric Company applauded the Rangers' help in protecting electric utilities and promised full cooperation. E.V. Caton to Morton, 3 November 1950, DHH, 326.042(D3).

21 Capt. E.D. McTavish to Chief of Staff, Winnipeg, 18 January 1952, DHH, 326.042(D3). On fears of communist subversion, see Reg Whitaker and Gary Marcuse, *Cold War Canada: The Making of a National Insecurity State, 1945-1957* (Toronto: University of Toronto Press, 1994) and Richard Cavell, ed., *Love, Hate, and Fear in Canada's Cold War* (Toronto: University of Toronto Press, 2004).

22 David Scandrett, "Gilbert George Faries," *Globe and Mail,* 23 March 2000; David Scandrett, telephone interview with author, 4 April 2012. See also Cecil Chabot, "Métis or Halfbreed or Whatever You Want to Call It" (paper presented at 7th European Social Science History Conference, Lisbon, Portugal, March 2008).

23 Acting GOC, Prairie Command to Army HQ, 27 April 1951, and reply, CGS to GOC, 3 May 1951, LAC, RG 24, acc. 1983-84/215, vol. 321, f. 2001-1999/0, vol. 2. The RCAF refused the army's requests for support in organizing efforts in Prairie Command. CGS to CAS, 9 July 1952, and reply, 18 July 1952, LAC, RG 24, acc. 1983-84/215, box 319, f. 2001-1999/0, vol. 5.

24 DMOP to Deputy Chief of the General Staff (DCGS) and marginalia, 17 May 1951; CGS to GOC, Prairie Command, 23 May 1951, LAC, RG 24, acc. 1983-84/215, vol. 321, f. 2001-1999/0, vol. 3. Cobb completely reorganized the Rangers in that command the next spring. Col. G.A. Turcot to Pers (Res), 22 October 1952, LAC, RG 24, acc. 1983-84/215, vol. 321, f. 2001-1999/0, vol. 4.

25 BGS (Plans) to CGS, 7 February 1949, DHH, 112.3M2(D49) vol. 3; Penhale to Army HQ, 18 October 1950, LAC, RG 24, acc. 1983-84/215, box 321, f. S-2001-1999/0, pt. 2. On Woolgar's

activities in early 1951, including successful recruiting at the Northwest Territories' forest warden meeting in Fort Smith, see DHH, 327.04(D1), vol. 1.

26 DMOP to VCGS, 20 September 1950; DMOP to CGS, 21 December 1950, DHH, 112.3M2(D49), vol. 3; BGS (Plans) to DGAP, 27 March 1951, LAC, RG 24, acc. 1983-84/167, vol. 4975, f. 3201-1999/0, vol. 2. On Penhale's relationship with Woolgar, see LAC, MG 31-G21, vol. 1, f. "Correspondence – Western Command Military Exercises, 1950."

27 "Newfoundland," *Canadian Army Journal* 2, 4 (1948): 27.

28 Kevin Major, *As Near to Heaven as by Sea: A History of Newfoundland and Labrador* (Toronto: Penguin, 2001), 375. See also J.N. Cardoulis, *A Friendly Invasion: The American Military in Newfoundland, 1940-1990, Volume 1* (St. John's, NL, 1990).

29 Quoted in John Parsons, *Probably without Equal: Frank Mercer and the Newfoundland Rangers – An Anthological Study* (Shearstown, NL: Grassy Pond Publishing, 2003), 78-79.

30 "Newfoundland," 30.

31 C.P. Stacey, *Six Years of War* (Ottawa: Queen's Printer, 1957), 180; G.W.L. Nicholson, *More Fighting Newfoundlanders: A History of Newfoundland's Fighting Forces in the Second World War* (St. John's: Government of Newfoundland and Labrador, 1969), 519-57; Darrin McGrath, Robert Smith, Ches Parsons, and Norman Crane, *The Newfoundland Rangers* (St. John's: DRC Publishing, 2005), 5; "Aircraft Detection Corps," 1944, Air Force HQ History, vol. 2, DHH, 80/395, A-12.

32 Major, *As Near to Heaven*, 374, 401.

33 David Bercuson, "SAC vs. Sovereignty: The Origins of the Goose Bay Lease, 1946-52," *Canadian Historical Review* 70, 2 (1989): 206-22.

34 On American interest in the Rangers, see Maj. J.R. Roberts to Nfld. Area Commander, 26 August 1950, DHH, 323.009(D94), and Capt. A.J. Shea to Nfld. Area Commander, 1 May 1951, DHH, 323.009(D96).

35 Major Roberts, "Report on a Visit to Northern Newfoundland and Labrador Carried Out by GSO II Nfld Area," 25 August 1950, and "Proposed Platoons in Nfld/Labrador," August 1950, LAC, RG 24, acc. 1983-84/215, box 321, f. S-2001-1999/0, pt. 1; list of platoon commanders ca. June 1951, DHH, 323.009(D96); "Recommendation for Appointment," Grubb, Frederick Charles Paul, 1 September 1950, DHH, 323.009(D95).

36 Roberts, "Report on a Visit to Northern Newfoundland and Labrador."

37 Ibid.

38 Confidential, GOC, Eastern Command to Army HQ, 15 January 1951, LAC, RG 24, acc. 1983-84/215, vol. 321, f. 2001-1999/0, vol. 2.

39 DMOP to VCGS, re: Cdn Rangers, 20 January 1951, LAC, RG 24, acc. 1983-84/215, vol. 321, f. 2001-1999/0, vol. 2.

40 Roberts for Dunn to Eastern Command, 22 February 1951, DHH, 323.009(D94). His date of birth is noted in Lt.-Col. E.W.H. Berwick to Eastern Command, 1 June 1955, DHH, 232.009(D150).

41 Brig. M.S. Dunn to Eastern Command, 1 June 1951, LAC, RG 24, acc. 1983-84/215, box 321, f. S-2001-1999/0, vol. 3. On communication systems, road and rail networks, and sea access, see Shea to Area Commander Nfld., 20 December 1951, DHH, 323.009(D96). On limitations to access, see also Dunn to Maj. J.R. McLaughlin, 27 February 1951, DHH, 323.009(D94).

42 Untitled list of Ranger officers, ca. June 1950, and Shea's reports on organizational tours, DHH, 323.009(D96). Along the way, Shea also reported on the "disquieting" presence of Jehovah's Witnesses in Newfoundland and their "pacifist and near-subversive nature." Shea to Newfoundland Area Commander, 3 May 1951, DHH, 323.009(D96).

43 Shea, "Report on Second Liaison Visit to Lewisporte, Notre Dame Bay," 1 May 1951; Shea, "Report on Liaison Visit to Clarenville, Newfoundland," 1 May 1951; Shea to Nfld. Area Commander, 25 June 1951, DHH, 323.009(D96).

44 Shea to Area Commander, 13 June 1951, DHH, 323.009(D96). On Cashin, see Diane P. Janes, "Cashin, Maj. Peter J.," in *Encyclopedia of Newfoundland and Labrador,* vol. 1, ed. Joseph R. Smallwood (St. John's: Newfoundland Book Publishers, 1967), 380-81.

45 Shea to Maj. J.R. McLaughlin, 21 September 1951, DHH, 323.009(D94).

46 Ibid.

47 Shea to Area Commander, Nfld. Area, 4 September 1951, 29 December 1951, DHH, 323.009(D96); Capt. J. Donnelly, "Quarterly Strength Return – Canadian Rangers, 31 December 1951," DHH, 323.009(D94). Shea learned, after he returned to Newfoundland Area Headquarters, that the director of military operations and plans had visited Eastern Command and explained that the distribution of arms and ammunition was unauthorized but that "it didn't matter!" Shea had assumed that the act of National Defence Headquarters sending rifles to Newfoundland implied authorization to distribute them. He was understandably perplexed. Shea to McLaughlin, 21 September 1951. On the submarine report, see Briefing for CGS, 28 September 1951, DHH, 112.3M2(D49), vol. 3, and Army Halifax to Director of Military Intelligence (DMI), 2 August 1951, LAC, RG 24, acc. 1983-84/215, vol. 321, f. 2001-1999/0, vol. 3. On Frieda, see Fred Gaffen, *Forgotten Soldiers* (Penticton: Theytus Books, 1985), 29.

48 Col. C.H. Cook to DCGS, 2 October 1951; CGS to GOC, Eastern Command, 23 May 1951; DMOP to DCGS, 26 July 195; Acting CGS to GOC, Eastern Command, 28 June 1951, DHH, 112.3M2(D49), vol. 3; Acting CGS to GOC, Eastern Command, 14 June 1951; GOC, Eastern Command to Army HQ, 17 July 1951, 26 July 1951 (and marginalia), LAC, RG 24, acc. 1983-84/215, vol. 321, f. 2001-1999/0, vol. 3. Based on Roberts's preliminary reconnaissance of Labrador in mid-1950, Canadian Ranger platoons were not given any responsibility for the Lake Melville area or the eastern approaches to Goose Bay. The large number of Canadian and American military personnel in the area would provide for their own security. "Report on a Visit," 25 August 1950.

49 Lt.-Col. T.A. Taylor to Maj.-Gen. W.H.S. Macklin, 25 April 1951, LAC, RG 24, acc. 1983-84/167, vol. 4975, f. 3201-1999/0, vol. 2. See also Taylor to Worthington, 24 April 1951, LAC, RG 24, acc. 1983-84/215, vol. 321, f. 2001-1999/0, vol. 3.

50 Col. E.C. Brown to Chief of Staff, Western Command, 26 April 1951, DHH, 327.049(D2).

51 Brown to Chief of Staff, Western Command, 26 April 1951, DHH, 327.049(D2); VCGS to Western Command, 30 April 1951, LAC, RG 24, acc. 1983-84/167, vol. 4975, f. 3201-1999/0, vol. 2; Vokes to VCGS, 30 April and 9 May 1951, and reply from Simonds, 3 May 1951, LAC, RG 24, acc. 1983-84/215, vol. 321, f. 2001-1999/0, vol. 2; Worthington to DMOP, 21 May 1951, and reply, 21 May 51, LAC, RG 24, acc. 1983-84/215, vol. 321, f. 2001-1999/0, vol. 3.

52 Taylor to Commander BC Area, 23 August 1951, DHH, 327.04(D1), vol. 1; GOC, Western Command to DMOP, 10 October 1951, LAC, RG 24, acc. 1983-84/215, vol. 321, f. 2001-1999/0, vol. 4. On BC reactions to his proposals, see "Defence Role Seen for Coast Rangers," *Victoria Colonist,* 20 May 1951, and "Good Chance for Rangers to Be Re-formed in B.C.," *Victoria Colonist,* 22 May 1951. Western Command was authorized to recruit 2,600 Rangers, 500 of whom were designated for Yukon and Northwest Territories.

53 Taylor to Commander BC Area, 23 August 1951.

54 DMOP to DCGS, 17 October 1951, LAC, RG 24, acc. 1983-84/215, box 321, f. S-2001-1999/0, vol. 3; Brown to HQ Western Command, 27 August 1951 and Acting CGS to GOC, Western Command, 23 October 1951, LAC, RG 24, acc. 1983-84/215, box 321, f. S-2001-1999/0, vol. 4. The intelligence staff officer at Western Command Headquarters who was responsible for the Rangers in Yukon and Northwest Territories also questioned Taylor's plans. Major Douthwaite worried that misguided expansionism in the south would lead the Rangers to fail everywhere. "I am strongly against forming a company or a platoon to [wartime] strengths just for the sake of having the bodies," he stated. If officers recruited the subunits to full strength, the Rangers' interest would quickly dissipate, and they would be ineffective

55 Megill to HQ Western Command, 18 December 1951, DHH, 327.049(D2).

56 Conference – Canadian Rangers – BC, HQ Western Command, 6 November 1951, DHH, 327.009(D207).

57 Ashby to Claxton, 18 December 1951, LAC, RG 24, acc. 1983-84/215, box 321, f. S-2001-1999/0, vol. 3. See other letters from British Columbians in the same file.

58 Minister of National Defence to E.D. Fulton, MP, Kamloops, 12 February 1952, LAC, RG 24, acc. 1983-84/215, box 321, f. 2001-1999/0, vol. 4. On Ashby, see *Driftwood* [Salt Spring Island], 17 November 1960, 2.

59 DMOP to DCGS, 7 February 1952, LAC, RG 24, acc. 1983-84/215, box 321, f. S-2001-1999/0, vol. 3.

60 Brig. W.J. Megill to Maj.-Gen. C. Vokes, 4 March 1952, DHH, 327.049(D2).

61 Megill to HQ Western Command, 18 March 1952, DHH, 327.049(D2).

62 Kenneth Coates and William R. Morrison, *Alaska Highway in World War II: The American Army of Occupation in Canada's Northwest* (Norman: University of Oklahoma Press, 1992), 179-80.

63 Lt.-Col. F.LeP.T. Clifford, "Report on a Visit to Northwest Highway System, 25 August-9 September 1946," 16 September 1946, DHH, 112.3M2(D276). For vivid descriptions of the route, see also Kenneth Coates, *North to Alaska* (Fairbanks: University of Alaska Press, 1992), 10.

64 "The Alaska Highway," 21 July 1949, DHH, 435.009(D43).

65 Stephen J. Harris, "'Really a Defile throughout Its Length': The Defence of the Alaska Highway in Peacetime," in *The Alaska Highway: Papers of the 40th Anniversary Symposium,* ed. Ken Coates (Vancouver, UBC Press, 1985), 121.

66 Ibid., 124-27. See also Sean M. Maloney, "The Mobile Striking Force and Continental Defence, 1948-1955," *Canadian Military History* 2, 2 (1993): 84.

67 The maintenance department operated about twenty small camps along the highway and several "roving crews" that laid gravel and repaired washouts. "The Alaska Highway," 21 July 1949, DHH, 435.009(D43). Civilian traffic on the North West Highway System was by convoy until the road was improved in the mid-1950s.

68 Col. E.C. Brown to Western Command HQ, April 1951, DHH, 327.009(D207).

69 A. Glenn to GOC Western Command, 10 January 1951, DHH, 327.04(D1) vol. 1.

70 Glenn to GOC Western Command, 16 April 1951, 12 May 1951, DHH, 327.04(D1) vol. 1.

71 Glenn to GOC Western Command, 28 May 1951; Douthwaite, memo to file, 4 June 1951; Public meeting held at Hudson's Hope, BC, 23 June 1951; Victor Peck to T.A.H. Taylor, 25 June 1951; K.B. Shaw to Western Command, 4 July 1951, DHH, 327.04(D1), vol. 1; K.B. Shaw to GSO II (Int.) Western Command, 20 October 1951, DHH, 327.04(D1), vol. 2. Ironically, Glenn became a strong convert to the Ranger idea and offered his services as a full-time training officer. The army refused his offer.

72 DCGS to DMOP, 10 June 1953; DMOP, minute to file, 19 June 1953, LAC, RG 24, acc. 1983-84/215, box 322, f. 2001-1999/0, vol. 6.

73 Acting CGS to GOC, Western Command, 9 October 1951; GOC, Western Command to DMOP, and marginalia, 12 November 1951; DCGS to VCGS, 7 December 1951, LAC, RG 24, acc. 1983-84/215, box 319, f. 2001-1999/0, vol. 5; Army HQ, SD 1, Letter no. 4401, 15 January 1952, LAC, RG 24, acc. 1983-84/215, vol. 321, f. 2001-1999/0, vol. 3.

74 Brig. H.W. Love to Western Command HQ, 22 September 1953, DHH, 327.049(D2). During the fall of 1951, when a soldier got lost in the bush north of the North West Highway System Camp at Mile 1202, Rangers with the Highway Maintenance Establishment formed an unpaid search party to find him during their off-duty hours. DHH, 327.049(D2).

75 K.B. Shaw to GSO II (Int.) Western Command, 3 November 1951, DHH, 327.04(D1), vol. 2. At the same time that the Dawson Creek company was created, 15 Company's Headquarters moved to Fort St. John. Joe Galibois was in command. The company had no place to hold lectures or meet, so Major Straubenzee arranged access to the Department of Transport's recreation hall. Maj. C.B. Van Straubenzee to District Controller of Air Service, 19 August 1953, DHH, 327.049(D2). Captain Galibois had recruited seventy Rangers in Fort St. John by mid-1952. "Part II Orders: No. 15 Company, Canadian Rangers, 14 June 1952," DHH, 328.009(D3).

76 Love to GSO II (Int.) Western Command, 7 October 1952, DHH, 328.009(D3). From the perspective of officials with the North West Highway System, Ranger service benefitted civilian employees because they could carry arms "and add to our meagre protective measures while continuing their normal highway work." Love to GSO II (Int.) Western Command, 7 October 1952, DHH, 328.009(D3).

77 Some head highway officials feared that, in the case of emergency, Ranger duties would interfere with normal maintenance operations. Emery found that these officials did "not lend the support that they would otherwise." As it stood, most of the "officer material" along the route occupied themselves fully with maintenance duties and were uninterested in the Rangers. Capt. W.M. Emery to Maj. C.B. Van Straubenzee, 5 December 1952, DHH, 328.009(D3).

78 Love to HQ Western Command, 28 January 1953, 23 October 1953; Love, "Reorganization Canadian Rangers," 6 November 1953, DHH, 327.009(D207); Van Straubenzee to Commander, North West Highway System, 19 August 1953, DHH, 328.009(D3); Capt. Galibois to HQ North West Highway System et al., 21 November 1953; Love to Command Record Officer, Western Command, 29 December 1953, DHH, 327.04(D1), vol. 3; GOC, Western Command to DMOP, 12 May 1953; CGS to Minister of National Defence, 23 July 1953, and GOC, Western Command to DMOP, 25 January 1954, LAC, RG 24, acc. 1983-84/215, vol. 322, f. 2001-1999/0, vol. 6.

79 Van Straubenzee to Maj. Claire White, 19 August 1953, DHH, 328.009(D3). On Mayo in this era, see Mayo Historical Society, *Gold and Galena: A History of the Mayo District* (Mayo, BC: Mayo Historical Society, 1990) and Aaro E. Aho, *Hills of Silver: The Yukon's Mighty Keno Hill Mine* (Madeira Park, BC: Lost Moose, 2006).

80 Lt.-Col. G.J.H. Wattsford, "The Strategic Importance of Canada," *Canadian Army Journal* 2, 4 (1948): 18.

81 See Gordon W. Smith, "Weather Stations in the Canadian North and Sovereignty," *Journal of Military and Strategic Studies* 11, 3 (2009): 2-7.

82 See, for example, Melanie Gagnon and Iqaluit Elders, *Inuit Recollections on the Military Presence in Iqaluit* (Iqaluit: Nunavut Arctic College, 2002), and P. Whitney Lackenbauer and Ryan Shackleton, "When the Skies Rained Boxes: The Air Force and the Qikiqtani Inuit, 1941-64," Working Papers on Arctic Security No. 4, Munk-Gordon Arctic Security Program and the ArcticNet Emerging Arctic Security Environment Project, Toronto, October 2012.

83 See Shelagh Grant, *Sovereignty or Security: Government Policy in the Canadian North, 1936-1950* (Vancouver: UBC Press, 1988) and P. Whitney Lackenbauer and Peter Kikkert, "Sovereignty and Security: The Department of External Affairs, the United States, and Arctic Sovereignty, 1945-68," in *In the National Interest: Canadian Foreign Policy and the Department of Foreign Affairs and International Trade, 1909-2009*, ed. Greg Donaghy and Michael Carroll (Calgary: University of Calgary Press, 2011), 101-20.

84 G.W. Smith, "The Transfer of Arctic Territories from Great Britain to Canada in 1880, and Some Related Matters," *Arctic* (1961), 53-73; Janice Cavell and Jeff Noakes, *Acts of Occupation: Canada and Arctic Sovereignty, 1918-25* (Vancouver: UBC Press, 2010).

85 Flight Lieutenant S.E. Alexander to AMOT, 7 January 1950, LAC, RG 24, vol. 5205, f. S-15-24-60. On Alexander's experiences, see "The Voyage of the 'Snowbird II,'" *Arctic* 2, 2 (1949): 91-97.

86 Alexander to AMOT, 7 January 1950. See also Alfred Johnson Brooks, House of Commons, *Debates (Hansard)*, 8 June 1950, 3404; 9 June 1950, 3408. Brooke Claxton explained to the House of Commons on 9 June 1950 that his government did not intend to give Inuit and Indians in the Far North "military training because in the nature of their living conditions they are fully occupied with survival." He explained, however, that Aboriginal people were "working very closely indeed with the armed forces in the north, and have been used extensively in transportation, construction, and the like. We have also borrowed to a great extent from their knowledge of northern living conditions, the first thing that forces operating in the north must learn." *Debates*, 3410. All of these considerations fit within the Rangers concept.

87 Charles Hendricks, "The Eskimos and the Defense of Alaska," *Pacific Historical Review* 54, 3 (1985): 271-95. See also Muktuk Marston, *Men of the Tundra: Alaska Eskimos at War* (New York: October House, 1969), and Lt.-Col. Thomas O. Blakely, "The Security of Alaska and the Tundra Army," *Military Review* 32 (1952): 3-12.

88 Col. N.T. Norris to Brig. H.E. Taber, 1 February 1952, LAC, RG 24, acc. 1983-84/215, vol. 321, f. 2001-1999/0, vol. 3.

89 Norris to Taber, 1 February 1952.

90 Blakely, "The Security of Alaska and the Tundra Army," 8.

91 Diamond Jenness, *Eskimo Administration: II* (Montreal: Arctic Institute of North America, 1964), 79.

92 See James Cantley, *Economic Report on Eskimo Affairs* (Ottawa: Department of Resources and Development, 1950).

93 R. Quinn Duffy, *The Road to Nunavut: The Progress of the Eastern Arctic Inuit since the Second World War* (Montreal/Kingston: McGill-Queen's University Press, 1988), 135.

94 Maj.-Gen. E.C. Plow to Army HQ, 5 May 1951, LAC, RG 24, acc. 1983-84/215, vol. 321, f. 2001-1999/0, vol. 2; Simonds to Plow, 5 May 1951, DHH, 112.3M2(D49), vol. 3.

95 Maj. F.B. Perrott to DMOP, 11 July 1951, LAC, RG 24, acc. 1983-84/215, box 321, f. 2001-1999/0, vol. 2. After Shea met in Labrador with James Houston and his wife (the pair were proceeding north to survey the "art and industry of the Northern Esquimaux"), he also requested their help. Shea to Assistant Adjutant and Quartermaster General, n.d., DHH, 323.009(D94).

96 Cook to DCGS, 11 July 1951, and reply, 12 July 1951, LAC, RG 24, acc. 1983-84/215, box 321, f. 2001-1999/0, vol. 2; Cook to Stevenson, 2 August 1951, DHH, 112.3M2(D49), vol. 3.

97 CGS to GOC, Eastern Command, 3 August 1951, DHH, 112.3M2(D49), vol. 3; CGS, SD 1, Letter no. 4307, 21 August 1951, LAC, RG 24, acc. 1983-84/215, vol. 321, f. 2001-1999/0, vol. 2.

98 Cook to Directorate of Staff Duties, 2 August 1951, LAC, RG 24, acc. 1983-84/215, box 321, f. 2001-1999/0, vol. 2; CGS to GOC, Eastern Command, 16 November 1951; CGS to R.H. Chesshire, 2 January 1952, and reply, 4 January 1952, LAC, RG 24, acc. 1983-84/215, vol. 321, f. 2001-1999/0, vol. 3; Shea to J.W. Anderson, 17 November 1952, DHH, 323.009(D95).

99 GOC, Eastern Command to DMOP, 17 April 1952, LAC, RG 24, acc. 1983-84/215, box 319, f. 2001-1999/0, vol. 5.

100 Eastern Command Operation Instruction no. 2, 19 May 1952, LAC, RG 24, acc. 1983-84/215, box 321, f. 2001-1999/0, vol. 4.

101 Army Engagement or Attestation Form for Peterloosie, 8 September 1952, copy courtesy of Capt. Conrad Schubert, 1 Canadian Ranger Patrol Group; Canadian Press, "Ranger Retires after 52 Years," 3 November 2004; Capt. Joanna Campbell, "Longest-Serving Canadian Forces Member Retires," CFNA News Details, 8 March 2005; "News Notes: Guardian,"

Maclean's, 15 November 2004. On Wilkinson's role, see Col. G.A. Turcot to Eastern Command HQ, 3 February 1953, LAC, RG 24, acc. 1983-84/215, box 319, f. 2001-1999/0, vol. 5. Wilkinson published an account of his year-long stay at an Inuit camp on northern Baffin Island as *The Land of the Long Day* (Toronto: Clarke Irwin, 1955) and worked as a northern service officer in the region until 1958.

102 Brooke Claxton, *Debates (Hansard)*, 25 May 1951, 3430-1.

103 Reserve Militia – Canadian Rangers, 2 February 1950, DHH, 112.3M2(D49), vol. 3; strength returns in LAC, RG 24, acc. 1983-84/215, box 321, f. S-2001-1999/0, vol. 4.

104 *Debates (Hansard)*, 8 April 1952, 1230-1.

105 Ottawa clarified official policy so that the Rangers would not have "responsibility for planning or directing local defence." Canadian Army Policy Statement no. 86, 6 December 1951, DHH, 000.1(D35).

Chapter 5: Exercising the Rangers, 1952-56

1 J. Anderson-Thomson memoirs, "No. 7 Company Canadian Rangers and DEW Line 1954 and 1955," 4-5, copy provided by 1 Canadian Ranger Patrol Group (CRPG). See also Randy Freeman, "Operation Bulldog," *Up Here*, May-June 2000, 53-55. "Yellowknife – Rangers Uphold Tradition," *Canadian Rangers News Letter* 9 (April 1955): 1-2, notes that "Captain Anderson-Thomson had just arrived back in Yellowknife from university to act as umpire, so most of the credit had to go to Lieutenant Red Anderson for his preparations and leadership while the company commander was away." Department of National Defence (DND), Directorate of History and Heritage (DHH), 327.04(D1), vol. 4.

2 Anderson-Thomson, "No. 7 Company," 5-6. See also Lt. C.E. Anderson to Maj. C.B. Van Straubenzee, 12 February 1955, and reply, February 1955, DHH, 327.039(D9).

3 Anderson-Thomson, "No. 7 Company," 6-7.

4 Ibid., 6-9. See also Maj. P.J. Carson, "Report on Exercise Bulldog III," 2 March 1955, DHH, 327.039(D9). In a later article, Anderson-Thomson wrote that "we beat off the invading force so often and so thoroughly that it was farcical." Part 15 in a series on Yellowknife's early days, *Yellowknifer*, 26 October 1983.

5 Prince of Wales Northern Heritage Centre (PWNHC), NWT Archives, Anderson-Thomson fonds, N 1986 012. For another glowing appraisal, see "Yellowknife – Rangers Uphold Tradition," *Canadian Rangers News Letter* 9 (April 1955): 1-2.

6 Anderson-Thomson, "No. 7 Company," 6-9.

7 Desmond Morton, *A Military History of Canada*, 4th ed. (Toronto: McClelland and Stewart, 1999), 238.

8 Bernd Horn, *Bastard Sons: An Examination of Canada's Airborne Experience, 1942-1995* (St. Catharines, ON: Vanwell, 2001), 79, 85.

9 *Victoria Colonist*, 10 September 1958, cited in Kenneth Eyre, "Custos Borealis: The Military in the Canadian North" (PhD diss., University of London, King's College, 1981), 180.

10 Donald Barry, ed., *Documents on Canadian External Relations*, vol. 18, *1952* (Ottawa: External Affairs and International Trade, 1990), 1201-3. In 1954, Canada took over the resupply of all joint Arctic weather stations except Alert. See G.W. Smith, "Weather Stations in the Canadian North and Sovereignty," *Journal of Military and Strategic Studies* 11, 3 (2009): 51-52. HMCS *Labrador* was commissioned into the Royal Canadian Navy in July 1954. J.M. Leeming, "HMCS Labrador and the Canadian Arctic," in *RCN in Retrospect, 1910-1968*, ed. J.A. Boutilier (Vancouver: UBC Press, 1982), 287.

11 Governor General Lord Alexander of Tunis personally asked Anderson-Thomson to assume this role at a meeting of "V.I.P.'s" in Yellowknife. "Ranger Arm Band and Beret of Captain John Anderson-Thomson (1900-1985)," biography from 1 CRPG.

12 John Anderson-Thomson, *Yellowknifer*, 26 October 1983.

13 Anderson-Thomson memoirs, "No. 7 Company," 2.

14 Ibid., 3. On Ranger contributions to local defence plans, see Maj. Van Straubenzee to officer commanding, 24 Field Squadron RCE, 28 January 1955, DHH, 327.039(D9).

15 Anderson-Thomson memoirs, "No. 7 Company," 4.

16 Anderson-Thomson memoirs, "The Year 1948 to 1953," 15-16; General Staff Officer (GSO) I, Western Command, to Commander, NWT&Y Radio System, 19 August 1953; *Canadian Militia Rangers Liaison Letter* 6 (2 September 1953): 2, DHH, 144.6(D1).

17 Capt. A.J. Shea to Maj. J.R. McLaughlin, 2 April 1952, DHH, 323.009(D96).

18 R.A.J. Phillips, "The Eastern Arctic Patrol," *Canadian Geographical Journal* 54 (May 1957): 9, 12.

19 On Ranger officer employment, see, for example "Notes for Ranger Liaison Sergeant," 20 June 1955, DHH, 323.009(D150). Major Van Straubenzee drew up detailed plans for the Rangers to defend vital installations at Port Radium, NWT. In a rare act of opposition, Eldorado Mining and Refining Company officials feared supporting a robust local defence program with heavy recruiting because they thought it would create alarm and dissuade would-be employees from working there. They consented only to a "nucleus of trusted staff officials" who would "earmark suitable individuals" to serve in a modest Ranger company. W.J. Bennett, the vice-president of Eldorado, was "not prepared to have this [Ranger] platoon carry out any effective training or preparation of defensive positions" because these activities would take away from company priorities. Major-General Vokes, displeased, complied with the request anyway. Van Straubenzee, "Appreciation of the Defence of Port Radium," ca. 1952-53, and Vokes to Army HQ, 13 February 1953, DHH, 327.009(D207); and Bennett, quoted in Robert Bothwell, *Eldorado: Canada's National Uranium Company* (Toronto: University of Toronto Press, 1984), 262.

20 *The Canadian Ranger: Liaison and Training Notes* 10 (December 1955): 6, DHH, 327.009 (D267).

21 Brig. H.W. Love to Western Command HQ, 22 September 1953, DHH, 327.049(D2).

22 Western Command, *Canadian Ranger News Letter* 8 (September 1954): 1, DHH, 327.009(D263). Despite the Rangers' success, headquarters feared that Rangers with no formal military approval, those not sworn in as special constables, would turn out with weapons. Headquarters reminded Rangers that if they "were not called out as soldiers by a competent military authority," they supported the police at their own risk. Vokes to Army HQ, 7 December 1955; Vokes, "Order no. 1: Canadian Ranger Role," ca. December 1955, DHH, 327.04(D1), vol. 4; "Western Command Orders: Canadian Army (Militia Rangers)," 18 June 1956, DHH, 326.009(D171).

23 Cox to Officer Commanding, Ranger HQ, 30 April 1952; Officer in Charge, Criminal Intelligence Branch, RCMP "B" Division, St. John's, Nfld., to Commander, Newfoundland Area (Army), 23 December 1952, and marginalia, DHH, 323.023(D1), vol. 1; Lt. W.S. Moores, TN14575, Cartwright, Labrador, to Ranger Officer, Nfld. Area Command, St. John's, 30 July 52, Library and Archives Canada (LAC), RG 24, DND, acc. 1983-84/215, box 399, f. S-9105-21/0.

24 "Bill" [Moores] to Capt. A.J. Shea, 28 May 1953; Shea to Chief of Staff, Royal Canadian Navy, 8 July 1953, DHH, 323.023(D1), vol. 1.

25 Ranger officers reported an unnamed ship drifting along the Lower North Shore in October 1954, a US transport aircraft that crashed in the Gulf of St. Lawrence in January 1955, and errant weather balloons off Blanc Sablon. See reports in DHH, 323.023(D1), vol. 1; Lt.-Col. P.C.R. Black to HQ, Eastern Command, 28 October 1954; Lt. M. Keeping to Shea, 25 January 1955; F.M. Cox to Shea, 27 January 1955, DHH, 323.023(D1), vol. 2; Annual Report, Canadian Rangers, Quebec Command, 30 September 1956, DHH, 324.009(D511).

26 A.J. Shea, *Canadian Rangers Newsletter* (21 December 1954), DHH, 323.009(D144).

27 *Canadian Militia Rangers Liaison Letter* 6 (2 September 1953): 1, DHH, 144.6(D1).

28 *Canadian Ranger Liaison Letter,* HQ Newfoundland Area, 3 January 1953, DHH, 323.009(D144). Shea was supported by Sergeant P.G. Marriott in 1955 and 1956. Marriott liaised with and resupplied the platoons in Newfoundland and Labrador while Shea went on the Eastern Arctic Patrol. Lt.-Col. W.A. Milroy to Newfoundland Area HQ, 16 November 1955, DHH, 323.009(D150); Milroy to Army HQ, 12 January 1956, DHH, 323.009(D261).

29 *Canadian Ranger Liaison Letter,* 3 January 1953.

30 Brig. G.E.R. Smith to G II (Int.), Eastern Command HQ, 13 November 1953, DHH, 323.023(D1), vol. 1.

31 Shea to GSO II, 23 November 1953, DHH, 323.023(D1), vol. 1.

32 Quebec Command to Canadian Army, 17 December 1952, DHH, 324.009(D512). In 1951, the general officer commanding, Eastern Command, assumed control over the Rangers in all of northeastern Canada, including Quebec. The following year, after responsibility for Mobile Striking Force's planning and operations transferred to Quebec Command, the Ranger liaison officer for Eastern Command complained that he was already overloaded with new responsibilities for Baffin Island. In late September 1952, command of the Rangers in Quebec reverted to Quebec Command. Memo, Vice Chief of the General Staff (VCGS) to Brigadier, General Staff (Plans), 9 March 1951, LAC, RG 24, acc. 1983-84/215, vol. 321, f. 2001-1999/0, vol. 2; Confidential cipher, G Ops, Army Halifax to Army Ottawa, 13 December 1951, LAC, RG 24, acc. 1983-84/215, vol. 321, f. 2001-1999/0, vol. 3; Director of Military Operations and Plans (DMOP) to Deputy CGS, 2 September 1952, LAC, RG 24, acc. 1983-84/215, box 319, f. 2001-1999/0, vol. 5.

33 Maj. P. Templeton to Chief of Staff, 22 March 1955, DHH, 323.023(D1), vol. 2.

34 Annual Report, Canadian Rangers, Quebec Command, 30 September 1956, DHH, 324.009(D511)

35 GOC, Eastern Command to DMOP, 3 February 1954; DMOP to DCGS, 15 April 1954; CGS to Deputy Minister, DND, 30 April 1954, LAC, RG 24, acc. 1983-84/215, vol. 322, f. 2001-1999/0, vol. 6.

36 Maj. P. Templeton to GSO I, Quebec Command, 27 July 1953; Templeton to GOC, Quebec Command, 10 August 1953, DHH, 324.009(D512). The Canadian Forces would implement a "patrol" system for similar reasons in the 1970s.

37 GOC, Quebec Command to DMOP, Army HQ, 30 September 1955, DHH, 328.009(D3); Annual Report, Canadian Rangers, Quebec Command, 30 September 1956, DHH, 324.009(D511).

38 Annual Report, Quebec Command, 30 September 1956. With the exception of Shefferville, there were no Ranger platoons in the Interior, but Templeton saw this as little cause for alarm because "natives, Indian and Eskimo, members of coastal platoons, cover most of the area in their annual hunting and fishing trips."

39 "Unsung Ranger Arctic Warfare Defenders in 'Guerilla Warfare' for Army," *Montreal Gazette,* 13 February 1954.

40 DMOP to DCGS, 20 April 1953, LAC, RG 24, acc. 1983-84/215, box 319, f. 2001-1999/0, vol. 5.

41 "Corr, instructions, reports re org & adm Rgrs," DHH, 327.009(D207). In 1953, Western Command boasted 56 percent of all Rangers, in companies ranging from Tofino to Yellowknife. *Canadian Militia Ranger Liaison Letter* 6 (2 September 1953): 1. By 1954, there was no specific Ranger officer in Prairie Command. The central staff carried out routine Ranger work and called upon Major Van Straubenzee to help when necessary. Col. G.A. Turcot to Worthington, 8 February 1954, LAC, RG 24, acc. 1983-84/215, box 322, f. S-2001-1999/0, vol. 6.

42 Annual Report, Quebec Command, 30 September 1956.

43 *The Rangers News Letter* 7 (1954): 1, DHH, 327.009(D263).

44 Vokes to Commander, BC Area, 30 June 1953, DHH, 327.009(D207).

45 Brig. W.J. Megill to Col. General Staff, Western Command HQ, 16 June 1955, DHH, 327.009(D207).

46 Vokes to Commander, BC Area, 30 June 1953.

47 "Companies in the News," *Canadian Ranger News Letter* 8 (September 1954): 2-4, and Command Canadian Ranger Officer (CCRO), Report on Visits to Canadian Rangers Companies Situated in the Interior of BC – 12-31 July 1954, DHH, 327.009(D267).

48 Maj. C.B. Van Straubenzee, "Thoughts on Training," *Canadian Ranger News Letter* 8 (September 1954): 5-6. Emphasis in original. On strengths and recruiting outlook, see Maj. C.B. Van Straubenzee, Canadian Rangers State Ending 1 June 54, DHH, 327.04(D1), vol. 3.

49 Major S.C. Waters to DMOP, 13 March 1951, LAC, RG 24, acc. 1983-84/167, vol. 4975, f. 3201-1999/0.

50 See "Training - Canadian Rangers," LAC, RG 24, acc. 1983-84/167, vol. 4975, f. 3201-1999/0. The annual training directive for 1952-53 also stated that the Rangers should be given "individual training" in patrolling and reporting, aircraft recognition, map use, field sketching, and ground observer corps duties. Captain Shea thought that the directive confused the Rangers with other parts of the army. Did it imply that every Ranger officer in Eastern Command should be given individual instruction and then "be in a position to pass their knowledge on to their men"? Shea found these expectations unrealistic. Shea to Area Commander, 14 May 1952, DHH, 323.009(D94). Literacy also proved an issue. Lieutenant-Colonel R.E. Nourse noted that some Rangers only spoke "in their native Indian dialect," which "considerably handicaps those charged with Ranger training as well as limiting the usefulness of the individual Ranger." Nourse to DMOP, 27 January 1954, LAC, RG 24, acc. 1983-84/215, box 322, f. S-2001-1999/0, vol. 6.

51 Maj.-Gen. E.C. Plow to Director of Military Training (DMT), 9 July 1952, LAC, RG 24, acc. 1983-84/167, vol. 4975, f. 3201-1999/0.

52 DMOP to DMT, 24 July 1952, and CGS to Eastern Command HQ, 31 July 1952, LAC, RG 24, acc. 1983-84/167, vol. 4975, f. 3201-1999/0.

53 Capt. A.J. Shea, Report on Training Exercise "Ambrose," Phase I (Baffin Island), 5 January 1953, and Training Exercise – Seagull, Phase II: Supplemental Report, 5 May 1954, DHH, 323.009(D148).

54 Col. R.M. Bishop, Canadian Rangers – Western Command, Exercise "Gabriel" I, Exercise Instructions, 5 May 1952, LAC, RG 24, acc. 1983-84/215, box 321, f. S-2001-1990/0, vol. 4.

55 *The Canadian Ranger Liaison Letter* 2 (19 June 1952): 1-2, LAC, RG 24, acc. 1983-84/215, box 321, f. S-2001-1990/0, vol. 4.

56 Detailed Estimate of Possible Enemy Lodgements in Canada, 29 June 1954; Extracts from Chiefs of Staff Committee, Minutes of the 569th Meeting, 2-3 November 1954, 577th Meeting, 22 March 1955, 593rd Meeting, 10 May 1956; Joint Planning Committee to the Chiefs of Staff Committee, "Defence against Enemy Lodgements in Canada," 7 February 1955; 577th Meeting of the Chief of Staff Committee, Item 2, 4 March 1955, DHH, 86/46. The chairman of the chiefs of staff reasoned that thermonuclear weapons used against cities would be much more disruptive and that once a war started there were no targets in northern Canada vital to Canadian defence. Indeed, the chairman speculated "that the significance of enemy lodgements had considerably decreased in the last ten years and, while still possible, was of a lower order of priority than before."

57 Horn, *Bastard Sons,* 80.

58 "Ranger Participation on Exercise Bulldog," *Canadian Militia Rangers Liaison Letter* 6 (2 September 1953): 3-4; and "Exercise 'Bull Dog': Lessons Learned," 119-30, "Lessons Learned, Winter Exercises, 1945-1954," DHH, 81/675. Names and initials from "Quarterly Strength Roster – No. 21 Company, Norman Wells, NWT," 31 March 1954, DHH, 327.04(D1), vol. 3.

59 "Oust Princess Pats, Van Doos Fly 2,000 Miles, Grab Airport," *Toronto Daily Star,* 16 February 1953.

60 Hitsman, "Canadian Rangers"; "Exercise 'Bull Dog': Lessons Learned," 119-30.

61 During Hot Dog II, local skirmishes with 1 Princess Patricia's Canadian Light Infantry along the North West Highway System allowed Rangers to practise their roles at Whitehorse (2 Company), Watson Lake (39 Company), Fort Nelson (38 Company), and Peace River (37 and 15 Companies). Although the idea of Rangers directly attacking an "enemy" of far greater strength was preposterous (and was permitted only to give more Rangers "some experience"), the Rangers learned a valuable lesson – that "in practice positive action would be limited to sniping, ambushing, or attacking much smaller forces using surprise as a main factor." Maj. P.J. Carson, "Report on Ranger Skirmishes, 18-21 Feb 54," DHH, 327.039(D9). See also "Ranger Participation on Ex Hot Dog II," *The Rangers News Letter* 7 (1954): 4-5, DHH, 327.009(D263).

62 They received training in weapons, fire and march discipline, map use and navigating, patrolling, demolition and booby traps, fieldcraft and camouflage, messages and reports, verbal orders, first aid, and camp routine, which they were expected to pass along to their home units. Maj. P.J. Carson to Western Command HQ, 27 February 1954, DHH, 327.039(D9).

63 See LAC, RG 24, vol. 22352, f. S-2001-1999/0, vol. 2; LAC, RG 24, acc. 1983-84/167, box 4975, f. 3201-1999/0.

64 Vokes to Army HQ, September 1954, DHH, 327.039(D9).

65 "Wally" to "Van," January 1955, DHH, 327.04(D1), vol. 4; Capt. W.F. Stott, "North West Highway System Ranger News Letter," 12 January 1955, DHH, 326.009(D171). Highway officials organized sporadic training with individual patrols. See, for example, "Exercise GEORGE," *Canadian Rangers News Letter* 9 (April 1955): 4; "Exercise BAKKE," *Canadian Ranger: Liaison and Training Notes* 10 (December 1955): 7-8; and "Exercise Beaver Dodge," DHH, 327.009(D301).

66 *Canadian Ranger: Liaison and Training Notes* 10 (December 1955): 1-6; Capt. H.C. Taylor, "North West Highway System Annual Service Rifle Competition 1956 – Report," 12 September 1956, DHH, 327.009(D301).

67 Maj. C.B. Van Straubenzee to Capt. H.C. Taylor, 7 September 1956, DHH, 327.009 (D301).

68 The deputy chief of the general staff told Stephenson that the military could not "avail ourselves of this kind offer of [the film] Board for security reasons." William Stephenson to DMOP, 26 February 1953; DMOP to DCGS, 21 May 1953; DCGS to National Film Board, 28 May 1953, LAC, RG 24, acc. 1983-84/215, box 319, f. 2001-1999/0, vol. 5.

69 "Unsung Ranger Arctic Warfare Defenders in 'Guerilla Warfare' for Army," *Montreal Gazette,* 13 February 1954.

70 *Ottawa Citizen,* 22 February 1954; "Exercise 'Loup Garou': Lessons Learned," 144-47, DHH, 81/675. Journalists also noted the mystique of Aboriginal people serving as defenders of their homeland, like Inuk trapper Tuktu during the army exercise Bulldog II in Baker Lake. "Cold War Exercise Fun for Eskimo Trappers," *Globe and Mail,* 13 December 1954. See also Exercise "Bull Dog II," 150-53, "Lessons Learned, Winter Exercises, 1945-1954," DHH, 81/675, and "Canadian Combined Forces Exercise Bulldog II, 1954," *Polar Record* 7, 51 (1955): 492.

71 Jim Senter, "Observer Says New Concept Needed to Ensure Canadians Can Deal Effectively with Invaders," *Hamilton Spectator,* 8 December 1954, quoted in Horn, *Bastard Sons,* 85. See also Bercuson, *True Patriot,* 245, and articles in DHH, 112.3M2.009(D264).

72 Brig. W.J. Megill to Western Command HQ, 14 October 1952, DHH, 327.009(D207).

73 Maj. L. Esmond, "Proposed Long-Range Company for Canadian Northwest," 10 June 1953, DHH, 327.009(D207).

74 See, for example, Canadian Army Policy Statement no. 86, 6 December 1951, DHH, 000.1(D35).

75 J.A. Flynn to R. Campney, 29 January 1955, and Maj. A.E. Smart, "Report on Cowichan Commando," 24 March 1955, LAC, RG 24, acc. 1983-84/215, box 321, f. S-2001-1999/0, vol. 2; Vokes to Army HQ, 13 April 1955, DHH, 327.049(D2); Director of Staff Duties, "The Cowichan Commandos," 20 April 1955, DHH, 112.3S2.003(D4); B. Kennelly to General Staff Section, 1 November 1956, and reply from Vokes, 15 November 1956, LAC, RG 24, acc. 1983-84/215, box 322, f. S-2001-1999/0, vol. 8. On the Cowichan Commandos, see R. Collins, "Jim Flynn's Private Army," *Maclean's,* 5 March 1955, 20-21, 43-46.

76 Kitimat had been a platoon in No. 12 Company. DMOP to DGPO, 26 January 1955; Brig. Moncel to Minister of National Defence, 14 June 1955, DHH, 112.3S2.003(D4).

77 DMOP to DGPO, 16 May 1955; Col. D.B. Buell to AOM, 22 February 1956; Buell to DMOP, 29 February 1956; Brig. G.C. Leech to VCGS, 8 March 1956; Maj.-Gen. N.E. Rodger to GOC, Western Command, 27 March 1956, LAC, RG 24, acc. 1983-84/215, box 322, f. S-2001-1999/0, vol. 7. The army had refused requests for the Rangers to play the role of local defence forces in both Newfoundland and Quebec. See DMOP to DCGS, 9 October 1952; Worthington to CGS, 28 July 1953; DMOP to DCGS, 30 July 1953; Chief of Air Staff to CGS, 2 September 1953; GOC, Quebec Command, to DMOP, 11 September 1953, LAC, RG 24, acc. 1983-84/215, box 319, f. 2001-1999/0, vol. 5.

78 DMOP brief in CAO 246-3 – Canadian Rangers, 25 July 1957, LAC, RG 24, acc. 1983-84/215, box 322, f. S-2001-1999/0, vol. 7. See also Lt.-Col. R.E. Nourse to DMOP, 1 December 1953, RG 24, acc. 1983-84/215, vol. 322, f. 2001-1999/0, vol. 6.

79 CAO 246-3 – Canadian Rangers, 17 February 1954, LAC, RG 24, acc. 1983-84/215, box 322, f. S-2001-1999/0, pt. 6.

80 Maj. P. Templeton to Chief of Staff, 22 March 1955, DHH, 323.023(D1), vol. 2.

81 Templeton to Chief of Staff, 22 March 1955; Templeton to Chief of Staff, Quebec Command, 26 July 1956, and "Canadian Rangers – Quebec Command: Ranger Assistance to MSF," Appendix L to Annual Report, 1956, DHH, 324.009(D511). Templeton flew in to take over the 1955 Ranger Refresher Course in Yellowknife after Major Van Straubenzee reacted to penicillin and had to be airlifted to Edmonton. *Canadian Rangers News Letter* 9 (April 1955): 4, DHH, 327.04(D1), vol. 4.

82 Templeton to Chief of Staff, 22 March 1955.

83 Templeton to Shea, 4 May 1955, DHH, 323.009(D150), vol. 2.

84 Ranger Information Bulletin, Newfoundland Area HQ, 3 June 1955, DHH, 323.023(D1), vol. 2.

85 Templeton to Chief of Staff, 26 July 1956.

86 Horn, *Bastard Sons,* 99.

87 Col. R. Kyle Jr. to Ranger Liaison Officer, Newfoundland Area HQ, 22 June 1954, DHH, 323.023(D1), vol. 1.

88 "Nineteen Years of Air Defense," Historical Reference Paper no. 11, Directorate of Command History, NORAD, Colorado Springs, 1965, 11.

89 Maj. D.H. Thorne, "The Mid-Canada Line," *Canadian Forces Communications and Electronics Newsletter* 1 (1982), 42.

90 Lt.-Col. R.E. Nourse to DMOP, 27 January 1954, LAC, RG 24, acc. 1983-84/215, box 322, f. S-2001-1999/0, vol. 6.

91 Col. G.A. Turcot to Maj.-Gen. F.F. Worthington, 8 February 1954, LAC, RG 24, acc. 1983-84/215, box 322, f. S-2001-1999/0, vol. 6.

92 J. Campbell to Ranger liaison officer, Prairie Command, 18 November 1958, DHH, 326.042(D3).

93 J.J. Honigmann, "Intercultural Relations at Great Whale River," *American Anthropologist* 54, 4 (1952): 512.

94 Annual Report, Canadian Rangers, Quebec Command, 30 September 1956, DHH, 324.009(D511). Cree hunters and trappers benefitted insofar as the unmanned radar sites in

the Interior, never locked, had food stocks to which they helped themselves. Toby Morantz, *The White Man's Gonna Getcha: The Colonial Challenge to the Crees in Quebec* (Montreal/Kingston: McGill-Queen's University Press, 2002), 194.

95 Journalist Lauchie Chisholm, quoted in Diamond Jenness, *Eskimo Administration II: Canada* (Montreal: Arctic Institute of North America, 1964), 95.

96 See P. Whitney Lackenbauer and Matthew Farish, "The Cold War on Canadian Soil: Militarizing a Northern Environment," *Environmental History* 12, 3 (2007): 920-50, and "High Modernism in the Arctic: Planning Frobisher Bay and Inuvik," *Journal of Historical Geography* 35, 3 (2009): 517-44.

97 Richard Morenus, *The DEW Line: Distant Early Warning, the Miracle of America's First Line of Defense* (New York: Rand McNally, 1957), 72.

98 J.D. Brannian, "Siting the DEWline Radar Stations," *Engineering Contract Record* 70, 7 (1955): 53-55, 171-78, 195-211; John Nicholas Harris, "National Defence and Northern Development" (master's thesis, Simon Fraser University, 1980), 89.

99 Joint Intelligence Bureau, Ottawa, Distant Early Warning Line: Military Geography Support Programme (ca. 1955), DHH, 79/82. See also Deputy Minister, DND, to Deputy Minister, Department of Northern Affairs and National Resources, 9 September 1954, LAC, RG 24, acc. 1983-84/215, vol. 399, f. S-9105-21/0.

100 J. Anderson-Thomson, part 16 in a series on Yellowknife's early days, *Yellowknifer*, 2 November 1983, A2; "Ranger Arm Band and Beret of Captain John Anderson-Thomson (1900-1985)," short biography provided by 1 CRPG.

101 Kevin McMahon, *Arctic Twilight: Reflections on the Destiny of Canada's Northern Land and People* (Toronto: Lorimer, 1988), 11.

102 Morenus, *DEW Line*, 138.

103 J.D. Ferguson, *A Study of the Effects of the Distant Early Warning Line upon the Eskimo of the Western Arctic of Canada* (Ottawa: Northern Research Co-ordination Centre, Department of Northern Affairs and National Resources, 1957), 3.

104 Quoted in Harris, "National Defence and Northern Development," 210.

105 A.J. Shea, "The Two Camps," *Canadian Army Journal* 10, 2 (April 1956): 65.

106 Shea, "Two Camps," 59. On "Charlie" Sageeaktuk, see D. Leiterman, "DEW Line Means End of Old Way of Life for 10,000 Eskimos in Canadian Northland," *Edmonton Journal*, 10 April 1956.

107 Shea to Templeton, 16 May 1955, DHH, 323.009(D150).

108 Pierre Berton, *The Mysterious North* (New York: Knopf, 1956), 234-35. On the military history of Iqaluit, see Melanie Gagnon and Iqaluit Elders, *Inuit Recollections on the Military Presence in Iqaluit* (Iqaluit: Nunavut Arctic College, 2002).

109 A.J. Shea, "Rangers of Frobisher," *The Beaver* 36, 3, outfit 287 (1956): 42.

110 Ibid., 43. The editor of *The Beaver* noted that the Inuit's ability to stand still for such a long period owed something to their hours of waiting patiently at breathing holes while hunting seals.

111 Shea, "Rangers of Frobisher," 42-43.

112 David Miller, "Canadian Rangers Stand on Guard," *News of the North*, 7 November 1979.

113 Vokes to VCGS, 4 June 1956, LAC, RG 24, acc. 1983-84/215, box 322, f. S-2001-1999/0, vol. 7.

114 Vokes to Army HQ, 4 April 1956, and DMOP, "Canadian Ranger Policy: Item 2(C) 14th CGS Conference with GOCs," 13 January 1956, LAC, RG 24, acc. 1983-84/215, box 322, f. S-2001-1999/0, vol. 7.

115 Undated press clipping (1950s), PWNHC, NWT Archives, N1986 012.

116 See strength returns in LAC, RG 24, acc. 1983-84/215, box 322, f. S-2001-1999/0, vol. 9.

117 Robert Taylor, "Eyes and Ears of the North," *Star Weekly Magazine*, 22 December 1956, 2-3.

118 Alex van Bibber, interview with author, Beaver Creek, YT, 17 June 2009.

119 *Debates (Hansard)*, 16 June 1955, p. 4870.

120 Bernd Horn and Michel Wyczynski, *Hook Up! The Canadian Airborne Compendium: A Summary of Major Airbourne Activities, Exercises, and Operations, 1940-2000* (St. Catharines, ON: Vanwell, 2003), 9; Sean Maloney, "The Mobile Striking Force and Continental Defence, 1948-1955," *Canadian Military History* 2, 2 (1993): 86. By 1957, the Mobile Striking Force was recast as the Defence of Canada force. It consisted of one company group from each of the three active force battalions – a "token company group." Eyre, "Custos Borealis," 168.

121 "Study Report: Northern Region Canadian Rangers," 27 May 1986, DND, Northern Region HQ, f. 5323-2(SSO R&C), 6.

Chapter 6: Shadow Army, 1957-70

1 Capt. A.J. Shea, "An Appreciation of the Situation of the Canadian Rangers in Eastern Command," 23 February 1960, Department of National Defence (DND), Directorate of History and Heritage (DHH), 323.009(D261).

2 Ibid.

3 Ibid.

4 Ibid.

5 "2,690 Canadian Rangers Keep Lookout for Foes," *Toronto Star*, 10 September 1958. See also "Rangers on Lookout for Enemy," undated clipping (September 1958), Prince of Wales Northern Heritage Centre (PWNHC), NWT Archives, f. N1986 012.

6 Maj.-Gen. F.F. Worthington to Lt.-Gen H.D. Graham, 11 June 1958, and reply, 20 June 1958, Library and Archives Canada (LAC), RG 24, Department of National Defence, acc. 1983-84/215, vol. 322, f. 2001-1999/0, vol. 9.

7 Maj.-Gen. F.F. Worthington, 11 August 1958, DHH, 326.042(D3). The position of colonel commandant was vacant in 1963, and no one was appointed in Worthington's place.

8 Lt. C.N.L. Westover, inspection report, 12 Company, Ocean Falls, BC, April 1958, LAC, RG 24, vol. 22352, f. S-2001-1999/0, vol. 2.

9 Ibid.

10 John R. Sperry, *Igloo Dwellers Were My Church: The Memoirs of Jack Sperry, Anglican Bishop of the Arctic* (Yellowknife: Bayeux Arts, 2001), 25; David Damas, *Arctic Migrants, Arctic Villagers: The Transformation of Inuit Settlement in the Central Arctic* (Montreal/Kingston: McGill-Queen's University Press, 2002), 73.

11 Penhale to Worthington, 24 March 1949, LAC, MG 31-G21, M.H.S. Penhale fonds, vol. 1, f. "Correspondence – Western Command and Personal, 1947-1949." See also Harold Webster, *Arctic Adventure* (Ridgetown: G.C. and H.C. Enterprises, n.d.).

12 Doug Holmes, "The North's Own Canadian Rangers," *Up Here,* February-March 1987, 60.

13 Sperry, *Igloo Dwellers,* 21-32; John R. Sperry, telephone interview with author, 17 December 2003.

14 Sperry, *Igloo Dwellers,* 26; Sperry interview. In our interview, Sperry reminisced about when he had discovered that some community members had two or three Ranger rifles, which they had won off other Rangers through gambling. Anecdotal evidence suggests that not all of the Rangers found the .303 useful. When Ross Gibson, the former RCMP constable at Resolute Bay, appeared before a Royal Commission on Aboriginal Peoples hearing in Ottawa on 17 June 1993, he recalled that "the Eskimo were not happy with the rifles that the rangers brought them." He was startled to see that, in one of his photographs, a Ranger rifle was used as a tent pole. "I don't think that [the Eskimo] were overly impressed with the rangers and I don't think sovereignty ever entered the Eskimo's mind," he noted. "I think survival is foremost in the Eskimo's mind." Royal Commission on Aboriginal Peoples (RCAP), *For*

Seven Generations: Final Report of the Royal Commission on Aboriginal Peoples, vol. 1, *Looking Forward, Looking Back* (Ottawa: Canada Communication Group, 1997), CD-ROM.

15 J.S. Matthiasson, *Living on the Land: Change among the Inuit of Baffin Island* (Peterborough, ON: Broadview, 1992), 54-55, 65. Matthiasson mistakenly attributed the source of the .303 rifles to the Ground Observer Corps, an unarmed civilian organization.

16 John Sperry, interviews with author, Yellowknife, NT, 19 December 2003 and 2 February 2009. The Oblate priests thanked Sperry by giving him a pair of moccasins. Rangers from 7 Company in Yellowknife eventually found Bourassa's plane.

17 Sperry interview, 17 December 2003. On dispersed settlement at Coppermine, see also Damas, *Arctic Migrants,* 75-78, and Sperry, *Igloo Dwellers.*

18 This discussion of Shea's 1958 tour is based on "Canadian Rangers: Journal of Eastern Arctic Patrol 1958," 22 September 1958, LAC, RG 24, acc. 1983-84/215, box 399, f. S-9105-21/0. On the Eastern Arctic Patrol, see P.S. Grygier, *A Long Way from Home: The Tuberculosis Epidemic among the Inuit* (Montreal/Kingston: McGill-Queen's University Press, 1997), 86-102.

19 Pierre Berton, *The Mysterious North* (Toronto: McClelland and Stewart, 1956), 235; Damas, *Arctic Migrants,* 72-74.

20 The relocation of Inuit from Port Harrison (Inukjuak) to Resolute and Grise Fiord in 1953 has generated significant political and scholarly debate, particularly over the motivations behind the move. Although government officials insisted that humanitarian reasons lay behind the decision, some Inuit residents and scholars assert that the primary motive was sovereignty – that these Inuit were used as human flags to bolster Canada's presence in the archipelago. See, for example, Frank Tester and Peter Kulchyski, *Tammarniit (Mistakes): Inuit Relocation in the Eastern Arctic, 1939-63* (Vancouver: UBC Press, 1994), and Alan Marcus, *Relocating Eden: The Image and Politics of Inuit Exile in the Canadian Arctic* (Hanover: University Press of New England, 1998). For a contrary perspective, see Gerard Kenney, *Arctic Smoke and Mirrors* (Prescott: Voyageur, 1994). The Rangers at Resolute told Shea that Sergeant Idlout had gone to Greenland on an "official mission," but they provided no additional information.

21 Shea also took care not to create divisions within communities. At Pangnirtung, he explained that he "was able to distribute the snapshots which I took last year and to take a few more, including one of quite a large group of the Rangers and another larger group of non-Rangers, just so they wouldn't feel left out of things." Shea, "Canadian Rangers: Journal of Eastern Arctic Patrol 1958," 22 September 1958.

22 On Frobisher Bay during this era, see J.J. Honigmann and I. Honigmann, *Eskimo Townsmen* (Ottawa: Canadian Research Centre for Anthropology, University of Ottawa, 1965) and S.M. Meldrum, *Frobisher Bay* (Ottawa: DIAND, 1975).

23 See, for example, Fred Kaplan, *The Wizards of Armageddon* (New York: Simon and Schuster, 1983) and Matthew Farish, "Frontier Engineering," *Canadian Geographer* 50, 2 (2006): 177-96.

24 James Eayrs, *In Defence of Canada: Peacemaking and Deterrence* (Toronto: University of Toronto Press, 1972), 372.

25 Richard J. Diubaldo and Stephen J. Scheinberg, *A Study of Canadian-American Defence Policy (1945-1975) – Northern Issues and Strategic Resources* (Ottawa: DND, 1978), 36-37.

26 Kenneth Eyre, "Forty Years of Military Activity in the Canadian North, 1947-87," *Arctic* 40, 4 (1987): 295.

27 Extract of Item II, Vice Chiefs of Staff Committee, Minute of the 48th Meeting, 12 December 1958; Vice Chief of the General Staff (VCGS) to Western Command, Quebec Command, Eastern Command, 9 January 1959; DGPO to VCGS, 9 January 1959, LAC, RG 24, acc. 1983-84/215, vol. 322, f. 2001-1999/0, vol. 9. The northern elements of the Ground Observer Corps were disbanded in 1963. See Air Marshal C.R. Dunlap to Minister of National Defence, 7 October 1963, DND, Canadian Rangers National Authority (CRNA), f. "Canadian Rangers 1970 and Before."

28 Western Command to Canadian Army, 13 January 1959; Eastern Command to Canadian Army, 15 January 1959; Quebec Command to Canadian Army, 29 January 1959, LAC, RG 24, acc. 1983-84/215, vol. 322, f. 2001-1999/0, vol. 9. On the Defence of Canada Force, see Bernd Horn, Michel Wyczynski, and Carlos Chagas, *Canadian Airborne Forces since 1942* (New York: Osprey, 2006), 23-25.

29 Brig. J.A.W. Bennett to VCGS and annexes, 10 November 1958; Notes on Chiefs of Staff Meeting with Minister of National Defence, 12 January 1959, DHH, 86/29; Director of Military Operations and Plans (DMOP), "Plan for Integration: Canadian Rangers and Ground Observer Corps," 24 February 1959; Western Command to Canadian Army, 21 May 1959, LAC, RG 24, acc. 1983-84/215, vol. 322, f. 2001-1999/0, vol. 9. Interestingly, if the RCAF asked the army to share the cost of an integrated organization, disbanding the Rangers would have increased the army's annual costs.

30 Van Straubenzee to HQ, BC Area, 9 June 1958, LAC, RG 24, vol. 2252, f. S-2001-1999/0, vol. 2, emphasis in original. Tellingly, the civil defence exercise Co-operation II in the Peace River area interrupted the Command Canadian Ranger Officer's tour of BC coastal settlements by rail, steamship, and chartered boat.

31 General Officer Commanding (GOC), Western Command to Army HQ, 11 June 1958, LAC, RG 24, acc. 1983-84/215, vol. 322, f. 2001-1999/0, vol. 9. On early provincial appeals to have the Rangers employed in civil defence, see C.R. Stein to Brig.-Gen. Kitching, 26 July 1955, and reply, 31 August 1955, LAC, RG 24, vol. 22352, f. S-2001-1999/0, vol. 2.

32 Andrew Burtch, *Give Me Shelter: The Failure of Canada's Cold War Civil Defence* (Vancouver: UBCP, 2012).

33 J.L. Granatstein, *Canada's Army: Waging War and Keeping the Peace* (Toronto: University of Toronto Press, 2002), 350-51.

34 Maj. A. Osland to Lt. E.A. Butler, 8 September 1959, PWNHC, NWT Archives, Anderson-Thomson fonds, N 1986 012.

35 Osland to No. 7, No. 8, No. 20, and No. 21 Companies, 25 October 1960, PWNHC, Anderson Thomson fonds, N 1986 012. See also Burtch, *Give Me Shelter*.

36 See, for example, Maj. E.F. Carron, "Canadian Rangers Diary Liaison Visits/61," entry for Southwest Coast, 26 November 1961, copy provided by 5 Canadian Rangers Patrol Group (CRPG).

37 See DHH, 323.009(D261) and LAC, RG 24, acc. 1983-84/215, box 399, f. S-9105-21/0.

38 Telegraph and DND minute sheet at 1 CRPG HQ, Yellowknife. On d'Artois's Arctic experience, see Bernd Horn, "A Military Enigma: The Canadian Air Service Company, 1948-1949," *Canadian Military History* 10, 1 (2001): 25, and Maurice Flint, *Operation Canon: A Short Account of the Life and Witness of the Reverend John Hudspith Turner* (London: Bible Churchmen's Missionary Society, 1949).

39 Kenneth Eyre, "Custos Borealis: The Military in the Canadian North" (PhD diss., University of London-King's College, 1981), 255. On the northern vision, see Morris Zaslow, *The Northward Expansion of Canada, 1914-1967* (Toronto: McClelland and Stewart, 1988), 332-51 and Philip Isard, "Northern Vision: Northern Development during the Diefenbaker Era" (master's thesis, University of Waterloo, 2010).

40 Eyre, "Custos Borealis," 180.

41 Larry Dignum, "Shadow Army of the North," *The Beaver* 39, 2, outfit 290 (Autumn 1959): 22-24.

42 John Anderson-Thomson to Maj. C.B. Van Straubenzee, 26 January 1958, PWNHC, NWT Historical Timeline, http://pwnhc.learnnet.nt.ca/.

43 Kitching to Quebec Command HQ, 28 May 1957, and 24 June 1957, and Col. W.C. Dick to Quebec Command HQ, 28 April 1957, DHH, 112.3S2.003(D4). In 1963, the regional administrator with the Department of Northern Affairs and National Resources contacted Western Command about "the need for the Eskimo to improve his proficiency with firearms

and thus ensuring a kill when hunting game for food, rather than the prevalent unnecessary game wastage because of their inability to make a sure kill." Army headquarters suggested increasing the strength of the Ranger company headquartered in Churchill by enlisting Inuit in platoons commanded by department representatives. As a result, the following year, Western Command requested permission to relocate the dormant platoons of No. 24 Company to Eskimo Point, Rankin Inlet, and Baker Lake. The chief of the general staff (CGS) in Ottawa withheld his decision. The policy on the Rangers had to be reviewed. VCGS to CGS, 22 April 1964; Canadian Army to Western Command, 30 April 1964, DHH, 112.3S2.003(D4).

44 Col. W.C. Dick to Deputy Chief of General Staff (DCGS), 26 February 1958, DHH, 112.3S2.003(D4); Maj.-Gen. J.V. Allard, SD 1, Letter No. 58/31, 24 April 1958, LAC, RG 24, acc. 1983-84/215, vol. 322, f. 2001-1999/0, vol. 9; Allard, SD 1, Letter No. 58/54, 1 August 1958, DHH, 326.042(D3). These were officially classified as "dormant sub-units."

45 Shea, "An Appreciation," 23 February 1960. The commander of Newfoundland Area agreed that inaccessible subunits and those toward which interest was lacking should be disbanded. These locations included Battle Harbour and Red Bay, Harbour Deep and Lewisporte, Lake Harbour, Cape Dorset, Pangnirtung, the entire No. 29 Company on Baffin Island, Hopedale, and Hebron. GOC, Eastern Command to Army HQ, DND, 22 September 1960, DHH, 323.009(D261).

46 Morres to HQ Eastern Command, 16 May 1960; GOC, Eastern Command to Army HQ, DND, 22 September 1960, DHH, 323.009(D261). Army headquarters also upheld the 1948 decision that place names should not be included in unit titles for security reasons. VCGS to GOC, Eastern Command, 2 November 1960, DHH, 323.009(D261).

47 GOC, Eastern Command to Army HQ, DND, 22 September 1960, and "Recommended Disbandments of Ranger Sub-Units," 16 May 1960, DHH, 323.009(D261).

48 Lt.-Col. J.M.E. Clarkson to Assistant Quartermaster General, 13 June 1963, LAC, RG 24, vol. 22337, f. S-ECS-1999/0, vol. 5; Carron to Gray, 2 July 63, LAC, RG 24, vol. 22335, f. C-ECC-1960-1999/0; Newfoundland Area to Eastern Command, 22 August 63, LAC, RG 24, vol. 22335, f. C-ECC-1960-1999/0.

49 "Ed" [Carron] to Gray, 27 February 1963 and 10 February 1964, LAC, RG 24, vol. 22337, f. S-ECS-2001-1999/0, vol. 6; Lt.-Col. G. Meharg to Directorate of Reserves-5 (DRES-5), "100 527 877 Maj. F.M. Cox Canadian Rangers," 29 January 1986, DND f. ARHQ: 5000-1 (COS RO). Racial criteria were still in place, however. The Rangers operational plan noted that "Eskimos will NOT be employed as Ranger Officers." "Newfoundland Area Operational Plan – Canadian Rangers," ca. fall 1964, LAC, RG 24, vol. 22337, f. S-ECS-2001-1999/0, vol. 6.

50 GOC, Eastern Command to Canadian Forces Headquarters (CFHQ), Director of Operations, 4 February 1966, LAC, RG 24, vol. 22335, f. C-EEC-1960-1999/0, vol. 7.

51 LAC, RG 24, vol. 22337, f. S-ECS-1999/0, vol. 5; LAC, RG 24, vol. 22337, f. S-ECS-2001-1990/0, vol. 6.

52 Carron to Area Commander, 10 February 1964, LAC, RG 24, vol. 22337, f. S-ECS-2001-1999/0, vol. 6.

53 Col. H.E.C. Price, Commander, Nfld. Area, to Eastern Command HQ, 9 April 1962, LAC, RG 24, vol. 22337, f. S-ECS-1999/0, vol. 5.

54 This restructuring simultaneously reduced the area of No. 34 Company, which Carron considered too big. Carron, "H.M.C.S. Thunder – Gaultois, Nfld – 16 October, 1961," copy at 5 CRPG, detachment HQ, Gander; and "Ed" [Carron] to Gray, 27 February 1963.

55 LAC, RG 24, vol. 22335, f. C-ECC-1960-1999/0.

56 LAC, RG 24, vol. 22337, f. S-ECS-2001-1990/0, vol. 6. Carron was replaced by Maj. J.E. Malone, who was replaced by Captain J.A. Latta in 1966. LAC, RG 24, vol. 22337, f. S-ECS-2001-1990/0, vol. 7. Neither left the mark of Shea or Carron.

57 Van Straubenzee to Capt. M.O. Lane, 29 January 1958, LAC, RG 24, vol. 22332, f. C-2001-1999/0, vol. 4.

58 LAC, RG 24, acc. 1983-84/215, vol. 322, f. 2001-1999/0, vol. 9.

59 C.H. Chapman, "Pacific Coast Militia Rangers: 135 Company Yukon Rangers," manuscript in possession of John Mitchell, Dawson.

60 See LAC, RG 24, vol. 22352, f. S-2001-1999/0, vol. 4.

61 Proceedings of Board of Officers, Vancouver, 27 January 1964, LAC, RG 24, vol. 22352, f. S-2001-1999/0, vol. 4. See also Brig. E.D. Danby, "Report of Visit: 4 Pl 14 Coy Canadian Rangers," 14 October 1964, LAC, RG 24, vol. 22352, f. S-2001-1999/0, vol. 4; Col. M.F. MacLachlan to Chief of the Defence Staff, 26 July 1966, DND, Canadian Rangers National Authority (CRNA), f. "Canadian Rangers 1970 and Before."

62 Proceedings of Board of Officers, Ocean Falls, 6 February 1964, LAC, RG 24, vol. 22352, f. S-2001-1999/0, vol. 4.

63 Proceedings of Board of Officers, Alexis Creek, 2 February 1964, LAC, RG 24, vol. 22352, f. S-2001-1999/0, vol. 4.

64 See examples in LAC, RG 24, vol. 22332, f. C-2001-1999/0, vol. 4. When one loaded weapon was found lying out in the countryside and the Ranger owner could not be contacted (he was out on his trapline), an officer noted: "We do not train Rangers. Leaving a loaded rifle lying around is in my estimation an individual lack of common sense and responsibility. Rangers are supposed to be mature sensible woodsmen who are familiar with the care and handling of weapons." Capt. T.R. Patrey to HQ, North West Highway System, 8 December 1961; undated memo, LAC, RG 24, vol. 22332, f. S-2001-1999/0, vol. 6.

65 H.V. George to District Assistant Adjutant and Quartermaster General, Camp Takhini, 3 September 1963, LAC, RG 24, vol. 22332, f. S-2001-1999/0, vol. 6. No. 39 Company officially disbanded in 1964.

66 Stephen Harris, "'Really a Defile throughout Its Length': The Defence of the Alaska Highway in Peacetime," in The Alaska Highway: Papers of the 40th Anniversary Symposium, ed. Kenneth Coates (Vancouver: UBC Press, 1985), 128. On the postwar highway, see Kenneth Coates, North to Alaska (Fairbanks: University of Alaska Press, 1992), 213-18, 224-26, 234-35.

67 DND (Army) to Western Command HQ, 13 March 1964, and marginalia, LAC, RG 24, vol. 22352, f. S-2001-1999/0, vol. 4.

68 "Strength Return – Canadian Rangers – 31 Mar 66," Annex A to ADS 2001-1999/0 (Trg), 26 July 1966, CRNA, "Canadian Rangers 1970 and Before."

69 J. Worsell, "Outpost Defenders 'Just a Bit Better Prepared,'" Canada Month, March 1964, 20.

70 Ibid.

71 Ibid. On closures at Whitehorse, see Eyre, "Custos Borealis," 249, 252-55.

72 R.J. Sutherland, "The Strategic Significance of the Canadian Arctic," in The Arctic Frontier, ed. R. St. J. Macdonald (Toronto: University of Toronto Press, 1966), 275.

73 Eyre, "Custos Borealis," 180-81; Melvin Conant, The Long Polar Watch: Canada and the Defense of North America (New York: Harper, 1962), 29; and Diubaldo and Scheinberg, Canadian-American Defence Policy, 41-42.

74 Colin Gray, Canadian Defence Priorities: A Question of Relevance (Toronto: Clarke, Irwin, 1972), 185. The 1964 Western Command Defence Plan mentioned the Canadian Rangers. See LAC, RG 24, vol. 22337, f. S-ECS-2001-1990/0, vol. 6.

75 Major L.R. Boyd, "Brief: Canadian Rangers," 29 November 1966, CRNA, f. "Canadian Rangers 1970 and Before." On Mobile Command, see Capt. J.R. Grodzinski, "Force Mobile Command," Army Doctrine and Training Bulletin 3, 1 (2000): 1-2.

76 See, for example, Gérard Duhaime, "La sédentarisation au Nouveau-Québec inuit," Etudes/Inuit/Studies 7, 2 (1983): 25-52; Damas, Arctic Migrants, 145, 162.

77 On resettlement in Newfoundland and Labrador, see Maritime History Archive, "'No Great Future': Government-Sponsored Resettlement in Newfoundland and Labrador since

Confederation," http://www.mun.ca/mha/; Noel Iverson and Ralph Mathews, *Communities in Decline: An Examination of Household Resettlement in Newfoundland* (St. John's, NL: Institute of Social and Economic Research, Memorial University, 1968); Parzival Copes, *The Resettlement of Fishing Communities in Newfoundland* (Ottawa: Canadian Council on Rural Development, 1972); David Courtney, "Newfoundland Household Resettlement Programs," in *Perspectives on Newfoundland Society and Culture,* ed. Maurice A. Sterns (St. John's: Memorial University of Newfoundland, 1974), 47-49; and Peter Gard, "Outport Resettlement 20 Years Later," *Canadian Geographic* 105, 3 (1985): 8-17.

78 See Cleophas Belvin, *Forgotten Labrador: Kegashka to Blanc-Sablon* (Montreal/Kingston: McGill-Queen's University Press, 2006), 143-44.

79 On changes in southeastern Labrador, see John Kennedy, *People of the Bays and Headlands: Anthropological History and the Fate of Communities in the Unknown Labrador* (Toronto: University of Toronto Press, 1995), 186-205.

80 Oz Dyson, Sam Morris, and Ed Sampson, interview with author, Hopedale, NL, 27 February 2006.

81 Gordon Foreman, interview with author, Harrington Harbour, QC, 13 April 2007. Captain Foreman recalled that the rifle and ammunition remained the main incentive through the 1960s and '70s.

82 Coretta Stacey, "A Knight's Tale," *The Nor'wester* 24, 16 (2002): 1, 8.

83 Gabriel Dionne, *In a Breaking Wave: Living History of the Lower North Shore* (Montreal: Les Missionaires Oblats de Marie Immaculée, 1988), 177; Louise Abbott, *The Coast Way: A Portrait of the English on the Lower North Shore of the St. Lawrence* (Montreal/Kingston: McGill-Queen's University Press, 1988), 114; and Belvin, *Forgotten Labrador*, 143-44.

84 Gordon Jones, interview with author, Chevery, QC, 12 April 2007.

85 David Gordon Anderson and Ernie Waye, interviews with author, Chevery, QC, 12 April 2007.

86 Foreman interview.

87 DHH, "History of Aboriginal Peoples in the Canadian Military," f. N-ON-7, John MacFarlane, telephone interview with Abraham Metatawabin and his son Ed (translator), Fort Albany, ON, 15 November 2001, transcribed by John Maclean. On the Mid-Canada Line station, see Leonard Tsuji, John Kataquapit, Billy Katapatuk, and Guy Iannucci, "Re-mediation of Site 050 of the Mid-Canada Radar Line," *Canadian Journal of Native Studies* 21, 1 (2001): 149-60, and Toby Morantz, *White Man's Gonna Getcha: The Colonial Challenge to the Crees in Quebec* (Montreal/Kingston: McGill-Queen's University Press, 2002), 194-95.

88 MacFarlane, interview with Metatawabin. Metatawabin explained that they did not anticipate a large Soviet invasion, only a raiding party with maybe ten canoes – the reference being to a historical episode when a French group blew up an English fort.

89 "A Paper on DND Policy in the Canadian North," 27 November 1968, updated 14 March 1969, DHH, 79/527, folder 2F.

90 "Review of 1968 Operations," April 1969, DHH, 79/527, folder 2C.

91 Col. R.A. Reid to Director Operations, 8 February 1968, CRNA, f. "Canadian Rangers 1970 and Before." Like other supporters at this time, Reid also recommended that the Rangers be organized in individual posts rather than "vastly dispersed companies." See also Maj. R. Liboiron to Lt.-Col. R. Bérubé, 7 November 1966, CRNA, f. "Canadian Rangers 1970 and Before."

92 "Minutes of a Conference to Discuss the Canadian Rangers Held at CFHQ at 1000 hrs, 24 Apr 69," 25 April 1969, DHH, 79/527, folder 2A. See also Director General Operations (Land) (DGOPSL), "Brief Concerning," 28 October 1969, DHH, 79/527, folder 2F; Canadian Rangers – Pacific Region, 29 February 1988, DND, f. MARP: 1901-2 (DRO), Esquimalt Military Museum, f. "Canadian Rangers."

93 DGOPSL, "Brief Concerning," 28 October 1969. A Canadian Rangers Working Group report prepared the same year recommended creating militia units to *replace* Ranger units.

These officers only suggested revitalizing the Rangers in areas without sufficient populations to support Primary Reserve units, such as the northern continental coast, Hudson Bay, and the High Arctic islands. Even there, they insisted, the Rangers would need to be brought under greater military control and "new Ranger posts established to ensure a token military presence." "Canadian Rangers Working Group Report," 1 May 1969, DHH, 79/527, folder 2A. The statistical basis and underlying assumptions for these bold plans were sketchy. In southern Canada, 3 percent of an urban population might reasonably volunteer for the militia. Nothing suggested this percentage should apply to the North, but planners cited it nonetheless, partly on the assumption that northerners had fewer activities that would compete for their time. But important differences remained between northern and southern communities. First, most "Whites" in northern settlements were transients. Second, the director general operations (land) asserted that "native northern peoples do not have a military tradition and are not amenable to the highly structured, performance-oriented, kind of life found in garrison military units." Third, and more appealingly, most northern males practised a lifestyle that made them admirably suited "for outdoor military activity." DGOPSL, "Brief Concerning," 28 October 1969, 7, and Annex D, "An Assessment of Recruiting Potential for Reserve Force Land Units in Northern Canada."

94 See Eyre, "Custos Borealis," 262, and House of Commons, *Debates (Hansard)*, 7 March 1969, 6337. On the lack of emphasis on national defence in the Northern Vision, see Isard, "Northern Vision."

95 "Northern Armed Force," ca. April 1969, John G. Diefenbaker Archives (JDA), MG 01/XI/B/22.2, vol. 44, f. "Arctic – The North [1967-74]." See also "n.g.g." (N.G. Guthrie), "Memo for Diefenbaker Re – Proposed Arctic Force, 3 April 1969," JDA, MG 01/XI/B/22.2, vol. 44, f. "Arctic – The North [1967-74]."

96 "Northern Armed Force" n.d., and marginalia, JDA, MG 01/XI/B/221, f. "Arctic – The North [1967-74]," notes that "*Civil servants rushed in* to say that there was such a force in Sup. Reserves Northern Rangers." Emphasis in original. See also "Eskimo Militia Going 27 Years," *Ottawa Journal*, 14 April 1969, clipping in CRNA, f. "Canadian Rangers 1970 and Before."

97 Scott Young, "The Shadowy Force on Guard in the Arctic," *Globe and Mail*, 14 April 1969, 7. Diefenbaker's papers suggest that he was oblivious to their continued existence until Young wrote his article.

98 Ibid.

99 Col. M. Turner to Chief of Defence Staff, 29 August 1969, DHH, 79/527, folder 2A.

100 Lt. J.A.C. Nuyens to Lt.-Col. B.J.S. Sutherland, 11 September 1969, DHH, 79/527, folder 2A.

101 "Report of the Steering Committee on the Canadian North," 25 November 1969, DHH, 79/527, folder 2H. On the potential contributions of "appropriately organized" Ranger units, see Report of the Steering Committee on the Canadian North, "Canadian Forces Policies Objectives and Activities in the Canadian North," December 1969, DHH, 73/1223/987, box 52, 7.

102 W.B.S. Sutherland, notes on Northern Steering Committee Meeting, 16 October 1969, DHH, 79/527, folder 2E.

103 Mobile Command (MOBCOM) to CFHQ, 5 May 1970, DHH, 79/527, folder 2E. The army gave Stirling three months to complete his preliminary study.

104 Maj. W.K. Stirling, "The Canadian Rangers: An In Depth Study," 5 August 1970, DND, Northern Region Headquarters, f. 5323-2 (SSO[L]) (hereafter "Stirling Report"). Stirling had recently completed a study on the reserves. See "Reserves Training: A New Approach," ca. January-March 1969, DHH, 79/527, folder 2A.

105 Dick Hill, for his part, emphasized that the government should not form separate or special programs for Native peoples: rather than perpetuating their colonization along ethnic lines,

"they should be treated simply as Northerners." For more on his vision for the North, see Hill, *Inuvik: A History, 1958-2008* (Victoria: Trafford, 2008).

106 This and the preceding paragraphs are based on the Stirling Report.

107 For a superb overview of these developments, see R. Quinn Duffy, *The Road to Nunavut: The Progress of the Eastern Arctic Inuit since the Second World War* (Montreal/Kingston: McGill-Queen's University Press, 1988).

108 Stirling Report, 16.

109 Ibid., 19.

Chapter 7: Sovereignty and Symbolism, 1970-84

1 Capt. Craig Mills, "Bannock Binds a Better Team," *Sentinel* 11, 2 (1975): 7-9.

2 Ibid.

3 Ibid. See also Canadian Forces, Northern Region, Exercise Nanook Ranger II: Exercise Report, 19 April 1974, Canadian Rangers National Authority (CRNA), f. "Canadian Rangers, 1974."

4 Report of the Steering Committee on the Canadian North, "Canadian Forces Policies Objectives and Activities in the Canadian North," 5 December 1969, Department of National Defence (DND), Directorate of History and Heritage (DHH), 73/1223/987, box 52, 11.

5 On this era, see Edgar Dosman, ed., *The Arctic in Question* (Toronto: Oxford University Press, 1976); Kenneth Coates et al., *Arctic Front: Defending Canada's Interests in the Far North* (Toronto: Thomas Allen, 2008), 93-109; and P. Whitney Lackenbauer and Peter Kikkert, *The Canadian Forces and Arctic Sovereignty: Debating Roles, Interests, and Requirements, 1968-1974* (Waterloo: Wilfrid Laurier University Press, 2010). On the legal issues, see Ted McDorman, *Salt Water Neighbours: International Ocean Law Relations between the United States and Canada* (Oxford: Oxford University Press, 2009), 49-84.

6 Kenneth C. Eyre, "Custos Borealis: The Military in the Canadian North" (PhD diss., University of London-King's College, 1981), 279 (quoting "Address to Canadian Naval Officers Association," *Montreal Star*, 2 March 1970).

7 Ibid., 261-66, 279.

8 Ibid., 266-67; Gen. F.R. Sharp, Chief of the Defence Staff (CDS) Directive D7/70: Establishment of Northern Command Headquarters, 16 March 1970, DND, f. S3120-13(CDS). On the Canadian Forces' establishment in the North, see DHH Library, Armed Forces News, Info Service, 1969, AFN167/69. Northern Region Headquarters was unique among the six designed regions of the Canadian Forces because it was not a joint functional or regional command. The commander was responsible to the chief of the defence staff for coordinating all of the Canadian Forces' activities in its area of responsibility. Canadian Forces Northern Region, "Northern Region Information" (pamphlet, ca. 1980), Canadian Forces Northern Area (CFNA), f. NA 1325-1 (PAffO).

9 "Canadian Rangers," 10 March 1970, DND, f. 1901-260/4(DMIL).

10 Maj. W.K. Stirling, "The Canadian Rangers: An In Depth Study," 5 August 1970, DND, f. NR 5323-2(SSO(L)). Copy provided by 1 Canadian Rangers Patrol Group (CRPG) HQ.

11 Director General Operations Land (DGOL), "Canadian Rangers," 10 March 1970, DND, f. V 1901-260/4(DMIL).

12 When created in 1966, Maritime Command assumed responsibility for the Royal Canadian Navy prior to unification (the navy disappeared as a distinct service in 1968) and for the air force's antisubmarine operations. David Bercuson and J.L. Granatstein, *Dictionary of Canadian Military History* (Don Mills, ON: Oxford University Press, 1992), 125.

13 Maritime Command (CANMARCOM) to Canadian Forces HQ (CANFORCEHED), 14 April 1970, DHH, 79/527 folder 2A. In April 1970, Lt.-Gen. M.R. Dare continued to support

Mobile Command's control of the Rangers. He believed "that this is the best alternative at present" and suggested to Maritime Command "that those in Newfoundland and Labrador should not be divorced from the remainder." Dare to Commander, Maritime Command, April 1970, DHH, 79/527, folder 2A. The change in direction undoubtedly owed to Withers's plans for Northern Region.

14 Lt.-Gen G.A. Turcot to Vice Chief of the Defence Staff, 4 September 1970, DND, f. 1901-260/4COMD.

15 See P. Whitney Lackenbauer and Peter Kikkert, "Building on 'Shifting Sands': The Canadian Armed Forces, Sovereignty, and the Arctic, 1968-72," in *Canada and Arctic Sovereignty and Security: Historical Perspectives,* Calgary Papers in Military and Strategic Studies, ed. P. Whitney Lackenbauer (Calgary: Centre for Military and Strategic Studies, 2011), 283-308.

16 Dare to Commander, Mobile Command, 18 November 1970, DND, f. V1901-260/ 4TD0258(DORL).

17 *Defence '71* (Ottawa: DND, 1971), 60; Annex C to V, 1901-260/4 (DORL), 22 February 1971, in DND, CRNA, f. Canadian Rangers 1971. Platoons at Port Harrison, Rupert House, Fort George, and Great Whale River in Quebec were made dormant. The Rangers likely never heard about this decision. The military made no official announcement regarding Yukon, but ammunition and support disappeared after 1969, when the sergeant who had been resupplying them moved to Ottawa. Chuck Hume, interview, Haines Junction, YT, 16 June 2009.

18 DHH Library, DND, Armed Forces News, Information Service, January-June 1970, AFN92/ 70; Major Mike Barr suggested that Withers "organized the nonsense of NRHQ to get himself promoted" – despite considerable opposition from Mobile Command. Quoted in Bernd Horn, *Bastard Sons: An Examination of Canada's Airborne Experience, 1942-1995* (St. Catharines, ON: Vanwell, 2001), 127-28.

19 Report of the Steering Committee, 5 December 1969.

20 On early Northern Region Headquarters (NRHQ) activities, see "Historical Report – Northern Region Headquarters 1970," entry 22 April 1970.

21 W.B.S. Sutherland to Col. Withers, 7 May 1970, DHH, 79/527, folder 2E.

22 Withers, "Concept of Operations – Canadian Forces Northern Region," 14 July 1970, 4, 6, DHH, 79/527, folder 59.

23 Maj. F.L. Berry to Commander, NRHQ, 20 July 1970, DND, f. 1901-2(CD Det), and Canadian Forces Detachment Whitehorse, "The Canadian Rangers – Yukon," 30 July 1970, DND, f. WHD 8/10, emphasis in original. Copies provided by 1 CRPG.

24 See J.D. Hamilton, *Arctic Revolution: Social Change in the Northwest Territories, 1935-1994* (Toronto: Dundurn, 1994), 93-114; and R. Quinn Duffy, *The Road to Nunavut: The Progress of the Eastern Arctic Inuit since the Second World War* (Montreal/Kingston: McGill-Queen's University Press, 1988), 226-35.

25 Berry to Commander, NRHQ, 20 July 1970; CF Detachment, Whitehorse, "The Canadian Rangers – Yukon," 30 July 1970. See also "Historical Report – Northern Region Headquarters: Whitehorse Detachment, 1970," entry 24 February 1970. In January 1971, Berry became Staff Officer Rangers and Cadets when NRHQ absorbed the Yellowknife Detachment.

26 S.M. Hodgson to Jean Chrétien, 25 August 1969, Library and Archives Canada (LAC), RG 85, Northern Affairs Program, vol. 1885, f. NR2626-16, pt. 10.

27 Berry to Commander, NRHQ, 20 July 1970.

28 CFNA Task Group on Rangers, Reserves, Cadets, 4 September 1970, 3-8.

29 Ibid. Although defence planners implied that an increased military presence in the North was necessary to assert Canada's sovereignty, External Affairs argued that this presence did nothing to establish the "legal validity of Canada's claims" in the Arctic. See Lackenbauer and Kikkert, "Building on 'Shifting Sands,'" and documents reprinted in their volume *Canadian Forces and Arctic Sovereignty.*

30 Berry, "Memorandum on Ranger Selection and Training for Northern Region Headquarters," 25 September 1970, DND, f. 5323-1 (CF Det); Withers to Director Operational Readiness Land (DORL), 30 October 1970, DND, f. NR 5323-1 (COS OPS). Copies provided by 1 CRPG.

31 Minister of National Defence, *Defence in the '70s* (Ottawa: DND, 1971), 18, 24. In November 1970, the chief of the defence staff directed Withers to prepare a detailed analysis of the organization and a *modus operandi* for Canadian Rangers within Northwest Territories and Yukon, a directive that fit with surging political interest in northern sovereignty and security.

32 Withers to All Officers, NRHQ, 15 July 71. See also Withers, "Defence Requirements 'North of Sixty,'" *Canadian Defence Quarterly*, 1, 1 (1971): 37-43.

33 Brig.-Gen R.M. Withers to All Officers NRHQ, 15 July 1971, DND, f. NR 3185-1. Because northern targets would differ from those in Europe and on the Atlantic in their low target density and low sensor-space ratio, they would require different response systems.

34 Stirling, "Study on the Canadian Rangers – Northern Service Unit (Rangers)," 28 January 1971, DND, f. NR 5323-2(SO OPS); "Historical Report – Northern Region Headquarters 1970," entry 9 November 1970. He described the existing Argus patrol flights as fleeting, and naval ships could only operate in ice-free conditions a few weeks of the year.

35 Stirling, "Study on the Canadian Rangers – Northern Service Unit."

36 See Lackenbauer and Kikkert, *Canadian Forces and Arctic Sovereignty*.

37 Stirling, "Visit Report – Alaska Army National Guard," 4 March 1971.

38 See, for example, Charles Hendricks, "The Eskimos and the Defense of Alaska," *Pacific Historical Review* 54, 3 (1985): 293.

39 Withers to All Officers, NRHQ, 15 July 1971.

40 Ibid.

41 For example, R.J. Orange, the MP for Northwest Territories, argued that the Rangers, "a very successful operation ... kept together primarily by a number of very dedicated officers," should be expanded with the establishment of Northern Command "so as to use the talents and knowledge of northerners for surveillance purposes and to assist the military." House of Commons, *Debates (Hansard)*, 21 May 1971, 6065.

42 Maj. F.L. Berry to Commander, NRHQ, 5 April 1971, DND, f. NR 5323-2(SO R&C).

43 Capt. D.C. Jones, "NRHQ Training Report: Ranger Training, Holman, Victoria Island, 31 July 71–14 August 71," 20 September 1971, CRNA, f. "Canadian Rangers, 1971." Frank Kuptana brought his thirteen-year old son, David, along for the training exercise. Father Tardy, the local priest in Holman, raised various concerns about NRHQ's planned Ranger force: tokenism, competition for the local labour pool, the effects of "an organization of white bosses and native followers," and "misunderstanding of the term leadership as it applies to the Eskimo." See also "Historical Report – Northern Region Headquarters 1971," entries 28 May 1971, 31 July 1971, 22 October 1971, 29 October 1971, and 18 November 1971; Advisory Committee on Northern Development, Annual Report, "Government Activities in the North – FY 1971/72," 85.

44 Jones, "NRHQ Training Report," 20 September 1971. Jones expressed surprise when Inuit referred several times to the Japanese as "the enemy," which indicated that they needed some training before they would be adept at reporting anomalies.

45 Jones, "NRHQ Training Report," 20 September 1971.

46 The Canadian Airborne Regiment even jumped and planted a flag at the North Pole during a May 1974 training exercise to simulate a response to a major air disaster. *Defence '72* (Ottawa: DND, 1972), 38; *Defence '74* (Ottawa: DND, 1974), 19; Lt.-Col. G.L. Simpson to DORL, 5 February 1970, 5 February 1970, DHH, 79/527, folder 2F.

47 Kenneth Eyre, "Forty Years of Military Activity in the Canadian North, 1947-87," *Arctic* 40, 4 (1987): 298; Eyre, "Custos Borealis," 284-86. These activities were vulnerable to budget

pressures. See, for example, Gerald Porter, *In Retreat: The Canadian Forces in the Trudeau Years* (Ottawa: Deneau and Greenberg, 1978), 55.

48　For details, see "Ranger Participation: Exercise Patrouille Nocturne," Appendix I to Annex B to NRHQ Historical Report for 1972. That the designated area complied with a request from the local Inuit hunters' association indicated the military's newfound attentiveness to environmental issues. At 3 P.M. on 17 January, five Ranger "trainees" set out on skidoo to the camp to mark a landing strip. Seven hours later, two returned to Frobisher and contacted Captain Jones. They explained that two soldiers in their party had lost contact and could not be found. The Rangers assumed that the lost pair had had technical problems with their skidoos, but they were not particularly alarmed. The soldiers had adequate camping equipment and rations, and they certainly knew how to survive on the land. Undeterred, Tommy Takpanie of Frobisher – "the unofficial leader of the group" – assured the staff officer responsible for the Rangers that he could still safely return to the training area and have the landing strip marked for 9 A.M. He completed his task as promised and impressed the officer: "This incident ... illustrate[s] the capability of the experienced hunters. Takpanie travelled a distance of 42 miles in a straight line (at least double that considering the rough terrain and lack of snow) in 13 hours. Five hours were spent constructing a snow house and resting. The temperature was – 45°F or lower with a headwind averaging 10 mph. The majority of this work was done in the dark. The missing persons were located the next day with a frozen carburetor." "Ranger Participation: Exercise Patrouille Nocturne," Appendix I to Annex B to NRHQ Historical Report for 1972.

49　Rick Michon, "Patrouille Nocturne," *Sentinel* 8, 4 (1972): 4.

50　Capt. D.C. Jones, "Canadian Ranger Participation Exercise Patrouille Nocturne," 16 February 1972, CRNA, f. "Canadian Rangers 1972." Jones and his wife died on a canoeing trip on the Coppermine River in late August 1972.

51　Jones, "Canadian Ranger Participation Exercise Patrouille Nocturne."

52　General Withers, email to author, 22 June 2008. The original headquarters on the site of the current Joint Task Force North Headquarters parking lot was known as the "Yellow Submarine," even after it was painted air force blue in 1976. "Recollections of David Sproule from His Tour at Northern Region HQ, Yellowknife, NWT, 1974-1977" (Vancouver, 2005), 1, copy provided by the author.

53　Withers, "Canadian Arctic Rangers (C Arctic R), 15 December 1971, DND, f. NR 1901-260/1(Comd). In 1975, NRHQ proposed the concept of "Arctic Air Rangers," patterned after the Alaskan Civil Air Patrol, to support search-and-rescue operations and to allow "normal scheduled and charter flights" to provide "para military presence and surveillance" throughout the North. Maj. K.C. Eyre, "Arctic Air Rangers: Concept Proposal," 29 September 1975.

54　Ramsay Withers interview, 25 June 2008.

55　"Historical Report – Northern Region Headquarters, 1971," entries 4 October 71, 16 December 71. Withers recalled: "When I went to CFHQ with our proposal for the Rangers the Director General Land Forces told me, 'that's not what we want, it's just a new CFAO' (definition, a new CF Administrative Order to clarify their status and entitlements!)": email to author, 22 June 2008.

56　Withers, "Reconstitution of the Canadian Rangers – Canadian Arctic Rangers," 22 September 1972, DND, f. NR 1901-260/1(Comd). See also Northern Region, Commander's Annual Review, 1 April 1971–31 March 1972. The House of Commons Standing Committee on External Affairs and National Defence (SCEAND) supported NRHQ's general plans to increase funding and facilities for the Rangers, "with a view to increasing its overall strength and effectiveness." See its report on *Defence in the 70s, Minutes and Proceedings,* 29 June 1972, 19:16-17.

57　DND, Submission for the Advisory Committee on Northern Development Annual Report, "Government Activities in the North – FY 1973/74," 3-4, and "FY 1974/75," 3.

58 Lt. D.A. Cossette, "Warships North," *Sentinel* 7, 9 (1971): 1-4.

59 Under new government policy, the navy's reordered priorities began with maintaining sovereignty through surveillance of coastal waters and ocean areas followed by collective defence of North America and the North Atlantic. Marc Milner, *Canada's Navy: The First Century* (Toronto: University of Toronto Press, 1999), 270-71.

60 *Defence 75*; Maritime Command (MARCOM) to Maritime Pacific Command (MARPAC), 3 March 1971, DND, CRNA, f. "Canadian Rangers, 1971."

61 Captain (Navy) A.L. Collier, "Maritime Command Briefing for the Board of Management," quoted in Porter, *In Retreat*, 40.

62 Maritime Command Directive – Canadian Rangers 1/71, 31 March 1971; Capt. C.R. Carpenter, Minutes of the DGLF Conference on the Canadian Rangers, 8 October 1971, DND, CRNA, f. "Canadian Rangers, 1971."

63 Maritime Command, Canadian Rangers, "Operational Concept," October 1970, Annex B, copy from 5 CRPG HQ, Gander.

64 Ibid., 11.

65 Ibid., Annexes F and J. The Maritime Command Canadian Ranger Battalion would include a staff of twenty-seven officers and twenty-six men, while the Canadian Ranger Independent Company in Maritime Pacific region would have a staff of seven officers and eight men. On Maritime Pacific plans, see CANMARPAC to RCEOC/CANMARCOM, 22 October 1971, DND, CRNA, f. "Canadian Rangers, 1971."

66 Maritime Command Operational Concept, October 1970, Annexes F and J.

67 Aide Memoire, "The Canadian Rangers," 21 November 1973, DND, f. 1901-260/4 (DMil).

68 Ibid.

69 Desmond Morton, *Canada and War: A Military and Political History* (Scarborough, ON: Butterworths, 1981), 190.

70 Deputy chief of the defence staff (DCDS) presentation to the Defence Management Committee (DMC) on the proposed reconstitution of the Canadian Rangers, no date (ca. November 1973), DND, f. 1901-260/4 (CLO).

71 J.L. Granatstein and Robert Bothwell, *Pirouette: Pierre Trudeau and Canadian Foreign Policy* (Toronto: University of Toronto Press, 1990), 235, and Douglas Bland, *Chiefs of Defence: Government and the Unified Command of the Canadian Armed Forces* (Toronto: Canadian Institute of Strategic Studies, 1995), 232-33.

72 Maj.-Gen R.A. Reid to DCDS, 12 April 1973, and Fifth Draft, Memorandum to the Cabinet, Reconstitution of the Canadian Rangers, November 1972. Copies provided by 1 CRPG.

73 DCDS presentation, ca. November 1973.

74 Brig.-Gen. J.A. Fulton to Chief of Land Operations, 28 March 1974, DND, CRNA, f. "Canadian Rangers, 1974"; "Chronology of Studies of Canadian Rangers," appended to D Res C4 to D Res C, 9 June 1978, DND, f. 1901-260/4 (D Res C 4); Northern Region, Commander's Annual Review 1 April 1971–31 March 1972, 2; Maj. R.S. McConnell, "The Canadian Rangers as Militia," 13 June 1979, DND, f. NR 5323-1. It was telling that DND's annual report for 1973 did not make any mention of the Rangers as an asset in Northern Region. See *Defence '73*, 56-58. Major Stirling could not comment on these proposals because he died in Yellowknife in December 1973. "Recollections of David Sproule," 1. General Jacques Dextraze apparently resurrected plans for an Arctic surveillance built around the Rangers in 1975, but the plans were never funded. Bland, *Chiefs of Defence*, 236.

75 "Recollections of David Sproule," 6.

76 Lemaire and Clarke based the Basic Ranger Course on the Royal Canadian Army Cadet Green Star Program. "Historical Report – Northern Region Headquarters 1973," 10 March 73; NRHQ, "Exercise Nanook Ranger IX: Training Program," Annex D to DND, f. NR 5323-3 (SSO R&C), 28 February 1978; "Historical Report – NRHQ 1979."

77 Col. W.B.S. Sutherland, "1971 White Paper on Defence Briefing Material for the Minister: The Canadian Rangers," 11 August 1971, DHH, 79/527, folder 2A.

78 "Brief for CDS: Northern Region Canadian Rangers," 6 March 1981, DND, f. 5323-1 (D Res).

79 Maj. S.J. Joudry, "Study Report: Northern Region Canadian Rangers," 27 May 1986, NR 5323-2 (SSO R&C), 8.

80 David Miller, "Canadian Rangers Stand on Guard," *News of the North,* 7 November 1979.

81 Joudry, "Study Report," 8.

82 The Rangers in the territories went from an effective strength of 163 in 1974 to 212 in 1976 without any formal recruiting program. NRHQ to DMIL, National Defence Headquarters, 11 April 1974, CRNA, f. "Canadian Rangers, 1974"; note in file, 1 July 1976, DND, CRNA, f. "Canadian Rangers, 1976." These figures suggest a decline from 1971 (when Mobile Command allegedly handed over control of 407 Rangers to Northern Region). This unreliable 1971 statistic was based on the last year of administrative activity in Eastern Area, in 1965, and in Western Command, in 1958. As Stirling's report showed, real effective strength was virtually nonexistent by 1970.

83 Jean Chrétien, *Northern Canada in the 70's* (Ottawa: DIAND, 1973). For a comprehensive reflection on the overlapping aims of DIAND and DND in this era, see J.S. Bryce, "Security Considerations in the Canadian Arctic" (master's thesis, Queen's University, 1975).

84 Eyre, "Forty Years," 298.

85 Maj.-Gen. David Huddleston, quoted in *The Arctic,* ed. Thomas Berger (Vancouver: Gordon Sproules, 1989), 179. See also G.G. Bell, "The Armed Forces and the Civil Authority," *Behind the Headlines* 31, 7-8 (1972): 1-14.

86 John Gellner, "The Military Task," in Dosman, *Arctic in Question,* 93.

87 Frances Abele, "Canadian Contradictions," *Arctic* 40, 4 (1987): 314-15.

88 A Canadian Airborne Regiment exercise planned for northeast of Yellowknife in 1976 was cancelled because the NWT commission was concerned that "no matter how effective militarily the exercise might be, Judge Berger and the Indian Brotherhood of the NWT (now the Dene Nation) would take the presence of large numbers of soldiers and equipment in the area as a 'show of strength' that had the potential to jeopardize the hearings." "Recollections of David Sproule," 4.

89 McConnell to Commander, CFNR, 7 November 1978, copy in possession of the author.

90 Ibid.; Brig.-Gen. C.E. Beattie to Chief Superintendent A.H. Buttler, G Division, RCMP, 13 December 1978, DND, f. NR 5323-2. See also NRHQ, untitled historical booklet, entries 31 July 1971, 18 November 1971, 13 January 1972, DND, f. NA 1325-1(PAffO).

91 In Canada, the provinces, territories, and municipalities have overall responsibility for ground and inland-water search and rescue (SAR), which they typically delegate to the local police force. In communities, RCMP search commanders are responsible for organizing and managing actual searches, including requesting assistance from volunteers. For a brief summary of these roles, see RCMP, "RCMP Search and Rescue," 15 December 2006, http://www.rcmp-grc.gc.ca/.

92 Questions about ground SAR policy persisted in the decades that followed. See, for example, Maj.-Gen. R.W. Lewis, "Visit to Northern Region Canadian Rangers, 30 November 1986," 1 CRPG, binder "Ranger Enhancement Papers, 1989-1994."

93 See, for example, McConnell, "The Canadian Rangers as Militia"; Brig.-Gen. J.B. Riffon, "Canadian Rangers Evaluation," 20 June 1980, DND, CRNA, f. "Canadian Rangers, 1980."

94 Director General Military Plans and Operations (DGMPO) to Commander, NRHQ, 4 February 1980; Brig.-Gen. M.L.A. Wiseman to Dist. List, 19 March 1980, DND, CRNA, f. "Canadian Rangers, 1980."

95 David Miller, "Canadian Rangers 'Stand on Guard,'" *News of the North,* 7 November 1979, C1.

96 Ibid.

97 Ibid.

98 Quoted in Brig.-Gen. Blake Baile, "Security and Sovereignty in Canada's North," *Proceedings of the National Northern Development Conference* (Edmonton: Northern Development Centre, 1982), 67.

99 After Brig. C.E. Beattie took over as commander, NRHQ, he submitted an evaluation report in December 1979 that recommended (as his predecessors had done) that the Rangers be reorganized and provided with more training, equipment, and a yearly maintenance grant of fifty dollars for each active Ranger. Briefing note for Director General Military Plans and Operations (DGMPO), "Canadian Ranger Program Expansion and Improvements," ca. June 1980, CRNA, f. "Canadian Rangers, 1980." He briefed several senior NDHQ staff on the proposal, including the vice and deputy chiefs of the defence staff and assistant deputy minister (policy). Although he received approval to pursue the idea and submitted a detailed implementation plan in April, the senior staff rejected it for being too extravagant. Joudry, "Study Report," 8.

100 Desmond Morton, *A Military History of Canada*, 4th ed. (Toronto: McClelland and Stewart, 1999), 261.

101 Capt. L. Palhazi to Staff Officer Regional Operations (SORO), Maritime Command Headquarters, 16 April 1984, acquired through Access to Information (ATIP); NRHQ to RCCWC/NDHQ, 5 May 1980, DND, CRNA, f. "Canadian Rangers, 1980." Tattersal insisted that trying to coordinate policy with Maritime Command before improving the staff situation in Yellowknife proved unrealistic.

102 Palhazi to SORO, 16 April 1984; NRHQ, Historical Report, 1981, 3-4.

103 Ken Spotswood, "The Raw Reality of Staying Alive," *Edmonton Journal,* 22 September 1981.

104 See, for example, Baile in "Open Forum Discussion," *Proceedings of the National Northern Development Conference,* 75. See also Lackenbauer and Kikkert, *Canadian Forces and Arctic Sovereignty.*

105 NRHQ, Historical Report, 1983, 4.

106 *Defence '82* (Ottawa: DND, 1972), 56.

107 Brian Mitchell, "Eskimo Point Rangers Honoured for Bravery," *News/North,* 20 April 1984.

108 NRHQ, Historical Reports, 1983, 4; 1984, 6. The four patrols declared inactive had not been trained in over two years.

109 Cossette, "Warships North," 4.

110 Porter, *In Retreat,* 59-61.

111 LANTREGHQ to RCCWC/NDHQ, 28 May 1980, CRNA, f. "Canadian Rangers, 1980."

112 Col. D.B. Ells to Director Reserves (DRES), 4 December 1984, 4-5, Atlantic Region Headquarters (ARHQ), f. 1901-260/4 (COS RO), 2-3. For a list of Ranger strengths and locations in Maritime Command in 1974, see RCCWC/NDHQ to Maritime Command HQ, 1 April 1974, CRNA, f. "Canadian Rangers, 1974." On Ranger liaison officers and resupply visits to Nain, see LAC, RG 24, H-2003-00872-1, box 5, f. "36 Coy 2 Pl."

113 Maritime Command reimbursed Ranger officers for modest travel expenses to meet with Rangers in their platoons. See, for example, Maj. H.L. MacFarlane to Director Compensation and Benefits Administration (DCBA), 31 December 1974, CRNA, f. "Canadian Rangers, 1974"; Maritime Command to RCCWC/NDHQ, 6 November 1975, CRNA. f. "Canadian Rangers, 1975." The Queen's Regulations and Orders were amended in 1975 to accommodate reimbursements to Ranger platoon commanders for recruiting, organizing, and training.

114 Mayor George N. Critchell to Palhazi, 13 December 1984, LAC, H-2003-00872-1, box 6, f. 1904-1 (1984); Lt.-Col G. Meharg to DRES-5, "100 527 877 Maj. F.M. Cox Canadian Rangers," 29 January 1986, f. ARHQ: 5000-1(COS RO).

115 Lt. Junior Roberts, interview with author, Gander, NL, 3 November 2008, and Jack Berry, telephone interview with author, Clarenville, NL, 26 March 2006; Austin Adams, interview with author, Clarenville, NL, 7 March 2006.

116 Maritime Pacific Headquarters to NDHQ, 10 April 1974, 24 June 1974, CRNA, f. "Canadian Rangers, 1974"; note in file, 1 July 1976, CRNA, f. "Canadian Rangers, 1976"; Rear Admiral A.L. Collier to Maritime Command, 21 December 1976; Lieutenant Commander G.E. Nicks to Director Reserves and Cadets, 9 June 1978, CRNA, f. "Canadian Rangers, 1977-1978"; Canadian Rangers – Pacific Region, 29 February 1988, MARP: 1901-2(DRO), Esquimalt Military Museum, f. "Canadian Rangers," 3-4. In 1971, Maritime Command seemed prepared to revitalize the Rangers along the Pacific Coast, but Maritime Pacific expressed little interest. See Maritime Command to Maritime Pacific, 3 March 1971, CRNA, f. "Canadian Rangers, 1971."

117 Canadian Rangers – Pacific Region, 29 February 1988, 4.

118 Pacific Region explained that this directive "would not introduce weapons where there were none already nor should it be construed as an overt act in contravention of any gun-control regulations" because the nineteen Rangers with outstanding rifles "were all hunters and outdoorsmen who already possess other hunting rifles." Pacific Region Headquarters to RCCWC/NDHQ, 23 October 1978, CRNA, f. "Canadian Rangers, 1977-1978."

119 Lt.-Col G.A. Gunton to DGLO, July 1974, CRNA, f. "Canadian Rangers, 1974."

120 Neil D. Greig to G.F. Anderson, Chief Policy Planning, NDHQ, 4 July 1974, CRNA, f. "Canadian Rangers, 1974."

121 Jacob Oweetaltuk to Army Rangers, Montreal, January 1977; Col. W.D. Wellsman to Oweetaltuk, 8 March 1977, CRNA, f. "Canadian Rangers, 1977-1978."

122 Maritime Command to RCCWC/NDHQ, 26 August 1977, CRNA, f. "Canadian Rangers, 1977-1978."

123 Northern Region had no responsibility in Eastern Region and would have been intruding on Mobile Command's jurisdiction. The latter, however, did not want control of Rangers, and the director general of military plans and operations in Ottawa was content "to let the Rangers 'seek their own level.'" Any threat was highly unlikely, and Mobile Command expressed no interest in investing in a Ranger liaison officer to train and administer the Rangers when Northern Region was willing to do so alongside its scheduled visits to Baffin Island. See CRNA, f. "Canadian Rangers, 1979."

124 The Rangers also persisted along the north shore of the Gulf of St. Lawrence east of Sept-Îles, although their common recollection is that they did little until the early 1980s. When veteran Rangers decided to retire, they commonly handed their weapons down to their sons, who assumed their place in the local platoons. Ranger Martin Conway of St. Paul River joined in 1981 when a military officer visited his father, who had been a Ranger since 1954. Because his father was in his seventies, the officer asked if anyone else could take his rifle. The father handed it over to Martin in his living room, and Martin signed up. He has been a Ranger ever since. Martin Conway, interview with author, St. Paul River, QC, 14 April 2007.

125 Col. D.B. Ellis to DRES, 4 December 1984, ARHQ, f. 1901-260/4(COS RO), 5, acquired through ATIP, describes Palhazi as "a single, thirty year old infantry officer who works well on his own."

126 Maritime Command, briefing for Director General Reserves and Cadets, 18 November 1983, acquired through ATIP; Capt. Richard Moore, "East Coast Rangers," *Sentinel* 20, 3 (1984): 7. On his high level of activity, see also Palhazi, "Canadian Rangers Training/Activity Plan Period 01 Jul-31 Dec 84," 5 April 1984, LAC, H-2003-00872-1, box 6, f. 1904-1 (1984), and slide show notes, ca. 1984, LAC, H-2003-00872-1, box 6, f. 1901-10, "Briefing Courses."

127 [Maritime Command HQ], briefing for DGRC, 18 November 1983.

128 "St. Anthony Resident Honoured for Contribution to Canadian Rangers," *Northern Pen (St. Anthony, NF)*, 25 September 1984, 8. On pay, see Ranger liaison officer to SORO, Atlantic Region HQ, 1 November 1984, LAC, H-2003-00872-1, box 6, f. 1901-1 (General).

129 Ellis to DRES, 4 December 1984, 4-5.

130 Lt. Junior Roberts interview.

131 Capt. L. Palhazi to SORO, Maritime Command HQ, 8 November 1984, LAC, H-2003-00872-1, box 6, f. 1901-1 (General).

132 Jack Berry, telephone interview with author, Clarenville, NL, 26 March 2006; also Austin Adams, interview with author, Clarenville, NL, 7 March 2006. Gord Anderson in Chevery shared this positive impression but noted that Palhazi and Captain Tony Lynch did not have "enough time to do what they should have" and had to rush through information and training. David Gordon Anderson, interview with author, 12 April 2007. One hundred and ten Rangers attended the four training seminars held in 1983 (15 percent of Maritime Command's Rangers) and 115 in 1984 (15.7 percent). Three hundred and thirty Rangers had been paid for attending a training seminar from 1981 to 1984, but many attended more than once. Ranger liaison officer to LANTREGHQ HALIFAX//SORO//, 1 November 1984, LAC, H-2003-00872-1, box 6, f. 1901-1 (General).

133 Dave Elms, "Canadian Rangers: 'Eyes and Ears of the Forces,'" *Northern Pen (St. Anthony, NF)*, 29 October 1985.

134 [Maritime Command HQ], briefing for Director General Reserves and Cadets, 18 November 1983; Palhazi to SORO, Maritime Command HQ, 26 October 1983, acquired through ATIP.

135 Moore, "East Coast Rangers," 7; Lt. Junior Roberts interview.

136 Palhazi to SORO, Maritime Command HQ, 26 October 1983, acquired through ATIP; Moore, "East Coast Rangers," 7. For an example, see, "Labrador Rangers Receive Medals," *Labradorian* (Happy Valley–Goose Bay) 10, 2 (January 1983).

137 Capt. L. Palhazi to SORO, Maritime Command HQ, 16 April 1984, LAC, H-2003-00872-1, box 6, f. 1775-1 (Visits).

138 Ellis to DRES, 4 December 1984, 2-3. The Rangers' education levels in Atlantic region were equally varied: some were former Canadian Forces officers and noncommissioned officers, others accountants, engineers, surveyors, wildlife officers, and even the superintendent of Terra Nova National Park, "who has 400 pers[onnel] working for him [and] has offered the use of his park accommodation and resources."

139 Palhazi to SORO, Maritime Command HQ, 16 April 1984, LAC, H-2003-00872-1, box 6, f. 1775-1 (Visits). As a general yardstick, Palhazi noted that the current strength of the Rangers in his area was roughly equivalent to an infantry battalion, "but the number of personnel dedicated to the command, control, training, administration and supply of an operational infantry battalion probably exceeds the one man Maritime Command Ranger Staff by several thousand percent."

140 "Vastness Limits Role to Showing Presence," *Globe and Mail*, 23 September 1971.

141 Wain King, "New Look for Arctic Patrols," *Ottawa Journal*, 3 April 1971. On how this message upset international lawyers, who insisted sovereignty was not in doubt, see Lackenbauer and Kikkert, "Building on 'Shifting Sands.'"

142 Canadian Rangers Evaluation Report, 6 December 1979, DND, f. 5323-1(Comd).

143 Eyre, "Custos Borealis," 300.

144 Foreman interview, 13 April 2007.

145 Law, Naval Officers Association of Canada, to Minister of National Defence, 22 February 1984, 14. Copy in possession of the author.

146 Canadian Forces Northern Region, "Northern Region Information," pamphlet, ca. 1980, 16-18, CFNA, f. NA 1325-1(PAffO).

147 Joudry, "Study Report," 3.

148 Capt. E.F. Reumiller, "Winter Warfare Instructor Course 8401," *Infantry Journal* 13 (Spring 1985): 9-10.

149 Ibid., 13-14.

Chapter 8: "The Most Cost-Efficient Program in the Canadian Forces," 1985-93

1 William Marsden, "With a 1940s Rifle, He Stands on Guard for Thee," *Montreal Gazette*, 5 October 1985.

2 Ibid.

3 On "the politics of ad hockery," see Rob Huebert, "A Northern Foreign Policy: The Politics of Ad Hocery," in *Diplomatic Departures: The Conservative Era in Canadian Foreign Policy, 1984-93*, ed. Nelson Michaud and Kim R. Nossal (Vancouver: UBC Press, 2001), 84. On the United States' decision to send the *Polar Sea*, see Huebert, "Polar Vision or Tunnel Vision? The Making of Canadian Arctic Waters Policy," *Marine Policy* 19, 4 (1995): 343-64.

4 See Huebert, "A Northern Foreign Policy," 86-91. For a fuller discussion, see Rob Huebert, "Steel, Ice and Decision-Making: The Voyage of the *Polar Sea* and Its Aftermath" (PhD diss., Dalhousie University, 1994). The navy had not entered Arctic waters since 1982.

5 House of Commons, *Debates (Hansard)*, 10 September 1985, 6462-64.

6 See, for example, Robert Fowler to House of Commons Standing Committee on National Defence, *Proceedings and Evidence*, 26 March 1987, 8:23-25.

7 George Erasmus, "Militarization of the North," *Information North*, Fall 1986, 1; Mary Simon, "Security, Peace and the Native Peoples of the Arctic," in *The Arctic: Choice for Peace and Security*, ed. Thomas R. Berger (Vancouver: Gordon Soules, 1989), 36, 67.

8 Kevin McMahon, *Arctic Twilight: Reflections on the Destiny of Canada's Northern Land and People* (Toronto: James Lorimer, 1988), 11, 126-28.

9 Kevin McMahon, "Strangers in the Land ... Again," *Peace and Security* 3, 1 (Spring 1988): 2-3.

10 McMahon, *Arctic Twilight*, 129-31.

11 Ibid., 131-32.

12 House of Commons Standing Committee on External Affairs and National Defence, *Minutes and Proceedings*, 17 September 1985, 28:48-49.

13 Ibid., 56-57. See also Gordon's comments in John R. Walker, "More Reliance on Inuit Suggested for Canada's Sovereignty in Arctic," *Ottawa Citizen*, 14 December 1985.

14 House of Commons Standing Committee on External Affairs and National Defence, *Minutes and Proceedings*, 17 September 1985, 28:50-51. See also her comments in Doug Holmes, "The North's Own Canadian Rangers," *Up Here*, February-March 1987, 61.

15 House of Commons Standing Committee on External Affairs and National Defence, *Minutes and Proceedings*, 17 September 1985, 28:55.

16 Brig.-Gen. J.E.L. Gollner, "Concept Paper – Canadian Forces Territorial Defence Regiment," 3 October 1989, copy provided by 1 Canadian Rangers Patrol Group (CRPG).

17 Maj. S.J. Joudry, "Study Report: Northern Region Canadian Rangers," 27 May 1986, Department of National Defence (DND), f. NR 5323-2(SSO R&C), 12.

18 Holmes, "The North's Own Canadian Rangers," 62-63.

19 Ibid., 60.

20 Christopher Wren, "Native Rangers Keep True North Free," *Globe and Mail*, 3 April 1986. This article first appeared as "Far North Has Militia of Eskimos," *New York Times*, 1 April 1986.

21 "Sub Sightings," n.d., released under Access to Information Policy (ATIP).

22 Miro Cernetig, "1-800 Call First Line Defence," *Globe and Mail*, 7 August 1991. This article followed William Claiborne, "Defending Canada with an 800 Number," *Washington Post*, 15 July 1991.

23 Peter Lesniak, "Subs, Rangers, Key to New Defense Plans," copy of undated article (ca. early 1990s) provided by 1 CRPG.

24 Northern Region Headquarters (NRHQ), annual report, 1985, 7-8.

25 Ibid., 1986, 7.

26 Malcolm Dunlop, "Nova Scotia Soldiers Awed by Arctic," *Halifax Chronicle-Herald,* 23 March 1987.

27 "Canadian Military Manoeuvres Highlight Sovereignty in Arctic," *Winnipeg Free Press,* 12 February 1987. See also Dan Leger, "Unique Sentries on Guard in Arctic," *Vancouver Sun,* 19 October 1987.

28 House of Commons Standing Committee on National Defence, *Minutes and Proceedings,* 26 March 1987, 8:20-21.

29 Minister of National Defence, *Challenge and Commitment: A Defence Policy for Canada* (Ottawa: Department of National Defence, 1987).

30 Holmes, "The North's Own Canadian Rangers," 62.

31 Annelies Pool, "Canadian Rangers to Be Expanded," *News/North,* 12 June 1987.

32 House of Commons Standing Committee on National Defence, 26 November 1987, 17:29-30.

33 House of Commons, *The Reserves,* Report of the House of Commons Standing Committee on National Defence (Ottawa: Queen's Printer, 1988). The army staffed a new Ranger rifle project from 1986 to 1993, and the chief of reserves and cadets signed off the statement of requirement in 1992, but the project failed because of cost and the project staff did not demonstrate a valid capability deficiency. Capt. J. Mills, briefing note to Director General Land Reserve Secretariat on the proposed Canadian Ranger Equipment Modernization Project, 31 August 2007, DND, f. 10001-1(DGL Res Sec).

34 NRHQ annual reports, 1987-89. Sanikiluaq, a community in the Belcher Islands, had been turned down when it requested a patrol a few years earlier because of the "low likelihood of military activity in the area." According to Major Joudry, the military preferred to devote its resources to strategically important locations along the Northwest Passage. Holmes, "North's Own Canadian Rangers," 63.

35 Capt. J.S. Kwasniewski to Staff Officer Regional Operations (SORO), Maritime HQ, 9 October 1986, DND, f. 7330-1(RLO).

36 Kwasniewski to SORO, 31 October 1985, DND, f. 7330-1(RLO); Capt. L.E. Ralph, Royal Canadian Air Cadets 842 Lions Squadron, Grand Falls, to Palhazi, 18 April 1985, and Lieutenant (Navy) Jim Walsh, 288 Royal Canadian Sea Cadet Corps, Gander, to Sgt. William Chafe, 20 May 1985, DND, f. 1085-20-1.

37 Kwasniewski to SORO, 13 February 1986, Library and Archives Canada (LAC), RG 24, Department of National Defence, H-2003-00872-1, box 6, f. 1775-1(Visits).

38 Lewis to Chief of the Defence Staff (CDS) et al., "Visit to Atlantic Region Canadian Rangers, 26 May 1986," DND, f. 1775-84/0 (C Res).

39 Ibid. See also Lewis, "Visit to NR Cdn Rgrs, 30 November 1986"; "Visit to Atlantic Region CR, 15-18 May 1986," LAC, RG 24, H-2003-00872-1, box 6, f. 1775-1(Visits).

40 Lt.-Col. G. Meharg to NDHQ/DRES-5, "100 527 877 Maj. F.M. Cox Canadian Rangers," 29 January 1986, Atlantic Region Headquarters, f. 5000-1(COS RO). For similar examples, see Capt. A.F. Lynch to Jobe Flowers et al., 27 September 1989, LAC, RG 24, H-2003-00872-1, box 5, f. 36 (North Labrador) Company.

41 Gordon Jones, interview with author, Chevery, QC, 12 April 2007. For example, Ernie Waye joined the platoon in 1985 when his father, who was a Ranger, decided to get out and asked Ernie to take his rifle. At twenty, Ernie was one of the youngest members of the company. Only a few years later, he was promoted to sergeant. Ranger Sergeant Ernie Waye, interview with author, Chevery, QC, 12 April 2007.

42 Sgt. Cyril Abbott, interview with author, 6 March 2006. Ranger Lieutenant Horace Lane, who joined in 1988, offered similar insights during an interview the same day in Lewisporte. As former Ranger Master Corporal Keith Matchem explained during an interview on

7 March 2006, the Rangers were not only unpaid, they were also expected to cover their own transportation costs in the late 1980s.

43 Kwasniewski to SORO, Maritime Command, Canadian Rangers, 1985-86 report, 9 October 1986. So did the company under Dunn, heralded as the "first functioning company." Points of meeting on 28 July 1987 between Major D.C. Iley and Capt. J.S. Kwasniewski, 20 August 1987, acquired through ATIP.

44 Canadian Rangers Atlantic Region, annual report, 1988-89, 28 April 1989, acquired through ATIP.

45 Kwasniewski, "Minutes of Canadian Ranger Atlantic Region Company Commanders Meeting," 14 May 1988," 16 May 1988, LAC, RG 24, H-2003-00872-1, box 6, f. 1901-1 (Orgs); Kwasniewski to SORO, 9 October 1986; Max Pickett, interview with author, Cape Freels, NL, 1 November 2008. Kwasniewski notes that a section of the Gander platoon conducted the first "field exercise" in Newfoundland and Labrador on 20 September 1986.

46 Canadian Rangers – Pacific Region, 29 February 1988, DND, f. "MARP: 1901-2 (DRO)," Esquimalt Military Museum, f. "Canadian Rangers," 8; Canadian Rangers Atlantic Region Training Directive, 1988-89, LAC, RG 24, H-2003-00872-1, box 1, f. 4500-1 (Trng), vol. 1; Canadian Rangers Atlantic Region, annual report, 1988-89, 28 April 1989, acquired through ATIP. Training in Labrador and along the Lower North Shore followed a different plan. Week-long sessions occurred in the spring before fishing season and in fall-winter after the fishing season, thus maximizing Ranger participation and minimizing the financial and human resources involved. In terms of pay, Northern Region enrolled its Rangers at the maximum incentive for privates while Maritime Command enrolled Rangers at the basic private rate of pay. This meant that, on average, Aboriginal people in the organization received higher pay than non-Aboriginal people (for the same job) at this time. Lt.-Col. W.J. Coupland to Staff Officer (SO) Rangers, Maritime Command; SO, Rangers and Cadets, NRHQ, Yellowknife; SO Reserve Operations, Pacific Region HQ, Victoria, 6 April 1988, LAC, RG 24, H-2003-00872-1, box 6, f. 1901-1 (Orgs).

47 Capt. A.F. Lynch, "Canadian Rangers Atlantic Region Annual Training Directive, 1990-91," February 1990, LAC, RG 24, H-2003-00872-1, box 1, f. 4500-1(Trng), v. 2.

48 Minutes of the Annual Company Commanders Meeting, 13-14 May 1989, LAC, RG 24, H-2003-00872-1, box 1, f. 1000-1 (General), v. 1.

49 Capt. A.F. Lynch to Officer Commanding No. 3 Platoon, No. 34 Company, 20 July 1989, LAC, RG 24, H-2003-00872-1, box 1, f. 5000-4(RLO).

50 Lt. H.T. Cole to Capt. J.S. Kwasniewski, 28 March 1988, LAC, RG 24, H-2003-00872-1, box 5, f. "35 Coy 2 Pl Churchill Falls." For various other examples, see Ranger liaison officer, *Ranger Newsletter,* 18 October 1989, LAC, RG 24, H-2003-00872-1, box 1, f. 1000-1(General), v. 1. In another example, four women Rangers from Nain – the first recorded women in the organization – participated in a long-range patrol exercise. The weather was awful, and snow houses proved warmer and more windproof than the military tents. Ranger liaison officer, *Ranger Newsletter,* 17 September 1990, acquired under ATIP. On these women, see also Canadian Rangers, Prospective Enlistments, 10 January 1990, LAC, RG 24, H-2003-00872-1, box 5, f. "36 Coy 2 Pl." Ranger Sergeant Gloria A. Collins is listed as a Ranger liaison clerk position working for the Ranger liaison office in St. John's in 1989, but I have found no additional information about her background.

51 For an introduction to the low-level flying dispute, see Marie Wadden, *Nitassinan: The Innu Struggle to Reclaim Their Homeland* (Vancouver: Douglas and McIntyre, 1991) and Peter Armitage and John Kennedy, "Redbaiting and Racism on Our Frontier: Military Expansion in Labrador and Quebec," *Canadian Review of Sociology and Anthropology* 26, 5 (1989): 798-817. The Innu still want nothing to do with the military at Goose Bay because of low-level flying controversy. Lieutenant Walter Joseph Anderson, interview with author, 22 February 2006. Anderson explained that the Innu and Inuit do not get along, and the Innu do not

support the claims of the Labrador Metis. Other members of the community corroborated his testimony.

52 Kwasniewski to SORO, 9 October 1986. For a representative sample of support for Primary Reserve and Regular Force training activities, see Canadian Rangers Atlantic Region, annual report, 1988-89, 28 April 1989, acquired through ATIP. Fifty Goose Bay residents signed up at the initial recruitment meeting in December 1985, and the military officially inducted twenty as Rangers early the following month. See LAC, RG 24, H-2003-00872-1, box 5, f. "35 Coy 3 Pl Goose Bay."

53 Walter Joseph Anderson interview.

54 Kwaniewski to Director Military Operations Co-ordination (DMOC), "Preliminary Surveillance Plans – Cartwright, Saglek," 25 November 1986, 7330-1 (RLO); notes from telephone conversations between Martin and Kwasniewski, 21 November 1986; Campbell and Kwasniewski, 21 November 1986; Web and Kwasniewski, 21 November 1986, acquired through ATIP.

55 Brig.-Gen. E.B. Beno to Chief Operational Planning and Force Development (COPFD), 23 August 1990, Canadian Ranger National Authority (CRNA), f. "Ranger Policy and Objectives."

56 Kwasniewski to SORO, 9 October 1986.

57 A Ranger documentary, filmed in 1990, began with an exercise featuring No. 31 Company Rangers in the Bonavista and Keels areas with soldiers from the 2nd Battalion, the Royal Newfoundland Regiment, who travelled from Stephenville and Corner Brook to give the film "the desired look." Filming resumed in Labrador, where soldiers from Secteur de l'est were "naturally gathered right to the nasties by the Rangers." *Ranger Newsletter,* 17 September 1990, acquired through ATIP.

58 Maj. D.C. Iley, "Military Paper: Future of the Canadian Rangers, 20 April 1989," DND, f. 201-260/4 (D Res 3-2), Esquimalt Military Museum, f. "Canadian Rangers." Iley thought this new, expanded organization would "allow for more contacts with civilians, assist in recruiting (long range), provide for a larger military lobby," and create opportunities for cadets who wanted to serve in remote regions. The list of new roles included teaching cadets, helping the Naval Reserve Maritime Coastal Defence Organization with coast watching and inshore surveillance, supporting land and air forces in the Territorial Defence Task Force, and assisting with local disaster operations such as oil spills and earthquakes. How many actually shared Iley's view – or would have supported his vision – is unclear. A few years before, Captain J.S. Kwasniewski had insisted that the Maritime Command Rangers preferred "the 'irregular' view of the reserve force." Capt. J.S. Kwasniewski to SORO, Maritime Command HQ, 13 February 1986, LAC, RG 24, H-2003-00872-1, box 6, f. 1775-1 (Visits). Australia's North-West Mobile Force (NORFORCE) is not structured or intended to be deployed away from its home region. Like the Rangers, "the regional nature of the unit allows access to what would be otherwise closed communities, engenders strong community support for their operations and facilitates access to unparalleled local knowledge." Unlike the Rangers, NORFORCE is the largest employer of indigenous people in both the Northern Territory and the Kimberley region. See "Defence Sub-Committee Visit to RAAF WLM, Darwin, East Timor and RAAF TDL," 15-19, online at http://www.aph.gov.au/. See also David Hancock, "Green Skin: Australia's Indigenous Army," *Australian Geographic* 93 (January-March 2009), online at http://www.australiangeographic.com/.

59 Brig.-Gen. J.E.P. Lalonde to Project Director Army Structure Implementation (PDASI), 23 May 1989, CRNA, f. "Ranger Policy and Objectives." Defence planners recognized that tying the Rangers to the territorial defence concept, even in a supporting role, "would necessitate a major revision of the present concept" and would require more resources.

60 Lt.-Col. Tattersal, untitled note on file, 24 January 1989, CRNA, f. "Ranger Strategy Paper."

61 Lt.-Col. W.H. Porter to Director General Reserves and Cadets (DGRC), "Canadian Rangers – CF Policy and Objectives," 28 May 1990, DND, f. 1901-260/4(D Res 6-2). Acquired through ATIP.

62 Lt.-Col. W.H. Porter to DGRC, 28 May 1998, DND, f. 1901-260/4, acquired through ATIP.

63 "The Rangers have and continue to serve a political/military purpose," Brigadier W.R. Dobson noted in July 1989. "The political aspect fits only the north or very sparsely settled areas of the country. That does not apply to the south." He insisted that military efforts in southern Canada should be directed towards the militia, not towards setting up competition from new Ranger units. He repeated the classic Primary Reservists versus Rangers debate but considered whether expanding the latter would generate "the adverse public perception of issuing rifles and ammunition to additional special segments of society." Dobson did, however, make an exception for sparsely populated areas along the BC Coast. Brig.-Gen. W.R. Dobson to Canadian Reserves and Cadets, 10 July 1989, CFNA, f. "Ranger Policy and Objectives."

64 Canadian Rangers – Pacific Region, 29 February 1988, 5, MARP: 1901-2(DRO), Esquimalt Military Museum, f. "Canadian Rangers." The Rangers' role and tasks had not changed much since the Second World War, and the military challenges posed by isolation and distance along the Pacific seaboard remained much the same. The vast majority of British Columbians lived south of fifty degrees latitude, seldom ventured north of that line, and had little awareness of northern issues. Although the population of BC had grown dramatically in the previous half century, development had largely occurred in a narrow southern belt and in isolated settlements based on resource extraction. At the same time, modern fish processing had led to the closure of canneries and the concentration of coastal residents into larger settlements. Iley, "Military Paper."

65 Canadian Rangers – Pacific Region, 29 February 1988. See also Chief of Staff Operations, Mobile Command, to Vancouver Militia Area, 29 April 1988, LAC, RG 24, H-2003-00872-1, box 6, f. 1901-1 (Orgs). To direct and guide them, Pacific Region requested a support staff of ten people, including two Ranger liaison officers and four sergeants as Ranger instructors.

66 Lt.-Col. W.H. Porter to DGRC, 28 May 1990, CRNA, f. "Ranger Policy and Objectives."

67 Brief for D Res Command, "Control and Organization of the Canadian Rangers (1947-1993)," CRNA, f. "Initial Planning Conference Enhancement of the Canadian Rangers."

68 Atlantic Region Headquarters (ARHQ) to DGRC, Ottawa, 16 January 1990, and Vice Admiral R.E. George to Deputy Chief of the Defence Staf (DCDS), 24 June 1990, Esquimalt Military Museum, f. "Canadian Rangers."

69 Major D.I. Hay, "The Canadian Rangers," 8 February 1991, Esquimalt Military Museum, f. "Canadian Rangers"; Wolf Christiansen, "Goodbye and Good Luck," The Ranger (4 CRPG) 8, 1 (Winter 2006): 2. See also Major Ian Hay, The Ranger 6, 1 (Winter 2004): 5.

70 Hay also noted that the company-platoon structure cost more and added no benefit because Ranger staff and patrols had adequate direct contact. Maj. A.K. Hamilton, Canadian Rangers (Pacific), Status Report, 12 June 1991, CRNA, f. "LFWA Rangers – SITREPS Annual Reports."

71 Captain Jim Miller, interview with author, Churchill, MB, 3 March 2009; Hay, "The Canadian Rangers," 8 February 1991. "The Ranger is a rugged self-reliant individualist who is intimately familiar with local terrain conditions," Hay's overview noted. "Rangers are integral members of their community and are prepared to serve their country in times of emergency."

72 Warrant Officer Dan Hryhoryshen, interview with author, Victoria, BC, 13 July 2005. On his background, see also "WO Dan Hryhoryhen [sic]," The Ranger 1, 1 (Winter 1999): 3-4.

73 Maj. A.K. Hamilton, Canadian Rangers (Pacific) Status Report, 12 June 1991. For descriptions of the various patrols and their host communities, see The Ranger (4 CRPG) 1, 1 (Winter 1999).

74 Dan Hryhoryshen interview.

75 In contrast to Northern Region, where instructors delivered a ten-day training package to each patrol once every two years, Hay wanted his instructors to visit each patrol three or four times annually.

76 Bill Leighton, interview with author, Nootka Island, BC, 16 July 2005.

77 Dan Hryhoryshen interview. The Ranger staff carefully allayed local concerns by explaining the local patrol's purpose and structure.

78 Jim Miller interview.

79 Tim Gallagher, "Happiness Is a Free Gun," *British Columbia Report*, 5 August 1991, 16. According to Gallagher, even the RCMP had concerns about accountability and the storage of the rifles, which Rangers normally kept in their homes. On Native blockades in BC, see Nicholas Blomley, "'Shut the Province Down': First Nations Blockades in British Columbia, 1984-1995," *BC Studies* 111 (Autumn 1996): 5-35.

80 J.L. Granatstein, *Canada's Army: Waging War and Keeping the Peace* (Toronto: University of Toronto Press, 2002), 379.

81 Douglas Bland, *Chiefs of Defence: Government and the Unified Command of the Canadian Armed Forces* (Toronto: Canadian Institute of Strategic Studies, 1995), 259; Adam Lajeunesse, "Sovereignty, Security and the Canadian Nuclear Submarine Program," *Canadian Military Journal*, 2007-08, 80-81.

82 Under this agreement, the United States agreed to obtain Canada's consent before operating icebreakers in waters that Canada claimed. See Canada-US Agreement on Arctic Cooperation, Ottawa, 11 June 1998, http://untreaty.un.org/unts/60001_120000/30/4/00058175.pdf.

83 Jeff Sallot, "True North Needs Less Guarding, Ottawa Decides," *Globe and Mail*, 18 September 1991.

84 "Minutes of the Commanding Officers Annual Conference, 16-17 March 1991," 9 May 1991, acquired through ATIP.

85 Maj. G.S. Rust, "Aide-Memoire on the Canadian Rangers," 3 January 1992, DND, f. 1901-260/4, 7. The Maritime Command budget for the Rangers had grown to nearly $1.7 million by 1992-93. Maritime Command, 1993 Annual Historical Report: Command Comptroller Branch – Finance, Annex G to MARC 1325-1 (NO2 ADMIN CO HQ), 29 March 1994, acquired through ATIP.

86 Brig.-Gen. J.E.L. Gollner to SSO, Rangers and Cadets, 1 April 1990, file NR 1901-2 (Comd). Emphasis in original. Copy provided by 1 CRPG.

87 Gollner to DCDS, 27 July 1990, CFNA, f. "CFNA Rangers-General." On growth plans, see also "Northern Ranger Expansion – Proposed Locations," 9 June 1988, LAC, RG 24, H-2003-00872-1, box 6, f. 1901-1 (Orgs).

88 Gollner to Gen. A.J.G.D. de Chastelain, 27 April 1990, 31 December 1990, NRHQ, f. 1000-2 (Comd). See also Massey Padgham, "Soldiers, Old Crow Rangers Join in Search," *Whitehorse Star*, 17 September 1987. In the summer of 1990, the Old Crow patrol provided a security piquet and assisted in evacuating the community when a forest fire threatened it. It earned the official recognition of the Yukon Government. Canadian Rangers, Brief for Maj. R. Bell, 10 June 1993. Copy provided by 1 CRPG.

89 2nd Lieutenant James Siamana, "Out on the Land," *Sentinel* 28, 4 (1992): 21.

90 "DHH History of Aboriginal Peoples in the Canadian Military," transcript of John MacFarlane telephone interview with Sgt. Vallee Saunders, Kuujjuaq, QC, 5 November 2001.

91 Brig.-Gen. Gellner to COPFD, 31 July 1990, CRNA, f. "Ranger Policy and Objectives."

92 Three previous attempts to create a patrol in Inuvik had been unsuccessful. Sergeant Mario Aubin explained to a local reporter in 1990 that job opportunities in the western Arctic made it difficult to attract and retain people who could devote time to Ranger training. The applicants he had recruited from the Inuvik Native Band led him, however, to correctly assume

that the military would eventually meet with success. Fred Huard, "Canadian Forces Recruiting More Northern Rangers," *Inuvik Drum,* 21 June 1990.

93   A few of the original Rangers in Inukjuak, who had been released in the early 1960s, rejoined alongside members of younger generations. Allie Ohaituk, interview with author, Inukjuak, QC, 26 August 2006.

94   There had never been any official announcement disbanding the Rangers in the territory, although ammunition resupply and support ended in 1969. "There was no shuttin' her down as far as I knew," Ranger Chuck Hume of Haines Junction recalled. As far as he was concerned, he carried right on through. Chuck Hume, interview with author, Haines Junction, YT, 16 June 2009.

95   William Morrison, "The 1200 Mile Village: The Alaska Highway and Settlement in the Far Northwest" (paper delivered to the Canadian Historical Association annual meeting, York University, May 2006).

96   Kenneth Coates and William Morrison, *Land of the Midnight Sun: A History of the Yukon* (Montreal/Kingston: McGill-Queen's University Press, 2005), 288, 292.

97   Brig.-Gen. Larry Gollner to CDS, 27 April 1990, NRHQ, f. 1000-2(Comd). The army had not conducted an exercise in Yukon since 1974.

98   Gollner to CDS, 30 April 1991, NRHQ, f. 1000-2(Comd). See also Lt.-Col. K.R. Sorfleet, "Comd Direction on Rangers and Cadets," 15 April 1991, 1 CRPG binder, "Ranger Enhancement Papers, 1989-1994."

99   Gollner to CDS, 30 April 1991.

100 Gollner to de Chastelain, 27 April 1990, and 31 December 1990, NRHQ, f. 1000-2 (Comd); Maj. M. Beztilny, "Northern Region Ranger Report," June 1990–May 1991, 5 July 1991, NRHQ, f. 4500-1(G3 R&C).

101 Yukon Situation Report, "Summary CFNA Cdn Rgrs as of 24 February 1993." Copy provided by 1 CRPG.

102 Canadian Rangers Brief for Maj. R. Bell, 10 June 1993.

103 Ranger Master Corporal Phil Morgan, interview with author, Whitehorse, YT, 15 June 2009; Maj. M.J. Winter, "Operations, Training, and Administration: Canadian Rangers in the Yukon and Northern British Columbia," 4 October 1994, 1 CRPG binder, "Ranger Enhancement Papers, 1989-1994." The Yukon Ranger Company, run out of the Whitehorse detachment at Boyle Barracks (now Cadet Camp Whitehorse), was modelled after the Atlantic Ranger companies but without Ranger officers.

104 Gollner to de Chastelain, 27 April 1990 and 31 December 1990.

105 Gollner to Chief of the Defence Staff, 30 April 1991.

106 "Yukon Sitrep" 24 February 1993. Audrey McLaughlin, Yukon MP and leader of the New Democratic Party, applauded the continued success and "great deal of community interest in participating in the Yukon Rangers." While in the territory in early March 1992, several people approached her about joining the Rangers. "Unfortunately," she noted, "there does not appear to be enough space to meet the demand." She acknowledged military cutbacks but also noted that the Department of National Defence was assuming Emergency Measures duties and saw "great potential" for the Yukon Rangers in this role. Audrey McLaughlin to Gen. de Chastelain, 11 March 1992, 1 CRPG binder, "Ranger Enhancement Papers, 1989-1994." CFNA had to remind the police and EMO in the territories that when they requested volunteer assistance from the Rangers in GSAR, the Rangers were serving as "individual volunteers" and not officially as Rangers or members of the Canadian Forces. Major D.V. Pittfield to Eric Bussey, 22 December 1993, 1 CRPG binder "Ranger Enhancement Papers, 1989-1994."

107 Gollner to de Chastelain, 27 April 1990.

108 "Summary CFNA Cdn Rgrs as at 24 February 1993." Copy provided by 1 CRPG.

109 Canadian Rangers, Brief for Maj. Bell, 10 June 1993, 12-13. The brief explained that the occasional negative attitude was heard in Yukon but was "almost non-existant in the NWT."

110 Brig.-Gen. P.J. O'Donnell to NDHQ, 7 July 1989, NRHQ, f. 3000-22 (Comd). Copy provided by 1 CRPG.

111 Canadian Rangers, Brief for Maj. Bell, 10 June 1993, 30-38.

112 Ibid.

113 NDHQ to G3 (Operations and Training Staff) Rangers and Cadets, CFNA, Yellowknife, 12 February 1993. Copy provided by 1 CRPG.

114 "Minutes of the Commanding Officers Annual Conference, 16-17 March 1991," 9 May 1991.

115 "Transfer of the Canadian Rangers to the Land Force: Implementation Plan," draft, CRNA, f. "Stewardship of the Canadian Rangers."

116 The James Bay and Northern Quebec Agreement created a complex administrative structure that included the Kativik Region, which had a southern land boundary "arbitrarily" drawn along the fifty-fifth parallel. Following major toponymic surveys with elders in the 1980s, Inuit of northern Quebec held a referendum and named the precise sociocultural region occupied and used by the Inuit "Nunavik." See Ludger Muller-White, "Shaping Modern Inuit Territorial Perception and Identity in the Quebec-Labrador Peninsula," in *Aboriginal Autonomy and Development in Northern Quebec and Labrador,* ed. Colin H. Scott (Vancouver: UBC Press, 2001), 33-40.

117 Land Force Quebec Area (LFQA) Sitrep, Annex B to "Minutes of Ranger Working Group Meeting," 25-26 May 1994, 20 June 1994, 4-5, DND, f. 3350-2 (G3 R&C). For statistics, see Maj. D.C. Iley, "Briefing Note for the Minister of National Defence on the Canadian Rangers in Quebec," 1 October 1991, CRNA, f. "SQFT-Canadian Rangers Creation 1993." The Sanikiluaq patrol on the Belcher Islands, while technically part of Northwest Territories and thus Northern Area, was placed under the command of Land Force Area Quebec for training and administration because all communications, transportation, and, "most importantly, hereditary and social ties" flowed from Sanikiluaq to the Ungava region. Canadian Rangers, Brief for Maj. R. Bell, 10 June 1993, 24-25.

118 Maj. M.U. Kelly, "Briefing Note for C Res and Cadets Rangers in SQFT," 19 February 1993, CRNA, f. "SQFT-Canadian Rangers Creation 1993"; Warrant Officer Pat Rizzo, telephone interview with author, 7 August 2009. Maj. Claude Archambault, the G3 (Operations and Training) Domestic Operations Officer at Land Force Quebec Area, was responsible for the Rangers from 1993-94 until they were transferred to the deputy chief of staff cadets. Maj. Claude Archambault, testimony, 22 February 2000, Standing Court Martial, St.-Jean, Quebec, 27, acquired through ATIP.

119 LFQA Sitrep, Annex B to "Minutes of Ranger Working Group Meeting, 25-26 May 1994," 20 June 1994, 4-5, DND, f. 3350-2 (G3 R&C).

120 Pat Rizzo interview.

121 Canadian Rangers Atlantic Region, annual report, 1988-89; Points of meeting on 28 July 1987 between Maj. D.C. Iley and Capt. J.S. Kwasniewski, 20 August 1987.

122 Sergeant Ernie Waye and David Gordon Anderson, interviews with author, Chevery, QC, 12 April 2007.

123 Ernie Waye interview. Initially, Blanc Sablon was going to be trained out of St. John's and everything west of St. Augustine out of Saint-Jean. This proposal raised concern, long-serving Ranger Captain Gordon Foreman in Harrington Harbour remembered, because it invited comparisons. He believed that the Ranger cell in Saint-Jean had wanted to eliminate the Rangers along the Lower North Shore in the early 1990s because it "only had interest in the North." Nevertheless, he successfully lobbied to keep the Lower North Shore patrols together under Quebec Area. Gordon Foreman, interview with author, Harrington Harbour, QC, 13 April 2007. Rizzo recalled that LFQA had remained skeptical about the Rangers' value until a Ranger passed along information about a submarine sighting to domestic

operations. This showed their value as an intelligence asset. Talk of shutting down patrols in the southern part of Quebec reflected financial constraints at LFQA in the 1990s. Pat Rizzo interview.

124 Pat Rizzo interview.

125 Gordon Foreman interview.

126 Pat Rizzo interview.

127 DND News Release, "Canadian Rangers Mark Double Celebration with 9000 Km Cross-Canada Trek," 13 January 1992; Canadian Armed Forces Northern Region Press Release, "NWT Leg of Exercise Baton Ranger Begins," 26 February 1992. Copies on file at Esquimalt Museum. See also 1 CRPG, f. "Ex Baton Ranger"; "La souveraineté canadienne dans l'Arctique," Le Soleil, 4 April 1992; Capt. Michael Mietzner, "Baton Ranger," Sentinel 28, 4 (1992) : 15-17; and Brig.-Gen. Pergat, "Canadian Forces in the North," 22 June 1992, excerpt in 1 CRPG binder, "Ranger Enhancement Papers, 1989-1994." See also Brig.-Gen. E. Beno to Commander Northern Region, 13 May 1992, file 1775-1(DGRC). This message was significant given the difficult national political context: commissions struck by the federal and Quebec governments to solve the constitutional riddle dominated the national agenda, and the eventual defeat of the Charlottetown Accord later that year revealed deep regional divisions in the country, as well as the unpopularity of the Conservative government.

128 Quoted in Richard Langlais, Reformulating Security: A Case Study from Arctic Canada (Göteborg, Sweden: Department for Interdisciplinary Studies of the Human Condition, Göteborg University, 1995), 151-53, 155-56, 190, 236.

129 Ibid., 151-53, 155-56, 190, 195-97, 202, 234.

130 Ibid., 195-97, 202, 234.

131 Inuit organizations jointly controlled land-use planning on remaining Crown lands, wildlife, environmental protection, and offshore resources with the federal government. For a basic overview, see R. Quinn Duffy, "Canada's Newest Territory," in Canada: Confederation to Present, ed. Bob Hesketh and Chris Hackett (Edmonton: Chinook Multimedia, 2001), CD-ROM.

132 See CBC Digital Archives, "Dene/Metis Ink Historic Land Claim Agreement," http://archives.cbc.ca/. The Tlicho (Dogrib) land claim and self-governance agreement received royal assent in 2005. The Dehcho's land claims remain unsettled. "Sam Gargan Elected New Dehcho grand Chief," CBC News, 23 June 2009. The Akaitcho Dene First Nations chose to negotiate fulfillment of their original treaty rights instead. NWT, Ministry of Aboriginal Affairs, "FAQ: Akaitcho Dene First Nations Lands, Resources & Governance Negotiations" (2000), http://www.gov.nt.ca/.

133 See Yukon, "The Umbrella Final Agreement, First Nations Final Agreements and Treaty Rights" (2008), http://www.eco.gov.yk.ca/landclaims/about.html. Canada reached final and self-government agreements with the following First Nations: Champagne and Aishihik First Nations (1995), Teslin Tlingit Council (1995), First Nation of Na-Cho Nyak Dun (1995), Vuntut Gwitchin First Nation (1995), Little Salmon/Carmacks First Nation (1997), Selkirk First Nation (1997), Tr'ondëk Hwëch'in (1998), Ta'an Kwäch'än Council (2002), Kluane First Nation (2004), Kwanlin Dün First Nation (2005), and Carcross/Tagish First Nation (2006). The Liard First Nation, Ross River Dena Council, and White River First Nation have yet to settle land claims.

134 See, for example, Graham White, "Treaty Federalism in Northern Canada," Publius 32, 3 (2002): 89-114.

135 Barry Zellen, "Gruben Foils Ranger Invasion of ISR," Tusaayaksat, 31 January 1991, 2; and Zellen, Breaking the Ice: From Land Claims to Tribal Sovereignty in the Arctic (Lanham: Lexington Books, 2008), 249-51. In 1989, for example, the Inuvialuit Land Administration approved a land-use permit for Ranger training in Sachs Harbour but refused to waive the access fee.

136 Zellen, *Breaking the Ice,* 251-52.

137 Ibid. 251-53.

138 Department of National Defence officials wanted to set aside land-use fees in light of the usual social and economic benefits accrued by isolated communities that hosted military exercises. "Comments on the Commander Northern Region Semi-Annual Report," Annex A to 1456-42 (DESP 5), 10 March 1992, CRNA, f. "CFNA Rangers – SITREPs Annual Reports." See also Vice Admiral L.E. Murray to CDS, Semi-Annual Report, Commander, Northern Area, 27 July 1992, 1 CRPG binder, "Ranger Enhancement Papers, 1989-1994." In February 1993, the Inuvialuit demanded application and access fees (approximately $100 for a Ranger exercise and up to $10,000 for a company-sized SOVEX). Consequently, DND held no sovereignty exercises in Inuvik, Aklavik, Tuktoyaktuk, Holman, Paulatuk, or Sachs Harbour. "Summary CFNA Cdn Rgrs as at 24 Feb 93." Copy provided by 1 CRPG.

139 The Inuvialuit Final Agreement Report, FY 96/97, Annex A to Maj. D. Galea to Director Claims and Aboriginal Government, 29 May 1997, CFNA, f. 1456-42-1 (G3).

140 CFNA, Annual Historical Report, 1994, 17; Kenneth Calder to CDS, 27 July 1992, DND, f. 1000-2(SPP-3); Gen. de Chastelain to Brig.-Gen. V. Pergat, 18 August 1992. Copies provided by 1 CRPG. Canadian Forces Northern Area consulted annually with mayors, Inuit organizations, tribal councils, renewable-resource councils, local chiefs, and land administrators about military activities conducted within other land claim settlement areas. Apart from the Inuvialuit, none sought land-use fees. See Galea to Director Claims and Aboriginal Government, 29 May 1997, and annexes.

141 Brent Morrison, "Rangers and Army to Train in Dawson Area," undated *Klondike Sun* article, ca. August 1993, Dawson Library clipping file.

142 "Ex Reliant Nordic," undated page from a 3rd Battalion Princess Patricia's Canadian Light Infantry report, ca. 1993, Dawson Library clipping file.

143 Ibid. The Rangers were similarly satisfied. Ranger Sergeant John "Mitch" Mitchell, interview with author, 13 June 2009, Dawson, YT.

144 Miro Cernetig, "Patriotism among the Icebergs," *Globe and Mail,* 2 July 1993.

145 Franklyn Griffiths, "Civility in the Arctic," in *Arctic Alternatives: Civility or Militarism in the Circumpolar North,* ed. Franklyn Griffiths (Toronto: Science for Peace/Samuel Stevens, 1992): 279-309.

146 Maj. M. Beztilny, "Northern Region Ranger Report Jun 90/May 91," 5 July 1991, NRHQ, f. 4500-1 (G3 R&C).

147 Gen. de Chastelain, "CDS Visit to NRHQ Yellowknife – 05 June 1990, 29 June 1990," 1 CRPG binder, "Ranger Enhancement Papers, 1989-1994."

148 Brig.-Gen. V. Pergat, "Northern Region Strategic Plan – 1992-97," 25 May 1992, CRNA, f. "CFNA Rangers – General."

149 J. Okalik Eegeesiak to Master Corporal Patterson, 26 October 1993; Maj. R. Bell to Eegeesiak, 28 October 1993, 1 CRPG binder, "Ranger Enhancement Papers, 1989-1994."

150 Audrey McLaughlin to de Chastelain, 11 March 1992; Canadian Rangers, Brief for Maj. R. Bell, 10 June 1993, 29. Copies provided by 1 CRPG. The name of Yukon Territory was changed officially to Yukon in 2003.

151 See, for example, Record of Decisions, Canadian Ranger Working Group, Whitehorse, YT, 23-24 February 1993, 1 CRPG binder, "Rgr/JCR Conf Feb 93-Feb 97."

152 Brig.-Gen. E.B. Beno, "Canadian Rangers Program – Long-Term Development, 9 August 1991," 1 CRPG binder, "Ranger Enhancement Papers, 1989-1994."

153 Ibid. Atlantic Region also "flirted with the idea of creating Ranger units along the coast of Nova Scotia in the anti-drug smuggling role," but it did not act on the plans.

154 Canadian Rangers Brief for Maj. R. Bell, 10 June 1993, 1 CRPG binder, "Ranger Enhancement Papers, 1989-1994."

155 Handwritten notes, "Rangers Working Group," 29 July 1993, and Capt. P.D. Chura, "Summary – Rgr Conf held 29 Jul 93," 6 August 1993, 1 CRPG binder, "Rgr/JCR Conf Feb 93-Feb 97."

156 Brief for Director of Reserves, "Control and Organization of the Canadian Rangers (1947-1993)," CRNA, f. "Initial Planning Conference Enhancement of the Canadian Rangers."

157 Col. J.R.P. Daigle to D Res, 21 February 1994, 1 CRPG binder, "Ranger Enhancement Papers, 1989-1994."

158 Daigle to D Res, 21 February 1994.

Chapter 9: Enhancement and the Junior Canadian Rangers, 1994-99

1 Department of National Defence (DND), Directorate of History and Heritage (DHH), "History of Aboriginal Peoples in the Canadian Military," f. N-ON-7, John MacFarlane, telephone interview with Abraham Metatawabin and his son, Ed (translator), Fort Albany, ON, 15 November 2001, transcribed by John Maclean.

2 John MacFarlane, interview with Metatawabin. Metatawabin's main concern was that airplanes flying overhead would not see lights or "evidence of land being in use" and would "go back home and say that area is uninhabited ... But we use that area, all the time."

3 Peter Moon, "In This Army, a Red Ball Cap Is Regular Gear," *Globe and Mail*, 14 November 1994.

4 "Canadian Rangers Ontario – South of 60 Degrees Study," May 1995, Canadian Rangers National Authority (CRNA), f. "Canadian Rangers – Inquiries – Historical Data."

5 "National Defence: Budget Impact" (Ottawa: DND, February 1994), i, 1-11; Lilly Goren and P. Whitney Lackenbauer, *The Comparative Politics of Military Base Closures* (Orono, ME: Canadian-American Centre, University of Maine, 2000).

6 See David Bercuson, *Significant Incident: Canada's Army, the Airborne, and the Murder in Somalia* (Toronto: McClelland and Stewart, 1996); John A. English, *Lament for an Army: The Decline of Military Professionalism* (Toronto: Irwin, 1998); and J.L. Granatstein, *Canada's Army: Waging War and Keeping the Peace* (Toronto: University of Toronto Press, 2002), 403-18.

7 Royal Commission on Aboriginal Peoples, *People to People, Nation to Nation* (Ottawa: Minister of Supply and Services, 1996), ix-xi, 10.

8 For two different perspectives, see Alan Cairns, *Citizens Plus: Aboriginal Peoples and the Canadian State* (Vancouver: UBC Press, 2000), and Tom Flanagan, *First Nations? Second Thoughts* (Montreal/Kingston: McGill-Queen's University Press, 2000).

9 Sarah Scott, "Native Rangers Put a New Face on Canada's Military," *National Post*, 14 June 2003. On the developments at Akwesasne, see Timothy Winegard, "The Forgotten Front of the Oka Crisis: Operation Feather/Akwesasne," *Journal of Military and Strategic Studies* 11, 1-2 (2009): 1-50.

10 Capt. D.M. Scandrett, "The Formation of the Canadian Rangers in LFCA," 30 May 1991; Scandrett to Major D. Iley, 12 June 1991, CRNA, f. "LFCA Canadian Rangers Creation 1993."

11 Major (ret'd) David Scandrett, telephone interview with the author, 4 April 2012.

12 Scandrett to Land Force Central Area (LFCA) HQ, Toronto, G3 Trg, G3 Ops, 18 June 1992, CRNA, f. "LFCA Canadian Rangers Creation 1993."

13 Scandrett, "Formation of the Canadian Rangers," 30 May 1991.

14 Scott, "Native Rangers Put a New Face on Canada's Military"; "Soldiers Learn in Role of Natives," *The Province* (Vancouver), 17 February 1995. Sault was sworn in as "Mishonis" (grandfather) of 3 Canadian Ranger Patrol Group (CRPG).

15 "Canadian Rangers LFCA Interim Trial Report," annex to the minutes of the Ranger Working Group, 25-26 May 1994, DND, f. 1901-260/0(D Res).

16 Scott, "Native Rangers," and David Scandrett interview. For an accessible introduction to First Nations culture in northwestern Ontario, see Rupert Ross, *Dancing with a Ghost:*

Exploring Indian Reality (Toronto: McClelland and Stewart, 1992). Ranger instructors in Quebec also visited patrols while wearing red sweatshirts and khaki pants. They did not want to appear too military when building relationships. Warrant Officer Pat Rizzo, telephone interview with author, 7 August 2009.

17 Interview with Capt. Harry Austen, Geraldton, ON, 9 July 2008. Austen served as the administration officer for the Rangers in northern Ontario from 1994 to 1997 before he left to spend five years as a senior instructor with the Ontario Workplace Safety and Insurance Board. He returned in October 2002 to take over 3 CRPG's PHASE program. "Junior Rangers' Safety, Abuse Programme Is Growing," 3 CRPG newsletter, May 2003.

18 Harry Austen interview.

19 Quoted in Moon, "In This Army."

20 Not all communities were receptive: some saw the Rangers "as just another sterile government force coming on to their land" and rejected them outright. Chris Hornsey, "Focus on Canadian Rangers," ca. 1994, newspaper clipping in CRNA, f. "Canadian Rangers – Inquiries – Historical Data."

21 "Canadian Rangers LFCA Interim Trial Report"; W.D. Harrison to Maj.-Gen. W.B. Vernon, 6 July 1994, CRNA, f. "LFCA Canadian Rangers Creation 1993." The LFCA's Ranger sergeant major went to Moosonee to act as a liaison between the new Ranger patrols, the communities, and various government agencies.

22 Scandrett, "Canadian Rangers Ontario: DGRC Working Group – Sitrep 95," 2 May 1995, DND, f. 1920-1 (OC Cdn Rang Ont); Maj. R. Smye to Maj. Y. Bouchard, email, 8 May 1995, CRNA, f. "Canadian Rangers–Ptl UIC."

23 Harry Austen interview. The Rangers also received the praise of the mayor of Geraldton and the chief of the Bearskin Lake First Nation for their actions during the evacuation.

24 Although the director of reserves in Ottawa assigned an officer part-time to the Ranger file and was the office of primary interest (OPI) within National Defence Headquarters, the director general reserves and cadets/director reserves only administered the Rangers on behalf of the vice chief of the defence staff (VCDS). Command rested with the VCDS, and operational command was delegated to Land Force Command and CFNA.

25 Record of Decisions, Canadian Ranger Working Group held at Whitehorse, YT, 23-24 February 1993, 1 CRPG, binder "Rgr/JCR Conf Feb 93-Feb 97." The creation of a Ranger Working Group was proposed in 1990. Maj. B.L. McLellan to Director of Reserves et al., 31 May 1990, CRNA, f. "Ranger Policy and Objectives."

26 Capt. P.D. Chura to Chief of Staff, "Summary – Rgr Conf held 29 July 1993," 6 August 1993, DND, f. 3350-2(G3 Rgr). "Our present representation in NDHQ lies with Maj[or] Sutherland who deals with rangers only half the time," Chura noted. "At the conference it was apparent that he has neither the interest [nor] the motivation for the job. Expressing a greater desire to conclude the meeting before lunch than to actually address any of the issues, Maj Sutherland left most of the participants with a bitter taste in their mouths."

27 Maj. R.D. Knight, "A Service Paper for Commander Canadian Forces Northern Area Discussing Increases to the Establishment of 1 Canadian Ranger Patrol Group," 20 July 1999, CFNA, f. 1920-1(CO). Copy provided by 1 CRPG.

28 Leblanc for Chief of the Defence Staff (CDS), 30 May 1995, DND, f. 1901/ 260/4(DGRC). To support these new patrols, CFNA requested two additional Ranger instructors.

29 Department of National Defence, *1994 Defence White Paper* (Ottawa: DND, 1994), 46.

30 Memorandum, "Project P9175: Canadian Ranger Enhancement Project," 1 July 1995, DND, f. 3136-5-P9175(DDAS 9).

31 COS, Northern Region Headquarters to G3 Rangers and Cadets, Northern Region Headquarters, 23 September 1993, email. Copy provided by 1 CRPG.

32 Leblanc for CDS, 30 May 1995, DND, f. 1901/ 260/4(DGRC). Col. (ret'd) Pierre Leblanc, telephone interview with author, Ottawa, ON, 18 July 2006. Leblanc's previous posting had

been as the Canadian defence adviser in India and Nepal. He cited the 1994 white paper, which opened the door to addressing "some current deficiencies" and "for expansion into some communities where the Rangers can make a significant contribution to the social fabric."

33 Leblanc, "Canadian Rangers Enhancement Project," 30 May 1995, DND, f. 1901/260/4(DGRC).

34 Lt.-Gen. P.J. O'Donnell to DGRC, 30 June 1995, DND, f. 3136-5-P9175(DDAS 9); "Project P9175," 1 July 1995; and Capital Project Summary, f. 3136-5-P9175, signed by David Collenette, 23 July 1995. The defence budget declined from 1994 to 1999. See Project Ploughshares Briefing 95/1.2, "1995-96 Military Spending: Monitoring the Downward Trend," and DND, "Canada's Defence Budget: 1993-2006," http://www.dnd.ca/site/Reports/budget05/back05_e. asp (last accessed 9 July 2007). Leblanc is convinced that his plans went unopposed because of their modest cost. Pierre Leblanc interview.

35 Canadian Forces Northern Area, *Historical Report*, 1995, 3.

36 Maj.-Gen. E.W. Linden to Commander, Land Force Command and Canadian Forces Northern Area , 30 January 1995, DND, f. 1901-260/4. See also Linden, "Enhancement of the Canadian Rangers Program," ca. 22 December 1994, 1 CRPG, binder "Ranger Enhancement Papers, 1989-1994."

37 Col. J.P.G. Leblanc, Canadian Rangers Enhancement Project, 30 May 1995, and Annex A, DND, f. 1901/260-4(DGRC). Leblanc considered the Rangers in the Arctic the most important, particularly those in the High Arctic islands because they represented a continuous government presence. He wanted to expand the number of patrols to increase coverage in the archipelago, but there were no communities without a patrol so this was not "doable." He considered awakening to this reality as "part of my education process." Pierre Leblanc interview.

38 Leblanc for CDS, 30 May 1995, DND, f. 1901/ 260/4(DGRC). Opening new patrols did not always proceed seamlessly. In 1996, for example, CFNA opened new patrols at Rae Lakes (fourteen Rangers) and Lutsel K'e (fifteen Rangers), but it encountered problems at Fort Liard related to infighting between community groups that prevented the formation of a patrol as planned. The Délįne patrol closed in December 1995 because of problems related to alcohol and a corresponding lack of leadership. In the summer, CFNA staff visited Watson Lake to try to reopen the patrol, which had been declared inactive the previous year, but a lack of interest in the community prompted its closure. Lieutenant (Navy) C.D. Purvis, Rangers Working Group, 13-14 November 1996, minutes, 3 December 1996, 1 CRPG, binder "Rgr/JCR Conf Feb 93–Feb 97."

39 Leblanc for CDS, 30 May 1995, Annex C. By 1995, fifteen Ranger patrols in CFNA had inspected thirty-eight North Warning System sites roughly three times per year (particularly to deter vandalism of old DEW Line infrastructure), with a budget of $274,000. Scandrett asked the DGRC to consider the other areas for the proposed communication and navigation equipment, but Leblanc refused. Col. J.P.G. Leblanc, Ranger Working Group Meeting, 3-4 May 1995, 11 May 1995, 1 CRPG, binder "Rgr/JCR Conf Feb 93–Feb 97."

40 Leblanc to Director General Policy Coordination (DGPC), 31 May 1995, DND, f. 1901-260/4(DGRC); Fax, "Rangers Enhancement Program," Chief Reserve and Cadets to Director General of Aboriginal Affairs, 30 November 1995; DND Backgrounder BG-96.043, "Update on Restructuring of the Reserves," 21 November 1996; Maj. B.A. Sutherland, minutes of Ranger Working Group Meeting, 25-26 May 1994, 27 May 1994, copy in 1 CRPG, binder "Rgr/JCR Conf Feb 93–Feb 97." The national working group decided to make the red-hooded sweatshirt an item for all Rangers in July 1993. When the Canadian Forces' supply system could not implement the directive fully, some staff officers procured shirts locally. Capt. P.D. Chura to COS, "Summary – Rgr Conf held 29 July 1993, 6 August 1993," DND, f. 3350-2 (G3 Rgr); Canadian Rangers LFCA Interim Trial Report, annex to the minutes of the Ranger Working Group, 25-26 May 1994, DND, f. 1901-260/0 (D Res). Officers encouraged the

Rangers in Atlantic area to go to the army surplus store to purchase their own uniforms, such as parkas. Ranger sweatshirts and t-shirts were available for purchase beginning in the late 1980s, but Rangers had to buy them – "and they were not cheap," Junior Roberts recalled. "It was a huge relief when they were provided for free." Lieutenant Junior Roberts, interview with author, Gander, NL, 3 November 2008. Ranger Sergeant Curtis Hicks made a similar point, explaining that they only got the ball cap for free. Interview with author, Musgrave Harbour, NL, 1 November 2008. Rangers Cyril Abbott and Keith Matchem explained that the original sweatshirts and t-shirts designed for the Rangers in Atlantic Canada cost twelve dollars and six dollars, respectively. Interviews with author, Bonavista, NL, 7 March 2006.

41 Personal interviews with Rangers across the country confirmed this observation. This clothing was delivered to each of the patrols by the summer of 1997. Some of these uniform purchases fared better than others. Bright orange safety vests, similar to those worn by work crews, failed to withstand the rigours of the climate and could not stand up to "any amount of normal wear and tear." The lettering peeled off (Rangers filled in missing letters with black markers); the "one size fits all" vests did not fit over most Rangers' parkas; the elastic and reflective material cracked in the cold (so the Rangers in Inukjuak used the reflective material for fishing); and buckles and pockets proved difficult to access and manipulate when placed over bulky clothing. By 1997, the military began to recall and replace the vests. DGRC, "CAN RAN 2000: A Review of the Canadian Rangers and of the Junior Canadian Rangers," 27 January 2000, 30-31 (hereafter CAN RAN 2000); members of the Inukjuak patrol, in discussion with author, August 2006. Similarly, the toques distributed to the Rangers were not warm enough to wear in the Arctic. Minutes of the 25-26 November 1998 meeting of the Ranger Working Group, 17 February 1999, DND, f. 1901-260/4(DGRC).

42 Northern Area Canadian Rangers Summary, June 1994–April 1995, 1 CRPG, binder "Rgr/ JCR Conf Feb 93–Feb 97"; Lt. Mark Gough, interview with author, Yellowknife, NT, 19 March 2000.

43 Martin Brouillard to Lt.-Cdr. Nicole Girard, "Memorandum on Sovereignty in the Arctic Re: Rangers, 14 June 2001," CRNA, f. "Sovereignty in the Arctic." Communications remained a concern, however, and some Rangers did not get paid for months when their patrol commanders neglected to send sovereignty patrol reports to headquarters or provided incorrect information about the Rangers who participated in the patrols. "Sovereignty Patrols," *Ranger Report* (1 CRPG) 6, 3 (1 April 2000): 17.

44 For example, when Keith Machem joined the Ranger platoon in Bonavista, his company commander simply instructed him to "just be available if you are ever called upon to assist the military." Until the mid-1990s, "the Ranger role was very obscure," he explained. "If anyone asked me what our role was, I would not have felt comfortable trying to explain what we did." Master Corporal Keith Matchem, interview with author, Bonavista, NL, 7 March 2006.

45 LFCA Headquarters, "Service Paper on LFC Canadian Rangers," 13 June 1995, DND, f. 4800-4-4 (G3), acquired through ATIP. See also Col. J.P.G. Leblanc to Distribution List, 16 February 1995, DND, f. 1901/260-4. The "South of 60" study noted that the territories "south of 70" had no sovereignty questions, which reinforced the point that the "north of 60" division was arbitrary from a technical sovereignty standpoint. The Rangers represented the only resource available to area commanders north of 50 in eastern Canada and north of 55 in western Canada. The study also noted that ground search and rescue would be much more difficult and expensive without Ranger volunteers participating in actual searches.

46 Special Commission on the Restructuring of the Reserves, *Report* (Ottawa: DND, 1995), 49. The commission predicated its recommendations for southern expansion on the Bold Eagle program, designed to recruit Aboriginal people in Saskatchewan into the Primary Reserve – "a laudable initiative [that had] thus far met with very limited success, producing

only a few reservists at remarkably high cost." If Bold Eagle was too costly per recruit to justify its existence, the commissioners suggested expanding the Rangers – "with its concept of operations and terms of service unchanged" – to absorb the Bold Eagle scheme. On the Bold Eagle youth development program, see http://www.army.gc.ca/.

47 Vice Admiral L.E. Murray, "Canadian Ranger Programme – A Strategic Overview (The Way Ahead)," 22 September 1995, 1 CRPG, binder "Ranger Enhancement Papers 1995." Rangers would provide "local assistance and advice to SAR activities," a cryptic phrase that did not refer to Rangers regularly conducting search and rescue "but rather to that level of general assistance and advice a local expert can reasonably be expected to offer to CF SAR teams." This confusing language, impenetrable to all but the most seasoned bureaucrats, sought to evade the long-standing policy problem of Ranger leadership and participation in search and rescue. "Canadian Rangers Role and Tasks," Annex A to Leblanc, "Canadian Rangers Enhancement Project," 30 May 1995, DND, f. 1901/260/4(DGRC).

48 See, for example, Col. J.H.P.M. Caron, "Comments on Canadian Rangers Studies," 8 August 1995, CRNA, f. "C2 Canadian Rangers Study 95."

49 Major B.A. Sutherland to DGRC, 13 June 1995, DND, f. 1901/260-1. The precedence of the patrol groups reflected the seniority of the various units, according to when they were first created in the 1940s.

50 The Rangers in Land Force Atlantic Area were commanded by the training and operations officer (G3 Ops and Plans) in Halifax, who exercised his control through the liaison officer in St. John's. The Ranger liaison staff consisted of the liaison officer, four Ranger instructors, a finance clerk, an administration clerk, and a unit quartermaster as of 1995. "Sitrep Canadian Rangers Atlantic," appended to Ranger Working Group, 3-4 May 1995, minutes, 15 May 1995, DND, f. 1901-260/0(D Res).

51 Capt. Eugene Squires, interview with author, Yellowknife, NT, 11 April 2008. Squires's previous posting had been in Croatia.

52 Ibid.

53 David Sorenson, "Canadian Rangers to Disband on Avalon," *The Express,* 20 September 1995, 3. For insight into Sherren's vision for the Rangers in Newfoundland more generally, see Capt. Nelson J. Sherren, "Canadian Rangers 32 Co., Notes on Improvements and Re-Organization," ca. June 1989, LAC, RG 24, H-2003-00872-1, box 1, f. 5000-4 (RLO). The marginalia on the document by Master Warrant Officer P.B. Dunne is telling.

54 Minutes of the Ranger Working Group Meeting, 12-13 December 1995, 22 December 1995, DND, f. 1901-260/0 (DGRC).

55 There were "no tears in the outports" when the company and "buddy platoon" in Gander shut down. Ranger Sergeant Curtis Hicks, interview with author, Musgrave Harbour, NL, 1 November 2008.

56 Eugene Squires interview.

57 Ranger Lieutenant Walter Joseph Anderson, interview with author, Goose Bay, NL, 22 February 2006.

58 Ranger Lieutenant Horace Lane, interview with author, Lewisporte, NL, 6 March 2006. Exceptions were Harry Martin, the company commander in Labrador who became patrol commander in Cartwright, and his second-in-command, David Clooney of Labrador City, who became a Ranger. The abolishment of the company structure also had the financial benefit of ending the expensive company commander meetings. Squires converted these savings to additional pay for the Rangers. Eugene Squires interview.

59 Rosemary Ommer, *Coasts Under Stress: Restructuring and Social-Ecological Health* (Montreal/Kingston: McGill-Queen's University Press, 2007), 5.

60 Situation Report Canadian Rangers Atlantic, ca. May 1995, 1 CRPG, binder "Rgr/JCR Conf Feb 93–Feb 97."

61 Col. J.A.L. Bujold, Ranger Working Group, 12-13 December 1995, 22 December 1995, meeting minutes, 1 CRPG, binder "Rgr/JCR Conf Feb 93–Feb 97."

62 The new patrols, stood up effective 1 April 1999, were set at twelve Rangers. Lt.-Col. C.T. Russell, "5 CRPG Situation Report as of 31 Oct 98," 23 November 1998, attached to minutes of the 25-26 November 1998 Meeting of the Ranger Working Group, 17 February 1999, DND, f. 1901-260/4(DGRC); Lt.-Col. B.G. Bailey, "5 CRPG Situation Report as of 31 Oct 99," 25 November 1999, attached to minutes of the 29 November–1 December 1999 Canadian Ranger and Junior Canadian Ranger Working Group Meeting, 6 March 2000, DND, f. 1901-260/5(Rgr-JCR 2).

63 Situation Report Canadian Rangers Atlantic, 10 November 1997, attached to minutes of the 13-14 November 1997 meeting of the Ranger Working Group, DND, f. 1901-260/4(DGRC).

64 Lt.-Col. K.A. Moher, "Canadian Rangers Atlantic Annual Operations and Training Directive 1996-97," 28 February 1996, 1 CRPG, binder "Rgr/JCR Conf Feb 93-Feb 97"; "Sitrep Canadian Rangers (Atl Region)," ca. November 1996, 1 CRPG, binder "Rgr/JCR Conf Feb 93-Feb 97." Staff scheduled training for the Nain and Hopedale patrols differently, with two training sessions of six days each given the logistics and cost involved in visiting remote Labrador communities.

65 Russell, "5 CRPG Situation Report as of 31 Oct 98."

66 "Sitrep Canadian Rangers Atlantic," appended to Ranger Working Group, 3-4 May 1995, meeting minutes, 15 May 1995, DND, f. 1901-260/0(D Res); Canadian Rangers Atlantic, "Significant Unit Events and Activities 1995," 1 CRPG, binder "Rgr/JCR Conf Feb 93–Feb 97."

67 "Rangers to Hold 4,000 Km Relay to Celebrate Cabot 500," *Evening Telegram,* 15 January 1997; and "Canadian Rangers Marking Cabot Anniversary with 4,000 Km Journey," *Northern Pen,* 21 January 1997.

68 Army Public Affairs press release, 13 January 1997, Centre for Newfoundland Studies, f. "Canadian Rangers."

69 Canadian Rangers, "Cabot 500 Relay," log book, copy on file at 5 CRPG HQ, Gander, Newfoundland. On 24 June, Lieutenant Cyril Abbott of Bonavista presented the ceremonial axe to Lieutenant-General Crabbe to pass along to Premier Brian Tobin and the people of Newfoundland and Labrador.

70 Meeting of the Ranger Working Group, 29 July 1993, 1 CRPG, binder "Rgr/JCR Conf Feb 93–Feb 97."

71 Bryan Pederson to Minister of National Defence, 24 February 1995, 1 CRPG, binder "Rgr/JCR Conf Feb 93–Feb 97."

72 See CRNA, f. "Canadian Rangers – Inquiries – Historical Data."

73 Lt.-Col. M.D. Capstick, "The Canadian Ranger Enhancement Program – Land Forces Western Area," 11 September 1996, and Maj. M.T. Vietch, "Briefing Note for Commander LFC, 'LFWA Ranger Enhancement Program,'" 20 November 1996, CRNA, f. "Rangers 1996"; "Canadian Ranger Pacific – Expansion Proposal," ca. July 1997, and Col. A.L. Bujold to VCDS, 9 November 1995, CRNA, f. "LFWA Restructure of Canadian Rangers Patrol." All of these communities had Royal Canadian Mounted Police (RCMP) detachments and had been stood up in 1993. National Defence Headquarters told Land Force Western Area that it first had to identify offsets and disband "redundant patrols" before creating new patrols that fit within the existing operations and maintenance budget.

74 Col. J.P.G. Leblanc, Ranger Working Group Meeting, 3-4 May 1995, 11 May 1995, and Lieutenant (Navy) S.V. Pokotylo, Ranger Working Group, 28-29 May 1996, meeting minutes, 12 June 1996, 1 CRPG, binder "Rgr/JCR Conf Feb 93–Feb 97."

75 Capt. Jim Miller, interview with author, Churchill, MB, 3 March 2009; Miller, "Farewell," *The Ranger* 5, 4 (Fall 2003): 5.

76 Canadian Rangers Pacific, annual report, attached to "Minutes of the 13-14 Nov 97 Meeting of the Ranger Working Group," DND, f. 1901-260/4(DGRC); "Exercise 'Teardrop,'" *The Ranger* 1, 2 (Spring 1999): 8; "Leadership RV (April 10 – 16/00)," *The Ranger* 2, 2 (Spring 2000): 5.

77 Jim Miller interview.

78 Capt. Jim Miller, "Introduction and Review of Leadership Theory," *The Ranger* 1, 2 (Spring 1999): 6.

79 Monique Giguère, "Au pays d'Agaguk: Le 'Davy Crockett' du Grand Nord," *Le Soleil*, 15 April 1996, A1. Translation by the author. "J'ai un pied dans l'Armée et un pied chez les Inuit." "Ils n'embarquent pas dans le système. C'est la liberté qu'ils aiment."

80 Warrant Officer François Duchesneau, interview with author, Inukjuak, QC, 23 August 2006, 28 August 2006.

81 Maj. Claude Archambault, testimony, 22 February 2000, Standing Court Martial, Saint-Jean, 14, 29, acquired through ATIP.

82 Maj. Carlo de Ciccio, "Les Rangers du SQFT à l'entrainement," *Servir* (BFC Montreal) 2, 8 (May 1996): 1, 3. Translation by the author. "Les membres de la presse ont été en mesure d'apprécier l'aide et les conseils des Rangers pour manger de la viande et du poisson crus gelés et pour dormir dans un igloo avec une température extérieure de moins 30°." "Ceci a permis à nos journalistes de constater que le mode de vie des Rangers Inuits se traduit par le terme 'Survie' pour les gens du Sud."

83 Jill Wherrett, *Aboriginal Peoples and the 1995 Quebec Referendum* (Ottawa: Library of Parliament, 1996).

84 André Noel, "Des Inuit participeront à un exercice militaire," *La Presse*, 28 March 1996. Translation by the author. "Ils agissent pour l'amour du pays." "La fierté chez les Inuit et leur sentiment d'appartenance au Canada, via l'armée canadienee." In 1996, six of the fourteen mayors in Nunavik were Rangers. Other patrol leaders included a Kativik school board executive, a Makavik offshore negotiator, a co-op manager, a conservation officer, and a substance abuse counsellor. Several Rangers worked for regional and local hunter support programs, and all were closely integrated into the social fabrics of their communities. "Ils portent fièrement l'uniforme et se sentent honorés de servir la population," Sergeant Mario Aubin noted. "Le choix des membres se fait par un comité de sélection nommé par la collectivité. Faire partie du groupe des Canadian Rangers est une marque de valeur." Mario Aubin, "Ce que les Inuit m'ont appris," *Dernière heure*, 21 September 1996, 38-39.

85 Monique Giguère, "Les Inuit ont peur d'un Québec souverain," *Le Soleil*, 18 September 1996. Forand was noncommittal.

86 Luc Chartrand, "Les séparatistes de la toundra," *L'Actualité*, 1 September 1996. "Cette loyauté se manifeste, entre autres façons, dans leur participation très enthousiaste à l'organisation des Rangers," Paul Bussières of Makivik Corporation explained to Chartrand.

87 He had first met the Rangers when responding to an avalanche at Blanc-Sablon, on the Lower North Shore, which required the army to detonate part of the mountain to safeguard the community. Presumably, this was the avalanche on 10 March 1995. See "Tempête sur Blanc-Sablon," *Le Midi-quinze* (Radio-Canada), 10 March 1995, http://archives.radio-canada.ca/.

88 See W.K. Barger, "Inuit-Cree Relations in the Eastern Hudson Bay Region," *Arctic Anthropology* 16, 2 (1979): 59-75. For Cree views on Quebec separatism, see Grand Council of the Crees, *Sovereign Injustice: Forcible Inclusion of the James Bay Cree into a Sovereign Québec* (Nemaska, QC: Grand Council of the Crees, Nemaska, 1995).

89 Lieutenant (Navy) C.D. Purvis, Rangers Working Group, 13-14 November 1996 meeting minutes, 3 December 1996, 1 CRPG, binder "Rgr/JCR Conf Feb 93–Feb 97." On Whapmagoostui,

see Naomi Adelson, "Gathering Knowledge: Reflections on the Anthropology of Identity, Aboriginality, and the Annual Gatherings in Whapmagoostui, Quebec," in *Aboriginal Autonomy and Development in Northern Quebec and Labrador,* ed. Colin H. Scott (Vancouver: UBC Press, 2001), 289-303.

90 Although Major R.D. Knight, the commanding officer in CFNA, worried about imposing ethnic quotas in patrols, the director general reserves and cadets affirmed that the Canadian Forces encouraged diversity and that "mixed patrols are an excellent example of multicultural integration." "Minutes of the 13-14 Nov 97 Meeting of the Ranger Working Group," and Maj. Claude Archambault, "Address Rangers," ca. November 1997 (attached to the minutes), DND, f. 1901-260/4(DGRC).

91 Archambault, "Address Rangers."

92 Mario Aubin, "Ce que les Inuit m'ont appris," *Dernière heure,* 21 September 1996, 38-39. Translation by the author. "Dans ces regions Nordiques, autant chez les Amérindiens que chez les Blancs, personne n'élève la voix. Chacun écoute ce que dit l'autre, et le plus âgé du group parle en dernier." "C'est aussi l'occasion pour les plus âgés des Inuit de transmettre aux plus jeunes les connaissances traditionelles de survie, de chasse et de pêche." "Nous respectons leur culture. Il n'est pas question de nous comporter en conquérants."

93 Scott, "Native Rangers."

94 Major B.A. Sutherland, "Draft Service Paper on the Organization, Establishment, Command, Control and Coordination of the Canadian Rangers," 18 May 1995, CRNA, f. "C2 Canadian Rangers – Study 95." LFCA Regular and Militia subunits started to come north to train with the Rangers in their communities for winter warfare, survival, and crosscultural training. Sappers from 1 CER came to Peawanuck and did construction, furnace repair, household plumbing, and field-engineering operations at forty below. 1 RCHA conducted winter warfare, boreal forest, and sea ice operations on the James Bay coast. Reservists came for summer survival and canoe training. David Scandrett interview.

95 Major Guy Ingram, interview with author, Geraldton, ON, 8 July 2008.

96 Ibid., and Harry Austen and David Scandrett interviews. Scandrett did not get along with Land Force Central Area and appealed directly to Ottawa rather than following the regional chain of command. He also told Ranger instructors to wear civilian clothing in northern Ontario rather than their uniforms in the hope that they would fit in better and develop trust and friendships.

97 James Morris to Hon. Doug Young, 24 February 1997, CRNA, f. "Canadian Rangers – Inquiries – Historical Data." The letter reported that the Nishnawbe-Aski Nation area had lost more than 140 youth to suicide, particularly young men between the ages of fifteen and twenty-five. At this time, the province of Ontario commissioned hearings into NAN Youth Suicide, which Scandrett attended. He incorporated the findings into the Ranger and Junior Canadian Ranger programs. David Scandrett interview.

98 "Canadian Rangers Ontario – South of 60 Degrees Study" (hereafter South of 60 Study) May 1995, CRNA, f. "Canadian Rangers – Inquiries – Historical Data."

99 Ibid. In this report, Scandrett described the Rangers as a "non-intrusive link to mainstream Canadian society that fosters and preserves native values" while concurrently acting as a vehicle for "nation building."

100 Col. J.P.G. Leblanc, Ranger Working Group Meeting, 3-4 May 1995, 11 May 1995, 1 CRPG, binder "Rgr/JCR Conf Feb 93–Feb 97."

101 South of 60 Study.

102 Sidney Linden, *Report of the Ipperwash Inquiry,* vol. 1 (Toronto: Ministry of Attorney General, 2007), 112; David Morrison to Douglas Young, 9 January 1997, CRNA, f. "LFCA Canadian Rangers Creation 1993"; Major David Scandrett, "Canadian Rangers Ontario – RWG96 SITREP," 26 May 1996; and Peter Cheney, "Why Our Soldiers Are Fighting Tears," *Globe and Mail,* 27 March 2001.

103 "Rangers Military Unit Elects Its Leaders," Canadian Press NewsWire (Toronto), 29 September 1996; and Guy Ingram interview.

104 On country space and community healing, see Cathrine Degnen, "Country Space as a Healing Place: Community Healing at Sheshatshiu," in *Aboriginal Autonomy and Development in Northern Quebec and Labrador,* ed. Colin H. Scott (Vancouver: UBC Press, 2001), 357-78.

105 Sylvie Poirier, "Territories, Identity and Modernity among the Atikamekw (Haut St-Maurice, Quebec)," in Scott, *Aboriginal Autonomy and Development,* 113. For a profound reflection on hunter-gatherers' place in the modern world, see also Hugh Brody, *The Other Side of Eden: Hunters, Farmers, and the Shaping of the World* (Vancouver: Douglas and McIntyre, 2001). On the conflict between schooling and traditional Inuit expressions of personhood, which socialize children to overcome egocentric concerns in the interests of group survival, see Anne S. Douglas, "'It's like they have two parents': Consequences of the Inconsistent Socialization of Inuit Children," *Inuit Studies* 33, 1-2 (2009): 35-54.

106 Richard G. Condon, "The Rise of the Leisure Class: Adolescence and Recreational Acculturation in the Canadian Arctic," *Ethos* 23, 1 (1995): 60.

107 Royal Commission on Aboriginal Peoples, *Choosing Life: Special Report on Suicide among Aboriginal People* (Ottawa: Royal Commission on Aboriginal Peoples, 1995). On the limitations of Aboriginal youth programs during this period, see Gerald Taiaiake Alfred, "A Review and Analysis of the Major Challenges and Concerns of Aboriginal Youth in Canada" (October 1995), and Leslie A. Pal, "Aboriginal Youth Policy" (March 1994), reports prepared for the royal commission.

108 Capt. J.N. Gri and Capt. S.A. Cameron, "Expansion of the NA Cadet Programme," 10 September 1992, CFNA, f. 1085-0. How could the military better support the needs of northern youth, foster northern development, and bolster public support? Gri and Cameron argued that the most appropriate leaders would be local people "who understand the strength of family and clan ties, the extended family situations from which the native youth often come, the importance of elders, the possibility of abuse of alcohol or physical abuse in the home, the unique strengths and vulnerabilities of native youth, and the need for spiritual and cultural guidance would do much to meet the needs of northern native youth." The formal requirements of the cadet program either dissuaded or prohibited many prospective northerners from assuming leadership roles. Nevertheless, constitutional uncertainty and growing support for Aboriginal self-government made it "the duty of the Canadian Forces to change or modify programs that they are mandated to support."

109 Ibid. Rangers had been involved with the cadets in Nain, albeit informally, since 1989. See "Nain Cadet Corps Requirements," 31 March 1989; Minutes of the Annual Company Commanders Meeting, 13-14 May 1989, LAC, RG 24, H-2003-00872-1, box 1, f. 1000-1 (General), vol. 1.

110 Maj. R.G. Bell, "Proposal to Trial a Junior Canadian Ranger Program," Briefing to the Chief of Reserves and Cadets, 23 March 1994, and Bell to Commander, CFNA, "Service Paper on the Establishment of a Canadian Forces Junior Ranger Program," 16 April 1996, 1-7, CFNA, f. 1085-0-1.

111 Northwest Territories Bureau of Statistics, "Paulatuk – Statistical Profile," http://www.stats.gov.nt.ca/community-data/Profile%20PDF/Paulatuk.pdf. On Paulatuk, see also "Environmental Impact for the Mackenzie Gas Project," vol. 4, part B, "Social Economic Baseline: Paulatuk Community Report," IPRCC.PR.2005.03 (April 2005), http://www.ngps.nt.ca/.

112 Bell, "Proposal to Trial," 4. During personal interviews, however, CFNA officials suggested that officers picked this particular site with the trial's failure in mind.

113 "The Junior Canadian Rangers Trial," attached to "Northern Area Canadian Rangers Summary: June 94–April 95," 1 CRPG, binder "RG R/JCR Conf Feb 93–Feb 97."

114 Maj. B.A. Sutherland, "Minutes of Ranger Working Group Meeting, 25-26 May 1994, 27 May 1994, copy in 1 CRPG, binder "Rgr/JCR Conf Feb 93–Feb 97."

115 Monique Giguère, "Les juniors rangers: Un antidote au suicide," *Le Soleil,* 18 September 1996. Translation by the author. "Les Junior Rangers, tu vas faire marcher ça!" "T'en auras pas!" See also Hélène Buzzetti, "(In)justice du Nord," *Le Devoir,* 4 August 2005.

116 Maj.-Gen. Roméo Dallaire to Commander, Land Forces, 8 February 1996, Secteur Québec de la force terrestre (SQFT, Land Force Quebec Area), f. 1085-11-5(SCEM Cad). The Kativik Regional Government allotted $5,000 to each patrol to assist in the introduction of the program, paid the return fares to Valcartier, and passed a resolution providing $45,000 to finance equipment (such as stoves, lanterns, tents, and sleeping bags). Lt.-Col. R. Chartrand, "Fiche préparée pour le GCMDT SQFT: Les junior rangers," 11 December 1995, 2; "Junior Rangers Nunvaik," Kativik Regional Government, 27 February 1998, quoted in CAN RAN 2000, 12.

117 Chartrand, "Fiche préparée pour le GCMDT SQFT," 2, Appendix A – Historique; Warrant Officer Pat Rizzo, telephone interview with author, 7 August 2009. On the opening ceremonies, see Monique Giguère, "Dans le mille avec les Junior Rangers!" *Le Soleil,* 18 September 1996, C1. Chartrand, "Fiche préparée pour le GCMDT SQFT," 3.

118 Undated note on Junior Canadian Rangers (JCR), ca. August 1999, in 1 CRPG, binder "1 CRPG Briefing." Captain Don Finnamore told me that the CFNA staff wanted the JCR pilot in Paulatuk to fail because it did not have sufficient manpower to run the program. They thought it had failed until the minister of national defence announced its official creation. Interview with author, Yellowknife, NT, 20 March 2000.

119 Rem Westland, email to author, 5 February 2004.

120 Canadian Forces General Message (CANFORGEN) 037/96, "Restructuring of the Reserves," 7 May 1996. The CFNA commander envisaged seven Junior Ranger patrols in his region in the short-term and up to twenty-eight patrols in the future. This plan would require more instructional staff, and he suggested a major to lead the program and a warrant officer for every seven Junior patrols. Major B.A. Sutherland, "Briefing Note for the VCDS: Proposed Junior Ranger Programme," 7 February 1996. Before the trial, Northern Area had anticipated the need for one full-time instructor for each increase of ten Junior Ranger patrols in the future. Bell, "Proposal to Trial," 4.

121 Sutherland, "Briefing Note for the VCDS."

122 Canadian Rangers – Ontario, "Young Ranger Program Business Plan," 7 March 1996, DND, f. 4500-9.

123 Giguère, "Les juniors rangers: Un antidote au suicide." Translation by the author. "Nos jeunes se conduisent mieux, ils font de meilleurs citoyens et apprennent à réagir éfficacement en situation de crise." On suicide in Aboriginal communities, see Royal Commission on Aboriginal Peoples, *Choosing Life.*

124 "Minutes of the 13-14 Nov 97 Meeting of the Ranger Working Group."

125 Giguère, "Dans le mille avec les Junior Rangers!" Translation by the author. "L'an dernier, je voulais commencer le programme avec deux patrouilles. On a fini par s'entendre sur trois. Kuujjuaq, Salluit et Povungnituk ont été créées. Cette année, j'en envisageais trois. Il y en a quatre: Tasiujaq, Kangiqsujuaq, Akulivik et Inukjuak. Je n'aime pas les échéanciers fermes qui ne laissent aucun jeu."

126 DGRC, "Synopsis Sheet: Junior Ranger Programme," ca. December 1996, DND, f. 3136-1(DGRC). See also Jocelyn Coulon, "Défense: Young réorganise la reserve," *Le Devoir,* 23 November 1996.

127 Jean Dupuis to Col. Chartrand, 27 February 1998, and Kativik Regional Government, Resolution No. 98-12, 26 February 1998, CRNA, f. "Rangers 1997-1998."

128 Tracy Kovalench, "Feds Boost Canadian Youth Funding," *Yellowknifer,* 22 July 1998. See also "We're Doing Things Nobody Else Can Do," *Ottawa Citizen,* 5 April 1998; DND press release, "Cadets, Junior Canadian Rangers and CF Reserve to Receive Additional Funding

for Youth Employment Initiatives," NR-98.55, 16 July 1998; Vice Admiral G.L. Garnett to DGRC, 12 November 1998, DND, f. 1901-260/1 (DFPPC 3-2). When the vice chief of the defence staff approved funding in October 1996, the implementation plan forecast twenty-one Junior Ranger patrols. Following Youth Initiative funding in July 1998, the forecasted number of patrols ballooned to seventy-one by 2000-01. Capt. C. Ferland, briefing note for the VCDS, "Junior Canadian Ranger Expansion," 17 May 1999, DND f. 1901-260/5 (DRes 2-3).

129 Sutherland, "Proposed Junior Ranger Programme," 7 February 1996.
130 "Junior Canadian Rangers," overview in *The Ranger Report* 5, 2 (1999): 12.
131 "1 Canadian Ranger Patrol Group SITREP as at 23 November 1998," CFNA, f. 901-1(CO 1CRPG).
132 "Minutes of the 13-14 Nov 97 Meeting of the Ranger Working Group."
133 For example, most of the Inuit youth at the 2001 summer camp in Whitehorse had never seen a horse or even large trees prior to their visit. Captain Chris Bergeron, interview with author, Yellowknife, NT, 20 April 2002.
134 "Minutes of the 29 November–1 December 1999 Canadian Ranger and Junior Canadian Ranger Working Group Meeting, 6 March 2000," DND, f. 1901-260/5 (Rgr-JCR 2).
135 "Minutes of the 13-14 Nov 97 Meeting of the Ranger Working Group."
136 Bell, "Service Paper," 16 April 1996.
137 Undated note on Junior Rangers, ca. August 1999, in 1 CRPG, binder "1 CRPG Briefing"; interview with Don Finnamore.
138 1 CRPG, "Brief for DGRC: Ranger/JCR Study," 25 October 1999, 1 CRPG, binder "1 CRPG Briefing."
139 Major D.I. Hay to Director of Reserves, 28 September 1999, DND, f. 1901-260/4 (OC). Similarly, 5 CRPG expressed concern that the Junior Rangers program would interfere with the cadets. When the director reserves encouraged them to consider establishing the Junior Rangers in Labrador communities with no cadet corps, they worried that, once Youth Initiatives funding ran out, they would be expected to pay for the program out of their operational budget. Director of Reserves 2 Maj. J.D.G. Chaplin explained that if the Junior Ranger program could show results to the Treasury Board, there would be a permanent baseline transfer to the department for the future conduct of the program. Minutes of the 25-26 November 1998 meeting of the Ranger Working Group, 17 February 1999, DND, f. 1901-260/4(DGRC). When Major Dan Hay, the officer commanding 4 CRPG, approached the cadet headquarters in Victoria, they informed him that they would support any community that wanted a youth program. According to this logic, the Junior Rangers were redundant. Maj. D.I. Hay to Director of Reserves, 28 September 1999, DND, f. 1901-260/4 (OC).
140 Email, Col. T. Gebert to Lt.-Cdr. K. Stewart, 29 March 1999; Director of Rangers/JCR, "Canadian Rangers/Junior Canadian Rangers" PowerPoint presentation, ca. 23 November 1999.
141 "Minutes of the 13-14 Nov 97 Meeting of the Ranger Working Group." On personnel issues, see also Capt. Claudia Ferland, "Briefing Note for the VCDS: Junior Canadian Ranger Expansion," 17 May 1999, DND, f. 1901-260/5 (DRes 2-3).
142 Overall command remained centralized at National Defence Headquarters (administered by the VCDS through the DGRC), with operational and administrative control of Rangers in the field delegated to the commander CFNA and to the chief of the land staff, who de-volved day-to-day responsibility for the Rangers to the land force areas. In Ottawa, the chief of the land staff assigned an officer to Ranger matters within the reserves and militia staff. The officer attended Ranger working groups on his behalf, staffed the allocation of funds between the vice chief of the defence staff and the areas, and monitored routine staffing between the director of reserves and the areas. As a Level 1 adviser, CFNA continued to communicate directly with the director. Chief of Review Services (CRS), "Review of the

Canadian Rangers [Draft]" September 2003, last amended 12 November 2003, CRNA, f. "CRS and CRNA Report" (hereafter CRS Review).

143 Captain Don Finnamore, interview with author, Yellowknife, NT, 20 March 2000.

144 Maj.-Gen. E.W. Linden, "Canadian Rangers/Junior Canadian Rangers," 12 March 1997, CRNA, f. "Rangers 1997-1998."

145 Minister Organization Order 97068, dated 24 November 1997, authorized the organization of 1 CRPG. I have not located similar records for the CRPGs under LFAs, but I presume that the authorizations would have been on or around the same date. The CRPGs were actually stood up in winter 1998. See CFOO 3685 – 1 CRPG, 23 February 1998, and presentation to Ranger Working Group 98 by 3 CRPG, attached to "Minutes of Canadian Ranger/JCR Working Group, November 1998." On 2 CRPG, see Archambault, testimony, 22 February 2000.

146 Don Finnamore interview; Dwayne Lovegrove, Speech, Parade of 1 CRPG, Official Ceremony, 2 April 1998, transcript held at 1 CRPG; fax, "Rangers Enhancement Program," 30 November 1995, 8-9. In 1 and 5 CRPGs, Regular Force commanding officers filled positions on the area staff, while a reserve major in a dedicated position commanded the other three patrol groups. The commanding officer of 4 CRPG was the chief of staff of 39 Canadian Brigade Group, but Major Ian Hay continued as officer commanding with responsibilities for day-to-day operations from headquarters in Victoria. "Opening Ceremony," *The Ranger* 1, 1 (Winter 1999): 1.

147 CRS Review, iv.

148 Archambault, testimony, 22 February 2000, 12-13, 16. Pat Rizzo described the situation in 1997: "Within our unit we were all scrutinized, we were all brought to question, we were all analyzed; dissected, not only the persons but the work itself, the files, the office, that whole atmosphere was under microscopic investigation ... It brought the stress level quite high ... Two persons of the unit were let go immediately, and that increased the workload for those who remained. So, we picked up their workload and carried on, but that didn't end; the investigation was still ongoing. So, we were like, walking on eggshells. Everything we did or said was being analysed." Sgt. Pat Rizzo, testimony, 22 February 2000, Standing Court Martial, Saint-Jean, 43, acquired through ATIP.

149 Pat Rizzo interview, 7 August 2009.

150 This was already the case in practice. See "Minutes of the 13-14 Nov 97 Meeting of the Ranger Working Group."

151 Pokotylo, "Ranger Working Group 28/29 May 1996 Meeting Minutes."

152 "Minutes of the 25/26 November 1998 Meeting of the Ranger Working Group."

153 Pierre Leblanc interview. Leblanc noted that once the Rangers in 1 CRPG learned about the parkas issued to Rangers in 2 CRPG, they immediately wanted them, too.

154 "Minutes of the 29 November–1 December 1999 Canadian Ranger and Junior Canadian Ranger Working Group Meeting," 6 March 2000, DND, f. 1901-260/5 (Rgr-JCR 2).

155 Maj. C. Archambault to Capt. M.J.C. Ferland, 13 September 1999, 1 CRPG, binder "1 CRPG Briefing." On plans for James Bay and Nunavik, see Canadian Rangers Situation Report, 2 CRPG, ca. November 1998, attached to minutes of the 25-26 November 1998 Meeting of the Ranger Working Group, 17 February 1999, DND, f. 1901- 260/4(DGRC). By the end of 1999, 2 CRPG Headquarters had grown to seventeen personnel. Archambault, testimony, 22 February 2000, 15.

156 Brig.-Gen. Robin Gagnon to vice chief of the defence staff (VCEMD), 13 April 1999, DND, f. 1085-1(GCmdt). Translation by the author. "Ne cesse de rejaillir favorablement sur les Forces canadiennes."

157 In 1998-99, for example, new Ranger patrols were added at Trout Lake and Wekweti in Northwest Territories and at Fond du Lac in Saskatchewan. CFNA, annual report, 1998-99, 12 July 1999, CFNA, f. NA 1630-2(COMD).

158 Email, Maj. R.D. Knight to Capt. M.J.C. Ferland, 13 September 1999, 1 CRPG, binder "1 CRPG Briefing." Knight desperately needed additional personnel in 1 CRPG. See "A Service Paper for Commander Canadian Forces Northern Area Discussing Increases to the Establishment of 1 Canadian Ranger Patrol Group," 20 July 1999, 1 CRPG, binder "1 CRPG Briefing."

159 Email, Capt. Guy Ingram to Maj. David Scandrett, 10 September 1999, acquired through ATIP.

160 Col. T.K.D. Geburt to VCDS, 17 May 1999, DND, f. 1901-260/5(D Res 2-3).

161 VCDS to CDS and Deputy Minister, "Junior Ranger Targets and Potential," 28 May 1999, and marginalia; Jim Judd to VCDS, 3 June 1999; Vice Admiral G.L. Garnett to LFQA and DGRC, 4 August 1999. Copies acquired through ATIP.

162 This motto was effective as of 24 June 1997. Minutes, "CR/JCR WG Meeting, Nov-Dec 1999," Appendix C, 1, copy provided by CRNA.

163 DHH, "History of Aboriginal Peoples in the Canadian Military," f. N-N-10, John MacFarlane telephone interview with Solomon Curley, Hall Beach, NU, 15 March 2002. The Rangers in CFNA also began to check local sites in 1992, looking for evidence of vandalism (a problem in many northern communities), damage by weather or animals, and possible fuel leaks. The North Warning System patrols varied from half days to six days. Canadian Rangers, "Brief for Maj R. Bell," 10 June 1993. Copy provided by 1 CRPG.

164 Eugene Squires interview. See also Bob Ferguson, "Rangers No Longer Missing Shots," Ottawa Citizen, 29 July 1990. Land Force Central Area did not complete because the Ontario Rangers were not proficient enough to complete, and Land Force Quebec Area did not find the competition economical and used the money for further patrol training. Lieutenant (Navy) C.D. Purvis, "Rangers Working Group 13/14 Nov 1996 Meeting Minutes," 3 December 1996, 1 CRPG, binder "Rgr/JCR Conf Feb 93–Feb 97." At the Canadian Forces Small Arms Competition (CFSAC), Rangers competed for three trophies: the Belzile Trophy for individual top shot, the Ranger Trophy for team competition, and the Ranger Cup for the falling-plates competition. Record of Decisions, Canadian Ranger Working Group, Whitehorse, YT, 23-24 February 1993, 1 CRPG, binder "Rgr/JCR Conf Feb 93-Feb 97."

165 MacFarlane, interview with Curley.

166 Ibid., supplemented with "Helicopter Crashes Near Hall Beach," Nunatsiaq News, 21 May 1998.

167 John Ralston Saul, "My Canada Includes the North," Globe and Mail, 9 March 2001.

168 "Op Nunavut – 1 Apr 99," Ranger Report 5, 2 (ca. 1999): 2-4; photo and caption, News North, 5 April 1999.

169 Jens Bartelson, A Genealogy of Sovereignty (Cambridge: Cambridge University Press, 1995), 30, 247.

170 CRS Review, 2.

171 Lt.-Col. Rory Kilburn, interview with author, Yellowknife, NT, 22 March 2000.

172 "1 Canadian Ranger Patrol Group SITREP as at 23 November 1998," CFNA, f. 901-1(CO 1CRPG).

173 Pat Rizzo interview.

174 Sgt. J.-F. Gauthier, telephone interview with author, 18 May 2006.

175 "Nunavik Rebuilding Initiatives Underway," Canada Newswire (Ottawa), 25 June 1999.

176 Knight to Ferland, email, 13 September 1999. In 1995-96, the Rangers under CFNA control had an operating budget of $1.7 million (out of $4.21 million total, or about 40 percent). In 1998-99, 1 CRPG had a budget of $2.2 million (out of $6.7 million total, or 33 percent). On real spending power in 1 CRPG, see "Rangers Enhancement Program," fax, 30 November 1995, 9, and 1 CRPG, SITREP, 23 November 1999, 7.

177 House of Commons Standing Committee on Foreign Affairs and International Trade, Canada and the Circumpolar World (Ottawa, 1997), ix, 100.

178 Department of Foreign Affairs and International Trade, *Government Response to Standing Committee on Foreign Affairs and International Trade Report, "Canada and the Circumpolar World"* (Ottawa, 1998), http://www.international.gc.ca/. The government's official response to *Canada and the Circumpolar World* noted: "Additionally, the cultural inter-play of service people serving in our North has an intangible benefit in promoting a sense of national awareness among the military and those northern residents who come in contact with the military ... A military presence in the North also provides Canada's Aboriginal peoples with an opportunity to serve their country and community through participation in the Canadian Rangers."

179 Department of Foreign Affairs and International Trade, *The Northern Dimension of Canada's Foreign Policy* (Ottawa, 2000).

180 Colonel J.G.P. Leblanc to CDS, 20 November 1998, CFNA, f. 3060-1(Comd).

181 *Arctic Capabilities Study*, June 2000, 9-10, DND, f. 1948-3-CC4C(DGSP).

182 For a solid overview, see Rob Huebert, "Canadian Arctic Security Issues," *International Journal* 54, 2 (1999): 203-29.

183 See, for example, David Pugliese's series of articles in the *Ottawa Citizen:* "Arctic Defence Costs Could Cripple Military," 8 December 2000; "Arctic Sovereignty at Risk: Military Warns North's Riches Open to Plunder by Foreign Lands," 7 December 2000. On the submarine sightings, see Maj. D. Gilbert to Director Land Reserves, 16 May 2000, CRNA, f. "Rangers 2000"; Warrant Officer R.C. Nickerson to CFNA HQ G2 et al., 8 July 1997, and Warrant Officer K. Rowe to CFNA HQ G2 et al., 24 November 1997, acquired through ATIP; and Sgt. B. Field to Sgt. P. Rizzo, 7 October 1999, CRNA, f. "Unusual Incident."

184 Miller, "Introduction and Review of Leadership Theory," 7.

Chapter 10: "Very Special Forces," 2000-06

1 Maj. D. Gilbert to Director Land Reserves, 16 May 2000, Department of National Defence (DND), Canadian Rangers National Authority (CRNA), f. "Rangers 2000." Gilbert worried that the raison d'être of the Rangers might "be lost to the implementation of these various initiatives," which ranged from leadership training, to harassment and abuse-prevention programs, to smoking policy and Ranger whistles.

2 Director General Reserves and Cadets (DGRC), "CAN RAN 2000: A Review of the Canadian Rangers and of the Junior Canadian Rangers," 27 January 2000 (hereafter CAN RAN 2000), 49.

3 CAN RAN 2000, 7-8.

4 Ibid., 16.

5 Vice Chief of the Defence Staff (VCDS), "Area Commanders Conference on Canadian Rangers and JCR Issues," 3 October 2003. Copy provided by CRNA.

6 CAN RAN 2000, 18.

7 D Res, "Annual Report #1 for FY 00-01 CAN RAN 2000," 1 June 2001 (hereafter CAN RAN Report No. 1). Major Ferland, the Junior Ranger project officer for the director general reserves and cadets until 1999, was the primary author of CAN RAN 2000. The Canadian Rangers–Junior Canadian Rangers coordination cell was established to direct policy, monitor the implementation of CAN RAN 2000 and the Junior Canadian Rangers program, and coordinate expansion plans.

8 "2001 Annual Historical Report – 5th Canadian Ranger Patrol Group," DND, f. 1326-1(LFAA HQ), January 2001; Terry Kruger, "Ranger Red," *Northern News Services*, 6 August 2001.

9 In 2004, DND issued three PCX 250 radios to each patrol with one antenna. Patrols in 1 Canadian Rangers Patrol Group (CRPG), which had been issued the SBX 11 radio in the previous decade, asked for these new radios as replacements. "Minutes of the 19-21 Oct 04

Canadian Rangers/Junior Canadian Rangers National Working Group," December 2004, DND, f. 1901-260/5(D Cdts 4-7-2) (hereafter CR/JCR NWG).

10 D Res, "Annual Report Number 5 for FY 04-05 CAN RAN 2000," September 2005 (hereafter CAN RAN Report No. 5).

11 "Minutes of the 27-29 Jan 04 CR/JCR NWG," February 2004, DND, f. 1901-260/4 (Rgr-JCR 3); D Res, "Annual Report Number 4 for FY 03-04 on CAN RAN 2000," August 2004 (hereafter CAN RAN Report No. 4).

12 CAN RAN Report No. 1. On Ranger requests, see, for example, Cindy MacDougall, "Rangers Seek More Gear," *Northern News Services*, 10 January 2000.

13 "Minutes of the 27-29 Jan 04 CR/JCR NWG."

14 Ibid.; D Res, "Annual Report #3 FY 02-03 CAN RAN 2000," 10 July 2003 (hereafter CAN RAN Report No. 3); CAN RAN Report No. 5. Rangers also received the old army crewneck sweaters, and some received old parkas and wind pants when they became available through the army system.

15 Glen Korstrom, "Recognizing Rangers," *Northern News Services*, 11 October 1999. The governor general wanted to recognize the Rangers in a public way, so he conceived the Special Service Medal (Ranger Bar). The Department of National Defence at first said no, anticipating that the government would not accept the proposal, but Colonel Pierre Leblanc insisted that as an initiative of the governor general it would probably go ahead. It did. Col. Pierre Leblanc, interview with author, Calgary, AB, 16 March 2000. 1 Canadian Ranger Patrol Group (CRPG) wanted the SSM (Ranger Bar) awarded to Ranger instructors. High-level officials and the Directorate of History and Heritage did not support this request. The rationale for the SSM Bar was to highlight special service with a branch of the Canadian Forces not eligible for other decorations, with the exception of the Canadian Forces Decoration (CD). "Minutes of the 14-16 Nov 2000 CR/JCR NWG," December 2000, DND, f. 1901-260/4 (Rgr-JCR 2-2); "Minutes of the 27-29 Jan 04 CR/JCR NWG." This decision upset instructors, who did not qualify even though they participated in more Ranger exercises than the Rangers. Why should a cook who served at Alert for a few months without once heading outdoors get an SSM while a Ranger instructor received no special recognition whatsoever? Instructors in all patrol groups raised similar questions during my interviews with them over the last decade.

16 Each Canadian Ranger Patrol Group (CRPG) nominated three recipients to receive the honour in the nation's capital. "Minutes of the 29 November–01 December 1999 CR/JCR NWG," 6 March 2000, DND, f. 1901-260/5(Rgr-JCR 2).

17 "Her Excellency the Right Honourable Adrienne Clarkson, Governor General of Canada and Commander-in-Chief of the Canadian Forces, on the occasion of the first presentation of Special Service Medals (SSM) to the Canadian Rangers, Rideau Hall, Ottawa, 14 February 2000," http://www.gg.ca/speeches/archive/rangers_e.html (last accessed 20 February 2000).

18 Dan Davidson, "Rangers Savoured Long-Overdue Recognition," *Whitehorse Star,* 15 March 2000; "Taking the Land by Warmth," *Toronto Star,* 23 December 2000.

19 Buzz Bourdon, "Canadian Rangers Honoured for Service," *National Post,* 15 February 2000.

20 Lieutenant Mark Gough, the Canadian Forces Northern Area (CFNA) public affairs officer, reaffirmed this perspective, contained in quotes in several territorial newspaper articles, during an interview in Yellowknife, NT, on 20 March 2000. Medal celebrations across the country reaffirmed this intimate connection. See, for example, Daniel MacIsaac, "Editorial: Standing on Guard," *Inuvik Drum,* 25 February 2000.

21 See, for example, Joseph Inge and Eric Findley, "Northern American Defense and Security after 9/11," *Joint Force Quarterly* 40, 1 (2006): 23-28.

22 The 5 CRPG Operations/Training cell also supported 9 Wing by providing camp cots and sleeping bags. "2001 Annual Historical Report – 5th Canadian Ranger Patrol Group,"

f. 1326-1(LFAA HQ), January 2001; "Minutes of the 14-16 Nov 01 CR/JCR NWG," October 2001, DND, f. 1901-260/4(Rgr-JCR 2-2).

23 Dawn Ostream, "Northern Military Role," *Northern News Service*, 15 October 2001.

24 Col. K.C. McLeod to VCDS, 1 December 2000, CFNA, f. NA 3000-1(Comd).

25 Canadian Forces Northern Area Headquarters, *Arctic Capabilities Study 2000: "True North Strong and Free,"* 2 December 2000, CFNA, f. NA 3000-1 (Comd), 2, 9-11.

26 Rob Huebert, "Climate Change and Canadian Sovereignty in the Northwest Passage," *Isuma* 2, 4 (2001): 92. Jane George, "Arctic Borders Need Tighter Control," *Nunatsiaq News*, 1 February 2001.

27 Terry Kruger, "The Thin Red Line," *Northern News Services*, 30 July 2001. 1 CRPG officially established a centralized operations cell in 2002. Previously, Ranger instructors alone dealt with the Rangers. Captain Rob Marois, interview with author, Yellowknife, NT, 22 April 2002.

28 Terry Kruger, "Ranger Red," *Northern News Services*, 6 August 2001. Warrant Officer Terry Cole explained that 1 CRPG gained structure after Laroche took over as commanding officer. He built relationships with the territorial governments and knew how to conduct business in communities. Terry Cole, interview with author, Musgrave Harbour, NL, 1 November 2008.

29 Dawn Ostrem, "Military Manoeuvres," *Northern News Services*, 21 August 2000. The *Arctic Capabilities Study* suggested that more sovereignty patrols, clothing, and equipment would enhance the Rangers' capabilities and boost their morale, and the new equipment distributed to patrols through CAN RAN 2000 did bring 1 CRPG "tremendous credibility from the Rangers themselves and the public in general." Dawn Ostrem, "Ranger Expansion Ahead," *Northern News Services*, 31 July 2000.

30 I participated in Operation Skookum Elan II, Quiet Lake, YT, March 2004. That same month, the first mass exercise took place in the Baffin region. It involved the Arctic Bay, Clyde River, Igloolik, Qikiqtarjuaq, and Pangnirtung patrols, which each sent four Rangers to meet at the Fox-3 North Warning Site 560 kilometres north of Iqaluit. Miriam Dewar, "Hot Shots Brave Baffin's Cold," *Nunavut News/North*, 5 March 2004; and Maj. Stu Gibson, "1 CRPG Annual Historical Report 2004," 13 April 2005, DND, Directorate of History and Heritage (DHH), f. 3685.

31 Major Yves Laroche, interview with the author, Cape Isachsen, NU, 17 April 2002. The cost of each sovereignty patrol was estimated at $10,500. Kruger, "Ranger Red." As attention shifted to "Type-5" enhanced sovereignty patrols, 1 CRPG decided that the original tempo of thirty SOVPATs (conducted by individual patrols in their area of operations) was overly ambitious and served "no utility" apart from proving a capability. The number was reduced to ten in 2003 and 2004. Captain Rob Marois, "Canadian Rangers Briefing," Yellowknife, 26 February 2004.

32 Stephanie Rubec, "Resolute Recruits," *Toronto Sun*, 29 April 2002.

33 Aaron Spitzer, "Canadian Forces Want Bigger Role for Nunavut's Rangers," *Nunatsiaq News*, 26 January 2001. Laroche expected the sovereignty patrols to involve four to eight Rangers who would spend about a week on the land. The scale quickly escalated beyond this projection.

34 Although human activity in the remotest parts of the Arctic Archipelago has been limited, other states have long recognized Canada's territorial sovereignty, which makes our legal position strong. Canada would only risk losing sovereignty if it abandoned the territory completely or tolerated the effective presence of another state in the archipelago as a competing sovereign. For a tight summary, see François Côté and Robert Dufresne, *The Arctic: Canada's Legal Claims* (Ottawa: Library of Parliament, 2008).

35 See, for example, John Mitchell, quoted in Adrian Humphreys, "Intrepid Rangers to Leave for Pole," *National Post*, 9 April 2002, A9.

36 Editorial, "Operation Ulu Sends the Right Messages," *Northern News Services*, 24 April 2000. See also James Cudmore, "Military Fails to Spot Polar Poachers in Double Operation: Charges Unconfirmed," *National Post*, 18 April 2000. Alexandria Fiord fell within the theoretical radius of the Grise Fiord patrol but could be accessed only by air. "We wanted to extend our area of influence ... go a little further than the Rangers' traditional hunting grounds," public affairs officer Lieutenant Mark Gough explained. "The whole purpose was so the Rangers would become familiar in a different area." Quoted in Kerry McCluskey, "Poacher Patrol," *Northern News Services*, 24 April 2000. Although Canada had tolerated traditional hunting by Greenland Inuit in the past, rumours of Inuit guiding and shuttling paying tourists across the international border (a practice that contravened Canada immigration, hunting, customs, and firearms laws) made the perceived threat more serious. Col. J.G.P. Leblanc to Deputy Chief of the Defence Staff (DCDS), December 1999, DND, f. NA 2100-4(Comd). Greenland's ambassador ridiculed Col. Leblanc's concerns that poachers from his country posed a threat to Canada's national security in the High Arctic. "Greenland Pooh-Poohs Poaching Claim," *Nunatsiaq News*, 30 March 2001.

37 Lt.-Gen. G.E.C. Macdonald to Maj. Yves Laroche, 1 May 2002, DND, DHH, 3685. Marking the sixtieth anniversary of the Rangers required tracing their lineage back to the Pacific Coast Militia Rangers, even though there was no official linkage between the two corps.

38 "Rangers Will Receive Medals," *Whitehorse Star*, 21 January 2003. Enhanced security patrols were also critical for staff training. Major Stu Gibson, interview with author, Yellowknife, NT, 27 February 2004.

39 Canada NewsWire, "Governor General's Canada Day Message," 29 June 2002.

40 The Haines Junction Ranger patrol had trained with 3 Princess Patricia's Canadian Light Infantry (PPCLI) on a sovereignty operation the previous year. The Rangers learned a lot from the soldiers, and they felt a real sense of camaraderie. Accordingly, twelve members of the patrol flew to Edmonton to provide an honour guard when soldiers of the 3 PPCLI Battle Group returned from Afghanistan in August 2002. Wade Istchenko to Capt. Conrad Schubert, email, 24 January 2005 (forwarded to me and used with permission); Sarah O'Donnell, "City Says 'Thank You' to Soldiers," *Edmonton Journal*, 10 August 2002. See also "A Little Glory for the Junction," *Whitehorse Star*, 1 August 2002. Members of the Haines Junction patrol not only take pride in their association with their Canadian Forces comrades but also maintain local awareness of the sacrifices they are making. Photos of all Canadian soldiers killed in Afghanistan hang on a wall of honour in its headquarters – the local bar. Visit to Haines Junction and meetings with the patrol, June 2009.

41 Sgt. Peter Moon, interview with author, Geraldton, ON, 8 July 2008. Even well-planned operations did not go as planned. In 2003, the Canadian Forces planned to conduct an enhanced sovereignty patrol on Prince Patrick Island but had to go to Banks Island instead. They could not clear the runway when a bulldozer, left in cold storage at Mould Bay when the weather station closed, failed to work, preventing the Hercules aircraft – carrying Rangers, equipment, and supplies – from landing. Instead, the Rangers established a base camp near Sachs Harbour and patrolled remote parts of Banks Island. "Patrol Redirected to Banks Island," *Whitehorse Star*, 2 April 2003.

42 These concerns were reflected in the ongoing debate between political scientists Rob Huebert and Franklyn Griffiths. See, for example, Huebert, "Climate Change and Canadian Sovereignty"; Griffiths, "The Shipping News," *International Journal* 58, 2 (2003): 278-82; Huebert, "The Shipping News, Part II," *International Journal* 58, 3 (2003): 295-308; and Griffiths, "Pathetic Fallacy," *Canadian Foreign Policy* 11, 3 (2004): 1-16.

43 Bob Weber, "Navy to Make First Arctic Patrol since 1989 Trip," *Whitehorse Star*, 30 July 2002. Narwhal Ranger – slated to involve a frigate, an entire company of soldiers, and a number of Auroras – was scaled back because of the Canadian Forces' commitments in Afghanistan, the Balkans, and the G8 Summit in Alberta.

44 Harry Sterling, "True North Strong – and Ours?" *The Gazette* (Montreal), 3 August 2002.

45 Joseph Brean, "Frozen Out," *National Post,* 15 February 2003.

46 James McNulty, "Canada's Military a Fading Shadow of What It Once Was," *Times-Herald* (Moose Jaw), 23 October 2004. Others include Barry Cooper and David Bercuson, "Privatized Defence Weakens True North," *Calgary Herald,* 1 October 2003; "Showing the Flag North of 60," *National Post,* 29 March 2004; "Guarding the Arctic," *Toronto Star,* 5 April 2004; and Chris Wattie and Carly Weeks, "U.S. Sub in Arctic Embarrassing, Opposition Says," *National Post,* 20 December 2005.

47 US Joint Chiefs of Staff, *Department of Defense Dictionary of Military and Associated Terms,* rev. ed. (Washington, DC: Department of Defense, 2005), 211.

48 Christine Kay, "Iqaluit Ranger to Get Medal," *Northern News Services,* 12 August 2002.

49 In 2004, Major Stewart Gibson predicted that each patrol would cost about $500,000. The following year, however, the projected cost for the long-range patrol reached 1 million dollars. In the end, it cost about $700,000. Greg Younger-Lewis, "Military Fails Disaster Response Test," *Nunatsiaq News,* 22 April 2005; Jack Danylchuk, "Arctic Flank Exposed," *Northern News Services,* 5 August 2005.

50 Adrian Humphreys, "Canada's Troops to Reclaim Arctic," *National Post,* 25 March 2004.

51 See P. Whitney Lackenbauer, *Canada's Rangers: Selected Stories, 1942-2012* (Kingston: CDA Press, 2013). "Without patrols like the patrol we're having, we don't necessarily have sovereignty here," Lieutenant-Colonel David Wheeler, the chief of staff in Yellowknife, declared to media in April 2004. "Without the Rangers up here, we would not have the footprints in the snow. Without the information they provide ... our knowledge ... would be very small." Greg Younger-Lewis, "National Defence Seeks Bigger Presence in the North," *Nunatsiaq News,* 16 April 2004.

52 Several interviewees used these terms to refer to these commanders. Collectively, they referred to them as "the Ranger mafia."

53 Major Guy Ingram, interview with author, Geraldton, ON, 9 July 2008. For example, a Ranger training guidance document was produced rather than a plan, and each patrol group set its training agenda according to its mission and tasks, as outlined by the areas. CAN RAN Report No. 1.

54 Warrant Officer Pat Rizzo, telephone interview with author, 7 August 2009.

55 Confidential interview; Warrant Officer François Duchesneau, interview with author, Inukjuak, QC, 30 August 2006.

56 2 CRPG, "Junior Canadian Rangers Performance Measurement Indicators: Area Annual Report," May 2005; François Duchesneau interview.

57 Pat Rizzo interview.

58 François Duchesneau interview. All staff at 2 CRPG were primary reservists hired on yearly contracts, and all instructors were bilingual. "Minutes of the 27-29 Jan 04 CR/JCR NWG."

59 François Duchesneau interview; "Minutes of the 19-21 Oct 04 CR/JCR NWG."

60 Junior Ranger expansion was half-hazard and "top-down," Junior Roberts recalled: "Not enough time and thought was put into things." The group stood up its first patrol in Red Bay within weeks of his appointment as coordinator. Two more patrols followed in the next two months. There were few directives on how patrols should operate, and there was no training plan indicating what should be taught, or how. "This put the cart before the horse," Roberts observed. Junior Ranger patrols were simply stood up and equipment sent to them. Rangers were also "a bit jealous" of the influx of tents and canoes intended for the Junior Rangers. Captain Ferland in Ottawa insisted that the Rangers and Junior Rangers were "completely separate entities" and were not to share equipment. Lieutenant Junior Roberts, interview with author, Gander, NL, 3 November 2008.

61 For example, eighty visits to thirty-three Junior Ranger patrols cost $824,118 in 2004-05. The total cost for the Junior Rangers in 1 CRPG was nearly $1.4 million that year. 1 CRPG, "Junior Canadian Rangers Performance Measurement Indicators: Area Annual Report," 10 June 2005.

62 CAN RAN Report No. 5.

63 CAN RAN Report No. 1.

64 He would, however, support a national-type Junior Ranger camp. "Minutes of the 19-21 Oct 04 CR/JCR NWG."

65 VCDS, "Area Commanders Conference."

66 Pat Rizzo interview.

67 Jane George, "Rangers Suffer from Their Own Success," *Nunatsiaq News,* 15 March 2002.

68 "3 CRPG Briefing Working Group Nov 00," CRNA, f. "Rangers 2001"; "3 CRPG Briefing to CRNA WG," October 2008. Copies provided by CRNA.

69 Peter Moon interview.

70 Ibid.

71 "'Outstanding' Response for Rangers in Kashechewan," *3 CRPG Newsletter,* November 2001.

72 "A Red Whistle for the North," *SAR SCENE* 12, 1 (Winter 2002): 7. 3 CRPG piloted the Red Whistle Program informally at Fort Albany First Nation in January 1996 and implemented it nationally in 2000. The Canadian Ranger Red Whistle Program, "10,000 Red Whistles," attached to "Minutes of the 25/26 November 1998 Meeting of the Ranger Working Group," 17 February 1999, DND, f. 1901-260/4 (DGRC); "Red Whistle Program Emphasizes Safety on the Land," *Ranger Report* (1 CRPG), n.d. (ca. 2000).

73 Peter Moon interview. See also "Lieutenant Governor's Book Program Ends on a High Note," *Canada NewsWire* (Ottawa), 28 February 2004; Miro Cernetig, "Operation Read Heads North," *Toronto Star,* 6 February 2004; Adrian Humphreys, "Viceroy's Goal Is to Fill Empty Bookshelves," *National Post,* 15 January 2004. 2 CRPG appears to have been the first to undertake this type of project. When elementary school students in Aupaluk asked the Rangers to gather French children's books for them, 2 CRPG delivered five hundred to the community. Odile Nelson, "Rangers Shower Books on Aupaluk," *Nunatsiaq News,* 11 July 2003.

74 "3 CRPG Briefing Working Group Nov 00."

75 "Canadian Rangers Demonstrate Their Trapping and Shooting Skills in the United States," *3 CRPG Newsletter,* May 2003; Ranger Sergeant Peter Moon, interview with author, Resolute, NU, 17 April 2002.

76 Pamela Martin, "Canadian Rangers, Aboriginal Reservists, Trained in Fort Knox Today," CTV News, 17 March 2002.

77 Peter Moon, "Canadian Rangers Are a Hit at Fort Knox," *3 CRPG Newsletter,* June 2002.

78 Martin, "Canadian Rangers, Aboriginal Reservists."

79 Adrian Humphreys, "'Very Special Forces' Head to Fort Knox," *National Post,* 13 March 2002.

80 Confidential interview. Scandrett explained to me that he had originally submitted weekly reports to LFCA, but officers there had told him that because National Defence Headquarters in Ottawa funded the Rangers, they did not want them. He insisted that it was only after he had departed as commanding officer that it was "crystallized that CRPGs actually fell under the LFAs." David Scandrett, interview, 4 April 2012.

81 David Scandrett interview, supplemented by Major Tim Byers, interview with the author, Victoria, BC, 10 August 2004, and email, Capt. Guy Ingram to Maj. David Scandrett, 10 September 1999, acquired through ATIP.

82 CAN RAN Report No. 1.

83 Maj. Ian Hay, "Change of Command," *The Ranger* (4 CRPG) 2, 4 (Fall 2000): 1; Alisha Sims, "Canadian Forces Putting 'Eyes and Ears' in the North," *Nickel Belt News* (Thompson, MB), 13 May 2002, 1; "Major Ian Hay," *The Ranger* 4, 2 (Spring 2002): 4; Major D.I. Hay, "4 CRPG Annual Historical Report 2002," 31 March 2003, DND, DHH, 3688.

84 Byers doubled as the patrol group's operations officer. He had been 4 CRPG's link to the army in his previous position at Land Force Western Area, so he was a natural fit. "Major Ian Hay," *The Ranger* 4, 2 (Spring 2002): 4; "Captain T.C. Byers," *The Ranger* 4, 2 (Spring 2002): 5.

85 Maj. D.I. Hay, "4 CRPG Annual Historical Report 2001," 31 March 2002, DND, DHH, 3688.

86 Tim Byers interview.

87 Master Warrant Officer Wade Jones, "Lac Brochet Patrol," *The Ranger* 4, 4 (Fall 2002): 10-12.

88 "JCR Officer's Assessment," Appendix 1 to Annex B, Maj. D.I. Hay, "4 CRPG Annual Historical Report 2002," 31 March 2003, DND, DHH, 3688; "Lac Brochet Junior Ranger Patrol," *The Ranger* 5, 3 (Summer 2003): 12.

89 CAN RAN Report No. 3.

90 Lt.-Gen. G.E.C. Macdonald to Chief of the Land Staff and Commander Canadian Forces Northern Area, 25 July 2003, DND, f. 5785-1(DRes). Regional commanders controlled the purse strings and the hiring of staff, and they adopted different procedures for releasing Rangers. While some patrol groups imposed a compulsory retirement age of sixty-five, others did not. There were no uniform standards when it came to compensation rates, including damage to Rangers' personal equipment while performing their duties. "Minutes of the 14-16 Nov 2000 CR/JCR NWG," December 2000, DND, f. 1901-260/4(Rgr-JCR 2-2).

91 Chief of Review Services (CRS), "Review of the Canadian Rangers [Draft]," September 2003, last amended 12 November 2003, (hereafter CRS Review), DND, CRNA, f. "CRS and CRNA Report," 22.

92 Macdonald to Chief of the Land Staff and Commander Canadian Forces Northern Area, 25 July 2003. The number of Ranger and Junior Ranger patrols and personnel ceilings had to remain within planned figures for fiscal year 2003-04.

93 CAN RAN Reports No. 3 and No. 5. The actual number of patrols exceeded 163 communities given that some patrols in weaker locations were amalgamated as subordinate sections in stronger patrols rather than being closed completely. Junior Ranger expansion was not discussed when the vice chief of the defence staff issued the Operation PAUSE directive in July 2003, but the DGRC issued further direction imposing a restriction on the expansion of JCR patrols that November. CAN RAN Report No. 5.

94 "Minutes of the 19-21 Oct 04 CR/JCR NWG."

95 Major C. Archambault, "2 CRPG Area Annual Report, JCR Performance Measurement Indicators, 2003-04," May 2004. "Notre parole ... en doute": translation by the author. See also "Minutes of the 19-21 Oct 04 CR/JCR NWG."

96 "Minutes of the 27-29 Jan 04 CR/JCR NWG." Major Byers had opened a detachment in Saskatchewan in 2003, providing for four headquarters in the patrol group that mirrored the domestic operation detachments in Land Force Western Area. When Operation PAUSE prevented 4 CRPG from opening new patrols in the province, the detachment was closed. Major Tim Byers, "4 CRPG Annual Historical Report 2003," 23 April 2004; "4 CRPG Annual Historical Report 2004," 7 March 2005, DND, DHH, 3688.

97 Guy Ingram interview, 9 July 2008; "Minutes of the 19-21 Oct 04 CR/JCR NWG." David Scandrett shared his nicknames with me during our interview. Normal summary investigation audits after Scandrett departed proved there were no financial problems with the unit. Scandrett interview, 4 April 2012.

98 Guy Ingram interviews, 8 and 9 July 2008, and Captain Mark Rittwage, interview with the author, Geraldton, ON, 10 July 2008. See also "Dinner Hails Ranger Group's First 10 Years,"

3CRPG Newsletter (September 2008), 17. Whereas Scandrett had recruited Ontario Provincial Police and Nishnawbe-Aski police officers into the Rangers, Lawrence discouraged them because, in times of emergency, they would be acting in a police capacity – meaning few Rangers and less leadership when it was most needed.

99 Interview with Warrant Officer David Gill, Musgrave Harbour, NL, 1 November 2008. 5 CRPG directed its efforts to identifying and releasing members who had expressed no interest in the Rangers and had not attended training sessions. It aimed to reach and maintain an effective strength of 750 Rangers. Lt.-Col. C.L. Corry, "5 CRPG Situation Report as of 15 October 2002," 15 October 2002, Land Force Atlantic Area, f. 1630-1 (CO).

100 "2005 Annual Historical Report – 5th Canadian Ranger Patrol Group," February 2005, f. 1326-2 (LFAAHQ); Captain Terry Stead, Rangers briefing, 31 October 2008. The employment of Canadian Rangers on full-time Class B terms of service within a CRPG Headquarters contravened Canadian Forces Administrative Order (CFAO) 2-8. After 31 March 2006, contracts to work in a CRPG Headquarters would not be renewed unless the individual transferred to an appropriate subcomponent of the Reserve Force (Primary Reserve, Supplementary Reserve, or Cadet Instructor Cadre). CAN RAN Report No. 4.

101 The Gold River patrol was an example. The closing of the local mill left "the community in a depressed state; many residents have moved out of the area to new jobs elsewhere." The patrol strength declined, but it retained "its original leadership and a strong nucleus of members, so there was never any question of whether or not they would still be able to cut. The question was more how much of their edge have they managed to retain as a result of losing so many members." "Gold River Patrol Training Exercise," *The Ranger* 3, 1 (Winter 2001): 7; author interviews with patrol members in Gold River, BC, July 2005.

102 Captain Jim Miller, interview with author, Churchill, MN, 3 March 2009. New instructors had to pass a ninety-day probationary period, Miller explained, but no one ever "failed."

103 Maj. Tim Byers, "CO's Corner," *The Ranger* 6, 2 (Spring 2004): 6; 6, 4 (Fall 2004): 5; and 7, 1 (Winter 2005): 7. As a desk officer at Land Force Western Area, Byers had originally viewed the Rangers as a waste of money. Given the lack of funding available for Regular Force exercises, even the small amount allocated to the Rangers in BC seemed a drain on already scarce resources. Before becoming commanding officer of 4 CRPG, however, he was exposed to the Rangers during a jump exercise into Yukon in 2003 and began to develop an appreciation for them. He grew to realize that they offered tremendous "bang for the buck." They accomplished a lot in terms of nation building and contributed to a state of readiness should disaster strike. Tim Byers interview.

104 Tim Byers, "CO's Corner," *The Ranger* 7, 1 (Winter 2005): 7.

105 Darryl Bazin interview; "Exercise Northern Run, Alberta Det, 4CRPG, Feb 16-26, 2005," *The Ranger* 7, 1 (Winter 2005): 1-6.

106 Interviews with Master Warrant Officer G.R. Westcott and Warrant Officer Kevin Mulhern, Yellowknife, NT, 26 February 2004.

107 David Gill interview.

108 Author interviews with 1 CRPG staff and instructors, Yellowknife, NT, 2004.

109 This corresponds with Rupert Ross's observations in *Dancing with a Ghost: Exploring Indian Reality* (Toronto: Penguin, 1992), 21-22.

110 Sgt. Joe Gonneau, telephone interview with author, 5 May 2006.

111 Kevin Mulhern interview.

112 P. Whitney Lackenbauer, "The Canadian Rangers: A Postmodern Militia That Works," *Canadian Military Journal* 6, 4 (2005-06): 49-60.

113 Capt. Rob Marois, "Rangers Briefing," 26 February 2004, and Kevin Mulhern interview. All Ranger sergeants in the eastern Arctic were male at that time.

114 "Intro – Canadian Rangers Training," http://www.rangers.dnd.ca/pubs/rangers/training/intro_e.asp (accessed 13 June 2006).

115 On the logic of training patrols as a group rather than expecting each Ranger to demonstrate specific competencies and skill levels (as per standard individual assessments in the South), see P. Whitney Lackenbauer, "Teaching Canada's Indigenous Sovereignty Soldiers ... and Vice Versa: 'Lessons Learned' from Ranger Instructors," *Canadian Army Journal* 10, 2 (2007): 66-81.

116 CRS Review.

117 CDS to VCDS, "Role, Mission, Tasks of the Canadian Rangers," 20 April 2004, acquired through ATIP. Colonel Tom Tarrant saw no need to develop significant equipment entitlement scales beyond what they already had.

118 CRS Review, iii-v, 11-15.

119 "Commentaires du SQFT sur les Rangers canadiens," 13 February 2004, DND, CRNA, f. "CRS and CFNA Report."

120 Ranger Master Corporal Anthony Elson, interview with author, Goose Bay, NL, 4 March 2006.

121 CDS to VCDS, "Role, Mission, Tasks of the Canadian Rangers," 20 April 2004.

122 Derek Neary, "A Ranger River Adventure," *Northern News Services,* 17 August 2001.

123 Pat Rizzo interview.

124 In 2004, this exercise included the navy's coastal defence ship HMCS *Goose Bay,* and the following year it traced a course from St. Anthony, Newfoundland, to Puvirnituq, Quebec. Lt.-Col. C.L. Corry, "5 CRPG Situation Report," 15 October 2002, Land Force Atlantic Area, f. 1630-1 (CO); Sgt. Jean-François Gauthier, telephone interview with author, 18 May 2006.

125 Capt. J.D. Murray, "BC Ranger Debt Consolidated SITREP," *The Ranger* 7, 2 (Spring 2005): 17; Myles Morrison, "Sovereignty Patrol off BC's West Coast," *The Ranger* 8, 1 (Winter 2006): 7-9.

126 Corry, "5 CRPG Situation Report."

127 "Rangers Help British Forces Test New Equipment," *3 CRPG Newsletter,* July 2005. See also Adrian Humphreys, "No Cold Like It for U.K. Marines," *National Post,* 1 February 2005. The Rangers struggled, however, to understand the distinctive accents and dialects of the British troops. "There's a real language barrier," Sergeant Sutherland said. "Half the time I don't know what they are saying. You have to listen very carefully."

128 See, for example, Lynn Lau, "British Soldiers Do Tuk Trek," *Northern News Services,* 18 March 2002.

129 See, for example, Ranger Master Corporal Baba Pederson of Kugluktuk, quoted in Darren Stewart, "Northern Watchers Honoured," *Northern News Services,* 5 March 2003.

130 See, for example, "Exercise Nootka Nomad," *The Ranger* 4, 2 (Spring 2002): 10-12; "Exercise Nootka Nomad II," *The Ranger* 6, 2 (Spring 2004): 1-5; "39 Brigade Group, Exercise Cougar Salvo '05," and WO Norm Swift, "Exercise Cougar Salvo 05," *The Ranger* 7, 2 (Spring 2005): 1-4.

131 "Rangers Participate in *Exercise Phoenix Ram* at Camp Wainwright," *The Ranger* 7, 4 (Fall 2005): 1-6; Ryan Calvery, "A Taste of Afghanistan in Alberta," *Northern Sentinel,* 23 November 2005, 7-8; "Local Rangers Train at Wainwright," *The Record* (Gold River), 30 November 2005; and "Rangers Receive Commander's Commendation," *Nickel Belt News,* 5 December 2005. These exercises gave the Rangers a chance to observe what soldiers do and, at the same time, helped to raise awareness about the Rangers in western Canada. Captain Darryl Bazin, interview with author, Churchill, MN, 3 March 2009.

132 Adrian Humphreys, "Canada's Troops to Reclaim Arctic," *National Post,* 25 March 2004; Chris Wattie, "Forces to 'Flex Muscles' in North," *National Post,* 27 March 2004.

133 Neils Christensen, "Successful Training," *Northern News Services,* 30 August 2004. See also Greg Younger-Lewis, "Senior Rangers Critical of Armed Forces," *Nunatsiaq News,* 27 August 2004; Vinnie Karetak (reporter), Wendy Mesley (host), "The Army, the Navy and the Air

Force Go North," CBC television, Sunday Report, 22 August 2004. Peter Kilabuk, a local MLA and Ranger, heralded the exercise a success because of local involvement and support. "This has a real positive impact ... because of what the land, the Rangers and the community have to offer," he said. Sara Minogue and Greg Younger-Lewis, "Military Bids Farewell to Panniqtuuq," *Nunatsiaq News,* 3 September 2004.

134 CDS to VCDS, "Role, Mission, Tasks of the Canadian Rangers," 20 April 2004.

135 Deputy Commanding Officer (DCO) to Commanding Officer, 1 CRPG, 24 August 2000, 1 CRPG, f. 1630-1; G2 INT&SECUR to G2, Canadian Forces Northern Area, 31 August 2000, acquired through ATIP. G2 is the acronym for the intelligence division at headquarters.

136 Lt.-Cdr. S.C. Bloom to N00 through N3, Maritime Forces Atlantic (MARLAND), 6 October 2000, DND, f. 3250-1 (LN31-3), acquired through ATIP. On submarine sightings near Pond Inlet the following summer, see David Pugliese, "The X-Files Come North," *Ottawa Citizen,* 18 August 2002.

137 Mark Rittwage interview.

138 "VCDS Area Commanders Conference," 3 October 2003.

139 Nathan VanderKlippe, "Arctic Called Tempting Terror Target," *Gazette* (Montreal), 19 September 2004.

140 Greg Younger-Lewis, "National Defence Seeks Bigger Presence in the North," *Nunatsiaq News,* 16 April 2004.

141 Nathan VanderKlippe, "Border Jumps Finds It Hard to Melt into Arctic," *Edmonton Journal,* 21 September 2006; Capt. Conrad Schubert, "Romanian Tourist Lands in Grise Fiord," *JTFN Northern Highlights,* December 2006.

142 They continued to conduct North Warning Site patrols in 1 and 5 CRPG inexpensively and effectively and collected information about local assets that a military commander might need to conduct operations in their area. Corry, "5 CRPG Situation Report." See, for example, "HMCS Goose Bay Visits Namesake Town," *Western Star* (Corner Brook), 7 August 2006; Sgt. G.J. Roberts, "Rangers Take to the Water Inspecting Canada's North Warning Radar Sites," *The Labradorian,* 5 September 2006.

143 CAN RAN Report No. 5.

144 Maj. Tim Byers, "4 CRPG Annual Historical Report 2003," 23 April 2004, DND, DHH, 3688; "Joint Exercise Completed with the French," *Western Star,* 27 August 2004; "Monster Search and Rescue," *Northern News Services,* 5 September 2005; "Terrace and Kitimat Patrols Joint Exercise with Coast Guard, Prince Rupert," *The Ranger* 6, 3 (Summer 2004), 11-13.

145 CAN RAN Report No. 1.

146 Joseph Hall, "Northern Patrol," *Toronto Star,* 18 June 2005, quoting Robert Gillies, a former sergeant in the Nishnawbe-Aski Police Service and a Ranger in Fort Albany.

147 Confidential interviews. See also Nunavik Briefs, "Man in Custody over Violent Death in Inukjuak," *Nunatsiaq News,* 19 December 2003.

148 "3 CRPG Briefing Working Group November 2000," CRNA, f. "Rangers 2001." The Canadian Forces counselling team flew into the community for three days at the request of Abraham Hunter, the band chief; Sergeant Jimmy Chapman, leader of the Peawanuck Canadian Ranger Patrol; and Master Corporal Linda Friday, the Canadian Ranger in charge of the Junior Canadian Ranger Patrol. They said the Canadian Rangers – who were involved in the search for Dennis, his fellow Junior Canadian Rangers, and others in the community – needed help with their grief. "We have an obligation to assist our Canadian Rangers, who are members of the Canadian Forces, when they undergo a traumatic event like this, as well as the Junior Canadian Rangers in Dennis's patrol. It shows that we care for them," Scandrett said. "When we help a small and very isolated community like Peawanuck in this way it shows them that we care for everyone in the community, too." Peter Moon, "Canadian Forces Help Stricken Community," *3 CRPG Newsletter,* November 2001.

149 For example, Glen Everitt, Dawson City's mayor, complained that he and his constituents had been shut out of the legal system after a crime wave swept through the community. He suggested creating camps for young offenders run by the Canadian Rangers. Michael Hale, "Dawson City Mayor's Court Presence Deemed 'Improper,'" *Whitehorse Star,* 7 April 2000. When a rash of property crimes swept local businesses in Rankin Inlet, the Ranger patrol considered starting up a "citizens on patrol" program in the hamlet. The RCMP applauded the idea. Chris Puglia, "Money Stolen from Hamlet," *Northern News Services,* 20 August 2003.

150 Daniel MacIsaac, "Editorial: Standing on Guard," *Inuvik Drum,* 25 February 2000.

151 Hall, "Northern Patrol." To give a sense of the frequency, Rangers in 1 CRPG participated in 164 volunteer ground search and rescues, one medical evacuation, and one emergency rescue in 1999-2000. CAN RAN 2000, 11.

152 See, for example, Darrell Greer, "Hunter Perishes on Land," *Nunavut News/North,* 5 February 2003.

153 For example, Rangers had a central role in the Kativik Regional Government's emergency plan for Nunavik. Jean-François Gauthier, telephone interview with author, 18 May 2006.

154 Warrant Officer P.T. Malcolm, "Exercise LONG REACH," *The Ranger* 7, 2 (Spring 2005): 18-19.

155 "Minutes of the 22-24 Oct 02 CR/JCR NWG," November 2002, DND, f. 1901-260/4 (Rgr-JCR 2).

156 Peter Moon, "Rangers Praised for Help in Evacuation," *3 CRPG Newsletter,* February 2003. Roy Sinclair, chief administrative officer for the municipality of Greenstone, wrote in a letter of thanks to 3 Canadian Ranger Patrol Group, "A few of the functions performed by the Rangers included, but were not limited to, provision of security, assistance in scheduling, general assistance to the Sandy Lake residents, co-ordination and organization of events with evacuation centre staff, assisting with transport issues, participation in daily briefing meetings, preparation of (aircraft) passenger manifests, assisting with the loading and off-loading of passengers, as well as liaising with other agencies involved in the evacuation."

157 Geraldton's fire chief, John J. Marino, observed that "The Rangers were the link from the community of Geraldton to the community of Sandy Lake," and they reassured elders who had never before left Sandy Lake. "The Rangers also acted as interpreters between their people and the evacuation staff, ensuring information was passed back and forth, whether it was directions or status reports on what was happening back in Sandy Lake, or identifying the needs and concerns of their people. Peter Moon, "Rangers Assist in Forest Fire Evacuation," *3 CRPG Newsletter,* October 2002.

158 Peter Moon, "Rangers Assist In Attawapiskat Evacuation," *The Voice* (Timmins), 1 June 2004; Adrian Humphreys, "Planes Rescue Cree from Rising River," *National Post,* 18 May 2002.

159 Peter Moon, "Kashechewan," *Wawatay News,* 17 November 2005. See also Chris Wattie, "Army Flies in Water Plant to Reserve," 31 October 2005; Carrie Kristal-Schroder, "More Flown from Reserve as Water Crisis Ebbs Away," *National Post,* 1 November 2005.

160 Peter Moon interview, 8 July 2008. Lt.-Col. Lawrence received a Chief of the Defence Staff commendation and Major Ingram a Canada Command Commendation for their leadership during Operation CANOPY. Maj. G.C. Ingram, "Annual Historical Report 2007 for 3 CRPG," 30 January 2008, DND, DHH, 3687.

161 Michelle Rodrigue, "Sanikiluaq Fire a Warning for Nunavut, MLA Says," *Nunavut News/North,* 5 May 2000; Kirsten Murphy, "From Fires to Funerals," *Nunavut News/North,* 2 April 2001.

162 DND, DHH, "History of Aboriginal Peoples in the Canadian Military," f. N-QC-8, John MacFarlane, telephone interview with Sgt. Alec Tuckatuck, Kuujjuarapik, QC, 21 November 2001.

163 Kirsten Murphy, "Printmaker Injured in Pangnirtung Storm," *Nunatsiaq News,* 7 February 2003.

164 Maj. Tim Byers, "4 CRPG Annual Historical Report 2003," 23 April 2004, DND, DHH, 3688.

165 Adrian Humphreys, "Officials Hope to Avoid Splitting Families Apart," *National Post,* 27 October 2005.

166 CDS to VCDS, "Role, Mission, Tasks of the Canadian Rangers." The document also noted that in some emergencies the Rangers could be employed as Canadian Forces assets when the solicitor general asks for assistance.

167 Hall, "Northern Patrol."

168 For examples of media profiles that make similar points regarding the Rangers' voluntarism, see Kathleen Lippa, "Hamlet Problems Don't Faze Him" (about Jack Himiack of Kugluktuk) and Neils Christensen, "Never Too Young to Get Involved" (about Bryan Simonee of Pond Inlet), both in *Nunavut News/North,* 9 August 2004. Accordingly, the Canadian Forces were competing with the municipalities, employers, and other volunteer organizations for their time. This explains why not all Rangers were available all the time – something that the army chain of command often misunderstood. Sergeant Milton Estrada, interview with author, flight from Kuujjuarapik to Montreal, QC, 1 September 2006.

169 Canadian Press, "Don't Dress as a Polar Bear," *Toronto Sun,* 25 October 2004.

170 "Vanderhoof Patrol," *The Ranger* 2, 2 (Spring 2000): 19.

171 "Port Hardy Patrol," *The Ranger* 1, 1 (Winter 1999): 14.

172 Kristen Murphy, "'Tis the Season for Iqaluit's Christmas Hamper Drive," *Nunatsiaq News,* 7 December 2001.

173 Lt.-Col. J.B. Morse, "5 CRPG Update," 1 October 2007, copy provided by CRNA.

174 "Canadian Rangers Blaze Quest Trail," *Whitehorse Star,* 8 February 2002.

175 Jason Small, "I Can't Do It Forever,'" *Whitehorse Star,* 10 March 2004; Dan Davidson, "Musher Slashes Record in Winning DeWolfe," *Whitehorse Star,* 24 March 2003; Dan Davidson, "Still Crazy Racing, after All These Years," *Whitehorse Star,* 22 March 2001.

176 "Sixth Annual Yukon River Quest Entry Deadline Set for May 26," *Whitehorse Star,* 6 April 2004; Mark Stevenson, "A Diary Etched by Ice and Wind," *National Post,* 29 April 2000; "The Truly Canadian Trail," *Canada News Wire* (Ottawa), 14 February 2000; Camille Hamilton and Janice Schultz, "The Hudson Bay Quest," *The Ranger* 6, 3 (Summer 2004): 9-10.

177 Petty Officer Paul Smith, interview with author, flight Toronto, ON, to Halifax, NS, 20 February 2006.

178 Juliet O'Neill, "Prince of 'Cool' Thrills Tiny Yukon Community," *Ottawa Citizen,* 30 April 2001; Chuck Tobin, "Snowman Part of Mayo's Warm Greetings," *Whitehorse Star,* 30 April 2001; Randy Boswell, "Royal Warmth in the Far, Far North," *Times-Colonist* (Victoria), 7 October 2002; "Queen Blesses Her Newest Territory," *Nunatsiaq News,* 11 October 2002 (online edition).

179 See, for example, Nathan VanderKlippe, "Arctic Memories of War," *Nunavut News/North,* 15 November 2001.

180 "Constance Lake Rangers Attend Unveiling of Aboriginal Veterans War Monument in Ottawa," *3 CRPG Newsletter,* November 2001.

181 From the CRPGs' standpoint, the expansion was partly pragmatic: the Junior Rangers originally meant hard money for patrol groups, whereas Ranger funding remained less secure.

182 Although the Rangers were overwhelmingly men, the Junior Rangers had a male to female ratio of 1.3 to 1 in 2005 (1,358 men; 1,030 women). 1 CRPG, "JCR Performance Measurement Indicators: Area Annual Report," 10 June 2005; 2 CRPG, "JCR Performance Measurement Indicators: Area Annual Report," May 2005; 3 CRPG, "JCR Performance Measurement Indicators: Area Annual Report," 13 June 2005; 4 CRPG, "JCR Performance

Measurement Indicators: Area Annual Report," 10 June 2005; 5 CRPG, "JCR Performance Measurement Indicators: Area Annual Report," 13 June 2005.

183 1 CRPG, "JCR Performance Measurement Indicators."

184 Maj. C. Archambault, "2 CRPG Area Annual Report, JCR Performance Measurement Indicators, 2003-04," May 2004. "Le programme comme tel est une nécessité pour tous nos villages et doit continuer. Le programme RJC est le seul programme dans le nord et endroits isolés à donner aux jeunes des communautés un sens de responsabilité, honnêteté, loyauté et uniformité." Translation by the author.

185 See, for example, various *Northern News Services* articles: Cindy MacDougall, "Rangers Seek More Gear," 10 January 2000; Andrew Raven, "Rangers in Fort Resolution," 21 July 2003; Neils Christensen, "Out on the Land," 16 August 2004; and John Thompson, "Ranger Teaches Skills to Youth," 27 June 2005.

186 "Junior Rangers Learning about Life," *North Island Gazette,* 20 March 2002, 3. They learned how to survive in cold weather, maintain a campfire without burning down a forest, eat safe plants, and work as a group. The Junior Rangers also picked up garbage on Malcolm Island. Not only did this instill a sense of voluntarism, Peter Gulitzine, the patrol commander from Sointula, BC, explained, but "a kid who has helped pick up garbage in the forest is less likely to throw beer cans on the ground when he or she gets older." "Junior Rangers Learning about Life," *North Island Gazette,* 20 March 2002.

187 Captain Anthony Lynch, telephone interview with author, May 2010.

188 Captain Chris Bergeron, interview with author, Yellowknife, NT, 20 April 2002. As was the case with the Rangers, regional resistance to standardization resulted in a "tool box" of Junior Ranger training guidance documents rather than a formal training standard and plan. CAN RAN Report No. 1; CAN RAN Report No. 4. 1 CRPG objected to having a formal policy to deliver the program because of differences among groups and even within the Territorial North. By contrast, 4 CRPG and 5 CRPG wanted a more formal outline and methodology for program delivery. "Minutes of the 14-16 Nov 2000 Canadian Ranger/Junior Canadian Ranger Working Group," December 2000, DND, f. 1901-260/4 (Rgr-JCR 2-2).

189 CAN RAN Report No. 5.

190 CAN RAN Report No. 1; Maj. Stu Gibson, "1 CRPG Annual Historical Report 2004," 13 April 2005, DND, DHH, 3685.

191 Bob Weber, "Rangers Less at Home on Their Range," *Globe and Mail,* 9 August 2004.

192 Hall, "Northern Patrol." Hall reported a cost of $150,000.

193 Rob Huebert, "Return of the Vikings," *Globe and Mail,* 28 December 2002. Commentators suggested that sovereignty claims relied on historical ownership and usage, a consideration that prompted Canadian Forces Northern Area to develop a surveillance plan that included annual sovereignty patrols to uninhabited parts of Canada's High Arctic. If Canada hoped to withstand legal challenges from potential adversaries such as Denmark, whose navy operated ice-strengthened frigates and cutters in the waters and had also visited the island to assert its claims, military officials believed that the Canadian Forces had to respond. Lieutenant (Navy) Russell, CFNA J2, "Canada-Denmark Sovereignty Issue," April 2003; Col. Norm Couturier to Deputy Chief of the Defence Staff, 10 May 2005, CFNA, f. 3000-1 (Comd), documents acquired through ATIP. Ranger Sergeant Jeffrey Quanaq relayed an oral history from one of the Grise Fiord residents who told of a villager who had lived on Hans Island for twenty years. Major K. Tyler, "Post Activity Report of Sovereign Inukshuk: Hans Island Type 4 Ptl, 11-19 Jul 05," 28 July 2005, f. CFNA 3000-28(J3), acquired through ATIP.

194 Sgt. Denis Lalonde to Commanding Officer, 1 CRPG, 19 July 2005, f. 3350-1-1(CO); Capt. J.Y.R. Chartrand, "Supplement to Type IV Patrol: Post Exercise Report Hans Island," ca. July 2005; Chartrand, "Exe FROZEN BEAVER," 22 June 2005, DND, f. 7605-1 (J4 Eng), acquired through ATIP. A week later, Bill Graham, minister of national defence, flew to the

island to plant a flag after a visit to Alert. See Bill Graham, foreword to Franklyn Griffiths, Rob Huebert, and P. Whitney Lackenbauer, *Canada and the Changing Arctic* (Waterloo: Wilfrid Laurier University Press, 2011), xx. For a critique of the Hans Island "Arctic flap" as a Grit smoke screen akin to the movie *Wag the Dog*, see Peter Worthington, "A Beaver That Roared," *Toronto Sun,* 29 March 2004.

195 Greg Younger-Lewis, "Military Fails Disaster Response Test," *Nunatsiaq News,* 22 April 2005.

196 CDS to VCDS, "Role, Mission, Tasks."

197 CRS Review.

198 Stephanie Rubec, "Resolute Recruits," *Toronto Sun,* 29 April 2002.

199 Arctic Climate Impact Assessment, *Impacts of a Warming Arctic: ACIA Overview Report* (Cambridge: Cambridge University Press, 2004).

200 Inuit Tapiriit Kanatami and Inuit Circumpolar Council (Canada), *Building Inuit Nunaat: The Inuit Action Plan* (Ottawa: ITK, 2006); Sheila Watt-Cloutier, "Connectivity: The Arctic – The Planet" (speech at Oslo Sophie Prize Ceremony, 15 June 2005), http://www.sophieprize.org/Articles/23.html.

201 CDS to VCDS, "Role, Mission, Tasks."

202 Hall, "Northern Patrol."

203 Warrant Officer Dan Hryhoryshen, interview with author, Victoria, BC, 13 July 2005.

204 "Minutes of the 19-21 Oct 04 CR/JCR NWG." The Armed Forces Council decided on 25 March 2004 that deputy chief of the defence staff group would assume responsibility for the Canadian Rangers effective 1 April 2005. This caused the vice chief of the defence staff to refocus its efforts from implementation of CAN RAN 2000 to preparing an action plan to transfer responsibility for the Rangers. When the new chief of the defence staff's vision for the Canadian Forces was unveiled in March 2005, however, this plan was suspended. For the same reason, the CAN RAN 2000 recommendation to review the Canadian Rangers organization in 2005 was delayed. CAN RAN Report No. 5. For a brief overview of CF Transformation, see Capt Vance White, "CF Transformation: From Vision to Mission," *Maple Leaf* 8, 31 (September 2005): 4. For the chief of defence staff's perspective, see Rick Hillier, *A Soldier First: Bullets, Bureaucrats and the Politics of War* (Toronto: HarperCollins, 2010).

205 Alexander Panetta, "PM's Promise to North," *Toronto Star,* 12 August 2004.

206 Bruce Campion-Smith, "Military Shopping List Growing," *Toronto Star,* 22 December 2004.

207 Canada, *Canada's International Policy Statement: Overview* (Ottawa: Department of Foreign Affairs and International Trade, 2005), 3.

208 Greg Younger-Lewis, "Rangers Get Enhanced Status in New Defence Policy," *Nunatsiaq News,* 29 April 2005. See also Terry Kruger, "New Eyes on the North," *Nunavut News/North,* 25 April 2005. The Canadian Rangers are mentioned twice in the policy statement. See *Canada's International Policy Statement: A Role of Pride and Influence in the World: Defence* (Ottawa: Department of Foreign Affairs and International Trade, 2005), 10, 20.

209 Jim Bell, "Expand Rangers, Tory Defence Critic Says," *Nunatsiaq News,* 9 September 2005. Both the Liberals and the Conservatives promised to expand the Rangers if elected. See CBC News, "North to Get Search-and-Rescue Aircraft from Liberals," 18 January 2006, http://www.cbc.ca/. During the election campaign, the Conservatives said they would recruit five hundred more Rangers. Sara Minogue, "Martin Slams Tory Plan to Protect Arctic," *Nunatsiaq News,* 20 January 2006.

Chapter 11: Sovereignty, Security, and Stewardship

1 Quoted in CBC North, "Military to Boost Rangers' Numbers across North," 28 May 2009.

2 Quoted in Bob Weber, "Arctic Patrol on Epic Trek," *Calgary Herald,* 1 April 2007.

3   On this notion, see Rob Huebert, "Canada and the Changing International Arctic," in *Northern Exposure: Peoples, Powers and Prospects in Canada's North,* ed. Frances Abele, Thomas J. Courchene, F. Leslie Seidle, and Francis St-Hilaire (Ottawa: Institute for Research on Public Policy, 2008), 1. For indications of popular support, see Ekos Research, *Rethinking the Top of the World: Arctic Security Public Opinion Survey – Final Report* (Toronto: Walter and Duncan Gordon Foundation and the Canada Centre for Global Security Studies at the Munk School of Global Affairs, January 2011).

4   Kathleen Harris, "Laying Claim to Canada's Internal Waters," *Toronto Sun,* 23 February 2007.

5   Speech from the Throne, 16 October 2007. See also Don Martin, "Invisible Force in the North; Rangers Guard Sovereignty with Old Guns, Radios," *National Post,* 26 October 2007.

6   Darrell Greer, "Commander Visits Rangers in Eight Communities," *Northern News Services,* 11 March 2009.

7   Standing Senate Committee on National Security and Defence, *Managing Turmoil: The Need to Upgrade Canadian Foreign Aid and Military Strength to Deal with Massive Change,* interim report (October 2006), 83.

8   See, for example, P. Whitney Lackenbauer, "Mirror Images? Canada, Russia, and the Circumpolar World" *International Journal* 65, 4 (2010): 879-97.

9   Franklyn Griffiths coined the label "purveyors of polar peril." Byers changed his tune abruptly in 2008 and became a strong proponent of Arctic cooperation. This shift fit with his close relationship with the Liberal and New Democratic parties. He ran as a candidate for the latter in the 2008 federal election. On these trends in a Canadian context, see Kenneth Coates, P. Whitney Lackenbauer, Bill Morrison, and Greg Poelzer, *Arctic Front: Defending Canada in the Far North* (Toronto: Thomas Allen, 2008); Michael Byers, *Who Owns the Arctic? Understanding Sovereignty Disputes in the North* (Vancouver: Douglas and McIntyre, 2009); and Franklyn Griffiths, Rob Huebert, and P. Whitney Lackenbauer, *Canada and the Changing Arctic: Sovereignty, Security, and Stewardship* (Waterloo: Wilfrid Laurier University Press, 2011).

10 Stephen Harper, "Expanding Canadian Forces Operations in the Arctic," 10 August 2007, http://pm.gc.ca/eng/media.asp?id=1785.

11 Prime Minister's Office, news release, "Prime Minister Announces Expansion of Canadian Forces Facilities and Operations in the Arctic," 10 August 2007, http://pm.gc. ca/eng/media. asp?id=1784.

12 In the North, some residents welcomed new infrastructure that could reduce transportation costs; others, such as Arctic Bay Ranger Sergeant Manasie Kilukishak, worried that the port and noise pollution associated with marine traffic could affect wildlife in the area. CBC Calgary, "Northerners Divided over Proposed Arctic Military Facilities," 13 August 2007.

13 Don Martin, "Invisible Force in the North," *National Post,* 26 October 2007.

14 Major D.C. Knowles, "Record of Discussion of the Canadian Ranger National Authority Working Group held in JTFNHQ Yellowknife 31 Jan–2 Feb 2007," March 2007, Department of National Defence (DND), f. 5030-1 (ACOS DGLRes Sec).

15 Bruce Valpy, "Operation Nunalivut 08," *Northern News Services,* 28 April 2008.

16 Kent Driscoll, "Where Only Rangers Tread," *Northern News Services,* 9 April 2007.

17 See, for example, Adrian Humphreys, "Defending the North," *National Post,* 7 March 2006; Philippe Morin, "Boots on the Ground," *Northern News Services,* 21 August 2006; John Thompson, "Military Mounts Its Most Ambitious Arctic Trek," *Nunatsiaq News,* 23 March 2007; Hon. Lawrence Cannon, House of Commons, *Debates,* 4 May 2009; Hon. Chuck Strahl, *Debates,* 16 November 2009; and Claude Bachand, *Debates,* 23 February 2009 and 4 May 2009.

18 "Quebec City's 400th Anniversary Tribute by Visitors from Northern Quebec," Canada NewsWire, 10 January 2008.

19 I participated in the last leg of the expedition from Points North Landing, Saskatchewan, to Churchill, Manitoba. On the expedition, see the special edition of *The Ranger* (January-March 2009). See also Tammy Scott-Wallace, "N.B. Native Takes a Chilling Trek," *Telegraph-Journal* (Saint John), 5 March 2009.

20 Four CRPGs were commanded by land force area commanders and 1 CRPG by the commander, Canadian Forces Northern Area. "There is no central executive above the Area level and no clear delineation of responsibility," the chief of review services observed in 2003. The director of reserves offered some central direction as chair of the Rangers' Working Group but did not have the power to enforce training standards, establishment levels, or policy. Directorate staff could generate policy and champion the Rangers in Ottawa, but their role was limited to "advising, assisting and warning." "CRS Review of the Canadian Rangers," draft, September 2003, iii-v, 17, DND, Canadian Rangers National Authority (CRNA), f. "CRS and CFNA Report."

21 The CRS Review recommended establishing the Canadian Ranger National Authority (CRNA) within the vice chief of the defence staff and director reserves (the least resource intensive option). The Armed Forces Council recommended in March 2004 that the deputy chief of the defence staff (DCDS) become the national authority in charge of Ranger issues. Lieutenant-General G.E.C. Macdonald to Chief of the Land Staff (CLS), "Future of the Canadian Rangers," 20 June 2004, DND, f. 5785-1 (DGRC). For concerns about this decision, see Brigadier-General J.G.M. Lessard to DCDS Group, "Chief of Staff Force Generation, Command and Control of the Canadian Rangers," 12 November 2004, Land Force Central Area (LFCA) Headquarters, f. 1901-1 (Comd). The planned transfer of command authority never took place, however, and the Canadian Forces announced a major overhaul of their command structure in June 2005. When CF Transformation dissolved the DCDS group in 2006, command and control of the Rangers was split between Land Force Command (the army) and Joint Task Force North (JTFN). Vice Admiral P.D. McFadden and Lieutenant-General A.B. Leslie, "Transfer Instruction – 1st Canadian Ranger Patrol Group from Canada Command/Joint Task Force North to Land Force Command," 15 October 2008, DND, f. 1950-3 (CRNA). The confusing command-and-control arrangements continued to bewilder journalists. See, for example, Karen Mackenzie, "Rangers to Expand under Army Command," *Northern News Services*, 20 August 2007. Canada Command was the "force generator" for the Rangers in 1 CRPG until 1 December 2008, when this responsibility fell to the chief of the land staff. Some interviewees suggested that Brigadier-General Christine Whitecross, the commander of JTFN until 2008, delayed the transfer because 1 CRPG was the only unit that she "owned" but that her replacement, Brigadier-General David Millar, immediately affected the transfer after he arrived.

22 Staff officers could work on force and policy development on behalf of the entire organization and "plug into proper homes" within the larger land staff. Major Guy Ingram, interview with author, Geraldton, ON, 8 July 2008.

23 Colin Campbell, "Canada's Ragtag Arctic Forces," *Maclean's*, 22 August 2006, 30-32.

24 See, for example, Randy Boswell, "Inuit Ask Ottawa for Authority to Keep Eye on Arctic," *Edmonton Journal*, 2 October 2009. The official website describes the Canadian Rangers as dedicated, knowledgeable members of the forces who "play an important role in advancing public recognition of Canada's First Nations and Inuit Groups." Quoted in Kenn Oliver, "Unsung Arm of Military Work for Common Good of the Nation," *The Labradorian*, 5 March 2007.

25 Sheila Watt-Cloutier, "Inuit, Climate Change, Sovereignty, and Security in the Canadian Arctic" (remarks presented to Canadian Arctic Resources Committee Conference, Ottawa, 25 January 2002).

26 Kerry McCluskey, "The Critical Role of the Canadian Rangers," *Naniiliqpita* (Nunavut Tunngavik Inc.), Winter 2006, 12-15.

27 See, for example, Paul Kaludjak, "Use the Inuit," *Ottawa Citizen,* 18 July 2007.

28 Franklyn Griffiths, "The Shipping News," *International Journal* 58, 2 (2003): 279.

29 Legislative Assembly of the Northwest Territories, *Hansard,* 2nd session, 16th Assembly, 12 June 2008, 1181.

30 Captain Terry Stead, the commander of the 5 CRPG detachment in Gander, explained that the basic army principle of reinforcing success, not trying to reinvent the Rangers, should guide the process. Capt. Terry Stead, "5 CRPG Rangers Briefing," Gander, NL, 31 October 2008. In a recent study, historian Barry Stentiford explains how the rise of the US National Guard and its incorporation of locally supported militia companies "brought increasing uniformity and professionalism to the militia as a whole" but undermined deep community connections. Better equipment and training did not offset the simple reality that increased federal military control made National Guard units local federal representatives rather than town institutions. As local community elites became less involved, the critical bond between unit and town was shattered. As a consequence, military service became "a federal and an individual concern" rather than a community one. Barry M. Stentiford, "The Meaning of a Name: The Rise of the National Guard and the End of a Town Militia," *Journal of Military History* 72 (July 2008): 728-29.

31 Lt.-Gen. M.J. Dumais, "Commander Canada Command Recommendation for the Expansion of Canadian Ranger Patrols," 20 March 2008, DND, Canada Command, f. 3440-2 (J3 Plans 7), referencing "VCDS Report on Plans and Priorities 07/08."

32 This ambiguity was not helped by the October 2007 speech from the throne, which reiterated that "the size and capabilities of the Arctic Rangers will be expanded to better patrol our vast Arctic territory."

33 Dumais, "Commander Canada Command Recommendation."

34 Capt. Conrad Schubert to Comd., JTFN, "Briefing Note – 1 CRPG Ranger Expansion," 22 October 2007, DND, 1 CRPG, f. 1920-1(DCO).

35 See the 2006 community profile at http://www12.statcan.ca/census-recensement/. The 2001 census listed five residents at Bathurst Inlet.

36 Schubert to Comd., JTFN, 22 October 2007. Northwest Territories had three communities with populations over three hundred that could support Ranger patrols (Norman Wells, Hay River, and Yellowknife–Detah–N'Dilo) and two in Yukon (Watson Lake and Faro).

37 Schubert to Comd., JTFN, 22 October 2007.

38 Brig.-Gen. G.J.P. O'Brien, "Canadian Ranger Expansion Update," 20 April 2010, DND, f. 1920-1 (CRNA).

39 Based on interviews in Northwest Territories and Yukon in 2009. I have chosen not to cite individuals in light of the sensitive nature of this material.

40 Capt. Neal Whitman, "1 CRPG Sit Rep," 29 October 2009. Copy provided by CRNA.

41 Lieutenant-Colonel Ian Pedley and Master Warrant Officer Bruce Dunn, interviews with author, Ottawa, ON, 17 February 2011.

42 "Les deux font la paire," *Servir* (Land Force Quebec Area) 16, 11 (2009): 3; "2nd Canadian Ranger Patrol Group" (presentation to CRNA WG [Working Group], October 2009 [copy provided by CRNA]). In 1980, in anticipation of erosion caused by the James Bay power project, 1,500 Cree were relocated from Fort George Island to the new town of Chisasibi on the mainland coast. The development of a sense of community in this "deliberately landscaped modern town" was difficult, however, and women found it more difficult to educate youth in the bush about Cree values. See Susan Jacobs, "Building a Community in the Town of Chisasibi," in *Aboriginal Autonomy and Development in Northern Quebec and Labrador,* ed. Colin H. Scott (Vancouver: UBC Press, 2001), 304-15.

43 The expansion plan for 2009-10 added a new Ranger section on Anticosti Island to the Havre-Sainte-Pierre patrol, and new patrols in Nemiscau, Mistissini, Oujé-Bougoumou, Waswanipi, and Fermont. "2nd Canadian Ranger Patrol Group," presentation October 2009.

44 3 CRPG Briefing to CRNA WG, October 2008; "3rd Canadian Ranger Patrol Group" (presentation to CRNA WG, October 2009); O'Brien, "Canadian Ranger Expansion Update." In 2009, 3 CRPG opened new patrols at the Eabametoong (Fort Hope), Kasabonika Lake, and Kingfisher Lake First Nations. Expansion is part of the army's "connecting-with-Canadians activity, particularly within targeted minority communities." Maj. K. Sproule, "JTFC/LFCA Response: 3rd Canadian Ranger Patrol Group Enhancements," April 2007, DND, f. 3121-2-1 (J5 Ops). Copy provided by CRNA.

45 The gaps were between Kitimat and Bella Coola and then Bella Coola and Port Hardy. Maj. W.C. LeClair, "Briefing Note for Comd Canada COM, BC Coastal Ranger Patrols," 4 October 2006, copy provided by CRNA.

46 Maj. T.C. Byers, "Request for Additional Canadian Ranger Patrols within Land Force Western Area, 2 March 2007," DND, f. 1901-1-2 (GSC).

47 4 CRPG, presentation to CRNA WG, ca. October 2007; 4 CRPG, presentation to CRNA WG, October 2009. Copies of slides provided by CRNA. Numbers had also dropped in 2004, after 4 CRPG had closed patrols in Chetwynd, British Columbia, and Little Grand Rapids, Manitoba, because of lack of interest. Major Tim Byers, 4 CRPG Annual Historical Report, 2005, 12 April 2006, DND, Directorate of History and Heritage (DHH), 3688.

48 Capt. Meades, "BC Det Comd's Sitrep," *The Ranger* 12, 3 (Summer 2010): 4.

49 WO Mike Gilliard, "Wollaston Lake DP1," *The Ranger* 12, 3 (Summer 2010): 7-8.

50 Lt.-Col. Tim Byers, "CO's Corner," *The Ranger,* 12, 3 (Summer 2010): 3.

51 Lt.-Col. Jamie Morse, "5 CRPG Canadian Ranger Program," briefing to CRNA WG, October 2009. Copy provided by CRNA.

52 For example, the founding of the Hamilton Sound patrol in central Newfoundland in April 2010 followed restructuring of the Lewisporte and Cape Freels patrols. Andrew Robinson, "Rangers Gain Hamilton Sound Presence," *The Beacon* (Gander, NL), 8 April 2010. "We looked at it and said right in the middle of these patrol areas is Hamilton Sound, or Gander Bay, where there's a lot of tiny communities where we don't have any Rangers," Lieutenant Junior Roberts noted. "We basically changed the boundaries so what was once covered by two is now covered by three." Andew Robinson, "Rangers Gain Hamilton Sound Presence," *The Beacon* (Gander, NL), 8 April 2010. See also Lt. G.J. (Junior) Roberts, "5 Canadian Ranger Patrol Group Continues to Expand," *What's New* (5 CRPG), January 2010.

53 It would silence critics who have chastised the Conservatives for failing to meet their Arctic sovereignty commitments. See, for example, Liberal Party of Canada, "Harper Conservatives' Latest Northern Strategy Announcement Amounts to Much Ado about Nothing," *States News Service,* 30 July 2009.

54 Major Jeff Allen, interview with author, Yellowknife, NT, 13 June 2011.

55 Maj. K. Sproule, "JTFC/LFCA Response: 3rd Canadian Ranger Patrol Group Enhancements," April 2007, DND, f. 3121-2-1 (J5 Ops). Copy provided by CRNA.

56 The government's northern strategy, outlined in the 2007 speech from the throne, "focused on strengthening Canada's sovereignty, protecting our environmental heritage, promoting economic and social development, and improving and devolving governance, so that northerners have greater control over their destines." On these speeches, see P. Whitney Lackenbauer, *From Polar Race to Polar Saga: An Integrated Strategy for Canada and the Circumpolar World* (Toronto: Canadian International Council, July 2009), and Klaus Dodds, "We Are a Northern Country," *Polar Record* 47, 4 (2011): 371-74.

57 Mary Simon, "Inuit: The Bedrock of Arctic Sovereignty," *Globe and Mail,* 26 July 2007. For a similar message, see Paul Berton, "Time to Stake Solid Claim over Arctic," *Toronto Sun,* 27 February 2007, and Mary Simon, "Inuit and the Canadian Arctic," *Journal of Canadian Studies* 43, 2 (2009): 250-60.

58 Jose Kusugak, "Stewards of the Northwest Passage," *National Post,* 3 February 2006.

59 Patricia Bell on CBC Radio, *The House,* hosted by Chris Hall, 12 August 2006.

60 CBC North, "Reaction Mixed to Senate Call for Stronger Canadian Ranger Presence," 11 May 2009.

61 Bruce Valpy, "Operation Lancaster Launched," *Northern News Services,* 21 August 2006.

62 Inuit Tapiriit Kanatami, "An Integrated Arctic Strategy," January 2008, 15, http://itk.ca/.

63 See Deborah Cowen, *Military Workfare: The Soldier and Citizenship in Canada* (Toronto: University of Toronto Press, 2008).

64 In 2008, it noted the publication of fifty-seven stories and ninety-five photos in newspapers and magazines; TV coverage on CBC, CTV, Global, and APTN; CBC Radio coverage; and the production of an *Army News* video on the Rangers in 3 CRPG. 3 CRPG, Briefing to CRNA WG, October 2008.

65 Guy Ingram interview.

66 Rangers in Haines Junction warned that 1 CRPG would start losing people if it started cancelling things such as shoots. Other Rangers said the patrol members would run these activities regardless of whether they got compensated. Observations by the author at the monthly patrol meeting, Haines Junction, YT, 16 June 2009. Rangers used to be paid in cash at the end of exercises. They had gone to direct deposit, but it now took months to get paid because headquarters was short-staffed. Larry Bagnell, MP for Yukon, also raised this issue in the House of Commons on 10 April 2008.

67 CBC News, "Canadian Rangers Pull Out of Yukon Quest," 10 November 2009, http://www.cbc.ca/. See also Annalee Grant, "Yukon Quest Plans Alternative as Canadian Rangers Step Down," *Whitehorse Star,* 10 November 2009.

68 Several Rangers said they would break and maintain trail and run shoots without instructor support or pay. Suzanna Caldwell, "2011 Yukon Quest Begins Today in Whitehorse, Yukon," *Fairbanks Daily News-Miner,* 5 February 2011. On the superiority of the trail put in by the Rangers compared to the Alaskan leg, see Justine Davidson, "Quest Stalwart Pushes All-Yukon Replacement Race," *Whitehorse Star,* 25 February 2011.

69 Gabriel Zarate, "A Simulated Apex Invasion," *Northern News Services,* 24 August 2009.

70 Robert Smol, "When Will We Get Serious about Arctic Defence?" CBC News, 11 May 2009, http://www.cbc.ca/. See also Robert Smol, "We're Not Serious about Arctic Defence," *National Post,* 27 August 2009.

71 James Raffan, "Policing the Passage," *Canadian Geographic* 127, 1 (2007): 43-47, 50-52, 54, 56, 58, 60.

72 John Ralston Saul, "The Roots of Canadian Law in Canada," *McGill Law Journal* 54, 4 (2010): 671-95. Saul is married to Adrienne Clarkson and, as her consort, visited many Ranger patrols during her tenure as governor general.

73 John Ralston Saul, "Listen to the North," *Literary Review of Canada,* October 2009, 3-5. His idea of re-enrolling Rangers in Primary Reserve battalions is rebuked by Geoff Hamilton in a letter to the editor, *Literary Review of Canada,* December 2009, 31.

74 The report cited Joseph Spears, who "believed that marine-capable Canadian Rangers would be useful in the areas of pollution response, marine SAR, security (naval boarding), climate change research, and in the exercise of jurisdiction in conjunction with other federal departments." Standing Senate Committee on Fisheries and Oceans, *Rising to the Arctic Challenge,* 12 March 2009.

75 Bob Weber, "Arm Icebreakers, Beef Up Rangers to Assert Canadian Control of Arctic: Senate," *Whitehorse Star,* 7 May 2009. In Rompkey's view, giving the Rangers enforcement powers would help the government beef up control of the Northwest Passage by monitoring small vessels and provide the Coast Guard with "the necessary muscle to enforce Canadian law." Bob Weber, "Clamp Down on Arctic Shipping, Beef Up Coast Guard Armament: Senate," *Waterloo Chronicle,* 14 December 2009. The government backgrounder that outlined Ranger expansion in August 2007 mentioned that the Rangers would also see an "enhancement of

transportation capabilities." As part of the Arctic Strategy Plan in 2007, Brigadier-General David Millar, the commander of Joint Task Force North, intended to formalize the task of water surveillance and search and rescue for the Rangers. This would require equipping specific patrols with boats. Captain Neal Whitman, "1 CRPG Sit Rep," 29 October 2009, provided by 1 CRPG. In a 2011 article, former Canadian Forces Northern Area commander Pierre Leblanc concurred that it is time to "think outside the igloo" and equip and train the Rangers for a maritime mission. See "Northwest Passage Unguarded: Thinking Outside the Igloo?" *FrontLine Defence* 3 (2011): 58-59. Commentators never discuss the practical issues of responsibility for these boats and how government ownership would affect the basic principle that the Rangers be "lightly equipped" and "self-sufficient."

76 Andrew Livingstone, "Make Rangers Reservists," *Northern News Services,* 20 May 2009. In this article, Dennis Bevington, the NDP member of Parliament representing the western Arctic, concurred that militarizing the Rangers and changing their mandate was the wrong approach to bolstering Arctic sovereignty. "Reservists can be called up for duty in Afghanistan," he warned. "The assumption was that Canadian Rangers were civil authority, search and rescue and giving capacity to the communities with linkage to the military. I think they can be enhanced within that concept without having to look at full militarization." See also CBC North, "Reaction Mixed to Senate Call for Stronger Canadian Ranger Presence," 11 May 2009. These concerns were not confined to the North. "If you try to turn the Rangers into the Primary Reserve," Major Tim Byers explained to me in Victoria on 13 July 2005, "it will die miserably." Making the Rangers more militaristic would kill it, Ranger Sergeant Curtis Hicks of the Cape Freels patrol in Newfoundland also told me during an interview in Musgrave Harbour on 1 November 2008.

77 Darrell Greer, "Not as Slow as Some May Think," *Kivalliq News,* 20 May 2009.

78 For a larger discussion of this theme, see Lackenbauer, *From Polar Race to Polar Saga.*

79 This quote opened Chapter 2.

80 Because many Reserve Force policies did not apply to the Rangers, the Armed Forces Council directed in April 2006 that the Rangers should form their own component of the Canadian Forces outside of the Reserve Force. Lt.-Gen. W.J. Natynczyk and Lt.-Gen. A.B. Leslie, "Canadian Rangers National Authority Transfer Instruction – Vice Chief of the Defence Staff to Chief Land Staff," 31 May 2007, DND, f. 1950-3 (1901-260/4 D Res).

81 Scott Taylor, "On the Road with the CDS," *Esprit de Corps* 16, 10 (2009): 14. In early 2011, the chief of the defence staff clarified that the Canada First Defence Strategy was intended to increase membership, not responsibilities. Jason Unrau, "General Visits 'the Eyes and Ears of Canada,'" *Whitehorse Star,* 12 January 2011.

82 Lt.-Gen. A.B. Leslie, "CLS Planning Guidance: Land Force Arctic Strategy," 9 March 2009, DND, f. 3000-1 (DLFD).

83 Lt.-Gen. A.B. Leslie, draft, "CLS Planning Guidance – Arctic Response," July 2009, DND, f. 3000-1 (A/DLFD). This Ranger contribution includes sovereignty patrolling and the majority of activities in extreme conditions.

84 Leslie, "CLS Planning Guidance: Land Force Arctic Strategy." The Rangers are cast as a "critical enabler and capability for operations in Canada's north." Brig.-Gen. G.R. Thibault, "Operationalization of Canadian Ranger Patrol Groups: Support to Canada Command," 16 October 2006, JTF(C) HQ, f. 4500-1 (COS), copy provided by CRNA.

85 Herb Mathisen, "Looking for Company," *Northern News Services,* 12 June 2009; Keith Doucette, "Forces to Set Up Permanent Reserve Unit in Yellowknife," *Waterloo Region Record,* 6 September 2008. 1 CRPG developed a concept plan with JTFN so that the unit could act as a rapid reaction force in the North. It was first tested during Operation Nunalivut 2011. This concept repackaged an existing capability, and the implications remained unclear at the time of writing. Jeanne Gagnon, "Speeding Up Response Time," *Nunavut News/North,*

28 March 2011; Capt. Neal Whitman, "1 CRPG Sit Rep," 29 October 2009, copy provided by CRNA; Captain Neil Whitmann, interview with author, Yellowknife, NT, 17 June 2011.

86 Captain Darryl Bazin, interview with author, Churchill, MB, 3 March 2009. See also Capt. Sheldon Maerz, "The First Survival School," *The Ranger* 7, 4 (2005): 9-11, and Lance Bushie, "Peace River Survival School," *The Ranger* 8, 1 (Winter 2006); 8. For appraisals, see Capt. Phil Chesne, "Learning to Survive with the Rangers," *Western Sentinel,* 24 January 2008; Major Tim Byers, "CO's Corner," *The Ranger* (4 CRPG) 10, 1 (Winter 2008): 6, and 12, 1 (Winter 2010), 3.

87 See, for example, Len Gillis, "Rangers Provide Wilderness Training for Canadian Soldiers in Timmins," *Timmins Times,* 4 March 2009.

88 Jeff Allen interview.

89 Editorial, "When Government Serves the Public Good," *Nunatsiaq News,* 3 November 2009. See also Jim Bell, "It Is Still the Best Protection You Can Get," *Nunatsiaq News,* 1 November 2009.

90 Major Luc Chang, "1 CRPG Briefing to CRNA WG," October 2008, copy provided by CRNA; Jeff Allen interview.

91 Guylaine Fortin, "Op TULUGAQ," *Bulletin Info Rangers* (2 CRPG) 13 (2007): 5; "Training," *Bulletin Info Rangers* 13 (2007): 2.

92 Guy Ingram interview. See also Brig.-Gen. G.R. Thibault, "Operationalization of Canadian Ranger Patrol Groups: Support to Canada Command," 16 October 2006, JTF(C) HQ, f. 4500-1 (COS), copy provided by CRNA.

93 Christie Blatchford, "Lifting the Veil on Native Youth Suicide," *Globe and Mail,* 4 January 2011. On a successful intervention, see Peter Moon, "Canadian Rangers, Police Save Suicidal Mother," *Northern Times* (Kapuskasing), 27 January 2011, and Morgan Ian Adams, "Local Military Man Hailed for Dramatic Rescue of Woman," *Enterprise-Bulletin* (Collingwood, ON), 10 February 2011.

94 Col. S.C. McQuitty, "Briefing Note to CLS on Command and Control of 1 CRPG," 24 April 2006, DND, f. 1310-1 (DGLRes); Lt.-Col. B.G. Derbach, "Briefing Note for Commander Canada Command – Subject: Transfer of Authority – 1 Canadian Ranger Patrol Group (1 CRPG)," 24 July 2006; Lt.-Gen. A.B. Leslie, "Transfer of Canadian Ranger National Authority to Command of Land Force Command – 1 Apr 07," DND, f. 1310-1 (CR Fin DGLRes). Within the land staff, the assistant chief of staff director general land reserve secretariat oversees four CRNA positions staffed by reservists: policy, training and equipment, human resources, and finance. Lt.-Gen. W.J. Natynczyk and Lt.-Gen. A.B. Leslie, "Canadian Rangers National Authority Transfer Instruction – Vice Chief of the Defence Staff to Chief Land Staff," 31 May 2007, DND, f. 1950-3 (1901-260/4 D Res).

95 "LFCO 11-99 – Canadian Rangers, 1 December 2010." Copy provided by CRNA.

96 Capt. Terry Stead, "5 CRPG Rangers Briefing," Gander, NL, 31 October 2008; "LFCO 11-99 – Canadian Rangers." Was this because older people were not considered elders unless they were Aboriginal? At one point in the discussion, officials in Ottawa proposed that only Aboriginal people could stay in past sixty-five years of age. Thankfully, they never adopted this racial criterion.

97 Some Rangers and Ranger instructors had expressed concern that some patrol commanders had been in their positions for too long. When Major Terry Stead proposed holding patrol leadership elections at the patrol commanders meeting, Rangers gave nearly unanimous approval. Patrols had to vote within the next year. Capt. Terry Stead, "5 CRPG Rangers Briefing." Sergeants voted in as patrol commanders would have a three-year term.

98 Brig.-Gen. I.C. Poulter, "Submission of Loss or Damage Claims for Personal Equipment Used in the Performance of Canadian Ranger Duties," 16 May 2008, DND, f. 7200-1 (CRHR). Previously, processing claims for damaged equipment took too long, making Rangers reluctant

to use their personal equipment. "2005 Annual Historical Report – 5 Canadian Ranger Patrol Group," 27 February 2006, f. 1326-2 (LFAAHQ). Even this standardization raised regional concerns. The commanding officer of a patrol group had the right to approve a claim in advance for damages up to one thousand dollars. Major Jeff Allen in 1 CRPG argued that this amount was unfair in his region, where Rangers often relied on ATVs and snow machines as their primary mode of transportation and thus for their livelihood. The average claim was more than a thousand dollars, prompting him to request authorization for a higher claim in advance. Interview with author, Yellowknife, NT, 13 June 2011.

99 Annex A to 7209-1 (Dres), 1 April 2003; Annex C to LFCO 11-99, 1 August 2009, copies provided by CRNA.

100 Master Warrant Officer Bruce Dunn, interview with author, Ottawa, ON, 17 February 2011. DAOD 5100-Canadian Rangers and DAOD 5511-0 Promotion, Seniority, Reversion and Relinquishment (to be issued) will provide national direction on day-to-day operations.

101 CRS 2003. Participants in the 2009 CRNA WG agreed that Rangers would be considered on duty when they were being paid or when authorized by the chain of command and that they were covered by the Queen's Regulations and Orders, Chapter 9, when travelling to and from a place of duty. Maj. Jim Mills, "Record of Discussion of the Canadian Ranger National Authority Working Group (CRNA WG) held in Ottawa, 29 Sep-1 Oct 2009," 2 November 2009, DND, f. 5030-1 (SO CR Pol DGLRes Sec).

102 Yumimi Pang, "Ranger Injured While Helping Dog Race," *Nunavut News/North,* 31 March 2008; CBC North, "Military to Investigate Accident Involving Canadian Ranger," 1 April 2008; Yumimi Pang, "Kimmirut Ranger Recovering," *Nunavut News/North,* 7 April 2008; Gabriel Zarate, "Making Ready for the Qimualaniq Quest," *Northern News Services,* 9 February 2009; Herb Mathisen, "Alone in the Snow with Broken Bones," *Northern News Services,* 15 September 2008.

103 Major Luc Chang, "1 CRPG Briefing to CRNA WG," October 2008. Copy provided by CRNA. Kootoo, the mayor of Kimmirut, died after he went missing on a caribou hunt in November 2011.

104 Paniloo died while hunting caribou for his tent group. He had served as MLA for the former Baffin Centre Riding in the Northwest Territories government from 1983 to 1987 and was a former mayor of Clyde River. Adrian Humphreys, "A Ranger's Final Patrol," *National Post,* 25 April 2007. On Paniloo's death, see also Hon. Larry Bagnell (Yukon, Liberal), Hansard, 23 April 2007. Paniloo's wife, Lucy Mingeriak, was eligible for the Memorial Cross, a medal for the next of kin given when soldiers die for their country. A second death of a Ranger on active duty – that of Corporal Charlie Sheppard of Flat Bay, Newfoundland, who died during a winter indoctrination exercise with the Second Battalion, Royal Newfoundland Regiment, in 2008 – confirmed the need for clear policies. 2Lt. G.J. (Junior) Roberts, "Tribute: Farewell to Ranger Cpl. Charles Sheppard," *Western Star* (Corner Brook), 5 March 2008.

105 Peter Moon, "Veterans' Grave Markers," *Northern Voice* (Cochrane, ON), 3 November 2009. In October 2009, the Last Post Fund presented the first headstones to deceased Rangers in Sandy Lake and Fort Albany. Major G.C. Ingram, "Annual Historical Report 2009 for 3 CRPG," 21 January 2010, DND, DHH, 3687.

106 Guy Ingram interview. Capt. Terry Stead made a similar point during our interview in Gander, NL, on 31 October 2008.

107 Maj. Jim Mills, "Record of Discussion of the Canadian Ranger National Authority Working Group (CRNA WG) held in Ottawa, 30 Sep-2 Oct 2008," 8 October 2008, DND, f. 5030-1 (SO CR Pol DGLRes Sec); Col. T. Tarrant, "Meeting of DRes Staff, CLS Representative, and Commanding Officers of CRPGs to Discuss the Future of the Canadian Rangers," 13 January 2006. Copy provided by CRNA. The 2007 working group agreed to an instructor-patrol ratio of one to four and to adjust the number of support positions in each patrol,

headquarters depending on the number of patrols supported by it. Knowles, Record of Discussion, March 2007.

108 O'Brien, "Canadian Ranger Expansion Update." The prime minister promised "to ensure that the necessary Command and Control systems are put in place to manage the expanded force." Stephen Harper, "Expanding Canadian Forces Operations in the Arctic," 10 August 2007, Prime Minister's Office, http://pm.gc.ca/eng/media.asp?id=1785.

109 4 CRPG, presentation to CRNA WG, ca. October 2007.

110 Land Forces Command also stated that it did not intend to redistribute 1 CRPG funding to the other patrol groups after 1 CRPG was transferred to army control. Knowles, Record of Discussion, March 2007.

111 Mills, Record of CRNA WG, 2 November 2009.

112 Lt.-Col. Tim Byers, "CO's Corner," The Ranger 12, 3 (Summer 2010): 3.

113 Lang explained to me that he intended to facilitate group training, encourage different patrols to meet with and learn from one another, have them operate outside of their local areas, and develop "une synergie." Major Guy Lang, interviews with author during a liaison visit to the Lower North Shore, Quebec, 10-14 April 2007. 2 CRPG appointed Ranger Warrant Officers with responsibilities for Hudson Bay, the Lower North Shore (two – a francophone and an anglophone), James Bay, Ungava Bay, and Hudson Strait. "Appointment of Regional Warrant Officers," Bulletin Info Rangers (2 CRPG) 15 (March 2008), 10. Because the position of warrant officer did not exist within the nationally authorized Canadian Ranger organization, authorities in Ottawa had no idea how 2 CRPG paid its warrant officers or "held" them, but they indicated this was an issue "between the CRPG and their area" commander. Lt.-Col. Ian Pedley, interview with author, 17 February 2011, Ottawa, ON. 3 CRPG also split its jurisdiction into four sub-areas of operation. 3 CRPG Briefing to CRNA WG, October 2008. Copy provided by CRNA.

114 Major G. Lang, "Mise à jour – 2 GPRC," ca. October 2007. Copy provided by CRNA. See also "2 CRPG Annual Historical Report 2010."

115 Daniel Rancourt, "Nakurmik!" Servir 16, 11 (2009): 3. "Mon plus grand défi, c'est de faire accepter les Rangers comme soldats. Les membres des Rangers sont responsables et sont capables d'être autonomes. Ils connaissent leur territoire, ils comprennent très bien leur mission et ils sont fiers de leur travail ... Moi, je les appelle mes 'Warriors.'" Translated by author. With all this strong soldiering language, he also reassured the Rangers that they were not expected to deploy overseas. Guylaine Fortin, "Op TULUGAQ," Bulletin Info Rangers (2 CRPG) 13 (March 2007): 5.

116 Mills, Record of CRNA WG, 2 November 2009.

117 Lt. G.J. Roberts, "5 CRPG Offers First Formal Training to Canadian Rangers," What's New (5 CRPG), September 2009.

118 Ranger Sergeant George Sutton of Milltown, quoted in G.J. Roberts, "Busy Weekend for Canadian Rangers of the Milltown Patrol," The Coaster (Harbour Breton, NL), 29 September 2009. See also Jennifer Geens, "New Rangers Graduate from Training Course," Northern News Services, 27 March 2009; Major Luc Chang, 1 CRPG Briefing to CRNA WG, October 2008; Lt. Shalako Smith, "Canadian Rangers Go Back to the Basics," The Labradorian, 20 July 2009; Emily Ridlington, "Nunavut Has Four New Canadian Rangers," Northern News Services, 26 February 2010.

119 Capt. Neal Whitman, "1 CRPG Sit Rep," 29 October 2009. Copy provided by CRNA.

120 Confidential interviews with three Ranger instructors in 1 CRPG in 2008 and 2009.

121 Jeff Allen interview. Indoctrination into the Rangers occurred in their home patrol.

122 Allen changed the Development Phase Two (DP2) training in 1 CRPG as well, making it more of a field course than a classroom-oriented one. Rather than gathering Ranger patrol leaders from across the three territories in one of the capitals (where the potential for distractions was ever-present), 1 CRPG ran individual courses for Ranger leaders in each territory, held in a

smaller centre. Rangers spent the first day in the classroom and the remainder in the field in small groups supported by a cadre of Ranger instructors. Jeff Allen interview.

123 Sgt. Jon Haines, "AMO Course – Breath Taking View," *The Ranger* 12, 3 (Summer 2010): 6.

124 Darryl Bazin interview.

125 On their roles, see P. Whitney Lackenbauer, "Teaching Canada's Indigenous Sovereignty Soldiers," *Canadian Army Journal* 10, 2 (2007): 66-81. In 2007, all five commander officers at the Canadian Ranger national working group agreed to try to reduce the instructor-to-patrol ratio from one to six to one to four. This reduction would heighten demands for new instructors even further. Maj. T.C. Byers, "Request for Additional Canadian Ranger Patrols within Land Force Western Area," 2 March 2007, DND, f. 1901-1-2 (GSC).

126 In 2007, 1 CRPG requested support from CRNA to increase its posting priority from six to at least five or four to address personnel shortfalls. Mills, Record of CRNA WG, 9 October 2007. It noted that further expansion would require at least two more Ranger instructors in the patrol group (assuming seven patrols per instructor). Capt. Conrad Schubert to Commander, JTFN, "Briefing Note – 1 CRPG Ranger Expansion," 22 October 2007, DND, 1 CRPG, f. 1920-1 (DCO).

127 Stephen Harper, "Expanding Canadian Forces Operations in the Arctic," 10 August 2007, http://pm.gc.ca/eng/media.asp?id=1785.

128 Ian Pedley and Bruce Dunn interviews. For example, 5 CRPG's budget rose from $2.5 million in 2008 to $4.2 million in 2009. Lt.-Col. Jamie Morse, "5 CRPG Canadian Ranger Program," Briefings to CRNA WG, October 2008 and October 2009. Copies provided by CRNA.

129 Guy Ingram interview.

130 "LFCO 11-99 – Canadian Rangers," 1 December 2010. Copy provided by CRNA. Rangers could freely invest this money in either maintaining or purchasing new personal equipment, which they could also use in their daily lives. This directive reinforced the principle that Rangers would be lightly equipped and self-sufficient and not dependent on the military for equipment and vehicles. Most of the Rangers I spoke to preferred increasing these allowances over (taxable) increases in pay. On the pay issue, see, for example, the editorial "Enhancing the Uniform," *Northern News Services,* 21 July 2008; Yvon Lévesque (Abitibi–Baie-James–Nunavik–Eeyou, BQ), *Hansard,* 13 June 2007; Hon. Larry Bagnell (Yukon, Liberal), *Hansard,* 4 November 2009.

131 Harper, "Expanding Canadian Forces Operations."

132 "Canadian Ranger Prioritized Individual Clothing and Equipment List as of 24 October 2007," DND, f. 10001-1 (DGL Res Sec).

133 The Rangers' current radios have limited range, cannot be operated on the move, and are unreliable in extreme conditions, which Rangers frequently encounter. CRNA WG, minutes, October 2007.

134 Maj. K. Sproule, "JTFC/LFCA Response: 3rd Canadian Ranger Patrol Group Enhancements," April 2007, DND, f. 3121-2-1(J5 Ops). Copy provided by CRNA. See also "New Equipment Will Soon Be Distributed," *Arctic Exposure: 1 CRPG Newsletter,* 1 March 2010, 9.

135 Capt. J. Mills, "Briefing Note to the CLS on the Proposed Canadian Ranger Equipment Modernization Project (CRMP) and Immediate Individual Equipment Requirements," 29 October 2007, DND, f. 10001-1 (DGL Res Sec), and Ian Pedley and Bruce Dunn interviews, 17 February 2011.

136 Mills, "Record of Discussion of CRNA WG, 30 Sep-2 Oct 2008."

137 Alexander Panetta, "Jean Dons Red Sweater on Her Arctic Visit," *Globe and Mail,* 14 April 2008.

138 For example, Sergeant Eddie McPherson, the patrol commander in Tulita, told a reporter that his biggest frustration was with "these antique guns ... It's hard to get parts for them. A lot of them have bent barrels." Tim Querengesser, "Embedded with the Canadian Rangers," *Up Here* 26, 7 (2010): 31.

139 Jason Unrau, "General Visits 'the Eyes and Ears of Canada,'" *Whitehorse Star,* 12 January 2011.

140 Capt. J. Mills, "Briefing Note to DGL Res on the Proposed Canadian Ranger Equipment Modernization Project (CRMP)," 31 August 2007, DND, f. 10001-1 (DGL Res Sec). Mills noted that very few modern "sport model" rifles would compare favourably to the Lee-Enfield. The calibre of the new rifle will be 7.62 mm/.308 Winchester, thus ending the historical connection between the Rangers and the .303 Lee-Enfield. Mills, "Record of Discussion of CRNA WG, 30 Sep-2 Oct 2008."

141 Ian Pedley and Bruce Dunn interviews. The rifle replacement is part of the formal Small Arms Modernization Project, an army project of which the Ranger rifle is only a small part. Delivery will be phased in over three years. Major Jim Mills, "Record of Discussion of the Canadian Ranger National Authority Working Group (CRNA WG) held in Ottawa, 29 Sep-1 Oct 2009," 2 November 2009, DND, f. 5030-1 (SO CR Pol DGLRes Sec). This timeline was confirmed the following year. See Lt.-Col. Tim Byers, "CO's Corner," *The Ranger,* Fall 2010, 5.

142 Neils Christensen, "Bringing Tradition to the Armed Forces," *Northern News Services,* 24 November 2003.

143 Darrell Greer, "Rankin Elder to Receive Governor General's Award," *Northern News Services,* 27 February 2008.

144 Darrell Greer, "First to Be Inducted," *Nunavut News/North,* 16 February 2009.

145 Jeff Allen interview.

146 On 21 August 2008, Peter MacKay, the minister of national defence, announced a $3.6 million expansion of the Junior Rangers to accommodate seventeen new patrols and five hundred additional youth by 2012-13. "Minister Mackay Announces Support for Junior Canadian Rangers," *Market Wire,* 21 August 2008.

147 Darrell Greer, "Commander Visits Rangers in Eight Communities," *Northern News Services,* 11 March 2009.

148 Captain Sharon Low, "Junior Canadian Rangers Participate in Remembrance Week," *Northern Frontline* (JTFN), Winter 2011, 10-14.

149 For examples of these themes, see Shelagh Beairsto, "Dinjii Kat Chih Ahaa: Gwich'in Notions of Leadership" (master's thesis, University of Manitoba, 1999).

150 Roxanna Thompson, "A Symbol of the North," *Deh Cho Drum,* 6 December 2007. Not all Rangers proved to be ideal role models. For example, Pingoatuk Kolola, a Ranger from 1994 to 2007, was discharged immediately from the Rangers after he was arrested for murdering an RCMP constable in Kimmirut. He received a life sentence in 2010. CBC North, "Accused in Nunavut RCMP Slaying Was Top Shot: Captain," 26 February 2010; CP, "Nunavut RCMP Shooter Says He Was Only Trying to Scare Officer When He Fired Gun," 5 March 2010; Chris Windeyer, "The Human Damage Caused by This Crime Is Incalculable," *Nunatsiaq News,* 11 March 2010.

151 Querengesser, "Embedded with the Canadian Rangers," 24.

152 See, for example, Frances Abele, "Confronting 'Harsh and Inescapable Facts': Indigenous Peoples and the Militarization of the Circumpolar Region" in *Sovereignty and Security in the Arctic,* ed. Edgar Dosman (London: Routledge, 1989), 189, and Mary Simon, "Militarization and the Aboriginal Peoples," in *Arctic Alternatives: Civility or Militarism in the Circumpolar North,* ed. Franklyn Griffiths (Toronto: Samuel Stevens, 1992), 60.

153 Darren Stewart, "Extreme Weather School," *Northern News Services,* 24 March 2003.

154 Eli Weetaluktuk, interview with author, Inukjuak, QC, 1 September 2006.

155 Andew Robinson, "Rangers Gain Hamilton Sound Presence," *The Beacon* (Gander, NL), 8 April 2010.

156 Najwa Asmar, "4 CRPG: Honour and Dedication," *Maple Leaf* 5, 20 (2002): 6.

157 Rancourt, "Nakurmik!" "Une très belle organisation, le rêve de tout commandant: 750 soldats déployés, dans 25 municipalités et communautés, un mélange de Cris, Inuits, Montagnais, Naskapis, de Blancs, anglophones et francophones, un 'chaudron' de cultures de qui nous pouvons apprendre beaucoup de choses." Translation by the author.

158 William Morrison, "The 1200 Mile Village" (paper presented at the annual meeting of the Canadian Historical Association, York University, Toronto, May 2006). Cited with permission.

159 Peter Kuniliusee, quoted in an interview with Petty Officer Paul Smith, flight from Toronto to Halifax, 20 February 2006.

160 For example, Peter Kulchyski insists that "regardless of the level of power provided to Aboriginal governments, every decision that is made following the dominant logic, in accordance with the hierarchical and bureaucratic structures of the established order, will take Aboriginal peoples further away from their own culture. Every decision that is made in the form appropriate to traditional cultures will be another step in the life of that culture": *Unjust Relations: Aboriginal Rights in Canadian Courts* (Toronto: Oxford University Press, 1994), 121.

161 Participant observation with the Inukjuak patrol, 22 August–1 September 2006.

162 Quoted in Louise Johncox, "We're in a Meltdown," *The Guardian,* 23 August 2007.

163 Franklyn Griffiths, "Camels in the Arctic?" *The Walrus,* November 2007, 46-61.

164 Pauloosie Attagootak, interview with author, Bylot Island, NU, 19 August 2010.

Bibliography

Unpublished Materials

BC Archives, Victoria, BC
British Columbia Legislative Assembly Sessional Clipping Books, Newspaper Accounts
   of the Debates, Microfilm Reel 15
James Edward Kingsley Diary (MSS 2516)
Newspaper indexes

Centre for Newfoundland Studies, St. John's, NL
Clippings files: "Canadian Rangers" and "Newfoundland Rangers"

City of Vancouver Archives, Vancouver, BC
Clippings file: "Canadian Rangers"

Dawson City Museum, Klondike History Library, Dawson, YT
Biography files: "'Chappie' Chapman"
Subject files: "Yukon Rangers," "War – World Wars I and II," "War – Veterans"

Department of National Defence
1 Canadian Rangers Patrol Group Headquarters, Yellowknife
4 Canadian Rangers Patrol Group, BC Detachment Headquarters, Victoria
5 Canadian Rangers Patrol Group Detachment Headquarters, Gander
Canadian Forces Northern Area/Joint Task Force North Headquarters, Yellowknife
Canadian Rangers National Authority, Ottawa
Directorate of History and Heritage (DHH), Ottawa
   Annual Historical Reports
      1st Canadian Ranger Patrol Group [Yellowknife, NT; UIC 3685], 2001-08, 2010
      2ᵉ Groupe de Patrouilles de Rangers Canadiens [Richelain, QC, UIC 3686], 2000-01,
         2003-08, 2010
      3rd Canadian Ranger Patrol Group [Borden, ON; UIC 3687], 2000-01, 2005-10
      4th Canadian Ranger Patrol Group [Victoria, BC; UIC 3688], 2000-09

5th Canadian Ranger Patrol Group [Halifax, NS; UIC 3689], 2000-01, 2003, 2005-09
  "History of Aboriginal Peoples in the Canadian Military" (interviews by John MacFarlane)
    N-QC-4: Sgt. Vallee Saunders, Kuujjuaq, QC, 5 November 2001
    N-QC-8: Sgt. Alec Tuckatuck, Kuujjuarapik, QC, 21 November 2001
    N-ON-7: Abraham Metatawabin and his son Ed (translator), Fort Albany, ON,
      15 November 2001
    N-N-10: Solomon Curley, Hall Beach, NU, 15 March 2002
  Kardex files
  Robert Lewis Raymont fonds (73/1223)
  Colonel W.B.S. Sutherland Office papers (79/527)

CFB Esquimalt Naval and Military Museum, Esquimalt, BC
Box 33, Pacific Coast Militia Rangers
Files: "Canadian Rangers," "Native Indians," "Japanese War Balloons"

John G. Diefenbaker Centre, Saskatoon, SK
MG 01/XI/B/22.2, vol. 44, f. "Arctic – The North (1967-74)"

Library and Archives Canada, Ottawa, ON
Brooke Claxton fonds, MG 32-B5
Ian Mackenzie fonds, MG 27, IIIB5
M.H.S. Penhale fonds, MG 31-G21
RG 2, Privy Council Office
RG 10, Department of Indian Affairs
RG 24, Department of National Defence
RG 85, Northern Affairs Program
RG 150, Ministry of the Overseas Military Forces of Canada

Library and Archives Canada, Regional Service Centre, Halifax, NS
RG 24-G-16-22. Subject files from Canadian Rangers, CFS St. John's

National Archives and Records Administration, College Park, MD
RG 59, State Department

Prince of Wales Northern Heritage Centre, Yellowknife, NT
NWT Archives
  Anderson-Thomson fonds, N 1986 012
  Research files

Personal Interviews

Colonel Pierre Leblanc, 20 March 2000, CFNA HQ, Yellowknife, NT
Lieutenant Colonel R.G. Kilburn, 22 March 2000, CFNA HQ, Yellowknife, NT
Lieutenant Mark Gough, 20 March 2000, CFNA HQ, Yellowknife, NT
Captain Don Finnamore, 20 March 2000, 1 CRPG HQ, Yellowknife, NT
Sergeant David McLean, 22 March 2000, Twin Otter flight from Chesterfield Inlet, NU,
  to Yellowknife, NT
Captain Conrad Schubert, 16 April 2002, 1 CRPG HQ, Yellowknife, NT
Colonel Kevin Macleod, 16 April 2002, CFNA HQ, Yellowknife, NT
Captain Christian Bergeron, 16 April 2002 and 20 April 2002, Yellowknife, NT
Captain Rob Marois, 22 April 2002, 26 February 2004, 1 CRPG HQ, Yellowknife, NT

Warrant Officer Kevin Mulhern, 26 February 2004, 1 CRPG Headquarters, Yellowknife, NT

Company Sergeant Major Gerry Westcott, 26 February 2004, 1 CRPG Headquarters, Yellowknife, NT

Sergeant Jeff Gottschalk, 27 February 2004, Yellowknife, NT

Colonel Norris Pettis, 27 February 2004, CFNA Headquarters, Yellowknife, NT

Major Stewart Gibson, 27 February 2004, 1 CRPG HQ Yellowknife, NT

Ranger Sergeant Cory Bruneau, 1 March 2004, Whitehorse, YT

Sergeant Martin St-Charles, 2 March 2004, Carmacks, YT; 12 March 2004, Whitehorse, YT

Sergeant William Lepatourel, 13 March 2004, Yellowknife, NT

Ranger Julian Tomlinson, 14 March 2004, Yellowknife, NT

Major Tim Byers, 10 August 2004, 4 CRPG HQ, Victoria, BC

Captain Jim Murray, 13 July 2005, 4 CRPG BC Detachment Headquarters, Victoria, BC

Warrant Officer Dan Hryhoryshen, 13 July 2005, 4 CRPG BC Detachment Headquarters, Victoria, BC

Lieutenant Sally Purdon, 13 July 2005, 4 CRPG BC Detachment Headquarters, Victoria, BC

Petty Officer Paul Smith, 20 February 2006, plane from Halifax to St. John's, NL

Sergeant Todd MacWirter, 21 February 2006, 5 CRPG Detachment Headquarters, Gander, NL

Warrant Officer Frank Power, 21 February 2006, CFB Gander, NL

Warrant Officer Dave Gill, 21 February 2006, CFB Gander, NL

Ranger Lieutenant Walter Joseph Anderson, 22 February 2006, Goose Bay, NL

Ranger Master Corporal Wilfred Lane, 26 February 2006, Postville, NL

Ranger Master Corporal Darryl Lovelace, 27 February 2006, Hopedale, NL

Ranger Sergeant Dean Coombs, 27 February 2006, Hopedale, NL

Ranger Master Corporal W.B. Andersen, 1 March 2006, Postville, NL

Sergeant Cyril Abbott, 6-8 March 2006, Gander and surrounding area, NL

Ranger Lieutenant Horace Lane, 6 March 2006, Lewisporte, NL

Ranger Master Corporal Curtis Hicks and Ranger Master Corporal Keith Guy, 6 March 2006, Musgrave Harbour, NL

Ranger Master Corporal Keith Matchem, 6 March 2006, Bonavista Peninsula, NL

Ranger Sergeant Austin Adams, 7 March 2006, Clarenville, NL

Sergeant Milton Estrada and Sergeant Neil McElligott, 1 September 2006, airplane from Kuujjuarapik/Whapmagoostui to Montreal, QC

Ranger Sergeant Ernie Waye, 12 April 2007, Chevery, QC

Ranger Gordon Jones, 12 April 2007, Chevery, QC

Ranger Lieutenant David Gordon (Gord) Anderson, 12 April 2007, Chevery, QC

Ranger Captain Gordon Foreman, 13 April 2007, Harrington Harbour, QC

Ranger Corporal Carrie Robertson, 13 April 2007, La Tabatière, QC

Ranger Sergeant Warren Letto, 14 April 2007, Lourdes de Blanc Sablon, QC

Mayor Lionel Roberts, 14 April 2007, St Paul River, QC

Ranger Martin Conway and Ranger Rick Thomas, 14 April 2007, St Paul River, QC

Ranger Sergeant John "Mitch" Mitchell, 10 August 2007; 13 June 2009, Dawson, YT

Pacific Coast Militia Ranger J.J. van Bibber, August 2007, Dawson, YT

Captain Eugene Squires, 11 April 2008, Yellowknife, NT

Colonel Craig McQuitty, Lieutenant Colonel Ian Pedley, Major Jim Mills, Chief Warrant Officer Dave Mahon, Master Warrant Officer Bruce Dunn, and Warrant Officer Annie Brassard, 24 June 2008, Ottawa, ON

General (retired) Ramsey Withers, 25 June 2008, Ottawa, ON

Major Guy Ingram, 8 and 9 July 2008, Geraldton, ON

Ranger Sergeant Peter Moon, 8 July 2008, Geraldton, ON
Captain Harry Austen, 9 July 2008, Geraldton, ON
Captain Mark Rittwage, 10 July 2008, Geraldton, ON
Captain Terry Stead, 31 October 2008, CFB Gander, NL
Warrant Officer Terry Cole, 31 October 2008, CFB Gander, NL
Lieutenant Junior Roberts, 3 November 2008, CFB Gander, NL
Ranger Corporal Doug Stern, 30-31 January 2009, Cambridge Bay, NU
Captain Jim Miller, 3 March 2009, Churchill, MN
Ranger Sergeant Phil Morgan, 15 June 2009, Whitehorse, YT
Haines Junction Ranger Patrol meeting, 16 June 2009, Haines Junction, YT
Ranger Chuck Hume, 16 June 2009, Haines Junction, YT
Ranger (retired) Alex van Bibber, 17 June 2009, Beaver Creek, YT
Captain Anthony Lynch, April 2010, flight from Alert, Nunavut, to Yellowknife, NT
Lt.-Col. Ian Pedley and Master Warrant Officer Bruce Dunn, 17 February 2011, Ottawa, ON
Major Jeff Allen, 13 June 2011, Ottawa, ON
Ranger Sergeant Jimmy Evalik, 21 August 2012, Cambridge Bay, NU
Ranger (retired) Paul Nochasak, 9 September 2012, Nain, NL
Ranger (retired) Zack Maggo, 9 September 2012, Nain, NL
Ranger (retired) Jacko Merkuratsuk, 9 September 2012, Nain, NL
Various confidential interviews, 2002-12

Telephone Interviews

Major David Scandrett, 18 April 2002, 22 October 2003, 6 April 2012
Ranger Lieutenant (ret'd) Rt. Rev. John Sperry, 19 December 2003
Ranger Lieutenant (ret'd) Jack Berry, 26 March 2006
Sergeant Joe Gonneau, 5 May 2006
Sergeant Jean-François Gauthier, 18 May 2006
Colonel (ret'd) Pierre Leblanc, August 2006
Warrant Officer Pat Rizzo, 7 August 2009
Captain Anthony Lynch, May 2010

Participant Observation

Operation Kigliqaqvik Ranger, Resolute and Cape Isaachsen, NU, April 2002
Colonel Kevin Macleod
Major Yves Laroche
Captain Rick Regan
Warrant Officer Kevin Mulhern
Sergeant Jim Martin
Ranger Sergeant Peter Moon
Thirty Rangers from the Yukon, Northwest Territories, and Nunavut

Ross River and Quiet Lake, YT, March 2004
Ranger Ryan Bob
Ranger Lloyd Caesar
Ranger Jason Chapman
Ranger James (Jim) Chapman
Ranger Rosemary Chapman
Ranger Amos Dick

Ranger Robin Dick
Ranger Pat Etzel
Ranger Daryl Fulton
Ranger Lonnie Jeffrey
Ranger Master Corporal Doris John
Ranger Dorothy John
Ranger Kim John
Ranger Gregory Keating
Ranger Doug MacPheat
Ranger Leithe Minder
Ranger Terry Olson
Ranger Sgt. Michael Powaschuk
Ranger Tom Smith
Ranger Dempsey Sterriah
Ranger Nancy Sterriah
Sergeant Denis Lalonde (Ranger instructor)
Fifty-two other Rangers from patrols in Yukon, including Ranger Sergeant Brian Murrell (Carmacks patrol); Ranger Leigh Knox (Carmacks patrol); Ranger Corporal Joseph O'Brian (Carmacks patrol); Ranger Sergeant Wade Istchenko (Haines Junction patrol)

Gold River and Nootka Island, BC, July 2005
Ranger Lona Bardal
Ranger Sandy Hall
Ranger Warren Hall
Ranger Glenn Haugen
Ranger Derrick Kasper
Ranger Marta Kasper
Ranger Terry Kellington
Ranger Bill Leighton
Ranger Sgt. Scott Patrick
Ranger Graham Roth
Ranger Master Corporal Chuck Syme
Warrant Officer Pete Malcolm (Ranger instructor)

Exercise "Goose Bay to Saglek," Goose Bay to Hopedale, Labrador, February-March 2006
Ranger Boyd Bessey (Churchill Falls)
Ranger Cpl. Abe Dyson (Cartwright)
Ranger Lieutenant Osman Dyson (Churchill Falls)
Ranger Master Corporal Anthony Elson (Cartwright)
Ranger Cpl. Dilbert Holwell (Cartwright)
Ranger Cpl. Sam Morris (Goose Bay)
Ranger Master Corporal Ed Sampson (Goose Bay)
Chief Warrant Officer Lou Kendell
Sergeant Rory Innes
Captain Terry Stead
Canadian Rangers from the Hopedale patrol

Inukjuak and Witch Bay, Nunavik, Quebec, August 2006
Ranger Cpl. Annie Alaku
Ranger Bobby Echalook

Ranger Johnny Echalook
Ranger Simeonie Elijassiapik
Ranger Charlie Elijassiapik
Ranger Cpl. Joshua Elijassiapik
Ranger Cpl. Betsy Epoo
Ranger Tamusie Kasudluak
Ranger Peter Kasudluak
Ranger Kitty Kritik
Ranger Cpl. Nancy Maina
Ranger Sgt. Simeonie Nalukturuk
Ranger Ituk Ningiuk
Ranger Simeonie Ohaituk
Ranger Markusie Ohaituk
Ranger Cpl. Allie Ohaituk
Ranger Master Corporal Jobie Oweetaluktuk
Ranger Daniel Oweetaluktuk
Ranger Irqumia (Smiley) Putulik
Ranger Minnie Weetaluktuk
Ranger Eli Weetaluktuk
Ranger Gabriel St-Cyr
Ranger Davidee Maina
Sergeant Antoine Duff (Ranger Instructor)
Warrant Officer François Duchesneau (Mission Element Warrant Officer, 2 CRPG)

Lower North Shore, Quebec, April 2007
Major Guy Lang
Captain Réjean Plourde
Sergeant-Major J.H.J.M. Themins
Ranger patrols in the following communities:
   Aguanish
   Blanc Sablon
   Chevery
   Harrington Harbour
   Havre St-Pierre
   La Romaine
   La Tabatière
   Natasquan
   Saint-Augustin
   St. Paul River

Op Nunalivut, Resolute and Eureka, Nunavut, April 2008
2 civilian scientists
4 CRPG staff
21 Canadian Rangers

Camp Loon, Junior Canadian Rangers Training Camp, Nakina, Ontario, July 2008
13 CRPG staff
30 incremental staff
32 Canadian Rangers
76 Junior Canadian Rangers

Op Nanook, Iqaluit, Nunavut, August 2008
8 Canadian Rangers from 1 CRPG
Sergeant Stephane Leduc (Ranger instructor)
Primary Reservists from northern Ontario

Cape Freels Patrol, Newfoundland, November 2008
Ranger Master Corporal Hedly Angell
Ranger Roger Chaulk
Ranger Wilford Cheater
Ranger Master Corporal Fraser Cooze
Ranger Cpl. Peter Dackers
Ranger Sgt. Curtis Hicks
Ranger Wayne Hicks
Ranger William Hicks
Ranger Dean Gillingham
Ranger Derrick Pickett
Ranger Cpl. Maxwell Pickett
Ranger Marvin Rogers
Ranger Cpl. Randy Wellon
Warrant Officer Dave Gill (Ranger instructor)

Tuktoyaktuk Patrol, Northwest Territories, January 2009
Ranger Master Corporal Emmanuel Adam
Ranger Derek Felix
Ranger David Nasogaluak
Ranger Douglas Panaktalok
Ranger Jesse Panaktalok
Ranger Richard Panaktalok
Ranger Cpl. Sam Pingo
Ranger Kevin St. Amand
Ranger Kurtis Wolki
Ranger Patrick Wolki
Ranger Sandy Wolki
Sergeant Tim Stanistreet (Ranger instructor)

Exercise Western Spirit, February-March 2009
Ranger Keith Antsanen
Ranger Modeste Antsanen
Ranger Gerald Azure
Ranger Raymond Bendoni
Ranger Pierre Bernier
Ranger Kevin Burke
Ranger Sgt. Lance Bushie
Ranger Andrée Couture
Ranger Norman Denedchezhe
Ranger Linda Denedchezhe
Ranger Ronnie Elliott
Ranger Every Farrow
Ranger Neil Flett
Ranger Camille Hamilton
Ranger Doug Holmes

Ranger Colleen Hornyak
Ranger Master Corporal Kevin Iles
Ranger Andy MacDougall
Ranger Sgt. Tom Nickel
Ranger Cherie Nickel
Ranger Master Corporal Bernie Olanski
Ranger Sheldon Olivier
Ranger Matt Ratson
Ranger Kelly Turcotte
Ranger Sgt. Maryanne Wettlaufer
Ranger Yancy Wood
Junior Canadian Ranger Kyle Dettanikeaze
Lieutenant-Colonel Ian Pedley
Major Tim Byers
Captain Doug Colton
Captain Jim Murray
Master Warrant Officer Dave Ames
Master Warrant Officer Darryl Bazin
Master Warrant Officer Bruce Dunn
Warrant Officer Jeff Belisle
Warrant Officer Dan Hryhoryshen
Warrant Officer Wade Jones
Warrant Officer Norm Swift
Jim Birrell (Manitoba Hydro)

Exercise Nanook 10, Resolute, Pond Inlet, and Bylot Island, August 2010
Ranger Uluriak (Star) Amarualik
Ranger Dennis Angnatsiak
Ranger Pauloosie (Paul) Atagootak
Ranger Caleb Sangoya
Lieutenant-Colonel Bill Kalogerakis
Major Allan Best
Captain Elizabeth Tremblay-Lewicki
Sergeant Billy Cornish (Ranger instructor)
28 soldiers with 2 platoon, Arctic Response Company Group, 32 Canadian Brigade Group

Nain Patrol, Labrador, September 2012
Ranger Margaret Andersen
Ranger Margaret (Peggy) Andersen
Ranger Joe Atsatata
Ranger Morrall Blake
Ranger Sgt. Henry Broomfield
Ranger Marie Dicker
Ranger Cpl. Fred Maggo
Ranger Levi Nochasak
Ranger Cpl. Kristopher Shiwak
Ranger Terry Smith
Ranger Master Corporal Steven Voisey
Ranger Master Corporal Sarah Webb
Sergeant Mike Rude (Ranger instructor)

Canadian Government Publications

Department of National Defence (DND). Annual Reports, 1949-1990.
–. *Challenge and Commitment: A Defence Policy for Canada*. Ottawa: Minister of Supply and Services, 1987.
–. *Canadian Defence Policy*. April 1992.
–. *1994 White Paper*.
House of Commons Standing Committee on External Affairs and National Defence. *Proceedings and Evidence*. 1972-73, 1981, 1985.
House of Commons Standing Committee on Foreign Affairs and International Trade. *Canada and the Circumpolar World*. Ottawa: Publications Service, 1997.
House of Commons Standing Committee on National Defence. *Proceedings and Evidence*. 1968, 1986-88.
Indian Affairs and Northern Development. *Looking North: Canada's Arctic Commitment*. Ottawa: Supply and Services, 1989.
Prime Minister's Office (PMO). *Backgrounder: Expanding Canadian Forces Operations in the Arctic*. 10 August 2007.
Royal Commission on Aboriginal Peoples (RCAP). *For Seven Generations: Final Report of the Royal Commission on Aboriginal Peoples*. 5 vols. Ottawa: Canada Communication Group (CCG), 1995.
Smith, Gordon W. "Territorial Sovereignty in the Canadian North: A Historical Outline of the Problem." Ottawa: Department of Northern Affairs and National Resources, 1963.
Standing Senate Committee on Fisheries and Oceans (SSCFO). *The Coast Guard in Canada's Arctic: Interim Report*. June 2008.
Yukon, Northwest Territories, and Nunavut Governments. *A Northern Vision: A Stronger North and a Better Canada*. 2007.

Newspapers and Magazines

Calgary Herald
Comox District Free Press
The Coaster (Newfoundland)
Dawson News
Edmonton Journal
Financial Post
Globe and Mail
The Gulf News (Port aux Basques)
Hamilton Spectator
Kamloops Sentinel
Klondike Sun
The Labradorian (Happy Valley-Goose Bay)
Maclean's
The Maple Leaf (DND)
Montreal Gazette
National Home Monthly (1943)
National Post
New York Times
Newfoundland Herald
News of the North
News North
Nor'Wester

Northern News Services Ltd. (Iqaluit)
Northern Pen (St. Anthony)
Nunatsiaq News (Iqaluit)
Ottawa Citizen
The Pilot (Lewisporte)
La Presse
The Ranger (Pacific Coast Militia Rangers)
The Ranger (4 CRPG)
The Record (Kitchener-Waterloo)
Safety Digest (Department of National Defence)
Sentinel: Magazine of the Canadian Forces
Le Soleil
Toronto Star
Tusaayaksat
Up Here
Vancouver News-Herald
Vancouver Province
Vancouver Sun
Victoria Times
The Western Star
Whitehorse Star
Winnipeg Free Press

Selected Secondary Sources

Abel, Kerry M., and Ken Coates, eds. *Northern Visions: New Perspectives on the North in Canadian History*. Peterborough, ON: Broadview Press, 2001.

Abele, Frances. "Canadian Contradictions: Forty Years of Northern Political Development." *Arctic* 40, 4 (1987): 310-20.

Abele, Frances, Thomas J. Courchene, F. Leslie Seidle, and France St-Hilaire, eds. *Northern Exposure: Peoples, Powers and Prospects for Canada's North*. Ottawa: Institute for Research on Public Policy, 2009.

Abbott, Louise. *The Coast Way: A Portrait of the English on the Lower North Shore of the St. Lawrence*. Kingston/Montreal: McGill-Queen's University Press, 1988.

Arctic Institute of North America. "Militarization in the North." Special issue, *Information North* 12, 3 (1986).

Aronsen, Lawrence R. "American National Security and the Defense of the Northern Frontier, 1945-51." *Canadian Review of American Studies* 14, 3 (1983): 259-77.

Bankes, Nigel D. "Forty Years of Canadian Sovereignty Assertion in the Arctic, 1947-87." *Arctic* 40, 4 (1987): 292-99.

Barman, Jean. *The West beyond the West: A History of British Columbia*. Rev. ed. Toronto: University of Toronto Press, 1996.

Belvin, Cleophas. *The Forgotten Labrador: Kegashka to Blanc-Sablon*. Montreal/Kingston: McGill-Queen's University Press, 2006.

Bercuson, David J. "Continental Defense and Arctic Security, 1945-50: Solving the Canadian Dilemma." In *The Cold War and Defense*, ed. K. Neilson and R.G. Haycock, 153-70. New York: Praeger, 1990.

–. *True Patriot: The Life of Brooke Claxton, 1898-1960*. Toronto: University of Toronto Press, 1993.

Berger, Thomas R., ed. *The Arctic: Choices for Peace and Security*. Vancouver: Gordon Soules, 1989.

–. *Northern Frontier/Northern Homeland: The Report of the Mackenzie Valley Pipeline Inquiry.* Vol. 1. Ottawa: Department of Supply and Services, 1977.

Berton, Pierre. *The Mysterious North.* New York: Knopf, 1956.

Bland, Douglas. *Chiefs of Defence.* Toronto: Canadian Institute of Strategic Studies, 1995.

Bone, Robert. *The Geography of the Canadian North: Issues and Challenges.* Toronto: Oxford, 1992.

Booth, Bradford, Meyer Kestnbaum, and David R. Segal. "Are Post-Cold War Militaries Postmodern?" *Armed Forces and Society* 27, 3 (2001): 319-42.

Bothwell, Robert. *Eldorado: Canada's National Uranium Company.* Toronto: University of Toronto Press, 1984.

Brice-Bennett, Carol. *Our Footprints Are Everywhere: Inuit Land Use and Occupancy in Labrador.* Nain: Labrador Inuit Association, 1977.

Brody, Hugh. *The Living Arctic.* Vancouver: Douglas and McIntyre, 1987.

–. *Maps and Dreams.* Vancouver: Douglas and McIntyre, 1981.

–. *The Other Side of Eden.* Vancouver: Douglas and McIntyre, 2000.

Burtch, Andrew. *Give Me Shelter: The Failure of Canada's Cold War Civil Service.* Vancouver: UBC Press, 2012.

Caforio, Giuseppe, ed. *Handbook of the Sociology of the Military.* New York: Springer, 2006.

Cairns, Alan. *Citizens Plus: Aboriginal Peoples and the Canadian State.* Vancouver: UBC Press, 2000.

Carney, Anne E. *Harrington Harbour ... Back Then.* Montreal: Self-Published, 1991.

Coates, Kenneth. *The Alaska Highway: Papers of the 40th Anniversary Symposium.* Vancouver: UBC Press, 1985.

–. *Best Left as Indians: Native-White Relations in the Yukon Territory, 1840-1973.* Montreal/Kingston: McGill-Queen's University Press, 1991.

–. *Canada's Colonies: A History of the Yukon and Northwest Territories.* Toronto: James Lorimer, 1985.

–. *North to Alaska.* Fairbanks: University of Alaska Press, 1992.

Coates, Kenneth, Whitney Lackenbauer, William Morrison, and Greg Poelzer. *Arctic Front: Defending Canada's Interests in the Far North.* Toronto: Thomas Allen, 2008.

Coates, Kenneth, and William R. Morrison. *The Alaska Highway in World War II: The American Army of Occupation in Canada's Northwest.* Norman: University of Oklahoma Press, 1992.

–. "The Federal Government and Urban Development in Northern Canada after World War II: Whitehorse and Dawson City, Yukon Territory." *BC Studies* 104 (1994): 25-67.

–, eds. *For Purposes of Dominion: Essays in Honour of Morris Zaslow.* Toronto: Captus University Press, 1989.

–. *The Forgotten North.* Toronto: James Lorimer, 1992.

–, eds. *Interpreting Canada's North: Selected Readings.* Toronto: Copp Clark, 1989.

–. *Land of the Midnight Sun: A History of the Yukon.* Montreal/Kingston: McGill-Queen's University Press, 2005.

Coates, Ken S., and Judith Powell. *The Modern North.* Toronto: Lorimer, 1989.

Conant, Melvin. *The Long Polar Watch: Canada and the Defence of North America.* New York: Harper, 1962.

Cotter, Jamie. "Developing a Coherent Plan to Deal with Canada's Conundrum in the Northwest Passage." *Journal of Military and Strategic Studies* 11, 3 (2009): 1-51.

Cowen, Deborah. *Military Workfare: The Soldier and Social Citizenship in Canada.* Toronto: University of Toronto Press, 2008.

Critchley, W. Harriet. "The Arctic." *International Journal* (Autumn 1987): 769-88.

Croteau, Pascal. "The Rangers of 2 Canadian Rangers Patrol Group." Army Lessons Learned Centre (ALLC) *Bulletin* 9, 4 (2003): 1-6.

Damas, David. *Arctic Migrants, Arctic Villagers: The Transformation of Inuit Settlement in the Central Arctic*. Montreal/Kingston: McGill-Queen's University Press, 2002.

Dickerson, Mark. *Whose North? Political Change, Political Development, and Self-Government in the Northwest Territories*. Vancouver: UBC Press, 1992.

Dignum, Larry. "Shadow Army of the North." *Beaver* (Autumn 1959): 22-24.

Dionne, Gabriel. *In a Breaking Wave: Living History of the Lower North Shore*. Trans. H. Miller and T. Marion. Rev. by W.E. O'Meara. Montreal: Les Missionaires Oblats de Marie Immaculée, 1988.

Dittmann, Paul. "In Defence of Defence: Canadian Arctic Sovereignty and Security." *Journal of Military and Strategic Studies* 11, 3 (2009): 1-77.

Diubaldo, Richard J. "The Role of the Arctic Islands in Defence." In *A Century of Canada's Arctic Island, 1880-1980*, ed. Morris Zaslow, 93-110. Ottawa: Royal Society of Canada, 1981.

Diubaldo, Richard J., and S.J. Scheinberg. *A Study of Canadian-American Defence Policy, 1945-1975: Northern Issues and Strategic Resources*. Ottawa: Department of National Defence, 1978.

Dosman, Edgar, ed. *The Arctic in Question*. Toronto: Oxford University Press, 1976.

–. *The National Interest*. Toronto: McClelland and Stewart, 1975.

––, ed. *Sovereignty and Security in the Arctic*. London: Routledge, 1989.

Douglas, W.A.B., Roger Sarty, and Michael Whitby. *No Higher Purpose: The Official Operational History of the Royal Canadian Navy in the Second World War, 1939-1943, Vol. 2, Part 1*. St. Catharines, ON: Vanwell, 2002.

Duffy, R. Quinn. "Canada's Newest Territory." In *Canada: Confederation to Present*, ed. Bob Hesketh and Chris Hackett. Edmonton: Chinook Multimedia, 2001. CD-ROM.

–. *The Road to Nunavut: The Progress of Eastern Arctic Inuit since the Second World War*. Montreal/Kingston: McGill-Queen's University Press, 1988.

Duhaime, Gérard. "La sédentarisation au Nouveau-Québec inuit." *Etudes/Inuit/Studies* 7, 2 (1983): 25-52.

Dziuban, Stanley W. *Military Relations between the United States and Canada, 1939-1945*. Washington, DC: Office of the Chief of Military History, Department of the Army, 1959.

Eayrs, James. *In Defence of Canada*. Vol. 3, *Peacemaking and Deterrence*. Toronto: University of Toronto Press, 1972.

–. *In Defence of Canada*. Vol. 4, *Growing Up Allied*. Toronto: University of Toronto Press, 1980.

Elliot-Meisel, Elizabeth B. *Arctic Diplomacy: Canada and the United States in the Northwest Passage*. New York: Peter Lang, 1998.

Enloe, H. Cynthia. *Ethnic Soldiers: State Security in Divided Societies*. Athens: University of Georgia Press, 1980.

Eyre, Kenneth C. "Custos Borealis: The Military in the Canadian North." PhD diss., University of London-King's College, 1981.

–. "Forty Years of Military Activity in the Canadian North, 1947-87." *Arctic* 40, 4 (1987): 292-99.

Farish, Matthew. "Frontier Engineering: From the Globe to the Body in the Cold War Arctic." *Canadian Geographer* 50, 2 (2006): 177-96.

Fenge, Terry. "Inuit and the Nunavut Land Claims Agreement: Supporting Canada's Arctic Sovereignty." *Policy Options* 29, 1 (2007-08): 84-88.

Gaffen, Fred. *Forgotten Soldiers*. Penticton: Theytus Books, 1985.

Garnier, Louis. *Dog Sled to Airplane: A History of the St. Lawrence North Shore*. Trans. H.A. Nantais and R.L. Nantais. Quebec, 1949.

Grace, Sherrill. *Canada and the Idea of North*. Montreal/Kingston: McGill-Queen's University Press, 2001.

Granatstein, J.L. *Canada's Army: Waging War and Keeping the Peace*. Toronto: University of Toronto Press, 2002.

Grant, Shelagh. "Arctic Wilderness and Other Mythologies." *Journal of Canadian Studies* 33, 2 (1998): 27-42.

–. *Sovereignty or Security? Government Policy in the Canadian North, 1936-1950.* Vancouver: UBC Press, 1988.

Gray, Colin. *Canadian Defence Policy: A Question of Priorities.* Toronto: Clarke, Irwin, 1972.

Grenier, John E. "'Of Great Utility': The Public Identity of Early American Rangers and Its Impact on American Society." *War and Society* 21 (2003): 1-14.

Griffiths, Franklyn. *Arctic Alternatives: Civility or Militarism in the Circumpolar North?* Toronto: Science for Peace/Samuel Stevens, 1992.

–. *A Northern Foreign Policy.* Toronto: Canadian Institute of International Affairs (CIIA), 1979.

–, ed. *Politics of the Northwest Passage.* Kingston/Montreal: McGill-Queen's University Press, 1987.

–. "The Shipping News: Canada's Arctic Sovereignty Not on Thinning Ice." *International Journal* 58, 2 (2003): 257-82.

Griffiths, Franklyn, Rob Huebert, and P. Whitney Lackenbauer. *Canada and the Changing Arctic: Sovereignty, Security and Stewardship.* Waterloo, ON: Wilfrid Laurier University Press, 2011.

Halliday, Hugh A. "Exercise 'Musk Ox': Asserting Sovereignty North of 60." *Canadian Military History* 7, 4 (1998): 37-44.

–. "Recapturing the North: Exercises 'Eskimo,' 'Polar Bear' and 'Lemming,' 1945." *Canadian Military History* 6, 2 (1997): 29-38.

Hamelin, Louise-Edmond. *Canadian Nordicity: It's Your North Too.* Trans. W. Barr. Montreal: Harvest House, 1978.

Hamilton, John D. *Arctic Revolution: Social Change in the Northwest Territories, 1935-1994.* Toronto: Dundurn Press, 1994.

Harris, Stephen J. *Canadian Brass: The Making of a Professional Army, 1860-1939.* Toronto: University of Toronto Press, 1988.

–. "'Really a Defile throughout Its Length': The Defence of the Alaska Highway in Peacetime." In *The Alaska Highway: Papers of the 40th Anniversary Symposium,* ed. Ken Coates, 119-32. Vancouver, UBC Press, 1985.

Hendricks, Charles. "The Eskimos and the Defense of Alaska." *Pacific Historical Review* 54, 3 (1985): 271-95.

Honigmann, John J., and Irma Honigmann. *Eskimo Townsmen.* Ottawa: Canadian Research Centre for Anthropology, University of Ottawa, 1965.

Horn, Bernd. *Bastard Sons: An Examination of Canada's Airborne Experience, 1942-1995.* St. Catharines, ON: Vanwell, 2001.

–. "Gateway to Invasion or the Curse of Geography? The Canadian Arctic and the Question of Security, 1939-1999." In *Forging a Nation: Perspectives on the Canadian Military Experience,* ed. Bernd Horn, 307-32. St. Catharines, ON: Vanwell, 2002.

Horner, G.L. "The North on Guard." *The Beaver* (March 1941): 6-7.

Huebert, Rob. "Canadian Arctic Maritime Security: The Return to Canada's Third Ocean." *Canadian Military Journal* 8, 2 (2007): 9-16.

–. "Canadian Arctic Security: Preparing for a Changing Future." *Behind the Headlines* 65, 4 (2008): 14-21.

–. "Canadian Arctic Security Issues: Transformation in the Post-Cold War Era." *International Journal* 54, 2 (1999): 203-29.

–. "Climate Change and Canadian Sovereignty in the Northwest Passage." *Isuma* (Winter 2001): 86-94.

–. "A Northern Foreign Policy: The Politics of Ad Hocery." In *Diplomatic Departures: The Conservative Era in Canadian Foreign Policy, 1984-93,* ed. N. Michaud and K.R. Nossal, 84-112. Vancouver: UBC Press, 2001: 84-112.

–. "Polar Vision or Tunnel Vision: The Making of Canadian Arctic Waters Policy." *Marine Policy* 19, 4 (1995): 343-63.

–. "The Shipping News Part II: How Canada's Arctic Sovereignty Is on Thinning Ice." *International Journal* (Summer 2003): 295-308.

–. "Steel, Ice and Decision-Making: The Voyage of the Polar Sea and Its Aftermath." PhD diss., Dalhousie University, 1994.

Hunter, T. Murray. "Coast Defence in British Columbia, 1939-1941: Attitudes and Realities." *BC Studies* 28 (Winter 1975-76): 3-28

Inuit Tapiriit Kanatami (ITK). "An Integrated Arctic Strategy." January 2008. http://itk.ca/.

Inuit Tapiriit Kanatami (ITK) and Inuit Circumpolar Council (Canada). *Building Inuit Nunaat: The Inuit Action Plan.* Ottawa: ITK and ICC, 2007. http://itk.ca/.

Jenness, Diamond. *Eskimo Administration II: Canada.* Montreal: Arctic Institute of North America, 1964.

Jockel, Joseph. *No Boundaries Upstairs: Canada, the United States, and the Origins of North American Air Defence, 1945-1958.* Vancouver, UBC Press, 1987.

Kennedy, John Charles. "The Changing Significance of Labrador Settler Identity." *Canadian Ethnic Studies* 20, 3 (1988): 94-111.

–. *People of the Bays and Headlands: Anthropological History and the Fate of Communities in the Unknown Labrador.* Toronto: University of Toronto Press, 1995.

Keshen, Jeffrey. *Saints, Sinners, and Soldiers: Canada's Second World War.* Vancouver: UBC Press, 2004.

Kingsley, James Edward. *Did I Ever Tell You About … The Memoirs of James Edward Kingsley of Parksville, British Columbia.* Parksville: J.E. Kingsley, n.d.

Kirton, John, and Don Munton. "Protecting the Canadian Arctic: The Manhattan Voyages, 1969-1970." In *Canadian Foreign Policy: Selected Cases,* ed. John Kirton and Don Munton, 206-21. Toronto: Prentice-Hall, 1992.

Lackenbauer, P. Whitney. "Aboriginal Peoples in the Canadian Rangers: Canada's 'Eyes and Ears' in Northern and Isolated Communities." In *Hidden in Plain Sight: Contributions of Aboriginal Peoples to Canadian Identity and Culture, Vol. 2,* ed. Cora Voyageur, David R. Newhouse, and Dan Beavon, 306-28. Toronto: University of Toronto Press, 2011.

–, ed. *Canada and Arctic Sovereignty and Security: Historical Perspectives.* Calgary Papers in Military and Strategic Studies. Calgary: Centre for Military and Strategic Studies, 2011.

–. "Canada's Northern Defenders: Aboriginal Peoples in the Canadian Rangers, 1947-2005." In *Aboriginal Peoples and the Canadian Military: Historical Perspectives,* ed. P. Whitney Lackenbauer and Craig Mantle, 171-208. Kingston, ON: CDA Press, 2007.

–. *Canada's Rangers: Selected Stories, 1942-2012.* Kingston, ON: CDA Press, 2012.

–. "The Canadian Rangers: Sovereignty, Security and Stewardship from the Inside Out." In *Thawing Ice – Cold War: Canada's Security, Sovereignty, and Environmental Concerns in the Arctic,* ed. Rob Huebert, 61-79. Bison Paper 12. Winnipeg: University of Manitoba Centre for Defence and Security Studies, 2009.

–. "The Canadian Rangers: A Postmodern Militia That Works." *Canadian Military Journal* 6, 4 (2005-06): 49-60.

–. "Guerrillas in Our Midst: The Pacific Coast Militia Rangers, 1942-45." *BC Studies* 155 (December 2007): 95-131.

–. "Right and Honourable: Mackenzie King, Canadian-American Bilateral Relations, and Canadian Sovereignty in the Northwest, 1943-1948." In *Mackenzie King: Citizenship and*

Community, ed. John English, Kenneth McLaughlin, and P. Whitney Lackenbauer, 151-68. Toronto: Robin Brass Studios, 2002.

–. "Teaching Canada's Indigenous Sovereignty Soldiers … and Vice Versa: 'Lessons Learned' from Ranger Instructors." *Canadian Army Journal* 10, 2 (2007): 66-81.

Lackenbauer, P. Whitney, and Andrew F. Cooper. "The Achilles Heel of Canadian Good International Citizenship: Indigenous Diplomacies and State Responses in the Twentieth Century." *Canadian Foreign Policy* 13, 3 (2007): 99-119.

Lackenbauer, P. Whitney, and Matthew Farish. "The Cold War on Canadian Soil: Militarizing a Northern Environment." *Environmental History* 12, 3 (2007): 920-50.

Lackenbauer, P. Whitney, and Peter Kikkert. *The Canadian Forces and Arctic Sovereignty: Debating Roles, Interests, and Requirements, 1968-1974.* Waterloo, ON: Laurier Centre for Military Strategic and Disarmament Studies/WLU Press, 2010.

–. "Sovereignty and Security: The Department of External Affairs, the United States, and Arctic Sovereignty, 1945-68." In *In the National Interest: Canadian Foreign Policy and the Department of Foreign Affairs and International Trade, 1909-2009,* ed. Greg Donaghy and Michael Carroll, 101-20. Calgary: University of Calgary Press, 2011.

Lackenbauer, P. Whitney, and Craig Mantle, eds. *Aboriginal Peoples and the Canadian Military: Historical Perspectives.* Kingston, ON: CDA Press, 2007.

Lackenbauer, P. Whitney, and Ryan Shackleton. "When the Skies Rained Boxes: The Air Force and the Qikiqtani Inuit, 1941-64." Working Papers on Arctic Security No.4, Munk-Gordon Arctic Security Program and the ArcticNet Emerging Arctic Security Environment Project, Toronto, 2012.

Langlais, Richard. *Reformulating Security: A Case Study from Arctic Canada.* Humanekologiska skrifter 13. Göteborg, Sweden: Department for Interdisciplinary Studies of the Human Condition, Göteborg University, 1995.

Lopez, Barry. *Arctic Dreams: Imagination and Desire in a Northern Landscape.* New York: Charles Scribner's Sons, 1986.

Loukacheva, Natalia. *The Arctic Promise: Legal and Political Autonomy of Greenland and Nunavut.* Toronto: University of Toronto Press, 2007.

MacDonald, A.G. "Men of the PCMR Reviving Frontier Tactics." *British Columbia Lumberman* 26 (1942): 53-55.

MacDonald, Brian, ed. *Defence Requirements for Canada's Arctic.* Vimy Paper 2007. Ottawa: Conference of Defence Associates, 2007.

MacDonald, R.St.J., ed. *The Arctic Frontier.* Toronto: University of Toronto Press, 1966.

Mackenzie, S.P. *The Home Guard: A Military and Political History.* London: Oxford University Press, 1995.

Major, Kevin. *As Near to Heaven as by Sea: A History of Newfoundland and Labrador.* Toronto: Penguin, 2002.

Maloney, Sean M. "The Mobile Striking Force and Continental Defence, 1948-1955." *Canadian Military History* 2, 2 (1993): 75-88.

Matthiasson, John S. *Living on the Land: Northern Baffin Inuit Respond to Change.* Peterborough, ON: Broadview Press, 1992.

McMahon, Kevin. *Arctic Twilight: Reflections on the Destiny of Canada's Northern Land and People.* Toronto: James Lorimer, 1988.

–. "Strangers in the Land … Again." *Peace and Security* [Canadian Institute for International Peace and Security] 3, 1 (1988): 2-3.

McRae, Donald M. "Arctic Sovereignty: Loss by Dereliction?" *Northern Perspectives* [Canadian Arctic Resources Committee] 22, 4 (1994-95): 4-9.

–. "Arctic Sovereignty: What Is at Stake?" *Behind the Headlines* 64, 1 (2007): 1-23.

–. "Arctic Waters and Canadian Sovereignty." *International Journal* 38, 3 (1983): 476-92.

Michon, Rick. "Patrouille Nocturne." *Sentinel – Magazine of the Canadian Forces* 8, 4 (1972): 1-11.

Mills, Craig. "Bannock Binds a Better Team." *Sentinel* 11, 2 (1975): 7-9.

Moore, Richard. "East Coast Rangers." *Sentinel* 20, 3 (1984): 7.

Morantz, Toby. *The White Man's Gonna Getcha: The Colonial Challenge to the Crees in Quebec.* Montreal/Kingston: McGill-Queen's University Press, 2002.

Morenus, Richard. *DEW Line: Distant Early Warning, The Miracle of America's First Line of Defense.* New York: Rand McNally, 1957.

Morrison, William R. "Eagle over the Arctic: Americans in the Canadian North, 1867-1985." *Canadian Review of American Studies* 18, 1 (1987): 61-85.

–. *Showing the Flag: The Mounted Police and Canadian Sovereignty in the North, 1894-1925.* Vancouver: UBC Press, 1985.

–. *True North: The Yukon and Northwest Territories.* Toronto: Oxford University Press, 1998.

–. "The 1200 Mile Village: The Alaska Highway and Settlement in the Far Northwest." Paper presented to the annual meeting of the Canadian Historical Association, York University, Toronto, Ontario, May 2006.

Morrison, William R., and Ken S. Coates. *Working the North: Labor and the Northwest Defense Projects, 1942-1945.* Fairbanks: University of Alaska Press, 1994.

Morton, Desmond. *Canada and War: A Military and Political History.* Toronto: Butterworths, 1981.

–. *A Military History of Canada: From Champlain to Kosovo.* 4th ed. Toronto: McClelland and Stewart, 1999.

–. "Providing and Consuming Security in Canada's Century." *Canadian Historical Review* 81, 1 (2000): 1-28.

Moskos, Charles C., John Allen Williams, and David R. Segal, eds. *The Postmodern Military: Armed Forces after the Cold War.* New York: Oxford University Press, 2000.

Neary, Peter. *Newfoundland in the North Atlantic World, 1929-1949.* Montreal/Kingston: McGill-Queen's University Press, 1988.

"Newfoundland," *Canadian Army Journal* 2, 3 (1948): 27-32.

Nicholson, G.W.L. *More Fighting Newfoundlanders: A History of Newfoundland's Fighting Forces in the Second World War.* St. John's: Government of Newfoundland and Labrador, 1969.

Ommer, Rosemary E., and Coasts Under Stress. *Coasts Under Stress: Understanding Restructuring and Social-Ecological Health.* Montreal/Kingston: McGill-Queen's University Press, 2007.

Ørvik, Nils. *Northern Development: Northern Security.* Centre for International Relations No. 1/83. Kingston, ON: Queen's University, 1983.

–. *Policies of Northern Development.* Kingston, ON: Queen's University, Department of Policy Studies, 1973.

Page, Robert. *Northern Development: The Canadian Dilemma.* Toronto: McClelland and Stewart, 1986.

Pearson, Lester. "Canada Looks 'Down North.'" *Foreign Affairs* 24, 4 (1946): 638-47.

Pharand, Donat. "Arctic Waters and the Northwest Passage: A Final Revisit." *Ocean Development and International Law* 38, 1-2 (2007): 3-69.

–. *Canada's Arctic Waters in International Law.* Cambridge: Cambridge University Press, 1988.

Phillips, Ivan E. "Salute to the Pacific Coast Militia Rangers." *Okanagan Historical Society 29th Annual Report* (1965): 149-50.

Phillips, R.A.J. *Canada's North.* Toronto: Macmillan, 1967.

Porter, Gerald. *In Retreat: The Canadian Forces in the Trudeau Years.* Ottawa: Deneau and Greenberg, 1978.

Pullen, Thomas C. "What Price Canadian Sovereignty?" *U.S. Naval Institute Proceedings* 113, 9 (1987): 66-72.

Purver, Ron. "The Arctic in Canadian Security Policy, 1945 to the Present." In *Canada's International Security Policy*, ed. David B. Dewitt and David Leyton-Brown, 81-110. Scarborough, ON: Prentice-Hall, 1995.

Rea, K.J. *The Political Economy of the Canadian North*. Toronto: University of Toronto Press, 1968.

Reumiller, E.F. "Winter Warfare Instructor Course 8401." *Infantry Journal* 13 (Spring 1985): 9-14.

Rohmer, Richard. *The Arctic Imperative*. Toronto: McClelland and Stewart, 1973.

Rompkey, Bill. *The Story of Labrador*. Montreal/Kingston: McGill-Queen's University Press, 2003.

Roy, Patricia E. "British Columbia's Fear of Asians, 1900-1950." *Histoire sociale/Social History* 13, 25 (1980): 161-72.

–. *The Oriental Question: Consolidating a White Man's Province, 1914-41*. Vancouver: UBC Press, 2003.

–. *The Triumph of Citizenship: The Japanese and Chinese in Canada, 1941-67*. Vancouver: UBC Press, 2008.

Roy, Patricia E., J.L. Granatstein, Masako Lino, and Hiroko Takamura. *Mutual Hostages: Canadians and Japanese during the Second World War*. Toronto: University of Toronto Press, 1990.

Sandwell, Ruth, ed. *Beyond the City Limits: Rural History in British Columbia*. Vancouver: UBC Press, 1998.

Sarty, Roger. *The Maritime Defence of Canada*. Toronto: Canadian Institute of Strategic Studies, 1996.

Scott, Colin H., ed. *Aboriginal Autonomy and Development in Northern Quebec and Labrador*. Vancouver: UBC Press, 2001.

Scott, E. "South Vancouver Island Rangers." *RCMP Quarterly* 17 (1951): 48-57.

Scott, James C. *Seeing Like a State: How Certain Schemes to Improve the Human Condition Have Failed*. New Haven: Yale University Press, 1998.

Shea, Ambrose. "Rangers of Frobisher." *The Beaver* 287 (Winter 1956): 42-43.

–. "The Two Camps." *Canadian Army Journal* 10, 2 (1956): 55-66.

Sheffield, R. Scott. *The Red Man's on the Warpath: The Image of the "Indian" and the Second World War*. Vancouver: UBC Press, 2003.

Sherwin, Tamara A. "From Total War to Total Force: Civil-Military Relations and the Canadian Army Reserve (Militia), 1945-1995." Master's thesis, University of New Brunswick, 1995.

Smith, Gordon W. "Weather Stations in the Canadian North and Sovereignty." *Journal of Military and Strategic Studies* 11, 3 (2009): 1-63.

Sperry, John R. *Igloo Dwellers Were My Church*. Yellowknife: Outcrop, 2005.

Stacey, C.P. *Arms, Men and Governments: The War Policies of Canada, 1939-1945*. Ottawa: Queen's Printer, 1970.

–. *The Military Problems of Canada: A Survey of Defence Policies and Strategic Conditions, Past and Present*. Toronto: Ryerson Press, 1940.

–. *Six Years of War: The Army in Canada, Britain, and the Pacific*. Ottawa: Queen's Printer, 1967.

Stanley, George F.G. *Canada's Soldiers: The Military History of an Unmilitary People*. Toronto: Macmillan, 1960.

Steeves, Kerry Ragnar. "The Pacific Coast Militia Rangers, 1942-1945." Master's thesis, University of British Columbia, 1990.

Stentiford, Barry M. "The Meaning of a Name: The Rise of the National Guard and the End of a Town Militia." *Journal of Military History* 72, 3 (2008): 727-54.

Stevenson, Michael D. *Canada's Greatest Wartime Muddle: National Selective Service and the Mobilization of Human Resources during World War II*. Montreal/Kingston: McGill-Queen's University Press, 2001.

–. "The Mobilisation of Native Canadians during the Second World War." *Journal of the Canadian Historical Association* 7 (1996): 205-26.

Strange, William. *Canada, the Pacific and War*. Toronto: Thomas Nelson and Sons, 1937.

Tester, Frank J., and Peter Kulchyski. *Tammarniit (Mistakes): Inuit Relocation in the Eastern Arctic, 1939-63*. Vancouver: UBC Press, 1994.

Urquhart, G.M. "The Changing Role of the Canadian Militia, 1945-1975." Master's thesis, University of Victoria, 1977.

Wattsford, G.J.H. "The Strategic Importance of Canada." *Canadian Army Journal* 2, 4 (1948): 17-21.

Whittington, Michael. *The North*. Toronto: University of Toronto Press, 1985.

Wilford, Timothy. *Canada's Road to the Pacific War: Intelligence, Strategy, and the Far East Crisis*. Vancouver: UBC Press, 2011.

Willett, Terry C. *Canada's Militia: A Heritage at Risk*. Ottawa: Conference of Defence Associations Institute, 1990.

Withers, R.M. "Defence Requirements 'North of Sixty.'" *Canadian Defence Quarterly* 1, 1 (1971): 37-43.

Wonders, William C., ed. *Canada's Changing North*. Toronto: McClelland and Stewart, 1971.

–, ed. *Canada's Changing North*. Rev. ed. Montreal/Kingston: McGill-Queen's University Press, 2003.

Wood, James. *Militia Myths: Ideas of the Canadian Citizen Soldier, 1896-1921*. Vancouver: UBC Press, 2010.

Worthington, Larry. *"Worthy": A Biography of Major-General F.F. Worthington*. Toronto: Macmillan, 1961.

Yelton, David K. "British Public Opinion, the Home Guard, and the Defense of Great Britain, 1940-1944." *Journal of Military History* 58, 3 (1994): 461-80.

Zaslow, Morris, ed. *A Century of Canada's Arctic Islands, 1880-1890*. Ottawa: The Royal Society of Canada, 1981.

–. *The Northward Expansion of Canada, 1914-1967*. Toronto: McClelland and Stewart, 1988.

Zellen, Barry Scott. *Breaking the Ice: From Land Claims to Tribal Sovereignty in the Arctic*. Lanham: Lexington Books, 2008.

Zimmerly, David William. *Cain's Land Revisited: Culture Change in Central Labrador, 1775-1972*. Newfoundland Social and Economic Studies No. 16. St. John's: Institute of Social and Economic Research, Memorial University of Newfoundland, 1975.

Index

Note: "(f)" after a page number indicates a figure; "(t)" after a page number indicates a table; and "(m)" after a page number indicates a map.

Chesshire, R.H., 147
Chesterfield Inlet (Igluligaarjuk), 295
Chevery, 319
Chibougamau, 93
Chilingarov, Artur, 438-39
Chipewyan, 96. *See also* Dene
Chisasibi, 451
Chrétien, Jean, 3, 6(f), 262
Chura, Capt. Paul, 331, 342
Churchill, 61, 121, 150(t), 173(f), 180, 190(t), 202, 207(f), 211-12(f), 219, 250, 425, 441
Churchill, Winston, 31
Churchill Falls, 296, 300, 302, 352, 462(f)
Ciccio, Maj. Carlo de, 357
civil defence, 9, 30, 144, 207, 209. *See also* home defence
civil-military relations, theories of, 18-24
Clarenville, 129, 214, 274, 277, 351
Clark, Brig.-Gen. S.F., 73
Clark, Joe, 285
Clarke, CSM Bob, 261
Clarkson, Adrienne, 389(f), 425
Claxton, Brooke, 61, 74, 78, 112, 114, 116, 118, 132, 135-36, 151
Clyde Inlet, 150(t)
Clyde River, 147, 149, 203, 464
coastal defence, 74, 304
Coasts Under Stress, 12, 488*n*29
Coates, Ken, 12, 16
Cobb, Rgr. Capt. W.J., 123-24
Collier, Capt. A.L., 254
Colt Canada 9mm pistol, 377
Colton, Capt. Doug, 406
command and control, 17, 64, 77, 79, 132, 141, 162-63, 213-17, 238-43, 261, 316-17, 371-73, 408, 413-14, 435, 439, 443
continental defence (expectations for Canada), 8-9, 61, 100, 143, 155, 179, 206, 294, 385; operations in Canada, 126, 161, 300. *See also* Distant Early Warning (DEW) Line; Mid-Canada Line
Cook, Col. C.H., 132, 147
Cook, Rev. H.G., 232
Cooper, James Fennimore, 34
Cooper, Sir Patrick Ashley, 89
Coppermine (Kugluktuk), 105-7, 197-201, 291, 310
Coral Harbour, 5, 146, 380
Corbett, Pte. Nick, 292

Cornett, Rgr. Lloyd, 41
corporate partnerships, 89-90, 98, 107, 121, 146, 159. *See also* Hudson's Bay Company (HBC)
Couturier, Col. Norm, 420
Cowen, Deborah, 15, 21
Cowichan Commandos, 174-76
Cox, Rgr. Les, 166
Cox, Rgr. Maj. Frederick M., 160, 213, 273-74, 298
CP-140A Arcturus, 343
Cree, 101, 122-23, 181, 222, 333, 357-58, 399, 404, 406, 422, 477
Curley, Rgr. Solomon, 376-78

Daigle, Col. J.R.P., 331-32
Dare, Lt.-Col. M.R., 83, 104
d'Artois, Maj. Guy, 210
Dawson City, 3, 45-47, 64, 67, 83-86, 104-5, 111, 150(t), 215, 218, 231, 311-12(f), 327-28, 425, 459(f)
Dawson Creek, 137-40, 159, 175, 179, 190(t), 231
Deacon, Maj. W.S., 242
de Chastelain, Gen. John, 309, 329
Deer Harbour, 129
"defence against help," 9, 60, 288
Defence Management Committee, 253, 258-59, 388
defence white paper: (1964), 219, 244, 258, 335; (1971), 244, 258; (1987), 294, 303, 308; (1994), 342-43
Dene, 2, 261, 267, 279, 309, 314, 324, 329, 369, 407
Denechezhe, Rgr. Lizette, 407
Denis, Rgr. Lt. Henry, 96,
Destruction Bay, 137-38, 142, 160, 190(t)
Diefenbaker, John G., 210, 226-27
Dignum, Larry, 210
Distant Early Warning (DEW) Line, 181-83, 191, 204(f), 206, 208, 210, 224. *See also* continental defence (expectations of Canada); North Warning System
Dodd, Brig.-Gen. Mark, 270
dogsled races, 351, 425
domestic operations, 7, 11, 371, 415-16, 421-24, 463
Douthwaite, Maj. C.R.R., 88, 97, 107-8
Dubeau, Rgr. Capt. Moise, 134, 166

Horn, Bernd, 9, 100
Howe, C.D., 186
Hryhoryshen, W.O. Dan, 306-8, 435, 468(f), 481
Hudson's Bay Company (HBC), 68, 70, 89-90, 98, 101-2, 113, 143, 197, 249, 430; employees as Rangers, 121-23, 146, 147, 172, 180, 202, 205, 243; lack of, 128
Hudson's Hope, 94, 139, 197
Huebert, Rob, 432, 435, 439

Igloolik, 295, 413
Ikkidluak, Rgr. Iola, 291
Ikkidluak, Rgr. Lucassie, 291
Ikuallaq, Rgr. Paul, 437
Îles de la Madeleine, 451
Iley, Maj. David, 302-3, 309, 342
Ingram, Maj. Guy, 359, 375-76, 403, 410, 455, 463, 465, 469
Innu, 300, 358. *See also* Montagnais; Naskapi
Innuksuk, Rhoda, 288
intelligence gathering, 107-8, 119-20, 182, 189, 193-94
interdepartmental cooperation, 107, 146-47, 351, 421, 461, 463. *See also* Royal Canadian Mounted Police (RCMPO)
Inuit, 2, 25, 207(f), 324, 379, 478; homeland, 24; Labrador, 93, 127, 168, 194-95, 351; lifestyle, 14, 102, 200, 267, 315; military impact on, 61, 286-87, 310, 355; and military service, 15, 103, 110, 120(f), 143-47, 193, 261, 227-28, 248-49, 252, 283, 412, 477; northern conditions, 146, 181, 182-86, 220, 232, 275, 284, 315, 362; Quebec, 281, 319, 356-58, 366-68; in Rangers, 2, 187, 235, 249, 250, 252, 270-71, 275, 289, 291; and sovereignty, 285-89, 291-92, 329, 336, 441, 446, 454-55, 470
Inuit Circumpolar Conference, 286, 446, 449
Inuit Tapiriit Kanatami, 454, 455
Inuit Tapirisat of Canada, 22, 288
Inukjuak, 275, 311, 357, 368, 429(f), 476-78(f), 481. *See also* Port Harrison
Inuvialuit, 24, 310, 324-27, 364
Inuvik, 226, 231(f), 270, 272, 311, 326
Ipperwash, 360-61, 401
Iqaluit, 272, 292, 322, 379-80, 397, 425, 436, 464. *See also* Frobisher Bay

Island Falls, 190(t)
Island Lake, 150(t), 180, 190(t)
Issigaitok, Rgr. David, 441
instructor. *See* Ranger instructor
Ittinuar, Rgr. Ollie, 472-74
Ivanhoe, 129

Jacobson, Rgr. Sgt. Jackie, 447
joint task forces, creation of, 444
Joint Task Force (Central), 452
Joint Task Force (East), 463
Joint Task Force (North), 26, 437
Joint Task Force (Pacific), 452
Joint Task Force (West), 452
Jones, MWO Wade, 407
Jones, Rgr. Dave, 232
Jones, Rgr. Gilbert, 221
Jones, Rgr. Gordon, 92, 221
Jones Sound, 329
Josephee, Rgr. Appa, 465(f)
Joudry, Maj. S.J., 282, 289
Junior Canadian Rangers, 11, 335, 336, 379, 407, 422, 424, 447, 455, 474-75; broadened mandate, 399-403, 410; creation of, 362-71; expansion of program, 374-76, 381-82, 384, 386-88, 409(f), 427(f), 451; role of Rangers in mentoring, 416, 426-28
Jutkas, Rgr. Marcel, 166

Kamloops, 52, 304
Kangiqsualujjuaq, 4-5, 378, 382
Kangiqsujuaq, 291, 321, 367-68
Kashechewan, 340, 403, 423
Kativik regional government, 365-66, 368
Kaunak, Rgr. Cpl. Manasie, 430
Keane, Lt.-Col. Bob, 57, 75-76, 80-81, 460
Keenainak, Rgr. Sgt. Simeonie, 419
Keeseekoowenin First Nation, 406
Kennelly, Lt. Brendan, 38, 43, 50-51, 174
Keno, 85, 142
Kenora, 77(t), 98, 150(t), 190(t)
Kerr, Master Corporal Lily, 390(f)
Kilburn, Lt.-Col. Rory, 380
Kincolith (Gingolx), 50-51, 306, 353
King, William Lyon Mackenzie, 28, 58, 62
Kippens, 349
Kitkatla, 49, 51, 306
Klemmer, Rgr. Sgt. Darrel, 2, 24
Klotz Lake, 356

search and rescue, 4-6, 11, 52, 63, 99, 159,
189, 197, 200-1, 216, 231, 242, 245, 255,
264-66, 270, 275, 288, 302, 310, 313, 319,
332, 334, 338, 340-41, 342, 360, 377, 378,
382, 389, 406, 416, 421-22, 455, 463
security: Cold War era, 8, 10, 117, 121-22,
177; culture, 21, 288; definitions of, 10,
321-22; human, 10-11, 286, 329, 383, 391,
434, 454; post 9/11, 391, 420-21; Second
World War, 8, 9, 27-30
security checks, 315, 321
Segal, David, 21
Sept-Îles, 90, 92, 172
Seven Sisters Falls, 121, 123, 150(t), 190(t)
Sewell, Rgr. Capt. Henry Arthur, 92-93
Shamattawa, 406
Shaw, Rgr. Capt. K.B., 139
Shea Capt. Ambrose J., 15, 128-31, 146,
148, 151, 161-62, 168, 176, 184-88, 192-95,
201-6, 211-14, 458, 468
Sherren, Rgr. Capt. Nelson, 349
ship sighting, 160, 384. *See also* roles
Simon, Mary, 22, 286, 454
Simonds, Lt.-Gen. Guy, 109, 111-12, 118,
133, 146
Simonie, Rgr. Sgt. Norman, 419, 446
Smithers, 97, 150(t), 166l, 90(f), 216
Smye, Maj. Russ, 360
Snare River, 96
Solandt, Dr. Omond, 89
Southport, 129
sovereignty, 2-4, 6-11, 224, 237, 242, 255,
262-64, 269, 281-82, 285, 330, 334, 357,
360, 383-85, 432-39; Arctic, 8, 143, 226,
228, 244, 360, 448-49, 454, 458; in Cold
War, 117, 143, 179, 210; Mobile Striking
Force and, 9; post–Cold War, 309, 343,
347; northern, 14, 23, 58, 60, 210, 292;
presence, 7, 8, 244, 255, 261, 270, 282-83,
286, 288-89, 347, 394, 437-38; theories
of, 22, 380. *See also* Canadian Rangers
(role of); "defence against help"; enhanced sovereignty patrols; *Manhattan*
(ship); *Polar Sea* (ship); United States,
in Arctic waters
Soviet Union (Union of Soviet Socialist
Republics), 9, 60, 78, 100, 119, 121-22,
126, 178, 217, 237, 255, 263, 285-87, 291;
and Arctic sovereignty, 294, 331; Inuit
in, 143, 194-95, 286; threat of attack by,

58, 116-17, 157, 169, 191, 206, 308. *See
also* Russia
Special Commission on the Restructuring
of the Reserves, 348
Special Service Medal (Ranger Bar), 123(f),
149(f), 223(f), 389, 390
Spence Bay (Taloyoak), 107
Sperry, Rgr. Lt. Rev. John R. (Jack),
198-201
Sproule, David, 259
Squirechuck, Rgr. Capt. Kit, 218
Squires, Capt. Eugene, 349, 351-52, 378
St. Anthony, 127-28, 150(t), 190(t), 213, 230,
277
St. Jones Within, 129
Stacey, C.P., 55, 58
standardization, 21, 318-19, 342, 400, 428,
464-66
Steering Committee on the Canadian
North, 225, 229, 237, 241
Steeves, Kerry, 51
Stephens, Rgr. Master Corporal Stanley,
417
Stephenson, William, 171
Stephenville, 273, 349
Sterling, Harry, 397
Stevens, G.R., 118-19
Stevenson, Alex, 146-47
Stewart, Jane, 382
Stewart, Rgr. Capt. J.P., 85
Stirling, Maj. W.K. Bill, 229-34, 238-40,
242-43, 245-47, 259, 397, 478
Strange, William, 27
Straubenzee, Maj. Casimir Bowen Van,
153, 160, 164-66, 168-69, 171, 180, 208-9,
215-16
Strid, Rgr. Cpl. Free Mitchell, 459f
Stuart, Lt.-Gen. Kenneth, 31, 36
submarine sighting, 127, 132, 160, 193, 201,
291, 384, 419
Sugluk. *See* Salluit
suicide, 335, 340, 361, 363, 365, 367, 369,
387, 454, 463
Sunnyside, 129
Sutherland, Lt.-Col. W.B.S., 226, 228-29,
239, 242
Sutherland, Maj. Brian, 348-49, 367, 369
Sutherland, Rgr. Master Corporal Florrie,
427
Sutherland, Rgr. Sgt. Albert, 417

STUDIES IN CANADIAN MILITARY HISTORY

John Griffith Armstrong, *The Halifax Explosion and the Royal Canadian Navy: Inquiry and Intrigue*

Andrew Richter, *Avoiding Armageddon: Canadian Military Strategy and Nuclear Weapons, 1950-63*

William Johnston, *A War of Patrols: Canadian Army Operations in Korea*

Julian Gwyn, *Frigates and Foremasts: The North American Squadron in Nova Scotia Waters, 1745-1815*

Jeffrey A. Keshen, *Saints, Sinners, and Soldiers: Canada's Second World War*

Desmond Morton, *Fight or Pay: Soldiers' Families in the Great War*

Douglas E. Delaney, *The Soldiers' General: Bert Hoffmeister at War*

Michael Whitby, ed., *Commanding Canadians: The Second World War Diaries of A.F.C. Layard*

Martin Auger, *Prisoners of the Home Front: German POWs and "Enemy Aliens" in Southern Quebec, 1940-46*

Tim Cook, *Clio's Warriors: Canadian Historians and the Writing of the World Wars*

Serge Marc Durflinger, *Fighting from Home: The Second World War in Verdun, Quebec*

Richard O. Mayne, *Betrayed: Scandal, Politics, and Canadian Naval Leadership*

P. Whitney Lackenbauer, *Battle Grounds: The Canadian Military and Aboriginal Lands*

Cynthia Toman, *An Officer and a Lady: Canadian Military Nursing and the Second World War*

Michael Petrou, *Renegades: Canadians in the Spanish Civil War*

Amy J. Shaw, *Crisis of Conscience: Conscientious Objection in Canada during the First World War*

Serge Marc Durflinger, *Veterans with a Vision: Canada's War Blinded in Peace and War*

James G. Fergusson, *Canada and Ballistic Missile Defence, 1954-2009: Déjà Vu All Over Again*

Benjamin Isitt, *From Victoria to Vladivostok: Canada's Siberian Expedition, 1917-19*

James Wood, *Militia Myths: Ideas of the Canadian Citizen Soldier, 1896-1921*

Timothy Balzer, *The Information Front: The Canadian Army and News Management during the Second World War*

Andrew Godefroy, *Defence and Discovery: Canada's Military Space Program, 1945-74*

Douglas E. Delaney, *Corps Commanders: Five British and Canadian Generals at War, 1939-45*

Timothy Wilford, *Canada's Road to the Pacific War: Intelligence, Strategy, and the Far East Crisis*

Randall Wakelam, *Cold War Fighters: Canadian Aircraft Procurement, 1945-54*

Andrew Burtch, Andrew, *Give Me Shelter: The Failure of Canada's Cold War Civil Defence*

Wendy Cuthbertson, *Labour Goes to War: The CIO and the Construction of a New Social Order, 1939-45*

Printed and bound in Canada by Friesens

Set in Garamond and Carta by Artegraphica Design Co. Ltd.

Cartographer: Jennifer Arthur

Copy editor: Lesley Erickson

Proofreader: Ruth Bradley-St-Cyr